FREEDOM IN THE WORLD

FREEDOM IN THE WORLD
The Annual Survey of Political Rights & Civil Liberties, 1996–1997

Freedom House Survey Team

Adrian Karatnycky
Survey Coordinator

Jessica Cashdan
Ha-Kyung Choi
Charles Graybow
Kristen Guida
Thomas R. Lansner
Arch Puddington
Boris Shor
Leonard R. Sussman
George Zarycky

Roger Kaplan
George Szamuely
General Editors

Tara L. Kelly
General Layout and Design

Transaction Publishers
New Brunswick (U.S.A.) and London (U.K.)

ISSN: 0732-6610
ISBN: 1-56000-354-5 (cloth); 0-7658-0422-0 (paper)
Printed in the United States of America

The Library of Congress has catalogued this serial title as follows:

Freedom in the world / 1978–
New York : Freedom House, 1978–
v. : map: 25 cm. (Freedom House Book)
Annual.
ISSN 0732-6610=Freedom in the World.
1. Civil rights Periodicals. I. R. Adrian Karatnycky, et al. I. Series.
JC571.F66323.4 05-dc 19   82-642048
AACR 2   MARC-S
Library of Congress [84101]

Contents

Foreword

The *Comparative Survey of Freedom* is an institutional effort by Freedom House to monitor the progress and decline of political rights and civil liberties in 191 nations and 59 related territories. These year-end reviews of freedom began in 1955, when they were called the *Balance Sheet of Freedom* and, still later, the *Annual Survey of the Progress of Freedom*. This program was expanded in the early 1970s, and has appeared in *Freedom Review* since 1973. It has also been issued in a more developed context as a yearbook since 1978.

Since 1989, the *Survey* project has been a year-long effort produced by our regional experts, consultants and human rights specialists. The *Survey* derives its information from a wide range of sources. Most valued of these are the many human rights activists, journalists, editors and political figures around the world who keep us informed of the human rights situation in their countries.

Throughout the year, Freedom House personnel regularly conduct fact-finding missions to gain more in-depth knowledge of the vast political transformations affecting our world. During these week-to-month- long investigations, we make every effort to meet a cross-section of political parties and associations, human rights monitors, religious figures, representatives of both the private sector and trade union movement, academics and journalists.

During the past year, Freedom House staff traveled to Azerbaijan; Bangladesh; Benin; Cambodia; Canada; Cote D'Ivoire; Cuba; Czech Republic; France; Germany; Haiti; Hong Kong; India; Indonesia; Israel; Jordan; Laos; Mexico; Nepal; Pakistan; Palestinian Authority-Administered Territories (Israel); Philippines; Russia; Singapore; Sri Lanka; Suriname; Switzerland; Thailand; Ukraine; and Vietnam. The *Survey* project team also consults a vast array of published source materials, ranging from the reports of other human rights organizations to often rare, regional newspapers and magazines.

This year's *Survey* team includes Adrian Karatnycky, the project coordinator Jessica Cashdan, Ha-Kyung Choi, Joshua Gordon, Charles Graybow (research coordinator), Kristen Guida, Thomas R. Lansner, Arch Puddington, Boris Shor, Leonard R. Sussman and George Zarycky. The general editors of *Freedom in the World* are Roger Kaplan and George Szamuely; the managing editor is Tara Kelly. This year's research associate was Eden Heinsheimer. This year's research assistants were Tamara Babiuk; Melissa Elwyn; Annie Gabriel; Amanda Gordon; Katherine Khamsi; Amina Luqman, Justin Okun; Nelson De Sousa; Clara Ward; and Michelle Wray.

Substantial support for the *Comparative Survey of Freedom* has been generously provided by the Lynde & Harry Bradley Foundation and the Smith Richardson Foundation.

Academic Advisory Board

Prof. David Becker, Dartmouth College

Prof. Daniel Brumberg, Georgetown University

Dr. Larry Diamond, Hoover Institution

Dr. Mark Falcoff, Resident Scholar, American Enterprise Institute

Dr. Charles Gati, Johns Hopkins University

Prof. Jeane Kirkpatrick, American Enterprise Institute

Dr. Seymour Martin Lipset, Institute for Public Policy, George Mason University

Dr. Alexander Motyl, Associate Director, Harriman Institute, Columbia University

Dr. Joshua Muravchik, Resident Scholar, American Enterprise Institute

Dr. Daniel Pipes, Editor, *Middle East Quarterly*

Prof. Robert A. Scalapino, Robson Research Professor of Government, Emeritus, University of California, Berkeley

Prof. Arthur Waldron, Professor of Strategy, U.S. Naval War College, and Adjunct Professor of East Asian Studies, Brown University

Specialists

Dr. Khalid Duran
Prof. Michael McFaul
George Melloan
Dr. Barnett Rubin
Prof. Arturo Valenzuela

The Comparative Survey of Freedom 1996-1997

Freedom on the March Adrian Karatnycky

Freedom made important strides around the world in 1996 as the number of Free countries grew from 76 to 79, the largest number since the Survey was launched in 1972. Nearly 42 percent of the countries in the world provide their citizens with a high degree of political and economic freedom and safeguard basic civil liberties. Fifty-nine countries—31 percent of the world total—are Partly Free, enjoying limited political rights and civil liberties, often in a context of corruption, a flawed justice system, ethnic strife, or war. Fifty-three countries, or 27 percent, are not free in which basic rights were suppressed and civil liberties denied. This year, there were 135 million more people lived in freedom than in 1995. In all, 1,250.3 million people (21.67 percent of the world's population) live in Free countries; 2,260.0 million people live in Partly Free countries (39.16 percent of the world's population); and 2,260.6 million people (39.17 percent) live in Not Free countries.

In contrast with this positive trend, many tyrannies maintained a stranglehold on their citizens. Genocide continued in Burundi, warfare erupted between Hutus and Tutsis in Eastern Zaire, the radical Taliban waged a war to expand its repressive control to two-thirds of Afghanistan, and the civil war in Tajikistan continued to claim many lives.

Freedom's advances

The year's new entrants into the ranks of Free countries are the Philippines, Taiwan, Romania, Bolivia and Venezuela.

The Philippines joined the ranks of Free countries due to a significant decline in rebel insurgencies and a reduction in the influence of the country's traditional ruling families, in part as a result of fundamental economic reforms undertaken by President Fidel Ramos. Taiwan, too, was a new entrant among the world's Free countries, having successfully completed its democratic transition to a competitive multiparty system with a free and fair presidential election in a setting of political pluralism. Romania's entry into the ranks of Free countries with a competitive multiparty system was affirmed in free and fair elections that saw opposition non-Communist forces come to power after seven years of rule by an elite that had its political roots in the deposed Ceausescu dictatorship.

Freedom in the World—1997

The population of the world this year is estimated at 5,771.0 billion persons, who reside in 191 sovereign states and 59 related territories—a total of 250 entities. The level of political rights and civil liberties as shown comparatively by the Freedom House Survey is:

Free: 1,250.3 billion (21.67 percent of the world's population) live in 79 of the states and in 44 of the related territories.

Partly Free: 2,260.1 billion (39.16 percent of the world's population) live in 59 of the states and 4 of the related territories.

Not Free: 2,260.6 billion (39.17 percent of the world's population) live in 53 of the states and 11 of the related territories.

A Record of the Survey
(population in millions)

SURVEY DATE	FREE		PARTLY FREE		NOT FREE		WORLD POPULATION
January '81	1,613.0	(35.90%)	970.9	(21.60%)	1,911.9	(42.50%)	4,495.8
January '83	1,665.1	(36.32%)	918.8	(20.04%)	2,000.2	(43.64%)	4,584.1
January '85	1,671.4	(34.85%)	1,117.4	(23.30%)	2,007.0	(41.85%)	4,795.8
January '87	1,842.5	(37.10%)	1,171.5	(23.60%)	1,949.9	(39.30%)	4,963.9
January '89	1,992.8	(38.86%)	1,027.9	(20.05%)	2,107.3	(41.09%)	5,128.0
January '90	2,034.4	(38.87%)	1,143.7	(21.85%)	2,055.9	(39.28%)	5,234.0
January '91*	2,088.2	(39.23%)	1,485.7	(27.91%)	1,748.7	(32.86%)	5,322.6
January '92	1,359.3	(25.29%)	2,306.6	(42.92%)	1,708.2	(31.79%)	5,374.2
January '93	1,352.2	(24.83%)	2,403.3	(44.11%)	1,690.4	(31.06%)	5,446.0
January '94	1,046.2	(19.00%)	2,224.4	(40.41%)	2,234.6	(40.59%)	5,505.2
January '95	1,119.7	(19.97%)	2,243.4	(40.01%)	2,243.9	(40.02%)	5,607.0
January '96	1,114.5	(19.55%)	2,365.8	(41.49%)	2.221.2	(38.96%)	5.701.5
January '97	1,250.3	(21.67%)	2,260.1	(39.16%)	2,260.6	(39.17%)	5,771.0

*The large shift in the population figure between 1991 and 1992 is due to India's change from Free to Partly Free.

In Bolivia, the end to a six-month state-of-siege introduced in 1995 signaled that democracy's return to the ranks of Free countries. Venezuela returned to its status as a Free country as social and political upheaval receded in 1995 along with the threat of the militarization of Caracas in the event of growing disorder.

Despite the fact that many war criminals indicted by an international tribunal remained at large, progress toward greater freedom was also registered in Bosnia, where an internationally-enforced peace process led to limited revival of civic life that accounts for the country advancing from Not Free to Partly Free. Sierra Leone was another country that made advances toward greater freedom. As a result of a successful national election and a cease-fire in a bloody civil war, the country exited the ranks of the Not Free states and is now Partly Free.

Setbacks

The year also saw serious setbacks for freedom. Slovakia slipped from Free to Partly Free as political terror against opponents of the ruling party and the actions of an increasingly authoritarian prime minister, Vladimir Meciar—who suppressed press freedoms and used extra-constitutional means in an attempt to unseat the country's president—eroded civil liberties and political rights. A deteriorating human and political rights climate under the tyrannical President Aleksandr Lukashenka signaled Belarus's entry into the ranks of the Not Free. Niger, which saw a military coup topple its electoral democracy, also joined this year's ranks of the Not Free. And Ecuador, where a new president exhibited authoritarian tendencies, exited from the ranks of Free countries and is now Partly Free.

In addition to these significant changes, a further 24 countries registered less dramatic gains in freedom without changing broad categories, while 9 countries saw a decline in freedom.

The most oppressive states

Seventeen states received Freedom House's lowest rating—7 for political rights and 7 for civil liberties. The most repressive of these were Iraq, North Korea, Cuba and Sudan. Other states judged among the world's least free were Afghanistan, Bhutan, Burma, Burundi, China, Equatorial Guinea, Libya, Saudi Arabia, Somalia, Syria, Tajikistan, Turkmenistan and Vietnam.

The Global Trend			
	Free	Partly Free	Not Free
1987	57	57	53
1997	79	59	53

Tracking Democracy	
Number of Democracies	
1987	69
1992	91
1997	118

Of the 17 least free countries, nine had Muslim majority populations. Four others—China, Cuba, North Korea and Vietnam—were among the world's few remaining one-party Marxist-Leninist dictatorships. While there has been significant progress toward freedom around the world in the last decade, 1,505.9 million people live in the 17 worst-rated and most repressive countries, 80 percent of them represented by China's 1.2 billion population.

The global trend

The broadening of freedom around the world indicates that democracy and the ideas of civil society are becoming a more permanent feature of the international landscape. Moreover, the number of Free societies has expanded in recent years, increasing from 72 in 1993 to 79 as 1996 drew to a close.

Nearly 22 percent of the world's population lives in Free societies in which a broad range of political rights and civil liberties are enjoyed; 39 percent of the world population lives in Partly Free countries in which basic rights are somewhat constrained as a consequence of government practice and/or as a result of the damage done to freedom by insurgencies, political terrorism, rampant corruption, and inordinate influence of the military on government and civic life; and 39 percent live in Not Free societies in which political rights are absent and civil liberties are systematically and massively abused.

Democracies

The year's survey also shows that the expansion of democracy is continuing. There are today 118 electoral democracies, the highest total in history, and a net gain of one new democracy in 1996. This means that the proportion of democracies in the world has expanded from a little over 40 percent a decade ago to 62 percent today. As significantly, 3,161.2 million people, 54.8 percent of the world's population, now live in electoral democracies. This year, three countries held generally free and fair elections and entered the ranks of democratic states: Ghana, Sierra Leone and Taiwan. Two electoral democracies were toppled in 1996: Niger, which saw a military coup sweep democratically elected leaders from power, and Zambia, where a high number of irregularities marred a presidential vote.

The progress registered in the number of electoral democracies around the world is remarkable. As the number of the world's democracies has increased in a decade from 2-in-5 to 3-in-5, the practice of democracy is becoming the global rule, rather than the exception. Today, a majority of the world's citizens expects to be able to vote for political leaders in free and fair elections. This set of expectations is also increasingly at work in countries where basic democratic rights are thwarted or denied.

In Armenia, hundreds of thousands have joined protests at the widespread falsification of election returns in that country's presidential elections. Serbian students, workers and intellectuals have taken to the streets in major urban centers to protest the government's annulment of municipal election results in late November, in which the opposition captured control of local government in Belgrade and other urban centers. Large protests calling for the restoration of democratic rule

The 17 Worst Rated Countries

Afghanistan
Bhutan
Burma
Burundi
China
Cuba
Equatorial Guinea
Iraq
Korea, North
Libya
Saudi Arabia
Somalia
Sudan
Syria
Tajikistan
Turkmenistan
Vietnam

The 5 Worst Rated Related Territories

East Timor (Indonesia)
Kashmir (India)
Kosovo (Yugoslavia)
Tibet (China)
West Papua (Indonesia)

have occurred in Burma, and calls for an open multiparty system fueled street protests in Indonesia. Such a deepening public commitment to democratic processes suggests that a decade of gradual expansion of electoral democracies shows no signs of reversal.

Over the years, some critics have derided electoral democracy, arguing that the emphasis of U.S. policy on promoting electoral processes results in "donor democracy"—a veneer of democratic practice to ensure good standing with the U.S. and other countries that provide foreign aid. Yet the record of the last decade's democratic transformations shows that something more profound is occurring around the world. Electoral democracy brings with it pressure for important additional liberties. For free and fair elections to take place, media that have some sense of objectivity and balancemust exist. Political parties also must offer voters a measure of choice. Electoral processes, furthermore, contribute to the emergence of non-governmental civic groups that promote voter participation and monitor elections, while at the same time strengthening civil society.

While electoral democracies do not ensure respect for the basic rights of their citizens, they offer the best climate in which basic freedoms can thrive. Of the world's 118 democracies, 79 are Free; the balance—39—are rated Partly Free, and in many cases confront insurgencies, ethnic and religious strife or the legacy of prolonged periods of dictatorial rule that arrested the development of civil societies and corrupted the legal and judicial systems. Yet despite these challenges, the vast majority of the Partly Free democracies, 27 of them, are what can be called "high partly free" countries.

Continuing momentum

What are the reasons for the continuing momentum in free societies and democracies?

One important reason for freedom's advance is the proliferation of new information and communication technologies. Innovations like the fax, desktop publishing, inexpensive printing capabilities and the Internet all have broken down the ability of the state to control access to uncensored information. They have created new conduits for democratic ideas and information from free societies. While the Internet is becoming subject to the "filtration" of politically sensitive material in China and other closed societies, it nevertheless is porous enough to be subversive of authoritarian ideas.

An equally important role has been played over the years by short-wave radio. Uncensored information and democratic ideas distributed by the foreign broadcast services of the U.S.-government funded Voice of America, Radio Marti, Radio Free Europe and Radio Liberty, as well as by the British Broadcasting Corporation, Germany's Deutsche Welle and Radio France Internationale, have all contributed to breaking the monopoly of information of many tyrannies. Satellite dishes, too, make it possible for hundreds of thousands of citizens in closed societies to receive televised information directly from the airwaves.

Globalization of the economic system has resulted in greater commerce and contact between market democracies and closed, statist societies. Democracy and rule of law, too, have been given impetus by the growing prosperity of many dynamic market economies. The emergence of more prosperous middle and working classes has created greater pressure for political reform. Entrepreneurs and other business leaders, eager to protect their property rights and ensure the dispassionate enforcement of contracts, are also a force is pressing for more open and accountable governance.

Another reason for democracy's spread is the effect created by its very example. The greater the number of democracies and free societies, the more likely it is that democratic ideas will cross borders through expanded trade, commerce and the flow of information. The economic success of many new democracies also exerts an influence on neighboring states, by serving as an attractive model of social, economic and political organization. The examples of Poland and the Czech Republic in the former Soviet bloc, the new dynamism of Chile's democracy in Latin America, and of the Philippines, Taiwan, and South Korea in the Asia/Pacific region are strengthening the case for democracy as a key component of successful economies and societies in the face of China, Singapore and other countries advocating authoritarian paths to economic development.

New democracies are also clearly exerting constructive influence on their more repressive neighbors. The Czech Republic's media are influencing the political evolution of neighboring Slovakia, where state control over the broadcast media is significant. In November, 1996, Ukraine, Lithuania and Poland, all young democracies, attempted to exert constructive diplomatic pressure on Belarus's president when he subverted basic democratic norms and constitutional rule. Russia's independent-minded telejournalists have also tried to report objectively about political repression in Belarus, with many of their broadcasts seen by Belarusian citizens who otherwise would be informed by state-controlled television and print media. And delegations of non-governmental groups and parliamentarians from neighboring democracies have traveled to Belarus to express solidarity with the country's democratic organizations and media.

South Africa—another young democracy— has taken the lead in seeking to exert political, diplomatic and economic pressure upon Nigeria's dictatorship. And democratic Mali's leaders spoke out against a recent military coup in neighboring Niger.

Another significant factor has been the commitment of resources by the U.S. and other G-7 countries to support democratic transitions, independent media, and the development of political pluralism in emerging democracies. Such aid programs, which began to proliferate in the early 1980s with the creation of the U.S. National Endowment for Democracy, have contributed to the strengthening of thousands of pro-democracy civic groups around the world. More recently, the U.S. Agency for International Development and the foreign assistance efforts of the European Union have dedicated resources to the strengthening of rule of law, democratic processes, independent media and civil society.

This is not to say clouds are not visible on the horizon.

Dictatorships are seeking ways of reasserting control over the flow of informa-

The Five Most Important Gains for Freedom in 1996

Freedom House has selected five events as the most significant events advancing the global tide of freedom in 1996. These were:

1) The awarding of the Nobel Peace Prize to two human rights advocates from East Timor, Bishop Carlos Filipe Ximenes Belo and human rights advocate Jose Ramos-Horta. By refocusing world attention on a much neglected part of the world, the Nobel Committee gave voice to hundreds of thousands of Timorese seeking national self-determination in the face of over two decades of Indonesian military occupation. The Nobel Committee's award also refocused international attention on the overall situation of human rights and political freedoms in Indonesia, whose economic growth has been accompanied by continuing repression.

2) The U.S.-led effort to bring peace to Bosnia. The deployment of an international military contingent anchored by the NATO alliance helped end bloodshed and established the basis for the reemergence of electoral democracy, while offering hope that a solution to the problems arising from the deep divisions between Bosnians, Serbs and Croats could be achieved.

3) The presidential election in Taiwan. The election of President Lee-Teng Hui was a milestone because of its implications for the people of Taiwan, and because it was an important signal to the mainland Chinese population that nothing in the Chinese tradition is incompatible with democratic values.

4) The triumph of electoral politics in Central and Eastern Europe. Free and fair elections were held for president in Russia, Moldova, Bulgaria and Romania, and for parliament in Romania and Lithuania. In most cases, voters rejected the ex-Communist and neo-Communist parties and opted for anti-Communist and non-Communist leaders. Moreover, ultranationalist parties and neo-fascist groups did quite poorly and receded as a political force in much of Central and Eastern Europe.

5) Nicaragua's rejection of the Sandinistas. The election of President Aleman in a vigorously contested process and the rejection by voters of Sandinista candidate Daniel Ortega was an important step toward the stabilization of democracy in a country with a long history of right-wing and left-wing dictatorship.

tion and news by jamming foreign broadcasts or pressuring foreign broadcasters to eliminate certain types of programs and news services. China's efforts to centralize the distribution of foreign news by channeling it through the state news agency, and to filter out politically sensitive web sites on the Internet, are also sources of concern.

Some disturbing signs also shown that, under new fiscal pressures and budget constraints, some democracies are retreating from their obligation to promote the free flow of ideas and democratic values. One component in this is the deep reduction in international spending for foreign broadcasting. The budgets of the U.S.-based Voice of America and Radio Free Europe and Radio Liberty have been drastically reduced. Canada has announced the closing down of its Radio Canada International broadcast service, and the budget of Britain's BBC has been severely cut.

Moreover, in a climate of reduced resources for foreign aid, many countries continue to direct foreign assistance to dictatorships rather than to the many worthy new democracies. Last year, for example, the third and fourth largest recipients of foreign aid for developing countries were China and Indonesia, two Not Free countries that massively and systematically repress their citizens and violate basic political and civil liberties.

Regional trends

Democratic dynamism and the expansion of free societies is a phenomenon that is present across all continents and in most cultures, underscoring that democracy and human liberty are not a Western construct but a universal aspiration. Nevertheless there are some important regional variations that deserve greater attention and a deeper understanding.

The Five Greatest Setbacks for Freedom in 1996

Five major events were identified by Freedom House as the greatest setbacks to freedom in 1996. These were:

1) The Taliban's march to power in Afghanistan. The expansion of control by the militant Taliban introduced a primitive regime of terror and severe restrictions against women to the capital, Kabul, and most of Afghanistan. The Taliban's fanatical leaders espouse a theory of Islam far more extreme than that preached by Iran's mullahs. A Taliban victory would signify that Afghanistan would be under a form of totalitarianism for the second time in recent history.

2) Saddam Hussein's invasion of the Kurdish region of Northern Iraq. The invasion, organized in cooperation with one Kurdish faction, strengthened the hand of dictator Saddam Hussein and set back hopes that the Kurds could peacefully resolve their factional differences under self-rule.

3) The widening zone of instability in Eastern Zaire, Rwanda, Uganda and Burundi. Ethnic conflicts between Tutsis and Hutus—encouraged and abetted by outside powers—claimed thousands of lives in 1996 and could, if unchecked, plunge a far wider part of Africa into turmoil and instability in the coming year.

4) The reemergence of a tyranny in Belarus. A new wave of repression and intimidation in Belarus, orchestrated by the country's megalomaniacal President Aleksandr Lukashenka, set back constitutional rule and the division of power in this East European state.

5) Chinese neo-nationalism. China's threats against Taiwan and its efforts to construct a powerful military force were coupled with the emergence of a new xenophobic nationalist ideology. As part of this new more aggressive mindset, China's leaders bullied and sought to censor foreign businesses, including American corporations.

As 1996 draws to a close, we can speak of democracy and freedom as being the dominant trends in the Americas, in Western Europe, and increasingly in the Asia/Pacific region. While substantial democratic evolution has taken place in Central Europe, in the former Soviet Union the picture is decidedly more mixed with a number of countries remaining Not Free. In Africa, too, Free societies represent a distinct minority of states. Moreover, no democracies exist in the Arab world and freedom is still an elusive goal for most predominantly Muslim societies.

In Africa, where there are 53 countries, 9 are Free (17 percent), 20 are Partly Free (37.7 percent), and 24 (45.3 percent) are Not Free. Moreover, just 18 states, a third of Africa's countries, are electoral democracies. New African entrants into the ranks of democracies are Ghana and Sierra Leone, while two countries—Niger and Zambia—exited from the ranks of democratic states.

In the Americas, 20 of the region's 35 countries are Free (57.1 percent of the regional total), 14 are Partly Free (40.0 percent), and one—Cuba—is Not Free. There are 31 democracies in the Americas, representing 89 percent of the region's states.

Western Europe is the only part of the world in which democracy is a universal phenomenon. All twenty-four of the region's countries are electoral democracies and Free societies in which basic civil liberties and political rights are respected.

In the former Communist countries of Central and Eastern Europe and the former USSR, democratic and market transitions are continuing and the strength of civil society and the private sector is on the rise. Nineteen of the region's 27 countries are democracies. This represents 70 percent of the region's states. Nine countries (33 percent) are Free, 11 countries (40.7 percent) are Partly Free and 7 (25.9 percent) are Not Free. But, despite progress in the five years since the collapse of the USSR, the picture remains bleak. While the three Baltic states are now both Free and democratic, among the twelve countries that are full or associated members of the Commonwealth of Independent States, (i.e. the republics of the former USSR minus the Baltic states), only four are electoral democracies. None of the 12 states is Free. Six—Armenia, Georgia, the Kyrgyz Republic, Moldova, Russia, and Ukraine—are Partly Free and six—Azerbaijan, Belarus, Kazakhstan, Tajikistan, Turkmenistan, and Uzbekistan—are Not Free.

An important trend in the region this year was the return to electoral office of anti-Communists and non-Communist political parties in elections in Lithuania, Romania, Bulgaria and Russia. Only in Moldova did a candidate of a post-Communist party win national electoral office.

With NATO enlargement on the agenda as 1996 drew to a close, the leading candidates for membership in the alliance—Poland, Hungary, and the Czech Republic—had all made stable and durable transitions to freedom and democracy.

While several vocal leaders in the Asia/Pacific region—in particular, Singapore's Lee Kuan Yew and China's Marxist-Leninist leaders—have sung the praises of authoritarian paths to prosperity and denounced Western democracies as an unacceptable model, trends in the region belie such claims. Indeed, the region has seen a number of democracies—Taiwan, South Korea, and the Philippines—registering high rates of growth. Notwithstanding claims by some regional leaders that democracy is incompatible with "Asian values and traditions," the proportion of democracies in the region, 24 of 38—63 percent—is higher than the global figure. With the addition of the Philippines and Taiwan, 16 of the Asia/Pacific region's states are Free (representing 42.1 percent of the regional total). Eleven are Partly Free countries (28.9 percent of the regional total), and 11 countries are Not Free (28.9 percent).

In the Middle East, of the region's 14 countries, one—Israel—is Free; three—Jordan, Kuwait and Turkey—are Partly Free, and ten are Not Free. Israel and Turkey are the region's two democracies.

In addition to these regional variations, Freedom House examined the state of freedom and democracy in the Arab world. Among the 16 states with a majority Arab population, there are no Free countries. Four majority Arab states are Partly Free and 12 are Not Free. Moreover, there are no democracies in the Arab world.

Within societies with a majority Islamic population, only one—Mali—is Free; 13 are Partly Free, and 29 are Not Free. Six countries with a predominantly Muslim (or traditionally Muslim) population are electoral democracies: Albania, Bangladesh, Kyrgyzstan, Mali, Pakistan and Turkey.

Propelling freedom's march

The continuing expansion of electoral democracy and the further expansion of Free societies suggests that five years after the collapse of the USSR and the end of the bi-polar superpower rivalry, the U.S. and other established democracies have an important opportunity to further accelerate freedom's forward progress. The years ahead will be crucial to determining whether the democratic momentum of recent years is sustained.

What mechanisms should the U.S. employ to help further advance the important progress toward democracy and freedom registered over the last two decades?

With the U.S. budget under pressure, new resources will be hard to come by. This will mean that tough choices need to be made in the allocation of funding for international affairs. The focus of such spending should be a commitment to propel the democratic tide of recent years, while meeting our humanitarian obligations to combat hunger and disease. Worthy programs and initiatives that deserve particular support are the National Endowment for Democracy; the programs of Radio Free Europe, Radio Liberty, Radio Marti, Radio Free Asia, and the Voice of America, the democracy and human rights oriented exchange and education programs of the U.S. Information Agency; and U.S. Agency for International Development programs that strengthen civil society and democratic processes. Many of these programs have suffered deep cuts in recent years and further cuts would damage their ability to make a significant difference in promoting democratic values. If new funds are unavailable, a larger portion of U.S. funding for Africa, the former Soviet Union, Asia and the Middle East should be devoted to programs that promote democratic ideas and educate new generations of democracy advocates.

Still, U.S funds for foreign assistance are not the only ones that are shrinking. Increasingly, many other advanced democracies are reducing government expenditures for foreign aid. Yet, while many new and struggling democracies are in need of support, foreign aid provided by our democratic allies is allocated to dictatorships that systematically suppress freedom. The third and fourth largest recipients of the democratic world's largesse last year were China and Indonesia, two of the world's most repressive states. Together, they received foreign aid of nearly $4 billion from established democracies.

While vigorous disagreement abounds about whether to impose economic and trade sanctions against repressive states, more consensus should be reached among the democracies over where foreign aid should be directed—to poor countries in acute need and to countries that respect basic democratic norms. The massive assistance recently provided to China and Indonesia does not meet such standards.

Yet despite the dramatic changes that have occurred in the world, no regular international forum discusses such key issues. The United Nations includes in its ranks many countries hostile to democratic values and democratic change and cannot serve this purpose. The same is true of large regional cooperation bodies which include both democratic governments and repressive regimes. And while there are security alliances made up of democratic states and economic forums made up of free-market economies, no international organization or forum composed of the world's democratic states focus on the promotion of peaceful democratic change. The establishment of a coordinating structure made up of democracies that commit significant resources to foreign assistance programs would provide a forum for the elected leaders of the democracies to discuss the opportunities and mechanisms for promoting and strengthening democratic transitions around the world. Such a forum could also enable democratic donor nations to target assistance to countries that are trying to play by the democratic rules and are protecting fundamental human rights.

While not a universal panacea, the global spread of electoral democracy is the best single hope for the enlargement of human freedom, the protection of fundamental human rights, and respect for the rule of law.

The challenge of expanding freedom and democracy will be more difficult in the years ahead, however. Many of the Not Free countries are working systematically to deny their citizens access to democratic ideas. As democratic values have spread to all corners of the world, dictators have found new mechanisms to suppress the democratic tide.

Countries that have proved particularly resistant to the global democratic tide are a handful of residual one-party Marxist-Leninist dictatorships—China, Vietnam, Laos, North Korea and Cuba. During the Cold War, the U.S. committed significant resources to efforts aimed at breaking the monopoly of information in the Soviet bloc and to supporting the flow of democratic ideas to these closed societies.

Today, however, few such initiatives by the U.S. are targeted at these residual Communist states. With the exception of Radio Marti, a small and underfunded Radio Free Asia, and a handful of small programs disseminating democratic literature, few resources are being committed to nurturing democratic values and democratic voices in these closed societies.

A new commitment should also be promoted to advance the spread of democratic values and assist democratic movements on the African continent, which has seen deep cutbacks in foreign assistance in recent years. Such pro-democracy programs could be undertaken in cooperation with Africa's new democratic states, including the Republic of South Africa.

A renewed commitment to promoting democratic values should be targeted at the former Soviet Union, where political rights and civil liberties have improved in several countries in recent years, but where durable transitions to broad-based freedoms have not been achieved.

To realize such initiatives will require leadership at home. Statements by President Bill Clinton, the secretary of state and the Congressional leadership reemphasizing the U.S. commitment to the spread of democracy are an important first step. So, too, would be the commitment of resources for international broadcasting to closed societies, enhanced funding for the National Endowment for Democracy, support for pro-democracy forces in closed societies, and funds to support reform in new and emerging democracies.

There is an historic opportunity to build a safer and more prosperous world by sustaining the global expansion of democracy that has been charted in Freedom House's annual surveys of recent years. U.S. leadership abroad will be essential if the global democratic momentum is to be sustained and deepened.

Adrian Karatnycky, president of Freedom House, is coordinator of the Comparative Survey of Freedom.

Russia: Transition Without Consolidation

Michael McFaul

I.

The historical facts of Russian politics over the last year appear to point to tremendous progress in making a democracy. There are milestones well worth noting in 1996, especially when compared to other periods: the upheavals of the early years of the new Russian state, the seventy years of totalitarian rule under the Communists, and the hundreds of years of autocratic government under the tsars.

• In December 1995, Russian citizens voted in parliamentary elections. In two rounds of voting in June and July 1996, voters elected a president. The vote for president was the first time in Russia's thousand year history that citizens selected their head of state.

• Despite calls for delay and postponement, these two elections were held on time and under the rule of law. These elections were the first to be held under laws drafted and approved through a democratic procedure by elected officials.

• Both of these elections were relatively free and relatively fair. In the parliamentary elections, strong evidence of falsification was reported in Chechnya and Dagestan, but these infractions were not sufficient to warrant objection to the results by any major political actor. In the presidential elections, Yeltsin grossly violated the campaign finance limits, the media openly propagated Yeltsin's cause, and counting irregularities again appeared in Chechnya and some other national republics. Most observers, however, agreed that these transgressions did not influence the outcome of the vote. Significantly, all the major actors accepted the election results.

• Large majorities of eligible voters participated in both of these elections. In the parliamentary elections, 65 percent of all eligible voters participated, while the turnout rates for both rounds of the presidential election approached an amazing 70 percent.

• When given the choice to vote for nationalists, Communists, or the current reform course, Russian voters overwhelmingly rejected the Soviet past or a fascist future and opted to support Boris Yeltsin. By a margin of ten million votes, Boris Yeltsin defeated his Communist challenger, Gennadi Zyuganov, in the second round of the presidential election. This electoral result defied the trend in the post-Communist world in which Communists have tended to win second elections.

• After Yeltsin's inauguration, the Communist-dominated parliament approved Boris Yeltsin's candidate for prime minister—Viktor Chernomyrdin—by an overwhelming majority. This, too, was a first, as Russia's elected parliament had never approved the executive's choice for prime minister under the procedures outlined in a legitimate constitution. Later in the year, the Duma passed the government's budget without major political conflict.

• The war in Chechnya has ended, at least temporarily. While resolution to the sovereignty issues in question have not been addressed, fighting has stopped. This conclusion to open warfare was the direct result of the presidential electoral process as both Boris Yeltsin and Alexander Lebed, another presidential candidate who then joined (albeit briefly) the Yeltsin government, pledged during their campaigns to end the war.

• Throughout the fall of 1996, dozens of gubernatorial elections were held throughout Russia. While evidence of falsification has tainted the results in some races, the vast majority were recognized as free and fair by all major participants. Significantly, and against most predictions entering the fall electoral season, incumbents supported by Yeltsin's government did not sweep these elections. Rather, the results have been more mixed, with independents, Communists, and even a few militant nationalists winning. Alexander Rutskoi, the former vice president who led the opposition against Yeltsin in October 1993, was elected governor in Kursk Oblast; and Yevgenii Mikhalov, a leader of Vladimir Zhirinovsky's nationalist Liberal Democratic Party of Russia, won in Pskov Oblast, demonstrating that these elections were not controlled from Moscow.

Remarkable achievements and pessimism

This series of democratic achievements is remarkable. Yet, no one in Russia seems impressed. On the contrary, elites, commentators and the public at large have grown noticeably more pessimistic about Russia's future since the conclusion of the presidential election in July 1996.

The magnitude of the wage arrears problem, estimated by Labor Minister Melikyan to be 42 trillion rubles in unpaid wages, coupled with the government's inability to collect taxes and the lack of economic growth, has fueled speculation of impending social upheaval. Beginning with walkouts by power workers in Primorskii Krai in August of 1996, wildcat strikes have increased throughout the country. Discontent within the military also appears to be growing, as the armed forces have not been immune from the government's inability to pay wages. In October 1996, General Boris Gromov, the former commander of Soviet armed forces in Afghanistan, warned that the armed forces were on the brink of collapse. Two weeks later, Defense Minister Igor Rodionov warned that the "extreme" economic and political instability may produce "unpredictable, catastrophic consequences" for the armed forces and for the country as a whole. Prime Minister Chernomyrdin was so worried about unrest within the military that he personally traveled to Ryazan to reassure paratroopers that their wages were coming. Analysts and politicians alike, including General Alexander Lebed, have speculated that the Russian military was nearing mutiny.

Others have predicted renewed tension between the center of the federation and its subjects. The ten richest regions of Russia have expressed their unwillingness to subsidize the budgets of the other seventy oblasts, krais, and republics through the inefficient centralized system of transfer currently in place. Instead, the more outspoken leaders of these donor regions, such as Moscow's mayor, Yurii Luzhkov, have called for a "new deal" between the federation subjects that would exclude the Russian federal government altogether. Because governors are now elected officials, the prospect of renewed tension between the center and the subjects of the federation seems to be growing.

Public opinion polls suggest that the same electorate that supported Yeltsin overwhelmingly in July does not believe that he or his government can deal with these crises. Yeltsin's approval rating has declined considerably since the 1996 summer ballot. In November, only ten percent of the Russian population trusted Yeltsin, down from 29 percent in June. More generally, mood polls conducted by the All-Russian Foundation for Public Opinion (VTsIOM) show that people are much less optimistic about the future than they were just months ago.

Taking into account these crises and these opinion poll numbers, many have concluded that the aforementioned milestones of democracy do not mean anything. For these analysts, Russian politics have not changed with the introduction of elections. The historical analogue of choice varies; for some, politics in Russia today looks like the late Brezhnev period, for others the Stalinist period, and for still others, tsarist days. But the basic premise remains the same—continuity with past authoritarian traditions is paramount, and change in the direction of liberalism is trivial.

How can we explain this divergence between apparent achievements in the process of democratization of the Russian political system and perceptions of the lack of progress? The heart of the answer is located in the nature of the Russian state. Russia's leaders have neither the will nor the capacity to meet the demands of Russia's citizens. This is because the state does not represent the interests of society as a whole, but rather reflects the interests of Russia's emergent capitalist class. In a sense, the state has been privatized by this nouveau riche class, thereby operating as an instrument of its new owners rather than the broader society. Consequently, the elections and rituals of a democratic polity more generally have only a temporary influence on the policy process.

Moreover, even if state rulers did respond to the interests of pluralist groups rather than merely the interests of corporate groups, the state still does not have the capacity to meet these demands. Just like the economy, the state collapsed in the fall of 1991. Since this simultaneous collapse of state and economy, Russian reformers rightly have devoted energy and resources to transforming the economy from a command system to a market. A commensurate reform program, however, has not been initiated to create a market-friendly, democratic state. Consequently, state reform has lagged considerably behind the market reform. This "bad" state constitutes one of the greatest impediments to deepening both political and economic reform.

To develop this argument about the centrality of the state to Russia's current impasse, this essay proceeds as follows. The next section defines the state and its characteristics, focusing in particular on state autonomy, interest intermediation between state and society, and state capacity. The next three sections then discuss each of the characteristics in detail. Section six concludes with observations of how this current equilibrium might change.

II. Measuring state power and effectiveness

The state is the set of government institutions that define and implement national policy. State power and effectiveness vary along three principal components: 1) state autonomy, 2) the kind of institutions of interest intermediation, and 3) state capacity. State autonomy refers to the state's ability to define preferences independent of society. The kind of interest intermediation dominant in a polity determines "in whose interest" the state acts. Pluralist institutions of interest intermediation favor mass-based groups, while corporatist institutional arrangements prefer small, well-organized economic interest groups. State capacity is a measure of the state's ability to implement preferences.

The Soviet/Russian state has undergone a tremendous transformation regarding these three parameters, migrating from a very capacious and autonomous state representing the interests of the Communist Party of the Soviet Union (CPSU) to a state with little autonomy or capacity representing the interests of big business. The following three sections explore this transformation in detail.

III. State collapse

The Soviet regime consolidated by Stalin was one of the most autonomous states of the twentieth century. Under Stalin, the Soviet state defined the creation of socialism (in one country) as its primary objective and then used coercion, violence, and mass murder to accomplish this task. Stalin's USSR was the paradigmatic definition of a totalitarian state. State policies were defined and implemented without reference to societal demands. Instead, only the interests of the Communist Party of the Soviet Union were served, to such an extent that the distinction between Party and state became meaningless. This omnipresent Party-state in turn blurred the lines between state and society as the Soviet regime penetrated virtually every sector and aspect of "private" life.

By 1991, this state no longer existed. While still totalitarian in structure, the Soviet state had weakened considerably throughout the Brezhnev years. Gorbachev's reforms further undermined the autonomy of the state to define and implement policy goals. Under Gorbachev, the main administrative agent of the Soviet system—the Communist Party—lost its "leading role," and no effective institution emerged to fill the void. Beginning in the fall of 1990, Boris Yeltsin and Democratic Russia directly challenged the sovereign authority of the Soviet regime on Russian territory. This revolutionary challenge gradually undermined the Soviet state. The absolute failure of the August 1991 coup attempt starkly exposed the state's weakness .

In the wake of the aborted August putsch, Yeltsin emerged as the most legitimate and powerful leader in Russia. He used this sudden profusion of political power to undermine many key components of the Soviet state. He banned the CPSU, assumed control of several Soviet institutions and subordinated them to the authority of the Russian state; and then abolished political institutions that competed with existing Russian institutions, including first and foremost the Soviet Congress of People's Deputies and the Soviet presidency. Finally, in December 1991, Yeltsin signed an agreement with his counterparts in Ukraine and Belarus effectively dismantled the Soviet state.

Yeltsin, however, refrained from further transforming the Russian state. Instead, he and his government opted to focus almost exclusively on economic transformation. He did not push the adoption of a new constitution, although a first draft of a new fundamental law produced by the Supreme Soviet Constitutional Commission (chaired by Yeltsin) had been circulated as early as October 1990. Yeltsin's new regime also did little to institutionalize its popular support in society. Yeltsin did not establish a political party or call for elections to stimulate party development. Despite repeated pleas from Democratic Russia, Yeltsin refused to call new elections in the fall of 1991, and postponed regional elections slated for the winter. Yeltsin also did not dismantle many Soviet-era governmental institutions, including, most importantly, the Supreme

Soviet and the Congress of People's Deputies. At the same time, Yeltsin did not insulate the state from societal pressures by erecting an authoritarian regime.

The Russian team of economic technocrats in charge of the government saw state reform as a nuisance to the more important task of creating a market economy. The state, in fact, was viewed as an enemy of neoliberal reform, as states were thought to use their powers to intervene, distort, and prey upon the market. If the state can be extricated from the economy, these theorists held, markets had a better chance of succeeding.

This attitude proved costly. Decisions, or the lack thereof, enacted by the Yeltsin government after the coup precipitated an even further weakening of an already feeble state. Fractures within the Russian state appeared both between different levels of government and between different branches of the central government, dramatically undermining the autonomy of the state as an independent actor. With no constitutional delineation of rights and responsibilities between central and local authorities, regional governments seized the moment of Soviet collapse to attain greater political and economic autonomy. The stalemate between different branches of the central government proved even more dire. Soon after ceding decree power to Yeltsin in November 1991, the Russian Supreme Soviet and the Russian Congress of People's Deputies began a campaign to reassert their authority as the "highest state organs." Even after Yeltsin's referendum victory in April 1993, the Congress continued to impede executive initiatives, constrain ministerial power, and pass laws contradicting Yeltsin's decrees. With no formal, or even informal, institutions to structure relations between the president and the Congress, the state virtually ceased to function. Yeltsin's dramatic actions in September and October 1993 reflected the degree to which Russia's government had stopped governing.

In his decree dissolving the Congress of People's Deputies, Yeltsin also called for immediate elections for a new parliament and a referendum to adopt a new constitution. This new basic law was ratified by the people in the December 1993 vote. After years of ambiguity Russia had a new set of formal rules for organizing politics, acceptable to the majority of the population and to all strategic political actors. Yeltsin's decree also called for elections to a new parliament, thereby establishing elections as the mechanism for empowering leaders. Subsequently, as mentioned above, Russian citizens voted in parliamentary elections both in 1993 and again in 1995, in presidential elections in the summer of 1996, and in gubernatorial elections throughout the fall of 1996. This sequence of elections signaled an important turning point in Russia's troubled transition to democracy. For the first time, strategic actors committed themselves to a set of rules governing political competition before they knew the results that these rules would produce. The institutionalization of elections as a way of selecting government officials also crowded out alternative, non-democratic models for determining who governs.

Progress regarding these formal electoral institutions, however, has not enhanced state autonomy. On the contrary, the Russian state today enjoys little autonomy from societal interests, but rather merely reflects the sum of societal forces. Not all societal interest groups, however, are represented equally. Russia's state is deeply penetrated and controlled by the interests of big business. As a general rule in society, smaller groups with narrow purposes are more likely to effectively organize than larger groups with broader agendas. Capitalist groups tend to be small in number and focused in their demands; for these groups, organization is easier than it is for their larger counterparts. Consequently, all of economic interest groups will not be represented equally. This imbalance is especially acute in Russia.

IV. Interest intermediation between state and society

Since January 1992, when Yeltsin's government initiated radical economic reform, the emergence of a market economy based on private property rights has stimulated the growth of a powerful and new "economic society." Three features of Russia's emerging capitalism are most significant to the development of interest articulation within the Russian state. First, capital is concentrated sectorally: Dynamic economic activity is located in trade and services, banking, and the export of raw materials, particularly oil and gas; production of manufactured goods of any sort has decreased steadily since 1990; small enterprise development, after a boom in the late Gorbachev era, has steadily decreased as a percentage share of GNP. Second, capital is concentrated geographically, with an estimated 80 percent of Russia's capital assets located in Moscow. Third, capital is closely tied to the state. Through privatization, the financing of state transfers, and the loans-for-shares program, Russian banks are still dependent on inside information and money from the state for profits. The intimate relationship between the state and the private sector is even more apparent in sectors exporting raw materials, as the state retains large equity stakes in all of these enterprises, and yet refuses to tax effectively these corporations.

A concentrated, centralized capitalist class, intimately if not parasitically tied to the state, already has left its mark on the preferences of the Russian state. Interest articulation and intermediation are dominated by a big business sector that crowds out other interest groups in lobbying the state. This sector's dominance over government leaders and the state was demonstrated most recently during the 1996 presidential election. While divided in the past over both political issues and markets, Russia's corporate bosses united during the presidential campaign to provide Boris Yeltsin with virtually unlimited resources and total control of the national media. During the campaign, these plutocrats also waged a successful effort to dismiss Yeltsin's original campaign team—headed by former first deputy prime minister Oleg Soskovets—and replace it with "their" campaign team, under the direction of Anatolii Chubais.

In return for this support, this small, well-organized interest group has enjoyed tremendous "representation" within the Russian state since the election. The most direct and obvious method of state control is through appointments. Russia's Prime Minister, Viktor Chernomyrdin, is the former chairman of Gazprom, Russia's largest company. With Chernomyrdin at the head of the government, the state has rarely acted against the interests of the oil and gas sector. Russian bankers are also well-represented in the current government. Their most powerful ally and representative is Anatolii Chubais, Yeltsin's current chief of staff. As the former head of the State Privatization Committee, Chubais has been closely tied to Russia's new financiers from the beginning. Allegedly as a condition of their financial support during the campaign, Russia's banking tycoons demanded that Chubais become chief of staff after the election. Some of these funders of Yeltsin's campaign were not content simply to have their representatives in government, but themselves wanted to try their hand in the "public" sector. Vladimir Potanin, the former head of the powerful financial group Oneksimbank, became deputy prime minister, and Boris Berezovsky, the head of Logovaz, was given the position of deputy chairman of the Security Council.

Like other presidential systems, Russia's superpresidentialism privileges big business lobbies and disadvantages mass based organizations that are better equipped to lobby legislatures than executives. The Duma, however, is not immune to Russia's business lobbies. A well-established system of bribe-taking has been formalized within the Duma in which business lobbies in the Duma pay cash directly to Duma deputies in return for votes. Less audaciously, big business lobbies also acquired tremendous influence over parliamentary factions by financing campaigns in the 1995 elections. In several cases, individual businessmen bought their positions on a party list. Zhirinovsky's Liberal Democratic Party was most open about offering Duma seats for money, but such transactions also occurred regarding the Yabloko and Our Home Is Russia lists.

The weakness of political parties

Big business enjoys hegemonic control over the Russian state in part because of the relative weakness of countervailing interest groups and institutions. Most importantly, Russia's party system remains extremely weak. In pluralist democracies, parties traditionally serve as the principal institution mediating societal interests within the state. In Russia, however, parties play only a marginal role in interest intermediation. While elections in Russia have produced positive signs of consolidation since 1993, the legacies of Russia's first failed transition still linger in regards to the development of a party system in Russia.

Russia still has too many ineffective parties and too few effective parties. In 1993, thirteen parties competed for seats on the PR list; in 1995, forty-three parties made the ballot. The 1995 parliamentary vote evidently promoted consolidation of party lists, as only four of these forty-three parties crossed the 5 percent threshold for entry into the Duma. However, all of these parliamentary parties have uncertain futures and poor records of representation.

Vladimir Zhirinovsky's Liberal Democratic Party of Russia (LDPR) has created an extensive network of regional offices and local organizers, but it remains unclear whether this organization is a cultist movement or a political party, as the organization would collapse almost instantaneously without Zhirinovsky. Our Home Is Russia, the political group founded by Prime Minister Viktor Chernomyrdin, is endowed with significant financial resources, government support, and modest regional organization, but easily could follow the fate of earlier "parties of power" in Russia and disintegrate. Grigorii Yavlinsky's Yabloko, the only reformist party not connected to the government that won parliamentary seats in both 1993 and 1995, most closely resembles a proto-party, complete with a parliamentary faction, grassroots regional organizations and internal democratic procedures. However, Yabloko's small faction in the parliament and near lack of penetration into government bodies outside of Moscow and St. Petersburg will assign this nascent party a marginal role in Russian politics in the near future. Only the Communist Party of the Russian Federation (CPRF) looks like a real, national party with a well articulated social base that will outlive its current leaders. Strikingly, however, the Communist party has not demonstrated a proclivity for legislating on behalf of its constituents as the Duma's largest faction. Since losing the presidential election in the summer of 1996, the CPRF has grown increasingly cooperative with the government, signaling a real rapprochement between old and new political elites—elites that both originated from the Communist Party of the Soviet Union.

Outside of the Duma, parties play virtually no role at all in aggregating, articulating or representing societal interests. Yeltsin is an "independent," while his executive administration is insulated from party influence. As in all presidential systems, Russia's strong executive system has downgraded the importance of political parties. Likewise, few executive leaders at the oblast, krai and republic level have open party affiliations. During the cascade of elections of regional executives in the fall of 1996, in which 52 leaders were chosen, political parties played only a marginal role in selecting and endorsing candidates. Several newly elected governors, including such prominent partisans as Aleksandr Rutskoi, renounced their party credentials after winning election. Most of the regional legislatures are dominated by local "parties of power" with no ideological affiliation and strong ties to local executive heads.

More generally, the limited number of elected offices and the low frequency of elections to these offices at the sub-national level of government have provided few opportunities for parties to play their organizing role during elections. A nascent party system has emerged in Russia, stimulated primarily by the PR component of the parliamentary electoral system; but this party system is still fragmented and Moscow-centric, and thereby peripheral to the organization and articulation of interests in Russia's political system.

The weakness of civil society

The void of mass-based representation left by Russia's weak parties has not been filled by other mass-based groups. Other economic actors are dwarfed by both the wealth and political organization of bankers, oil and gas exporters, and their allies. Directors of formerly state-owned enterprises, once a relatively unified lobby, have now fractured into several sectoral and regional industrial organizations. Civic Union, the electoral bloc most firmly identified with this economic group, garnered only 1.9 percent of the popular vote in 1993, prompting many factory managers to gravitate back to the "party of power" (Chernomyrdin's bloc and Yeltsin's campaign) as the only political organization worthy of investment. Paradoxically, then, enterprise directors throughout a wide variety of industrial sectors have had a confluence of political interests in the short run, with both old money from raw material exporters and new money from Russia's financiers and bankers. Some enterprises of the military industrial complex have formed alliances with opposition parties and lobbies such as the CPRF and Congress of Russian Communities, but the influence of this segment of Russia's economic society has steadily declined since 1992.

Small businesses and start-up companies have been hurt the most by the kind of capitalism emerging in Russia. Exorbitant taxes, inflation, the lack of liberalization at the local level, the mafia, and the consolidation of large financial groups exerting monopoly control over many markets have created a very unfriendly environment for small businesses. Consequently, this economic interest group—the backbone of many consolidated democracies—is weak, disorganized, and depoliticized in Russia.

Labor is also disoriented and disorganized in the midst of Russia's economic transformation. Old Soviet trade unions, once a tool of control for the Soviet Communist Party, have been slow to reorganize to meet the new challenges of capitalism. The Federation of Independent Free Trade Unions (FNPR), a consortium of sectorally-based unions claiming over 50 million members, in most cases still identifies with the interests of directors rather than workers. As the interests of management and labor diverge, the FNPR has gradually lost its credibility with both groups, making it a politically inconsequential. In the 1996 presidential elections, the FNPR did not endorse a candidate, nor have truly independent trade unions filled the void. The Independent Union of Miners, the coalition of strike committees that brought the Soviet government to its knees in 1991, lost its independence and credibility by consistently siding with the Yeltsin government over the last five years. Wildcat strikes, particularly in coal regions and the Far East, persist, raising some speculation that Russian labor finally has started to remobilize; the lack of national organization however suggests that these strikes will remain isolated instances.

More generally, participation in overt political activity by civic groups may have peaked as early as 1990 as part of the nationwide anti-communist movement. Since then, independent civic groups have played less and less a role in the organization and conduct of state policy for several reasons. First, the ability of civic groups to articulate and lobby for their interests vis-a-vis the state in Russia's post-Communist era has been impeded by the same factors retarding party development more generally—structural changes in the economy and society, delayed development of pluralist institutions (especially the weakness of representative institutions), and the commensurate ascendancy of executive power. Second, the civil society that was emerging in the latter years of the Soviet Union was undercut by the shocks of Russia's economic revolution. As with the labor movement, Russia's new market-embedded society has not sufficiently consolidated to develop market-embedded social organizations. Additionally, post-communist grass roots organizations have no financial resources, as the "middle class"—the financier of most civic groups in the West—has not yet emerged in Russia. Third, famous anti-Communist civic groups such as Memorial (a nationwide grassroots organization dedicated to commemorating the victims of Stalinism) lost their raison d'etre in the post-Communist era. The Chechen war briefly mobilized human rights leaders and organizations, but the low level of mass participation in their protest acts underscored the fact that post-Communist Russian society in January 1995 had developed a new set of concerns and interests different from Soviet society in 1991.

The development of a vibrant post-Communist civil society is further hampered by the sequence and kind of consolidation of Russia's political institutions. The suspension of party development from 1991 to 1993 served to keep civic groups out of state politics. If the party system is underdeveloped, then the ability of civic organizations to influence the state is also impaired. By the time parties began to play a more substantial role in politics after the 1993 parliamentary elections, the disconnection between political society and civic society was nearly total: civic organizations saw no benefit from participating in the electoral process while political parties discerned no electoral benefit from catering to allegedly small and ineffective civic groups. Instead of a civil society concerned with influencing the state, Russia has developed an "a-civil" society concerned with insulating itself from the state.

The absence of the rule of law

Historically, in the evolution of other democracies, well-organized business interests have assumed disproportionate influence over the state during periods of rapid industrialization or capital accumulation. Mass-based interest groups typically gained access to the state much later. In the United States, excluded mass-based groups—minorities, women or labor—fought for enfranchisement through the independent courts system. This key set of independent institutions does not exist in Russia. The Soviet legacy, of course, has impeded the development of rule of law, as the Soviet Communist regime accorded the courts no autonomy whatsoever. Since 1991, the idea of an independent judiciary has been supported in theory by virtually every major political force in Russia, but only a few positive steps have been made.

Russia's first Constitutional Court relinquished its authority as arbitrator between the president and parliament in 1993, when the head of the Court, Valerii Zorkin, unequivocally sided with White House defenders during the October 1993 crisis. For a year thereafter, the Court ceased to function, and convened again only after Yeltsin had expanded the number of justices to dilute the voice of his opponents. Since reconvening, the Court has made few important decisions.

At lower levels, courts are revamping slowly to deal with the new challenges of a market economy. Institutionalization of a legal system to protect property rights, govern bankruptcy procedures, enforce contracts and insure competition has only just begun. The adoption of the Civil Code (hailed as Russia's "economic constitution") by parliament constituted a first step towards creating these institutions, but only a first step. In the corporate legal context, laws on disclosure are weak and not enforced, general accounting procedures have not been codified, procedures for shareholder and proxy voting are ambiguous, and institutions governing the payment of dividends do not exist. Consequently, stockholders have little access to information about enterprises in which they have invested. "Rule of law" also has become weaker regarding criminal and civil matters. The combination of a weak state and incompetent judicial system has produced a sense of anarchy in Russia, a situation alien and frightening to a population accustomed to a powerful authoritarian state. Popular cries for law and order, in turn, threaten to undermine individual liberties and human rights.

State capacity

The strength of big business, the weakness of political parties, labor, and civil society, and the virtual absence of rule of law have combined to allow the Russian state to act in the interests of Russia's richest. This configuration has impeded not only democratic consolidation regarding political transformation, but has also blocked a deepening of economic reform. Most importantly, this small group of financiers and resource exporters has used its dominance over the state to discourage direct foreign investment, its greatest enemy. Perhaps most amazingly, this economic clique has forced the costs of stabilization onto Russian laborers. Where else in the world is inflation controlled by simply not paying wages for months at a time. Obviously, the preferences of mass-based interest groups find little voice in Russia's contemporary state configuration.

However, even if these mass-based interest groups were articulated, organized and influential, Russia's contemporary state still would have little capacity to act upon their interests. This observation seems counterintuitive, as the Russian state on paper appears bigger and more extensive than most states in developed capitalist democracies. These figures, though, tell little about the state's actual capacity to execute policy decisions. Neither parliamentary laws nor presidential decrees are enforced since the state has little coercive capability against—or legitimacy within—society. For similar reasons, the state has not been very successful at collecting taxes. The state's capacity to act shrinks commensurately to its revenue base. The most respected and capacious state institutions in Russia are located at the lowest levels of government, providing another impediment to state action at the federal level.

The consequences of this declining state capacity in Russia have been dramatic. Basic services traditionally provided by the Soviet/Russian state, such as security, welfare and education, are no longer public goods. Employees of the state must negotiate and strike just to be paid for work already completed. At the same time, corruption within the government remains rampant.

Conclusion

The Russian state has neither the will nor the ability to act upon citizen preferences. To the extent that it functions at all, Russia's state primarily serves the interests of a small group of business elites in Moscow. Pluralist institutions of interest intermediation are weak, mass-based interest groups are marginal, and institutions that could help to redress this imbalance—such as a strong parliament or an independent court system—do not exist. Under these conditions, elections appear ritualistic, bearing little impact on conduct or operation of the state. During a brief campaign period, candidates may seem responsive to popular interests, but once in office a different set of preferences—the preferences of big business—takes precedence. Under these conditions, it should not be surprising that opinion polls demonstrate a strong distrust in the government and a lack of optimism about the future.

To argue that the state has neither the will nor the capacity to meet the expectations of its citizens does not mean that the situation is unstable or that crisis, breakdown, or revolution is inevitable. On the contrary, weak states dominated by big business and insulated from societal pressures have existed for decades in other countries. Russia might be no different.

Three factors can alter this situation. First, and least likely, leaders currently in control of the state could turn against those that helped bring them to power and instead begin to attend to the interests of mass-based groups. Yeltsin is the one political actor in the current state with the capability to carry out a painful and destabilizing reform of the state from within. Perhaps thinking about his place in history, Yeltsin could initiate such a radical internal reform. So far, however, there are few signs that Yeltsin is prepared to initiate such changes, as his health problems have diminished his imprint on the conduct of his own government.

Second, an exogenous shock could come from society, forcing the state to change. For instance, sustained strikes in strategic industries could have crippling consequences for the current government, as they did for the Soviet regime in 1991. Weak states have little capacity to absorb even relatively minor crises. The situation in Primorskii Krai in the fall of 1996 is illustrative. The elected governor of this region, Evgenii Nazdratenko, is considered one of the most authoritarian of all Russia's governors. He and his government enjoy an intimate relationship with PAKT, a local big business consortium. In the fall of 1996, however, Nazdratenko had to scramble for his political life after workers at the local power station went on strike to demand back wages. Moscow sided with the striking workers and threatened to remove Nazdratenko if he did not pay the wages immediately. While the governor kept his job in the end, the crisis illustrated that even powerful and elected governors can be quickly undermined by organized mass action.

Third, new elections might bring to power new leaders of mass-based groups, not beholden to big business, with the will to use the state to serve the interests of a wider segment of the population (both Roosevelts, in the United States, used government this way). Currently, Alexander Lebed has positioned himself as the person most likely to initiate state reform on behalf of all voters. Ultimately, the current equilibrium will change only when the state can be deployed to destroy monopolies, tax profit-makers, and provide a more favorable environment for market competition. While a slow process, this change is most likely to happen through the ballot box.

When understood in this longer time framework, the elections of 1995 and 1996 may have more far-reaching consequences than were immediately apparent. By helping to establish elections as the most likely instrument of change and reform, these may indeed be milestones that will provide the means for democratic renewal in Russia in the future.

Michael McFaul is an Assistant Professor of Political Science at Stanford University and a Senior Associate at the Moscow Carnegie Center.

The non-Russian States: Soviet Legacies, Post-Soviet Transformations

Alexander J. Motyl

Five years after the Soviet Union's break-up, most of the non-Russian successor states are a mess. While the unbounded optimism of 1989-1991 was understandable, post-Soviet transformations could not avoid being affected by a "totalitarian legacy" that must be understood if it is to be transcended. Not surprisingly, reform has been tentative, change has been directionless, and improvements have been painstakingly slow.

Freedom House surveys support this gloomy conclusion. While most of the East-Central European and Baltic states have been "free" since the early 1990s, the newly independent states still are, as of 1996, either "not free" (Belarus, Azerbaijan, Kazakstan, Uzbekistan, Turkmenistan, and Tajikistan) or "partly free" (Ukraine, Moldova, Georgia, Armenia, and Kyrgyzstan), and virtually none had a different score from the year before. Indeed, if there is any trend since 1991-1992, it is toward fewer political rights and civil liberties. Most of the non-Russian states have equally dismal economic scores, which enhance the overall impression of glacial movement, if not complete stasis.

Western observers generally blame non-Russian policy makers for the absence of fundamental change. There is a kernel of truth in the charge that they lack vision and political will, but it misses the larger point. The institutional legacies inherited from the Soviet Union have precluded—thus far—desired changes, while inclining non-Russian policy makers toward undesirable forms of political and economic behavior.

The non-Russian successor states did not, after all, come from nowhere. Each had the status of a nominally independent polity within the world's only totalitarian empire. The Communist Party of the Soviet Union (CPSU) and the secret police, the KGB, reigned supreme in an all-encompassing totalitarian system that permitted only pro-Soviet and pro-Communist institutions to exist. The public activities that characterize democracy, rule of law, civil society and the market were taboo. In turn, the imperial structure of the Soviet bloc privileged the Party-state apparatus housed in Moscow, ensured that the Party-state elite was either Russian or Russified, and deprived the non-Russian republics and East Central European satellites of sovereignty.

Not all Soviet-dominated states experienced the same degree of totalitarian intrusiveness and imperial rule. The East-Central Europeans—Poles, Czechs, Slovaks, Hungarians, Bulgarians, and Romanians—were most autonomous, possessing ready-made elites, armies, police forces, courts, borders, and bureaucracies, even if inefficient ones. Many of them also had elements of civil society and the market: churches, underground media, political movements, "flying universities," and privately held farms and shops.

The majority of non-Russian Soviet republics were least autonomous, completely lacking states, elites, civil society, rule of law, and the market. For a variety of histori-

stan, Uzbekistan, and Belarus have constructed veritable cults of personal-

ia, Armenia, Moldova, Kyrgyzstan, and Ukraine have made somewhat more
ut they, too, continue to face enormous problems. Secessionist movements
ia and South Ossetia, warlordism in the "stable" parts of the country, and
collapse have brought Georgia, despite President Eduard Shevardnadze's
ions, to its knees. Armenia is committed to a costly policy of mini-imperi-
gorno-Karabakh, while its president, Levon Ter-Petrossian, has been will-
er with election procedures in order to remain in office. Moldova remains
ussia's muscle-flexing 14th Army and a secessionist republic in the trans-
gion. Kyrgyzstan is experiencing a Russian brain drain, is surrounded by
ctatorships, and has a president, Askar Akaev, with increasingly authori-
ncies. Ukraine seems stable, but, despite not unimpressive reform efforts
t Leonid Kuchma, the economy still requires massive restructuring before
living standards and ensure long-term stability.

this panorama, several issues deserve special attention: state building and
cratization and civil society; economic reform and corruption; and nation
d ethnic conflict. An analysis of current trends suggests that not only are
markets, and civil society still far off in the future, but that, in the process
get from here to there, the non-Russian states may even be derailed from
ed transitions. When one considers this sobering prospect together with
Russia is unlikely to become a market-oriented democracy anytime soon,
bability of instability in the post-Soviet political space must be consid-
ingly high.

ding and elites

essing issue facing all of the non-Russian states is, arguably, state build-
democratization and economic reform. Genuine democracy and genuine
clusters of institutions and not merely sets of participatory attitudes and
ial dispositions, require a political base—an effective administrative appa-
working government—in order to be viable. Indeed, policy making
mplementing of any kind, be it with respect to the administration of
e maintenance of law and order, or taxation, requires states. Finally, state
together with militaries, police forces, border guards, and the like, en-
to sustain themselves internationally, to preserve their security, and to

above, however, none of the non-Russian republics inherited state appa-
bureaucracies were shapeless and oriented on directives from Moscow;
es were either undermanned or nonexistent; and their elites were trained
ers vertically, from Moscow, and lacked the horizontal institutional ties
requisite of functioning states and effective elites.

all the proto-elites that came to power in the republics were committed
ates, establishing authority, acquiring power and extending their politi-
the provinces, the malfunctioning economic and political systems they
ctively undermined their state-building efforts. In turn, marginal suc-
ilding had profound consequences for a variety of other transformative

cal reasons, the Baltic republics—Estonia, Latvia, and
mediate position between East-Central Europe and th
a category of its own, as the core of the empire and th
In sum, identifiable clusters of Soviet-bloc countries
cies that shaped the range of subsequent possible bel

The East-Central Europeans and the Balts were b
successfully complete, their transitions to democracy
political wherewithal to begin its transitions, but not
that its own institutional legacies created. The non-F
advantaged; thus, they were least likely to initiate ch;
the course.

Soviet legacies

The institutions constituting democracy, rule of la
state are what the non-Russian republics did not inh
then, *did* they inherit? First and foremost, the remr
viet economy; in particular, a structure whose functi
a center that no longer existed and on centrally de
too, collapsed with the collapse of the USSR. Seco
ized economy, which meant that economic power
industrial plants who, as a result, could assume eve
and, oftentimes, national politics.

Third, the non-Russian republics remained ho
cal of the Soviet period. Now as then, political co
gional groupings of Communist old-boy networks
the "Dnipropetrovsk mafia" that served Leonid Bre;
although party systems were woefully undevelop
did stand out, retaining much of its influence at all
former republican branches of the CPSU.

These legacies combined to create a partic
amalgam. Dilapidated economies, powerful mana
Communist *apparatchiks* fused into closed networ
taining a status quo that enabled them to live off
sites of power. To have expected such elites to
recommended by Western advisors was utterly
reformers among them to succeed in pushing th
hensively was no less unrealistic, as the oppositi
task envisioned—the simultaneous construction
of law, and civil societies—was historically unp

Thus, while surviving Soviet institutions we
necessary and desirable, these changes were so
able under the best of conditions. Small wond
changed only marginally.

Within these general trends there are substan
Tajikistan, Turkmenistan, Belarus, and Azerbaij
political systems are least open, their economies
are most inclined to clan-based authoritaria:

Turkmen
ity.

Geor
progress,
in Abkha
economic
best inter
alism in N
ing to tam
home to F
Dniester
unstable c
tarian tene
by Preside
it can rais

Withi:
elites; den
building a
democracy
of trying t
their inten
the fact tha
then the pi
ered distre

State bu

The most p
ing, and no
markets, as
entrepreneu
ratus and a
and policy
territories,
apparatuses
able politie;
survive.

As note
ratuses. The
their ministi
to receive o
that are a pr

Althoug
to building s
cal reach int
inherited eff
cess at state
goals.

Democratization and civil society

The shapelessness of the non-Russian states precluded the development of genuine democratic institutions on the one hand, while encouraging clan politics and presidential authoritarianism on the other. All of the non-Russian states developed presidencies, parliaments, parties and constitutions, but for the most part these proto-institutions remained amorphous arenas within which Soviet-era personalities, bosses and clans could compete for power and riches. Naturally, even feeble institutions and manipulated elections are significant departures from the totalitarian past. Moreover, the fact that relations between parliaments and presidents were stalemated in most non-Russian states did produce a *modus vivendi* that, over time, could lay the foundations for genuine rules of the game.

In the short run at least, these developments seemed unlikely to grow institutional roots, precisely because the formlessness of political life permitted the worst vestiges of the Soviet past to establish a formidable political and social presence in the system as a whole. Thus, in the absence of state-like institutions able to enforce rules of the game, the field was open for the best organized forces—political bosses, regional and ethnic clans, former Communist apparatchiks, and coalitions of industrial managers and regional power holders—to seize control of the emerging polities. Genuine democracy could not really take hold, because these forces were strong enough to absorb democratic reforms and to tailor emerging democratic institutions to their own ends.

No less important, in all of the non-Russian states—as indeed in many East-Central European states and Russia as well—presidents tended to accumulate enormous powers, while the political systems as a whole acquired increasingly presidential, if not quite authoritarian, tendencies. Neither trend was surprising. Given the institutional formlessness and deadlock at the core of most of the governments, powerful politicians could rise above the fray and, like Napoleon III, achieve Olympian stature. Because parliaments were pitted against presidents in undefined circumstances, presidents naturally had the upper hand in confrontations. Their capacity to act as willful actors stood in sharp contrast to the divisiveness of parliaments, which resembled raucous agglomerations of individuals with no sense of party discipline and little commitment to actual institution building. If presidents were reformers, the authoritarian tendency could be packaged as political will, but even then, the price, potentially, is high.

Given the emergence of strong executives facing weak legislatures, presidents had every incentive to bypass parliaments and to form alliances with regional power brokers—the clans that ran bits and pieces of the countries. Clan politics did have a positive side, permitting regional elites to circulate and, possibly, to develop feelings of state legitimacy. Less auspiciously, however, such alliances also stood to transform states into under-institutionalized systems ruled by combinations of strong men, regional mafias, and local bosses.

Fortunately, the autonomous institutions that comprise civil society could and did develop even under such conditions. Churches, clubs, parties, newspapers and NGOs were a welcome development, but, being confined to the nonpolitical nooks and crannies of life, their impact was largely social, cultural, and intellectual. Civil society, like public opinion, was too removed from the corridors of power, and lacked the institutional channels to influence decision-makers who plied their trade in the arena of the state. As one Russian scholar put it last summer: "The state used to repress civil society in Soviet times. Now the state just ignores us. Which is worse?"

Economic reform and corruption

The weakness of the state, the prevalence of strong presidents and clan politics, and the irrelevance of civil society left their greatest mark on the economy and economic reform. In general, radical economic reform was inconsistent with the interests of the power holders, all of whom had a stake in the continuation of a dilapidated system that permitted them to live off the polity, economy and society in comfortably parasitic fashion. Even where coalitions of policy makers could agree on radical change, they were generally incapable of pushing it to its logical conclusion—not necessarily for lack of political will or intelligence, but precisely because their own political will and intelligence encouraged a sober appreciation of the possible.

The formlessness of the state meant that centrally generated laws and decrees had little influence outside the capital cities, and more often than not, in the capitals as well. As a rule, genuine reforms were therefore confined to macroeconomic issues, largely because monetary and fiscal policy was the exclusive prerogative of central policy makers and did not presuppose an effective state for its implementation. Privatization inevitably proceeded far more slowly than envisioned, because regional bosses either resisted it or, alternatively, used such laws as pretexts for expropriating the assets they already controlled.

The scope for crime and corruption was thus enormous. The economic assets formerly controlled by the Soviet party-state now devolved automatically, either to the managers that ran them or to emerging clans or mafia structures that had the resources and experience to seize them. Even if, as seems likely, the non-Russian economies eventually bottom out and begin growing, the prime beneficiaries of growth will most likely not, in general, be the masses. Rather, political elites, regional clans, and criminal forces will exploit institutional formlessness to pursue their own interests without regard for the well-being of the population in general.

Russia may be a harbinger of things to come. Economic revitalization seemed to go hand in hand with economic criminalization and the continued misery, if not immiseration, of broad segments of the population. By the same token, the rich oil and gas deposits possessed by Azerbaijan, Turkmenistan, and Kazakstan are a mixed blessing. They will increase the revenues available to these states, but they may also transform them into Third World *rentier* states, with coupon-clipping elites inclined to extravagant life-styles as well as the construction of fragile political systems susceptible to breakdown in response to sudden changes in world market prices.

Nation building and ethnic conflict

Building a coherent sense of nationhood on such weak foundations may have been a hopeless task. Neither a weak state, a feeble civil society nor an enervated economy could promote feelings of national solidarity or legitimacy. Native culture, native language and ethnic roots had some intrinsic appeal, but that was limited, as most populations had been thoroughly sovietized and had poorly defined notions of who they were. Although some states maintained a commitment to "civic nationalism" for some time after 1991—Ukraine, Kyrgyzstan and possibly Kazakstan come to mind—this commitment was mostly due to the fact that, with large Russian-speaking populations, they had no choice. In general, the construction of bona fide nations, whether of the civic or ethnic variety, moved along at a snail's pace.

The low level of political, social and economic institutionalization, the declining economy, the emergence of regional bosses and clans, and the lack of an overarching national identity encouraged subnational ethnic groups to serve as the focal points of political and economic mobilization, and guaranteed that ethnic competition and conflict would be the order of the day. In Moldova, Russian generals mobilized the 14th Army and the Russian-speaking population against Cisinau. In Ukraine, Crimean Russians demanded independence, while Crimean Tatars demanded civil and human rights. In the Caucasus, the Armenians claimed Nagorno-Karabakh, the Abkhaz rebelled against Georgia, and the South Ossetians insisted on autonomy. In Kazakstan and Kyrgyzstan, Russians grumbled about autonomy and rights, while in Tajikistan clan leaders mobilized groups with regional loyalties against the government in Dushanbe.

Prospects for the future

Most worrisome for all the non-Russian states is the fact that countervailing forces are either absent or unlikely to kick in with any great force for some time to come. In other words, most of them will remain under-institutionalized, and authoritarian leaders will maintain their alliances with regional clans and local mafias; most economic benefits will go to a minority of the population, and corruption will be endemic; nations will remain amorphous, and ethnic conflict will not go away. In sum, the non-Russian states appear to be trapped on an inertial path that promises continued stagnation and decay for the foreseeable future.

None of this bodes well for democracy, civil society, rule of law, and the market, not to mention stable, normal relations among the non-Russians, and between them and Russia. On the one hand, their shapelessness will make it difficult for the non-Russian states to translate formal treaties and good intentions into genuine political and economic relationships. On the other hand, the fact that Russia has such overwhelming power, possesses a comparatively powerful state, and seems committed to a vision of manifest destiny translates into the virtual certainty that it will, either try to reassert—or be pushed into reasserting—its influence over the non-Russian states. Russia may succeed or it may fail, but neither outcome is likely to promote stability and security in Eurasia.

Alexander J. Motyl is associate director of Columbia University's Harriman Institute and a member of the Survey of Freedom Advisory Board.

East-Central Europe and the Baltics: Westward, Ho?

George Zarycky

Since the fall of postwar Marxist-Leninist regimes in the late 1980s, the political pendulum in East-Central Europe and the Baltics has swung over a broad spectrum. It moved in the early 1990s from anti-Communist ex-dissidents to ex-Communist and nationalist populist coalitions, whose variegated elements defied ideological labels at a time of profound transition. In 1996, even as societies remained divided over the pace, character, and social consequences of market reforms, Communist-era culpability, and ethno-national questions, the political plumb line appeared to be somewhere over the center. Ex-Communists fared poorly in elections in the Baltics, Albania, the Czech Republic, Romania, Bulgaria, and Slovenia. Extremist parties on the left and right remained peripheral, and ex-Communists in power in Poland and Hungary acted more like West European social democrats than Stalinists. Governments observed—with exceptions—basic democratic procedures, while civil societies continued to consolidate. Western-oriented trade and foreign policies aimed to speed integration into Europe's economic and security structures.

Most states recognized that conditions for membership in Western institutions—the Council of Europe, the EU, NATO, the OECD—required a measure of political stability, resolution of intra-state ethnic and border disputes (i.e. the Hungary-Romania border agreement), respect for human rights and civil liberties, and implementation of IMF guidelines to dismantle command economies. For the war-torn states of the former Yugoslavia, it also meant adherence to the Dayton Accords and, for Croatia and Serbia, foreign and domestic pressures for more open, democratic societies. Though economic conditions were uneven in the region, and in some places quite bad, market reforms and democracy continued to gain ground.

Positive trends

Encouraging news came from the southeastern corner of the old Soviet bloc. Romania and Bulgaria, long stigmatized as the region's political and economic laggards, moved to catch up with their more prosperous and democratic Visegrad neighbors (Poland, Hungary, the Czech Republic and, for the moment, Slovakia and Slovenia). Former Ceausescu toady Ion Iliescu was voted out as president of Romania, and the center-right Democratic Convention (CDR) trounced the ruling ex-Communist Party of Social Democracy in parliamentary elections. In Bulgaria, Peter Stoyanov of the Union of Democratic Forces (center-right) soundly defeated his ex-Communist challenger from the ruling Bulgarian Socialist Party (BSP). The fractious BSP cut loose Prime Minister Zhan Videnov, who resigned in late December.

Serb President Slobodan Milosevic was besieged by weeks of massive student-led protests after nullifying opposition victories in local elections. As the year drew to a close, the normally quiescent Orthodox Church called for a negotiated solution, and the federal army said it would not fire on peaceful demonstrators. Leaders of Montenegro, the long-suffering junior partner in rump-Yugoslavia, supported the demonstrators and asserted their independent-mindedness. Not surprisingly, Serb nationalists in Bosnia, who blame Milosevic for betraying their cause, also called on him to recognize local election results. Increasingly isolated, Milosevic hoped that control of the federal Yugoslav parliament by the Socialists and their allies would allow him to be elected federal president of Yugoslavia when his term as Serb president expired in 1997. He conceded opposition victory and offered some economic relief to workers and the rural population to keep them on the sidelines. With Milosevic no longer indispensable to the U.S. Bosnia peace effort, Washington and Europe have put pressure on him to compromise; otherwise, he risks reimposition of sanctions and jeopardizes aid from Western financial institutions like the IMF and World Bank. Yugoslavs are tired of being international pariahs living in a depressed, largely statist economy, and Milosevic's intransigence could set the stage for a wrenching, potentially violent transition period.

Bosnia: mixed signals

In Bosnia, over three years of carnage and ethnic cleansing stopped. But complex elections mandated by the Dayton Accords were marked by irregularities, new federal structures remained ineffectual, the Croat-Muslim federation existed only on paper, heavy arms had not been turned over, and hundreds of thousands of refugees neither voted nor repatriated. Croat refused to abide by municipal elections in Mostar, and violently discouraged non-Croatian refugees from returning to their homes. The pre-election period saw intimidation of candidates opposed to the major nationalist parties, as the OSCE allowed the ruling nationalist parties to run local election commissions. In Republika Srpska, the ruling Serbian Democratic Party harassed opposition candidates and barred access to local radio and television. In Croatian-dominant western Herzegovina, the Croatian Democratic Union kept a tight reign on the opposition. And President Izetbegovic's ruling Party for Democratic Action (SDA), which allegedly received campaign financing from Iran, used strong-arm tactics and media control to pressure opponents. A fragmented information system allowed nationalist parties of the different entities to obstruct the free flow of information and propagate their nationalist platforms.

The 60,000-man IFOR (Implementation Force) was to be replaced by a scaled-down STAFOR (Stabilization Force), with American troops strength reduced from 16,000 to some 8,500. A $100 million U.S plan to train and equip the Muslim Croat Federation was held up until Bosnian President Alija Izetbegovic reluctantly dismissed Defense Minister Hasan Cengic, who had close ties to Iran. While the Dayton Accords and elections did lead to the development of rudimentary democratic mechanisms, by year's end the conventional wisdom was that the voting merely reflected a de facto partition that would eventually be accepted by the international community, which wanted to avoid interminable and expensive peace-keeping. Yet, there were some hopeful signs. Opposition parties did better than expected in Republika Srpska. Bosnia's government was expected to convene in early 1997, with the multi-ethnic parliament picking a cabinet. A special conference in Brussels was slated to discuss funds for reconstructing Bosnia. One thing is certain: the ultimate resolution of the conflict will take years to achieve, and nothing permanent will be accomplished without U.S. and European engagement at every level of the process.

Now some bad news

Slovakia's mercurial prime minister, Vladimir Meciar, continued his bitter power struggle with President Michal Kovác, spurned dialogue with the opposition, increased his power over parliament and regional government, and meddled with press freedom and cultural expression. So while the OECD reported the country would achieve one of the highest levels of economic growth and the lowest inflation rates of any country in East-Central Europe for 1996-97, the U.S. and Europe rebuked Slovakia's sluggish democratic development, thus postponing its inclusion in the EU and NATO. The opposition was polarized between rightist parties that organized "Save Slovakia" rallies and the post-Communist Party of the Democratic Left, whose stated priority was helping citizens hard hit by economic and social difficulties.

Albania's President Sali Berisha and his Democratic Party rigged parliamentary elections, but a fairer local vote, progress in market reforms, improved relations with Greece, and Berisha's refusal to back secession demands by Albanian minorities in Kosovo and Macedonia squelched speculation that the country might be expelled from the Council of Europe. But at year's end, the collapse of several "pyramid schemes," some with ties to the government, led furious investors into the streets, in the most serious challenge to Berisha's rule.

Croatia remained in the hands of ailing authoritarian President Franjo Tudjman and the ruling Croatian Democratic Union (HDZ), split between hard-line nationalists and moderate reformers. Tudjman's refusal to recognize the election of an opposition-dominated Zagreb city council, the government's failure to fully cooperate with the Hague war crimes tribunal, and official pressure on the media delayed Croatia's entry into the Council of Europe. Tudjman's failing health, the lack of an anointed successor, and increased public disaffection with heavy-handed, one-man rule presages a heated presidential race in late 1997.

Throughout the region, governments grappled with the conundrum of modifying social welfare, health and pension programs to meet IMF deficit targets, while placating citizens hurt by the social dislocations of economic transition. And while most economies performed reasonably well, segments of the population—the old, poor, redundant workers—were left behind. Moreover, corruption, links (real or perceived) between government, businesses and organized crime, and the social inequities that accompanied reforms unevenly carried out could not but have political consequences.

Battles for media control raged across the region, with partisan squabbling between those in power and the opposition over press legislation and the staffing of all-important TV and radio oversight boards. Electronic media, the main source of information and, as such, a powerful political asset, was the big prize. Governments resorted to legal and extra-legal means to weaken the free press, including arbitrary taxation policies, libel laws, regulations on foreign ownership, state control of distribution and publishing facilities, and levels of government subsidies. Opposition groups were denied equal access to state media throughout the region, and journalists of state-run media faced dismissal, detention or law suits if they strayed too far from the government line. The state's power to cancel programs and suspend broadcasting licenses on flimsy pretexts was abused in several countries. The press faced the most intimidation in Albania, Bosnia, Croatia, Serbia and Slovakia, but the challenge to de-politicize media was an issue in virtually every country. Nevertheless, the relentlessness of the information age and economics led to the proliferation of private television and radio stations in Estonia, Poland, Hungary, the Czech Republic, Latvia, Lithuania, Romania, Macedonia and Slovenia. The Internet also linked the region to the rest of the world. When Serb authorities shut down independent station B-92, the station's plight and news of the demonstrations in Belgrade went out on the net.

Politics: center-left, center-right

In 1996, politics in much of East-Central Europe gravitated toward the center. Old ideological divisions were not entirely subsumed by the exigencies of modernization, economic restructuring and European integration. Moderate right-wing parties made headway in several countries, and nationalism remained a unpredictable dynamic in the region.

Romania's voters elected Emil Constantinescu of the center-right Democratic Convention of Romania (CDR) and a parliament dominated by the CDR, the Social Democratic Union of former Prime Minister Petre Roman and the Hungarian Democratic Federation of Romania (UDMR). Far-right parties, such as the Party of Romanian National Unity (PUNR) lost ground, partly because Hungary and Romania, under Western pressure, signed a pact recognizing the inviolability of their respective borders and vowing to treat minorities according to "European" standards. The former mayor of Bucharest, Victor Ciorbea of the National Peasant Party-Christian Democratic (PNTCD), became prime minister. A lawyer and former independent trade unionist, Ciorbea promised faster economic reform, and a more transparent government, and said Romania should apply for NATO membership.

The opposition inherited a broken-down economy, a business elite dominated by ex-Communist *apparatchiks* and former officers of the Securitate (secret police), an obsolete infrastructure, half-baked privatization and incomplete commercial laws. But with more legislators from the entrepreneurial and professional classes, agricultural wealth, oil reserves, a potential market of over 23 million and a pro-Western foreign policy, there is now a chance for growth and increased Western investment. Seven years after the fall of Ceausescu, Romanians are too inured and realistic to expect overnight miracles, but at year's end a regional poll showed that 61 percent of Romanians thought they would be better off in 1997 than in 1996, the highest "optimism index" among the countries surveyed.

In Bulgaria, voters replaced outgoing opposition President Zhelyu Zhelev with Peter Stoyanov of the UDF. Significantly, Bulgarian Business Bloc leader Georges Ganchev, a free-marketeer, finished a strong third. A mismanaged economy plagued by corruption, financial and banking crises, dwindling foreign-exchange reserves, skyrocketing interest rates and hyperinflation splintered the BSP. Reformers formed the Alliance for Social Democracy (OSD) around popular ex-Foreign Minister Georgi Pirinski. The opposition called for public demonstrations against the BSP at year's end, pressing for early parliamentary elections (not due until 1998) and insisting that a new government gain the confidence of international financial institutions.

With the old *nomenklatura* in control of much of the economy, the Russian mafia gaining influence, and rising poverty and public frustration, any new government faces a rough road. The future depends on re-orienting Bulgaria away from Russia toward the West, and President Stoyanov has pledged to bring the country closer to NATO and the EU and to implement sweeping reforms. The BSP and its allies are likely to cobble together a ruling coalition, escalating the likelihood of confrontation with a restive public and a galvanized and angry opposition.

The incumbent ex-Communist/center-left coalitions came under pressure in the region's most economically successful states—Slovenia, Hungary and Poland. In Slovenia, the ruling Liberal Democratic Party (LDS), which can trace its roots to the League of Communists and the former Communist youth organization, lost seats in the 90-member National Assembly in November elections. In January, the LDS coalition had lost its absolute parliamentary majority when the former-Communist United List of Social Democrats, with 14 seats, left the coalition. In the parliamentary vote, the rightist Slovenian People's Party won 19 seats, and the ultra-conservative's Social Democrats (SDSS), led by controversial former defense minister Janez Jansa, took 16. By year's end, a new government had not been formed.

Nationalist rhetoric notwithstanding, Slovenia's economy, which has shown positive growth since 1993, and its trade policies are oriented toward the EU. Nevertheless, the right has exploited concerns about foreign ownership of assets, dimming the prospects of rapid privatization and discouraging foreign investment.

In Hungary, the former Communist Hungarian Socialist Party and its coalition partner, the Alliance of Free Democrats, have adopted essentially center-right positions, implementing a severe austerity program aimed at slashing state spending on social welfare while boosting privatization policies the former governing party, the populist Hungarian Democratic Forum (MDF), was unwilling to adopt. In October, the government was rocked by the so-called "Tocsik affair," a highly damaging scandal over illegal payments to a consultant by the state privatization agency. The opposition, led by the Young Democrats (FiDeSz) which raised the issue in parliament has tried to position itself as a right-center alternative. The MDF has split into a more right-wing party and the Democratic People's Party made up of MDF intellectuals. Hardships resulting from the austerity plan have bolstered the hopes of the anti-foreigner, populist Independent Smallholders Party.

With a fragmented opposition and one of the most privatized and rapidly-evolving economies in Europe, Hungary is on the way to membership in the EU and NATO, making it unlikely that the country will soon veer from its centrist course.

In Poland, the ruling Democratic Left Alliance (SLD, ex-Communists) was shaken by the resignation in January 1996 of Prime Minister Josef Oleksy, after allegations that he collaborated with Soviet, and later Russian, intelligence. The SLD and its coalition partner, the Peasant Party (PSL), bumped heads over privatization and local government administration. In June, the Solidarity trade union movement and some 30 smaller, mainly rightist, parties established the Solidarity Electoral Action (AWS) to oust the SLD in 1997 parliamentary elections. Polls late in the year showed that AWS enjoyed 23 percent support, compared to 19 percent for the SLD. Other important parties were the conservative Movement for the Restoration of Poland, headed by former Prime Minister Jan Olszewski; the left-centrist Freedom Union, the largest parliamentary opposition group, led by ex-Prime Minister Tadeusz Mazowiecki; and the intensely nationalist Confederation for an Independent Poland.

It is difficult to predict the 1997 elections. Even with a comparatively robust, recovering economy, Poles, particularly pensioners and workers, and certain professional categories which are still on state payrolls, are fed up with the SLD's unkept promises, while others view the privatization policy as allowing a substantial part of the economy to be taken over by former Communist apparatchiks. In this context, it seems likely that Poland will probably move to the right, but the country's commitment to market reforms, democracy and membership in the European Union will be largely unaffected.

In the Czech Republic, Prime Minister Vaclav Klaus's three-party right-of-center coalition led by his pro-market Civic Democratic Party (ODS) won just 99 of 200 parliamentary seats in June elections, down from some 120 in the 1992 vote. Voter discontent with the prime minister's arrogant assertion that the country had no alternative to his policies led disaffected workers and former communists to vote for the center-left Social Democrats led by Milos Zeman, which won 61 seats. The right-wing, xenophobic Republican Party won 18 seats (8 percent). The Communists fell from 35 to 22 seats.

In July, the renewed center-right coalition, two seats short of an overall majority, received a parliamentary vote of confidence after the Social Democrats walked out just before the vote. As a concession, Zeman was named parliamentary chairman. The Social Democratic victory was short-lived; inter-party squabbling led four deputies to vote with the government on a balanced budget for 1997, even though the party had campaigned on a platform of deficit spending to avoid cuts in health and welfare programs. In November, the ruling coalition won 52 of 81 seats in the newly created Senate. Only 30 percent of the electorate bothered to vote, however, compared to 76 percent in the general election.

Despite macro-economic stability, the Czech economy had problems, particularly in regulating the banking and financial sector and in reforming the stock exchange. There are signs that the vibrant economy may be slowing down. But after six years of non-Communist governance, the country's democracy seems the most secure in Central Europe.

The baltics: moving on

The salient political event in the Baltics was the electoral defeat of the ex-Communists in Lithuania by a center-right coalition spearheaded by the Homeland Union under Vytautus Landsbergis, who led the country to independence as leader of the Sajudis popular front in 1990. Homeland and its ally, the Christian Democrats, won 86 of 137 seats, with the ex-Communist Lithuanian Democratic Party dropping from 75 seats to 12. In December, the new parliament, chaired by Landsbergis, overwhelmingly approved Prime Minister Gediminas Vagnorius's program focusing on economic growth, tax cuts, rooting out corruption, and integration with the EU and NATO.

The new government faced an increasingly apathetic public. The 55 percent election turnout was the lowest in three elections, suggesting dissatisfaction with politics in general among Lithuanians. In 1992, the ex-Communists won by promising to increase government spending on social programs amid economic difficulties caused by the collapse of the Soviet trading bloc and Russia's cut-off of energy. Four years later, the Homeland Union's populist campaign painted the Democrats as the party of the new economic elites that profited from insider deals while the rest of the country suffered and banks collapsed. Now, the new government must revive a stagnant economy while adhering to a program that would slow privatization.

Politics in Latvia and Estonia were highlighted by realignments of ruling coalitions. In October 1995 elections to Latvia's 100 seat parliament, pro-market ex-Communists Latvia's Way, which ruled in coalition with its ally the Farmers Union, saw its percent of the vote total halved to 15 percent. After much wrangling, parliament voted to approve the government of non-affiliated businessman Adris Skele, who forged an ideologically diverse and shaky six-party coalition. In 1996, the powerful Saimneks (roughly, Masters of Your Own Home), led by Ziedonis Cevers, a former leader of Latvia's Komsomol and interior minister of the first post-Communist government, merged with the Latvian Democratic Party, Latvian Unity Party and the Republican Party, giving it 27 deputies. The party is an eclectic mix of free-marketeers, centrists and technocratic ex-Communists. With parliament's June re-election of President Guntis Ulmanis, a strong advocate of close cooperation with the EU and NATO, Latvia, though polarized, will likely steer a centrist course. One problem that Latvia faces is that recurrent bank crises have dramatically slowed foreign investment and the economy flattened in response. In addition, an EU report criticized corruption at all levels of the Latvian government and the country's large "informal" economy.

In Estonia, the center-left government of Prime Minister Tiit Vahi and his Coalition Party/Rural Union Alliance, which scored a major victory over the conservative Pro-Patria/Estonian National Independence coalition in 1995, collapsed after the Reform Party left the ruling coalition to protest a cooperation agreement between Vahi and the Center Party. In 1995, the Center Party had left the ruling coalition and brought down the government after its leader, Edgar Savisaar, then interior minister, resigned after a bugging scandal. In December 1996, Vahi formed a minority government approved by President Lennart Meri, who was re-elected by parliament in September after months of delay due to political infighting.

Despite having six governments since independence in 1991, Estonia emerged with a vibrant, privatized economy with annual growth rates of 4 to 6 percent and an enviable unemployment rate of 2.3 percent. Estonia's low-tax, low-regulation, low-safety net Thatcherite model and its proximity to Finland have provided a relatively good standard of living. Grousing has been limited to pensioners and ethnic Russians who must learn Estonian to become citizens.

Communism and nationalism: spent forces?

Just a few years ago, the big regional story was the return of the Communists, which raised the specter of renewed repression and rollbacks of market reforms. In 1996, politics in East-Central Europe tended toward the center. Somewhat paradoxically, ex-Communists in Hungary and Poland were more free-market, free-trade and pro-Western than their populist-nationalist and far-left opponents. Time, generational shifts, and the lure of the market clearly have marginalized the Communist old guard. Some, like Meciar in Slovakia, Milosevic in Serbia, Tudjman in Croatia and, until his ouster, Iliescu in Romania, wrapped themselves in the mantle of authoritarian nationalism. But throughout the region, the ex-Communist priviligentsia used the old-comrade network, corruption and vague commercial laws to become the new entrepreneurial elite, spurring resentment among those hard-hit by changes in the rules of the economy. This resentment still runs deep, which partly explains the strong showing of rightist parties in polls and elections, particularly in rural areas.

While it is likely that right-wing parties will do well in the near future, persecution of ex-Communists is unlikely given their adaptability and economic clout, especially given the reluctance of the first post-Soviet governments to pursue de-Communization. The Czech Republic's lustration laws, aimed at excluding senior Communist officials from holding certain political or public offices, were attacked by human rights groups and never assiduously enforced. Slovakia stopped enforcing them in 1992. In 1996, the Czech government refused to ask the Supreme Court to ban the neo-Stalinist Party of Czechoslovak Communists because it did not present a danger to democracy according to Prime Minister Klaus. Bulgaria's so-called Panev laws met similar resistance. In 1996, prosecutors in Bulgaria canceled the trial of nineteen former Communists charged with diverting state funds, and in February the BSP-dominated parliament scrapped laws preventing former communists from holding higher academic posts.

Former Communist party leaders went on trial in Lithuania for the 1991 killing of unarmed civilians by Soviet troops, and in Latvia eight former Party members were indicted for lying about their political activities after the Party was outlawed in January 1991. In Poland, a parliamentary commission drafted a lustration law in late 1996 requiring that all state officials declare in writing whether they were in or collaborated with the secret service in 1944-1990. Slovakia passed a watered-down bill on the "immorality and illegitimacy" of the Communist-era regime. Only Albania made a concerted effort to try to jail Communist-era officials, leading to charges that President Berisha was engaging in a witch-hunt to silence his main opposition.

In this context, communism is not so much a spent force as a refurbished one. As democratic institutions and market reforms become entrenched and peaceful electoral transitions become the norm, chances for reversion to discredited command economies and totalitarian values diminish with every passing year.

The destabilizing power of nationalism is more problematic, particularly in multi-ethnic states. But international monitoring, diplomacy and troops have contributed to defusing some potentially troublesome spots. For years, there were predictions that Kosovo would explode; it hasn't. There were fears Macedonia's Albanians would secede, but crafty politics by Macedonian President Kiro Gligorov, Albanian President Berisha's refusal to support Albanian separatists, and the presence of U.S. troops have kept a lid on the situation. In relatively homogeneous states like Hungary, Poland, Slovenia and the Czech Republic, extreme nationalists remained on the fringe. The success of the xenophobic, anti-Gypsy, and anti-democratic Republican Party in the Czech elections, however, with its assertion that the country is controlled by a Communist-dissident mafia, make it clear that the social factors that play to extremism—class polarization, economic dislocation, poverty, the influx of foreign business interests—must be addressed by all governments.

In countries with large national minorities, there were signs in 1996 that the implementation of democratic processes, human rights norms, the rise in civil society and, the prospect of membership in the European Union had taken the edge off ethnic tensions and tempered irredentist impulses. In Bulgaria, which in the late 1980s persecuted the Turkish minority, the Turkish-based Movement for Rights and Freedoms remained an important swing vote. In Romania, the support of the Hungarian Democratic Federation of Romania would allow the new non-Communist parliament to control about 60 percent of the seats in both legislative chambers. Hungary and Romania signed a historic border and minority rights agreement, and other territorial disputes, such as Baltics sea borders, are being settled through negotiations. Furthermore, the United Nations is mediating the status of Eastern Slavonia in Croatia, captured and ethnically cleansed by Serbs.

Of course, problem spots remain. Slovakia's controversial language and "protection of the republic" legislation has alarmed the country's large Hungarian minority while jeopardizing applications to join the EU and NATO. In Macedonia, Albanians protested the closing of a private Albanian university and the jailing of its dean, but the situation remained peaceful. Italy and Slovenia which, with Croatia, control the former Italian territory of Istria, bickered over Rome's insistence that Italian citizens or their descendants who left the region are entitled to land restitution. The dispute held up Slovenia's admission as an EU associate member.

Given the character and history of the region, nationalist passions remain a combustible factor. Bosnia served as a sobering cautionary lesson on how quickly these passions can be aroused and how destructive, destabilizing and undemocratic they can be.

Looking ahead

There are reasons for optimism regarding the future of East-Central Europe. Over the last six years, the political culture in much of the region has evolved from paternalistic one-party dictatorships to pluralistic, more open societies. A generation has come of age at a time when the habits of democracy have taken root, but they are by no means firmly anchored in history or tradition. The post-Communist landscape is fraught with factors that hamper democracy's growth. While centrist-pragmatic forces have made impressive headway, rapid sociopolitical changes have contributed to political polarization that still strains the fabric of fledgling societies. Depressed economies, widespread institutionalized corruption, organized crime and ethnic tensions can still erode public faith in democratic regimes and impede economic liberalization. The authoritarian temptation still lingers.

It is up to the West to keep the momentum for democratic change from flagging. Western financial aid, technical assistance and values, as well as diplomatic pressure and firepower over the past six years, have contributed to establishing the framework for the rule-of-law, civil society and economic growth. Continued U.S. and Western engagement is indispensable for preserving long-fought, hard-won gains.

George Zarycky is Central and Eastern Europe Area Specialist for Freedom House.

Central Asia:
Problems of Wealth,
A Wealth of Problems   Barnett R. Rubin

In 1996, Central Asia more clearly than ever became the object of a new form of international rivalry, particularly in the renewed regional contest over Afghanistan. Some analysts referred to this rivalry as a new "Great Game," harking back to the term made famous by Rudyard Kipling and Lord Curzon to describe Russian-British rivalry in the area a century ago. And it is surely true that in the civil war between the Taliban movement and the forces under the command of Ahmed Shah Massoud, foreign powers played a role—Pakistan's support to the Taliban was critical. The stakes today, however, are different: not the reach of distantly based empires, but the viability of nearby states which recently became independent, and the control of trade and pipeline routes to connect the region to the world market. Direct military and administrative control of territory plays less of a role, and the Central Asians themselves are now major players as they were not a century ago.

And, yet, certain aspects of the region's politics are better understood by reference to the Great Game than to the Cold War. Though nineteenth century Britain was a constitutional monarchy and Russia an autocracy, the ideological difference between these systems played little role in their competition, just as the ideological differences among today's outside contenders—Russia, Iran, Pakistan, Afghanistan and, more distantly, the United States—play a limited role. The collapse of the USSR, with the subsequent opening of borders, has reinserted Central Asia, so long captive within a closed Soviet empire, into its position in the larger region, including Russia, China, and the Muslim states to the south.

The economic stake

The immediate economic stake is access to the world's largest sources of oil and natural gas outside of the Organization of Petroleum Exporting Countries (OPEC). Since economic interest rather than ideological alignment is the main force underlying the rivalry, alignments can be fluid. Iran and Russia are allied in their approach to Caspian and Central Asian oil, favoring Iran as the main southerly route, while Pakistan, Saudi Arabia and the U.S. favor an alternate route through Afghanistan. While the Central Asian states have different international orientations, in particular toward Russia, their attitudes toward the conflict over pipeline routes are essentially pragmatic: they stand to benefit from any southern export route and they have not lined up clearly on one side or the other.

In one respect, however, faint echoes of the Cold War can be heard. As Uzbekistan distances itself from Russia, the U.S. has become an alternative patron. But as many countries have learned from experience, dealing with the U.S. involves trying to read contradictory signals. Security concerns and economic interests become intermingled with suggestions that a liberal government, mindful of human rights, would get more respect—and help—from Washington. American engagement brings with it some notions of human rights and political liberalization, but—and here are the Cold War echoes—American assurances give regimes the idea that they can resume patterns of repression.

The new states of Central Asia became independent by default. They were expelled from the USSR by the Slavic states and found themselves thrust into new roles with little preparation. None of these ethnically defined "national republics"— Kazakstan, Kyrgyzstan, Turkmenistan, Uzbekistan and Tajikistan—had ever been independent. The pre-Russian history of the region consisted of dynastic and Islamic expansion and contraction in counterpoint with tribal resistance, not the establishment of nation-states. While most of the republics developed movements of ethnic and religious revival during perestroika and experienced some incidents of protest and inter-ethnic violence, none had a well-developed nationalist movement.

The first priority of these newly independent states was to form national political systems, modes of rule that would establish them as sovereign actors both domestically and in the international community. They had to define a new relationship with Russia and the outside world. Despite nominal independence, these states remained tied to Russia through the "hard wiring" of decades of investment in infrastructure: economic relations, transport, communications and security, as well as education, language, and even personal and family links. At the same time, the new states eagerly seized on the opportunity to diversify the external relations that independence afforded.

No aspect of international relations had greater importance than economics. The collapse of the USSR meant the loss of budgetary subsidies, which ranged from around 20 percent for energy-rich Turkmenistan and Kazakstan to as high as 50 percent for Tajikistan. The republics also lost sources of raw materials and markets for their industries, which produced mostly intermediate goods, especially for the vast Soviet defense establishment. They hoped that they could make up for these losses by selling oil and natural gas to foreign markets, and by attracting foreign investment to revitalize their industries and rebuild their infrastructure.

Security also posed a major problem. Portions of the former Soviet military and security forces remained in each of these states. In a clear demonstration of the sheer newness of the situation in Central Asia, political leaders, in power and in opposition, could sincerely say that they did not know whether the Russians should be viewed as their allies or as the principal threat to their national security. All joined the Commonwealth of Independent States, though Turkmenistan has announced a doctrine of neutrality and therefore declined to participate in CIS joint military activities; and Uzbekistan has sought to balance Russian power with a strong relation to the U.S. All but Tajikistan, still torn by a civil war, also joined NATO's Partnership for Peace.

Furthermore, as long as they were republics of the USSR, these states' external borders were closed and the region to which they belonged well-defined. Today, the five former Soviet Central Asian republics are not simply part of the post-Soviet space; they are also becoming part of a new, enlarged area of international interaction. On issues of security and economics their relations with Iran, Afghanistan, Pakistan and China are key. The events in Afghanistan, for instance, were triggered in part by the Pakistan-Iran rivalry, thus leading to major changes in Central Asia's security and economies. And not only did Chinese pressure lead to restrictions on the activities of

Uighur activists, but China is quietly becoming one of the largest sources of foreign investment and trade in the region outside of the energy sector.

Finally, the domestic challenge of statehood has meant establishing a definition of citizenship, defining the role of ethnicity or nationality in a particular state, and creating new institutions of authority, governance, and participation. Here, too, different tendencies have emerged, though strong presidencies with few checks on their powers are a regional trend. The protection of political rights and civil liberties remains precarious in the region. Threats of ethnic and religious strife, pressure from neighboring countries, and the need for stability in times of economic transformation are often cited as reasons for limits on political activity and even for violent repression.

The current situation

Five years after independence, while certain measures have been taken toward regional integration, Central Asia is characterized by diversity. A number of differences are identifiable.

Although Turkic Central Asia has been stable since independence, civil war in Tajikistan has continued and is closely related to the situation in Afghanistan. The Tajiks are as populous in northern Afghanistan as in their own country and speak a variety of Persian (known in Afghanistan as Dari) as their main language. The Tajik civil war, like the Afghan war, began as an ideological conflict between those favoring and those opposing the Soviet system. After the collapse of the USSR, however, both conflicts changed into multi-sided ones among coalitions from different regions with different foreign backers. The combatants have somewhat differing ideologies, but these are less important than regional and ethnic allegiances. Currently, the government of Tajikistan is controlled by a faction from Kulab province backed by Russia, which also maintains about 25,000 troops and border guards in the country, ostensibly for peacekeeping. Uzbekistan, Kazakstan and Kyrgyzstan also maintain a token military presence as part of the border guards or peacekeepers. Uzbekistan played a leading role in bringing the current government to power but has lost influence to Russia. The main opposition, drawn from other regions of the country (Garm and the Pamir mountains), includes democrats, Islamists and nationalists, and is largely based among the Tajik refugee population in northern Afghanistan, which receives support from international Islamist groups.

Within the past year, a third faction emerged in Khujand (Leninabad) province in the north. This more fully developed region, from which the Soviet-era leaders of Tajikistan came, called on Kulabi fighters to defend it from the opposition in 1992, but then lost power. Its leaders now demand a separate seat at the negotiating table and recognition as a power in their own right. They have support from Uzbekistan.

The civil war in Tajikistan, accompanied by social disintegration and economic breakdown, has brought with it pervasive violence beyond the battle fields, which the government is unable to contain—especially since it participates in it. Assassinations and disappearances of political figures are common. Within the past year, several well known Khujandi intellectuals were assassinated, a representative of the opposition on a U.N.-sponsored joint commission disappeared after being abducted from his hotel, and several journalists were killed. No one has been arrested; nor has any information explaining any of these incidents been released by the government. Russian troops are also victims of assassination in Dushanbe. The violence is complicated by the fact that Tajikistan has also become a major transit route for drugs smuggled out of Afghanistan. All political groups, including Russian troops, are involved in this trade, one of the few ways available to pay for the war. Consequently, it is difficult to distinguish purely political assassinations from those related to criminal activities.

Despite repeated cease-fire agreements, violence increased toward the end of the year. At the same time, leaders of the Islamic opposition and the government met in December to put the finishing touches on a peace agreement. According to some reports, the capture of Kabul by the Pakistani-backed Taliban led the Russian security establishment to reconsider the idea of a political accord in Tajikistan. A compromise that would bring the opposition out of Afghanistan, where they would be subject to further radicalization, now seemed the lesser risk. President Emomali Rakhmonov and opposition leader Sayed Abdullo Nuri signed a peace agreement in Moscow on December 23, but at this writing it is impossible to determine if it will be implemented.

International orientation

Five years after independence, the international orientation of the states of Central Asia began to diverge and stabilize. Tajikistan remained a Russian protectorate in all but name, with its security precariously protected by Russian troops and its budget more dependent on Russian subsidies (70 percent, by some accounts) than during Soviet times. The other states, to varying degrees, had begun to mark their differences with Russia, though these did not follow the simplistic cultural lines predicted by some in the immediate aftermath of independence, with Turkic states gravitating toward Turkey and Tajikistan toward Iran.

Kazakstan, with its large Russian population mostly living in several northern oblasts adjacent to Siberia, had to maintain close relations with Russia simply to assure its existence as a state. Turkmenistan, however, defined itself as a neutral country and hoped to use its vast oil wealth as a magnet for investment. It declined to participate in CIS military exercises, distanced itself from Russia's concern about the Taliban, and actively pursued economic cooperation with Iran. Iran placed great importance on its relations with Turkmenistan, the only Central Asian country with which it shares a border, and thus, key to Iran's plan to become the major outlet to the world market for Central Asia's hydrocarbons and other products. In April, Iran established the first rail link between Central Asia and the countries to its south, effectively linking the region to the Persian Gulf. (See below on the politics of energy.)

Uzbekistan, however, went the furthest in demarcating an independent position. In June, President Islam Karimov visited Washington and met with President Clinton. Significantly, Karimov then left Washington for meetings with businessmen in Houston and Denver. As a result of this visit, Uzbekistan turned over to the U.S. detailed information on its economy, including data previously regarded as Soviet state secrets, leading to a protest from Russia.

The visit highlighted Uzbekistan's attempts to establish close relations with the U.S. as a counterbalance to Russia. The establishment of seemingly permanent Russian bases in Tajikistan and the rise of nationalism as a force in Russian politics seems to have convinced Karimov even further that Russia had become a threat to the independence of the Central Asian states. Lacking a border with Russia or a large ethnic Russian population, Uzbekistan, as the most populous Central Asian state, could try to use American support to become the dominant regional power. Karimov had been seeking a visit to Washington for years but had been denied it on human rights grounds. Apparently, he agreed to make at least cosmetic improvements in return for the visit, but these appear not to have been sustained.

The idea of a strategic relationship with Uzbekistan found some supporters in the U.S., where the Russophilia of the immediate post-Soviet era was wearing thin. Though the Organization for Security and Cooperation in Europe engaged in some quiet diplomacy in support of human rights, most states and international organizations praised the country's independent path.

Energy and the international market

If there is a new "Great Game" in Central Asia, it is being played out over control of the transit routes from the oil and gas fields in the region. Kazakstan and Turkmenistan are potentially major oil producers (though not in the same league as the major suppliers in the Persian Gulf), and Uzbekistan and northern Afghanistan also have significant gas reserves. Under the Soviet system, all the energy systems of the region were under tight central control, and all pipelines were structured so as to ensure this control. Control of the energy infrastructure of the former Soviet Union remains one of Russia's most important sources of leverage over the successor states. Even energy-rich Kazakstan and Turkmenistan are dependent on Russia for refining and transit and have so far not realized the benefits they anticipated from economic independence.

In 1996, however, competition over the southern transit routes for Central Asian energy and trade heated up. As mentioned, Iran established the first link between its rail network and that of Central Asia (via Turkmenistan). It also established a free-trade zone on the border with Turkmenistan. Specifically in the energy area, it concluded agreements with both Kazakstan and Turkmenistan on what are known as "swap deals." Even with the rail link, it is still prohibitively expensive to transport Central Asian oil and gas to Iranian ports and oil terminals on the Persian Gulf, as the proposed pipeline has not been completed, in part because the U.S. has blocked all international financing for it. Most of Iran's oil and natural gas resources, however, are located on the Persian Gulf, in the southwest of the country, and it is expensive to transport them to consumers in the north. Under the agreements, Kazakstan and Turkmenistan will deliver oil and gas to northern Iran, in return for which Iran will export an equivalent amount of its own production from the south on behalf of the Central Asian countries. This indirect route constitutes the first link between Central Asian and Persian Gulf hydrocarbon resources.

Iran's main rivals for this trade—Pakistan and Saudi Arabia—reacted strongly. While there were indigenous Afghan factors and ethnic and security considerations at work, plans for oil and gas pipelines from Turkmenistan to Pakistan and then to East Asia, the world's fastest growing energy market, were vital reasons that the Taliban movement in Afghanistan received such significant external support. It also partly explains the mild U.S. reaction to the movement.

In the spring of 1996, the U.S. oil company Unocal and the Saudi company Delta made public plans for oil and gas pipelines from Turkmenistan to Pakistan via the Afghan cities of Herat and Qandahar, both under Taliban control. An Argentine firm, Bridas, and the South Korean conglomerate Daewoo also proposed plans for the pipelines. It proved impossible, however, to obtain financing for the pipeline as long as the war continued and, specifically, the government and the pipeline route were controlled by different forces. At that time the government was controlled by the mainly Tajik forces of President Burhanuddin Rabbani and military commander Ahmad Shah Massoud.

The Taliban capture of Kabul in September appeared to open new possibilities. Unocal welcomed the Taliban victory in a public statement and also signed a deal with Uzbekistan for oil and gas exploration. Meanwhile, the Pakistan interior minister, Nasirullah Babar, the Taliban's chief sponsor, flew to north Afghanistan several times to meet with the ethnic Uzbek warlord who controlled access to Uzbekistan and most of Afghanistan's gas reserves. By December, a major delegation of the oil companies involved visited the region, where they announced that the Russian firm Gazprom, as well as Pakistani and Japanese investors, would also participate in the pipeline deal. While distancing itself from the Taliban, the U.S. government welcomed the potential pipeline as contributing to peace in Afghanistan. Not coincidentally, it would also prevent Iran from monopolizing the southern trade routes. Iran, however, together with Russia and some Central Asian states, supported the coalition of Uzbek, Tajik and Shia forces that continued to oppose the Taliban and controlled most of Afghanistan's border with Central Asia. With Iranian support, in November and December, these forces pressed west toward the area from which the proposed pipeline would enter Afghanistan from Turkmenistan. Their goal was Herat, over which Russian-supported Iranian forces had fought British-Indian and Afghan forces in 1837, and control of which was now key to any pipeline project.

Political freedom and human rights

In the immediate aftermath of independence, Central Asia seemed to be bifurcated between the democratic states of Kazakstan and Kyrgyzstan (the only country where the president was not a former Soviet official) and the dictatorships of Turkmenistan, Tajikistan and Uzbekistan. The situation is more complex, however. Respect for democracy and human rights varies greatly among the five states, but all the states of the region have learned that outsiders are more interested in oil wealth than in democracy.

All five states have moved toward strong presidential regimes with few checks on executive power, weak legislatures and judiciaries, and some limits on press freedom, especially when it comes to the "honor of the president." In a way, President Emomali Rahmonov of Tajikistan probably has the most limited power, because of Tajikistan's collapse into violent anarchy rather than the rule of law. Even in Kyrgyzstan, still the most liberal of the republics, several journalists and opposition figures were jailed briefly in the past year for slandering the president, academician Askar Akaev. A few such incidents have also occurred in Kazakstan in recent years, where President Nursultan Nazarbaev nonetheless tolerates some harsh criticism in the press. Kazakstan's politics are now only marginally democratic; its 1995 parliamentary elections, for instance, held after an autocratic dissolution of the parliament and a constitutional rewrite sponsored by the president, were marred by massive irregularities. In Kyrgyzstan the increasingly impotent parliament was nonetheless duly elected. In both Kazakstan and Kyrgyzstan, however, the rule of law was generally observed in political and civil relations between the state and citizens, despite horrendous prison conditions, harassment of the opposition (especially in Kazakstan) and other ills. This does not appear to be the case with respect to economic relations, especially in Kazakstan, where massive corruption and favoritism in the awarding of contracts and privatization opportunities have aroused public resentment.

At the other extreme, Turkmenistan is a fully authoritarian personalized dictatorship. Portraits of the ruler, Turkmenbashi (Guide of the Turkmen) Saparmurad Niyazov, are omnipresent, and his will appears identical with state policy. There is no opposition, no independent civic groups, and no free press. Turkmenistan is the only post-Soviet state that continues to imprison dissidents in psychiatric hospitals. The one public demonstration that occurred in the history of independent Turkmenistan, in the summer of 1995, was forcefully suppressed. The only known anti-government demonstrations in 1996 took place in prisons, where the prisoners demanded humane prison conditions and judicial review of their harsh sentences.

The most interesting case is Uzbekistan. President Islam Karimov, too, monopolizes power in his person, but he presides over a more complex and somewhat flexible system. While direct opposition to the government is forbidden and major dissident figures are in exile, some independent and critical civic activity is permitted at the margins.

In 1996, these margins shifted in a confusing and uncertain manner, apparently under the impact of Karimov's new relationship with the U.S. On the eve of his U.S. visit, Karimov freed eighty-five prisoners, including five political dissidents. He permitted several initiatives related to human rights monitoring, and granted permission to Human Rights Watch/Helsinki, the New York-based human rights group, to establish an office in Tashkent. The parliament's human rights commission began work and issued a report which, while glossing over major abuses, did contain some surprisingly frank comments. The government also sponsored a supposedly nongovernmental Committee for the Defense of Human Rights. More surprisingly, during his visit to Washington, Karimov met exiled human rights activist Abdumannob Pulatov and agreed to allow him to return to Uzbekistan. In September, Pulatov presided without incident over the organizing congress of the banned Human Rights Society of Uzbekistan in Tashkent, though he soon returned to the U.S.

Contrary trends also continued, however. In an as yet unexplained incident, the director of the HRW/Helsinki office was detained and mistreated by the police. The Human Rights Society's application for official registration had still not been accepted by mid-December, and dissidents and independent journalists continued to be harassed and arrested. In November, the son of a leading opposition figure, Karimov's former deputy, was assaulted and badly beaten by unknown assailants,m in a throwback to the regime's practice of several years ago. In February, a Russian-speaking journalist was found murdered. No one was arrested in connection with the murder, and in the context of Karimov's continued attacks on the freer and more independent Russian media, this incident sent a chilling message. Islamic activists in the Ferghana Valley were also harassed and beaten.

Throughout the region, concern over ethnic challenges motivated some repression. The Kazakstan government limits the political activity of Russian nationalists, especially Cossacks, as well as Kazak nationalists with a more Islamic orientation. Tajik religious leaders seem to be subject to particular surveillance in Uzbekistan. Uzbekistan, Kyrgyzstan and Kazakstan, apparently under Chinese pressure, prevented Uighurs from organizing political or nationalist organizations. During the past year, this Turkic-Muslim group engaged in a number of protests in northwest China, which the Uighurs call East Turkestan, leading to strong Chinese repression.

There is a close, though not simple, relation among the various problems faced by these new states and their human rights practices. Despite the concentration of power in the presidencies, all the rulers of the area feel somewhat insecure. The bases of their legitimacy are weak. Their economies have yet to recover from the shock of Soviet dissolution, though only Tajikistan remains in full collapse. The new constitutions are not yet fully working. Afghanistan remains a source of violence, drugs and weapons. It has also become an object of rivalry among outside powers seeking access to the wealth of Central Asia.

These conditions are hardly propitious for the protection of human rights. While excesses such as the cult of personality in Turkmenistan result partly from policy decisions by individual dictators, many deeply-rooted obstacles to free and open societies still remain in this region, including economic decline that pits groups against each other, a heritage of autocracy from pre-colonial, Russian and Soviet times, and a lack of basic legal institutions and people with the skills to run them. The interest of outside powers in the region's wealth and strategic importance means that the rulers receive some scrutiny, but it also means that foreign governments and companies have incentives to flatter rather than pressure them. Governments also benefit from their "secularism" and portray themselves as bulwarks against a largely non-existent fundamentalist threat.

However, the partial successes of Kyrgyzstan and Kazakstan, as well as the halting and reversible changes in Uzbekistan, show that improvement is possible, and that international pressure and engagement can push it forward. The U.S. and other foreign powers cannot bring about massive historical change in this region by fiat, but engagement with democratic forces and selective pressure can and should affect the long process of transformation.

Barnett R. Rubin is director of the Center for Preventive Action, Council on Foreign Relations. The Council on Foreign Relations takes no institutional position on policy issues, and this article is the sole responsibility of the author. I would like to thank Erika Dailey for her assistance, though she, too, bears no responsibility for the views expressed herein or for any errors.

South Asia: Venal Politicians, Grassroots Heroes

Charles Graybow

In South Asia, the welfare of ordinary citizens has too often been subjugated to the greed and shortsightedness of their leaders. In a region that boasts some of Asia's most open societies, oldest political parties and enduring political institutions, there is widespread resentment of ruling classes which are, for all intents and purposes, above the law. Ultimately, this threatens to make ordinary citizens cynical not only about politicians but also about democratic politics.

Five of South Asia's seven countries are formal democracies–India, Bangladesh, Pakistan, Nepal and Sri Lanka. They have a population of 1.24 billion people, of whom over three fourths are in India. In South Asia, only Bhutan and the Maldives are under repressive rule.

Yet, throughout the region, widespread corruption and a weak rule of law undermine elected legislatures, courts and other democratic institutions, leading to considerable civil liberties violations. These include trafficking of women and children for prostitution, violence against women, illicit child labor, and a climate where security forces and police too often violate rights with near impunity, not only in Kashmir and other sensitive areas but also in daily, mundane encounters between police and civilians, on the streets and in detention centers and jails.

In most of South Asia, the challenge is to reform political systems that have largely failed to provide clean government, and to promote economic development in a region where, according to UNICEF, in 1995 almost two-thirds of all children were undernourished and fewer than half completed five years of primary education. Rajiv Gandhi, the late Indian prime minister, once estimated that 85 percent of all development money directed towards the poor in his country was skimmed off before it reached them. What South Asian governance lacks is "accountability."

According to the New Delhi-based weekly magazine *Outlook*, at least thirty-nine members of India's parliament have criminal cases pending against them, including allegations of rape, kidnapping and murder. In northern Uttar Pradesh, India's most populous state with 146 million people, dozens of candidates for the country's April-May 1996 parliamentary elections had prison records, including several organized crime leaders. Pakistan's English-language press regularly carries stories of murder, kidnapping and other serious charges against politicians. Bangladesh and Pakistan, which are still shaking off the legacy of years of military rule, and Nepal, which has been ruled as an absolute monarchy for most of its history, face the additional challenge of consolidating democracies that only emerged in the last decade.

Grassroots pressures...

Yet South Asia is also one of the more politically dynamic regions in the world. Citizens vote in high numbers and regularly throw out the party in power. Grassroots nongovernmental organizations (NGO) are robust and outspoken. The press is independent and vigorous. An agitational political culture makes moot the talk, popular with authoritarian elites in Malaysia and Singapore, of "Asian values" being somehow antithetical to universal rights.

By far, the greatest pressures for political and social reform come from the thousands of grassroots NGOs across the region; these are in the vanguard in educating women, minorities and other disadvantaged groups about their rights, providing basic health services in areas neglected by authorities, organizing garment workers and other laborers, assisting refugees and street children, and monitoring human rights violations. These NGOs are in turn tapping into solid support among ordinary citizens for basic rights and political pluralism. In the process, these NGOs have become the bedrock of a civil society that is increasingly vigilant against arbitrary official action and is championing the aspirations of disadvantaged groups. It is not surprising that in Bhutan and the Maldives, categorically the least free countries in the region, repressive rulers tolerate few elements of civil society.

Unfortunately, many South Asian politicians, officials, landowners and businessmen consider NGOs to be threats rather than partners in progress. NGOs are providing groups that have been traditionally marginalized with new opportunities for political, economic and social advancement, and this threatens to shake up entrenched political and financial interests. Although NGOs generally operate freely in the democratic countries, authorities often disparage their work and occasionally harass activists, particularly those monitoring and publicizing human rights violations.

More serious harassment comes from party activists, religious extremists, and agricultural landlords and industrialists. In Bangladesh, Islamists have called for a holy war against NGOs working to improve literacy and provide health care, family planning assistance and other aid to women, and have burnt hundreds of girls' schools. Thugs hired by the garment industry have attacked the offices and staff of the nonpartisan Bangladesh Independent Garment Workers Union. In India, NGOs are harassed in rural areas by wealthy landowners and militant groups.

As with their colleagues throughout the world, South Asian NGO activists working in strife-torn areas or on particularly controversial issues occasionally place their own lives in jeopardy. In May 1996, Parag Kumar Das, a journalist and the general secretary of the respected Manab Adhikar Sangram Samiti human rights organization in the northeastern Indian state of Assam, which is locked in a cycle of atrocities by insurgent groups and crackdowns by security forces, was killed in Guwahati, apparently by a separatist faction backed by security forces. Asma Jahangir, the chairperson of the independent Human Rights Commission of Pakistan and one of her country's leading human rights lawyers, has faced numerous death threats from Islamists for representing women and religious minorities in sensitive cases.

...and activism from above

Another key catalyst for reform has been the emergence in several countries of independent high courts that are acting as checks on arbitrary executive authority and establishing basic standards of accountability. In India, the Supreme Court is cracking down on corrupt politicians, and lower courts have handed down convictions in several sensitive human rights cases. In opinion polls, citizens rate the Supreme Court as the most trusted institution in the country.

Because politicians, bureaucrats and police often work together to obstruct investigations, many of these cases only reach the courts after ordinary citizens file public interest suits. Most notably, in January 1996, India's Supreme Court responded to public interest litigation by ordering authorities to investigate a long dormant scandal involving $18.3 million in laundered money, given by a prominent business family to top politicians and bureaucrats between 1988 and 1991 for help in landing industrial contracts. By late February, twenty-five politicians from most major parties had been charged in the *hawala* (black money) scandal, including seven cabinet ministers. The Court's critical support for the Election Commission's enforcement of campaign codes helped make the April-May national elections the cleanest in the country's history. In the fall, investigations mandated by lower courts led to criminal charges being filed against former Prime Minister P.V. Narasimha Rao in three separate cases. Lower courts also handed down the first convictions for murder during anti-Sikh rioting in 1984.

In 1996, the Supreme Court in Pakistan issued key rulings aimed at consolidating judicial independence. A March ruling stipulated that senior judges could only be appointed in consultation with the chief justices and only according to merit, while a December ruling requires the president to also consult with the prime minister on top judicial appointments.

To be sure, the lower courts in South Asia's democracies remain largely inaccessable to the poor, are hugely backlogged and are subject to manipulation by politicians and other well-connected persons. Moreover, the activism of India's top courts may not be emulated elsewhere in the region any time soon. But the fact that the apex courts in the five South Asian democracies have established their independence means that there are now real counterbalances to executive power. Senior justices in the other democracies may eventually become emboldened by the Indian model and respond to public outrage over abuses of official power.

A confrontational political culture

South Asian politics are often characterized by their volatility. Sumit Ganguly, a professor at Hunter College in New York, noted in the *New York Times* in August 1996 that the struggle against British colonial rule on the subcontinent earlier in the century has shaped a confrontational political culture in India, Bangladesh and Pakistan. Even in Nepal, which was never colonized, several veteran pro-democracy leaders joined Indian freedom fighters in the anti-colonial Quit India movement in the early 1940s.

Ganguly believes that this legacy differentiates these countries from authoritarian Southeast Asian nations such as Malaysia and Singapore, which achieved independence through fairly non-confrontational processes. It most likely explains the limited support for authoritarian rule in the region. In India, a national opinion poll taken prior to the 1996 parliamentary elections found 68 percent of those surveyed agreeing that the country cannot be better governed than by "parties, assemblies or elections." This is up from 44 percent when the poll was last taken in 1971. Responses such as this, plus the high turnouts for elections, indicates that most voters may be frustrated with politicians but still want to participate in and improve the political process.

The reverse side to the anti-colonial legacy is that today there is often little faith in the notion of a loyal opposition. "So you don't like higher cooking oil prices or bus fares?" asked Ganguly. "You don't debate it in the context of parliament but resort to looting shops or burning buses."

In parts of India and Nepal, a *bandh*, a shutdown of shops and businesses, is routinely organized as a means of political protest. Similarly, citizens in these areas often surround government officials or buildings or block roads in order to raise issues with recalcitrant or indifferent local authorities. These civil disobedience techniques may be the only recourse in societies where lower courts, local authorities, parliaments and other formal institutions are often unresponsive to the poor. Unfortunately, peaceful protests and demonstrations too often are manipulated by political parties as shortcuts to achieving political goals. At the more extreme end, politics in Bangladesh and Pakistan frequently descend into street clashes and violence.

A secular triumph

India's April-May national elections were the region's leading political development in 1996. With nearly all major parties tainted by the hawala scandal, none could afford to make corruption an issue. In fact, many Indians seemed to be inured to the venality of their political class. Pre-election opinion polls showed most voters were mainly concerned with unemployment, inflation, power and water supplies and other local issues.

The right-wing Hindu nationalist Indian People's Party (BJP) and its allies took 196 of the 543 elective seats in a hung parliament, while the ruling Congress Party, which had governed India for all but four years since independence, stumbled to its lowest number of seats ever with 140. The biggest swing went to fourteen regional, lower caste and Muslim-based parties, including BJP allies and Congress splinters, which won 103 seats. These parties now hold the balance of power in parliament.

In May, the BJP briefly formed a minority government that resigned after failing to attract secular allies. On June 1, the United Front, a coalition of thirteen leftist, centrist, regional and caste-based parties, took power under H.D. Deve Gowda, the chief minister of Karnataka state.

Despite the BJP's plurality, the party failed to expand beyond its support base of urban, upper caste Hindus and its stronghold in five northern and western Hindi-speaking states and Delhi. The party's 21 percent share of the popular vote matched its total in the 1991 elections. While this figure may be uncomfortably high in a secular society, it shows that a clear majority of voters rejected the BJP's appeals to *Hindutva* (Hindu ethos) and anti-Muslim sentiments.

Other key developments, the decline of the Congress Party and the continued rise of regional and caste based parties, were closely related. In the decades following independence, the Congress Party, shaped by Jawaharlal Nehru's and Mohandas K. Gandhi's vision of a secular, inclusive society, portrayed itself as the benefactor of the lower castes and *dalits* (downtrodden, ex-untouchables), who together form 70 percent of the population; the party also claimed to represent religious minorities and other disadvantaged groups.

But for all the party's grand claims, Congress governments invested relatively little in basic health and primary education. In the late 1980s, parties representing lower castes and dalits began making headway in populous Uttar Pradesh. This coincided with economic reforms initiated by Congress Prime Minister P.V. Narasimha Rao in 1991, which had the effect of decentralizing political and economic power to the state level. With more to offer voters at the state level, regional and caste-based parties began to tap into the alienation that many poor and low-caste voters felt from the Congress and other mainstream parties. The Congress Party also lost the support of Muslim voters who blamed Rao for failing to protect them from communal violence in the aftermath of the destruction of a sixteenth century mosque at Ayodhya in Uttar Pradesh in late 1992.

What is now the most fragmented parliament in India's history may be a harbinger of an era of coalition politics. Yet this is not necessarily bad. The regional and caste-based parties have integrated many voters more fully into the political process. In recent years, regional parties won control of legislatures in Andhra Pradesh, Tamil Nadu and other states by making unrealistic populist promises of larger subsidies for rice, water and other goods. Once in power, financial realities have forced them to make more sober policy decisions.

While the development of parties along regional interests was more or less expected, the rise of caste-based parties has received more critical attention. Following independence in 1947, it appeared that the retrograde force of caste would be swept away by the modernization of Indian society. Yet caste continues to be a social fault line, although, as author Amitav Ghosh noted after election, its religious significance has largely been subordinated to its political role.

To some, caste-based parties allow numerically superior, historically disadvantaged groups to finally obtain their fair share of political power. To others, it heralds, as the Calcutta *Statesman* disparagingly opined, "the parceling out of the State–primarily in the form of government jobs, bureaucratic appointments, chairmanships of public sector units–to various caste interests depending on their strength in the legislature." Ultimately, the challenge for these parties is to advocate responsible policies aimed at providing equal opportunities for their supporters.

A setback to freedom

While clean elections, a more inclusive political process and an activist judiciary were positive developments in India, there was growing cause for concern in Pakistan in 1996. President Farooq Leghari drew widespread approval when he dismissed Benazir Bhutto's government on November 5 on charges of corruption, undermining the judiciary by largely rejecting its rulings on judicial appointments, and sanctioning extrajudicial killings in the southern city of Karachi. But by year's end, a caretaker government headed by Meraj Khalid had failed to bring corruption charges against Bhutto and other leading politicians. Yet even if Bhutto and, perhaps, opposition leader Nawaz Sharif are disqualified from contesting elections called for February 3, 1997, more systemic problems, which are having a corrosive effect on efforts to consolidate democratic gains, will need to be addressed.

Political power largely remains concentrated in a powerful landowning agricultural elite, popularly known as "feudals." The country's present electoral districts were drawn in 1984, based on a 1981 census. Since then there has been a significant demographic shift from rural to urban areas. Consequently, wealthy landowners hold a disproportionately high number of seats in parliament and are able to shape fiscal and economic policies to their advantage and subvert efforts at political reform. According to the *Far Eastern Economic Review*, in 1995-96, agricultural landowners paid only $79,000 in wealth taxes, or 0.0036 percent of the direct taxes collected. Meanwhile, foreign exchange reserves, at some $800 million at the end of 1996, are barely enough to pay for four weeks of imports.

Islamists continue to undermine Pakistan's secular foundations by demanding a broad application of the 1979 Hadood Ordinances, which introduced elements of *Shari'a* (Islamic law) into the penal code; harassing judges in trials involving often spurious allegations of blasphemy against Islam; and threatening human rights activists. Meanwhile, the government, which supported the Taliban's rise to power in neighboring Afghanistan in part as a means of securing trade routes to Central Asia, watches warily as the fundamentalists consolidate power in what is now the world's most radical theocratic state. The army, which has ruled for nearly half of Pakistan's fifty years of independence, remains a powerful political force. A military coup seems unlikely, but the armed forces may demand some sort of formal political role.

Confronting a legacy of military rule

Making the ruling class more accountable is also a key concern in Bangladesh, where politics became bogged down in recriminations and accusations in March 1994 when the three leading opposition parties walked out of parliament, accusing Khaleda Zia's ruling Bangladesh National Party (BNP) government of corruption and, later, of rigging a key by-election. By the fall of 1994, politics had descended into street level confrontations between supporters of rival political parties, who were often poor people lured into the streets by modest payoffs, and between demonstrators and the police.

At the heart of the confrontation is an intense personal rivalry between Zia and Sheikh Hasina Wajed, the leader of the main opposition Awami League. Sheikh Hasina's father, Sheikh Mujibur Rahman, was assassinated in 1975 by army officers, and she believes that Zia's husband, who later ruled the country before being assassinated in 1981, played a role in her father's murder.

The BNP easily won elections that the opposition boycotted in February 1996. A series of debilitating general strikes in March that cost the country $80 million per day convinced Zia to cede power to a caretaker administration. The Awami League won the ensuing June 12 elections with 146 out of 300 elective seats in parliament and formed a minority government.

By mid-summer, Sheikh Hasina's new Awami League government and the BNP again appeared to be headed toward confrontation. The authorities arrested a senior serving army officer, three retired senior army officers, and six others for alleged links to the assassination of Sheikh Mujibur Rahman twenty-one years ago. As in many other nations that are confronting a legacy of human rights abuses committed during military rule, Bangladesh's leaders face the sensitive issue of whether democratic consolidation would best be served by bringing the accused to justice or by focusing on reconciliation.

Democracy subverted. . .

Sri Lankan President Chandrika Kumaratunga took office in August 1994, pledging to usher in an era of media liberalization, end the country's civil war that has killed at least 40,000 people since 1983, and abolish the powerful presidency in favor of a parliamentary system. Midway through her term she has not only failed to follow through, but has adopted some of the authoritarian tactics of her predecessors.

Kumaratunga's government has filed several criminal defamation cases against newspaper editors, and from April to October 1996 imposed a blanket censorship on coverage of the civil war in the north and east, where the Liberation Tigers of Tamil

Eelam (LTTE) have been fighting for a separate Tamil homeland in the predominantly Sinhalese country. An August 1995 proposal to devolve authority to new regional councils has been rejected by both the LTTE and Sinhalese hardliners.

In April, the government extended emergency rule, which gives security forces sweeping powers of arrest and detention, to the entire country. Local elections have been repeatedly postponed, even though the security situation in much of the country is far less volatile than in the north. Throughout the country, the army routinely detains young Tamil men for questioning. Defense spending is at its highest level ever.

In Nepal, premier Sher Bahadur Deuba of the Nepali Congress (NC) party held together his three-party ruling coalition in 1996, but faces a potential leadership challenge from former premier G.P. Koirala, who won election to the NC presidency in May. In February, the radical Communist Party of Nepal (Maoist) launched a "people's war" in several midwestern hill districts. By mid-November, terrorist attacks and police shootouts had killed sixty-two people and wounded dozens of others.

Like other countries on the subcontinent, Nepal faces the challenge of reforming a corruption-ridden political system that siphons off money targeted for development spending. In the absence of an activist judiciary, there is little chance that the very politicians and bureaucrats who are feeding at the trough will take decisive action. In 1996, the Deuba government further politicized an already partisan bureaucracy by placing some sixty "advisors" in key positions and creating twenty-four top civil service posts. In addition to creating yet more opportunities for graft, the move further strains the country's already precarious finances.

...and democracy denied

The most repressive country in South Asia is the Himalayan kingdom of Bhutan, one of the world's last absolute monarchies. In the late 1980s, King Jigme Singye Wangchuk's government, dominated by the minority Tibetan-descended Drukpas, began arbitrarily tightening citizenship requirements and enforcing dress and language codes based on Drukpa culture.

This ethnic purity campaign reached a brutal peak in the early 1990s when the army raped and tortured ethnic Nepalese villagers, burnt their homes and forcibly expelled tens of thousands from the country. There are now some 90,000 Bhutanese refugees living in eight camps in southeastern Nepal, and perhaps 15,000-20,000 more in India and elsewhere in Nepal. The formation in 1994 of the Druk National Congress, an exile group comprised of ethnic Sarchops from eastern Bhutan, showed that the issue is not a Drukpa-Nepalese rivalry; rather, it is a basic struggle for freedom from absolute rule.

In Bhutan, rule is based on power rather than law, basic freedoms are denied, and southern Bhutanese continue to face official discrimination, harassment and restrictions on cultural expression. South Asia's best-known political prisoner, Tek Nath Rizal, is a southern Bhutanese who was given a life sentence in November 1993 under a 1992 National Security Act legislated three years after his imprisonment. In a sign of the regime's inflexibility on repatriating the refugees, in August 1996 authorities forcibly deported fifty southern Bhutanese who had re-entered the country seeking to deliver a petition to the king. Earlier in the year, hundreds of refugees were detained by Indian police during several attempts to march peacefully to the Bhutan border.

The Maldives, a string of low-lying atolls in the Indian Ocean, is a somewhat more tolerant and open society, but with strict limits. President Maumoon Abdul Gayoom has served since 1978 under a tightly-controlled system where the president wields powerful executive powers but is indirectly elected. There are valiant independent journalists in the Maldives, but most have spent time in jail for their reporting. In 1996, the best known of these journalists, Mohammed Nasheed, served several months in jail over a 1994 article criticizing the procedures used for legislative assembly elections.

The Kashmiri tragedy

Finally, there is Kashmir. The region broadly known as Kashmir consists of land that today is the Indian state of Jammu and Kashmir, Pakistan's Azad (Free) Kashmir and Northern Areas, and Chinese-controlled regions.

But the conflict in Kashmir, which has claimed 20,000 lives since an insurgency against Indian rule began in December 1989, centers on "the Valley," a lush region in the heart of Jammu and Kashmir, India's only Muslim-majority state. The state's September 1996 elections, the first since 1987, were neither free nor fair, with Kashmiris whipsawed between Indian soldiers coercing them to vote and militants agitating for a boycott. The pro-India Muslim Conference easily captured a majority of the eighty-seven seats in the state assembly.

Earlier in the year, Human Rights Watch reported that the Indian government was arming irregular militias to carry out counterinsurgency operations. The militias have attacked journalists, human rights activists and medical workers with impunity, while regular security forces continue to commit extrajudicial executions, rape and torture. Militants continued to launch indiscriminate attacks that killed or injured hundreds of civilians in 1996.

Women and children at risk

Political reform, while important, will not ease the appalling condition of many women and children in South Asia. Exploitation of women and children in the region is a well-organized enterprise. Millions of children under fifteen are working in carpet, garment, glass, and brick kiln factories, as agricultural and construction workers, and as domestic help. Most work long hours in dangerous conditions for little or no wages. The solution to child labor is not merely to move children out of the factories. In the mid-1990s, tens of thousands of garment workers in Bangladesh and carpet weavers in Nepal were thrown into the streets by factory owners concerned with negative publicity in the Western media. The only viable, long-term alternative to child labor is to provide new schools, subsidies for tuition, and stipends to help children support their families.

The revelation in June 1996 by the International Confederation of Free Trade Unions (ICFTU) that the souvenir soccer balls for the Euro 96 championship had been made by child laborers in the northeastern Pakistani town of Sialkot brought fresh outside attention to the issue. In November the world soccer governing body agreed to a "code of practice" to stop its contractors and subcontractors from using child labor. The code includes a program to set up schools for children who lose their jobs and provide "transitional economic support" for parents. In Bangladesh, a 1995 Memorandum of Understanding committed garment factory owners to transfer child workers under fourteen years old into new schools sponsored by UNICEF and other agencies, which will also provide the children with a monthly $7.50 stipend. Such programs are welcome but will only be effective if vigorously enforced through independent monitoring.

Major cities in South Asia have thousands of street children. In Nepal, many work as ragpickers and street vendors in Kathmanu, Biratnagar, and other cities. A November 1996 Human Rights Watch report detailed illegal detentions, beatings and torture of street children by police in India.

Trafficking of women and children for prostitution is carried out across international borders by networks of agents who operate with the complicity of border guards and other local officials. In India, tens of thousands of Nepalese women and children are held in debt servitude, forced to work as prostitutes and subjected to rape, beatings and other torture.

The Karachi-based Lawyers for Human Rights and Legal Aid estimates that in recent years, some 200,000 women and girls from Bangladesh have been trafficked by organized networks to Pakistan, where they are sold as sex workers or domestic servants. Some 2,000 *victims* of trafficking are detained under criminal charges for entering Pakistan illegally or for engaging in extramarital sex. In Sri Lanka the child prostitution business caters to the perversions of mainly European sex tourists. In October, local human rights groups reported that orphanages are now supplying children to the island's sex tourism industry.

Another concern is violence against women, including rape, domestic violence and dowry-related incidents, which is perpetuated by traditional norms inimical to women's welfare and by the failure of police and the judicial system to investigate, arrest and prosecute offenders. In India, several thousand women are burnt to death, driven to suicide or otherwise killed, and countless others are similarly harassed, beaten and deserted by their husbands in dowry disputes each year. In rural Pakistan, women are still killed for alleged adultery under traditional norms that permit "honor" killings.

The consequences of a (mostly) cold war

Despite these and other pressing social problems, bitter regional rivalries divert development money into military budgets. A South Asian nuclear war is a specter hanging over the region and, in this context, China is a key player. India and Pakistan have fought three wars since 1947, while India and China fought in 1962. The Indian-Pakistani rivalry over Kashmir is, of course, the critical tension. Fought from the inhospitable heights of the Siachen Glacier in Kashmir, where artillery fire is traded almost daily, to the debating halls of the United Nations in New York and Geneva, the rivalry has considerable humanitarian consequences on both sides. In Pakistan, the army consumes 26 percent of the budget, and this will not be touched even as social programs are cut back under an IMF-led austerity program.

In late 1996, there were limited moves toward easing regional tensions. In November, China and India pledged to demilitarize disputed Himalayan border areas, although no timetable was set. China may also be moving toward recognizing India's 1975 annexation of the disputed Himalayan region of Sikkim. An easing of Sino-Indian tensions could encourage a limited reproachment between India and Pakistan, which receives Chinese arms and nuclear technology. In December, India and Bangladesh eased a festering dispute by signing a thirty year deal on sharing water from the Ganges River. Some analysts believe that water sharing could be part of an eventual solution in Kashmir, where several major rivers originate.

democrats vs. autocrats

Authoritarian leaders in East Asia–and their Western apologists–delight in comparing India to China to point out the supposed shortcomings of democracy in promoting economic growth in developing countries. But the oft repeated refrain that "it is better to be born a peasant in China than a poor villager in rural India," while cavalierly overlooking China's egregious human rights record, also misunderstands the relationship between economic freedom and economic growth. In this regard, India's embrace of autarkic, control-bound economic policies after independence was the greatest barrier to development, not its democratic practices. There is also little evidence to back the claim that authoritarian governments are better positioned to enact tough economic reforms. Governments in both India and China lack the will to dismantle loss-making state enterprises for fear that mass layoffs would provoke social unrest.

In the long run, economic development requires a strong rule of law to ensure that contracts will be enforced, and that the rules of doing business will not be arbitrarily changed. In this regard, South Asia's democracies, for all their faults, are categorically ahead of China. What is needed now in South Asia are sensible development policies, including a greater share of educational spending allocated to primary schooling, closer governmental cooperation with NGOs and, of course, less corruption.

Hopeful signs do exist.. According to the United Nations Development Program, net enrollment at the primary school level in South Asia increased from 48 percent to 79 percent between 1960 and 1991. In Bangladesh, the Grameen (Village) Bank, which in the mid-1970s was the world pioneer in microlending to the rural poor, now has a rural credit network that covers more than two million borrowers in more than half of Bangladesh's 68,000 villages, with most loans under $100. The loans, of which 93 percent are to women, are used to buy modest tools or other materials to start small businesses.

A third of its borrowers have been lifted from poverty, and the Grameen model is being copied worldwide from developing countries to inner-city Chicago. The Grameen bank and similar institutions, as well as the region's grassroots NGOs, are at the forefront of efforts to build freer societies.

Charles Graybow is Asian Affairs Specialist at Freedom House.

East Asia: Peace and Prosperity, and Some Democracy
Robert A. Scalapino

East Asia continues to display the three basic political systems characteristic of this century. Four Asian states—China, North Korea, Vietnam and Laos—proclaim themselves socialist in Leninist form.

A larger number of states can be defined as authoritarian—pluralist in nature, with politics controlled and constrained in varying degree, but with existing civil societies apart from the state possessing some autonomy, and mixed economies in which the market plays an important role. This category ranges from the hard authoritarianism of Burma to the soft authoritarianism of Singapore, with nations such as Indonesia occupying the middle range. There is much in Asian history and political culture that supports authoritarianism: the weak role of law; the primacy of leaders over political institutions; and the elevation of the collective over the individual.

The Asian democracies also contend with this heritage, although with favorable economic conditions at home and a sympathetic global environment, they have recently increased in number: Japan, South Korea, Mongolia and Taiwan in Northeast Asia; the Philippines, Malaysia and Thailand in Southeast Asia.

Leninism in East Asia is under siege, as developments in China illustrate. Despite the efforts of China's third and fourth generation Communist leaders to keep ideology at the forefront, enthusiasm for Marxism-Leninism continues to wane. Chinese citizens, especially youth, are primarily interested in making money—materialism and the pragmatism that accompanies it dominate the scene.

Thus, a new approach is being used in an effort to insure loyalty and cohesion: militant nationalism is now featured, heralding China's rich traditions as well as its contemporary strengths. One hears more about Confucius and Sun Yat-sen than about Marx. The insistence on the absolute sovereignty of the nation-state and the angry charges of interference in China's internal affairs are recurrent. Some of China's educated youth are riding the nationalist wave with avidity since it resonates both with the rising current of self-confidence and the lingering residue of insecurity.

Meanwhile, China's new leaders cautiously seek to consolidate a more collective leadership system than has existed in the past. President Jiang Zemin is seen as "the core" and is consolidating his power, but responsibilities for governance are divided, and consultation with diverse interest groups is required. Deng Xiaoping has done his nation a great service in dying by inches, thereby enabling an adjustment to take place with his imprimature still available, yet an era is coming to a close. The last of the old Chinese revolutionaries are leaving the stage. The complex trends with respect to Chinese domestic politics were clearly illustrated in 1996. On the one hand, the eleven year sentence meted out to Wang Dan for advocating greater political freedom, and other repressions sent a clear signal that "people's democracy" did not include certain people. The dictatorship of the Communist party was to be respected. On the other hand, village elections and meaningful debates in the National People's Assembly testified to the growth of diversity, a product of rapid economic growth. Today, speech in China is relatively unrestrained if you trust the person to whom you are speaking; Chinese citizens, however, are not free to write or engage in public displays of dissent.

The major political issues on the Chinese horizon are clear: Collective leadership or a future all-powerful leader following serious factional struggles? An institutionalized federal system allocating power among center, region, province and locality, or power distribution based haphazardly upon the prevailing power balance? Leninism is slipping, but China is not likely to move toward democracy in the foreseeable future. The trend is toward authoritarian-pluralism.

The concern of China's neighbors is not that of a collapsed or chaotic China, but of a China reaching major power status armed with a nationalistic determination to regain its traditional empire and exert regional leadership. Thus, the reversion of Hong Kong on July 1, 1997, and its aftermath, will be watched with great interest, as will trends in the ever delicate China-Taiwan relationship. Greater China, now increasingly evident in economic form, may assume political dimension. Or China could live up to its word, and abide by the five principles first enunciated in 1954 and endlessly repeated thereafter: mutual respect for each nation's territorial integrity and sovereignty; nonaggression; non-interference in each other's internal affairs; equality and mutual benefit; and peaceful coexistence. Such behavior would indeed be exemplary, and would require certain PRC adjustments, at least in the interpretation of its neighbors. The evidence from 1996 was inconclusive.

Problems in North Korea

North Korea presents a radically different picture. In the midst of deep economic problems, this nation has neither a president nor a party secretary two-and-a-half years after the death of Kim Il Sung. The evidence, though sparse, indicates that Kim Jong Il, backed by both military and civilian elites, firmly holds power, perhaps awaiting more favorable domestic conditions before assuming the appropriate titles.

The religious aura that surrounds North Korean politics is striking. Kim Il Sung is not dead. He has been reborn in his son, and how can one challenge the Great Leader? The ideological reliance rests almost entirely on a combination of cult of personality and nationalism of an historic xenophobic type. Marx and Lenin are rarely mentioned, and *juche,* self-reliance, together with the sacred words of the Great Leader, constitute the bible of the Democratic People's Republic of Korea.

Here, a Stalinist system—both politically and economically—lives on;. yet reality has penetrated a portion of the elite. The commitment to more acitvely seek selective economic changes can be clearly seen in 1996, in the bid for foreign investment and in heralding the existence of Special Economic Zones in the northernmost part of the country. Some relaxations in the collective agricultural system have also been signaled.

Many predict North Korea will collapse, with efforts to abandon economic autarky too late, too limited. Others suggest that one should not underestimate the capacity of a long-enduring people and a tightly knit elite to tough it out with minimal changes, whatever the sacrifices. Still others see North Korea evolving gradually in the same direction as China, and ultimately achieving a "soft landing," enabling North-South relations to improve and avoiding the horrendous costs to the South of an early collapse.

The past year has seen little progress in the latter direction, despite the continuance of the KEDO project aimed at preventing DPRK nuclear weapon development by providing a light water reactor system for energy production. U.S.-DPRK talks on such matters as an exchange of liaison missions were stalled, especially after North Korea sent a submarine carrying infiltrators into South Korea, touching off an international incident and heightening hard-line sentiment in South Korea. At year's end, however, after intensive negotiations between the U.S. and the DPRK, the North expressed "deep regret" for the submarine intrusion, and promised to "make efforts to insure that the incident will not recur, and work with others for durable peace and stability on the Korean peninsula."

This rather amazing step, suggesting the urgent needs that the North has for improved economic and political relations, may lead to an acceptance of the four-party dialogue proposed earlier by South Korea and the United States. It may also lead to a resumption of KEDO operations on schedule and advances in the bilateral dialogues between the DPRK and ROK and the DPRK and the U.S. Given the many hopeful signs of the past that faltered, one must be cautious, but recent clouds seem to be lifting.

The two Leninist states of Southeast Asia—Vietnam and Laos—evidenced a combination of change and continuity in 1996. Vietnam held its Eighth Congress of the Communist Party from June 28 to July 1, and Party Secretary Du Muoi, in his closing remarks, outlined the tasks for the party faithful: maintain socialism while engaging in *doi moi* (reform) and adhering to Marxism-Leninism together with the Thought of Ho Chi Minh; struggle against political liberalism which promotes instability and against external interference in Vietnam's domestic affairs; maintain Party leadership and democratic centralism; and build a market economy within state socialist management. These themes, which reflect China's stated goals, represent the political objectives of the VCP.

The effort to keep the Vietnamese people in line was evident in the arrest of two Buddhist monks charged with activities injurious to the states, and in the broad campaign against "subversive and immoral" publications and videos.

Yet troubles and uncertainties have grown. A generational change is at hand with no clear succession in place. Furthermore, as in China, despite party efforts, "spiritual pollution" is currently projected as a rising menace, with younger generations indifferent to ideological appeals. Here too, nationalism is prominently utilized—although care must be taken not to allow its anti-China dimension to be displayed too openly.

Vietnam's economy, still moving ahead, displays certain problems. The government has tightened controls in an effort to stem corruption; the legal foundation for investors remains precarious; and while Vietnam's growth rate remains strong and the country continues to attract many foreign investors, warning flags are up.

Laos has leaned to Thailand economically and to Vietnam politically in recent years. In 1996, there were numerous signs that this small landlocked country was seeking greater contact with its Southeast Asian neighbors and participation in ASEAN. The government also appealed to expatriate Laotians for aid in economic development. Politically, however, there were no significant changes, with an older generation of leaders led by President Nouhak Phoumsavan determined to preserve the socialist order.

Economic change, including the importance of the market domestically and enhanced contact with market economies, is now accepted—with varying restraints and degrees of reluctance—by all the Asian socialist states. In turn, challenges to the old political values have emerged. To combat the ideological decline, nationalism is brought to the fore. The shift from Leninism is unlikely to be stopped, however. Diversity is both the inevitable partner of development and the enemy of monolithism. As noted, the political transformation of Asian Leninism is not likely to be toward democracy; rather, as is already apparent, it will be toward authoritarian-pluralism.

What of the authoritarian-pluralist Asian states? For Indonesia, 1996 marked the thirtieth anniversary of the "New Order" under President Suharto, who hailed the economic accomplishments of the past three decades and strongly criticized both Communism and "the multiparty system." The former had "masterminded" the 1996 rebellion, he asserted; and while defeated, lingered on in the society in certain forms. Liberal democracy was conducive to so much instability that both development and independence had been jeopardized in the years following Dutch withdrawal.

Less than three weeks before the president's speech, Jakarta had witnessed a serious riot as a result of the effort to oust Megawati Sukarnoputri, President Sukarno's daughter, as leader of the Democratic People's Party, the principal opposition group; many are convinced that this effort had the covert support of the government. Deaths were few, but property destruction was extensive.

Behind this riot lies a rising resentment of the current political scene, especially on the part of a portion of the young, educated urbanites. Corruption and privilege, symbolized by the deep involvement of the First Family in various business deals, and the centralization of authority in the hands of one individual whose decisions with respect to power holders are final, has bred a mixture of cynicism, indifference and antagonism.

Meanwhile, Indonesia continues its annexation of East Timor, where an estimated 200,000 East Timorese have perished as a result of Indonesia's brutal occupation in 1979. Indonesia's government was greatly discomforted when two East Timor activists, Bishop Carlos Filipe Ximenes Belo and Jose Ramos-Horta, were awarded the Nobel Peace prize. To mitigate the impact, in July, the Indonesian government announced the opening of a branch office of the National Commission on Human Rights in Dili.

Despite restiveness, the Indonesian government does not appear to be in danger of being toppled. A strong economy, the relative unity of the military, and the absence of a credible opposition suggest that dissidence will be contained. President Suharto, seventy-five and in good health, may well run for a seventh five-year term in 1998. The issue of transition looms, however. An aging leader, accustomed to power, rarely provides in advance for his succession, and despite the rise of certain individuals like Research and Technology Minister B.J. Habibie, palace favorites come and go. Thus, an undercurrent of political unhappiness combined with uncertainty as to the timing of change will continue to mark Indonesian politics.

Burma's repressive SLORC

The challenges facing Burma are vastly more serious, although they may be contained by a tough military junta determined to stay in power. This past year, the State Law and Order Restoration Council (SLORC), Burma's governing body, made it clear that it intended to promote economic development through foreign assistance and seek full participation in such regional bodies as ASEAN. The economic situation, however, remains shaky despite some advances in foreign investment. Inflation is very high, depressing living standards still further. The trade imbalance is serious, with a progressive accumulation of foreign debt.

On the political front, the SLORC runs one of the most repressive countries in the world (in fact, Freedom House, in its most recent *Survey*, ranks Burma among the 17 worst-rated countries in the world), and shows few signs of relaxation. Its method is to crack down severely, then loosen restraints. Thus, earlier in the year, prior to the oppositionist National League for Democracy (NLD) party convention in May, more than 250 members were arrested, and a larger number were incarcerated in late September when the party attempted to hold a second congress. Barricades were also put up around the home of NLD leader Aung San Suu Kyi, and for a time she was prohibited from speaking to her followers, but in October, the detainees were released and the barricades removed. Suu Kyi herself gives speeches in front of her residence and frequently writes for and communicates with foreign sources. Yet, on November 9, a mob attacked Suu Kyi's motorcade, and strong evidence suggested that the attack had the government's blessing since security forces watched but took no action.

The SLORC's brutal politics and the strong international opposition to its repressive tactics have raised problems for ASEAN members, some of whom have hoped to admit Burma to full membership in 1997. In November, the ASEAN seven agreed that Burma, Cambodia and Laos should become members simultaneously, with no date set. The Philippines and Thailand had earlier indicated that Burma was not "technically prepared." Others, such as Malaysia, have argued that membership would assist in Burma's evolution. The evidence from 1996 suggests that the SLORC is determined to keep elements like the NLD under control.

Singapore presents a different picture. While this city-state faces increased economic competition from its neighbors with respect to port facilities and joint high-tech ventures, the prospects for the economy are relatively good. Meanwhile, the People's Action Party (PAP), as in the past, provides efficient, honest government.

Here, the transition from charismatic to technocratic leadership has already taken place, with Senior Minister Lee Kuan Yew busy advising other governments on their appropriate course, while Prime Minister Goh Chok Tong runs the Singaporean city-state. In recent years, the PAP has seen its share of the vote decline, but the opposition is weak. Nevertheless, to cement its supremacy in the coming elections, the government is proposing electoral changes that would enlarge the multi-member districts, winner take all. Single-seat wards would be cut from 21 to 8.

It is not easy to be an oppositionist in Singapore. Fund raising and organizational efforts meet difficulties since loyalty to the PAP has its rewards. Libel suits are initiated for slips of tongue by oppositionists, and the nongovernmentally controlled media is under careful surveillance. The judicial system is subordinate due to executive appointment rights. All is legal. Singapore represents soft authoritarianism at its most effective.

Asian democracies

Fifty years have passed since democracy was restarted in Japan (from roughly 1918 to 1931, Japan had what was termed Taisho Democracy—until 1925 when Emperor

Taisho died—followed by the Showa era, during which competitive parties existed, elections were held, and the Parliamentary system was functional), and its roots seem firmly planted. Nonetheless, in 1996, Japanese politics experienced complex problems. Early in the year, Social Democrat Tomiichi Murayama, minority head of a shaky coalition, resigned the prime ministership, with the post passing to Ryutaro Hashimoto. Once again, the Liberal Democratic Party was at the helm, although in coalition with the Social Democrats and another small party, Sakigake.

At this point, Japan had had four prime ministers in three years, and a stable party system seemed elusive. Then followed Hashimoto's dissolution of the Diet and the October 20 election, in which the LDP won 38.6 percent of the vote and 239 seats, slightly less than a majority of the 500 seats. Only 59.6 percent of eligible voters cast ballots, a very low number for Japan. The principal opposition party, the New Frontier Party (NFP), afflicted with internal divisions, garnered 28 percent of the vote and 156 seats, fewer than previously. The LDP coalition partners fared badly, with the Social Democrats dropping from 30 to 15 seats and Sakigake obtaining only 2 seats. A new reformist group led by younger figures, the Democratic Party, obtained 52 seats. The Communists moved from 15 to 26 seats, largely because they could claim to be clean—and no one thought of them as truly Communist.

In effect, the election revealed an electorate that was deeply split, but with a plurality seeing Hashimoto and his party as the force that could combine stability and reform. After talks with the old coalition partners, Hashimoto created a minority LDP government, with the others pledged only to support the government on specific policies, a loose political union. The new cabinet was strongly traditional, with the old LDP factions represented and most key posts going to long-established politicians.

Was this a cabinet that could effect the comprehensive administrative reforms pledged? Would these politicians tackle the thorny issues of deregulation and bureaucratic downsizing? Many observers, in and out of Japan, expressed doubts. Hashimoto himself, however, insisted that these actions would be his highest priorities, and promised that a blue-ribbon commission composed of businessmen and academics, excluding bureaucrats, appointed by and answerable to him, would make its recommendations in 1997, with proposals to be presented to the Diet in 1998 and effectuated in 2001.

The future of the Japanese party system remains in doubt. Some see indications that the old 1955 one-and-a-half party structure will return, with the LDP the dominant force, and all others in a perennial minority position. Others believe that in the course of the next few elections, a genuine two-party system will emerge, with others being minor actors. Some see a lengthy continuance of coalition politics, making resolute action on either domestic or foreign policy difficult. Political weakness increases the possibility of the survival of bureaucratic supremacy. Yet bureaucratic inflexibility, together with the cartelized industrial structure, has increasingly raised questions about Japan's future competitiveness. Hence, important elements of the business community and media are now championing reforms. The "iron-triangle"—the bond connecting parties, bureaucracy and business—if not broken, is currently bent. Moreover, the scandals of the past, some of them touching such powerful organs as the Ministry of Finance, coupled with the slow and spotty recovery from the recession, have disillusioned many Japanese, providing additional support for reform. As Hashimoto himself said after the election, his capacity to execute the promised reform program (together with the course of the Japanese economy) will determine his place in history.

Foreign policy figured little in the October election. Subsequently, Hashimoto has spoken of the need to strengthen relations with China and the U.S. The former will require a major effort since Sino-Japanese relations have recently sunk to their lowest level in recent years, with the Senkaku (Daiyu) island issue, visits to Yasukuni Shrine, charges of renewed "Japanese militarism," among other matters, on the table.

In addition, signs are that a more assertive Japan is on the horizon, with younger generations for whom World War II is history determined to improve Japan's regional and global position. Here too, nationalism, in various forms, is rising.

Cooperation with the U.S., however, is on the upswing, especially in the security realm, with economic issues handled separately to the extent possible, and continuously negotiated. As the year ended, an agreement reducing U.S. land usage on Okinawa was reached, and as the earlier Clinton-Hashimoto joint statement indicated, the guidelines restricting Japanese commitments to regional and international peace-making and peace-keeping will be reviewed in the context of a continuing Japan-U.S. alliance.

Across the Korea Straits lies another democracy, the Republic of Korea. For South Korea, 1996 was a truly traumatic year. Two former presidents, Chun Doo-hwan and Roh Tae-woo, are in jail. The former was originally sentenced to death, now commuted to life imprisonment; the latter, originally sentenced to life imprisonment, now reduced to seventeen years. The crimes for which they were convicted include corruption, and in the case of Chun, masterminding the attacks upon the existing government in 1979-1980. Throughout the year, moreover, key figures in government and business were charged with accepting or giving funds illegally. The ministers of defense and health were forced to resign, along with many lesser officials.

When he came to office in 1993, President Kim Young-sam pledged that his three principal tasks would be to eradicate corruption, restore national discipline and revitalize the economy. With one more year in office, he has a very considerable distance to go.

Perhaps South Korea epitomizes a problem much broader in scope. Over many centuries' evolution, and not without flaws, Western politics has come to be based essentially upon legalism. Despite efforts in that direction, especially in recent years, politics in much of Asia is based upon reciprocity. If the principle "one hand washes the other" prevails, corruption will constitute a natural mode of operation, binding formal and informal politics together.

Another problem confronting South Korean democracy is the deep regionalism that pervades politics, notwithstanding the relatively small size of the country and the homogeneity of its people. In part, this may be due to developmental differences, and the governor of North Cholla province has launched a growth campaign to keep his province abreast of the advanced regions.

In August, student riots broke out in and around the Yonsei University campus in connection with the call of the *Hanchongnyon* (Korean Federation of Student Councils) for South Korean youth to meet with their Northern counterparts at Panmunjom on the occasion of National Liberation day. The government responded with numerous arrests and subsequent jail sentences ranging from eight months to three years, applying the National Security Law. In fact, student radicalism in South Korea is at a low ebb. The average student is career oriented and relatively indifferent to politics, although here too, nationalism has been rising, in some cases manifesting an anti-American tone.

Meanwhile, the era of the three Kims (Kim Young-Sam, Kim Dae-jung, and Kim Jong-pil) is drawing to a close, although it will be extended for a few years more. What younger individuals will emerge in the future, and will they strengthen South Korea's still fragile democracy? Despite the problems, South Korea's era of military coups appears over. The weakening of the economy due to slower growth, rising prices, and a negative balance of payment signals the need for some important reforms, as in Japan. Yet the economy is not in deep trouble; growth was about 6.9 percent in 1996 and is projected to be around 6.4 percent in 1997.

Developments in North Korea, of course, could have a dramatic impact on the South Korean domestic scene. A North Korean collapse would create the problem of absorbing some 23 million people living at one-eighth the level of their Southern compatriots, and having known only a hard authoritarian political system. War would be horrendous to all parties. As 1996 came to an end, North-South contact was extremely minimal. Nonetheless, it appears that the KEDO project will continue, even if delayed, and the South's best hope remains that of a North Korean "soft landing."

South Korean cooperation with the United States, sorely tested during 1996, is destined to continue. Meanwhile, closer relations are being forged with the other major Northeast nations, including China and Russia. Mounting trade with the former and military exchanges with the latter characterized events in 1996. On balance, South Korea's international standing is strong.

Taiwan's recent democracy

Another recent democracy is Taiwan, a society which, like South Korea, emerged from an authoritarian-pluralist system to a democratic order in rapid stages. The presidential elections of March 1996 were highly significant, primarily because they provided a test both of Lee-Teng-hui and of the PRC's recent hard-line policies, including military threats. Lee won handily, with 54 percent of the vote in a four-way race, and most observers believe that his margin was increased as a result of China's policies.

While Taiwan's politics have generally been stable since the March elections, developments in the fall presage new complexities. In October, staunch advocates of independence broke away from the Democratic Progressive Party (DPP), the party historically holding that position, and formed the Taiwan Independence Party (TAIP). In its 1991 platform, the DPP had advocated Taiwan's independence, but on the condition that this was first supported by a nation-wide plebiscite. Strictly speaking, according to Republic of China law, parties are prohibited from advocating a separation of national territories, but this law was never applied to the DPP. Will it be used against the TAIP?

Observers debate the impact of the split on the DPP, but most feel that it will redound to the advantage of the Kuomintang. The DPP has been able to count upon roughly 25-30 percent of the vote, but in the last election, the issue of independence was downplayed in favor of domestic issues such as KMT corruption, mismanagement and an uneven economy. Indeed, in 1995, the DPP advanced a "New Theory," claiming that since Taiwan had never been governed by the Mainland, it was already independent; hence, attention should be directed toward other matters, including the eradication of provincialism and the advance of multiparty cooperation.

Lee and KMT demonstrated convincingly in the 1996 elections that they had positioned themselves closest to voter sentiment on the China issue. The official position is that the party supports a "One China" policy and eventual reunification, but that will come only when mainland China has become democratic. Meanwhile, two separate political entities exist, each with its own government; and the ROC deserves international recognition, given its economic and political accomplishments.

A small party largely composed of Mainland first and second generation refugees had earlier broken away from the Kuomintang to form the New Party, a party supportive of more active measures to promote unification. Beyond formal party divisions, a continuing cleavage exists between Taiwanese, making up some 85 percent of the population, and Mainlanders, who constitute most of the remaining citizens. While not discussed publicly, this cleavage has long existed and shows limited signs of diminution.

Lee's goal is naturally greater internal unity. In mid-December, he convened a National Development Conference, with all of the political parties initially participating. Among the recommendations was one for virtually eliminating the provincial government, transferring its powers to the center. The KMT and DPP agreed on this proposal, but the New Party left the conference and Governor James Soong resigned in protest. Beijing has not yet expressed itself, but if the recommendation is adopted in its present form, the Taiwan national government would be the solo player, a situation not likely to please PRC leaders.

Political freedom in Taiwan today is more extensive than at any time in its history. The key issues lie elsewhere. International recognition of the ROC has steadily shrunk, and at year's end, South Africa announced that it would accede to the PRC demand and break diplomatic relations with the ROC, thereby removing Taiwan's most important diplomatic tie. Hence, the quest for identity is understandable. Lee's efforts, symbolized by "vacation diplomacy," his 1995 Cornell University visit, attempts to get a U.N. seat and extensive financial commitments to those who might be supportive, characterize the drive for greater recognition. Success, however, is likely to remain limited.

Meanwhile, in the aftermath of PRC missile exercises and a low ebb in PRC-Taiwan relations, Beijing appears to be following a new tactic: united front policies, centering upon the cultivation of Taiwan economic groups, but accepting unofficial political dialogues as well. An eighty-member Taiwan trade delegation was received in Beijing in late August, with discussions extending over ten days. More surprisingly, an unofficial PRC group composed of academics and others went to Taiwan in the fall to discuss and observe local politics. For its part, Taiwan announced in November that it was relaxing the rules for Mainland reporters to visit Taiwan for up to two years.

Despite these developments, however, there is no sign that the fundamental issues separating the two governments are en route to being resolved. Economic intercourse will continue to grow, with direct trade a probability. But on the political front, the PRC formula of "One Country, Two Systems" is not likely to be acceptable to the great majority of Taiwanese people, and the PRC seems precluded from advancing a new thesis such as Confederation due to domestic political considerations. Thus, recurrent PRC-Taiwan tension will remain a matter of concern to all Asia/Pacific nations.

To the east of the Korean peninsula, across northeast China, lies the Republic of Mongolia, another of Asia's new democracies, with its lengthy dependence on the

Soviet Union severed. The major event of the year came on June 30, with the surprise electoral victory of a democratic coalition, ousting the Leninist Mongolian People's Revolutionary Party from power. The MPRP, which had been dominant in Mongolian politics since the country's founding in 1921, relinquished power without a struggle, an historic development. The new coalition garnered 47 of the 76 Great Hural (parliament) seats, with the National Democratic Party obtaining 34 seats, and the Social Democratic Party, 13. Voter participation was a phenomenal 87 percent. The new prime minister, M. Enkhsaikhan, pledged to lead a vigorous economic reform program.

By the end of the year, the new government had to acknowledge that the opening stages of the reform have been harsh, especially upon the urban poor. Prices have risen steeply and unemployment is massive. At local levels, the old Communist-era officials often remain in office, bewildered by the changes. Perhaps in part because of the economic trends, the MPRP won the local elections in October, with 65 percent of the vote. Clearly, Mongolia's political future will hinge on whether the economic transition can soon benefit a majority of its people.

Meanwhile, the three prominent Southeast Asian democracies each had an eventful year. The Philippines, under the Ramos administration, continued in its efforts to catch up economically with other ASEAN members, through reforms aimed at a more market-driven system and attacks on the cartel-monopoly system of the past. Growth reached over 6 percent in 1996, a record. However, the challenges remain substantial, since the oligarchic nature of Philippine society, and the huge gap between the privileged and the masses, especially the rural poor, remains largely intact.

Economic gains have been aided by political stability. Former military dissidents have largely been brought into the fold; the Communists—now bitterly split—are no longer a major factor; and in June 1996, an agreement was reached with Nur Misuari, chairman of the Moro National Liberation Front (MNLF), to create a new body—the Southern Philippines Council for Peace and Development. In September, with Ramos's support, Misuari was elected governor of the autonomous Mindanao region (Autonomous Region of Muslim Mindanao), first established in 1989. A threat from the more militant elements of the Moro secessionist movement continues, but the steps taken in the past year are promising.

The country looks increasingly to Asia despite its ties to the United States. Hosting the APEC conference enabled the Philippines to play a larger role than usual, and on some issues, such as new membership in ASEAN, its voice was heard. The process of Asianization—now germane to all of the states in the region—is underway.

In Malaysia, a strong leader, Prime Minister Mahatir Mohamad, is now completing his sixteenth year as head of government. His party, United Malays National Organization (UMNO), dominates the political scene, winning 64 percent of the vote in the 1995 elections. As the October party conference of 1996 illustrated, however, strong factionalism exists within UMNO. While Anwar Ibrahim, Mahatir's forty-nine-year-old deputy, is widely regarded as heir apparent, his faction lost certain key contests for party posts. Moreover, Mahatir has given no indication he will retire when his term ends in 1999.

Is Malaysia a democracy, or should it be classified as an authoritarian-pluralist state? Syed Husin Ali, president of the opposition Parti Rakyat Malaysia, would use the latter categorization; but in education, cultural activities and the media, considerable freedom exists, and opposition parties operate with few restraints. The economy is flourishing and there exist largely self-imposed restraints on the part of ethnic groups and Islamic fundamentalists.

In foreign policy, Mahathir continues to be an active participant in ASEAN, with a quizzical attitude toward APEC. His anti-West attitude has not been abandoned, but it depends upon the circumstances; on economic matters, he had no qualms about seeking interaction.

Malaysia's neighbor to the north, Thailand, is another democracy, albeit one with a less than wholesome reputation. Coalition politics is the rule in Thailand. The Banharn Silapa-archa government, regarded as both corrupt and inept, resigned in early November after sixteen months in office; and on November 17 a general election was held with the New Aspiration Party headed by General Chavalit Yongchaiyudh garnering 125 seats, and the Democrat Party, 123 .

All observers agreed that vote buying was rampant, especially in the rural northeast, where the NAP is strongest. Bangkok, on the contrary, provided Chuan Leekpai's Democrats—generally seen as the least tainted party—with an overwhelming majority. Chavalit has formed another coalition government, and promises to tackle the problems of a somewhat shaky Thai economy by giving extensive authority to a team of technocrats. He has also promised to undertake political reform, with the first step being the election of a Constitution Drafting Assembly that will amend the constitution so as to curb vote-buying and corruption. These are not new pledges, and skepticism runs high.

Thailand's foreign policy has been characterized by support for ASEAN, a tilt toward the U.S. despite quarrels over economic issues, and increasing interest in a Natural Economic Territory (NET) that encompasses portions of Malaysia and Indonesian Sumatra. Thailand will continue to seek extensive economic involvement in continental southeast Asia.

One Southeast Asian nation, Cambodia, defies political classification at present. Fears are widespread—not without some justification—that Cambodia is a failing state despite the external efforts that have been expended. As events in 1996 made clear, the key problem currently is not the Khmer Rouge. The Communists openly split during the year, with Ieng Sary and his soldiers breaking away from the Pol Pot elements, and most of the troops being brought into royalist military ranks.

The central problem lies in the rivalry and hostility between the two prime ministers in Phnom Penh. First Prime Minister Rannariddeh, son of King Sihanouk, is an individual of amiable disposition and questionable ability. Second Prime Minister Hun Sen is sharp, determined, and according to some, willing to use whatever means necessary to achieve and hold power. His influence within the military appears strong. Sihanouk remains a key figure in preserving some degree of stability, but with health problems, his influence may have waned. Corruption is widespread and most reform programs lag.

When the vast, heterogeneous region of East Asia is carefully examined, there is reason for cautious optimism as we enter 1997. The risks of a major power conflict are at the lowest ebb in this century, with the large states concentrating mainly on domestic problems. Economic growth, while likely to slow, will continue to make East Asia a pace-setter in the immediate future. The rigid ideological barriers to contact, once so prevalent, are largely gone. Even the remaining Leninist societies display greater diversity and some degree of openness, North Korea excepted.

Authoritarianism is still a strong political force, but it comes in many varieties. Meanwhile, democratic institutions have survived, and, notwithstanding such problems as money-politics and citizen apathy, are unlikely to be overturned, except in rare instances. Most importantly, peace and prosperity are feasible goals, with regional institutions and mechanisms, formal and informal, now gaining strength as organs of communication and negotiation on many fronts.

Robert A. Scalapino is Robson Research Professor of Government Emeritus at the University of California, Berkeley and a member of the Survey of Freedom Advisory Board.

Africa: Between Failure and Opportunity

Thomas R. Lansner

Africa is slowly sloughing off decades of failure and economic decay. But any optimism that Africa is moving toward sustained democratic development must be tempered by acknowledgment of the enormity of its needs in almost every area, from education and health care to economic investment to competent governance. These challenges are neither peculiar to Africa nor impervious to solution, once the political will to change takes hold. This essay describes some of the year's most important events in Africa. They include the long-predicted but ill-prepared-for crisis in Africa's Great Lakes region, setbacks for democratization and human rights in several countries and the consolidation of fundamental freedoms in others. To put this continental survey in perspective, however, it is useful to first offer some discussion of political and economic policies within and toward Africa.

Sustainable democratic development

While Africa is a major recipient of international aid in the form of development assistance and loans, sub-Saharan Africa receives less than 2 percent of all international direct investment. Few wealthy Africans invest in their own lands; capital flight from resource-rich African countries remains a costly hindrance to development. While lack of infrastructure is an important disincentive, conditions that breed instability deserve greater blame. Many of the booming "dragon" economies of East Asia thirty years ago boasted GDPs no greater than many African countries at the time.

Africa's current crises are neither congenital nor insoluble, but are often caused or intensified by incompetent administrations pursuing bad policies. These can be reversed. Industrialized countries that offer aid to Africa should insist on policy changes that create conditions to grow open societies and open markets.

An African platform for sustained democratic development must include several basic points:
- Respect for human rights and fundamental freedoms;
- Accountability and transparency in public affairs and the rule of law;
- Democratization and decentralization in decision-making;
- Free markets and economic reform;
- The end of hegemonic spheres of influence.

This platform is not only the core of the struggle for human rights and democratization in Africa; it also embodies the continent's best hopes for establishing long-term economic growth, which is spurred and nurtured by the rule of law. Countries which pursue such policies should be encouraged with increased economic assistance and debt relief. It is clear that some countries such as Ghana, Botswana and South Africa are realizing domestic peace and growth as fundamental freedoms grow. It is precisely where such freedoms are denied, in such countries as Zaire, Kenya or Nigeria, that prospects remain bleakest, and where predictions of upheaval and collapse may prove accurate.

Great lakes region: bad to worse?

Zaire is the outstanding example of how African politics can go from bad to worse. The country is richly endowed with natural resources, but was left after gaining independence from Belgium in 1961 with few educated people and little physical infrastructure. Three-and-a-half decades of parasitic dictatorship, which the West tolerated because it viewed Zaire as a base for maintaining influence in Africa during the Cold War, has left the country worse off than at independence. President Field Marshal Mobutu Sese Seko's kleptocracy squandered an entire nation's wealth. In December, Mobutu briefly returned from prostate cancer treatment in Switzerland to face a spreading rebellion and economic collapse.

The dictator's medical infirmities have apparently yet to impair his shrewd ability to divide and co-opt critics both at home and abroad. Although his regime still turns to crude repression, it faces a growing civil society and independent media. Elections are tentatively set for July 1997 after a delay of over one year, but it is unlikely that the political or logistical conditions for a free and fair electoral process—which must have substantial international moral and financial backing to succeed—can be realized by that date. Today, the country faces the possibility of its physical dismemberment. The central Kasai provinces have seceded for all practical purposes, and Mobutu's manipulation of the Rwandan crisis backfired. Mobutu offered sanctuary to the Hutu militias responsible for the Rwandan genocide—perhaps with encouragement from Paris—only to find ethnic Tutsi in eastern Zaire rise up and rout his ill-trained and unmotivated army. At year's end, a wide swathe of Zaire's eastern frontier was under control of Tutsi-led rebels supported by Rwanda, and the possibility of Zaire's breakup, with unpredictable consequences for the country and the region, suddenly became an urgent rather than theoretical concern.

Meanwhile, in Rwanda, the ruling Rwanda Patriotic Front (RPF) had reason to be satisfied with Mobutu's misfortune. Through the first eight months of the year, the RPF, led by the country's Tutsi minority, which seized power in 1994 after a five year guerrilla struggle, repelled raids by Zaire-based Hutu militias. Rebel advances in eastern Zaire dispersed the militias and created a friendly buffer zone along the frontier. The defeat of the militias also sparked a reverse exodus of most of the approximately 2 million Hutu who fled Rwanda in mid-1994. The fate of hundreds of thousands who fled deeper into Zaire is unclear. In December, Tanzania closed refugee camps on its territory, violating international law by forcibly repatriating Rwandans with barely a ripple of international protest.

How these refugees reintegrate into Rwandan society and are treated by RPF authorities will help determine Rwanda's civil peace for years to come. By year's end, at least 2,500 returnees had been arrested on suspicion of taking part in the April-July 1994 genocide. In late December, the first trial for genocide began in Rwanda's courts, and a U.N.-authorized court in Arusha, Tanzania, had also begun proceedings.

About 90,000 genocide suspects are crammed into prisons and temporary detention centers throughout Rwanda. Their fate has sparked an important international debate on questions of justice and impunity in post-conflict situations. While some people advocate "reconciliation and no revenge" as the fastest route to national healing, others insist there can be "no peace without justice." A movement to establish an international criminal court with jurisdiction over international crimes has gathered many prominent supporters.

In Burundi, with an ethnic divide similar to neighboring Rwanda's (both countries are roughly 85 percent Hutu and 15 percent Tutsi), a brutal guerrilla war marked by excesses on both sides continues. In July, a coup by the Tutsi-controlled army eliminated most vestiges of a democratic transition begun five years ago. Major Pierre Buyoya, who first seized power in 1987 but left office in 1993, is again president. The growing ethnic war has claimed over 150,000 lives and threatens to descend into savagery that could match Rwanda's 1994 genocide. In a rare show of cooperation, Burundi's neighbors imposed economic sanctions aimed at forcing the country's Tutsi-dominated military to restore at least a power-sharing arrangement with Burundi's Hutu majority. Buyoya's September decree reversing the ban on political parties and restoring parliament had little apparent effect in either loosening sanctions or reducing attacks by Hutu guerrilla groups.

The region's tumult reflects a basic conundrum facing many African countries: how to impose modern state structures on multi-ethnic societies that mainly possess only the formal attributes of nationhood. Africa's colonial boundaries are still largely considered inviolable for fear of opening a Pandora's box of secessionism and irredentism. Yet the respect for diversity found in the rule of law and human rights that best buttresses a multi-cultural society remains notably absent in many African countries.

Real elections and democratic consolidation

Elections generally viewed as free and fair returned to power former military dictators in Madagascar and Benin; and to varying extents some other former military leaders legitimized their rule through victories from crediblepolls. In several other countries, the electoral process was blatantly manipulated to allow coup-makers to clothe themselves in nominal civilian legitimacy. Among the year's most successful elections:

• Benin's March polls saw the ex-general and president, Mathieu Kerekou, defeat incumbent Nicéphore Soglo. The election was also notable for other reasons. Kerekou triumphed through an ethnic coalition that allied traditional rivals from the north and south of the country. Plus, the entire electoral process was marked by a civility which can be largely credited to an extensive civic and voter education campaign conducted by Beninese nongovernmental organizations with international support. This included many programs over broadcast media and thousands of in-person presentations that reached even remote areas. The access to state media by all political parties and many civic groups greatly enhanced the public credibility of the entire electoral process.

• Madagascar's former dictator Admiral Didier Ratsiraka's December 29 victory in a second round presidential run-off election against impeached President Albert Zafy capped a year of political turbulence in Madagascar, played out almost entirely without violence. Zafy was impeached by parliament on corruption charges in July, after more than three years of tension between the president and the national assembly.

• Ghana's December 1996 presidential and legislative elections returned President Jerry Rawlings and his National Democratic Congress party to another four years in power. The polls were free and fair according to international observers, but were also marked by the incumbents' heavy use of state media and patronage. The elections included an extensive civic education campaign, as well as international assistance with registration and other electoral procedures.

• Sierra Leone's election to replace an army junta in March, together with a November 30 pact with rebels that halted a vicious six-year guerrilla war, renewed prospects for peaceful democratic development in a country which only a year ago appeared on the edge of disintegration. It was the country's first open multiparty elections in two decades. Despite the new government's electoral credentials, media repression has heightened; the country's democratic transition appeared very fragile, vulnerable to threats such as an army coup foiled by President Ahmed Tejan Kabbah in September. The peace pact raised hope that a tenuous February cease-fire with the rebel Revolutionary United Front would take permanent hold. The war had taken about 10,000 lives and displaced over a million people

• Cape Verde President Antonio Mascarenhas Monteiro won a second five-year term in an unopposed February election that drew only a sparse turnout among this island nation's 400,000 people. The low participation was variously ascribed to voter fatigue after parliamentary and local polls in the two preceding months and to preparations for a major religious festival. Despite the lack of enthusiasm displayed for the presidential poll, Cape Verde's transition to multiparty democracy, begun in 1991, now seems well under way.

• Uganda's first elected government in nearly fifteen years took office in 1996, in voting that restricted formal political party participation but was deemed by most observers generally free and fair. President Yoweri Museveni, after over a decade as Uganda's president, won an electoral mandate with 74 percent of the vote against his only serious rival, Democratic Party head Paul Ssemogerere. The May election was denounced by oppositionists as fraudulent, and most boycotted legislative elections the following month. Critics complained that Museveni used state resources and media to support his candidacy. Most observers believe Museveni would have won handily even with party participation, and pollwatchers described the electoral process as transparent, despite minor irregularities.

• In the tiny Indian Ocean island nation of the Federal Islamic Republic of the Comoros, Mohamed Taki, of the National Union for Democracy, won Presidential elections in a second round March run-off. In October, a new constitution that increases the impact of Islamic law in everyday life was adopted by an 85 percent vote in a referendum.

In several other countries, democratic consolidations continued or peace processes took stronger hold. Even in countries with apparently successful transitions, however, institutionalization of the democratic process remains tenuous. The litmus test for entrenchment of democratic change can often be seen in the performance of an independent judiciary and free media.

• This test is so far being met successfully in South Africa, where a new constitution became law in December after being amended by the Constitutional Assembly. The new constitution includes provisions to protect human rights, including freedom of expression and assembly.

As in Rwanda, the question of justice in dealing with the excesses of the recent past is causing tensions. Former defense minister General Magnus Malan was acquitted of murder charges, but some former security officials have been convicted. Other trials are in the works. Nobel peace laureate and recently retired Archbishop Desmond Tutu is leading public hearings of the official Truth and Reconciliation Commission. Numerous officials of the former white minority regime have appeared before the panel, admitted wrongdoings and requested amnesty. Bishop Tutu has threatened to resign unless members of the African National Congress (ANC) who undertook terrorist acts or committed extrajudicial killings during the liberation struggle do the same.

• Mozambique's four-year transformation from decades of war and repressive rule continued in 1996, and Angola enjoyed its least violent year in three decades, though prospects for a lasting peace remained tenuous. A United Nations-monitored peace agreement reached in November 1994 is being implemented by 7,000 U.N. peacekeepers and 1,000 U.N. civilian officials.

• The Central African Republic's (CAR) elected government was badly shaken in 1996 by three army mutinies, the second of which, in May, garnered broad popular support and was suppressed only by French military intervention.

• In the Congo, security and human rights conditions deteriorated amidst intense political maneuvering among the country's several regional/ethnic-based parties; these make up the ruling and opposition coalitions ahead of scheduled August 1997 elections in which President Pascal Lissouba will seek a second five-year term. A brief army-pay mutiny in February, regional militia actions and the banning of private media slowed a trend toward increased security and respect for human rights.

Elections surreal: Repression and generals in mufti

The countries cited in the preceding section allow relative optimism and offer genuine hope for fundamental freedoms. But in several countries, including Chad, the Gambia and Niger, the electoral process has been subverted to clothe army coup-makers in civilian legitimacy that places little restraint on repressive rule. And in a few countries, like Zambia, tenuous democratic transitions have been eroded by unfair elections or increased repression.

• President Idriss Déby's July victory in Chad's first multiparty election was marred by irregularities that sharply devalued Déby's mandate and seriously eroded confidence in the electoral process. The flawed results were condoned by France, and accepted by some observer groups as legitimate. Other groups denounced the polls, noting the disqualification of several credible challengers, intimidation of opposition activists and manipulation of the vote count.

• In Equatorial Guinea, a February presidential election saw President Teodoro Obiang Nguema M'basogo declared winner of a contest that was neither free nor fair. Nearly all power remains concentrated in the hands of ethnic Fang people, particularly Esangui clansmen related to President Obiang. Despite this, the president's renewed seven-year mandate, however flawed, may allow a slight easing of the most overt repression. New wealth from oilfields is unlikely to soon ease the economic despair of the country's 400,000 people.

• In the Gambia, Yahya A.J.J. Jammeh was proclaimed victor of deeply flawed September presidential elections two years after seizing power in a military coup. The most formidable opposition candidates were barred from running, and the army employed violence and intimidation and made heavy use of state resources to promote the recently retired Colonel Jammeh's candidacy. The army's intention to retain effective power was so blatant that even the Commonwealth and the Organization of African Unity, usually quite loose in their election-observation standards, refused to send observers.

• In Gabon, President Omar Bongo neared the end of his third decade as ruler of this small oil-rich Central African nation. Strongly backed by his army and by France, which maintains a garrison in Gabon, Bongo's rule remains personal, despite the formal trappings of democracy. The ruling party won overwhelmingly in December parliamentary elections marked by violence, confusion and charges of fraud.

• Mauritania's gradual liberalization stalled in 1996, as October elections, generously described as rife with "imperfections," saw the military-backed ruling Social Democratic Republican Party take all but one of 79 National Assembly seats against a divided opposition. Media censorship continues. Mauritania's political divisions run along racial and ethnic lines. Discrimination against the country's black African minority and reports of de facto slavery affecting tens of thousands of people persist. Yet greater political activity, open discussion and criticism of the government was tolerated, even if President Maaouya Ould Sid Ahmed Taya seems little inclined to allow any real challenge to his expected 1998 re-election bid.

• In Niger, an army coup toppled the democratically-elected government in January, ousting President Mahamane Ousmane and shattering the country's fragile transition to representative rule. In July, coup leader Colonel Barre Mainassara Ibrahim was proclaimed victor of elections so plagued by irregularities as to be meaningless as a test of popular will.

• Africa's longest-serving leader, President Gnassingbé Eyadéma, reasserted nearly full control over the Togolese government after parliamentary by-elections and party defections gave him a working majority in the country's National Assembly. The main opposition party chose to boycott the polls, when, in violation of an earlier agreement, the interior ministry rather than an independent authority ran the elections.

• Zambian President Frederick Chiluba was proclaimed victor of a second five-year term of office in an election rejected by independent monitors and opposition parties as neither free nor fair. The ruling Movement for Multiparty Democracy (MMD) also renewed its dominance over parliament as most opposition parties boycotted the polls. The November vote was held under a new constitution adopted five months earlier that barred the most credible opposition candidate, former President Kenneth Kaunda, and weakened the judiciary. Problems in voter registration and other irregularities plagued election preparations, and state resources and media were mobilized to support Chiluba and the MMD. Several international observer groups refused to monitor the polls.

• President Robert Mugabe and his Zimbabwe African National Union-Patriotic Front (ZANU-PF) party swept to a deeply-flawed presidential election victory in March that reflected state powers of patronage and repression as the country edged closer to becoming a de facto one-party state. ZANU-PF's firm grip on parliament, security forces and the media, electoral laws that strongly favor the ruling party, and decreasing parameters for free expression further entrenched autocratic rule.

• President Daniel arap Moi continues to rule through a combination of state patronage, media control and repression as he prepares for December 1997 presidential and legislative elections that he and his Kenya African National Union are expected to dominate. Moi's already formidable prospects are buoyed by the existence of only a fractious opposition. While a wide range of political parties and civil society groups are demanding constitutional and other reforms before the coming elections, have denounced widespread corruption and condemned Moi's media repression and other human rights abuses, few signs of their uniting to present a single challenger are evident.

• In Cameroon, sweeping opposition victories in local elections were met by increasing repression and measures aimed at eviscerating resistance to President Paul Biya's authoritarian rule. Constitutional amendments adopted in December 1995 concentrated even more power in the presidency and only nominally strengthened a compliant judiciary. A sustained assault on the independent media continued, and the regime deployed physical and administrative intimidation in an effort to cripple opposition political parties in advance of presidential and parliamentary elections set for 1997.

• Ethiopia's democratic transition remained hobbled in 1996, as the ruling Ethiopian People's Revolutionary Democratic Front government not only intensified attacks against the independent media but increased harassment of political opponents. The repression further devalued the important step achieved in 1995, of realizing at least the form of democratic governance in polls described as generally free and fair, despite an opposition boycott.

Despots dig in; wars go on

In several countries, little effort is given to honoring even the pretense of electoral democracy. Sudan, Africa's largest country in area, and Nigeria, the continent's most populous, are each ruled by harsh juntas. The situation in both Liberia and Somalia is near anarchy, and Swaziland's royal family sought to maintain the continent's only absolute monarchy.

• Nigeria's military junta maintained its timetable to return the country to at least a semblance of civilian rule by late 1998, apparently unperturbed by international criticism that remained mostly rhetoric. The only effective tool to pressure the generals to respect human rights and restore democracy, an embargo on petroleum exports which provide three-quarters of the national budget, was left untouched by Western nations whose companies earn large profits from pumping Nigeria's oil. The assassination, in broad daylight in June, of the wife of Moshood Abiola, the imprisoned victor of 1993's democratic presidential election,atop a series of other political murders and continuing repression, was not enough to convince the United States, Britain, Holland, France and other countries to endanger corporate profits by angering the military regime.

Reports by the U.N., Amnesty International and other human rights groups describe Nigeria as a place where the judicial system is made a mockery by military tribunals and decrees, where arbitrary arrest, torture and summary executions are commonplace, and where free expression and free media are muzzled. Striking unions have been banned, and new political parties allowed to register only under stringent conditions. Rampant lawlessness, corruption and drug-trafficking mark the rule of General Sani Abacha, who seized power in a palace coup in November 1993. The U.S. Justice Department also reported that thousands of Americans have fallen prey to swindles that sometimes involve Nigerian government officials. But perhaps the most successful and insidious has been the multi-million dollar public relations campaign, mounted by American lobbying firms hired by Abacha, to improve the murderous dictatorship's image in Washington, and to deflect international pressure on the regime.

• Sudan is suffering Africa's longest and bloodiest war; civil war and massive human rights abuses continue to wrack the country. Widespread slavery persists in parts of the country, as genocidal campaigns against minorities continues. Sudan's ruling dictatorship, dominated by Arab Islamic fundamentalists, seeks to subjugate the country's black African minority and secular and democratic forces. New fighting flared along the Eritrean frontier, as the U.S. and Sudan's neighbors supported armed opposition groups. Sudanese president and prime minister Lieutenant-General Omar Hassan Ahmed al-Bashir, claimed electoral legitimacy in heavily manipulated March elections which gave him and the ruling party sweeping victories.

• In Liberia, the worst fighting of the country's seven-year civil war raged through the capital, Monrovia, for seven weeks in April and May, leaving much of the city in ruins and at least 1,500 people dead. Refugees fled into the bush or onto the high seas in overcrowded ships that were repeatedly refused safe haven in neighboring countries. An August statement by the country's Catholic bishops condemned the various factions responsible for prolonging the war and summed up the situation well, declaring: "Violence as a way of life has been and continues to be institutionalized. There is no respect for human life or for private or public property. Morality seems to be something of the past."

• Somalia's leading warlord, Mohammed Farah Aideed, died in battle in August, briefly raising hopes for a lasting peace in the war-ravaged country. However, a ceasefire negotiated in October almost immediately disintegrated amid clashes in the divided capital, Mogadishu. Clan-based factions fought over territory, control of sea and airports, and the country's banana trade. In some areas, harsh Islamic law brought a semblance of draconian order, but chances for Somalia to become a modern unified state are diminishing. The northern portion of the country, which was once British Somaliland, maintained its self-declared independence, although it, too, was wracked by internecine strife.

• In Guinea, the after-effects of a February army mutiny that nearly ousted long-serving President Lansana Conté are still being felt. The rebellion was accompanied by widespread looting and destruction in the capital, Conakry. But Conté, who seized power in a 1984 coup and was declared victor in a gravely flawed December 1993 election, rallied loyal troops and has reasserted control.

• Swazi King Mswati III acceded to demands by trade unionists and multiparty advocates for constitutional revisions in Africa's last absolute monarchy after strikes and demonstrations led to violence early in the year. For decades, Swaziland was a regional oasis of calm, as war and turmoil raged in neighboring Mozambique and South Africa. Now, the tiny kingdom of less than one million people has southern Africa's only unelected government. The king named a twenty-nine-member constitutional review panel in July, but traditional chiefs are unlikely to quietly accept reform.

Maghreb: radical islam and repression

The Maghrebian lands stretching across the northern coast of Africa are a geographically and culturally distinct portion of the continent, facing some challenges apart from sub-Saharan Africa. Most important is the rise of militant Islamic groups dedicated to the creation of theocratic states. Such groups also exist in several Sahelian states just south of the Sahara, but nowhere in black Africa do they possess the cohesion or support to launch a serious bid for power. Their strength in the Maghreb is considerable, arising from dissatisfaction with repressive rule and difficult economic conditions as much as from deep religiosity. To counter the Islamist threat, the Maghreb's secular but authoritarian regimes are increasing security cooperation, prompting closer ties even between long-time rivals Morocco and Algeria, and between Tunisia and Libya.

• Most affected is Algeria, whose 29 million people suffered another year of bloody internecine conflict, as Islamist radicals employed terrorism in their armed struggle against a brutally repressive military-dominated regime that voided the results of democratic elections in 1992. President Lamine Zeroual's plan for a return to civilian rule, including parliamentary elections in 1997, is as yet rejected by leading political parties, as well as by the armed opposition. A new constitution approved by a referendum in November expands presidential powers and bans Islamic-based parties.

• In Libya, Islamist groups and other foes of Colonel Mu'ammar al-Qadhafi stepped up attacks on security forces, as the most serious threat to Qadhafi's rule since he seized power in a 1969 coup. Qadhafi handed more power to the military and ordered populist "purges" against black-market traders in an effort to curb Islamist influence.

• In Morocco, King Hassan II continued to implement his vision of turning the kingdom into a limited democracy through a September referendum that approved decentralization and a new bicameral legislature. The country's human rights performance showed gradual improvement, but problems remain. King Hassan and his heir-apparent, Prince Sidi Mohamed, strengthened ties with France, which views Morocco as a crucial ally against rising Islamist power in the Maghreb. In Western Sahara, Moroccan obstruction continued to block preparation for a referendum on nationhood or integration into Morocco. The plan's failure to date raises fear of a return to the bloody guerrilla war that ravaged the territory from 1976 until a 1991 cease-fire. Yet, direct talks between top Moroccan officials, led by Crown Prince Sidi Mohamed and Interior Minister Driss Basri and the Popular Front for the Liberation of Saguia el-Hamra and Rio de Oro (Polisario) in October, and the release of sixty-six Polisario prisoners, raised hopes that a negotiated solution to the long stalemate could still be achieved.

• Tunisian President Zine el-Abidine Ben Ali maintained a repressive stability and a firm grip on power in 1996, stifling dissent and harshly suppressing signs of Islamic radicalism, whose proponents are waging armed rebellions in neighboring Algeria and Libya. As many as 2,000 suspected Islamists remain in detention, and two leading oppositionists and a human rights activist were imprisoned on dubious charges in 1996. President Ben Ali has also achieved a modicum of popular support through steady economic growth and promotion of social benefits and women's rights. Elections are closely managed affairs, however, as demonstrated by Ben Ali's ruling Constitutional Democratic Rally party's victory in all but six of 4,090 seats contested in May municipal elections.

Moving the debate: rights & consent

The survey above outlines some genuine achievements as well as many grim realities in Africa. Yet even when considering the subversion of electoral processes and the denial of human rights, it is important to remember that the basic terms of debate over governance in Africa is evolving toward respect for fundamental freedoms. Stronger civil societies are emerging in many countries, forging ties beyond race, religion and ethnicity. African leaders are increasingly accepting that domestic peace demands the consent of their citizenry. They are also coming to realize that a prosperous future requires looking beyond national boundaries that often make little geographic, demographic or economic sense.

The international community must do its best to support countries which adopt policies to help themselves, and should not hesitate to sanction countries which do not. Interference that props repressive regimes should not be tolerated. In December, donors earmarked $5 billion for a dozen of Africa's poorest countries—and tied the aid to those countries' commitment to serious reforms. This should also be a prerequisite for debt relief of any of the over $300 billion African nations owe to international creditors. The continent clearly needs international assistance. But as the past three decades have shown, even massive aid may mean little if there is global forbearance for despots and kleptocrats.

Thomas R. Lansner is Africa specialist for Freedom House.

The Middle East: Islamists on the March   Khalid Durán

Nineteen-ninety-six was characterized by the continuous advance of Islamism ("Muslim Fundamentalism") in much of the Muslim world. This progress has little to do with Islamist performance, achievements or heightened attractiveness. On the contrary, much has happened to turn people away from Islamism. Several drawbacks occurred in 1996 to make Islamist advances seem unlikely:

1. *Islamists did not achieve any military victory.* In Afghanistan, they were driven out of Kabul by the Tálibán, traditionalist Muslims who might appear to be fundamentalist, but who are, in fact, strangers to the international Islamist movement. In Algeria, Islamist terror did not lose momentum, but neither was it able to overturn the regime. The Islamist regime in Sudan suffered military reverses against the Southern insurgents who were joined by military units and politicians from the North. In Kashmir, the Indian occupation forces gained the upper hand against the mostly Islamist guerrillas. In Israel, the Islamist resistance could have taken the shape of spectacular terrorist exploits against Israel's new Likud government, but terrorism declined from the year before.

On the contrary, violence and fighting, especially the internecine warfare in Afghanistan and Algeria, gave Islamists a negative image, causing dismay even in their own ranks.[1]

2. *Islamists did not enjoy resounding election victories.* Islamists cannot even claim victory in Turkey, where 21 percent of the vote made them the strongest party, still dependent on finding a coalition partner with whom to govern. In Bangladesh, Islamists suffered a devastating defeat, almost disappearing from the political scene. The 40 percent Islamists got in the Kuwaiti elections in the fall of 1996 is the highest percentage Islamists have ever obtained in free and fair elections but, nonetheless, they have a clear majority of 60 percent against them. Besides, the Islamist camp in Kuwait is so fractious that it can scarcely be considered as one bloc.

3. *Islamists are not yet short of finances, but neither is there much new funding to substitute for sources that are drying up.* Rival state subsidies—Iran/Saudi Arabia—have decreased, making Islamists more dependent on donations from private sympathizers.

4. *No new charismatic Islamist leadership has emerged.* Sudan's Hasan Al-Turábí, who in 1995 still looked like a rising star about to establish an *Islamist Internationale*, is in poor health and has lost steam. His crown prince, Ráshid Al-Ghannúshí of Tunisia's Islamist party An-Nahda, is making every effort to present himself to his British hosts as a moderate, a kind of "Muslim Democrat." That may be sensible politics, but it

does not inspire those who think of him as a revolutionary. Mustafa Mashhúr, who was made the new head of Egypt's Muslim Brethren and their international office, faces a rebellion from younger cadres. They revolt against a closed society which the party assumed under a bureaucratic leadership, now in their seventies and eighties. Turkey's Necmettin Erbakan aspires to a larger role, but he is a manager, a party boss, not an ideologue—not even an intellectual.

5. *Islamism has not seen the ideological breakthrough many had hoped for.* Many Islamists are carried by a somewhat mystical belief that there is more to their ideology than meets the eye. They go along with all the talk about the superiority of Islam over any other ideology or "man made system," convinced that the specialty and effectiveness of Islamism will eventually unfold. In the meantime, the slogan "Islam is the Solution" has not lost its appeal, but neither has anything happened to make it more meaningful.[2]

It may be said, then, that the 1996 Islamist advance took place more by default than by design. The important point is that the pressures are so many and exist in so many places that they become overwhelming, reinforcing one another. For this reason, three or four reversals for Islamism count less than three or four Islamist advances. An analysis of developments in several countries may shed some light on how Islamists have been helped to numerous successes, all their failures notwithstanding.

Bosnia and Turkey: European betrayal, Islamist gains

Before the outbreak of the war in April 1992, Bosnia was anything but a fertile ground for Islamism. Muslim identity had remained strong because it was equated with Bosnianism; Islam stood for national rather than religious identity. However, since the Serb aggressors made ample and brutal use of Christian symbolism and declared their land-grabbing a Crusade for the defense of Christianity against Islam, Bosnians were pushed into an Islamist corner. Initially, there was much resistance to such a trend, foreign *mujahidin* were not welcome. Many government officials and other citizens who today seem won over to the Islamist cause were at first emphatic that this was not a conflict between Christians and Muslims, but between ultranationalists from Serbia and Bosnian pluralists. As late as 1995, a national congress abolished the political category *Musliman,* which Tito had introduced to designate the Bosnian nationality. "We have been Muslims for several hundred years, but Europeans for thousands of years," was a common complaint of Bosnians whenever they were referred to as Muslims. Vice-President Ejub Ganíc went as far as to say that Bosnia was reestablished after 500 years of foreign domination—since the Ottoman (Muslim) conquest in 1463. In 1994, Ganíc joined the pro-Iranian faction within the government. The disappointment over the abandonment of Bosnia by Europe became overwhelming.

The partitioning of the country on a 51 to 49 percent basis was accepted under duress, but is not taken as final by Bosnian Muslims. Those "Bosnian Serbs" who fought for Serbia constitute less than 20 percent of the overall population of the country, because many "Bosnian Serbs" stayed on the government side, as personified by General Divjak, who became a hero of the defense of Sarajevo against Serb separatists. At least half of those 20 percent separatists are relative newcomers, mostly settled in Bosnia after the establishment of Communist Yugoslavia in 1945.

The U.S. policy of allowing Islamist Iran to help Bosnians with arms (instead of openly rejecting the arms embargo) had a paralyzing effect on Bosnian pluralism, because it became next to impossible for Bosnians to take an open stand against Iran and Islamism, their sense of gratitude being too strong.

The betrayal of pluralist Bosnia and the country's drift into the Islamist camp had a far-reaching effect on the entire world of Islam. Islamists everywhere point to the plight of Bosnia as evidence of non-Muslim hostility toward Muslims *qua* Muslims.[3] Secularists face a difficult task defending themselves against this argument. Bosnia's former foreign minister and then prime minister, Dr. Haris Silajdzíc, himself an Islamic scholar but an avowed secularist, obtained barely 14 percent of the vote in the elections of 1996, despite the fact that as prime minister (until 1995) he was immensely popular.

That the Bosnian tragedy would have profound repercussions on Muslims around the world was not hard to predict and, yet, the effects seem to have been grossly underestimated by decision-makers in Western Europe and the United States. The relative inaction of the governments of major Muslim states was registered with some surprise. Lack of analysis of this phenomenon might have contributed to misjudgments.[4] Margaret Thatcher's warnings, in July 1992, that Bosnia was a time bomb, were not heeded. Subsequent developments proved her right, and the repercussions are just beginning to show.

Thus, although Bosnia is Europe, it is a major factor in the Middle East. Turkey, the Middle Eastern country closest to the scene, was the first to be affected by the Bosnian events. Some 5 percent of Turkey's roughly 60 million people are of Bosnian origin, but their influence on Turkish politics exceeds their number, because many belong to the educated class. As refugees from earlier anti-Muslim pogroms in Yugoslavia (especially around 1948) they are receptive to Islamist propaganda. Since the outbreak of the Bosnian war, Islamists have been the most vocal group in Turkey, demanding military action to save Bosnia. This factor contributed to the emergence of the Islamist Refah Partisi ("Welfare Party") as the strongest party (21 percent of the vote) in the Turkish elections of December 1995. The Welfare Party's subsequent rise to power greatly enhanced the prestige of Islamists everywhere. Whether in Morocco, Egypt or Kuwait, Islamists are euphoric over developments in Turkey. Even those who spurn democracy as an insidious Western machination celebrate the Turkish example, where free and fair elections led to the formation of an Islamist government.

While the Islamist election victory in Turkey was partly the voters' response to Western treachery in Bosnia, it also was the result of European discrimination against Turkey itself. Had the previous Turkish government received stronger support from the European Union, the Refah Partisi might have received significantly fewer votes. Turkish resentment of the European Union runs very deep, and needed an outlet.

Iran/Sudan: closer cooperation

In June 1989, Sudanese Islamists grabbed power through their cadres in the military. Only a few months later, they began to woo the clerical regime in Tehran. This incurred them the wrath of Saudi Arabia, but the Iranians were not as forthcoming as expected. Sudan, an extremely poor country, was an expensive proposition for an Iranian regime itself suffering severe economic hardships. Besides, the Shi'i clerics want Sunni Islamists to accept their leadership; they are less interested in propping up a Sunni counterpart to Shi'i Iran. The Irani-Sudani alliance took years to come into full swing until, in 1996, it was properly cemented. President Rafsanjani visited Khartoum, once again, with a huge entourage, concluding numerous agreements on economic support and military cooperation. This Islamist axis was caused largely by U.S. sanctions—which are not enough to bring down the Sudanese and Iranian governments, but enough to make them look to each other for support.

Afghanistan/Pakistan: How "fundamentalists" are fabricated

In Afghanistan, Islamists seemed severely beaten after the Tálibán, a religious movement created in Pakistan, pushed them out of Kabul. In fact, the Islamist "government" practiced a tactical retreat. Its forces are likely to recuperate, especially since they have the support of India, Iran and Russia. The United States and Russia have been working at cross purposes, with both sides showing themselves to be equally inept, as if they had no Afghanistan experience. Russian leaders called the Tálibán advance a threat,[5] failing to understand that this movement had a very limited horizon and none of the expansionist ideology that caused the Islamist government in Kabul to give the Russians so much trouble in Tajikistan since 1991. Fears of an American hold on the resources of formerly Soviet Central Asia are obviously the determining factor for such off-track analyses of the Tálibán as the fundamentalist danger from the South.

Washington seemed originally supportive of efforts by the Bhutto government in Pakistan to substitute Islamist Hikmatyár with the traditionalist Tálibán.[6] Hikmatyár had been the favorite of Pakistan's Islamist military dictatorship, and now the secularist Bhutto government joined the Afghan race with its own horse, the Tálibán. Hardly had the Tálibán captured Kabul when they were criticized in Washington for being "fundamentalists." This was hilarious inasmuch as Islamists around the world were furious with the U.S. for allegedly having introduced those non-fundamentalists into Afghanistan.[7]

A possible explanation for the misunderstanding was the restrictions imposed by the Tálibán upon women—the only way they could think to put an end to daily incidents of rape and the sale of tens of thousands of Afghan women to neighboring countries by the previous rulers.[8] Curiously, the Islamists (viz. the government of President Rabbání and Prime Minister Hikmatyár) were rarely criticized for those crimes; instead, attention was diverted from their inhumanity to the puritanism of the Tálibán. Islamists could now pose as liberators of Afghanistan from the yoke of the "fundamentalists."

With the fall of the Bhutto government in November, the Tálibán were left in the lurch. The most likely option for them was to submit to one of the Islamist factions and become "fundamentalists" for real. This would mean an end to U.S. plans for running a gas pipeline and a super-highway from Turkmenistan through Afghanistan into Pakistan in order to circumvent Iran.[9]

And the dismissal of Bhutto's government meant a second lease on life for Islamists in Pakistan, where they have never won more than 6 percent of the vote, but always have had a disproportionately high influence because of their entrenchment in the bureaucracy, especially military intelligence. The West did not grab the opportunity offered by Bhutto to turn Pakistan into a front line state against Islamism in general, and Iran in particular.

Israel/Egypt: Iran profits from Israeli fears

In Israel, Islamists received a boost as a result of Israeli elections that brought to power a new Likud government. The Israeli actions aimed at limiting the Oslo peace process were so damaging to the Palestinian Authority under Arafat that the Islamist organizations, Hamás and Islamic Jihád of Palestine, could afford to sit back and let the dynamics of the situation work in their favor.

Arab-Israeli relations stand little chance of improvement, because the positions are too wide apart and a suicidal determination for self-sacrifice exists on both sides. Islamists are the ones to benefit most from expected clashes, one of which may well be the catastrophic collision zealots on both sides look to with eschatological expectations. This has rarely been so evident as during 1996. Dozens died over a matter of archeology when the Likud government opened a Hasmonean Tunnel in the old city of Jerusalem. The real issue, however, was not the tunnel, but Jerusalem as a capital. Had Prime Minister Netanyahu and Mayor Ehud Olmert not reiterated their unwillingness to share the city with the Palestinians, there would almost certainly have been less fighting over opening the tunnel for tourism.

For the Middle East peace process, 1996 was a step backward. In 1995, the Arab world found itself in the grip of a liberating movement, as for the first time in decades the Arab-Israeli conflict receded into a less than secondary position. Constructive issues such as social and economic development began to occupy center stage. 1996 witnessed a reversal, with talk of another Israeli war with Syria, and possibly even with Egypt. This went so far as to propel Damascus, so far the most determined anti-Islamist regime, to mend fences with its opposition and invite fugitive leaders of the Syrian Muslim Brethren back home, among them Dr. Isám Al-Attár, who used his German exile of twenty-eight years to turn the little border town of Aachen into Europe's foremost bastion of Islamism.

In retrospect the clashes may look like little more than the forebodings of a devastating storm. It cannot be ruled out that attempts to derail the Israeli-Palestinian peace process was the big Islamist coup in 1996. Much evidence indicates that the terrorist attacks early in the year were sponsored by Iran in order to prompt a backlash among Israelis that brought Likud to power. All along, Khomeini's successors have been determined to sabotage the peace process and exacerbate Israeli-Palestinian antagonism. The "Mullacracy" in Tehran has never left any doubt that it is prepared to sacrifice thousands of Palestinians in order to deal some blows to Israel, and vicariously to the U.S. Tehran has enough leverage with Hamás, and especially with the Islamic Jihad of Palestine, to manipulate such developments. What appears as an unmerited Islamist advance might in fact be the result of a skilful Khomeinist trap into which both Palestinians and Israelis fell all too easily. The continuous clashes on the West Bank are an even bigger boost to Islamism than the rape of Bosnia.

In Egypt, Islamists suffer from divisiveness. A section of the Muslim Brotherhood Party attempted to establish a new political party that might be classified as "Muslim Democrat," an analogy to the Christian Democrats in Europe. Many of the younger generation broke away earlier but in the opposite direction; that is, they joined the underground movements Al-Gihád and Al-Gamá`a Al-Islámiya under the leadership of Shaikh Umar Abdu-r-Rahmán (Omar Abdel Rahman). The final break of the young moderates with the ossified leadership of the Muslim Brethren occurred in October 1996, after it had lingered for two years.[10]

All the same, the overall following of Egypt's Islamists did not shrink. They thrive on disappointment with President Mubárak's leadership. In 1996, this disaffection continued to increase, and not only because of the constantly deteriorating quality of life. Palestinian developments led to a new anti-Israeli fury among all classes of Egyptians and, accordingly, to increased receptivity to the jihád slogans of the Islamists.

From Saudi Arabia to the U.N.: A new wave of anti-Americanism

In Saudi Arabia the Islamist opposition to the House of Saud has made steady progress, facilitated by the regime's inability to reform itself; but also because of disillusionment with the country's pro-American orientation, which is unpopular because of U.S. support for Israel. The Qana massacre in Lebanon, where Israeli bombs killed children in a U.N. compound, is scarcely known in the U.S., but it was a watershed experience for Arabs. The U.S. veto against a condemnation of Israel for this act, and the subsequent U.S. opposition to U.N. General Secretary Boutros-Ghali, allegedly because of his support for the condemnation, gave rise to a new anti-Americanism in much of the Muslim world and beyond, especially in Africa.

The ancient symbolism of a battle between the forces of darkness and light—Satan and the Angel in Islamic terminology—has been translated into a 1996 wrestling match between Madeleine Albright and Boutros-Ghali. The antagonistic pair became the favorite topic of cartoons in the press of the Arab and Muslim countries.[11] This is remarkable in view of the fact that until 1995 Boutros-Ghali was unpopular, and for the Islamists he was one of the principal villains because of his inaction in Bosnia and some undiplomatic remarks regarding the conflict as a "rich man's war." Islamists have been quick to capitalize on the new symbolism, turning the once vilified Copt Boutros-Ghali into a hero of just causes—a mujahid.

A peculiar effect of this rage over U.S. opposition to a second term for Boutros-Ghali as secretary general of the U.N. is that some Islamists have taken up the cudgels on behalf of the world organization. Whereas previously they mostly reviled the U.N. as a pawn in the hands of the United States and allied big powers, they are now enumerating its modest achievements and issue appeals to "Save the U.N."[12]

Bangladesh: The Islamist diaspora grows by leaps and bounds

Free and fair elections in Bangladesh resulted in a clear victory for Hasína Wájid and her secularist Awámí Party. The Islamist Jamá'at-e Islámí did not even get 3 percent. The new prime minister immediately began proceedings against the assassins of her father, Shaikh Mujíbu-r-Rahmán, under whom Bangladesh acquired independence in 1971. The assassination had been carried out by a group of Islamist army officers who are now being hunted down.

Thus, Bangladesh may be considered the exception to the rule. Here, there is no Islamist advance. However, the Bangladesher Jamá'at-e Islámí has large numbers of its cadres abroad, especially in Britain, Canada and the U.S. The diaspora is wealthy and well-organized. The defeat in the election was certainly a disappointment, but it did not cause damage.

In the United States, Islamists are very much on the march, fortifying existing institutions and creating new ones. As the U.S. Muslim community grows wealthier, the Islamist minority also thrives, especially since they are the best organized. One might say that they are the most corporate among Muslims in the U.S. In 1995, opponents launched what may have been, worldwide, the most forceful campaign against Islamism, culminating in the PBS documentary *Jihad in America*, a campaign that reverberated throughout 1996. All the same, it did not cause Islamists much harm. In part, the campaign was counter-productive, because a concerted Islamist propaganda effort succeeded in making many non-Islamist Muslims believe that it was linked to the Israeli right at a time when the Likud was seen as anti-peace. For this reason, many Muslims, and even some anti-Islamists among them, sympathized with Palestinian terrorists. The episode proved that Islamists are so firmly established in the U.S. that they are able to run an effective propaganda war on American soil. Their campaign proved that they have become truly competitive—at least in the domain of disinformation.

Wishing to honor the U.S. Muslim community, President Clinton invited representatives to the White House on the occasion of an Islamic holiday. While most Muslims acknowledged the good will behind this gesture, many were stunned by the choice of guests, mostly Islamist hardliners, who turned the event into a propaganda boost for their cause.

Algeria/Morocco: Islamists feed on the reservoir of unemployment

Algeria witnessed a stalemate between the government and the Islamists. Because of the regime's inability to reform, the government's 1995 gains against the insurgents have not been broadened. None of the old army brass has been eased out, and the privileges of a corrupt ruling class have scarcely been curtailed. The Islamists cannot wage war, because their arms supplies have been reduced. An Islamist take-over, as predicted by the *Economist* and others, is out of question. The regime, however, seems unable to curb the urban terrorism carried out by the insurgents. Although most Algerians are fed up with the violence, Islamists have no shortage of new recruits. Among the masses of unemployed, Algerian frustration has turned to despair, and that has helpd Islamism to recuperate.

In Morocco a growing Islamist underground thrives for reasons similar to those in Algeria and Egypt: masses of young people have received education, but no jobs.

It may sound like a platitude, but all North Africa is seething with discontent, primarily of an economic nature. Therefore, Islamists can afford to offer nothing more than empty slogans; they can even afford to commit blunder after blunder. Despite their failures, they are bound to grow.

Without comprehensive and energetic reforms, repression is only a temporary cure. In 1996, only Tunisia made a serious effort to tackle the issue, by taking stern measures against Islamists while at the same time achieving economic progress, enacting educational reforms and creating jobs.

Whereas in 1995 it looked as if Islamism had reached its peak and Islamists were beginning to lose ground in one country after another, 1996 witnessed a further Islamist advance. It may not have been spectacular, but it was unmistakable, and significant enough to make other developments recede from the limelight. Moreover, it was an indication of what the future has in store, because the advance is likely to continue. There is nothing to indicate that the economic conditions in Morocco, Algeria or Egypt will improve any time soon. Accordingly, the army of unemployed youth is bound to grow and the already unbearable housing shortage will almost necessarily lead to riots. Any rise of food prices is certain to spark "bread riots" of the type already witnessed in earlier years in Jordan, Egypt, Tunisia, Algeria and Morocco. The difference this time is that Islamists are lying in wait to channel spontaneous uprisings into purposeful movements of revolution against the existing order.

Notes

1. See Isam Abdu-l-Hakím, "Summer of Initiatives," *Al Muslimún;* No. 554; September 15, 1995, p. 3. *Al-Muslimún* is an Islamist Weekly of Saudi inspiration, published in Arabic from London.

2. An awareness of this intellectual standstill can be encountered even in the columns of an Arabic-language magazine published by the Salafís, a particularly extreme brand of Islamists, in the United States. See Ahmad BinMuhammad Al-Isá, "Look out for Slogans," *As-Sirátu l-Mustaqím;* No. 40; Ramadán 1415, p. 11: "Islamist thought has become stagnant, using slogans and generalities. It has not been able to proceed beyond the initial stages of the resurgence, despite the fact that the resurgence has left those initial stages behind and has become a worldwide phenomenon...[Islamism] should not be left to remain standing still like a statue in our intellectual life."

3. See the editorial, "The Injustice meted out to the Muslims of Bosnia in War and Peace," in the Kuwaiti Islamist magazine *Al Mujtama;* No. 1177; November 28, 1995, p. 9:

4. Many governments of Muslim countries have come to look at such conflicts from a very different angle. They are primarily apprehensive of Islamist internationalists who move from battlefield to battlefield (Afghanistan-Kashmir-Bosnia-Chechnya) to gain experiences which are ultimately to be used against governments in their home countries. See "Is there an Afghan Pattern?" *TransState Islam;* Vol. 1, No. 4; Washington, D.C., Spring 1996, p. 28.

5. See the report by Sámí Ammára, "Lebed: For Russia the Danger Comes from the South, not from the West," *Ash-Sharq Al-Ausat;* No. 6527; London, October 11, 1996, p. 12.

6. The Taliban are the creation of Mauláná Fadlu-r-Rahmán (Fazlur Rehman), a religious leader and party boss aligned with Bhutto against the Islamists. Falu-r-Rahmán's Jam'iyatu l-ulamá (a religious association and political party) runs hundreds of Koranic schools in Pakistani camps of Afghan refugees. It is the students (tálibán) of those schools that provide the ladership of the Taliban movement in Afghanistan.

7. See Ahmad Mansúr, "America's New Role in Afghanistan," *Al Mujtama;* No. 1211; Kuwait, August 6, 1996, p. 29. Likewise Khalid Baig, "Taleban: The 'Good Fundamentalists'?" *Pakistan Link;* Inglewood, CA, October 4, 1996, p. 4.

8. See Michael Pohly, *Krieg und Widerstand in Afghanistan* (Berlin: Das Arabische Buch, 1993). This Ph.D. dissertation on War and Resistance in Afghanistan, submitted to the Institute of Iranian Studies at Freie Universität Berlin, is as yet the most comprehensive and perceptive study of the Islamist role in Afghanistan.

9. See Lally Weymouth, "Drugs and Terror in Afghanistan," the *Washington Post,* November 12, 1996, p. A25.

10. See "The Muslim Brethren faced with the most dangerous internal Crisis," *Al-Wasat;* No. 251; London, November 18, 1996, pp. 22-24. *Al-Wasat* is a weekly newsmagazine in Arabic, usually well-informed and with a high standard of reporting. Incidentally, the party founded by the Muslim Brotherhood's breakaway moderates is also called *Al-Wasat* (The Middleground).

11. For instance *Al-Hayát,* London, November 21, 1996, p. 17. *Al-Hayát* is the leading international Arabic daily newspaper.

12. See the press release "Save the UN!" by *Just World Trust,* a Malaysia-based, pro-Iranian organization, Penang, Malaysia, October 23, 1996, signed by Dr. Chandra Muzaffar, director, *Just World Trust,* and S.N. Mohamed Idris, coordinator, Third World Network.

Khalid Durán is editor of TransState Islam.

Western Europe:
A Union of Opportunity George Melloan

Any discussion of the grand historic enterprise called European Union is apt to dwell on the problems it faces. There are indeed many, some of them cultural, some procedural and some deriving from the fact that the peoples of Europe seem to be more inclined to demand a devolution of power, even within the existing nation states, than to support an envisioned supra-national government in Brussels.

But, as a preface to discussing these and other problems, it is useful to look at the progress Europe has made over the last decade, either by design or happy circumstance, in the realm this essay addresses—the expansion of human freedom. My definition of freedom is a broad one. Most particularly, it includes economic freedom—the ease with which people, goods and capital can move across borders—as well as freedom of thought and expression.

If we look at Europe as a whole, and not just at those fifteen countries that constitute the European Union, the progress on all counts has been phenomenal. This is, of course, primarily due to the disintegration of the oppressive power structure that allowed the Kremlin to exercise control over the lives of over 300 million people who were trapped within the confines of the Soviet Empire. It further reflects the reconstruction along more democratic lines of most of the twenty-two independent European states that have emerged out of that empire. Finally, it reflects the continued progress being made by what we for so long have referred to as Western Europe in reducing the importance of national borders.

Indeed, the total dismantling of passport control and customs posts is underway on the common borders of the ten EU countries that so far have signed the Schengen Agreement, a forerunner of the broad EU commitment to open borders. The process of opening borders is well advanced. Motorists now sail across the Dutch-German or German-Belgian borders, to pick two examples, unimpeded by stop signs or barrier gates. The old control posts that still remain are empty. Scandinavian countries may soon merge their own open-borders system into the Schengen system.

The major exception to open physical borders is the United Kingdom, which also is the principal skeptic on some other unifying measures, especially the single currency envisioned by the December 1991 Maastricht Treaty. But the UK is mainly concerned that some EU measures might abridge already existing English freedoms, not about expansion of freedoms as such. It remains a bastion of parliamentary procedure and free-market capitalism, and has been in the forefront of those European countries favoring reduced barriers to movement of capital and goods.

Melting national borders

The melting away of national border restrictions in a part of the world where heavily fortified borders are a recent memory is perhaps the most dramatic manifestation of greater freedom in Europe. People moved freely around Europe in the Middle Ages, before the advent of what we now call nationalism, but with little security from the depredations of bandits or warring princes. Nationalism, which some historians see as having had its origins in the French Revolution, provided greater security within the boundaries of newly formed European nation states. But it also resulted in the creation of national borders and new restrictions on travel and commerce. More seriously, the definition of "national" territories often resulted in the division of peoples who found their most important sense of identity in culture and ethnicity, which more accurately constitute nationhood, than in nation-states created arbitrarily by war or treaty.

This made Europe an unsettled place, contributing to jealousies that fomented two bloody world wars in the twentieth century, and to more partitions and divisions that further complicated the problems of national identity. To cite one of the most dramatic cases, Poland, which was one of the original victims of Nazi and Soviet aggression, was simply picked up by the Russians at the end of the World War II and moved half its width westward. This left a large Polish population in what is now Belarus (one of the major exceptions to the expansion of freedom in Europe) and an ethnic German population in Poland. These treaty-created anomalies exist all over Europe—ethnic Hungarians in Romania, Germans in the Czech Republic, Germanic people in Alsace and the Tyrol. In light of this, it is no wonder that many people in Europe strongly favor the erasure of national borders.

From nationalism to supra-nationalism

It can be argued that since World War II, advanced nations all over the world have been moving from nationalism toward supra-nationalism in response to the tragic consequences of extreme nationalism, specifically the mass destruction of lives and property during the two world wars. The United Nations, multilateral lending and economic development agencies, and such organizations as NATO and the Western European Union, are manifestations of supra-nationalism, growing out of the strong sentiment for stronger supra-national, or at least multilateral, institutions that built up during World War II. U.S. presidential candidate Wendell Willkie wrote a visionary book titled *One World* during the war. World federalism was promoted by other visionaries.

These ideals did not overcome nationalism in any revolutionary sense, but there has been a gradual erosion. The U.S. has seen fit since World War II to try to work through the U.N. to restore peace in troubled regions, thus trying to make amends for what many saw as the post-World War I "mistake" of not giving adequate support to the League of Nations. The U.N. has been a far from perfect supra-national instrument, but its imprimatur served well in Desert Storm. Bosnia is a different story, but in that case the West ultimately turned to another supra-national or multinational body, NATO.

It is not surprising that Europe, whose peoples have been among the foremost victims of the excesses of nationalism, should now be in the forefront of the movement toward supra-nationalism; and that the politicians of Europe, particularly successive leaders of Germany and France, have made such a strong commitment to the European Union.

Broadening vs. deepening

A key issue during this process has been the question of broadening vs. deepening. Both France and Germany have sought to deepen the union so as to insure that there will never be another war between their two peoples. This implies harmonization of policies within the union, not only in economic and social terms, but even to the extent of having common EU policies toward the outside world. This implies a common defense and foreign policy. But an imperative is also seen to broaden the union, so as to take in new members who want to join, particularly the newly free countries of central and eastern Europe. These countries, newly free of Moscow, feel that they will have greater protection from a future revanchist Russia, should one emerge out of the still strong nationalist passions within that country, if they can gain membership in those two major western European clubs, the EU and NATO.

Both broadening and deepening present problems for the EU. The problem with deepening is, of course, Europe's complex multi-culturalism. The leaders of France and Germany have preached deepening for years, beginning with Konrad Adenauer and Charles de Gaulle, but the German and French people still speak separate languages and thus cannot converse freely with each other. The French like wine and the Germans like beer. The French prefer Bizet and the Germans Wagner. The French like bouillabaisse and the Germans rindfleisch. Multiply the cultural preferences of fifteen nationalities speaking eleven different languages and you get some idea of the problems of deepening. The use of English as a common language has been spreading in Europe, thanks to the powerful influence the U.S. and, to a lesser degree, the British have on world culture through the export of movies and television. But even as national leaders argue on behalf of deepening, they resist erosion of national cultures. It will be a long time before Europe accepts a supra-natural culture as well as a supra-national political institution, and the importance of that should never be underrated.

A single market

It does seem possible at this point that some countries of Europe will adopt a common currency, the Euro, at the beginning of the next century; and that will further simplify commerce and travel, contributing toward the gradual homogenization of what is now a highly heterogeneous continental population. The advances made toward creating a single European market should not be discounted, either, in its cultural impact, as products and services are exchanged more freely across national borders. With the lowering of national barriers, trade in goods and services is by consequence freer, although not entirely outside the reach of various non-tariff barriers such as product standards and the like. And trade in services seems likely to continue making progress as well, even though national policies in such fields as banking and insurance still constitute important barriers, not to mention the natural inhibitions arising from the language problem.

The language problem should not be exaggerated, although it is the fundamental cultural barrier to the opening up of the European continent to the free exchange of goods and ideas. Aside from its importance in breaking down cultural barriers, English has come to be the preferred language of commerce and tourism throughout the world, particularly in the realm of banking and financial services, and that influence is perhaps more evident in Europe than anywhere else.

But, of course, part of the resistance to broadening the European Union has been the likely effect it will have on deepening. If fifteen countries with eleven languages are a barrier to deepening, imagine the problem when Poles, Czechs, Hungarians and Slovenes are added to the mix. There are also serious policy problems for the European Union. The countries of central Europe are still heavily agricultural, which would make their entry a burden on the EU Common Agricultural Policy (CAP), through which it pays massive subsidies to farmers. The solution to that problem, obviously, is to abandon the CAP, but this is not easy to do politically, not least because cross-subsidization is seen by Europe's leaders as an important way to bind the nations of the community together and persuade them to do the bidding of the European Commission.

Nonetheless, concerns about future European security, plus the importunings of the nonmember nations, seem to be tilting the balance toward broadening at the expense of deepening. That is the logical choice, since the problems of broadening are far more simple than those of deepening.

Aside from the official efforts in Brussels to bring the European Union under a single set of regulations and laws and to provide its people with a common currency, another influence is coming to bear on Europe and, indeed, on most of the world. As nations have signed away their prerogatives to tax or otherwise control trade through regional and multilateral trade agreements such as the Uruguay Round, and have correspondingly eliminated most of their controls on capital movements, the power of government has diminished in several ways, one example being, the ability to employ inflation of the national currency as a means of covering government deficits—the so-called unseen tax. To do that in today's open world is to invite a sudden capital flight and the serious consequences such flight has for the banking system and the value of the government's bonds. The open European and global trading system also acts as a curb on inflation in that the supply of goods and tradable services is less limited to those produced or supplied from within a nation's boundaries. The supply side of the supply-demand equation is thus augmented with a consequent restraint on price increases.

So Europeans, along with the people of many other advanced countries, have yet another freedom that they did not have a decade or two ago, greater freedom from the pernicious effects of inflation. While that might be regarded as peculiarly an economic freedom, it is not easy or necessary to separate freedom into its component parts. It is liberating to be rid of the insidious effects inflation has on savings and living standards, just as it is exhilarating to have access to an uncontrolled press and television; or just as it is a boon to human dignity to not be subject to the whims of petty officials or, worse, the late night knock on the door.

The gradual shift toward liberalization

To return to Europe from this discussion of broader trends, a word or two is in order about where Europe stands today in its gradual shift toward liberalization, and particularly about the issue of whether the countries of Central and Eastern Europe are to be a part of that liberal order. To a degree, some already are. East Germany no longer exists, of course, and its people are being gradually assimilated by Germany and the

European Union. Poland, the Czech Republic and Hungary, along with the former Yugoslav republic of Slovenia, have become free-market democracies and are bidding to upgrade their associate status with the EU to full membership. Slovakia is faring well enough economically but remains politically unstable.

The former Soviet republics are a mixed bag, with Ukraine still struggling for post-Communist reform and Belarus still stuck somewhere in the 1950s, both politically and economically. The Baltic states aspire to be a part of the West to reduce the economic and political power their big neighbor, Russia, still exerts in various subtle ways over them. And then, of course, there is Russia itself, which has made enormous progress toward establishing democratic institutions, but still suffers from dangerous instability because of the absence of reliable law enforcement and the consequences of the government's difficulty in raising revenues, primarily because of a punitive tax system that has engendered an almost country-wide taxpayer revolt.

It is in the context of these happenings in the East that the European Union, which is, of course, the continent's rich nation club, is faced with issues that have confronted it ever since it was comprised of only six nations and was little more than a customs union. Not the least is how to broaden and deepen at the same time. This will be a gradual process and it could even fail if Europe makes the mistake of handing Brussels too much arbitrary and undemocratic power, thereby creating resentment and reviving nationalist fervor. But there can be no denying that the Europe of today is a far freer and better place than the Europe of a decade ago, and light years better than the Europe that emerged from the chaos of World War II.

George Melloan is deputy editor (international) of the Wall Street Journal, *and author of the weekly column, "Global View."*

The United States: Ambivalent Power, Ambivalent Democracy Joshua Muravchik

The United States of America was the first modern democracy and the first state erected on the premise that its reason for being was to secure the God-given rights of its citizens. Two hundred and twenty years after the founding of the republic, freedom in America is so firmly rooted as to make one wonder whether an annual review of freedom in America is a meaningful exercise. And yet, the American destiny is a permanent test of freedom as the founding—and guiding—principle of a regime. It therefore requires examination.

Lately, however, the question has been whether America is *too* free. This question has been put pointedly by representatives of various Asian regimes whose caucus within the United Nations has challenged the prevailing international standards of human rights on the grounds that these are distinctly "western." The claim that such norms are inapplicable to Asian societies rings hollow, because most Asian governments freely signed various international human rights treaties, and at least some Asian states, like post-War Japan, have good human rights records—and much to show for them. But when these Asian spokesmen focus on the high level of crime and decadence in America and other western societies, their argument gains more bite.

Indeed, many Americans are concerned about the same things. In 1996, Robert Bork's *Slouching Toward Gomorrah,* decrying "moral anarchy" in America, leapt to the top of bestseller lists. Bork rejects the "popular notion that expanding the sphere of liberty is always a net gain." "Extremes of liberty and the pursuit of happiness court personal license and social disorder," he says. This erosion of moral standards is exemplified by wanton displays of sex and violence in public entertainment. Bork challenges the body of contemporary American legal doctrine that protects all of this as free expression, but among American legal scholars his voice is clearly in the minority.

Protection for children
The issue changes, however, when it comes to children. The law holds that children require special protection. And it recognizes that while children have rights, these are not identical to those of adults. Several issues in the news in 1996 revolved around proposed restrictions on the activities of children or on those of adults in their interactions with children. Legislation was passed providing for the use of "V" chips in home televisions by which parents might restrict what their children can view. Some localities adopted curfews restricting the hours during which teenagers could be out unaccompanied by adults (measures intended both for the protection of the youth and of others from the youth). These statutes continue to be challenged in the courts, and

their legality remains at issue. In addition, President Clinton spoke out in favor of strict prohibitions on the sale and advertising of cigarettes to minors, and for requiring schoolchildren to wear uniforms.

A particularly heated controversy has developed over efforts to restrict dissemination of offensive materials to minors over the internet. Civil libertarians argue that individual expression is protected, regardless of whether or not it is offensive, and that those who post messages electronically cannot be held accountable if minors read them. But others point out that the protection of children has long been recognized as a legitimate constraint on free expression.

Another subject of high controversy is abortion. This issue illustrates the truth that perfect respect for rights is impossible. Even if a society reaches that happy state in which it is free from any arbitrary authority, circumstances still remain in which rights conflict with one another. The abortion wars in America are waged between two "right" campaigns: "right to life" and "right to choose." Only zealots on either side would be unable to see a degree of validity in the claims of the other. Who would deny, in principle, that women should govern their own reproductive functions or that the unborn should be protected? But these rights cannot both be fully guaranteed.

Probably the most politically salient issue on which the question arises of whether America suffers from an overabundance of freedom is criminal law enforcement. Crime repeatedly appears at or near the top of the list of issues that American say most concern them, and there can be no doubt that the experience or fear of crime has diminished the quality of life for many Americans. For many decades, civil libertarians fought for ever more perfect protections of the rights of those accused of lawbreaking. The impetus for this was easy to understand. The persecutions of tyrants often masquerade as justice. Historically, the growth of freedom unfolded in large part in the form of protections of the rights of the accused: trial by jury, habeus corpus, due process, proscription of cruel or unusual punishment.

No system, however, can prevent all error. A system that goes to extremes to assure that no innocent individual is ever punished will necessarily let many guilty individuals go free. Anglo-American legal tradition strongly prefers the escape of the guilty to the punishment of the innocent; hence the presumption of innocence and the requirement of proof beyond a reasonable doubt. This results from the belief that a greater menace to the liberties of the citizen inheres in the awesome power of the state than in the depredations of other citizens. Nonetheless, liberties may be infringed upon by private individuals. When the Declaration of Independence says that just government is created in order to secure the rights of the citizenry, it cannot mean only that government must protect the people from itself, but that it must protect them from each other and from outsiders as well.

In practice many Americans who fear going out at night, have come to feel that their freedoms are infringed by criminals. A substantial consensus has gathered for firmer law-enforcement and surer punishment. The crystallization of this consensus was evident in the 1996 U.S. election campaign. For many years, the Republicans have presented themselves as the party of law and order, while the Democrats have been more protective of defendants. But in 1996, Democrat Clinton aggressively and successfully competed with the Republicans as the champion of law and order, taking credit for Federal funding of local police forces.

Money and politics

Issues of this kind arise in a society in which fundamental freedoms are very safe from challenge. However, the experiences of 1996 also brought home one glaring weakness in the political liberties enjoyed by Americans: the role of money in the U.S. electoral process. The year ended with clouds hanging over both House Speaker Newt Gingrich and President Bill Clinton. Both cases involved the solicitation or handling of political funds. These episodes illustrated the potential for corruption inherent in a system that compels politicians to solicit large sums in order to campaign for office.

Even in the absence of what we might call formal corruption—an explicit barter of cash for political favors—this situation is troubling. Wealthy businessmen who made large contributions to Democratic coffers were rewarded with private audiences with the president. Clinton's spokesmen eventually acknowledged that various of these businessmen pressed policy matters with Clinton (such as turning a blind eye to China's human rights violations), but they insist that Clinton remained uninfluenced by the meetings. Perhaps this is so, but influence is a nebulous thing. Who among us can be sure about which of our encounters influence us and which do not? The inescapable fact is that those with six-figure sums to spend can tell their thoughts directly to the president; the rest of us cannot. This cannot but derogate the quality of our democratic processes, which are predicated on a principle of civil equality. (Adding insult to injury, some of those who purchased privileged relationships with the president were not even citizens.)

An additional aspect of the distorting effect of money on America's democratic process was illustrated by the presidential campaigns of Steve Forbes and Ross Perot. These are both accomplished men, but their role in the presidential race was secured not by their talents but by their ability to spend tens of millions of dollars out of personal fortunes. Their electoral presence illustrated a perverse anomaly in current electoral law. The Congress aimed to reduce the political impact of private money when it passed the campaign finance reform that placed a $1,000 ceiling on individual contributions to federal campaigns. The effect of this was distorted when the Supreme Court ruled that a citizen's right to spend money on his own behalf was a form of speech protected by the Constitution, but did not extend this principle to expenditure on behalf of others. As a result, those few Americans with fortunes big enough to spend scores of million of dollars on a whim, and with a yen for office, can buy themselves a very considerable advantage in a presidential race. Other aspirants cannot counterbalance this through the generosity of a small number of wealthy backers. They can only compete by securing thousands of modest-sized donations. Few potential competitors have any hope of doing that. Even among the few who might accomplish the feat, some have no stomach for it. This may have been what led such putative presidential candidates as Dick Cheney, Jack Kemp and Bill Bennett to remove themselves early from the 1996 race. All in all, a large part of the energy of an election campaign revolves around the exigencies of raising money, except for those few candidates in the position of a Forbes or a Perot.

Power and influence

The largest questions about America are not about the health of freedom in America but about America's willingness to extend itself on behalf of freedom elsewhere. The spread of freedom over the past 220 years owes much to the American example and to American power. The American revolution inspired the French revolution and also some Latin American actions. American influence after the two world wars rang down the curtain on the colonial era. American occupations democratized Germany and Japan. American power was essential to the defeat of the mighty totalitarian despotisms of the twentieth century.

When the last of them succumbed, America breathed a sigh of relief and experienced a yearning to be free of the heavy burdens of international leadership. "It's time to be nicer to ourselves," said Congressman Barney Frank, capturing the spirit of the moment. Since then, there has not been a resurgence of 1920s-style isolationism, but there has been a palpable sentiment for America to play a more modest role abroad. A *Times-Mirror* poll found that only 7 percent of Americans wanted the country to play "no leadership role," but not many more—10 percent—wanted it to be the "single world leader." The vast majority—78 percent—opted for the comfortable middle position in favor of a "shared leadership role." When this group was pressed further, only one third said America should be the "most active of the leading nations," while two thirds preferred it to be "no more or less active than other leading nations."

America, however, is not just another "leading nation"; it is far and away the most powerful and influential. If it is only as active as other leading nations, then it will fail to shoulder the responsibilities that fall inevitably to the "sole superpower."

This lesson was driven home by the example of Bosnia ,which was a kind of test for the notion that America should play no more than a shared leadership role. If any other nations are capable of sharing leadership with America, it would be the wealthy and powerful democracies of Western Europe. And if there is any locus where they could demonstrate this capacity, it is in Europe itself. When Yugoslavia began to come undone in 1991, America was feeling sapped from its effort to drive Iraq from Kuwait. Hence, a trans-Atlantic agreement was reached: the European Union, rather than America, would take the lead in confronting the Yugoslav crisis. "This is the hour of Europe, not...of the American," declared Luxembourg's Foreign Minister Jacques Poos, chairman of an EU delegation to Belgrade.

Over the next four years, Europe's futility in Croatia and Bosnia demonstrated that it was helpless without America. Only when America finally stepped to the fore was some semblance of peace achieved through the Dayton Accords. The military provisions of the Accords were largely fulfilled in 1996, thanks to the emplacement of American and European forces. However, the political and humanitarian provisions remained largely dead letters due to the reluctance of the international force to take on police functions. America's own continued ambivalence about its role was exemplified both by President Clinton's decision to extend the duration of the American military mission in Bosnia, and by his delay in announcing this manifestly necessary step until after the November election. Clinton, moreover, cut the size of the U.S. contingent roughly in half, apparently in order to demonstrate that he was in the process of "bringing the boys home," even though newspaper interviews with soldiers and officers on the scene revealed their profound misgivings about a reduction in numbers.

American ambivalence was also on display during the crisis over refugee camps in Zaire. While France and other European states clamored for international action to avert another humanitarian disaster in Central Africa, America held back until Canada proclaimed its willingness to lead an international force. Some U.S. officials claimed that our government had actually planted that thought with the Canadians; whether or not this is so, America announced its willingness to participate in a Canadian-led force, although changing circumstances on the ground in Zaire obviated the mission.

In many other parts of the world, America demonstrated in 1996 that although it is ambivalent about its leadership role, it is far from turning its back on the world. America sent two air-craft carrier battle groups to the Taiwan Straits in response to mainland China's attempt to intimidate Taiwan by conducting "missile tests" in its direction. President Clinton declared his intention to see NATO begin to admit new members from central or eastern Europe in 1999, and he was challenged on this by his Republican opponent only for not choosing an earlier deadline. The U.S. State Department continued to play a pivotal role in the Middle East peace negotiations. And America took military action, albeit small-scale, in response to Saddam Hussein's dispatch of forces to Iraqi Kurdistan.

The budget crisis

The questions surrounding America's leadership role arose not only from the ambivalence of public opinion, however, but also from the federal budget crisis. The mushrooming costs of entitlement programs placed mounting pressure on all domestic accounts, and foreign affairs proved to be the most vulnerable. Huge defense cuts (amounting to roughly a 40 percent drop from the height of the Reagan buildup) were feasible because of the disappearance of the Soviet threat. But deep cuts in other foreign policy programs may jeopardize America's effectiveness in coping with a range of post-Cold War challenges. For example, budget cuts have forced the State Department to close dozens of overseas posts. These included posts in Indonesia, Egypt and Turkey, arguably America's three most important allies in the Islamic world. What sense does this make at a time when moderates in the Islamic world are beset by fanatics who see America as "the great Satan"?

The degree of leadership that America is willing to offer will inevitably have a profound impact on the progress of freedom in the world. But it is not just a matter of how much leadership America exerts. There is also a question of the degree to which America devotes its energies to the cause of global freedom, as opposed to more narrow national goals. In this realm, too, America continued to demonstrate ambivalence in 1996. While enforcing the peace in Bosnia, America hung back from trying to enforce human rights by protecting Bosnian civilians seeking to return to homes from which they had been driven or by arresting those indicted for war crimes. America insisted on pushing forward with national elections in Bosnia, nominally a step of democratization. The real purpose of the elections, however, seemed to have been to create a framework to facilitate a U.S. withdrawal; and Bosnia's most credible democrats urged that the elections be delayed until conditions were in place that would make them a meaningful democratic exercise.

Likewise, in respect to China, 1996 saw the long-delayed launching of Radio Free Asia. But the main thrust of U.S. policy toward China in 1996 was to try to secure friendlier relations between the two governments, even at the cost of downplaying Beijing's increasingly brazen abuse of political dissidents and its ham-fisted measures to crush the seedlings of democracy in Hong Kong as a prelude to the reassertion of Chinese sovereignty there.

In the nations of the former Soviet empire, U.S. policy seemed to be guided for the most part by a strong appreciation for the importance of democratization. The centerpiece of this approach was the not very subtle effort to facilitate the triumph of Boris Yeltsin in Russia's presidential election. The glaring exception to this policy in Washington's relations with Eastern Europe was Serbia. There, because U.S. policy-makers viewed President Milosevic as a guarantor of the Dayton accords, little protest was made over his depredations against democracy until massive popular demonstrations against Milosevic persuaded Washington to stiffen its line towards him.

The greatest impediment to America's activities on behalf of freedom is the same as that which impeded all aspects of its foreign policy: budgetary stringency. The accounts that fund those American activities most directly aimed at nurturing freedom have been particularly hard hit by budget cuts. Overseas broadcasting has been curtailed, the U.S. Information Agency has had to lay off hundreds of employees, foreign aid has been reduced or eliminated to scores of countries and, once again, the National Endowment for Democracy faced legislative threats to its very existence despite its outstanding record. The sums involved are paltry when measured against the budget deficit, but they account for a significant share of America's international activities.

Worse still, with the president and the Republican leaders of Congress agreed on a target year of 2002 for achieving a balanced budget, the foreign affairs accounts are penciled in for additional cuts of 30 percent. This would strike a body blow against the conduct of U.S. foreign policy, and it would amount to a substantial abdication of America's role in nurturing freedom around the world.

Joshua Muravchik is a Resident Scholar at the American Enterprise Institute and a member of the Survey of Freedom Advisory Board.

Latin America and the Caribbean: Toward a Democratic Culture

Arturo Valenzuela

There is reason for optimism about the continued progress of democratic consolidation in Latin America and the Caribbean despite the many challenges facing the Hemisphere. In 1996, all of the nations of the Americas were governed by chief executives and legislatures elected by the citizenry in more or less free and fair contests. The only glaring exception was Cuba, a political anachronism, where the thirty-six-year-old dictatorship of Fidel Castro hardened its rule. The Hemispheric trend away from military rule and dictatorship has led to the longest period of constitutional government in history. As the twentieth century comes to a close, the democratic ideals of the Enlightenment appear to be more secure in the Americas than in any other region of the world, including much of Christian Europe.

In Latin America, fifty-three presidential elections have taken place since 1980. In every country, presidents have been succeeded by their duly elected successors, often in representation of opposition parties. In Freedom House's 1996 Survey of Freedom, nine of the thirty-five countries in the Western Hemisphere improved their standing on measures of political rights and civil liberties. Only one, Ecuador, was downgraded, due to concern over the election of a president known for authoritarian proclivities. It remains to be seen, however, whether Abdula Bucaram's tenure will prove to be a setback to Ecuadoran democracy, or whether he will follow the example of other populist leaders who surprised observers by governing with discipline and moderation once in office.

The general trend toward the establishment of democratic governments in Latin America and the Caribbean should not obscure significant variations in the democratic experience of the region. The challenges of democratic consolidation and the danger of democratic reversal are far greater in countries with weak or non-existent democratic traditions than in those with a long history of representative institutions.

The English-speaking states of the Caribbean, independent for only a few decades, have managed for the most part to deal with the extraordinary challenges of economic development in multiethnic societies while preserving the institutions of British parliamentary democracy.

In Latin America, three countries—Colombia, Costa Rica and Venezuela—avoided the interruption of constitutional rule that swept the hemisphere in the 1960s and 1970s when military regimes sought to check the growth of populist and leftist movements. Others, notably Chile and Uruguay, recovered democratic traditions that had developed over several generations. The end of authoritarian rule led to a process of redemocratization far less complex than the process of democratic construction facing countries with little or no democratic traditions.

Before the 1990s, Haiti, Paraguay, Mexico and most of the countries of Central America had never, or rarely, experienced free and competitive national elections.

Other countries, including Argentina, Brazil and Peru, had a mixed record of democratic interludes followed by authoritarian periods. Despite numerous elections this century, only in 1995 did Argentines witness the first transfer of power from one elected leader to another since 1916.

During 1996, significant steps towards democratic consolidation were taken in three of the countries with the weakest democratic records in the region: Haiti, Paraguay and Guatemala. In January 1996, ten years to the day after the overthrow of the Duvalier dictatorship, President Aristide stepped down as head of state to make way for his constitutionally elected successor, the first such transition in Haitian history. The elections were marred by disorganization, voter abstention and the weakness of opposition parties. Nevertheless, the selection of a new president, congressional authorities and local governments, and the establishment of far reaching programs to rebuild the security forces, the justice system and the national economy, represented a sea-change for a country that had been mismanaged by a self-serving military clique.

In Paraguay, President Juan Carlos Wasmosy, the first head of state to be elected in free and competitive national elections (1993), faced a serious threat to constitutional rule when the commander of the Paraguayan army refused to accept the president's order to step down in April. General Lino Oviedo had repeatedly sought to influence national policy, openly clashing with the president over issues unrelated to national security. Swift and strong support from the international community, opposition from constitutionalist officers and a groundswell of support for the president from broad elements of Paraguayan civil society, strengthened the president's hand and forced the general to abandon his post.

In the aftermath of the confrontation, Wasmosy was able to purge many officers wedded to the view that a military career is a stepping stone to political power and privilege. Although Wasmosy remains a weak president, Paraguayan democracy was strengthened by the popular mobilization in defense of the constitution and the personnel changes within the armed forces.

Shortly after the crisis, the MERCOSUR countries (Brazil, Argentina, Paraguay and Uruguay, later joined by Chile as an associate) adopted a "democracy clause" barring membership of any country where the constitutional order is disrupted.

MERCOSUR thus added its voice to that of the Organization of American States (OAS), which, after the adoption of the historic Resolution 1080 in 1991, has made the defense of democracy one of the cardinal objectives of the regional organization. The OAS played a key role in the reversal of the coup that overthrew President Aristide in Haiti in 1991, and the return to constitutional normality after threats to democracy in Peru and Guatemala in 1992 and 1993, respectively.

Guatemalan peace, finally

The peace accord between the Guatemalan government and the guerrilla movement signed on December 29, 1996, is an extraordinary milestone for Guatemala and the Americas. Set in motion by the Esquipula's Declaration of August 1987, through which the Central American governments sought to establish a lasting peace in the region, the accord marks the end of the longest civil insurrection in the Hemisphere. The guerrilla movement first emerged after the CIA aided the 1954 overthrow of the elected government of Jacobo Arbenz, an event that served as a catalyst for the development of guerrilla movements from Cuba through Central and South America that spurred harsh governmental repression and resulted in the loss of tens of thousands of lives.

The peace negotiations led to the formal signing of a cease-fire and an agreement on "Constitutional Reform and Electoral Procedures." This accord builds on earlier agreements, including commitments to promote political participation, defend indigenous and human rights, address social, economic and land issues, and reintegrate displaced persons into Guatemalan society.

Like the peace settlements in other countries, the accord calls for the peaceful incorporation of the guerrilla movement into the political life of the country, reforms in the military, modernization of the executive and legislative branches and a strengthening of the judicial process. Brokered with U.N. mediation, the peace negotiators were actively supported by a group of "friends" that included the United States, Mexico, Spain, Norway, Venezuela and Colombia, as well as "sectoral" groups consisting of business, indigenous and human rights organizations. Guatemalans can now look forward to former combatants working together within the democratic process to build a better society.

The peace accord, forged over several years, is a testament to the enormous progress Central America has made since President Oscar Arias of Costa Rica brokered the peace plan that led the countries of the region to opt for the ballot box rather than the bullet in seeking to resolve the still daunting challenges they face. Today, for the first time in almost half a century of conflict, the countries of El Salvador, Nicaragua, Guatemala and Honduras are at peace while struggling to consolidate more open and participatory societies.

Less dramatic but equally far-reaching events contributed to democratic progress in the region. Nicaragua, like Haiti, witnessed its first ever transfer of power from one freely elected leader to another. In the Dominican Republic, President Joaquín Balaguer kept his word by holding early elections to compensate for allegations of fraud in his 1994 victory, leading to the election as president of an opposition party figure representing a new generation.

Although candidate access to the media and campaign financing remain controversial issues, Mexico has made enormous strides in guaranteeing impartial elections for the first time in history. These strides are the product of a difficult but largely successful process of inter-party consultations that led to significant agreements for political and institutional reform between Mexico's once dominant Partido Revolucionario Institucional (PRI), the Partido Acción Nacional (PAN) and Partido de la Revolución Democrática (PRD). At the same time, opposition forces continued to make considerable headway in state and local elections viewed as largely fair and legitimate. The principal Mexican opposition party now governs 45 percent of the populations at the local level, and stands a strong chance of winning the mayoralty of Mexico City in the first free and open elections for that post. From a one party state, Mexico, despite daunting social and political challenges, is moving rather quickly to a more open and competitive political process with a far more open and critical press than in the past.

Brazil, Latin America's largest country, has managed to maintain economic stability under the leadership of Latin America's great contemporary statesman, Fernando Henrique Cardoso. Discussions of constitutional reform that would enable Cardoso to stand for reelection for a second term is evidence of the success of his government and not, as some detractors would hold, a move towards elected authoritarianism. It is highly unlikely that Mr. Cardoso's predecessors would have been reelected had they been able to seek a second term, a generalization that would also apply to President Menem in Argentina and President Fujimori in Peru. The success of incumbents in Latin America is a fairly new phenomenon in the region and should be viewed as a tribute to the growing process of democratic consolidation, not as a throwback to the politics of the past.

Fighting corruption and money laundering

At the international level, the nations of the America's, through the OAS, adopted the Inter-American Convention Against Corruption, becoming the first region of the world to press for change in domestic legislation and international practices to combat corruption and money laundering, a significant scourge of democratic governments. Propelled by Latin American states as part of the Summit of the Americas implementation process, the convention is a manifestation of the increased collaboration of hemispheric nations in addressing issues of common concern.

Critics of this "optimistic" interpretation of democratic development in the Hemisphere argue that elections have meant little to the average citizen, and that democracy remains a shallow artifact in a continent still characterized by massive poverty and sharp inequalities. However, these critics seriously underestimate the extraordinary importance of the right for average citizens to have a say in choosing their leaders in more open and free societies. Few Chileans, Nicaraguans, Haitians, Brazilians or Peruvians, who turned out in large numbers in critical contests that defined the direction of their nations, would argue that elections are irrelevant exercises. And few would defend the view that their citizens were better off in the 1970s or 1980s under repressive authoritarian regimes racked by civil strife and official impunity. Although a regional survey noted that only 27 percent of respondents were satisfied with the way democracy was functioning in Latin America, only 20 percent said that they were not satisfied at all, with the rest of those surveyed preferring an intermediate formulation.

Pessimists argue further that the new era of democracy has not led to significant social progress. It is true that average per capita income for the region as a whole remains below 1980 levels, that the Americas have the highest degree of inequality of any continent, and that 45 percent of the region's 481 people live in poverty.

For most people, however, living conditions have been improving. The political success of Presidents Alberto Fujimori in Peru, Carlos Menem in Argentina, Fernando Henrique Cardoso in Brazil and Gonzalo Sanchez de Lozada in Bolivia, is due in no small measure to their ability, either as presidents or as ministers in previous administrations, to reign in inflationary spirals that had devastated the standards of living of citizens in all walks of life. In 1995, inflation rates for Latin America and the Caribbean were at their lowest level in twenty-five years.

Furthermore, although painful, fiscal discipline and market reforms, which were thought impossible under elected governments, have placed most countries on a solid road to recovery. With the exclusion of Argentina and Mexico, both devastated by the 1995 Mexican peso crisis, per capita GDP grew for the fourth straight year while regional trade reached record levels. Moreover, the Mexican economy headed towards a strong recovery in 1997, belying fears that the Mexican crisis would continue to threaten regional growth.

It is important to underscore, however, that democracy per se does not provide solutions to social and economic problems. Democracy is a system of governance based on the notion that authority is generated by the choice of the citizenry. Through constitutionally defined rules and procedures, a divided citizenry can agree to disagree peacefully at the ballot box, and the resulting preferences are reconciled through the institutions of representative democracy. If a democratic government fails to respond to the aspirations of a majority of citizens, the solution is not a change of regime, but the election of an alternative government. The critics of weak or misguided democratic governments should not confuse the institutions and practices of democracy with the political incumbents of the moment. Democracy, as a system of government, is policy neutral.

It is equally important to stress that the consolidation of democratic institutions does not take place overnight. In all societies, democratic institutions are continuously evolving and subject to improvement. Democratic consolidation, however, can only occur within the framework of democratic governance. It is also misleading to argue that democracy can only work where prior democratic values have emerged, i.e., that the problem with Latin America is a value system inimical to democracy inherited from Catholic Spain's colonial rule. The successful cases of democratic consolidation in Latin America, such as Chile and Uruguay, belie that proposition.

Democratic values evolve from democratic practices honed through years of open electoral competition where, by definition, the rights of minorities and oppositions are respected and guaranteed. Democratic practices precede the advent of widespread democratic values; they do not stem from them.

It follows that democracy is learned in democracy, even if, at the outset, democratic institutions are fragile and incomplete. The challenge for Latin America is not to despair at the shortcomings of nascent democracies, but to strive to consolidate democratic institutions and deepen democratic practices without resorting to extraconstitutional solutions.

The challenges of representation, accountability and efficacy

Representative government in Latin America, as in much of the contemporary world, faces a series of difficult challenges. For the sake of simplicity, these can be referred to as the challenges of representation, accountability and efficacy.

The challenge of representation goes to the core of democratic legitimacy. How best can the will of the people as expressed in the ballot box be translated into effective and legitimate representation? A critical first step, which most countries in the region have put behind them, is the establishment of fair and impartial elections. Many citizens, however, don't identify with their representatives; indeed, they might not even know who they are. Voters frequently confront lists with large numbers of candidates who seek to represent large districts on a proportional basis. These candidates often live in the capital and owe their nomination to party leaders, not local activists. In several countries, such as Mexico and Ecuador, term limits make it impossible for representatives to get to know their regions and provide them with effective representation.

Complicating matters is the weakness of national legislatures vis-a-vis executives, the product of a long tradition of de facto governments that ruled by decree. Presidents often feel pressured to bypass legislatures when they cannot count on majorities in Congress.

Of the fifty-three elected presidents since 1980, only twenty enjoyed legislative majorities, making divided government the norm in Latin America. This contributes to the perception of governmental paralysis and partisan wrangling that undermines the image of politicians and governmental institutions. It is instructive that the more successful governments in the region, those able to hammer out often difficult legislative agendas and implement often unpopular programs, either had strong majority representation of the president's party in Congress (Mexico, Argentina and Peru) or were able to establish presidential majorities through successful governing coalitions (Chile and Bolivia).

Finally, democratic authorities continue to be challenged by military establishments that enjoy considerable autonomy from the representatives of the people. Although the incidents in Paraguay were a dramatic indication of military autonomy, military rumblings have been heard in Venezuela and Colombia. In Chile, and to a lesser extent in Brazil and Uruguay, military establishments negotiated an extraordinary degree of autonomy from congressional and executive oversight in the transition to democracy. Chile's president cannot remove the armed forces commanders who serve for fixed terms in office, and is severely limited in his ability to appoint new commanders.

Reforms of the electoral system, the strengthening of parties and coalition politics, a greater role for national legislatures, and greater civilian oversight of the military are important steps that need to be taken to address the challenges of more legitimate democratic representation.

Also important are moves to decentralize authority and create more viable forms of representation at the local level. Chile and Colombia's very different experiments with more effective local government and Bolivia's efforts to increase local and indigenous participation are cases in point. The growing vitality of state politics in federal governments in Argentina, Mexico and Brazil, encouraged by victories of opposition forces, is also contributing to the revitalization of representation closer to the people.

The challenge of accountability has received much attention as political and governmental leaders have been accused in country after country of profiting from public office for personal gain. Two presidents, Fernando Collor de Melo in Brazil and Carlos Andrés Perez in Venezuela, were impeached after being charged with personal corruption, and former elected presidents in Honduras, Guatemala, Mexico and Bolivia have been charged with serious violations of the public trust. In Colombia, President Samper has been accused of accepting money from narcotics traffickers for his campaign, while avoiding impeachment due to the support of legislators also charged with receiving bribes from drug kingpins. Official corruption extends to the judiciary and regulatory agencies, including many involved in the privatization process that has led to a transfer of state resources into private hands.

It is difficult to argue, however, that corruption is more serious today than during periods of authoritarian rule. No president had even been impeached in Latin America before Collor and Perez were. If it was addressed in the past, corruption served as a pretext for reformist military officers to justify a military coup, thereby undermining further the rule of law. More often than not, corruption went undiscovered or was not subject to sanction. The growing acknowledgment of corruption in the region is due in part to the growing capacity of open societies to uncover corruption and hold public officials to account.

Corruption is best addressed by open and competitive politics, by oversight from opposition forces and the strengthening of representation, particularly legislatures. It also requires fundamental reforms in the judicial system and law enforcement agencies which need modernization, better training and better salary levels.

The downsizing of the state, the process of privatization, and more effective international conventions to address bribery and other crimes will contribute to reducing the opportunities for corruption while increasing its cost. Over the long haul, however, the full implementation of the rule of law can only come with the continued strengthening of democracy itself, with the capacity of the citizenry to provide, through representative institutions, an open and free press and nongovernmental organizations, the oversight functions of a democratic society.

The challenge of governmental efficacy refers to the weakness of state institutions throughout the region. Although state structures have been downsized in most countries, drastically reducing massive fiscal deficits and government waste, the state continues to have a vital role in society. Antiquated and inefficient state institutions undermine the state's capacity to regulate the private sector, collect revenues and administer critical programs.

In particular, Latin American states have not adequately responded to the rising tide of criminal violence and social inequality in the region that has undermined confidence in national leadership. Social dislocation spawned by economic change, combined with a rise in drug-trafficking and criminal organizations and the availability of inexpensive fire arms, have pushed the murder rate to six times the world average. In most countries, there is an urgent need to reform corrupt and inefficient police organizations and to strengthen the judicial system.

At the same time, a far greater effort is required to address the problems of poverty and marginality. More imaginative programs that draw on the combined resources of the public, private and nongovernmental sectors need to be targeted toward the poor. Also, even the most developed countries of the region require far greater investment in basic and secondary education to prepare citizens for the more competitive and technologically sophisticated employment opportunities of the future. This requires more effective state institutions, at the national and local level, with better trained and paid civil servants, more fully accountable to elected officials and the citizenry at large.

Despite these daunting challenges, the countries of the Americas are moving in the right direction. In country after country, fledgling democratic institutions are being supported or held to account by a growing network of secondary associations that are enriching civil society. Most countries are struggling to introduce needed reforms to strengthen democratic institutions and procedures. Plus, the nations of the Americas have shown their strong determination to collectively seek mechanisms to improve representative institutions, while safeguarding against democratic reversals.

The advent of democratic governments has not solved all of the problems of society. But open societies are proving to be better stewards of individual liberties, freedoms and opportunities than the authoritarian experiments of the right or left that failed to deliver on their promises. The lesson for the Americas is that the problems of society, and indeed the problems of democracy itself, must be addressed within the framework of constitutional democracy, and not through a reversion to the ad hoc regimes of the past.

Arturo Valenzeula is professor of government and director of the Center for Latin American Studies at Georgetown University. He served as Deputy Assistant Secretary of State for Inter-American Affairs in the first Clinton administration.

Press Freedom: Democracy, Yes; Press Freedom, Maybe

Leonard R. Sussman
and Kristen Guida

With the rising tide of democracies in 1996, press freedom increased slightly in 39 countries, but was marginally reduced in 52 others. Often, insecure leaders tightened the screws on journalists for exhibiting "too much freedom." Significant improvement in press freedom was recorded in five countries, major declines in six. At year's end, 2,374 million people lived in 63 countries without a free press, 2,249 million in 57 countries with a partly-free press, and only 1,148 million in 67 countries with a free press.

Press freedom simply means the state does nothing to hinder journalistically balanced, politically unrestricted reports based on diverse sources of public and private information.

A dangerous trade

An Algerian man wounded during the murder of his brother, a radio commentator, would hardly be comforted to learn fewer journalists were slain in 1996 than in the previous year. In Algeria, where more than 60 journalists have been murdered by Islamic extremist rebels in the last three years, the toll last year was ten; in 1995, 26. Mohammed Guessab, who ran "Radio Koran" on the government radio station, was gunned down in August while driving with his two brothers in a suburb of Algiers. One brother was shot, the other killed along with Mohammed.

Worldwide, 37 journalists in 19 countries were murdered last year; 62 in 1995. In 1996, another 45 were kidnapped or "disappeared," 349 arrested in 54 countries; and 273 others were physically assaulted or tortured in nearly 50 countries. Given the 1,820 reported cases of violations against journalists in 116 countries, it would be difficult to persuade anyone, least of all victims like Guessab's surviving brother, that press freedom increased at all in 1996: 1,445 cases were recorded the year before.

Though the murder rate of journalists declined in 1996, according to the Freedom House Survey, cases of harassment doubled. Such violations can be as detrimental to the content and quality of journalism as physical attack. Seventy-three death threats against journalists in 23 countries in 1996 were crude but effective forms of persuasion. Self-censorship becomes endemic after governments threaten to enforce restrictive press laws or ban criticism of political leaders. The word leaks out that critical reporting, investigative journalism or even fairly balanced reportage is dangerous.

Last year, only 21 percent of all countries saw some enlargement in press freedom, compared with 45 percent the previous year. Ironically, this virtual reduction occurs despite the record number of states—118—with democratic systems of governance. In many of these, leaders are reluctant to free the media of formal or subtle controls. In a period of transition, uncertain leaders timidly test liberalizing policies only to retreat when they believe new journalistic freedoms challenge political power.

Tanzania is an example. This East African state, which held its first multiparty election in 1995, permitted scores of newspapers to begin publishing. Journalists expected to report the voting. When official results hiking the ruling party's slate did not match tallies provided by local vote supervisors, newspapers reported the discrepancy. Some papers were banned, and journalists were barred from further employment. Some thirty papers were expected to fold in 1996 because of high government taxes on newsprint. The government has also blocked many papers from receiving advertising revenues. Although independent broadcast services were recently permitted, state-run television will be the only nationwide network.

Press freedom ratings

Of 187 countries, only five significantly improved their press-freedom standard in 1996. Benin, Ecuador, Madagascar and Mongolia went from Partly Free to Free; Ghana moved from Not Free to Partly Free.

Six countries significantly declined in press freedom: Brazil and Hong Kong went from Free to Partly Free, and Bahrain, Niger, Croatia and Zambia moved to Not Free from Partly Free.

To determine press freedom rankings, Freedom House employs twenty criteria, examining four basic categories: each country's laws and administration, political impact on the content of journalism, economic influence and actual violations of press freedom directed at journalists or their institutions. After such assessments, domestic journalism is termed Free, Partly Free, or Not Free.

There was movement within these categories. Thirteen countries with a Free press improved their standing: Austria, Belgium, Canada, Colombia, Costa Rica, Germany, Greece, Japan, South Korea, Latvia, Lithuania, Namibia and Taiwan. Among the Free, 14 declined slightly: Australia, Chile, Cyprus, Grenada, Ireland, Mali, Poland, Slovenia, Solomon Islands, Spain, Trinidad and Tobago, United Kingdom, United States and Uruguay.

The U.S., with the world's most diverse news media, received the smallest reduction in the survey for trends regarded as troublesome. The new Telecommunications Act deregulated major systems, encouraging massive buyouts and mergers of large communications networks. These could reduce the number and kind of news flows available to the public, while placing fewer gatekeepers at the news flow switches. The new Federal Aviation Authority authorization act empowers the agency to "ensure" that media organizations do not "intrude on the privacy of families of passengers" in airline accidents—an act of compassion mixed with potential censorship. And, again, the CIA authorized the use of U.S. journalists for covert activities abroad "in extraordinary circumstances"—a shadow cast over American reporters serving overseas. Increasingly, too, privatization of government services puts under private bans information formerly accessible to journalists and the public through the Freedom of Information Act.

Among countries with a Partly Free press, 15 gained within the category: Congo, Dominican Republic, Haiti, Bulgaria, Lebanon, Macedonia, Malawi, Nepal, Nicaragua, Palestine, Paraguay, Peru, Philippines, Sao Tome & Principe, and Uganda. The Partly Free press declined in 23 countries: Antigua & Barbuda, Argentina, Armenia,

PRESS FREEDOM VIOLATIONS — 1996
(and cumulative figures since 1982)

	[] countries	Total 1982-96
A. Killed	46 [20]	768
B. Kidnapped, Disappeared, Abducted	47 [18]	342
C. Arrested/Detained	372 [55]	3437
D. Expelled	6 [5]	421

A. Algeria 11; Angola 1; Bangladesh 2; Cambodia 1; Colombia 1; Cyprus 1; Guatemala 2; Honduras 1; India 2; Indonesia 1; Ireland 1; Mexico 3; Pakistan 1; Philippines 2; Russia 11; Tajikistan 1; Thailand 1; Turkey 1; Ukraine 1; Uzbekistan 1.

B. Algeria 1; Argentina 1; Cambodia 1; Cameroon 1; Colombia 2; Cuba 2; Ethiopia 2; Guatemala 1; India 21; Iran 1; Mexico 2; Moldova 1; Niger 1; Nigeria 2; Pakistan 2; Paraguay 1; Poland 1; Russia 4.

C. Albania 37; Algeria 9; Azerbaijan 2; Bangladesh 2; Belarus 9; Bosnia 5; Brazil 3; Bulgaria 2; Burundi 4; Cameroon 7; Central African Republic 1; China 17; Colombia 2; Cuba 36; Equatorial Guinea 2; El Salvador 1; Ethiopia 22; France 5; Gambia 8; Ghana 6; Guinea 6; Haiti 4; Indonesia 3; Iran 1; Israel 4; Ivory Coast 1; Jordan 11; Kenya 2; Lebanon 6; Liberia 5; Malaysia 10; Mali 1; Niger 10; Nigeria 10; Pakistan 2; Palest. Terr 3; Peru 2; Russia 2; Rwanda 4; Serbia 6; Sierra Leone 9; South Africa 10; South Korea 3; Sri Lanka 7; Sudan 5; Tonga 4; Trinidad & Tobago 1; Turkey 41; Turkmenistan 1; Uganda 2; Ukraine 1; Uruguay 2; Yemen 3; Zaire 2; Zambia 8.

D. China 2; Gambia 1; Guinea 1; Nigeria 1; Zaire 1.

		Total 1987-96
E. Charged, Sentenced, Fined	179 [61]	640
F. Beaten, Assaulted, Tortured	281 [50]	1422
G. Wounded in Attack	16 [2]	354
H. Threatened	77 [24]	688
I. Robbery, Confiscation of Materials or Credentials	114 [46]	695
J. Barred from Entry or Travel	44 [20]	406
K. Harassed	214 [62]	1251
L. Publication or Program Shut Down	343 [20]	652
M. Publication or Program Banned, Censored, or Suspended.	103 [37]	755
N. Home Bombed, Burned, Raided, or Occupied	21 [14]	105
O. Publication or Program Bombed, Burned, Raided or Occupied	64 [31]	282
Total Violations		1927 [120]

—Compiled by Kristen Guida, research assistant

Bangladesh, Comoros, El Salvador, Ethiopia, Honduras, India, Jordan, Lesotho, Mexico, Morocco, Mozambique, Romania, Russia, Senegal, Slovakia, Sri Lanka, Thailand, Tonga, Ukraine, and Zimbabwe.

Small gains in the Not Free category were shown in eleven nations: Bosnia, Cameroon, Mauritania, Nigeria, Rwanda, Sierra Leone, Somalia, Tajikistan, Tunisia, Vietnam, and Zaire. Further declines were noted in 15 Not Free countries: Albania, Azerbaijan, Belarus, Cambodia, Cuba, Egypt, Gambia, Guinea, Kazakhstan, Liberia, Malaysia, Moldova, Serbia, Turkey, and Yemen.

No discernible change in press freedom was noted in the 85 other countries surveyed. Of these, 36 are Free, 16 Partly Free, and 33 Not Free.

Regional assessments reveal the disparity of press freedom worldwide. Of Africa's 53 nations, 7 (13 percent) boast a Free press, 19 (36 percent) a Partly Free press, and 27 (51 percent) a Not Free press. In 49 Asian nations (including the Middle East), the press is Free in 6 (12 percent), Partly Free in 14 (29 percent), and Not Free in 29 (59 percent). In Europe (West and East), of 38 countries, 27 (71 percent) enjoy a Free press, 6 (16 percent) a Partly Free press, and 5 (13 percent) have a Not Free press. Eighteen Latin American and Caribbean countries have a Free press (55 percent), 14 (42 percent) have a Partly Free press, and 1(3 percent) has a press that is Not Free. Both North American countries boast a Free press. Oceania has 9 (75 percent) countries with a Free press and 3 (25 percent) countries with a press that is Partly Free.

The following table shows regional changes within categories and changing categories of press freedom.

Changes 1995 to 1996

	One Category to Another		Within Categories			
	Impr.	Dec.	Impr.	Dec.	Unchanged	#
Africa	3	2	13	12	23	53
Asia	1	2	9	13	25	49
Europe	0	1	9	12	15	38
Lat. Am/Carib	1	1	7	10	14	33
North Amer.	0	0	1	1	0	2
Oceania	0	0	0	3	8	12
Total	5	6	39	51	85	187
%	3%	3%	21%	27%	46%	100%

Leonard R. Sussman is Senior Scholar for International Communications at Freedom House. Kristen Guida is a Researcher at Freedom House.

Introduction to Country and Related Territory Reports

The *Survey* team at Freedom House wrote reports on 191 countries and 16 related territories.

Each report begins with brief political, economic, and social data. This information is arranged under the following headings: **polity, economy, political rights, civil liberties, status, population, purchasing power parities (PPP), life expectancy,** and **ethnic groups.** There is also a brief explanation of **ratings changes and trends** since the last yearbook. When actual events changed the rating or trend, a succinct explanation follows. Readers interested in understanding the derivation of the ratings in this *Survey* should consult the chapter on methodology.

More detailed information follows in an **overview** and in an essay on the **political rights** and **civil liberties** of each country.

Under **polity**, there is an encapsulated description of the dominant centers of freely chosen or unelected political power in each country. Most of the descriptions are self-explanatory, such as Communist one-party for China or parliamentary democracy for Ireland. Such non-parliamentary democracies as the United States of America are designated presidential-legislative democracies. European democratic countries with constitutional monarchs are designated parliamentary democracies, because the elected body is the locus of most real political power. Only countries with powerful monarchs (e.g. the Sultan of Brunei) warrant a reference to the monarchy in the brief description of the polity. Dominant-party polities are systems in which the ruling party (or front) dominates government, but allows other parties to organize or compete short of taking control of government. There are other types of polities listed as well. Among them are various military and military-influenced or -dominated regimes, transitional systems, and several unique polities, such as Iran's clergy-dominated parliamentary system. Countries with genuine federalism have the word "federal" in the polity description.

The reports label the **economy** of each country. Non-industrial economies are called traditional or pre-industrial. Developed market economies and Third World economies with a modern market sector have the designation capitalist. Mixed capitalist countries combine private enterprise with substantial government involvement in the economy for social welfare purposes. Capitalist-statist economies have both large market sectors and government-owned productive enterprises, due either to elitist economic policies or state dependence on key natural resource industries. Mixed capitalist-statist economies have the characteristics of capitalist-statist economies plus major social welfare programs. Statist systems have the goal of placing the entire economy under direct or indirect government control. Mixed statist economies are primarily government-controlled, but also have significant private enterprise. Developing Third World economies with a government-directed modern sector belong in the statist category. Economies in transition between statist and capitalist forms may have the word transitional"in the economy description.

Each country report mentions in which category of **political rights** and **civil liberties** Freedom House classified the country. Category 1 is the most free and category 7 is the least free in each case. **Status** refers to the designations free, partly free, and not free,"which Freedom House uses as an overall summary of the general state of freedom in the country.

The ratings of countries and territories that are different from those of the previous year are marked with an asterisk (*). The reasons for the change precede the "Overview" of the country or territory.

Each entry includes a **population** figure that is sometimes the best approximation available. For all cases in which the information is available, the *Survey* provides **life expectancy** statistics.

Freedom House obtained the **Purchasing Power Parities (PPP)** from the U.N. Development Program. These figures show per capita gross domestic product (GDP) in terms of international dollars. The PPP statistic adjusts GDP to account for real buying power. For some countries, especially for newly independent countries, tiny island states, and those with statist economies, these statistics were unavailable.

The *Survey* provides a listing of countries' **ethnic groups**, because this information may help the reader understand issues, such as minority rights, which the *Survey* takes into account.

Each country summary has an **overview** that describes such matters as the most important events of 1996 and current political issues. Finally, the country reports contain a section on **political rights** and **civil liberties**. This section summarizes each country's degree of respect for the rights and liberties that Freedom House uses to evaluate freedom in the world. These summaries include instances of human rights violations by both governmental and nongovernmental entities.

Reports on related territories follow the country summaries. In most cases, these reports are comparatively brief and contain fewer categories of information than one finds in the country summaries.

Beginning in 1995-96, we are including reports only for 15 related territories rated "Partly Free" and "Not Free," and for the U.S. territory of Puerto Rico, which has a civil liberties situation of particular concern. However, ratings are provided for all 59 related territories.

Afghanistan

Polity: Competing war- **Political Rights:** 7
lords, traditional rulers, **Civil Liberties:** 7
and local councils **Status:** Not Free
Economy: Mixed-statist
Population: 21,472,000
PPP: $800
Life Expectancy: 43.7
Ethnic Groups: Pashtun (38 percent), Tajik (25 percent), Hazara
(19 percent), Uzbek (6 percent)
Capital: Kabul

Overview: The Taliban militia's capture of Kabul in late September 1996, following a two-year offensive, has placed two-thirds of Afghanistan under the group's rigid Islamic rule and subjected women to draconian restrictions.

King Zahir Shah ruled Afghanistan from 1933 until his cousin deposed him in a 1973 coup. Following a 1978 Communist coup, the Soviet Union invaded in December 1979 to install a pro-Moscow Communist faction. After a decade of battling foreign-backed *mujahideen* guerrilla fighters, the Soviet army withdrew its last troops in 1989.

Following the April 1992 overthrow of the Communist government, the mujahideen began fighting each other. Gulbuddin Hekmatyar's radical fundamentalist Hizb-i-Islami (Islamic Society) drew support from the Pashtuns, who have ruled Afghanistan for most of the past 250 years. The Jamiat-i-Islami (Islamic Society), headed by Burhanuddin Rabbani, was based in Afghanistan's large Tajik minority. In December 1992 a Grand Council of tribal elders and militia commanders elected Rabbani as interim president, although five of the nine major mujahideen factions boycotted the vote, including Hekmatyar's Hizb-i-Islami.

Rabbani, whose government exercised little authority outside the capital, refused to step down after his mandate expired in June 1994. During the summer a new militia, supported by Pakistan and organized around radical theology students disgusted with the continued fighting and the rape and banditry plaguing the country, took up arms and began disarming local militia commanders around the southern city of Kandahar.

By February 1995, the Pashtun-based Taliban had ousted Hekmatyar's troops, many of whom come from a rival Pashtun sub-clan, from their foothold near southeastern Kabul. By September, the rebel group, their ranks swollen with defectors from the government army and other militias, had conquered much of southern and western Afghanistan.

After months of fighting, on September 26, 1996, the Taliban captured Kabul. Although the group set up a six-member provisional *shura*, or ruling council, real power rested with a former mujahideen fighter, Mullah Mohammed Omar, in Kandahar. In mid-October Ahmad Shah Masood, the military commander of the ousted government, formed an anti-Taliban alliance with Uzbek warlord Rashid Dostum, who commands a well-equipped militia and runs a de facto state near the northern Uzbekistan border. Subsequent fighting on the plain north of Kabul caused numerous casualties among Tajik villagers but failed to dislodge the Taliban from the capital. The UNHCR expressed concern that the conflict was turning into all-out intra-ethnic war.

Political Rights and Civil Liberties: No democratic processes exist at any level in Afghanistan. The country is partitioned among the Taliban, who at the end of 1996, ruled some 65-70 percent of the territory; Uzbek warlord Rashid Dostum, who held five northern provinces; and former government military commander Ahmad Shah Masood, who controlled the Panjshir Valley and territory in the northeast. The tiny Shiite Hazara community also controls a small territory in central Afghanistan.

The Taliban's territorial consolidation has reduced incidents of rape, banditry, extortion and looting by troops of the former government and the factional militias. However, beginning with the Taliban's initial assault on the capital in March 1995, the group has resorted to the indiscriminate artillery, rocket and air attacks practiced by the other militias that have killed 25,000 residents of Kabul since 1992. In 1996 the Taliban also carried out brutal reprisals against Shiite and Tajik villagers for allegedly supporting rival militias.

The Taliban administers its territory through local *shura*, or councils, composed of appointed senior officials who rule by decree. Ad hoc judiciaries preside over summary trials that lack due process rights. Punishments are based on the group's interpretation of Shari'a, or Islamic law, and include public execution of murderers and allegedly corrupt local officials, amputation of a hand and a foot of thieves, and the stoning to death of adulterers.

Almost immediately after entering Kabul, the Taliban seized former Communist president Mohammad Najibullah and his brother from their refuge in a United Nations compound, tortured them and hung their bodies from a traffic post. Several thousand residents of Kabul have reportedly been arbitrarily arrested on suspicion of aiding the ousted Rabbani government.

By Taliban decree, women are barred from working, cannot leave their homes unless accompanied by a male relative and are required to wear the *burqa*, a one-piece garment covering the entire body with only a mesh opening for the eyes. Taliban soldiers beat women for minor violations. The restrictions have forced the suspension of medical care and relief services provided by women, and have caused additional hardship for the 25-30,000 war widows in the capital who now have no source of income. The Taliban have also closed girls' schools and forced men to pray in neighborhood mosques five times each day.

Outside areas of Taliban control, justice is administered arbitrarily according to Islamic law and traditional customs. Rival groups carry out torture and extrajudicial killings against their opponents and suspected sympathizers.

Uzbek warlord Rashid Dostum rules his territory near the northern Uzbekistan border through the National Islamic Movement (NIM), essentially an outgrowth of his militia, based at Mazar-i-Sharif. The NIM mini-state has its own flag, airline and currency.

Freedom of speech, press and association is sharply restricted throughout the country. The key faction leaders control their own broadcast facilities and newspapers. Few if any civil institutions exist, and there is no known trade union activity.

Roughly 85 percent of the population is Sunni Muslim, and the Shiite minority that forms most of the remainder has faced particularly harsh treatment by the Taliban and other factions. Sikhs and Hindus are often randomly attacked, and thousands have fled the country. There are several thousand Tajik refugees in northern Afghanistan.

Freedom of internal movement is hampered by the continued fighting and by the estimated ten million uncleared landmines strewn across the country. Some two million Afghans are internally displaced, many living in camps in and around the eastern city of Jalalabad, and more than two million others are refugees, primarily in Iran and Pakistan. The Taliban have placed a ban on emigration, although many members of Kabul's middle class have clandestinely fled to Pakistan.

Albania

Polity: Presidential-   **Political Rights:** 4*
parliamentary democracy **Civil Liberties:** 4
Economy: Transitional   **Status:** Partly Free
Population: 3,,282,000
PPP: $2,200
Life Expectancy: 72.0
Ethnic Groups: Albanians (two main ethnic/linguistic
groups: Ghegs, Tosks, 95 percent), Greeks (3 percent)
Capital: Tirana
Ratings Change: Albania's political rights changed from 3 to 4 because of ballot fraud and a post-election crackdown on anti-government protesters.

Overview: Allegations of ballot fraud by President Sali Berisha's ruling Democratic Party (DP) marred parliamentary elections in May 1996, and a post-election crackdown on anti-government protesters raised concerns in this Balkan country on the Adriatic coast. By year's end, the collapse of so-called "pyramid"investment schemes threatened the savings of millions and social stability.

Albania gained independence in 1912 after 450 years of Ottoman rule. It was annexed by Italy in 1939. A one-party Communist regime was established in 1946 under World War II partisan Enver Hoxha, who died in office in 1985. In 1990, Ramiz Alia, Hoxha's successor as first secretary of the Albanian Party of Labor (Communist), was elected president of the Socialist Party (PS), renamed Communists. In the 1992 elections for the 140-member People's Assembly, Berisha's DP captured 97 seats; the PS, 38; the Social Democratic Party, 7; the Union for Human Rights of the Greek Minority, 2; and the Republican Party, 1. Lawmakers elected Berisha president. Alexander Meksi was named prime minister.

The defeat of a government-backed constitution by referendum in November 1994, and the passage in 1995 of the so-called "genocide law" barring former high-ranking Communists from running for office until 2002, led to charges by the opposition that President Berisha and the DP were, as one critic put it, "institutionalizing political revenge" and abusing power.

By February 1996, 32 former leaders were imprisoned for crimes of the Communist regime. A new election law rushed through parliament over opposition protests restructured the electoral commissions to the advantage of the government, and gave the president sole power to approve changes to voting districts. Political tensions flared in April, when 35 Socialist Party members, including SP General Secretary Gramoz Ruci, and several other leading opposition figures were banned from running for election by a government-appointed "verification" commission set up to enforce the genocide law. The SP accused the government of selective enforcement, noting that President Berisha himself was a privileged heart surgeon under the old regime and treated senior officials, including Enver Hoxha.

The May 1996 election plunged the country into political turmoil amid allegations of fraud by Albanian and international monitors. The Central Election Commission announced that the DP had won. Riot police were used to quell opposition protests in Tirana, opposition figures were detained and rallies were banned. The SP, as well as the centrist Democratic Alliance and the Social Democrats, threatened to boycott parliament.

October's local elections for over 300 communes and 43 municipalities were not monitored by officials from the Organization of Security and Cooperation in Europe (OSCE), which pulled out after the government tried to cut the number of observers. The Council of Europe, which coordinated monitoring, reported no serious infractions, findings disputed by the opposition. The DP won over 58 percent of commune seats and over 60 percent of city halls, including Tirana. The Socialists won only 6 percent of city halls and commune seats, down from over 50 percent in 1992.

Political Rights and Civil Liberties:

Albanians can change their government through elections but the 1996 parliamentary elections were rife with irregularities, according to Albanian and international observers. The electoral law was restructured to favor the government, give the president sole power to change electoral districts and make it more difficult for smaller parties to enter parliament.

There is a multi-party parliamentary opposition, but the "genocide law" bars former high-ranking Communists, including leading members of the opposition, from running for office.

In September, four Albanians were sentenced to 12-18 months in prison for founding a Communist Party and trying to overthrow the government by violence. The same month, nine senior officials of the Communist era were sentenced (five in absentia) to up to 20 year's imprisonment on charges of political persecution of dissidents under the "genocide law." Among those imprisoned under the law was Ramiz Alia, the country's first democratically-elected president in 1990 and former Communist Party leader. Former prime minister and PS leader, Fatos Nano, sentenced to nine years in 1993 for corruption (but widely regarded as a political prisoner), remained behind bars despite international protests.

The regime has used financial constraints, legal barriers and a highly restrictive press law to hinder the development of a genuinely free press. Among provisions susceptible to abuse are requirements for editors-in-chief; guidelines for the confiscation of press publications; and measures which allow a prosecutor to remove a publication from circulation on the basis of broad, poorly defined criteria. The law restricts access to information that can be regarded as a state secret. A 1995 penal code criminalized insulting official foreign representatives and public officials, including judges. Penalties include fines or prison terms of up to three years.

State Radio and Television, a government agency, controls all broadcasting. State-controlled television violated the electoral law by failing to allot equal time to the opposition. After post-election protests, state-controlled television refused to show violence by police against protesters and opposition leaders. Journalists have acknowledged that government pressure and fear of persecution have made them reluctant to cover such issues as government corruption. In the months prior to the elections, Albania's largest daily, *Koha Jone*, was harassed by authorities. In January, the paper was accused of collaborating with the Serbian secret police, although no supporting evidence was ever disclosed. In February, authorities detained the entire staff of the paper. Other journalists were arbitrarily detained and, in some cases, beaten.

The 1995 penal code enhanced defendant's rights and reduced sentences, but the executive branch has interfered with the judiciary. The Association of Judges of Albania has criticized government organs that "directly affect the independence of the judicial powers."Arbitrary restrictions on freedom of assembly have been enforced, including a ban on public gatherings in the wake of the controversial parliamentary elections. In March 1996, parliament adopted a new civil code as part of an effort at judicial reform.

Religious activity is unrestricted in this predominantly Muslim country with Orthodox and Catholic minorities. A special religious affairs office monitors proselytizing by Christian groups from abroad.

The Independent Confederation of Trade Unions of Albania (BSPSH) is an umbrella organization for a number of smaller unions. A federation with links to the Socialist Party, the Confederation of Unions, a successor to the official Communist-era group, has few members. In January 1996, a survey of Albanian women by the women's group Refleksione found a high rate of violence against women.

Algeria

Polity: Civilian-military **Political Rights:** 6
Economy: Statist   **Civil Liberties:** 6
Population: 29,006,000 **Status:** Not Free
PPP: $5,570
Life Expectancy: 67.3
Ethnic Groups: Arabs (75 percent), Berbers (25 percent)
Capital: Algiers

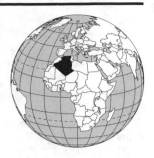

Overview: Islamist radicals continued their campaign of terror this year, even as the security services restored order to most urban areas. The violence, in which over 55,000 people have been killed, eased somewhat in 1996 amidst signs of economic recovery. However, economic recovery did not impact positively on the average person's standard of living. Censorship of security information has made an accurate count of the victims impossible. President Lamine Zeroual's plan to move toward multi-party democracy, including parliamentary elections in 1997, is as yet rejected by leading political parties, as well as by the armed opposition. A new constitution, approved by a referendum in November, expands presidential powers and bans religion from the political arena. Participation in this referendum, as well as in last year's presidential election, suggests Algerians, unlike the organized opposition, agree with Zeroual that voting is a step toward civil peace.

Algeria's violent political climate intensified in 1992 after the army canceled the second round of democratic parliamentary elections, in which the Islamic Salvation Front (FIS) had already taken a commanding lead. FIS's avowed aim to install theocratic rule under *Shari'a* law would have destroyed many constitutional protections Algerians had enjoyed since winning independence from France in 1962 after a bloody struggle. Three decades later, the National Liberation Front (FLN) that led the fight against the French still held power. By 1992, however, two-thirds of the popuation had been born after independence, and the FLN's popularity had long faded. Economic stagnation, housing shortages, unemployment and other social ills broadened support for opposition parties.

A state of emergency followed the voiding of the 1992 polls; thousands of FIS supporters were detained; and the armed rebellion began. President Chadli Benjedid was forced from office, and in 1993 Major-General Lamine Zeroual was appointed president. Zeroual gained some legitimacy for his tenure in the November 1995 election that was restricted to regime-approved candidates but nonetheless drew an impressive 75 percent turnout. He has sought compromise with moderate Islamic leaders while pursuing a ruthless campaign to crush clandestine Islamist groups. Among the fundamentalists' favorite targets are soldiers, policemen and government officials, but all of civil society is under threat. Anyone uncommitted to an Islamist state is considered fair game, including unveiled women, Christians, and foreigners. Journalists, trade unionists, academics and magistrates are special targets of Islamist death squads, often murdered in a calculated and cruel manner meant to maximize the slayings' terroristic impact.

Government security forces have responded brutally as well. Extrajudicial killings are allegedly common, beyond the thousands of militants who have died in armed clashes. Many suspected militants or supporters are detained and some reportedly tortured.

Political Rights and Civil Liberties: In 1992 Algerians lost their right to freely choose their government in democratic elections. Constitutional changes in 1989 began Algeria's transition to a multiparty system after nearly three decades of one-party rule. The new constitution, amended by referendum, permits political parties if they are not based on religious or regionalist programs.

The civil war has severely curtailed freedom of expression. Nearly 60 journalists have been murdered by Islamist terrorists. In February a massive car bomb destroyed or damaged the National Press Building in Algiers, killing two journalists.

The regime is equally unrelenting in its efforts to bend the press to its point of view, albiet in a far less brutal fashion. It directly controls broadcast media and some newspapers, has threatened and arrested reporters and editors and closed some newspapers. The regime has almost unlimited power under the declared emergency and the anti-terrorist decree. All reports relating to the insurgency must be passed by government censors. In September, a cartoonist and two editors of the French-language daily *La Tribune* were given suspended prison sentences for publishing a cartoon the court said mocked the national flag. Publication of other newspapers such as *La Nation,* whose editor, Salima Ghozali, is the only woman in such a position, has been suspended.

Public debate is limited by both Islamist terror and government strictures. Public assemblies that do not back the government are not permitted, but legal opposition parties need no permits to hold meetings; nongovernmental organizations must be licensed. The Algerian League for the Defense of Human Rights has offered public findings on the human rights situation, but the official government human rights monitoring body had made only confidential reports.

Torture and killing of suspected Islamists is allegedly widespread. The International Committee of the Red Cross has no access to thousands of suspected Islamists convicted of crimes or held on suspicion of fundamentalist activity. Members of the Berber minority, who predominate in the northeastern Kabylie region, are also targeted by extreme fundamentalists because of their more relaxed interpretations of Islamic practice. Religious freedom, guaranteed by the constitution, is clearly under threat by the fundamentalists. The Armed Islamic Group (GIA) has publicly declared Christians, Jews and polytheists to be targets. In May, seven French Trappist monks were murdered after being held captive for two months, and on August 1, the Roman Catholic bishop of Oran, Pierre Claverie, an outspoken opponent of all violence, was also killed.

Women also suffer discrimination under some laws, including the *Shari'a*-based family code, as well as under traditional practices. Trade union rights are protected and nearly two-thirds of the labor force is unionized. An FIS-allied union has been banned, but strikes and other union activity are legal, and take place. A government report claims that 400 trade unionists were murdered by Islamists in 1994-95.

Algeria is saddled with $32 billion in foreign debt. Its economy is still strongly dominated by state enterprises, especially in the chemical sector which earns most of the country's export income, but the government has pledged a serious privatization effort to begin in 1997. The government has reduced tariffs and government production subsidies. Despite continuing violence and uncertainty, Western oil companies have announced major new investments.

Andorra

Polity: Parliamentary democracy
Economy: Capitalist
Population: 66,000
PPP: na
Life Expectancy: na
Ethnic Groups: Spanish (61 percent), Andorran (30 percent), French (6 percent)
Capital: Andorra la Vella

Political Rights: 1
Civil Liberties: 1
Status: Free

Overview: Andorra was established as a sovereign parliamentary democracy and a member of the United Nations in 1993 when it ratified and approved a constitution. Since 1278, the six parishes of Andorra, under the joint control of France and the bishop of Urgel in Spain, has existed as an unwritten democracy without official borders. The General Council (parliament) functioned in various legislative and executive capacities under the supervision of the co-princes since 1868.

The Council of Europe recommended in 1990 that the principality adopt a modern constitution in order to attain full integration into the European Union. After extensive negotiations, French President Francois Mitterand and Bishop Joan Marti i Alanis agreed to grant full sovereignty to Andorra. Under the constitution, these co-princes continue as heads of state, but the head of government retains executive power.

Andorran politics are dominated by five major parties, none of which controls the General Council. Efforts to modernize and liberalize the economy continue, driven by pressure from the EU. As Andorra has no currency of its own (francs and pesetas circulate instead), inflationary pressures are felt from prices in France and Spain. Andorra's duty-free status continues to attract large numbers of tourists, though limits have been placed on duty-free allowances as a result of EU negotiations. The vibrant economy also attracts many immigrants and foreign workers, which in turn drives up the public debt for education, health care, and maintenance of infrastructure. Increasing debt and the status of native Andorrans as a minority of the population have led to stringent citizenship requirements and political inequality for immigrants.

Political Rights and Civil Liberties:

Andorrans can change their government democratically. The Sindic (President), subsindic and members of the General Council are elected in general elections held every four years. The new constitution equalized representation in parliament by mandating that half of its representatives be elected by parish, and half selected from nationwide lists.

The judiciary is independent. Citizens enjoy the right to due process, the presumption of innocence and the right to legal counsel - including free counsel for the indigent.

The constitution proclaims respect for the promotion of liberty, equality, justice, tolerance, and defense of human rights and human dignity. Torture and the death penalty are outlawed. There have been no documented cases of police brutality.

The constitution prohibits discrimination based on birth, race, sex, origin, religion, disability, opinion, language or any other "personal or social condition." However, many rights and privileges are granted only to Andorran citizens. Citizenship is attained through lineage, marriage, birth, or after 30 years of living and working in the country. Dual citizenship is prohibited, and immigrant workers are not entitled to social benefits. Non-citizens are allowed to own 33 percent of the shares of a company.

Freedom of assembly, association and religion is guaranteed. The new constitution legalizes trade unions for the first time, though no labor unions exist at present.

The constitution guarantees freedom of expression, communication and information, but allows for laws regulating the right of reply, correction and professional confidentiality. The domestic press consists of two daily papers and one weekly. There is local public radio and television as well as easy access to print and broadcast media from neighboring countries.

The Roman Catholic Church is guaranteed the "preservation of the relations of special cooperation with the State in accordance with the Andorran tradition." However, the Church is not subsidized by the government. The practice of other religions is respected but subject to limitations "in the interests of public safety, order, health or morals, or for the protection of the fundamental rights and freedoms of others."

There are no restrictions on domestic or foreign travel, emigration, or repatriation. Andorra has a tradition of providing asylum for refugees although there is no formal asylum policy. Requests are considered on an individual basis.

Women were granted full suffrage in 1970, and though there are no legal barriers to their political participation, social conservatism makes it difficult for women to gain access to the political world. Only two cabinet-level posts have been held by women.

Angola

Polity: Presidential-
legislative
Economy: Statist
Population: 11,469,000
PPP: $674
Life Expectancy: 46.8
Ethnic Groups: Ovimbundu (37 percent),
Kimbundu (25 percent), Bakongo (13 percent), others
Capital: Luanda

Political Rights: 6
Civil Liberties: 6
Status: Not Free

Overview:
Angola enjoyed its least violent year in three decades in 1996, but prospects for a lasting peace remained tenuous. A United Nations-sponsored peace agreement reached in November 1994 is being implemented by 7,000 UN peacekeepers and 1,000 U.N. civilian officials. Yet delays in integrating fighters of the rebel National Union for Total Independence of Angola (UNITA) into the government army, and UNITA leader Jonas Savimbi's continued political procrastination, is imperiling the peace pact. Diamonds and oil, sources of potential wealth, cannot be exploited efficiently in present conditions, and Angola is one of the most destitute countries in Africa.

On November 11, 1975, 14 years of anti-colonial bush war ended, and with it five centuries of Portuguese presence in Africa. But Angola's ethnic-based rivals were armed by East and West, and 15 more years of fighting followed, with Cuban and South African involvement on opposing sides. Large-scale covert American aid bolstered UNITA's fortunes, but produced no clear victor.

With the Cold War's end the United Nations became deeply involved in the Angola peace process, with mixed results. It was hoped that U.N.-supervised elections in September 1992 would end the long-running war. Despite many irregularities, international observers described the voting as generally free and fair. President Jose Eduardo dos Santos, leader of the Popular Movement for the Liberation of Angola (MPLA), led by a wide margin in the first round of voting. After UNITA leader and presidential candidate Savimbi rejected this defeat and refused to enter a second-round run-off, the war resumed in October 1992.

Hundreds of thousands of people died in combat and of starvation and disease before the latest tenuous peace accord was reached in 1994. In August, Savimbi reversed his decision to accept a newly-created post as vice-president. Continuing uncertainty hinders economic reconstruction. Human rights violations by both rebel and government forces continue. Savimbi's reluctance to accept fully the peace accord may arise from commercial as well as political motivations; his control of diamond fields in northeastern Angola reportedly earns UNITA as much as $500 million annually.

In the oil-rich and little-developed northern enclave of Cabinda, sporadic violence by secessionist guerrilla groups continued through 1996. Several attempts at negotiation produced offers of limited revenue sharing by the central government. Limited Cabindan autonomy may also be granted, but it is certain that any government in Luanda would not allow independence to an area whose oil exports bring about $700 million per year to the central treasury.

Political Rights and Civil Liberties: The 1992 presidential and legislative elections allowed Angolans to freely elect their own representatives for the first time. UNITA's return to war precluded the second round run-off required when neither presidential candidate won an outright majority, but President dos Santos took office nonetheless. The MPLA dominates the 220-member national assembly. Opposition deputies attend but the assembly remains largely a rubber-stamp to the MPLA executive. Local elections planned for 1994 never took place. It is not certain that the Angolan people will be free to change their government through the ballot box in the future.

The political process has been subsumed by the military contest between the MPLA and UNITA. Until the basic issue of war and peace is resolved, broader popular participation, especially from the rural areas, will be problematical.

Media operate freely in Luanda, but are under constant threat from the government. Journalists have been threatened, harassed and even murdered, and the government keeps tight reign on the broadcast media. In UNITA-controlled areas, there is even less opportunity for media access.

Across the countryside, an enormous number of land mines are sown, many haphazardly. Decades of guerrilla war left many weapons in the hands of bandits. Reimposing civil authority will be difficult even if there is a genuine peace. In some areas, local courts operate regarding civil matters and petty crime, but an overall lack of training and infrastructure inhibit judicial proceedings.

Women's rights are protected legally, but societal discrimination remains strong, particularly in rural areas. Religious freedom is generally respected. Constitutional guarantees protect freedom of assembly and labor rights, although an implementation of legislation and administrative procedures to allow free trade union activities is lacking. Some independent unions are operating, however, and several strikes have resulted in negotiated settlements. Nearly all organized labor activities are concentrated in Angola's cities, and the vast majority of rural and agricultural workers remain outside the modern economic sector.

The state is still deeply involved in the country's limited economic activity, which is largely confined to extractive industries. Corruption and black marketing are widespread.

Antigua and Barbuda

Polity: Dominant party
Economy: Capitalist-
statist
Population: 100,000
PPP: $5,369
Life Expectancy: 74.0
Ethnic Groups: Black (89 percent), other (11 percent)
Capital: St. John's

Political Rights: 4
Civil Liberties: 3
Status: Partly Free

Overview:
Antigua and Barbuda is a member of the British Commonwealth. The British monarchy is represented by a governor-general. The islands gained independence in 1981.
Under the 1981 constitution, the political system is a parliamentary democracy, with
a bicameral parliament consisting of a 17 member House of Representatives elected
for five years, and an appointed Senate. In the House there are 16 seats for Antigua
and one for Barbuda. Eleven senators are appointed by the prime minister, four by
the parliamentary opposition leader, one by the Barbuda Council and one by the
governor-general.

Antigua and Barbuda has been dominated by the Bird family and the Antigua
Labour Party (ALP) for decades. Rule has been based more on power and the abuse
of authority than on law. The constitution has consistently been disregarded and the
Bird tenure has been marked by corruption scandals. A commission headed by prominent British jurist Louis Blom-Cooper concluded in 1990 that the country faced
"being engulfed in corruption."

In 1994 Vere Bird, the patriarch of the most prominent family and prime minister, stepped down in favor of his son Lester. In the run-up to the 1994 elections
three opposition parties united to form the United Progressive Party (UPP). Labor
activist Baldwin Spencer became UPP leader, and Tim Hector, editor of the outspoken weekly *Outlet,* deputy leader. The UPP campaigned on a social-democratic
platform emphasizing rule of law and good governance.

In the election the ALP won 11 of 17 parliamentary seats, down from 15 in
1989. The UPP won five, up from one in 1989. The Barbuda People's Movement
(BPM) retained the Barbuda seat, giving the opposition a total of six seats. Despite
unfair conditions, the UPP opted to accept the outcome because it believed that
political momentum was now on its side.

After taking office as prime minister, Lester Bird promised cleaner, more efficient government. But his administration continued to be dogged by scandals. In
1995 Bird's brother, Ivor, was convicted of smuggling cocaine into the country, but
was let off with a fine.

With the nation facing a huge per capita foreign debt, Bird imposed a structural
adjustment program in 1995. Tax hikes and fiscal tightening sparked labor strikes
and demonstrations. In late summer Hurricane Luis struck the islands. While Bird
looked for international aid, the UPP claimed the storm had set development back
a decade. In September 1996 Bird sacked Finance Minister Molwyn Joseph over
accusations that he helped a friend evade customs duties on an imported car.

Political Rights and Civil Liberties: Constitutionally, citizens are able to change their government by democratic means. The 1994 elections, however, were neither free nor fair because the balloting system did not guarantee a secret vote; the ruling party dominated the broadcast media and excluded the opposition; the voter registration system was deficient; the voter registry was inflated by possibly up to 30 percent with names of people who had died or left the country; and the electoral law allows the ruling party to abuse the power of incumbency with impunity.

Political parties, labor unions and civic organizations are free to organize. There is an Industrial Court to mediate labor disputes, but public sector unions tend to be under the sway of the ruling party. Demonstrators are occasionally subject to harassment by the police, who are politically tied to the ruling party. Freedom of religion is respected.

The judiciary is nominally independent but weak, and subject to political manipulation by the ruling party; it has been nearly powerless to address corruption in the executive branch. There is an intra-island court of appeals for Antigua and five other former British colonies in the Lesser Antilles.

The ALP government and the Bird family control the country's television, cable and radio outlets. During the 1994 elections, the opposition was allowed to purchase broadcast time only to announce its campaign events. The government barred the UPP from the broadcast media through a strict interpretation of the country's archaic electoral law, which prohibits broadcast of any item "for the purpose of promoting or procuring the election of any candidate or of any political party." Meanwhile, the ALP rode roughshod over the law with a concerted political campaign thinly disguised as news about the government.

The government, the ruling party and the Bird family also control four newspapers, including *Antigua Today*, an expensively produced weekly established in 1993 as an election vehicle for Lester Bird. The opposition counts solely on the *Daily Observer*, a small but vocal 12-page publication, and the weekly *Outlet,* which the government is continually trying to throttle, albeit unsuccessfully, via intimidation and libel suits.

Argentina

Polity: Federal presiden-
tial-legislative democracy
Economy: Capitalist
Population: 34,684,000
PPP: $8,350
Life Expectancy: 72.2
Ethnic Groups: European (mostly Spanish and Italian, 85
percent), mestizo, Indian, Arab
Capital: Buenos Aires

Politic Rights: 2
Civil Liberties: 3
Status: Free

Overview:

President Carlos Saul Menem faces the possibility of a two-year lame-duck period—a very long time in volatile Argentina—following the 1997 congressional elections. Unemployment, continued corruption, economic adjustment fatigue and weariness with an administration that has been in office for seven years have eroded popular support for the president and his allies, and renders opposition gains likely.

The Argentine Republic was established after independence from Spain in 1816. Democratic rule was often interrupted by military takeovers. The end of authoritarian rule under Juan Peron (1946-55) led to left-wing violence and repressive military regimes. Argentina returned to elected civilian rule in 1983.

Most of the 1853 federal constitution was restored in 1983. As amended in 1994, it provides for a president elected for four years with the option of re-election for one term. Presidential candidates must win 45 percent of the vote to avoid a runoff. The legislature consists of a 257-member Chamber of Deputies elected for six years, with half the seats renewable every three years, and a 72-member Senate nominated by elected provincial legislatures for nine-year terms, with one-third of the seats renewable every three years. Two senators are directly elected in the Buenos Aires federal district.

Peronist party leader Menem won a six-year presidential term in 1989, defeating Eduardo Angeloz of the incumbent, moderate-left Radical party. Menem discarded statist Peronist traditions by implementing, mostly by decree, an economic liberalization program.

In 1993 Menem made a deal with Radical leader Raul Alfonsin for a series of constitutional amendments, including an end to the prohibition on presidential re-election—Menem's main aim—a four-year presidential term and measures to limit the inordinate power of the presidency.

The 1995 election was contested by Menem, Senator Jose Octavio Bordon, a Peronist defector at the head of the new center-left Front for a Country in Solidarity (FREPASO), and Radical Horacio Massaccesi, a lackluster provincial governor. Menem, struggling with an economic crisis sparked by the Mexican peso devaluation, effectively played the fear card, declaring the choice was between "him and chaos."

Menem captured nearly 50 percent of the vote against about 30 percent for Bordon and 17 percent for Massaccesi. The Peronists gained a narrow majority in both houses of Congress.

Continued social unrest over the highest unemployment rates in modern Argentine history - approximately 17 percent for most of 1996 - and the growth and deepening of poverty, led to several national strikes in August, September and December.

Corruption, according to most polls the second most important issue of public concern following unemployment, retains its corrosive force. In 1995, bribery charges were levelled against a local subsidiary of IBM and officials of a state-owned bank. In 1996 illegal arms sales to Ecuador led to the resignation of the Defense Minister. Charges of malfeasance in office have been lodged against the former presidential candidate for the opposition Radical Party, and ex-provincial governor, Eduardo Angeloz. These cases were unique in that they led to judicial proceedings.

On December 18, President Menem signed three decrees making employment regulations more flexible. The resort to decrees is yet another sign of weakness in the governing coalition and the failure to institutionalize democratic political procedures.

Political Rights and Civil Liberties:

Citizens can change their government through elections. Constitutional guarantees regarding freedom of religion and the right to organize political parties, civic organizations and labor unions are generally respected.

However, the separation of powers and the rule of law have been undermined by President Menem's authoritarian ways and his manipulation of the judiciary. Legislative attempts to challenge Menem in court have been blocked since 1990, when Menem pushed a bill increasing the number of Supreme Court justices from five to nine through the Peronist-controlled Senate and stacked the court with politically-loyal judges. In December 1995 Menem used the Peronist-controlled Senate to put yet another crony on the Supreme Court.

Menem has used the Supreme Court to uphold decrees removing the comptroller general and other officials mandated to probe government wrongdoing. Overall, the judicial system is politicized and riddled with the corruption endemic to all branches of the government, creating what Argentines call "juridical insecurity." Despite more than two dozen major corruption scandals and the resignations of at least that many senior government officials since 1989, no investigation has ended in a trial. Polls show that more than 80 percent of Argentines do not trust the judicial system.

Since their condemnation of Menem's 1990 pardon of military officers convicted for human rights violations committed in the "dirty war," human rights groups have been subject to anonymous threats and various forms of intimidation. In 1993 the Inter-American Commission on Human Rights of the Organization of American States determined that the 1990 pardons were incompatible with Argentina's treaty obligations under the American Convention on Human Rights. Revelations, in early 1996, of previously unknown lists of victims of military repression led the Chief of the Army to apologize on television. In April, the Catholic Church hierarchy published its own self-criticism, admitting that it had not denounced illegal repression with sufficient force.

Newspapers and magazines are privately owned and vocal, and reflect a wide variety of viewpoints. Television and radio are both private and public. But Menem's authoritarian style has been particularly evident in his antagonism toward the media, which has created a climate in which journalists have come under increasing attack. Journalists and publications investigating official corruption are the principal targets. They have also been subjected to a libel-suit campaign and cuts in government advertising.

In 1995 international pressure kept the government from passing a series of restrictive press laws. But intimidation, including death threats and illegal searches, continued with impunity. Prominent journalist Guillermo Cherashny was shot and wounded in June, the most recent among dozens of attacks against reporters investigating government corruption in recent years.

There continue to be frequent reports of arbitrary arrests and ill-treatment by police during confinement. Police brutality cases rarely go anywhere in civil courts due to intimidation of witnesses and judges. Criminal court judges are frequent targets of anonymous threats.

The still unsolved 1994 car-bombing of a Jewish organization in Buenos Aires provided Menem with an excuse to establish by decree a security super-secretariat, encompassing the foreign, interior, intelligence and defense ministries and answerable directly to the president. Critics charged that Menem was less concerned about terrorism than about being able to confront chronic social unrest in the provinces.

The Catholic majority enjoys freedom of religious expression. The 250,000-strong Jewish community is a frequent target of anti-Semitic vandalism. Neo-Nazi organizations and other anti-Semitic groups remain active.

Labor is dominated by Peronist unions. Union influence, however, has diminished because of corruption scandals, internal divisions, and restrictions on public-sector strikes decreed by Menem to pave the way for his privatization program.

Armenia

Polity: Dominant party **Political Rights:** 5*
Economy: Mixed-statist **Civil Liberties:** 4
(transitional) **Status:** Partly Free
Population: 3,768,000
PPP: $2,040
Life Expectancy: 72.8
Ethnic Groups: Armenian (93 percent), Azeri (3 percent)
Capital: Yerevan
Ratings Change: Armenia's political rights rating changed from 4 to 5 because 1996 presidential elections were rife with irregularities.

Overview: In September 1996, President Levon Ter-Petrossian defeated former Prime Minister Vazgen Manukian of the National Democratic Union, in a vote labeled as "flawed" and rife with irregularities by international observers. The vote came just over a year after nine parties, including the largest opposition group, the Armenian Revolutionary Federation (ARF-Dashnak), were banned from parliamentary elections, ensuring the dominance of the president's ruling Armenian National Movement (ANM).

This landlocked, predominantly Christian Transcaucus republic was ruled at various times by Macedonians, Romans, Persians, Mongols and others; it was obtained by Russia from Persia in 1928. Prior to their defeat in World War I, Ottoman Turks controlled a western region, and between 1894 and 1915, engaged in a systematic campaign of genocide. The Russian component came under Communist control and was divided, with eastern Armenia becoming a Soviet Socialist republic in 1922 and western Armenia remaining part of Turkey. Armenia officially declared independence from the Soviet Union on September 23, 1991. About a month later, Ter-Petrossian, a former human rights activist, was elected president.

Before the 1995 parliamentary elections, the government-controlled Central Election Commission arbitrarily excluded certain parties and candidates. Though there are over 40 registered parties, by election day only 13 parties/blocs had emerged and/or survived the election registration process to contest the 40 seats allocated for proportional voting. All but 10 of the legislature's 190 seats were filled, with the president's Republican bloc controlling an estimated two-thirds of the seats. About 54 percent of eligible voters reportedly took part in the vote, but 411,743 ballots cast in proportional voting—or about 25 percent—were declared invalid. The opposition charged that it was denied equal access to the state-run electronic media, in violation of the electoral laws. After the vote, the president reappointed Hrant Bagratian as prime minister.

A new constitution was appproved by referendum. It provides for a weak legislature and the strongest presidency among the Organization on Security and Co-operation (OSCE) states. The president can dissolve parliament, appoint and dismiss the prime minister, appoint all judges and members of the constitutional court, and declare martial law.

In 1996, corruption, poor administration and economic conditions were key issues for voters. Former Prime Minister Manukian, President Ter-Petrossian's chief opponent, ran on a pro-market platform and promised to return the country to parliamentary rule.

Nine candidates competed in the September elections. The state-appointed Central and Regional Election Commissions, with 160 Ter-Petrossian loyalists, announced that the president won 51 won percent of the vote to Manukian's 42 percent. The results sparked three days of protests by over 100,000 demonstrators in Yerevan. Ruben Kakobian, a parliamentary deputy, was beaten and seriously injured after his arrest by a group of men that allegedly included Defense Minister Vazgen Sarkisian.

The November 10 local elections, which were boycotted by the opposition, were deemed free and fair by the Council of Europe, which acknowledged that some irregularities did occur but did not affect the outcome.

Other issues facing the country were economic privation and the unresolved conflict with Azerbaijan over the Armenian enclave of Nagorno-Karabakh. The government's 1997 economic program called for a continuation of the structural reforms, launched in 1993, aimed at encouraging competition and making enterprises cost-effective. The United Nations Development Program (UNDP) reported in January that only four percent of the population was able to meet their family's daily needs. In the Nagorno-Karabakh conflict, a May 1994 ceasefire held through most of 1996. Negotiations launched four years ago by the OSCE Minsk group continued intermittently with little progress.

Political Rights and Civil Liberties: Armenians can elect their government. In the 1995 parliamentary elections and the 1996 presidential vote were fraught with irregularities and charges of fraud that marred the democratic process.

While the criminal code has largely been carried over from the Soviet era, the new constitution enshrined the presumption of innocence and gives people the right not to incriminate themselves or testify against their spouses or close relatives. The trial of 31 prominent figures from ARF-Dashnak accused of treason and attempting to overthrow the government continued in the Supreme Court. The trial has been marked by several serious inconsistencies and persistent violations of the defendants' rights to due process. Generally, defendants' access to attorneys has been restricted, and the lawyers themselves reported harassment, intimidation and beatings.

The media faced government interference. The Justice Ministry revoked the registration of the daily *Azg* (Nation) published by a branch of the Ramkavar Party, then reconstituted its board, which published a pro-government version of the paper. The move touched off protests from independent journalists and anti-government politicians, and the old *Azg* management sued the ministry. A court ruled in favor of the original board of directors. A Yerevan court banned publication of the daily *Lragir* for three months for articles advocating Armenia's annexation of regions in southern Georgia. The Noyan Tappan news agency reported that 300 to 440 mass media outlets have been stripped of their licenses, and that only about 10 percent of the registered mass media are functioning "more or less normally." State television and radio gave the opposition limited access during the election campaign in contravention of election law, according to the independent European Institute for the Media. Independent television is making some inroads, with nine nongovernmental stations on the air. Most private publications operate under severe economic constraints as a result of increases in the costs of newsprint and production.

Freedom of religion in this overwhelmingly Christian country is generally respected, though the government has periodically launched campaigns against Protestant sects and the Bahai. Freedom of assembly was temporarily suspended in the wake of post-election demonstrations by the opposition.

Nearly 80 percent of Armenian workers belong to trade unions, nearly all of which were established during the Soviet era. Under the 1992 law on employment, workers are guaranteed the right to form unions, while a January 1993 presidential decree entitles workers to strike, as does the new constitution. There are several small independent unions. While deeply engrained attitudes make Armenia a male-dominated society, employers are prohibited by law from discriminating against women. The law is frequently violated in practice, and women face obstacles to advancement. Unemployment among women is several times higher than among men. A women's party placed second in the parliamentary elections.

Australia

Polity: Federal parliamentary democracy
Economy: Capitalist
Population: 18,342,000
PPP: $18,530
Life Expectancy: 77.8
Ethnic Groups: European (95 percent), Asian (4 percent), Aboriginal (1 percent)
Capital: Canberra

Political Rights: 1
Civil Liberties: 1
Status: Free

Overview:

The center-right Liberal/National Parties coalition won the March 1996 federal elections, ending 13 years of Labor Party government. The coalition, led by Prime Minister John Howard, won 94 of the 148 seats in the House of Representatives and 37 of the 76 seats in the Senate, gaining the largest majority in Australian electoral history.

The British claimed Australia in 1770. In January 1901 six states formed the Commonwealth of Australia, adding the Northern Territory and capital city of Canberra as territorial units in 1911. The Queen of England is the nominal head of state and is represented by the governor-general, who holds executive power in this parliamentary democracy. The directly elected bicameral parliament consists of a 76 member Senate, drawing 12 members from each state plus two each from the capital and the Northern Territory, and a 148-member House of Representatives.

Since World War II political power has alternated between the center-left Labor Party and the conservative coalition of the Liberal Party and the smaller National Party. Prime Minister Bob Hawke led Labor to four consecutive election victories between 1983 and March 1990, and introduced measures to liberalize the economy. In December 1991, during a deep recession, then-Treasurer Paul Keating unseated Hawke in a confidence vote among Labor MPs.

High unemployment rates (about 9 percent), low growth and high interest rates were a concern for the electorate. The coalition's campaign platform revolved around privatization and labor market reform.

Political Rights and Civil Liberties:

Australians have the democratic means to change their government. Fundamental freedoms are respected in practice. The judiciary is fully independent of the government.

Australia's major human rights issue is the treatment of its indigenous population of approximately 230,000 Aborigines and 28,000 Torres Straits Islanders. A 1991 Royal Commission Report found Aborigines incarcerated at a rate 29 times higher than that of whites, often because they could not afford a fine or were denied bail for minor offenses. Gaps in nutrition, life expectancy and child mortality rates between the indigenous and white populations are the highest in the developed world. The government has taken positive measures, including the launching of a national Aboriginal health program and the opening of "bail hostels" so that Aborigines suspected of minor crimes are not denied bail for lack of a fixed address. However, deaths of Aboriginal people in police custody persist. Twenty-one deaths by hanging, physical injuries and fatal cardiovascular injuries were recorded during a 12-month period ending July.

The new conservative government has questioned the "accountability" of federally-funded indigenous groups, particularly the Aboriginal and Torres Strait Islander Commission (ATSIC), pledging to appoint a "special auditor" to address allegations of financial irregularities and claims of general mismanagement. This decision has spawned criticism for undermining Aboriginal claims to "self-determination."

The practicality of the 1993 Native Title Act became another issue of possible contention. In June 1992 the High Court formally overturned the concept of *terra nullius* (no man's land), which from a legal standpoint had considered Australia to have been vacant when the British settlers arrived. The Mabo Decision (after claimant Eddie Mabo) formally recognized that Aboriginal groups inhabited the land prior to the British arrival, and that native titles to the land would still be valid in government-owned areas, provided the indigenous people had maintained a "close and continuing" connection to the land. However, since many groups have been pushed off their traditional land, in practice only about 10 percent of Aborigines would be able to take direct advantage of the law.

The Act leaves uncertain the extent to which pastoral leases negate native title claims, a matter which has drawn considerable concern in the mining industry. If a native title is registered on a portion of land, mining progresses only after a lengthy negotiation process.

Refugees are kept in detention until their asylum applications have been decided, a legal process that can take several years. Domestic violence is common. The Law Reform Commission reports that women face discrimination in the judicial system.

Australian trade unions are independent and vigorous with a membership of 33 percent of the workforce. In an effort by the coalition government to increase productivity, the Workplace Relations Bill, a radical revision of previous labor and industrial laws, is expected to be enacted by next year. This legislation is meant to encourage individual contracts between workers and employers and to undermine standards set by collective bargaining.

Austria

Polity: Federal par-
liamentary democracy
Economy: Mixed
capitalist
Population: 8,077,000
PPP: $19,115
Life Expectancy: 76.3
Ethnic Groups: German (99 percent), Slovene, Croat
Capital: Vienna

Political Rights: 1
Civil Liberties: 1
Status: Free

Overview:
Austria's ruling coalition (Christian Democrats and Social Democrats) faced unprecedented gains by Jorg Haider's nationalist Freedom Party in the country's first European elections held in October 1996. The Freedom Party won 28 percent of the vote, just 60,000 fewer votes than Chancellor Franz Vranitzky's Social Democrats, who took 29.1 percent. In traditionally socialist Vienna, the Freedom Party increased its representation by seven seats, and now holds 29 of the 100 seats in the municipal council. It is estimated that half of blue-collar workers voted for the far right in a display of disaffection with recent austerity measures taken by the government to meet European Union economic integration criteria. An anti-Semite who last year lauded the decency of veterans of Adolph Hitler's Waffen SS and is often accused of harboring neo-Nazi sympathies, Haider has played to working class anger and to the fear that European integration will exacerbate unemployment, bankruptcies and takeovers.

The right-wing extremist group Bajuwarian Liberation Army (BLA) is suspected in a renewed campaign of bomb threats that began in October. Claiming responsibility for some 20 letter bombs since December 1993, including one that killed four gypsy men last year, the BLA is alleged to have threatened to kill eight prominent figures in Austria and abroad. Chancellor Franz Vranitzky's name appeared on the list of targets sent by the BLA to a current affairs magazine.

The Republic of Austria was established in 1918 after the collapse of the Austro-Hungarian Empire, and reborn in 1945, seven years after its annexation by Nazi Germany. Occupation by the Western Allies and the Soviet Union ended in 1955 under the Austrian State Treaty, which guaranteed Austrian neutrality and restored national sovereignty.

The two leading parties, the Christian Democratic Austrian People's Party (OVP) and the Social Democratic Party (SPO), have governed the country in coalition for ten years. The October 1994 federal elections brought in Social Democrat Franz Vranitzky as chancellor and OVP members Thomas Klestil and Wolfgang Schussel as president and vice-chancellor, respectively. The coalition fell over budget disputes in October 1995, and snap elections were held in December. In early March, 1996, the coalition was reassembled with an agreement to govern Austria for the next four years.

In February, in an effort to fulfill the budgetary and other conditions established under the Maastricht Treaty, the government implemented a two-year cost-cutting program to slash the deficit by the end of 1997. Taxes were raised, while a number of social benefits, including maternity allowances, early retirement privileges and student subsidies, were cut. Discontent among workers is rife as foreign and domestic firms cut thousands of jobs.

As of October, 57 percent of Austrians surveyed blamed European integration for the country's economic woes. Economists assert that the government has not adequately explained the benefits of EU membership to the public, and insist that joining the economic bloc simply exposed Austria's already deep-seated problems of poor competitiveness, a stifling bureaucracy and lavish government spending.

But the results of the mid-October elections for the European Parliament and the Vienna city council indicate there is widespread "Euro-skepticism." The "Haider phenomenon" reflects real social discontent, as well as the failure of the political class to explain where Austria is heading. However, Austrian democracy is stable.

Political Rights and Civil Liberties:

Austrians can change their government democratically. The country's provinces possess considerable latitude in local administration and can check federal power by electing members of the upper house of parliament. Voting is compulsory in some provinces. The independent judiciary is headed by a Supreme Judicial Court and includes both Constitutional and Administrative courts.

Nazis are prohibited by a 1955 State treaty from exercising freedom of assembly or association. All Nazi organizations are illegal, but Nazis do enjoy sympathy and membership in the Freedom Party. A 1992 law officially outlawed Holocaust denial as well as approval or justification of Nazi crimes against humanity in public. Austrian police tend to enforce anti-Nazi statutes more enthusiastically when extremists attract international attention.

The Austrian media are free, but rarely-invoked restrictions on press freedom concerning public morality and national security are extant. Nazi propaganda and Holocaust denial are also prohibited in the media. The Austrian Broadcasting Company (ORF), which controls radio and television, is state-owned but protected from political interference by a broadcasting law. The government decided in 1989 to end the ORFs monopoly by licensing private broadcasting. However, the launching of the first commercial radio station, scheduled for 1995, was derailed by a constitutional court decision to review the regulations. Increased competition from German satellite cable has put a financial strain on the two ORF television stations.

Women have held about 10 percent of Federal Assembly seats, while more than twice that number serve in provincial government. Women are still prohibited by law from working at night in most occupations. Nurses, taxi drivers and a few other occupations are exempted from this ban. The European Court of Justice in 1994 ruled that a sex-based prohibition of nighttime work is not permissible. The Government has been given until 2001 to adapt its legislation to gender-neutral European Union regulations, and is due to report in 1997 on its progress. Women generally earn 20 percent less than men, and are not allowed in the military.

Trade unions have an important and independent voice in the political, social, and economic life of the country. Fifty-two percent of workers are organized in 14 national unions, all belonging to the Austrian Trade Union Federation. Although the right to strike is not explicitly provided for in the Constitution or in national legislation, it is universally recognized.

Azerbaijan

Polity: Dominant party
Economy: Statist
transitional
Population: 7,409,000
PPP: $2,190
Life Expectancy: 70.7
Ethnic Groups: Azeri (82 percent), Russian (7 percent),
Armenian (5 percent)
Capital: Baku

Political Rights: 6
Civil Liberties: 5*
Status: Not Free

Ratings Change: Azerbaijan's civil liberties rating changed from 6 to 5 because of a nascent but expanding civil sector.

Overview:
President Gaidar Aliyev consolidated his hold on power in 1996 with the dismissal of Prime Minister Faud Guliyev and the resignation of Speaker of Parliament Rasul Guliyev. Key issues included agreements to exploit the country's vast oil wealth and negotiations over Nagorno-Karabakh, controlled by Armenian forces after seven years of war.

Persia and the Ottoman Empire competed for Azeri territory in the sixteenth century, with the former gaining control in 1603. The northern sector, ceded to Russia in the early nineteenth century, joined Armenia and Georgia in a short-lived Transcaucasia Federation after the 1917 Bolshevik Revolution. It proclaimed its independence the following year, but was subdued by the Red Army in 1920. In 1922 it entered the Soviet Union as part of the Transcaucasian Soviet Federal Republic, becoming a separate Soviet Socialist republic in 1936.

Azeris voted for independence in a 1991 referendum. Hard-line Communist Ayaz Mutabilov was elected president. The 360-member Supreme Soviet, elected in 1990 in fraudulent elections, was dominated by Communists; the anti-Communist, nationalist Azerbaijan Popular Front (AzPF) under Abulfaz Elchibey, held some 40 seats. After months of turmoil the Supreme Soviet created a National Council, a fifty-seat legislature, half of whose members were picked by the president, half by the opposition. In June 1992, Elchibey was elected president. In October 1993, after setbacks in Nagorno-Karabakh and Russian destabilization, Aliyev was elected president in a vote boycotted by the AzPF and declared "undemocratic" by Western observers.

In the 1995 the parliamentary elections, five leading parties and 600 independent candidates were banned. Alieyev's Yeni Azerbaijan (New Azerbaijan) won 78 percent of the vote, taking 18 of 25 seats reserved for political parties; the AzPF, though banned, won 2 seats. A new constitution strengthened the already wide-reaching power of the president. The Organization for Security and Cooperation in Europe (OSCE) said the balloting was "not free and fair," while the Council of Europe said the vote was marred by "irregularities and clear cases of fraud."

In September 1996, the political council of the ruling Yeni Azerbaijan called for a special session of parliament to review the conduct and performance of Speaker Guliyev and to investigate charges of corruption. The speaker, who reportedly made millions of dollars in the oil industry, had clashed with Aliyev over the slow pace of economic reform. He was replaced by Murtuz Nadjaf Alesqerov, deputy chairman of Yeni Azerbaijan. Earlier, President Aliyev had replaced Prime Minister Guliyev with First Deputy Prime Minister Artur Radizade.

In October, parliament ratified a June contract, between the State Oil Company of Azerbaijan (SOCAR) and a consortium consisting of Russia's Lukoil, British Petroleum, Norway's Statoil, Turkey's TPAO, Elf Aquitaine and the National Iranian Oil Company, to develop the Shah Deniz field. Parliament passed a legislative package of agrarian reforms with significant land redistribution and privatization. The reforms also provide the right of foreign leasing and utilization of agriculture, but bars foreigners from purchasing land.

A cease-fire in Nagorno-Karabakh held through 1996, but negotiations mediated by the OSCE's Minsk group made little headway toward a final settlement.

Political Rights and Civil Liberties: Azerbaijan's citizens do not have the means to change their government democratically, as the November 1995 parliamentary vote was fraudulent. The new constitution gives the president control over the government, legislature and judiciary.

Some 43 political parties, though legal, face restrictions, harassment, and arbitrary decisions by the state election commission. The Social Democratic Party reported that there are over 2,500 political prisoners in Azerbaijan. The independent Institute of Peace and Democracy accused the government of maintaining a special jail in the basement of the Special Department of President's Office where detainees are interrogated and tortured.

The government limits the press to "constructive criticism" and censorship is common. In January, a new law was announced requiring all media to re-register with authorities, a tactic aimed at intimidating opposition press. In March, two journalists lost their accreditation to cover parliament. In July, censors demanded the names, addresses and telephone numbers of all journalists employed by opposition newspapers. Authorities suspended the publication of the Turkish-owned daily *Avrasya* because of articles on Iranian-Azeri relations. The first 1996 issue of the opposition *Azadlyg* was banned for including an article critical of President Aliyev's announcement of an amnesty for military deserters. Throughout the year, opposition newspapers were published with blank spaces in place of censored articles. In June, the acting Minister of Justice sent a letter to all regional executives saying that commercial television and radio stations should be closed. Commercial television stations in several cities were shut down.

Freedom of assembly and association have been periodically curtailed, and several demonstrations were brutally broken up by police in 1996.

There is no state religion, though most Azeris are Shiite Muslims. In May, the U.S. Commission on Security and Cooperation in Europe sent a letter to President Aliyev to protest the denial of church registration to a Protestant sect. There are significant Russian and Jewish minorities who can worship freely. Continued persecution of the small Kurdish minority and the Lezgin people has been reported. In July, 300 members of the nationalist Lezgin Sadval organization seized four Azerbaijani police officers along the Russian border. They demanded the release of one of their leaders, Nariman Ramazanov, jailed by Azeri authorities for allegedly taking part in a 1994 bombing of a Baku metro station. The Lezgin traditional homeland is divided between Azerbaijan and Dagestan (Russia).

The judiciary is not independent and is structured like the old Soviet system. The president appoints judges and has substantial influence over the judicial branch.

The only significant labor organization remains the post-Communist Azerbaijan Labor Federation, which depends on government support. The largest independent union, dominated by reform Communists, is the oil workers' union, which represents about 85,000 workers, about 80 percent of workers in that industry. In July, oil workers at a Caspian facility went on strike over wages, food and safety. Cultural norms and the Karabakh war have led to discrimination and violence against women, but in Baku and cosmopolitan areas women can be found in universities, business and government.

Bahamas

Polity: Parliamentary democracy
Economy: Capitalist-statist
Population: 280,000
PPP: $16,180
Life Expectancy: 73.2
Ethnic Groups: Black (85 percent), European (15 percent)
Capital: Nassau

Political Rights: 1
Civil Liberties: 2
Status: Free

Overview:
The privatization program of Prime Minister Hubert Ingraham proceeded in 1996, with the government preparing to offer local and foreign investors a stake in its electricity and telecommunications companies, as well as a partnership with the national airline, Bahamasair. Efforts to reduce government involvement in the economy stem from losses and mismanagement incurred during the 25-year administration of former Prime Minister Lynden Pindling.

The Commonwealth of the Bahamas, a 700-island nation in the Caribbean, is a member of the British Commonwealth. It was granted independence in 1973. The British monarchy is represented by a governor-general.

Under the 1973 constitution, a bicameral parliament consists of a 49-member House of Assembly directly elected for five years; and a 16-member Senate with nine members appointed by the prime minister, four by the leader of the parliamentary opposition and three by the governor-general. The prime minister is the leader of the party that commands a majority in the House.

After 25 years in office, Pindling's Progressive Liberal Party (PLP) was ousted by Ingraham and the Free National Movement (FNM) in the 1992 elections. The PLP had been dogged for years by allegations of corruption and high official involvement in narcotics trafficking. Ingraham, a lawyer and former cabinet official, was expelled by the PLP in 1986 for his outspoken attacks on corruption. He became leader of the FNM in 1990.

Ingraham vowed to bring honesty, efficiency and accountability to government. Pindling, at the time the Western hemisphere's longest-serving elected head of government, relied on his image as the father of the nation's independence.

But many voters were born after independence and many workers had been left unemployed as a result of a protracted economic downturn. The PLP and the FNM are both centrist parties, but the FNM is more oriented toward free enterprise and a philosophy of limited government.

With 90 percent of the electorate voting, the FNM won 32 seats in the House of Assembly to the PLP's 17. Pindling held his own seat and became the official opposition leader.

Upon taking office, Ingraham appointed a Commission of Inquiry to investigate the Pindling government. In 1995 the commission detailed widespread mismanagement and malpractice in the national telephone and airline companies.

Political Rights and Civil Liberties:

Citizens are able to change their government through democratic elections. Unlike previous balloting, the 1992 vote was relatively free of irregularities and fraud. In 1992 indelible ink was used for the first time to identify people who had voted.

Constitutional guarantees regarding the right to organize political parties, civic organizations and labor unions are generally respected, as is the free exercise of religion. Labor, business and professional organizations are generally free. Unions have the right to strike and collective bargaining is prevalent.

There are a number of independent rights groups, who have documented the increase in recent years of violent crime and police brutality. Rights groups also criticize the "subhuman conditions" and overcrowding in the nation's prisons. The Fox Hill prison remains filled to more than twice its intended capacity.

There are an estimated 25,000 to 40,000 Haitians living illegally in the Bahamas. Tight citizenship laws and a strict work permit system leave Haitians in limbo and with few rights. The influx has created social tension because of the strain on government services. In 1995 the Bahamas reached an agreement with Haiti on a program of repatriation of illegal Haitian immigrants. A similar agreement with Cuba facilitated the return of 34 illegal Cuban immigrants in November.

Full freedom of expression is constrained by strict libel laws. Unlike its predecessor, the Ingraham government has not made use of these laws against independent newspapers. It has amended media laws to allow for private ownership of broadcasting outlets. For the first time, two newspaper companies have been awarded licenses to operate private radio stations; many applications to start cable television stations are pending.

The judicial system is headed by a Supreme Court and a Court of Appeal, with the right of appeal under certain circumstances to the Privy Council in London. There are local courts, and on the outer islands the local commissioners have magisterial powers. Despite anti-drug legislation and a 1987 agreement with the United States to suppress the drug trade, there is evidence that drug-related corruption and money-laundering remain a problem, although to a far lesser extent than during the Pindling years. In late 1995 the government finally introduced anti-money-laundering legislation.

Bahrain

Polity: Traditional monarchy
Economy: Capitalist-statist
Population: 590,000
PPP: $15,500
Life Expectancy: 71.7

Political Rights: 7*
Civil Liberties: 6
Status: Not Free

Ethnic Groups: Bahraini (63 percent), Asian (13 percent), other Arab (10 percent), Iranian (8 percent)
Capital: Manama
Ratings Change: Bahrain's political rights rating changed from 6 to 7 because of the government's heavy-handed crackdown on continuing opposition.

Overview:

Internal dissent and violent civil unrest in this Persian Gulf archipelago, ruled by the Al Khalifa family since 1782, reached dangerous levels. Opposition forces have faced stiffened government resolve and a propaganda campaign blaming Iran for the unrest. Human rights organizations, including Amnesty International, have accused police forces of using torture. Women and children are also reportedly subject to arbitrary arrest and abuse. Approximately 28 people have been killed since 1994; Shiite opposition groups argue that the actual number of deaths is much higher.

Although a constitutional monarchy was established following independence from the United Kingdom in August 1971, the 1973 constitutional provision for an elected assembly was suspended in August 1975. At that time the National Assembly, consisting of the cabinet and 30 popularly elected members, was dissolved, ostensibly for debating "alien ideas." The current Emir, Sheikh 'Isa ibn Salman Al Khalifa, assumed power in 1961, and rules along with his brother, Prime Minister Khalifa ibn Salman Al Khalifa, and his son, crown prince Hamad ibn 'isa Al Khalifa. In December 1992 the government created a 30-member *majlis al-shura*, a consultancy council consisting of appointed business and religious leaders. It has met several times but has little legislative power.

On December 5, 1994, Shiite cleric Sheikh 'Ali Salman and several Sunni former members of parliament who had urged 20,000 Bahrainis to sign a petition calling for the reinstitution of parliamentary rule, freedom of speech and the release of political prisoners, were arrested. These arrests sparked clashes between Shiites and Saudi-backed police forces in the capital, Manama, as well as throughout the city's poorer suburbs. Many Bahraini Shiites, who make up 70 percent of the population, are barred from obtaining certain jobs and resent the presence of a large foreign (primarily South Asian) work force, which dominates low-to middle-income jobs. Since December 1994, protests have become increasingly violent. According to opposition sources some 4,000 dissidents, including Abdul-Amir Al-Jamri===symbol of the opposition===have been arrested. Schools including the university have been centers of discontent. In June 1995 military officers were appointed as Minister of Education and Dean of the University, and university staff were banned from talking to the media. Foreign diplomats have since been refused entry into the heavily- policed compound.

This continuing crackdown and the reintroduction of capital punishment did not stop either terrorism or discontent. Four hundred people were arrested following the March 1996 firebombing of a restaurant frequented by South Asians in Sitra (a poor village outside Manama and an opposition stronghold), which led to the deaths of seven Bangladeshis. Three of the eight suspects brought to trial were sentenced to death. In April 1996, 'Isa Ahmad Hasan Qambar was executed by firing squad for killing the chief corporal at the Ministry of the Interior. According to Amnesty International, the trial ignored internationally accepted human rights standards. Widespread protests followed the execution, the first since 1977, and police used tear gas and rubber bullets to disperse the large, predominantly Shiite crowds. Certain districts were sealed off and every vehicle was systematically searched.

There were several bombings over the next few months in hotels and local as well as foreign businesses, resulting in millions of dollars in damages but leading to few casualties. Internal security forces, made up of Pakistani and Indian mercenaries and led by former British colonial policeman Ian Henderson, conduct regular sweeps and tightly control activity around the mosques.

Political Rights and Civil Liberties: Bahrainians cannot change their government democratically. Political parties are prohibited, and all opposition leaders are currently imprisoned or exiled. The emir rules by decree and appoints all government officials, including the fifteen-member cabinet, the urban municipal councils and the rural *mukhtars* (local councils). The only political recourse for citizens is to submit petitions to the government, and to appeal to the emir and other officials at *majlises*, which are regularly scheduled audiences. The ruling party belongs to the Sunni Muslim minority which dominates top government positions. The majority Shi'a Muslims face discrimination in employment and social services, and are generally barred from the army and police.

The Interior Ministry monitors some communications, and maintains informal control over most activities through pervasive informant networks. Agents can search homes without warrants, as has been the case primarily in Shiite communities since civil unrest began in late 1994.

The 1974 State Security Act permits the government to detain individuals accused of "anti-government activity," which can include participation in peaceful demonstrations and membership in outlawed organizations, for up to three years without trial. Ordinary trials feature due process safeguards, but defendants tried in security courts do not enjoy such guarantees. Tough new anti-violence laws were announced in March 1996, under which any person found to have committed a crime linked to anti-government protests will be automatically brought before the state security court without the possibility of appeal.

Freedom of speech is sharply restricted. Privately owned newspapers refrain from criticizing the regime, while radio and television are government-owned and present official views only.

Women face fewer restrictions than in other Islamic countries, but wage and job discrimination continue. Islamic *Shari'a* courts rule on matters of divorce and inheritance, occasionally rejecting divorce requests. Women have begun to take part in protests as a result of the government's response to dissent, calling for political reform through the signing of petitions. They have since been pressured to apologize or lose their jobs.

Islam is the state religion, but Christians, Hindus, Jews and others are generally permitted to worship freely. The 1963 Bahraini Citizenship Act denies full citizenship to some 3,000-5,000 Persian-origin Shi'as, known as *bidoon* (those without). Bidoon are restricted in business activities, and have difficulty obtaining passports and government loans.

No independent labor unions exist. Workers do not have the right to bargain collectively or to strike. The government has instead created Joint Labor-Management Consultative Committees (JCC), composed of worker and employer representatives. Foreign laborers and non-industrial workers are underrepresented in the 16 JCCs. The 1974 Security Law restricts strikes deemed damaging to worker-employer relations or the national interest, and few strikes occur.

Bangladesh

Polity: Parliamentary democracy
Economy: Capitalist-statist
Population: 119,823,000
PPP: $1,290
Life Expectancy: 55.9

Political Rights: 2*
Civil Liberties: 4
Status: Partly Free

Ethnic Groups: Bengali (98 percent), Bihari (1 percent), various tribal groups (1 percent)
Capital: Dhaka
Ratings Change: Bangladesh's political rights rating changed from 3 to 2 because the country held its freest election in June.

Overview: The opposition Awami League won elections in June 1996, ending a two-year political impasse marked by partisan violence and paralyzing general strikes.

Bangladesh won independence in December 1971 after a nine-month war with the occupying West Pakistani army. Following 15 years of often turbulent military rule, the country's democratic transition began in December 1990, after weeks of pro-democracy demonstrations, with the resignation of General H.M. Ershad.

The February 1991 elections brought the Bangladesh National Party (BNP) to power with Khaleda Zia as prime minister. A national referendum in September ended the powerful presidency in favor of a parliamentary democracy with a largely ceremonial head of state. In March 1994 the opposition began a parliamentary boycott to protest official corruption and alleged vote-rigging in a by-election.

In November 1995, following more than a year of street clashes and violent strikes, the president dissolved parliament and called for early elections on the advice of premier Zia. The opposition Awami League boycotted the flawed February 1996 elections. The BNP won handily, but on March 30, after weeks of general strikes and mounting violence, Zia resigned and agreed to fresh elections under a neutral, caretaker government, as authorized by a newly-passed constitutional amendment.

At the June 12 elections, held with a 73 percent turnout, the Awami League won 146 of the 300 contested parliamentary seats (30 additional seats are reserved for women), and subsequently formed a government under Sheikh Hasina Wajed with the support of ex-president Ershad's Jatiya Party, which had 32 seats. The BNP took 116 seats, with the remainder going to smaller parties and independents.

Political Rights and Civil Liberties:

Bangladeshis can democratically change their government, although a weak rule of law continues to undermine civil liberties protections. The June 1996 elections, rated by international observers as the freest in the country's history despite some violence and irregularities, set a precedent for voting to be held under a neutral caretaker government, as authorized in a March constitutional amendment.

By contrast, the February polls were marred by widespread violence, looting of polling stations, and ballot-rigging by the governing BNP. The weeks prior to the vote were marked by escalating gun battles and bomb and arson attacks on party and newspaper offices in Dhaka, Chittagong and other major cities and towns. The police and the paramilitary Bangladesh Rifles responded by firing indiscriminately at demonstrators on several occasions and arresting suspected opposition supporters, while failing to arrest BNP militants for violent acts. In early 1996 the army frequently engaged in indiscriminate beatings, arbitrary arrest and torture of villagers during an ostensible crackdown on illegal weapons.

The police routinely torture suspects, leading to several deaths each year, and abuse of prisoners in the lowly Class "C" cells is widespread. Those responsible are rarely punished. In the southeastern Chittagong Hill Tracts (CHT), where since 1973 the Shanti Bahini rebel group has been fighting for greater autonomy for the Chakmas and other indigenous Buddhist hill tribes, the security forces are accused of rape, torture and illegal detention of villagers.

The Zia government frequently used the 1974 Special Powers Act, which allows for detention without charge or trial for 30 days, to detain opposition supporters. The judiciary has shown independence at the higher levels but overall is susceptible to government pressure, and weakened by a severe backlog of cases and rampant corruption. The criminal code allows for the "safe custody" incarceration of girls who have escaped from brothels but cannot return home.

Women face discrimination in health care, education and employment opportunities. Domestic violence is common. In rural areas a *shalish*, an informal council of fundamentalist leaders, often imposes floggings and other sanctions on women accused of moral offenses. Fundamentalists have attacked female nongovernmental organization (NGO) activists and schools run by NGOs.

NGOs estimate that organized networks, often with the complicity of local authorities, have trafficked as many as 20,000 women and children out of the country in the past ten years for prostitution, mostly to Pakistan. Child maids or servants in urban households face sexual abuse. In rural areas poor girls are sometimes "sold" into marriage to older men.

The country's diverse and generally outspoken print media face sectarian and political harassment. Prior to, and following, the February elections, newspaper offices were attacked; journalists were beaten by police and party enforcers and several were arrested; and at least one journalist was killed after police opened fire on demonstrators. BNP activists, police and others attacked dozens of journalists in a series of incidents between August and late September. In August the magistrate of Kushtia district shut down a weekly that had published articles about corruption. Islamic fundamentalists have ransacked newspaper offices and beaten journalists.

Most publications are heavily dependent on the government's 80-90 percent share of the total advertising revenue, and in practice, advertising apportionment and allocation of subsidized newsprint are politically slanted. Broadcast media are state-owned and coverage favors the party in power.

Islam is the official religion. Hindus are subject to random violence and discrimination. Members of the Garos and other tribal minorities say the authorities frequently displace them for development projects. Nearly 80 percent of the 270,000 Rohingya Muslim refugees who fled from Burma in 1992 have been repatriated, but from January-May 1996 about 10,000 new refugees had arrived.

Most unions are heavily politicized and are not true labor advocates. Civil servants are barred from joining unions and cannot engage in collective bargaining. Formation of new unions is hampered by high requirements for employee approval, and by restrictions on organizing by unregistered unions. Labor laws are rarely enforced and permit workers suspected of union activities to be transferred. Thugs have attacked officials and members of the nonpartisan Bangladesh Independent Garment Workers Union.

Barbados

Polity: Parliamentary democracy
Economy: Capitalist
Population: 263,000
PPP: $10,570
Life Expectancy: 75.7
Ethnic Groups: Black (80 percent), European (4 percent), mixed (16 percent)
Capital: Bridgetown

Political Rights: 1
Civil Liberties: 1
Status: Free

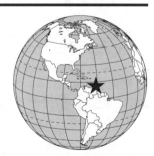

Overview: **A** member of the British Commonwealth, Barbados achieved independence in 1966. The British monarchy is represented by a governor-general. The government is a parliamentary democracy with a bicameral legislature and a party system based on universal adult suffrage. The Senate is comprised of 21 members, all appointed by the governor-general; 12 on the advice of the prime minister, two on advice of the leader of the opposition, and the remaining seven at the discretion of the governor-general. A 28-member House of Assembly is elected for a five-year term. Executive authority is vested in the prime minister, who is the leader of the political party commanding a majority in the House.

Since independence, power has alternated between two centrist parties, the Democratic Labour Party (DLP) under Errol Barrow, and the Barbados Labour Party (BLP) under Tom Adams. Adams led the BLP from 1976 until his death in 1985. Adams was succeeded by Bernard St. John, but the BLP was defeated. This returned Barrow to power in 1986. Barrow died in 1987 and was succeeded by Erskine Sandiford, who led the DLP to victory in the 1991 elections.

Under Sandiford, Barbados suffered a prolonged economic recession as revenues from sugar and tourism declined. By 1994, the economy appeared to be improving, but employment was still at nearly 25 percent. Sandiford's popularity suffered and he was increasingly criticized for his authoritarian style of government. He lost a no-confidence vote in parliament when nine BLP legislators were joined by four DLP backbenchers and one independent legislator who had quit the DLP. Sandiford called for new elections and gave up the leadership of the DLP, which elected David Thompson, the young finance minister, to replace him.

In the 1994 election campaign, Owen Arthur, the economist elected in 1993 to head the BLP, promised to build "a modern, technologically dynamic economy," create jobs and restore investor confidence. The BLP won 19 seats, the DLP eight and the New Democratic Party (NDP), a disaffected offshoot of the DLP formed in 1989, one.

Voter participation dipped to 60 percent, down from 62 percent in 1991 and 76 percent in 1986. According to one local analyst, the trend reflected "a growing disenchantment with voting, particularly among the youth where the scourge of unemployment is greatest."

In his first year, Arthur seemed able to combine a technocratic approach to revitalizing the economy with savvy politics. He also appointed a number of promising young cabinet officials. By mid-1995, unemployment was down to 20.5 percent, the lowest level since 1990. It has dropped steadily since then.

Political Rights and Civil Liberties: Citizens can change their government through democratic elections. Constitutional guarantees regarding freedom of religion and the right to organize political parties, labor unions and civic organization are respected.

Apart from the parties holding parliamentary seats, other political organizations abound, including the small left-wing Workers' Party of Barbados. There are two major labor unions and various smaller ones, and all are politically active and free to strike. Human rights organizations operate freely.

An agreement between employers and the Workers' Union early in 1996 provided a 5-6 percent pay increase for about 4,000 hotel workers, though economic forecasters predicted that the industry would see job losses as a result. In 1994, women made up 47 percent of the labor force.

Freedom of expression is fully respected. Public opinion expressed through the news media, which are free of censorship and government control, has a powerful influence on policy. Newspapers are privately owned, and there are two major dailies. Private and government radio stations operate. The single television station, operated by the government-owned Caribbean Broadcasting Corporation (CBC), presents a wide range of political viewpoints. The highlight of the 1994 election campaign was the first-ever televised debate between the major candidates.

Recent applications to establish new television stations in Barbados have not been approved by government. According to *Caribbean Week*, Arthur claimed that none of the applications received was based on broad enough ownership to ensure that the interest of the masses would be maintained. The government is reportedly finalizing an Information and Communications policy.

The judicial system is independent and includes a Supreme Court that encompasses a High Court and a Court of Appeal. Lower court officials are appointed on the advice of the Judicial and Legal Service Commission. The government provides free legal aid to the indigent.

The high crime rate, much of it fueled by an increase in drug abuse and trafficking, has given rise to human rights concerns. The police are alleged to use excessive force during arrests and interrogation. A counternarcotics agreement signed between the United States and Barbados in late 1996 will provide funding for the Barbados police force, the coast guard, customs and other ministries, for a broad array of programs to combat drug-related crime.

In 1992 the Court of Appeal outlawed the practice of public flogging of criminals. Also in 1992, a Domestic Violence law was passed to give police and judges greater powers to protect women.

Belarus

Polity: Presidential-
dictatorship
Economy: Statist
transitional
Population: 10,297,000
PPP: $4,244
Life Expectancy: 69.7

Political Rights: 6*
Civil Liberties: 6*
Status: Not Free

Ethnic Groups: Belarusian (78 percent), Russian (13 percent), Polish (4 percent), Ukrainian (2 percent), Jewish (1 percent)
Capital: Minsk
Ratings Change: Belarus's political rights and civil liberties ratings changed from 5 to 6 because of a deteriorating human and political rights climate.

Overview: President Alyaksandr Lukashenka has reintroduced censorship, banned independent trade unions, reimposed the use of Soviet-era textbooks and national symbols, ignored the Supreme Court when it overturned his decrees, limited the rights of candidates in parliamentary elections, and sought reintegration with Russia. The president's constitutional draft would give him virtual dictatorial control of the government without parliamentary checks.

Present-day Belarus was part of the tenth-century Kievan realm. After a lengthy period of Lithuanian rule, it merged with Poland in the sixteenth century. It was absorbed into the Russian Empire after Poland was partitioned in the eighteenth century, and it became a constituent republic of the USSR in 1922. With the collapse of the Soviet Union, nationalist-minded centrist Stanislaw Shushkevich became head of state as well as chairman of the Communist-dominated Supreme Council. After parliament ousted Shushkevich in 1994 and created the post of president, elections were held and won by Lukashenka, a populist, former state farm director and chairman of parliament's anti-corruption committee.

The Soviet-era parliament was supposed to fill the vacuum until the fall elections, but it did not meet until September. Ignoring the constitution, the president ruled by decree. He stripped deputies of their parliamentary immunity and threatened to impose presidential rule.

The first several months of 1996 saw mass anti-government demonstrations in Minsk. On March 24, special security forces broke up a demonstration of 40,000 people protesting the signing of integration agreements with Russia; 20,000 participated in a rally on April 2, the day of the signing. Warrants were issued for the arrests of Belarus Popular Front (BPF) leaders Zyanon Paznyak and Syarhei Naumchyk for organizing the protests. The two fled to the Czech Republic, and applied for asylum in the U.S. in July. Over 50,000 took part in a demonstration on April 26 to mark the tenth anniversary of the Chernobyl nuclear disaster and protest the president's authoritarian policies.

In late July, President Lukashenka announced his intention to extend his term and amend the country's constitution by holding a national referendum on November 7, the anniversary of the Bolshevik revolution. The amendments extend the presidential term from five to seven years and give the president the right to annul decisions of local councils, set election dates, call parliamentary sessions and dissolve parliament. The president would also appoint judges; five of the 11 Constitutional Court members, as well as the chief justice; and Central Election Commission officials. Parliament would be restructured into a bicameral legislature made up of a house of representatives with 110 deputies and a senate, with the president appointing one-third of the senators.

The proposed constitutional changes united several parliamentary parties and factions from across the political spectrum into a large anti-presidential bloc led by Speaker Syamyon Sharetsky, among them communists, agrarians, social democrats and the BPF. But the president retained the support of some 60 deputies, making it difficult to garner the two-thirds majority needed for impeachment. In August, the legislature rescheduled Lukashenka's referendum to November 24, the day of parliamentary by-elections, and decided to hold a counter-referendum on its own version of a new constitution that would abolish the presidency. Lukashenka said he would refuse to change the referendum date.

The president convened an extra-parliamentary All Belarusian Congress to debate his draft constitution, and on October 19, 5,000 delegates hand-picked by the president overwhelmingly supported the president's constitution and called on parliament to rescind its decision for a counter-referendum. The president also announced that he supported the November 24 date. A week earlier the Constitutional Court had ruled that Lukashenka's referendum would not be legally binding if it were not held on the date set by parliament. Opinion polls showed that only 15 percent of voters favored the parliamentary constitution; fifty percent of eligible voters are needed to pass the referendum. A Moscow-brokered compromise between Lukashenka and parliament collapsed on November 22, one day after it was signed. It had called on Lukashenka to nullify his decree making the referendum binding, and on parliament to withdraw its request to the Constitutional Court to start impeachment proceedings. On November 24, 70.5 percent of voters approved Lukashenka's constitution.

Political Rights and Civil Liberties:

Belarus citizens cannot change their government democratically, and President Lukashenka has instituted de facto presidential rule. A parliamentary quorum was not reached until December 10, 1995, after several rounds of elections deemed neither free nor fair by European observers, who cited restrictions on media access, the barring of posters and limits on campaign financing. In 1996, the constitutional crisis threatened to give the president totalitarian authority.

Although legal, opposition parties face harassment. In addition, they are denied access to the state-run media and their publications are banned. In July, two leading BPF activists sought asylum in the U.S. after warrants were issued for their arrests.

Freedom of the press is strictly curtailed. The media law facilitates government closure or suspension of publications, and the press faces censorship. The country's one independent radio station, Radio 101.2, was closed by the authorities in August. In October, the opposition newspaper *Svaboda* was threatened with suspension. At least seven independent or opposition journalists were arrested and at least 12 assaulted, according to Western sources. Since August, at least nine independent or opposition papers were targeted by tax authorities for alleged infractions. In September, the government froze the bank accounts of several non-state periodicals and papers. State journalists were banned from broadcasting live coverage of anti-government rallies. State radio and television ignore stories unfavorable to the president's policies. In November, the U.S. Commission on Security and Cooperation in Europe accused the president of imposing a "virtual information blockade" through control of radio and television.

Limits have been arbitrarily placed on the freedom of speech and assembly. Following protests in the spring, President Lukashenka banned all anti-government rallies. Seven Ukrainians remained imprisoned for participating in a demonstration, and for the first time since the end of Stalin's regime, a poet, Slavimir Adamovich, was imprisoned for literary activity.

Even though 80 percent of the country is ethnically Belarusian, the Belarusian-language education system is being dismantled; Russian was restored as an official language in 1995. Freedom of religion is guaranteed by law and usually respected in practice. Catholics (with strong links to Poland) and Jews have complained of government foot-dragging in returning church property and synagogues.

The judiciary is not independent and remains a remnant of the Soviet era.

In 1995, the president banned the activity of the independent Free Trade Union of Belarus, which led to a transport workers strike. Several strike leaders were arrested and sentenced to brief terms of forced labor. Women's organizations have been established to document discrimination and abuses. There are no legal restrictions on the participation of women in politics and government, though social barriers to women in the public arena exist.

Belgium

Polity: Federal par-
liamentary democracy
Economy: Capitalist
Population: 10,176,000
PPP: $19,540
Life Expectancy: 76.5

Political Rights: 1
Civil Liberties: 2*
Status: Free

Ethnic Groups: Fleming (55 percent), Walloon (33 percent),
mixed and others, including Moroccan, Turkish and other
immigrant groups (12 percent)
Capital: Brussels
Ratings Change: Belgium's civil liberties rating changed from 1
to 2 because allegations of official incompetence and complicity
in several high-profile criminal cases has undermined popular
confidence in the judiciary and police forces.

Overview: Charges of judicial incompetence and government corruption at the highest levels, the discovery of a pedophile ring,
and the murder of a former deputy prime minister roiled
Belgium's political establishment.

In September 1996, the government announced its intention of looking into allegations of a cover-up in the five year investigation of the 1991 murder of former
Socialist deputy prime minister André Cools. There were also a number of other
political scandals, including the Augusta bribes affair that led to the resignation of
four Belgian ministers and Willy Claes, secretary-general of NATO.

A sordid pedophile case involving the kidnapping, trafficking and murder of at
least six young girls has further undermined the credibility of the country's judicial
institutions. The principal suspect, Marc Dutroux, is a convicted rapist who was
released after serving only three years of a 13 year sentence. He is also said to have
been involved in a car theft and drug smuggling racket involving police complicity.
Spontaneous demonstrations and wildcat strikes were set off in October following
the Belgian Supreme Court's dismissal of the case's chief investigating judge.

Tens of thousands of public servants carried out strikes and mass protests in
late 1995, in opposition to government austerity measures and privatization plans
driven by the Maastricht criteria for the single European currency. Despite the protests, Christian Democratic Prime Minister Jean-Luc Dehaene and his center-left
coalition survived a May 1996 no-confidence vote in parliament over plans for an
employment pact with unions and business. In addition, parliament granted the
government special powers to legislate by decree in certain areas of policy. The
new policy calls for reforms of the costly social security system, and for the reduction of unemployment by half by 2002 through limits on salary increases, to keep
such increases in line with Belgium's main trading partners.

Modern Belgium dates from 1830, when the territory broke away from the Netherlands and formed a constitutional monarchy. Today, the largely ceremonial monarchy symbolizes the increasingly fragile unity of this ethnically diverse country.
Ethnic and linguistic antagonism during the 1960s prompted a series of constitu-

tional amendments in 1970-71, and again in 1993, conferring a considerable degree of power on regional councils at the expense of the central government. A 1993 amendment formally transformed the country into a federation of the three regions of Flanders, Wallonia and bilingual Brussels, with the German-speaking area also accorded cultural autonomy. The same year, parliament adopted an amendment establishing three directly-elected regional assemblies with primary responsibility for housing, transportation, public works, education, culture and the environment. The weak central government continues to oversee foreign policy, defense, justice, monetary policy, taxation and the management of the budget deficit.

Political parties are split along linguistic lines, with both Walloon and Flemish parties ranging across the political spectrum. However, the dominance of three major groupings—Social Democrats, Christian Democrats and Liberals—has declined with the emergence of numerous small ethnic parties and special interest groups. The latest political and criminal scandals have exacerbated tensions in the country, with militant Flemish separatists blaming the French-speaking officials and increasing their demands for the formation of a separate state.

Political Rights and Civil Liberties:

Belgians can change their government democratically. Non-voters are subject to fines. Political parties generally organize along ethnic lines, with different factions of the leading parties subscribing to a common platform for general elections. Each ethnic group has autonomy in its region. However, constitutional disputes arise when members of one group are elected to office in another territory but refuse to take competency tests in the dominant language of that region.

While freedom of speech and of the press is guaranteed, Belgian law does prohibit some forms of pornography and all incitements to violence. Libel laws have some minor restraining effects on the press, and restrictions on the right of civil servants to criticize the government may constitute a slight reduction in freedom of speech. Autonomous public boards govern the state television and radio networks and ensure that public broadcasting is linguistically pluralistic. The state has permitted and licensed independent radio stations since 1985. In a September 1996 investigation of funding sources, however, Belgian police raided the offices and homes of several Kurdish institutions and exiles, including the licensed Kurdish MED-TV television station in Brussels.

There is freedom of association and religion. Christian, Jewish and Muslim institutions are state-subsidized in this overwhelmingly Roman Catholic country, and other faiths are not restricted. Immigrants and linguistic minorities argue that linguistic zoning limits opportunity. Belgium has taken important steps toward sexual equality, including the prohibition of sexual harassment.

The independent judiciary has come under attack due to the latest series of scandals, and demands for a complete shake-up of the criminal justice system have been made from all segments of society. In an unusual move that went beyond his constitutional role, King Albert II supported calls for a overhaul of Belgium's justice system in September. This move reflected the crisis of confidence in the rule of law, an essential prerequisite for participation in the European economic and monetary union.

Belize

Polity: Parliamentary democracy
Economy: Capitalist
Population: 215,000
PPP: $4,610
Life Expectancy: 73.7
Ethnic Groups: Mestizo (44 percent), Creole (30 percent), Maya (11 percent), Garifuna (7 percent)
Capital: Belmopan

Political Rights: 1
Civil Liberties: 1
Status: Free

Overview: In 1996 Belize's Maya ethnic minority voiced discontent over the government's decision to develop land to which they hold ancestral claim. The Belize government challenged the right of the Privy Council in London to hear death row appeals. Drug trafficking and government corruption were on the rise.

Belize is a member of the British Commonwealth. The British monarchy is represented by a governor-general. Formerly British Honduras, the name was changed to Belize in 1973. Independence was granted in 1981.

Belize is a parliamentary democracy with a bicameral National Assembly. The 29-seat House of Representatives is elected for a five-year term. Members of the Senate are appointed: five by the governor-general on the advice of the prime minister; two by the leader of the parliamentary opposition; and one by the Belize Advisory Council.

The government changed hands three times since independence between the center-right United Democratic Party (UDP) and the center-left People's United Party (PUP). In the 1993 elections the UDP and National Alliance for Belizean Rights (NABR) formed a coalition, winning 16 of the 29 seats in the House of Representatives. Suffrage is universal; women hold a number of appointed positions—including three of the nine Senate seats—but very few popularly elected ones.

In January 1996 nine death row prisoners received a reprieve from the Privy Council in London, rekindling Belizean government resentment of British involvement in domestic matters. The Belize constitution affords death row convicts the right to such an appeal; the current government lacks the necessary majority to amend the constitution.

Political Rights and Civil Liberties: Citizens are able to change their government democratically. There are no restrictions on the right to organize political parties. Civil society is well established, with a large number of nongovernmental organizations working in social, economic and environmental areas. There is freedom of religion and the government actively discourages racial and ethnic discrimination.

In general, the judiciary is independent and nondiscriminatory, and the rule of law is respected. However, judges and the director of public prosecutions must negotiate the renewal of their employment contracts, rendering them vulnerable to political influence. In addition, narcotics cases often go on for years while defendants are free on bail. One possible reason for this is the close link between government ministers and defense lawyers in such cases. The U.S. State department drew attention to this practice in a 1996 report.

The Belize Human Rights Commission is independent and effective. Human rights concerns include the plight of migrant workers and refugees from neighboring Central American countries, and charges of labor abuses by Belizean employers. Most of the estimated 40,000 Spanish-speakers who have immigrated since the 1980s do not have legal status. Some have registered under an amnesty program implemented in cooperation with the United Nations High Commissioner for Refugees. Reports continue of mistreatment of migrant workers, however.

Prison conditions do not meet minimum standards. The government opened a new facility in 1993 to alleviate overcrowding. However, this new prison, which houses death row inmates, provides in some cases one bed for six inmates, non-working toilets, and inadequate protection from weather.

More than half of the 21,000 Belize Maya Indians live in the Toledo district, where they form nearly two thirds of the population. Despite their claim to be the original inhabitants of Belize, they have no secure title to their ancestral lands which have been targeted by foreign investors. This land, for thousands of years, has provided Maya Indians food, medicinal plants, building materials and hunting grounds. In 1996 the Maya Indians organized demonstrations and took legal steps to block government negotiated logging contracts. They also opposed the paving of a major road to afford businesses access to the area.

Belizeans have suffered from an increase in violent crime, much of it related to drug trafficking and gang conflict. In February 1996 the U.S. government added Belize to its list of major drug transit countries despite the anti-crime measures undertaken in 1995, which included the adoption of a quick-trial plan.

There are six privately owned newspapers, three of which are subsidized by major political parties. The press is free to publish a variety of political viewpoints, including those critical of the government. Belize has a literacy rate of over 90 percent. Radio and television are saturated with political advertising during elections. Fourteen private television stations are in operation, including four cable systems. There is an independent board to oversee operations of government-owned outlets.

Labor unions are independent and well organized, and have the right to strike, but the percentage of the workforce that is organized has declined to 11 percent. Disputes are adjudicated by official boards of inquiry and businesses are penalized for failing to abide by the labor code.

Benin

Polity: Presidential-
parliamentary democracy
Economy: Statist-
transitional
Population: 5,574,000
PPP: $1,650
Life Expectancy: 47.8
Ethnic Groups: Aja, Barriba, Fon, Yoruba (99 percent)
Capital: Porto-Novo

Political Rights: 2
Civil Liberties: 2
Status: Free

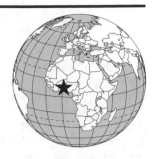

Overview: Benin's former Marxist military dictator Mathieu Kerekou returned to power in open elections that further consolidated the country's five-year old democracy. Adrien Houngbedji, a long-time opposition leader once jailed and tortured under President Kerekou's military regime, became prime minister. Defeated incumbent President Nicephore Soglo promoted conditions for a free and fair election, but failed to build a winning coalition among Benin's main ethnic groups and accepted defeat gracefully.

The modern state of Benin was once the center of the ancient kingdom of Dahomey, and took that name upon independence in 1960 after six decades of French rule. A succession of coups and counter-coups ended when General Kerekou seized power in 1972. Kerekou changed the country's name to Benin in 1975 and pursued a program based on nationalism and Marxist-Leninist economic policies through the Benin People's Revolutionary Party (the only one with legal status). Benin's Marxist economy was no more successful than the Soviet economy; by 1989, the country was essentially bankrupt and facing mounting internal unrest. Kerekou began the transition to a multiparty system. He was defeated in presidential elections by Soglo in March 1991. The country's human rights record has improved dramatically since, and civil society and free institutions are generally flourishing.

President Kerekou won a 52.5 percent victory in the March presidential polls, after a vigorous campaign notable for its lack of violence. Many nongovernmental organizations were active in the months before the vote in promoting a peaceful election through rallies, pamphlets and street theater. State-controlled radio and television broadcast continual appeals for peaceful campaigning.

Kerekou's victory was realized through an alliance of previously bitterly opposed politicians heading ethnically-based parties. The new government is effectively a coalition of these parties, as is the legislative majority in the national assembly, which triumphed in the March 1995 elections by winning 49 seats in the 89-member National Assembly. Former President Soglo's Benin Renaissance party is the largest single parliamentary party, with 20 seats.

Benin's second free presidential poll suggests that a democratic tradition may be taking root in the country. Historically, the country has been divided between ethnic groups in the north and south, and these remain the bases of the current political parties. The army is dominated by ethnic northerners recruited by Kerekou during his 18 years in power. Still fragile, Benin's democracy is an example for all

Africa, and particularly for the authoritarian regimes in neighboring Burkina Faso, Niger, Nigeria and Togo.

Political Rights and Civil Liberties: Benin's citizens freely elected their government in 1991, in the country's first genuine multiparty elections. Legislative polls in March 1995 went smoothly and returned an opposition majority. The March 1996 presidential contest was marked by some irregularities, but was free and fair. The president is limited to two five-year terms and national assembly members may serve an unlimited number of four-year terms. There is universal adult suffrage and voting is by secret ballot.

Freedom of expression, guaranteed by the constitution, is respected. Broadcast media are state-owned, but opposition voices have access and reports critical of the government are aired. Independent radio and television stations may begin operating in 1997. The independent and pluralistic print media include party-affiliated newspapers; they publish articles highly critical of both government and opposition leaders and policies. Foreign periodicals are easily available.

Freedom of assembly and association are respected, with permits and registration requirements treated as routine formalities. Numerous nongovernmental organizations are active and suffer no governmental interference. Several focus directly on human rights work, among them Centre Afrika-Obata, the League for the Defense of Human Rights in Benin, and the Study and Research Group on Democracy and Economic and Social Development (Gerrdes). Religious freedom, guaranteed by the constitution, is respected.

The judiciary is generally considered independent, though lacking in staff and training. Prison conditions are harsh; severe overcrowding and lack of medical care and proper diet cause unnecessary deaths among prisoners. The deployment of soldiers in a major anti-crime drive late in 1996 raised some fears of civil rights violations.

Legal rights for women are often not enforced, especially in rural areas and in family matters where traditional practices prevail. Women generally have fewer educational and employment opportunities. The right to organize and join unions is guaranteed by the constitution. Strikes are legal and collective bargaining widely used in labor negotiations. There are several labor federations, some of which are affiliated to political parties. The formal sector of Benin's economy remains small: about 80 percent of the workforce is found in rural areas working subsistence farm holdings.

President Kerekou has so far shown no inclination to revive his discredited Marxist economic policies. Privatization programs have reduced the state's stake in the economy, and efforts to raise agricultural production continue.

Bhutan

Polity: Traditional monarchy
Economy: Pre-industrial
Population: 842,000
PPP: $790
Life Expectancy: 51.0
Ethnic Groups: Ngalung, Sarchop, Nepalese, others
Capital: Thimphu

Political Rights: 7
Civil Liberties: 7
Status: Not Free

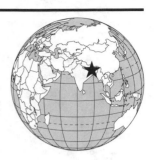

Overview:

In 1996 political rights and civil liberties in Bhutan remained severely circumscribed. In August the authorities deported 50 Bhutanese refugees who had re-entered the country to petition the king on behalf of the more than 90,000 refugees living in southeastern Nepal and 15,000 others living in India.

The Wangchuk dynasty was installed in 1907 by the British, and since then has ruled this Himalayan land as an absolute monarchy. In 1972 the current monarch, Jigme Singye Wangchuk, succeeded his father to the throne. The 150-member National Assembly meets irregularly, and in practice has little independent power. Every three years 100 National Assembly members are chosen by village headmen, while 10 seats go to religious groups and 40 are appointed by the king.

Since the late 1980s the government, dominated by the minority Tibetan-descended *Ngalung Drukpa* ethnic group, has persecuted Nepali-speaking citizens, also known as Southern Bhutanese. After a 1988 census showed Southern Bhutanese to be in the majority in five districts in the south, the government began applying a discriminatory 1985 Citizenship Act to strip thousands of Southern Bhutanese of their citizenship.

The Citizenship Act confirmed the primary basis for citizenship to be residence in Bhutan in 1958, the year in which the kingdom extended citizenship to most Southern Bhutanese. But to prove citizenship, Southern Bhutanese now had to show a land tax receipt for 1958, which amounted to asking a largely illiterate population to produce a document that had been of little importance when issued three decades earlier. The Act also required both parents to be Bhutanese citizens to grant citizenship to persons born after 1958, whereas previously only the father needed be a Bhutanese national.

Between 1989-92 soldiers forcibly expelled tens of thousands of Southern Bhutanese from the country, and the government arrested thousands more as "anti-nationals." Officials forced many expelled to sign "voluntary migration forms" that forfeited their land and property. Bhutan claims that most of the refugees were illegal immigrants, but according to the Nepalese government 97 percent of the refugees possess proper identity cards or alternate documentation of Bhutanese citizenship, such as tax receipts or health certificates.

In June 1994 dissidents from a third ethnic group, the Sarchop community in eastern Bhutan, launched the Druk National Congress (DNC) in exile in Nepal to press for democratic reforms. In late May 1995 the DNC organized an underground campaign of pro-democracy wall posters calling for basic rights. In August a court sentenced Colonel Tandin Dorji, the chief of police and a brother-in-law of the DNC chairman, to a three-year prison sentence for alleged negligence over a jailbreak, an action widely seen as politically motivated. On August 15-16, 1996, the government forcibly deported 50 Bhutanese refugees who had re-entered the country to march to Thimpu, the capital, to petition the king to resolve the refugee situation.

Political Rights and Civil Liberties:

Bhutanese lack the democratic means to change their government. The king wields absolute power, and policymaking is centered around the king and a small group of Buddhist aristocratic elites. The National Assembly has become a forum for diatribes against the Southern Bhutanese, who hold a disproportionately small number of seats. Despite National Assembly rules mandating twice-yearly regular meetings, since 1988 the body has met irregularly. Political parties are de facto prohibited, and none exist.

The rule of law is nonexistent. Between 1989-92 the army and police committed grave human rights violations against Southern Bhutanese, including arbitrary arrests, beatings, rape, destruction of homes, and robbery. The Royal Bhutan Army maintains a strong presence in the south and arbitrarily searches homes, harasses residents, and threatens and intimidates local officials.

State-organized "village volunteer groups," armed robber gangs and militants from the Bodo tribal community and separatist groups in the northeast Indian state of Assam are also responsible for rights abuses in southern Bhutan.

The king appoints and can dismiss judges, and the rudimentary judiciary is not independent. Several detainees and prisoners have reportedly died in custody in recent years due to torture and poor conditions. Amnesty International estimates that as of mid-1995 44 political prisoners were in custody, with a further 70 on trial. The country's most famous dissident, Tek Nath Rizal, was sentenced in November 1993 to life imprisonment under a 1992 National Security Act legislated three years after his imprisonment.

Freedom of speech is restricted and criticism of the king is not permitted, except indirectly during National Assembly discussions. The state-owned weekly, *Kuensel*, the country's only regular publication, is a government mouthpiece and frequently runs articles biased against the Southern Bhutanese. Since 1989 the kingdom has banned satellite dishes. There is no freedom of association for political purposes, although some business and civic organizations are permitted.

The sixth Five Year Plan (1987-92) introduced a program of "One Nation, One People," that included the promotion of *Driglam Namzha*, the national dress code and customs of the ruling Ngalungs. A January 1989 Royal Decree made this Driglam Namzha code mandatory for all Bhutanese, although enforcement is sporadic. The government also banned the Nepali language as a subject of instruction in schools.

Southern Bhutanese are required to obtain "No Objection Certificates" from the government to enter schools, take government jobs and sell farm products. In practice NOCs are frequently denied. Many of the southern schools and hospitals closed by the authorities in 1990 have yet to reopen.

The Druk Kargue sect of Mahayana Buddhism is the official state religion. Buddhist *lamas* (priests) wield political influence. Most Southern Bhutanese are Hindus; due to persecution they lack the means to worship freely. Independent trade unions and strikes are not permitted.

Bolivia

Polity: Presidential-
legislative democracy
Economy: Capitalist
Population: 7,623,000
PPP: $2,510
Life Expectancy: 59.7

Political Rights: 2
Civil Liberties: 3*
Status: Free

Ethnic Groups: Quechua (30 percent), Aymara (25 percent),
other Indian (15 percent), mestizo and other Indian (25-30 percent), European
(5percent)
Capital: La Paz (administrative), Sucre (judicial)
Ratings Change: Bolivia's civil liberties rating changed from 4 to 3 due to the end of
the six-month state-of-siege in 1995.

Overview: In 1996 Bolivian President Gonzalo Sanchez de Losada's
privatization plans provoked widespread protests and
caused his party's popularity ratings to drop prior to national elections due in mid-1997.

After achieving independence from Spain in 1825, the Republic of Bolivia
endured recurrent instability and military rule. The armed forces, responsible for
over 180 coups in 157 years, have stayed in their barracks since 1982, when with
the restoration of the 1967 constitution a civilian government was elected.

The constitution provides for the election every four years (five years beginning in 1997) of a president and a Congress consisting of a 130-member House of
Representatives and 27-member Senate. If no candidate receives an absolute majority of votes, Congress chooses the president from among the three leading contenders. Starting in 1997, the outcome will be decided by a runoff between the top
two candidates.

Bolivia's principal parties are Sanchez de Losada's center-right Nationalist
Revolutionary Movement (MNR), the conservative National Democratic Action
(ADN) and the social-democratic Movement of the Revolutionary Left (MIR). The
MIR's Jaime Paz Zamora became president in 1989 at the head of a MIR-ADN
coalition. His term was marked by corruption scandals and social unrest.

In 1993 the MIR-ADN candidate was the former dictator and retired general
Hugo Banzer. Sanchez de Losada, the planning minister in a former MNR administration (1985-89), was the MNR candidate. He took 33.8 percent of the vote to
Banzer's 20 percent. Two populists, talk-show host Carlos Palenque and beer mag-
nate Max Fernandez, won 13.6 and 13.1 percent, respectively. Antonio Aranibar of
the leftist Free Bolivia Movement (MBL) took 5.1 percent.

The MNR won 69 seats in the bicameral legislature. Sanchez de Losada secured the backing of the Civic and Solidarity Union (UCS), which won 21 seats,
and the MBL, which won seven, by offering them cabinet posts. The three-party
coalition elected Sanchez de Losada president. Running-mate Hugo Cardenas, an
Aymara Indian, became vice president, the first indigenous person in Latin America
to hold such high office.

In his first two years Sanchez de Losada initiated a sweeping privatization program and, under U.S. pressure, stepped up coca eradication. These measures were assailed by labor unions and coca growers. Early 1995 saw a series of labor strikes and mass protests. Sanchez de Losada imposed a six-month state of siege that allowed him to repress protests and implement his policies by decree. The MNR fared poorly in local elections in December.

Sanchez de Losada's privatization program, particularly a plan to auction the state-owned oil and gas monopoly, brought regular street protests in 1996. During the year some opinion polls showed nearly three-quarters of those surveyed disapproving of the government's performance.

Political Rights and Civil Liberties:

Citizens can change their government through elections. In 1991 a new electoral court consisting of five relatively independent magistrates was created, and a new voter registration system was implemented. Presidential, senatorial and legislative elections are scheduled for June 1, 1997.

Political parties range from fascist to radical left. There are also a number of indigenous-based peasant movements. The languages of the indigenous population are officially recognized, but the 40 percent Spanish-speaking minority still dominates the political process.

The constitution guarantees free expression, freedom of religion and the right to organize political parties, civic groups and labor unions. Unions have the right to strike.

In 1995, however, labor rights and many civil liberties were suspended during a six-month state of siege imposed by the government to quell protests against its economic and coca-eradication policies. Strikes and demonstrations were violently repressed and hundreds of labor activists were arrested. After the state of siege was lifted, the government put troops in the streets in response to renewed protests and a number of people, including two children, were killed in violent clashes. Labor unrest, often violent, continued in 1996. In March authorities detained hundreds of protesters who clashed with police during a strike by teachers, public health workers, miners at state-owned factories, and other state employees.

Strong evidence abounds that drug money has been used to finance political campaigns and buy government officials, including police and military personnel. The drug trade has also spawned private security forces that operate with relative impunity in the coca-growing regions. Bolivia is the world's second largest producer of cocaine, after Peru.

A U.S.-sponsored coca-eradication program has angered peasant unions representing Bolivia's 50,000 coca farmers. In 1995 their peaceful protests and demonstrations were violently repressed by security forces, and hundreds, possibly thousands, were arrested in the course of the year. A May 1996 Human Rights Watch report stated that government forces, particularly troops of the Mobile Rural Patrol Unit, continue to commit serious human rights abuses during coca eradication efforts in the Chapare, a tropical lowland region, including excessive use of force, arbitrary detentions and suppression of peaceful demonstrations.

The emergence of small indigenous-based guerrilla groups has caused an overreaction by security forces against legitimate government opponents.

The judiciary, headed by a Supreme Court, is the weakest branch of government. Despite recent reforms it remains riddled with corruption, and subject to the compromising power of drug traffickers. The creation of a Constitutional Tribunal and a "people's defender" branch have not yet led to any marked improvement.

Government-sponsored as well as independent human rights organizations are in existence. Their reports indicate an increase, in recent years, in police brutality, including torture during confinement. Intimidation against activists has been reported. Prison conditions are poor, and nearly three-quarters of prisoners have not been formally sentenced.

The press, radio and television are mostly private. Journalists covering corruption stories are occasionally subject to verbal intimidation by government officials, arbitrary detention by police and violent attacks. A number of daily newspapers publish, including one sponsored by the influential Catholic church. Opinion polling is on the rise. Eight years ago there was no television, but now there are more than 60 channels, a development which has had an impact on recent political campaigns. Voters reacting to information on television were less predictable than in the past, when they gave their votes to well-known national figures.

Bosnia-Herzegovina

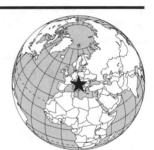

Polity: Presidential-parliamentary democracy (transitional)
Economy: Mixed-statist (severely war-damaged)
Population: 3,588,000
PPP: na
Life Expectancy: na
Ethnic Groups: Pre-war—Slavic Muslim (44 percent), Serb (33 percent), Croat (17 percent)
Capital: Sarajevo

Political Rights: 5*
Civil Liberties: 5*
Status: Partly Free

Ratings Change: Bosnia-Herzegovina's political rights and civil liberties ratings changed from 6 to 5 because progress toward freedom was registered as an internationally-enforced peace process led to a limited revival of civic life.

Overview: In 1996, voters from Bosnia-Herzegovina's two entities, the Moslem-Croat Federation and Republika Srpska, elected a national government and local bodies on September 14 under the provisions of the 1995 U.S.-brokered Dayton Agreement that ended four years of war. Nationalist parties representing the three main ethnic groups dominated the vote, consolidated their hold in separate territories and cast doubt on Bosnia's viability as a multi-ethnic state.

While the Organization for Security and Cooperation in Europe (OSCE) certified the poll results, five conditions for elections specified in the Dayton agreement were not met—a politically neutral environment; the right to vote in secret without intimidation; freedom of expression; freedom of association; and freedom of movement. Municipal elections were canceled twice because of vote-rigging and other irregularities, as displaced Serbs applied for ballots in Serb-occupied places where there had been a Muslim majority.

The worst fighting since the Dayton Accords flared up on November 12 between Serbs and Muslims trying to return to their former homes in Republika Srpska. A $100 million U.S. plan to equip and train the Muslim-Croat Federation army was put on hold because Bosnian President Alija Izetbegovic failed to dismiss Defense Minister Hasan Cengic for alleged close ties with Iran. The 60,000-strong, NATO-led international peace force (IFOR), originally set to withdraw by year's end, will remain in reduced strength through 1997.

Bosnia-Herzegovina became one of six constituent republics of Yugoslavia in 1945. As Yugoslavia began to unravel, multiparty parliamentary elections in September 1990 were won by three nationalist parties representing ethnic constituencies. After a 1992 referendum boycotted by Serbs favored secession, President Izetbegovic declared independence on March 3, leading to the outbreak of war. By year's end, Serbs controlled over 70 percent of the country. "Ethnic cleansing" had killed or displaced hundreds of thousands of Muslim, Croat and Serb civilians. The European Union-UN Vance-Owen plan, calling for partition of Bosnia into 10 autonomous provinces, was widely criticized and never implemented. Over 20,000 UN peacekeepers could not deter aggression.

In 1994, a U.S.-brokered ceasefire between warring Bosnian Croats and Muslims established a Muslim-Croat Federation. In 1995, Croatia recaptured West Slavonia and Krajina. NATO launched air strikes on Serb forces after a mortar attack on Sarajevo. Serb control was reduced from 70 to 50 percent of Bosnian territory, and Serb leaders agreed to a cease-fire. On November 21, the presidents of Bosnia, Croatia and Serbia initialed the Dayton Accords. Key provisions included a united Sarajevo; internationally-supervised elections; a constitution calling for a loose federative state with semi-autonomous Muslim-Croatian (51 percent) and Serb (49 percent) entities, a rotating presidency and the assignment of posts by nationality; UN-supervised disarmament; and the introduction of Implementation Force (IFOR) troops. Indicted war criminals, including Bosnian Serb President Karadzic and General Ratko Mladic, would be barred from public office.

In 1996, implementation of nation-building provisions proved difficult. While IFOR separated combatants by establishing and enforcing zones of separation, tensions and distrust between Muslims, Croats and Serbs hindered full compliance with the accords. Refugees trying to return home were met by violence. In March, with Sarajevo due to revert to the Bosnian government, Serbs in the Grbavica district were terrorized by Serb authorities and gangs who burned buildings and forced them to flee. Strains in the Muslim-Croat Federation continued. When June elections in the divided city of Mostar gave a Muslim-Serb coalition control of the city council, officials in Croat western Mostar rejected the results, and "Herzec-Bosna," the self-proclaimed Croat statelet within the Muslim-Croat Federation, was nominally dismantled in the summer.

Over 27,000 candidates and 47 parties registered for the September 14 elections. Voters from the Muslim-Croat Federation and Republika Srpska voted for a national government consisting of a collective presidency (one Muslim, one Croat, one Serb), as well as for a House of Representatives of Bosnia-Herzegovina---the lower chamber---consisting of 42 members, 28 directly elected by voters in the Federation and 14 by residents of Republika Srpska. A House of the People would consist of 15 delegates, 10 from the House of Representatives of the Federation and five from the National Assembly of Republika Srpska, both to be elected that day.

The pre-election period saw intimidation of opposition parties and the barring of refugees from returning to their homes to vote. The OSCE allowed members of the ruling nationalist parties to run all the local election commissions. In the Republika Srpska, the ruling Serbian Democratic Party (SDS), was led by presidential candidate and Speaker of the Bosnian Serb Parliament, Momcilo Krajisnik. Having replaced Karadzic, an indicted war criminal barred from running, Krajisnik harassed opposition candidates and prevented them from getting access to local radio and television. In the Muslim-Croat Federation, the Croatian Democratic Union (HDZ)—a counterpart to Croatia's ruling HDZ—led by presidential candidate Kresimir Zubak also kept a tight rein on the opposition in western Herzegovina. President Izetbegovic's ruling Party for Democratic Action (SDA) used strong-arm tactics and media control to pressure opposition. After Haris Silajdzic, the former Bosnian prime minister and head of the multi-ethnic Party for Bosnia-Herzegovina, was attacked at a June rally, international election officials ruled that the violence had been organized by local police working with the SDA, and struck seven of the party's candidates from the slate.

Prior to the vote, NATO and the UN designated 19 "secure voter routes" to protect Bosnian voters returning to their homes to vote. About half of Bosnia's 2.9 million eligible voters were refugees. Under the plan, refugee voters returning to Republika Srpska could only cross internal ethnic boundaries in 730 buses organized by the Muslim-Croat Federation, or in private vehicles carrying over eight people. But with NATO refusing to protect Muslims who wanted to vote in their Serb-controlled former towns, only 14,700 of an eligible 150,000 Muslim voters chose to cross the line. Officials from Serbia's ministry for refugees told tens of thousands of Serb refugees living in Serbia that if they voted in the towns they had lived which were now under Croat-Muslim rule, they would lose refugee status.

As expected, Izetbegovic, Krajisnik and Zubak were elected to the three-member presidency; Izetbegovic, who received the most votes, became chairman of the presidency. In the race for the 28 Federation members of the House of Representatives of Bosnia-Herzegovina, the SDA won 16 seats; the Croat Democratic Party, 8; the Party for Bosnia-Herzegovina, 2; and the United List (a joint ticket grouping five multiethnic parties), 2. Of the 14 Republika Srpska seats, nine went to the Serb Democratic Party, and three to the SDA, and the People's Union for Peace took two. The Presidency of Republika Srpska went to Biljana Plavsic of the SDS, a hardline Karadzic ally. In the 83-member National Assembly of Republika Srpska, the SDS took 45 seats; the SDA, 14; the People's Union for Peace, 10; and the Serbian Radical Party, 6, with smaller parties taking one or two seats. Seventeen Muslim deputies and one Croat were elected. In the 140-member House of Representatives of the Federation, the SDA won 78 seats; the HDZ, 36; the United List, 11; and the Party for Bosnia-Herzegovina, 10. The term for all legislative bodies is two years.

International monitors reported irregularities such as voting lists remaining incomplete, refugees not being provided with bus transportation, and refugee polling places being unmarked. The OSCE certified the elections "free and fair" despite objections from the SDA and some international NGOs that the preconditions set in the Dayton accords were not met.

In October, Serb member of the presidency Momcilo Krajisnik boycotted the opening of the all-Bosnian legislature and refused to sign a loyalty oath to Bosnia-Herzegovina. By mid-November, the collective presidency still had not agreed on a government. Meeting in Paris on November 14, U.S. and European officials warned that economic aid would be cut off in two years if peace had not taken hold.

Political Rights and Civil Liberties: Citizens of Bosnia and its constituent entities can elect their government under the constitution stipulated in the Dayton Agreement. The 1996 elections, however, failed to meet key preconditions such as freedom of movement and free media.

Political parties are allowed to organize; some 47 participated in the September voting. Opposition parties were harassed by the three ethnic ruling parties.

Radio-Television (RTV) of Bosnia-Herzegovina is controlled by the SDA and promotes party politics. The director of Croatian RTV Mostar is staunchly anti-Muslim and opposes reunification. In Republika Srpska, the Serbian RTV network controls local television studios and radio stations, all of which use Serbian RTV newscasts and follow a pro-Serbian political agenda. The Bosnian government resisted plans by the international community to link the frequencies of five independent private stations into a network, the Open Broadcasting Network, for objective election coverage. The fragmented information system allows national parties of the different entities to obstruct the free flow of information and to advocate their nationalistic platforms. Three putatively independent dailies operate in Sarajevo, though *Dnevni Avaz* is controlled by the SDA. On October 28, representatives of indepedent papers and radio in Republika Srpska met to discuss coordinating marketing, forming a journalists' union and establishing an independent printing house. Independent papers have been denied access to the government-owned printing office, radios have been threatened with losing licenses and frequencies, and journalists have faced dubious libel charges by government officials. With few exceptions, opposition candidates were denied access to most major media.

Freedom of movement across entity boundaries remains constricted, and refugees who have attempted to return home have been attacked. Repatriation remains an unresolved major issue.

Muslims, Catholic Croats and Orthodox Serbs practice their religions in areas they control. Mosques, churches and cemeteries were intentionally targeted in war zones.

The rupture of the federal state led to the fragmentation of a functioning national judiciary, which has yet to be rebuilt. Croats and Serbs have established local court systems in areas they control.

Trade unions exist, but their functions have been limited by economic and social dislocation. Women bore a terrible burden during the war, victimized by rape, poverty and dislocation, particularly in rural areas. The Bosnian government guarantees equal rights for women in terms of education and employment.

Botswana

Polity: Parliamentary democracy and traditional chiefs
Economy: Capitalist
Population: 1,531,000
PPP: $5,220
Life Expectancy: 65.2
Ethnic Groups: Tswana and Baswara (95 percent), Kalanga, Kgagaladi, European
Capital: Gaborone

Political Rights: 2
Civil Liberties: 2
Status: Free

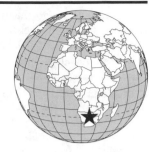

Overview:

Botswana maintained its reputation as one of Africa's few multiparty democracies in 1996 with improved respect for women's rights and the formal appointment of an independent election commission. A puzzling arms procurement drive, and concerns over the treatment of indigenous Baswara, or N/oakwe ("red people"), however, clouded an otherwise positive picture.

For the three decades since Botswana gained independence from Britain in 1966, the country has been ruled by elected governments. Elections have become increasingly free and fair. The opposition Botswana National Front (BNF) made a strong showing in the October 1994 national assembly elections, winning 13 of 35 seats contested. The new independent election commission, which has a life of ten years, may put an end to accusations that the Botswana Democratic Party (BDP)—in power since independence—has manipulated elections in its favor. The next elections are set for October 1999. Botswana has long been a model of stability in troubled southern Africa, but its purchase of attack jets and armored vehicles in 1996 while it faced no identifiable internal or external threats, raised regional tensions and diverted resources sorely needed for development.

Political Rights and Civil Liberties:

Botswana's citizens choose their government through open legislative elections that international observers consider generally free and fair. The national assembly elects the president to serve a concurrent term. Opposition electoral gains in 1994 indicate a more open system is taking hold, and the scheduled 1999 elections under the newly-constituted Independent Election Commission could challenge the ruling BDP's long tenure in power. Botswana's strong human rights record is one of Africa's best. A strong bill of rights is generally respected by the government. However, several potentially repressive laws regarding sedition, and detention without trial (under the National Security Act), remain on the books. They are rarely used but are a lingering threat to freedom of expression and political activity. Political discussion is possible through a free media, though the government retains control of the broadcast media that is crucial to reaching rural areas.

Treatment of the country's Baswara, or N/oakwe ("red people"), is under increasing scrutiny. Widespread discrimination and abuse of N/oakwe people is alleged, including forcible evictions from their traditional lands. Only about 3,000 N/oakwe still live traditional nomadic lives as "bushmen" in the central Kalahari desert. About 45,000 others have been resettled in villages or work as farm laborers, often under difficult conditions. N/oakwe activists are demanding land rights and permission to hunt on traditional lands, much of which are now game preserves. The case of Baswara from the Xade settlement in the Central Kalahari Game Preserve has attracted international attention.

The status of women has also been criticized. In January 1996, the Citizenship Act was amended to remove the provision barring Botswana citizenship to the children of female citizens married to foreigners. Married women must receive their husbands' permission to receive a bank loan, and women face traditional discrimination, especially in rural areas.

Workers' rights to strike and to bargain for wages are restricted, and concentration of economic power has hindered labor organizing. Reports of official corruption persist, but there is a general trend towards more openness in governance. A new law adopted in 1996 calls for the president, members of the cabinet and parliamentarians to declare their assets.

Brazil

Polity: Federal presidential-legislative democracy
Economy: Capitalist-statist
Population: 160,523,000
PPP: $5,500
Life Expectancy: 66.5
Ethnic Groups: European (53 percent), black mixed (46 percent), Indian (less than 1 percent)
Capital: Brasilia

Political Rights: 2
Civil Liberties: 4
Status: Partly Free

Overview: In 1996 Brazilian president Fernando Henrique Cardoso persuaded a divided congress to pass some elements of his economic reform program. Land disputes highlighted the need for reform in a country with one of the world's most inequitable distributions of wealth.

After gaining independence from Portugal in 1822, Brazil retained a monarchical system until a republic was established in 1889. Democratic rule has been interrupted by long periods of authoritarian rule, most recently under military regimes from 1964 to 1985.

Elected civilian rule was reestablished in 1985 and a new constitution was implemented in 1988. It provides for a president elected for four years, a bicameral Congress consisting of an 81-member Senate elected for eight years and a 503-member Chamber of Deputies elected for four years.

Civilian rule has been marked by constant corruption scandals, one of which led to the impeachment by Congress of President Fernando Collor de Mello (1989-92). Collor resigned and was replaced by his vice-president, Itamar Franco, whose weak, feckless administration prompted rumors of a military coup.

In early 1994 the fiery Luis Ignacio "Lula" da Silva of the leftist Workers' Party (PT) was the frontrunner in a field of eight presidential candidates. Cardoso, Franco's finance minister and a market-oriented centrist, cobbled together a center-right, three-party coalition centered around his own Social Democratic Party (PSDB). He put an anti-inflation plan into effect in July, and within months inflation had plummeted from 50 percent to less than 2 percent. The campaign turned around as Cardoso, backed by big media and big business, jumped into the lead.

In October 1994 Cardoso won the presidency with 54 percent of the vote, against 27 percent for Lula. The Senate was left divided among 11 parties and the Chamber of Deputies among 18. Cardoso's three-party coalition did not win a majority in either branch.

Cardoso spent 1995 cajoling and horse-trading for the congressional votes needed to carry out his economic liberalization program. Progress was slow as the Congress remained a gridlock-prone labyrinth of overlapping special interests and corrupt patronage machines. In the fall Cardoso's government was rocked by a bribery and phone-tapping scandal. There were a number of high-level resignations.

Cardoso had to make political concessions, including agreeing to refinance part of Sao Paulo's debts, to get Congress to pass a watered-down version of the government's reforms of the ailing social security system in late March 1996. In April Cardoso indicated that he favored a constitutional amendment to drop the one-term limit so as to allow him to run for re-election in 1998.

In 1996 land issues were high on the political agenda. In January Cardoso announced presidential decree 1775, which allows states, municipalities and non-Indians to challenge, at the federal level, proposed demarcations of Indian lands. Following the decree, miners and loggers, seeking to establish new land claims, increased their encroachments on Indian reservations. More than 400 claims were filed under the decree by the end of the year; most were ultimately rejected, but at least one reservation lost land. In another development, the Landless Workers Movement, representing landless villagers, continued to occupy mostly fallow land in rural areas to pressure the government to settle rural families. The activism frequently engendered violent conflicts, leading to the death of several villagers.

Political Rights and Civil Liberties: Citizens can change governments through elections. The 1994 elections were relatively free, but there were irregularities in northeastern states and in Rio de Janeiro, and also evidence that candidate Cardoso benefited from government support.

The constitution guarantees freedoms of religion and expression and the right to organize political and civic organizations. However, a national breakdown in police discipline and escalating criminal violence, much of it fueled by the burgeoning drug trade, have created a climate of lawlessness and general insecurity in which human rights are violated with impunity on a massive scale.

Brazil's police are among the world's most violent and corrupt. Although nominally commanded by elected officials, the police in each state get military training and are under the jurisdiction of military courts, in which they are rarely held accountable. In August 1996 Cardoso signed legislation giving civilian courts jurisdiction in cases where police commit homicide against civilians; by year's end, this and other key elements of the government's National Human Rights Plan had not been passed by the Senate. Military police use the inefficiency and corruption of the local civil police as an excuse to justify their tactics of simply eliminating suspected criminals.

Brazil's numerous independent rights organizations have documented killings by military police and systematic abuse and torture in police detention centers. Conditions in Brazil's packed, violence-plagued penal system are wretched, and the military police are responsible for quelling disorder.

Vigilante "extermination squads," linked to the police and financed by local merchants, are responsible for thousands of extrajudicial killings yearly. Violence, including disappearances, against the 35 million children living in poverty---at least 20 percent of whom live on the streets of burgeoning urban centers---is systematic. Up to five street kids a day are murdered in Brazil, according to researchers at the University of Sao Paulo, yet very rarely are their killers caught. About 80 percent of the victims are of African descent.

The climate of lawlessness is reinforced by a weak judiciary. Brazil's Supreme Court is granted substantial autonomy by the constitution. However, the judicial system is overwhelmed (with only 7,000 judges for a population of more than 150 million), and vulnerable to the chronic corruption that undermines the entire political system. It has been virtually powerless in the face of organized crime.

Since 1994 the federal government has occasionally deployed the army in Rio de Janeiro's 400 slums, most of which have been taken over by drug gangs in league, or in competition, with corrupt police and local politicians.

There is little public confidence in the judiciary, so poorer citizens have resorted to lynchings, with hundreds of mob executions reported in the last three years.

Violence caused by land disputes continues unabated. Brazil's large landowners control nearly 60 percent of arable land, while the poorest 30 percent share less than 2 percent. Every year dozens of activists, Catholic church workers and rural unionists are killed by paramilitary groups and hired killers in the pay of large landowners, with very few cases brought to court. In April police in El Dorado de Carajas in the Para state opened fire on landless squatters, killing 19.

Continued reports of forced labor of thousands of workers by ranchers surface in the Amazon and other rural regions, often implying the complicity of local police. Forced labor is against Brazilian law, but the judicial response remains indifferent at best.

Rubber tappers and Indians remain targets of violence, including killings, associated with Amazon development projects initiated under military rule and with the gold rush in the far north. The constitution grants land rights to Brazil's quarter of a million Indians, but the government has only reluctantly tried to stop incursions by settlers and miners into Indian reserves.

Violence against women and children is endemic, much of it occurring in the home. Protective laws are rarely enforced. In 1991 the Supreme Court ruled that a man could no longer kill his wife and win acquittal on the ground of "legitimate defense of honor," but juries tend to ignore the ruling. Forced prostitution of children is widespread.

Industrial labor unions are well-organized, politically connected and many are prone to corruption. The right to strike is recognized and there are special labor courts. Hundreds of strikes have taken place in recent years against attempts to privatize state industries. Child labor is prevalent and laws against it are rarely enforced.

The press is privately owned. There are dozens of daily newspapers and numerous other publications throughout the country. The print media have played a central role in exposing official corruption, which has led to intimidation and violence.

Radio is mostly commercial. Television is independent, and a powerful political instrument. Roughly two-thirds of the population is illiterate, while 85 percent of households have television sets. The huge TV Globo is a near-monopoly and has enormous political clout. Three much smaller networks operate, as do educational channels.

Brunei

Polity: Traditional monarchy
Economy: Capitalist-statist
Population: 304,000
PPP: $18,414
Life Expectancy: 74.3
Ethnic Groups: Malay (64 percent), Chinese (20 percent), others (15 percent)
Capital: Bandar Seri Begawan

Political Rights: 7
Civil Liberties: 5
Status: Not Free

Overview: Located on the northern coast of the Southeast Asian island of Borneo, Brunei became a British protectorate in 1888. The 1959 constitution provided for five advisory councils: the Privy Council, the Religious Council, the Council of Succession, the Council of Ministers and a Legislative Council. In 1962 the leftist Brunei People's Party (PRB) took all ten of the elected seats in the 21-member Legislative Council; late in the year British troops crushed a PRB-backed rebellion. The sultan then assumed constitutionally-authorized emergency powers for a stipulated two-year period. These powers have been renewed every two years since then, and elections have not been held since 1965. Sultan Haji Hasanal Bolkiah Mu'izzadin Waddaulah ascended the throne in October 1967.

The country achieved independence in January 1984. The sultan serves as prime minister and has nearly complete authority over the country. Currently only the Council of Ministers, composed largely of the sultan's relatives, and the Legislative Council, with all members appointed by the sultan, are convened. In 1985 the government recognized the moderate Brunei National Democratic Party (PKDB), followed a year later by the offshoot Brunei National United Party (PPKB). In 1988, however, the sultan ordered the PKDB dissolved and detained two of its leaders for two years, reportedly after the party called on the sultan to hold elections. The PPKB currently has fewer than 100 members and wields no influence.

In February 1995 Abdul Latief Chuchu, one of the two ex-leaders of the PKDB who had been detained from 1988-90, formed the Brunei National Solidarity Party. Chuchu resigned as president of the party later that year, after warnings from the government not to become involved in political activity.

Political Rights and Civil Liberties:

Citizens of Brunei, a hereditary sultanate, lack the democratic means to change their government. Nearly all political power is wielded by the sultan and his inner circle of relatives. Since 1992 there have been local elections for village chiefs, who serve life terms. All candidates must have a knowledge of Islam (although they may be non-Muslims) and cannot have past or current links with a political party. The only other means of popular political participation is through petitions to the sultan. The constitution does not protect the freedom of speech, press, assembly or association, and these rights are restricted in practice. Criticism of the government is rare due to the threat of sanction. A government commission is in the process of reviewing the 1959 constitution, although its exact mandate is unclear.

A 1988 law mandates corporal punishment for 42 criminal offenses, including drug-related crimes. Police have broad powers to make arrests without obtaining warrants. The Internal Security Act (ISA) allows the government to detain suspects without trial for renewable two-year periods. There have been no new detentions under the ISA since 1988, but there are several political prisoners still in jail for their role in the 1962 rebellion.

The judiciary is independent of the government. Hong Kong provides judges for the High Court and the Court of Appeals. Defendants enjoy adequate procedural safeguards, with the notable exception of the right to trial by jury. The only private newspaper practices self-censorship by avoiding discussion of religious issues and of the sultan's paramount political role. Sensitive articles and photographs in foreign periodicals are often censored. The one television station is state-owned and does not offer pluralistic views.

Since 1991 the government has been asserting the primacy of Islam through a national ideology of Malay Muslim Monarchy (MIB), which, it claims, dates back more than 500 years. The government frequently refuses non-Muslims permission to build new places of worship, and has closed some existing ones. Other restrictions on non-Muslims include bans on proselytizing and on the importation of religious books or educational materials, restrictions on religious education in non-Muslim schools and a requirement that Islamic education and MIB be taught at all schools. The ethnic Malay majority enjoys advantages in university admission and employment. Most Chinese were not granted citizenship when the country became independent, and the rigorous Malay-language citizenship test makes it difficult for them to be naturalized. Women face discrimination in divorce, in inheritance matters, and in obtaining equal pay and benefits. Muslim women are strongly encouraged to wear the *tudong*, a traditional head covering, although there is no formal sanction against those who do not. Foreign servants are occasionally beaten or otherwise treated poorly.

Citizens can travel freely within the country and abroad. The government must approve of all trade unions, but does not interfere in their affairs. Three exist, but they cover just 5 percent of the workforce and have little influence. The constitution neither recognizes nor denies the right to strike, and in practice none occur.

Bulgaria

Polity: Parliamentary
democracy
Economy: Mixed statist
transitional
Population: 8,380,000
PPP: $4,320
Life Expectancy: 71.2

Political Rights: 2
Civil Liberties: 3*
Status: Free

Ethnic Groups: Bulgarian (86 percent), Turkish
(9 percent), Roma (4 percent), Macedonian
Capital: Sofia
Ratings Change: Bulgaria's civil liberties rating changed from 2 to 3 because of
increasing restraints on the media.

Overview: Petar Stoyanov of the opposition Union of Democratic
Forces (UDF) won the presidential election after a November 3, 1996 run-off, defeating the candidate of the ruling
ex-Communist Bulgarian Socialist Party (BSP), Ivan Marazov.

The election took place against the background of the unsolved September murder of Andrei Lukanov, Bulgaria's first post-communist prime minister (1989-91),
and a member of the BSP's social democratic wing who had criticized Prime Minister Zhan Videnov for his reluctance to reform the economy, and accused the government of massive corruption.

Occupied by the Ottoman Turks from 1396 to 1878, Bulgaria achieved independence in 1908. Allied with Nazi Germany in World War II, it was "liberated" by
the Soviet Red Army in 1944. Between 1954 and 1989 the country was in the grip
of Communist Party strongman Todor Zhivkov, who was forced to resign one day
after the fall of the Berlin Wall in November 1989.

The BSP won the parliamentary elections of December 1994 after a period of
non-party government led by Prime Minster Lyuben Berov. The BSP took 125 seats;
the fragmented UDF, 69; the Popular Union, 18; the Turkish-based Movement for
Rights and Freedom (MRF), 15; and the pro-market Bulgarian Business Block, 13.

In the first round of the 1996 presidential elections on October 29, Stoyanov
gained 44 percent of the vote, and Marazov 26.9 percent. Both the first and second
rounds of the election were called "free and fair" by international monitors.

In 1996, the main issue facing the Videnov government was improving the
economy, which lagged behind the rest of East-Central Europe. With BSP support
coming mostly from pensioners and the poor, the government was reluctant to cut
state subsidies and institute privatization. Communist-era holdovers control much
of privatized business, and corruption is rampant.

With foreign debt payments due, the currency (the lev) collapsing and requirements for support assistance from the International Monetary Fund (IMF) unmet,
the government has promised to close dozens of money-losing state enterprises,
throwing thousands out of work. However, by the end of September, the lev had
lost two-thirds of its value and inflation was running at nearly 20 percent a month.
The Central Bank tripled its interest rate to 300 percent.

Corruption and organized crime remain problems, and the Russian mafia is very active in Bulgaria. The murder of former Prime Minister Lukanov highlighted such activities. Though he allegedly had information on corruption in the Videnov government, Lukanov himself had amassed millions of dollars as a member of one of the shadowy economic groups tied to the state.

Political Rights and Civil Liberties:

Bulgarians can change their government democratically. The 1994 parliamentary elections and the 1996 presidential vote were free and fair. The constitution establishes a multiparty democracy. Over 160 parties exist, though many of them are inactive.

The media are proscribed from acting "to the detriment of the rights and reputations of others." In February, correspondents of the national dailies *Trud* and *24 chas* were arrested in southern Bulgaria and charged with libel for reporting on local corruption. Virtually all print media are in private hands, and about 1,400 publications operate countrywide. Over 60 private radio stations are broadcasting and three private national television broadcasters have been licensed. In July, the director-general of state-run Bulgarian National Television was dismissed by parliament after being accused of "disrespect for political forces." Some BSP legislators said he did not report favorably on the Videnov government.

In July parliament passed a controversial law on the electronic media, which was vetoed by then-president Zhelev and sent to the Constitutional Court for review in September. The law would allow the parliamentary majority to exercise absolute control over the state media and enable it to restrict the operation of the private media. The law would be implemented by the National Radio and Television Council. Seven members would be appointed by parliament and two each by the president and parliament. Political parties, trade unions, religious organizations and non-profit groups would be barred from broadcasting their own programs. However, political parties in parliament would have the right to two monthly nationwide five-minute addresses on state television. The Council would have the power to cancel programs and suspend licenses.

There is free public discussion, and no significant restrictions of freedom of association or assembly. Freedom of worship is generally respected, although the government regulates churches and religious institutions through the Directorate of Religious Beliefs. A 1994 law on registration led to 39 mostly Protestant associations losing their status as "juridical entities," thus barring them from re-registration. Human rights groups charged that the law violated Articles 12 and 13 of the constitution, which guarantee religious freedom and a separation of church and state. There were reports of discrimination against Turks, Roma (Gypsies) and Pomaks (ethnic Bulgarian Muslims).

Under the constitution, the judiciary is guaranteed independence, and equal status with the legislature and executive branch. A 1994 law stipulating that judges should have at least fifteen years' experience, thereby insuring that Communist-era holdovers remained on the bench, was declared unconstitutional. The Constitutional Court has struck down a number of government measures. Judges and prosecutors have discriminated on the basis of ethnicity in criminal procedures.

Bulgaria has two large labor union confederations, the Confederation of Independent Trade Unions (KNSB), a reform oriented movement that evolved from the

Communist-era union, and Podkrepa, an independent federation founded in 1989. Workers have the right to strike. Some 11,000 coal miners went on strike on March 20.

A 1995 United Nations-sponsored report ranked Bulgaria twentieth among 116 surveyed countries in women's opportunity to exercise power. The advanced rating in "women's opportunity for participation in political and economic decision-making" is due to the relatively large share of educated women holding administrative and managerial positions.

Burkina Faso

Polity: Dominant party **Political Rights:** 5
Economy: Mixed statist **Civil Liberties:** 4
Population: 10,623,000 **Status:** Partly Free
PPP: $780
Life Expectancy: 47.5
Ethnic Groups: Mossi, Gurunsi, Senufo, Lobi, Bobo, Mande, Fulani
Capital: Ouagadougou

Overview: Burkina Faso's political life continues to be dominated by President Blaise Compaoré and his ruling Organization for Popular Democracy/Labor Movement (ODP/MT) party. Burkinabé civil society is increasingly vibrant, however, and opposition political parties and independent media operate with little hindrance. Compaoré's flamboyant lifestyle and allegations of corruption have evoked discontent in the formal sector. The mostly agricultural population has benefited little from a fragile economic recovery.

Compaoré is the most recent of a string of Burkinabè soldiers to install himself as president at gunpoint since the country received independence from France in 1960 as Upper Volta. Compaoré's 1987 coup was the culmination of internecine strife within a junta that had seized power in 1983. The struggle for power included the murder of charismatic populist President Thomas Sankara and 13 of his closest associates. More Sankara supporters were executed two years later.

The Compaoré regime has left its bloody beginnings behind. Multiparty structures were introduced in a new 1991 constitution. However, the presidential election that followed in December 1991 was marred by widespread violence and an opposition boycott. Only about 25 percent of registered voters chose to cast ballots, and Compaoré was declared victor of the non-contest with a reported 85 percent of the vote. Legislative elections also drew a small turnout in May 1992, despite opposition participation, and the ODP/MT took 79 of 107 seats in the Assembly of People's Deputies.

Municipal elections in February 1995 were free and fair according to international observers, but made only a small dent in the ODP/MT's overall control. Opposition parties remain weak and divided as the 1997 legislative elections and 1998 presidential polls approach. Further local elections and decentralization are planned for the next two years. Despite the ruling party's dominance, repression has eased, although security forces sometimes engage in excesses with impunity.

Political Rights and Civil Liberties:

While Burkina Faso's 1991 constitution provides for free, multiparty elections, none have taken place. Serious irregularities, considerable violence and an opposition boycott marked the 1991 presidential vote. Legislative elections the next year went forward with opposition participation, but were not open enough to be considered fair. President Compaoré still holds most power, along with the ruling ODP/MT, whose top leaders were prominent in the military-dominated juntas that ruled the country from 1983-91. Few of the other 60 political parties have any meaningful influence. The Alliance for Democracy and the Federation (ADF), which holds five parliamentary seats, may run its leader, Herman Yaméogo, as a presidential candidate in 1998.

The increasing democratization of the last few years is perhaps most apparent in the vigorous independent media. A degree of self-censorship still prevails, but there are none of the broad libel and defamation laws to which other authoritarian African countries have resorted. Private radio stations and newspapers function with little interference from the government, and publications highly critical of the government are part of wide public debate.

Freedom of assembly is constitutionally protected and generally respected, with required permits usually issued as a matter of routine. Many non-governmental organizations operate openly and freely, including the Burkinabè Movement for Human Rights and Peoples (MBDHP) and several other human rights-oriented groups. The MBDHP has protested police brutality, which often goes unpunished. In May the shooting of a villager sparked anti-government rioting. No state religion is mandated and religious freedom is respected.

The Burkinabè judiciary lacks resources and training, but is considered generally independent in matters of civil and criminal law. Political cases are more susceptible to government influence. Legal limits on detention, search and seizure are routinely ignored by police, and national security laws allow a variety of special powers of arrest and surveillance. Prison conditions are very difficult and sometimes life-threatening, with overcrowding, poor diets and scant medical attention.

In rural areas, traditional courts often evoke customary law that discriminates against women to resolve civil and family disputes. Legal and constitutional protections for women's rights are lacking. Educational and wage employment opportunities for women are most limited in the countryside, and women hold few better-paying positions in the formal sector. Few women serve in parliament or senior government posts. Female genital mutilation is still common, despite a government campaign against the practice.

Workers in essential services are barred from joining unions, but most other workers enjoy a broad range of legal protections, including the right to strike. Several labor confederations and independent unions bargain with employers and conduct various job actions.

The government received considerable international debt relief in 1996, and hopes economic growth will reach 5 percent in 1997. Widespread perception of governmental corruption resulted in 1995 legislation that produced only nominal reassurance of government probity, with senior officials required to disclose their assets only in confidential documents filed with the supreme court. Allegations against senior officials persist, however, despite the appointment in May of a national ombudsman tasked with cleaning up the civil administration.

Burma (Myanmar)

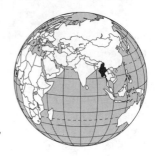

Polity: Military   **Political Rights:** 7
Economy: Mixed statist **Civil Liberties:** 7
Population: 45,976,000 **Status:** Not Free
PPP: $650
Life Expectancy: 57.9
Ethnic Groups: Burmese (68 percent), Karen (7 percent),
Shan (9 percent), Rakhine (4 percent), others
Capital: Rangoon

Overview: In 1996 Burma's ruling military junta twice carried out mass detentions of members of the National League for Democracy (NLD), the party headed by Nobel Laureate Aung San Suu Kyi that won free elections in 1990. On the eastern frontier the army forcibly expelled tens of thousands of villagers from their homes during counterinsurgency operations against ethnic-based rebel groups.

Following Japanese occupation in World War II, Burma achieved independence from the British in 1948. The army overthrew an elected government in 1962 amidst an economic crisis and threats from ethnic rebel groups.

During the next 26 years General Ne Win's Burmese Socialist Program Party (BSPP) turned one of Southeast Asia's richest countries into an impoverished backwater. In September 1988 the army cracked down on massive, peaceful pro-democracy demonstrations, killing some 3,000 people. Army leaders General Saw Maung and Brigadier General Khin Nyunt instituted military rule under the State Law and Order Restoration Council (SLORC). In July 1989 the SLORC placed Aung San Suu Kyi, the secretary general of the NLD and the country's foremost pro-democracy campaigner, under house arrest.

At the first free elections in three decades in May 1990, the NLD won 392 of the 485 parliamentary seats, while the SLORC-sponsored National Unity Party, the successor to the BSPP, won just 10. The SLORC refused to recognize the results and jailed hundreds of NLD members, including several elected MPs.

In 1992 the SLORC carried out a series of superficial liberalizations, including replacing hardliner Saw Maung with General Than Shwe as prime minister and junta leader and lifting a nationwide curfew. In January 1993 the SLORC opened a national convention to draft a constitution formalizing the military's leading role in politics. By June the tightly-controlled convention had drafted guidelines for a system with a president drawn from the army and holding broad executive powers, and granting the military one-quarter of the parliamentary seats.

In July 1995 the SLORC released Suu Kyi after six years of house arrest, but the generals subsequently rejected her calls for a dialogue on a democratic transition. In late November the junta reconvened the constitutional convention after a seven-month hiatus but the NLD, which had participated in earlier rounds, pulled out of the process. In 1996 the junta launched broad crackdowns on the NLD. In late May the authorities arrested 268 elected NLD MPs and supporters trying to attend the party's first congress since the 1990 elections. In late September the authorities detained upwards of 800 NLD supporters on the eve of a new party congress.

Since 1989 the SLORC has signed cease-fire deals with 15 ethnic-based rebel armies in the border areas. For decades these rebel armies have fought the central government for greater autonomy. The deals allow the armies to keep their weapons and territory, and many have entered the opium trade.

In January 1995 the army captured the headquarters of the Karen National Union (KNU), the strongest of the insurgent groups still active, in southeastern Karen state. In 1996 sporadic fighting continued between the KNU and the SLORC-backed Democratic Karen Buddhist Army, which launched several attacks on Karen refugees, church groups and schools. Meanwhile, in early May the army began burning and looting villages in eastern Karenni state, forcing thousands of ethnic Karenni from their homes. The army apparently sought to deprive the Karenni Nationalities People's Party, the second major active rebel group, of civilian support.

In another development, in January 1996 druglord Khun Sa "surrendered" to the government along with most of his 10,000-strong Mong Tai army in northeastern Shan state. Khun Sa reportedly received amnesty, the right to maintain a militia, and control over a smaller Shan territory.

Political Rights and Civil Liberties:

Burmese citizens cannot change their government democratically. The rule of law is nonexistent. Freedom of speech, press and association is severely restricted; trade unions, collective bargaining and strikes are illegal; and at least 1,000 political prisoners are in custody. The government is dominated by the majority Burman ethnic group and discriminates against minority groups through a strict citizenship law, and through language and other cultural restrictions.

Many of the most serious rights violations occur in border areas populated by ethnic minority groups. The army is responsible for arbitrary beatings and killings of civilians; the use of civilians as porters and human minesweepers under brutal conditions (with soldiers sometimes killing porters who are too weak to work, or executing those who refuse to become porters); summary executions of civilians who refuse to provide food or money to military units; the arrest of civilians as alleged insurgents or insurgent sympathizers; and rape of women by soldiers.

In July Human Rights Watch/Asia reported that the army had forced 70,000 people from their homes in Shan and Karenni states since March. Several thousand Karenni fled to Thailand, joining some 100,000 mostly Karen refugees already living in camps along the border. Several Karenni villagers were reportedly killed for disobeying an order to relocate from their homes by June 7. Dissidents reported that at least 150 Karenni died of illnesses in July at an army relocation site. Nearly one million residents of Rangoon, the capital, have been forcibly relocated to seven squalid satellite towns. In 1995 residents of Pagan, a tourist site, were forced to build new homes and relocate to a newly-created village.

Nearly 80 percent of the 270,000 Rohingya Muslim refugees from southwestern Arakan state who fled to Bangladesh in 1992 have been repatriated, but from January to May 1996, new army abuses against the minority group had forced about 10,000 to flee to Bangladesh. Thousands of Burmese women and young girls, many from ethnic minority groups, have been trafficked across the Thai border by criminal gangs to work in brothels.

Throughout the country the junta uses forced labor for building roads, railways and other public works, as well as beautification projects related to the official "Visit Myanmar Year" beginning in 1996. The laborers toil under harsh conditions and receive no compensation; in addition, they often must pay for their transportation, as well as bring their own food and tools and rent bulldozers.

There are persistent, credible reports of the use of forced, unpaid labor by Burmese military units protecting the construction of a foreign-financed natural gas pipeline that will transport offshore natural gas across Burma's southern peninsula to Thailand. The military units, who are using the forced labor to build infrastructure associated with the project, are also accused of rape and extrajudicial killings of villagers. Ethnic Karen rebels have launched several attacks on security forces and pipeline workers, and in June Radio Australia reported that at least ten ethnic Karen villagers had been killed by the army in retaliation for a rebel attack.

The Directorate of Defense Services Intelligence (DDSI) routinely searches homes, intercepts mail, and monitors telephone conversations. Universities are closely monitored. NLD members and other activists face difficulty in traveling around the country.

The judiciary is wracked by corruption and is not independent. Political trials do not meet minimum international standards of due process. Prison conditions are abysmal and torture of both criminals and political prisoners is routine. In late March 21 political prisoners received additional jail terms of five to 12 years each for trying to bring outside attention to their conditions. In June, James Nichols, an honorary consul in Burma for several European countries, and a friend of Suu Kyi, died in mysterious circumstances in prison after serving six weeks of a three-year sentence for unauthorized possession of fax machines. Reuters reported that the army forced officials at Rangoon's Roman Catholic Cathedral to cancel a planned memorial service.

The 1975 State Protection Law (as amended in 1992) permits detention without trial for up to five years. In 1996 detention and imprisonment of dissidents continued. Most of the 268 NLD members arrested in late May were released, but by early September an additional 60 people had been detained on political grounds. More than 30 people, including several who had been detained in the May crackdown, were sentenced to up to ten years imprisonment for peaceful acts including distributing pro-democracy pamphlets, videotaping impoverished conditions in the countryside, and distributing and viewing videotapes of Suu Kyi's public addresses.

Outdoor gatherings of five or more people are prohibited. In September the SLORC for the first time barred the weekly speeches to supporters that Suu Kyi had been making at her compound since her release from house arrest in July 1995. Following the May 1996 NLD congress these speeches had been attracting upwards of 10,000 people. In response the government organized pro-SLORC rallies and ceremonies in which attendance was compulsory for members of households, students and civil servants.

In a move clearly aimed at the NLD, on June 7 the junta announced decree 5/96, which authorized the Home Ministry to ban any organization violating the law against public gatherings or obstructing the drafting of a new constitution by the state-controlled national convention. The broadly drawn decree provides for jail terms of five to 20 years for anyone aiding activities "which adversely affect the national interest." In early October the government subjected unauthorized possession of a computer with Internet access ability, or the transmission of political or economic materials via the Internet without permission, to jail terms of between seven and 15 years.

Many of the 300 monks arrested during a violent October 1990 crackdown on monasteries remain in detention. Religious centers are closely monitored. Christians and Muslims have trouble openly practicing their religion, and the government occasionally orders their places of worship demolished.

Burundi

Polity: Civilian-military **Political Rights:** 7*
Economy: Statist **Civil Liberties:** 7
Population: 5,943,000 **Status:** Not Free
PPP: $670
Life Expectancy: 50.3
Ethnic Groups: Hutu (85 percent), Tutsi (14 percent),
Twa (pygmy) (1 percent)
Capital: Bujumbura
Ratings Change: Burundi's political rights rating changed from 6
to 7 because of a July military coup.

Overview: A July coup brought retired army Major Pierre Buyoya, a Tutsi, to power for a second time amidst a worsening conflict that has claimed thousands of lives and threatened to lead to massacres that could match Rwanda's 1994 genocide. Most Hutus have been driven from the capital, Bujumburi, and guerrilla fighting and abuses by both sides afflict the countryside. In a rare show of unified action, Burundi's neighbors imposed economic sanctions aimed at forcing the country's Tutsi-dominated military to restore at least a power-sharing arrangement with the Hutu majority. Buyoya's September decree legalizing political parties and restoring parliament had little apparent effect in either loosening sanctions or reducing attacks by Hutu guerrilla groups.

Burundi gained independence from Belgium in 1962 under a system that left political and military power mostly in the hands of the country's Tutsi minority. Waves of ethnic killings both by and against the country's ethnic Hutu majority have repeatedly torn the country since, sometimes sparked by similar ethnic confrontations in neighboring Rwanda. In 1987, Major Buyoya mounted his first coup, which was widely welcomed, against President Jean-Baptiste Bagaza. In June 1992, the Tutsi dominated Unity for National Progress (Uprona) party agreed to multiparty elections which were held one year later. Winning over 60 percent of the vote, Melchior Ndadaye, leading the Burundi Front for Democracy (Frodebu), defeated Major Buyoya to became the country's first Hutu president, also leading his party to a large victory in legislative elections.

Burundi's democratic transition was aborted in October 1993 when President Ndadaye and several other senior officials were murdered by Tutsi soldiers. Ethnic violence since has left more than 160,000 people dead. In April 1994, Ndadaye's successor, Cyprien Ntaryamira, was killed in a still-unexplained plane crash with Rwanda President Juvenal Habyarimana. The event marked the start of the anti-Tutsi genocide in Rwanda, and provoked more killings in Burundi. In October 1994, a forum of political and civic leaders chose Hutu politician Sylvestre Ntibantunganya as Burundi's new president under a power-sharing arrangement among the main political parties. Ntibantunganya was unable to impose control over a deteriorating situation in which he had little control over the country's Tutsi-led army, and even less control over various Hutu guerrilla forces (the most active are the Front for National Liberation, the National Council for the Defense of Democracy and Hutu People's Liberation Party) or the local militias and death squads from both groups.

Political Rights and Civil Liberties: In June 1993, Burundi citizens freely elected their president and legislative representatives to five year terms by secret ballot in the country's first open multiparty elections.

But the murders of Presidents Ndadaye and Cyprien Ntaryamira eventually led to the creation of a coalition government, which was overthrown by Major Buyoya in July. The national assembly, banned after the coup, is now nominally restored, but many of its members have fled the country.

Many of the newspapers published in Burundi's capital, Bujumbura, are little more than propaganda organs bankrolled by extremist parties and filled with ethnic diatribes and crude incitements to violence. A 1992 press law allows many restrictions of publications, but in practice is not enforced. Self-censorship is practiced by journalists who fear attacks or reprisals because of their reporting. Several journalists have fled Burundi after receiving death threats. Radio broadcasts are far more effective at reaching people, especially in the countryside, and have been a favorite mobilizing tool for Hutu radicals. International NGOs have helped set up independent local radio stations to broadcast non-partisan programs. There is little government interference in religious practice, or in the formation of political parties or associations, although private militias have been known to target even non-violent activists. The Burundi Human Rights Association (ITEKA), like other NGOs, cannot function effectively in the militarized and dangerous conditions that prevail in the country. The barely functioning judicial system is widely distrusted by the Hutu majority because of Tutsi predominance among judges and court officials.

Legal and customary discrimination affect women in Burundi. Inheritance laws allow women to be dispossessed; they also find it very difficult to find sources of credit. Their opportunities for education are fewer than men's, especially in the countryside; and even with laws providing for equal pay for equal work, few opportunities exist for women to advance in the formal sector. Violence against women is reported, but only anecdotal accounts of its prevalence are available.

Workers' rights to form unions are guaranteed by the constitution, and the labor code provides the right to strike. The sole labor confederation, the Organization of Free Unions of Burundi, has been independent since the emergence of the multiparty system in 1992. Most union members are civil servants and have bargained collectively with the government.

Cambodia

Polity: Monarchy, constituent assembly, and Khmer Rouge occupation
Economy: Statist
Population: 10,861,000
PPP: $1,250
Life Expectancy: 51.9
Ethnic Groups: Khmer (90 percent), Vietnamese (5 percent), Chinese (1 percent)
Capital: Phnom Penh

Political Rights: 6
Civil Liberties: 6
Status: Not Free

Overview: In 1996 co-premier Hun Sen's Cambodian People's Party (CPP) continued its authoritarian consolidation of power.

Cambodia achieved independence from France in 1953 under King Norodom Sihanouk. In 1970 premier Lon Nol ousted Sihanouk in a U.S.-supported bloodless coup. The Maoist Khmer Rouge seized power in April 1975 and subsequently caused as many as two million deaths through executions, overwork and starvation in a genocidal attempt to create a classless agrarian society. Vietnam invaded in December 1978 and installed the Communist Khmer People's Revolutionary Party (KPRP).

In 1982 Sihanouk, the Khmer Rouge and former premier Son Sann joined their armies against the KPRP. Several rounds of talks yielded a peace accord in Paris in October 1991. In May 1993 the country held free elections under United Nations protection, although the Khmer Rouge refused to participate. Voting for a 120-seat National Assembly gave the royalist opposition United Front for an Independent, Neutral and Free Cambodia (FUNCINPEC), headed by Prince Norodom Ranariddh, a Sihanouk son, 58 seats; Prime Minister Hun Sen's governing CPP, the successor to the KPRP, 51; Son Sann's Buddhist Liberal Democratic Party (BLDP), 10; and Moulinaka, a FUNCINPEC offshoot, 1.

In June 1993 a brief CPP-backed secessionist movement in seven eastern provinces convinced FUNCINPEC to share power with the ex-Communists, who still dominated the army and the bureaucracy. A compromise reached in September made Prince Ranariddh first prime minister and Hun Sen second prime minister. Sihanouk returned to the throne he abdicated in 1955 under a new constitution stipulating that the king "reigns but does not rule."

In October 1994 the government sacked outspoken reformist Finance Minister Sam Rainsy. In November 1995 the authorities ruled Rainsy's newly-formed Khmer Nation Party (KNP) illegal on technical grounds. In late November police arrested Prince Norodom Sirivudh, a reform-oriented FUNCINPEC leader, on trumped-up charges of plotting to kill Hun Sen. Sirivudh went into exile, but in February 1996 a court sentenced him in absentia to ten years imprisonment.

In early August 1996 Ieng Sary, the second most important Khmer Rouge leader, defected along with two commanders and some 4,000 troops. In the fall Hun Sen, overriding Prince Ranariddh's objections to embracing one of the leaders of the 1975-78 genocide, appeared ready to allow Ieng Sary to remain in control of territory in northwest Cambodia and possibly participate in the 1998 elections.

Political Rights and Civil Liberties: Cambodia's political and human rights situation has steadily deteriorated since the country held its freest elections ever in May 1993.

The CPP, nominally the junior member of the coalition government, effectively runs the country through its control of the army, the police, the administrative bureaucracy, the judiciary and the provincial and village posts. The CPP has carried out politically-related murders with impunity. Official corruption is widespread and the country is becoming a regional center for money-laundering and the drug trade.

In 1994 the government formally outlawed the Khmer Rouge, which is weakened by defections and a loss of external support. The group rules its territory in a brutal manner, denying basic rights, banning Buddhist religious practices and confiscating private property. Dozens of civilians have been killed since the 1991 peace treaty as a result of indiscriminate shelling by both the army and the Khmer Rouge.

The rule of law is especially weak in the countryside. Regular army soldiers and Khmer Rouge guerrillas carry out rape, extortion, banditry and extrajudicial killings with impunity. A UN report leaked in August 1994 described a reign of terror by army units in northwestern Cambodia that included the extrajudicial execution of 35 civilians.

The CPP has blocked the planned establishment of a judicial council to decide the constitutionality of new laws. The judiciary is not independent of the government; due process rights fall short of international norms; and torture of detainees is routine. Prisons are dangerously overcrowded and unsanitary, and inmates are frequently abused.

Journalists are routinely harassed and threatened, and there have been no convictions in the cases of three journalists murdered since 1993. On February 8, 1996, gunmen shot and seriously wounded Ek Mongkol, a broadcaster on a FUNCINPEC-owned radio station who had criticized government inaction over alleged Vietnamese incursions into eastern Cambodia.

The July 1995 press law permits the government to suspend publication of a newspaper for up to one month without a court order, authorizes fines for broadly-drawn offenses, and permits the courts to invoke criminal sanctions against the media. In February 1996 the authorities suspended the anti-monarchist *Republic News* for one month.

In June 1996 the government rejected the KNP's request to set up a radio station, and in July it suspended authorization of new radio or television stations, citing crowded airwaves. The authorities also indefinitely suspended the establishment of any new newspapers.

Harassment against the KNP in 1996 included a January police raid on party headquarters in Phnom Penh; the May 18 murder of Thun Bunly, a KNP official and former newspaper editor; and in June the forcible prevention of the opening of a pair of party offices in central Kandal province, and an attack by thugs on a new office in eastern Prey Veng province. Meanwhile, on May 15 a mob looted a FUNCINPEC office in the northern town of Ratanakiri, and several days later police unlawfully entered the homes of several FUNCINPEC leaders in Siem Reap province.

In April the Interior Ministry ordered all political parties except the four represented in parliament to suspend their operations pending re-registration. Although in May the government annulled this order, it apparently left intact a clause ordering provincial authorities to report on the activities of nongovernmental organizations and aid agencies.

The constitution refers only to the rights of the ethnic Khmer majority, complicating the legal status of the estimated 200-500,000 Vietnamese residents. The Khmer Rouge has massacred scores of Vietnamese villagers in recent years.

Domestic violence is common. Several thousand street children live in Phnom Penh and child prostitution is increasing. Trade union activity is minimal and labor laws are rarely enforced. In late October the U.S.-based AFL-CIO cited Cambodia for child labor, forced labor, physical abuse of workers, denial of overtime wages, and poor working conditions.

Cameroon

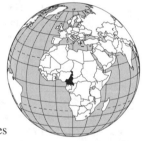

Polity: Dominant party
Economy: Capitalist
Population: 13,609,000
PPP: $2,220
Life Expectancy: 56.3
Ethnic Groups: Adamawa, Bamileke, Beti, Dzem, Fulani, Mandari, Shouwa, other—over 100 tribes and 24 languages
Capital: Yaounde

Political Rights: 7
Civil Liberties: 5
Status: Not Free

Overview: **P**resident Paul Biya's authoritarian rule was challenged by decisive victories by opposition parties in local elections in 1996. Constitutional amendments adopted in December 1995 have concentrated even more power in the presidency and only nominally strengthened a compliant judiciary. A sustained assault on the independent media continued, and the regime used physical and administrative intimidation to try to cripple opposition political parties in advance of presidential and parliamentary elections set for 1997.

Cameroon's population is distributed not only among nearly 200 ethnic groups, but also divided among people who use English or French as a second language. Cameroon was a German colony from 1884 until 1916. After being seized in World War I and administered by Britain and France, distinct Anglophone and Francophone areas were reunited in an independent country in 1961. About a quarter of Cameroon's 13 million people are Anglophone, and this linguistic distinction is, arguably, the country's most potent political division. The uncertain delineation of the country's western frontier sparked clashes with Nigeria on the oil-rich Bokassi Peninsula, a dispute now under consideration by the International Court of Justice.

Cameroon was ruled from independence under a repressive one-party system until 1992, when President Biya agreed to hold multiparty elections. Biya's Cameroon People's Democratic Movement (CPDM) won the largest number of seats after a truncated parliamentary campaign in March 1992 that was boycotted by the main opposition party, the Social Democratic Front (SDF), whose leader, John Fru Ndi, charged serious irregularities in election preparation. The presidential election that returned Biya to office in October 1992 was even more clearly fraudulent. Biya imposed a state of emergency to quell widespread protests and detained opposition candidate Fru Ndi for three months.

The fragmented opposition has renewed its efforts to present a united front for the 1997 elections, although this is complicated by the country's linguistic divide and the existence of about 100 mostly small parties. These rivalries bolster Biya, presently serving a one-year term as chairman of the Organization of African Unity.

Political Rights and Civil Liberties: Cameroon is constitutionally a multiparty republic, but its citizens have been unable to change their government by democratic means. The 1992 legislative and presidential elections were marked by serious irregularities and outright fraud, and cannot be taken to genuinely represent the will of the people. The National Assembly meets for only two months each year. The president rules by decree and the parliamentary opposition is largely superfluous to the lawmaking process.

Nearly all power is held by President Biya and a small coterie of ruling CPDM members, mostly from the president's own Beti ethnic group. Biya's sweeping decree power and the executive's control of the judiciary offer little legal recourse to Cameroonians seeking justice in their country's courts. The judiciary is part of the executive branch. Provincial and local administrators are appointed by the government. The courts and the local administration are often corrupt and subject to heavy political influence from the center.

Biya sought to subvert opposition gains in the January 1996 municipal elections by appointing a new layer of local administrators reporting directly to the president. There is little confidence that the 1997 presidential and parliamentary elections will be free or fair. All elections are conducted by the Ministry of Territorial Administration, dominated by the ruling CPDM. The leaders of the opposition parties complain of irregularities in voter registration and a lack of access to state-run broadcast media, and have demanded the creation of an independent election commission. The regime has also restricted opposition activities by refusing to allow or breaking up political meetings.

The lack of free media has political consequences. The regime maintains a tight monopoly on broadcasting, crucial in a largely rural country with low literacy. It also censors, suspends and shuts down independent publications, and in 1996 the regime's harassment of the independent media intensified. A 1990 press law formalized pre-publication censorship. New legislation in 1995 complicated licensing procedures. It also expanded government seizure and banning powers "where there is conflict with the principles of public policy," and against publications that endanger "public order" or violate undefined "accepted standards of good behavior/values." Publications are suspended and individual editions are occasionally confiscated, or arrive filled with blank spaces where censors ordered cuts. In October, journalist Eyoum Ngange of the newspaper *Le Messager* was sentenced to a year's imprisonment, and his editor, Pius Njawe, to six months, for "defamation" against President Biya. In August, another editor, Paddy Mbawa of the daily *Cameroon Post,* was released from jail after serving 11 months, but faces seven more charges. Also in August, *La Détente* publisher Samuel Eleme and his assistant Gaston Ekwalla were each imprisoned for five months, and the newspaper was suspended for six months. A number of other journalists were convicted on libel charges and sentenced to prison terms ranging from five to 24 months.

Intimidation and arrests of opposition activists, as well as anyone engaged in advocacy and social work, continued, but numerous nongovernmental organizations still operated, including the Organization for Freedom of the Press in Cameroon, the National League for Human Rights, the Organization for Human Rights and Freedoms, the Human Rights Clinic and Education Center and the Association of Women against Violence. Freedom of religion is generally respected, but most other civil liberties remain at risk. Indefinite pretrial detention is permitted after a warrant is issued.

Members of President Biya's Beti ethnic group often receive preference in employment, and English-speakers complain of systemic discrimination that divests them of a real voice in government. Indigenous pygmy peoples often work under conditions that amount to slave labor. Reports of actual slavery persist from the country's northern areas, where traditional chiefs still hold many powers and even run their own courts and prisons, which have been used against the regime's political opponents. Prison conditions there and in government prisons are reportedly extremely harsh.

Women are often denied inheritance and land ownership rights even where these are codified. Wife-beating and violence against women in general are reportedly widespread. Many laws contain unequal provisions and penalties based on sex.

The 1992 labor code permits trade union formation, but some provisions of the code have never been implemented and many government workers are not covered. The Confederation of Cameroonian Trade Unions(CCTU) is technically independent, but the government intervened to oust its leader in 1994 when he attempted to pursue policies that displeased the ruling party. The regime created another labor confederation, the misnamed Union of Free Trade Unions of Cameroon (USLC), to undercut union independence further.

Corruption and the lack of independent courts limit business development in Cameroon, and have deterred new investors and slowed the release of international financial support. The country enjoys income from petroleum, forests and other natural resources, but has been unable to meet IMF and World Bank targets for economic reform.

Canada

Polity: Federal
parliamentary democracy
Economy: Capitalist
Population: 29,965,000
PPP: $20,950
Life Expectancy: 77.5

Political Rights: 1
Civil Liberties: 1
Status: Free

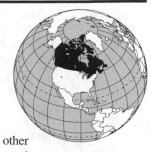

Ethnic Groups: British (40 percent), French (27 percent), other
European (20 percent), Asian, aboriginal or native (Indian and
Inuit) (1.5 percent), Caribbean black, others
Capital: Ottawa

Overview: While separatist sentiments among Quebecois remained
strong after last year's divisive referendum on independence
for the province, Quebec Premier Lucien Bouchard focused
on more pressing economic issues in 1996. Equally taken with economic matters,
Prime Minister Jean Chretien's Liberal Party government began scaling back
Canada's welfare system.

Colonized by both France and Great Britain in the seventeenth and eighteenth
centuries, Canada came under the control of Britain with the Treaty of Paris in 1763.
After granting home rule in 1867, Britain retained a theoretical right to overrule the
Canadian Parliament until 1982, when Canadians established complete control over
their own constitution. The British monarch remains nominal head of state, represented by a ceremonial governor-general appointed by the prime minister.

**Political Rights
and Civil Liberties:**
Canadians can change their government democratically.
Due to government canvassing, Canada has nearly 100
percent effective voter registration. Prisoners have the
right to vote in federal elections, as do citizens who have
lived abroad for less than five years. In the 1993 elections, the government held
three days of advance voting for people unable to vote on election day.

A federal law prohibiting the broadcasting of public opinion poll results two
days prior to and during federal elections was upheld in 1995. However, a 1988
Tobacco Products Control Act limiting all forms of cigarette advertisement was
struck down as a violation of free speech. Other limitations on expression range
from unevenly enforced "hate laws" and restrictions on pornography to rules on
reporting. The media are generally free, although they exercise self-censorship in
areas such as violence on television.

Civil liberties are protected by the federal Charter of Rights and Freedoms, but
limited by the constitutional "notwithstanding clause," which permits provincial
governments to exempt themselves from applying individual provisions within their
jurisdictions. Quebec has used the clause to retain its provincial language law, which
restricts the use of English on outdoor commercial signs. The provincial governments, with their own constitutions and legislative assemblies, exercise significant
autonomy. Each has its own judicial system as well, with the right of appeal to the

Supreme Court of Canada.

In May, Canadian legislators voted overwhelmingly to amend the constitution to outlaw discrimination based on "sexual orientation," adding that term to a list under the Human Rights Act of 1977 that includes age, sex, race, religion and disability. The vote was hailed by gay rights activists as "an important step," while conservative groups voiced concerns that the measure would "start down the slippery slope" towards the official sanctioning of gay marriage. The government stressed the limited nature of the change, and emphasized that the legislation was not intended to give legal status to same-sex marriage.

Despite a series of cuts in 1996 aimed at balancing the national ledger, Canada continues to boast a generous welfare system that supplements the largely open, competitive economy. Property rights for current occupants are generally strong, but increasing Indian land claims have led to litigation and strained relations between the government and Canadian Indians. Increased dissatisfaction with the state of Indian affairs in Canada was voiced by the Assembly of First Nations, the nationwide organization representing the estimated 600,000 Indians who live on 633 reservations in Canada, in the wake of a government-conducted poll that suggested that Canadians' attitudes toward Indians was hardening. Ovide Mercredi, national chief of the Assembly, called for Indians to emulate French-speaking Quebec in pushing for greater sovereignty.

Trade unions and business associations are free and well-organized.

Religious expression is free and diverse, but there has been some controversy in recent years concerning religious education. Many provinces have state-supported religious school systems that do not represent all denominations. Legislation in Newfoundland to reform the system, creating nondenominational schools and eliminating religious affiliation as a criterion for hiring teachers, has met resistance from religious groups who fear it will set a precedent making all church-run school systems vulnerable to court challenges. Other controversies center on government recognition of holy days, particularly in regard to closing schools and government offices for Muslim observances.

Despite restrictions announced in 1994, the flow of immigrants into the country remains strong. Canada has expanded the opportunities for political asylum to include refuge on the grounds of spousal abuse and sexual orientation.

Cape Verde

Polity: Presidential-par-
liamentary democracy
Economy: Mixed statist
Population: 403,000
PPP: $1,820
Life Expectancy: 64.9
Ethnic Groups: Creole (71 percent), black (28 percent),
European (1 percent)
Capital: Praia

Political Rights: 1
Civil Liberties: 2
Status: Free

Overview:

President Antonio Mascarenhas Monteiro won a second five-year term in an unopposed February election that drew only a sparse turnout among this island nation's 400,000 people. The low participation was variously ascribed to voter fatigue after parliamentary and legislative polls in the two preceding months, and to preparations for a major festival. Despite the lack of enthusiasm displayed for the presidential poll, Cape Verde's transition to multiparty democracy, begun in 1991, now seems successful.

In the December 1995 multiparty legislative elections, only the second since gaining independence from Portugal in 1975, the ruling Movement for Democracy (MPD) was returned to power, winning 59 percent of the vote and 50 of 72 seats. Prime Minister Carlos Alberto Wahnon de Carvalho Veiga has continued with free market policies which may stimulate development in one of Africa's smallest and poorest nations. His new administration, however, has been tainted by allegations of high-level corruption.

The MPD's renewed mandate came after a 1991 landslide victory in the first democratic legislative elections after 16 years of Marxist, one-party rule by the African Party for the Independence of Cape Verde (PAICV). Cape Verde was the first former Portuguese colony in Africa to abandon the Marxist political and economic system. It has attracted foreign investment through tax incentives and has enjoyed rising exports and tourism. Extensive plans for infrastructure improvements have recently been implemented to assist in private-sector development. Cape Verde has few exploitable natural resources, and must rely heavily on food imports. Many citizens work abroad, and their remittances, along with foreign aid, are an important source of national income.

**Political Rights
and Civil Liberties:**

Cape Verdeans are able to change their government by democratic means in open elections. The president and members of the National People's Assembly, including six representatives chosen by citizens living abroad, are elected through universal suffrage. Elections since the 1991 transition to multiparty democracy have been free and fair. The new constitution adopted in 1992 greatly reduced the formal powers of the presidency, leaving it little authority other than to delay ratification of legislation, propose amendments and dissolve parliament after a vote of no confidence. Popular referenda are permitted in some circumstances, but may not challenge individual liberties or the rights of opposition parties.

There are no reported political prisoners in Cape Verde, and two human rights groups, the National Commission of the Rights of Man and the Cape Verdean League for Human Rights, operate openly.

The judiciary is independent, comprised of a Supreme Court and regional courts that generally adjudicate criminal and civil cases fairly, though sometimes with long delays. Defendants are presumed innocent until proven guilty, and trials are public, with free legal counsel provided to indigents. Judges must lay charges within 24 hours of arrests. The police, until 1994 controlled by the military, are now a separate institution answerable to civilian authority.

The freedom of peaceful assembly and association is guaranteed and respected. Workers are free to form and join independent unions without restriction. Union members possess the constitutional right to strike and the freedom to affiliate with international organizations.

The vast majority of Cape Verdeans belongs to the Roman Catholic Church. The constitution requires the separation of church and state. Religious rights are respected in practice.

Freedom of expression and of the press is guaranteed, and generally respected in practice. Newspapers and other publications may be established without authorization. National Assembly sessions, including sharp attacks by opposition members, are broadcast live via radio in their entirety. However, the most widely read newspaper, along with radio and television, is state-controlled, and criticism of the government is restrained by self-censorship reinforced by fear of demotion or dismissal. Government officials have so far unsuccessfully also sought to use libel charges to silence opposition newspapers.

Discrimination against women persists, despite legal prohibitions against gender discrimination as well as provisions for social and economic equality. Especially in rural areas where illiteracy is high, many women neither know their rights nor possess the means to seek redress. There is less pay for equal work, exclusion from traditionally male professions and allegedly common but little-reported domestic violence. There are also serious concerns about child abuse and the prevalence of child labor. Local nongovernmental organizations, with international assistance, have recently mounted campaigns to promote women's civil and human rights, along with awareness about child abuse.

Central African Republic

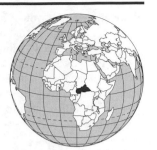

Polity: Presidential-par-
liamentary democracy
Economy: Capitalist-
statist
Population: 3,274,000
PPP: $1,050
Life Expectancy: 49.5
Ethnic Groups: Baya (34 percent), Banda (27 percent),
Mandja (21 percent), Sara (10 percent)
Capital: Bangui

Political Rights: 3
Civil Liberties: 5*
Status: Partly Free

Rating Change: The Central African Republic's civil liberties rating changed from 4 to 5 because mutinous soldiers caused the security situation in the capital to deteriorate, and indications mounted that unrest is spreading along ethnic lines.

Overview: The elected government of the Central African Republic (CAR) was badly shaken in 1996 by three army mutinies, the second of which, in May, garnered broad popular support and was suppressed only by French military intervention. Economic problems and corruption have prompted numerous strikes, hampered multiparty governance and showed the CAR's renewed democracy to be fragile. A national conference held in August brought pledges of army reforms and better administration. However, even with half his six-year term of office remaining, President Ange-Félix Patassé appears politically paralyzed. New and nominally independent Prime Minister Jean-Paul Ngoupande heads the cabinet of a "national unity government" dominated by the ruling Central African People's Liberation Movement (MLPC) party. The main opposition alliance, the Central African Combined Democratic Opposition (Codepo), has refused to follow several smaller parties into the government.

The Central African Republic, a Texas-sized country of just 3.3 million people, gained independence from France in 1960 after a history of colonial exploitation terrible even for the times. Colonel Jean-Bedel Bokassa seized power in 1966 and imposed an increasingly bizarre personal dictatorship upon the renamed Central African Empire. French support waned only after Bokassa began murdering schoolchildren; French troops ousted him in 1979. His French-installed successor lost favor in Paris and was deposed by General André Kolingba in 1981. Kolingba introduced the facade of civilian rule, and eventually agreed to introduce a multiparty system which led to democratic elections in 1993. The effects of autocratic rule still linger, however, and the country's media, judiciary and civil service are far from real independence.

International lenders and investors whose funding is crucial to the impoverished CAR were shaken by the massive looting and destruction that accompanied the army mutinies. France's intervention to preserve the Patassé government met popular anger, marked by the burning of the French cultural center. France maintains two garrisons in CAR that are crucial for its intervention capabilities throughout the region. Reports in 1995 indicated the CAR has been used as a staging point for retraining and rearming Hutu extremists who fled Rwanda in 1994.

Political Rights and Civil Liberties:

In 1993, the CAR's people chose their government in open and democratic elections under the 1986 constitution for the first time. President Patassé's victory was not matched by a clear triumph for his party in the 85-seat national assembly, and his MLPC party's uncertain mandate has created tensions and a weak coalition with several smaller parties. There are over 20 officially registered parties.

A national referendum in December 1994 adopted a new constitution that promises judicial and legislative autonomy and safeguards the multiparty system. Parliamentary elections set for August 1998 and the following year's presidential contest will test the strength of the new institutions. Ethnic divisions may divert attention from issues and could provoke further armed intervention in the political process.

The state dominates the broadcast media; opposition activities are sometimes reported but rarely given prominence. The only licensed private radio stations are music- or religion-oriented. Private print media have suffered little direct interference from the new government, and at least a dozen newspapers publish with various regularity. In September, however, Marcel Mocoapi, director of the daily *Le Novateur,* was detained for questioning after criticizing judicial conduct. In 1995 an opposition newspaper editor was jailed for two years on charges of insulting President Patassé. Other strongly partisan newspapers publish political statements and critiques from various parties. But the independent print media have no sound financial base to guarantee their independence, and in a vast country with low literacy, they carry little impact beyond the capital, Bangui.

Open public discussion is permitted, and freedom of assembly, while constitutionally guaranteed, is not always honored by authorities. Public meetings must be registered 48 hours in advance. At least 23 officially registered political parties are active in varying degrees. Many other nongovernmental organizations, including human rights groups such as the Central African Human Rights League and the Movement for the Defense of Human Rights and Humanitarian Action, operate without interference. Religious freedom is respected, although religious groups must register with the government and the broad prohibitions against "fundamentalism" could provide scope for official restrictions on worship.

Judicial institutions suffer from lack of training, corruption and political interference. Legal restrictions on searches and detention are often ignored. Police brutality is also a serious problem, and conditions for prisoners, including large numbers of long-term pre-trial detainees, are extremely difficult.

Constitutional guarantees for women's rights are not reflected in reality. Especially in rural areas, educational, employment and other economic opportunities for women are far less than those available to men. Societal discrimination in many areas relegates women to the status of second-class citizens. Female genital mutilation is still practiced.

The CAR's formal economic sector is small. The government is the largest single employer, and government employee trade unions have been especially active. The labor code protects the right of all workers to form or join unions of their choice. Five labor federations compete for union affiliates. Unions may call strikes, but only after a conciliation process. While collective bargaining is not specifically protected, unions have negotiated wage agreements, although the government still sets wage guidelines in consultation with employers and unions.

Economic opportunity is limited by the country's low level of development. However, output and prices for the agricultural commodities which bring most of the county's export earnings have revived. Prime Minister Ngoupande is trying to meet the demands of the World Bank and other international lenders and donors by instituting civil service reforms and more rational financial and economic planning.

Chad

Polity: Interim legislature (military-dominated) (transitional)
Economy: Capitalist
Population: 6,543,000
PPP: $690
Life Expectancy: 47.7
Ethnic Groups: Arab, Bagirmi, Sara,Wadai, Zaghawa, Bideyat Gorane, 200 distinct groups
Capital: N'Djamena

Political Rights: 6
Civil Liberties: 5
Status: Not Free

Overview:

President Idriss Déby's July victory in Chad's first multiparty election was marred by serious irregularities that eroded confidence in both the electoral process and Déby's mandate. The election was strongly supported by France, and accepted by some observer groups as legitimate. Other groups denounced the polls, noting the disqualification of several credible challengers, the intimidation of opposition activists and manipulation of the vote count. Legislative elections scheduled for December were postponed until early 1997.

Chad's transition towards a genuine multiparty system remains tenuous. A trend toward greater openness faltered due to repression and government violence. While peace pacts brought an uncertain calm to several areas of the countryside, the brutal guerrilla conflicts continued to cause suffering in other parts.

Since achieving its independence from France in 1960, Chad has been in a state of almost constant war. External interference and clan rivalries have exacerbated ethnic and religious differences. The country is roughly split between Nilotic and Bantu Christian farmers who inhabit the country's south, and Arab and Saharan peoples who occupy vast areas in the north.

Chad's 6.5 million people are comprised of over 200 ethnic groups, but the army, and thus today its political life, is dominated by members of two small groups—the Zaghawa and the Bideyat—from President Déby's northeastern region. The security forces are not subject to the rule of law and constitutional authority, and it is not clear that the formality of President Déby's flawed transformation into an elected leader will change this.

In June and July 1996, Chadians voted for their president in multiparty elections for the first time. France helped, deploying soldiers stationed in Chad for logistical assistance. It is impossible to ascertain if President Déby's victory, with 69 percent of the vote, was credible. Seven of the 13 candidates eliminated in the first round urged their supporters to boycott the run-off to protest alleged irregularities.

Opposition efforts to organize suffered from intimidation and harassment by the National Security Agency (ANS) and other security agencies, and counting of absentee ballots was particularly suspect. State control of broadcast media allowed little exposure for dissenting views, especially important in a vast country where most people can neither read nor afford to buy the few newspapers available.

Political Rights and Civil Liberties:

Chad knows no tradition of peaceful and orderly transference of political power. President Idriss Déby himself first gained power through the gun, overthrowing Hissein Habré in December 1990. Déby lifted the ban on political parties in 1993, convening a national conference that included a broad array of civic and political groups, including his own Patriotic Salvation Movement (MPS), which controlled the transitional parliament. Over 60 political parties are now registered. Thirty form the Republican Front, which backs President Déby, and the Coordination of the Democratic Opposition (COD) alliance comprises 17 parties.

The human rights situation in Chad is grim. Amnesty International called for an impartial investigation into the assassination on August 16 in the capital, N'Djamena, of opposition politician Bichara Digui. The group also demanded an end to what it described as widespread violence with impunity by Chadian security forces, and urged France to seek to curb such excesses. In 1995, Amnesty called on the United States, France and China to end all weapons sales to Chad, which was a major recipient of Western arms aid during its border wars with Libya in the 1980s. Some of the worst violations are blamed on Déby's elite presidential guard, and tens of thousands of Chadians have fled their country to escape the violence.

In 1996, President Déby reached peace pacts with several of the two dozen or more armed factions conducting rebellions of varying intensities against his government. In August, a faction of one of the most significant southern rebel groups, the Armed Forces for the Federal Republic, renounced the armed struggle and formed a political party, the Patriotic Front for Democracy. It is hoped that the settlement can reduce abuses in the southern districts where many of the worst human rights abuses have been reported.

A number of such agreements have been made in the past, however. Banditry contributes to the pervasive insecurity; Chad's long and porous borders are not easily policed, and trade in weapons is rife among the nomadic Sahelian peoples. In a May 1995 report, Amnesty International charged that over 1,500 civilians have been murdered by government forces over the past five years.

Several human rights groups operate openly and publish findings critical of the government. Investigations by international human rights groups have also been allowed, but their findings have been dismissed. The record on labor rights is also mixed. Few Chadians participate in the formal economy and union membership is low, but the right to organize and to strike is generally respected—yet the Federation of Chadian Unions (UST) was banned for four weeks after denouncing the conduct of the presidential election.

Freedom of religion is generally respected in Chad, although religion remains one of the markers dividing the society. Women's rights, however, are protected neither by traditional law nor in the penal code. The traditional practice of female genital mutilation is commonplace. The literacy rate for women is very low, and few educational opportunities are available, especially in rural areas.

Chile

Polity: Presidential-
legislative democracy
Economy: Capitalist
Population: 14,470,000
PPP: $8,900
Life Expectancy: 73.9
Ethnic Groups: Mestizo, Spanish, other European, Indian
Capital: Santiago

Political Rights: 2
Civil Liberties: 2
Status: Free

Overview:

Constitutional reforms proposed by President Eduardo Frei in August 1995 were defeated by the Chilean Congress in April. The reforms were intended to eliminate some of the most egregious features of the 1980 constitution imposed by the military dictatorship under President Augusto Pinochet, such as the provision for nine appointed senatorial seats occupied by Pinochet designees until 1998.

The Republic of Chile was founded after independence from Spain in 1818. Democratic rule predominated in this century until the 1973 overthrow of Salvador Allende by the military under Pinochet.

The 1980 constitution provided for a plebiscite in which voters could reject another presidential term for Pinochet. In 1988, 55 percent of voters said "no" to eight more years of military rule, and competitive presidential and legislative elections were scheduled for 1989.

Following the 1989 and 1994 constitutional reforms, presidents are elected for six years. There is a bicameral Congress with a 120-member Chamber of Deputies elected for four years and a Senate with 38 senators elected for eight years, with eight appointed by the government for eight years.

In 1989 Patricio Aylwin, the candidate of the center-left Concertacion for Democracy, was elected president over two right-wing candidates, and the Concertacion won a majority in the Chamber. But with eight senators appointed by the outgoing military government, it fell short of a Senate majority.

Aylwin oversaw a broadly representative, remarkably clean government that was responsive to a wide social base—but efforts to reform the constitution, so as to prevent Pinochet and other military chiefs from remaining at their posts until 1997, were stopped by the right-wing Senate bloc.

Frei, a 52-year-old businessman, was the Concertacion candidate in the December 1993 elections and won easily over right-wing candidate Arturo Alessandri. Frei vowed to establish full civilian control over the military, but like Aylwin he did not have the numbers in Congress. In 1993 the Concertacion lost a Senate seat and two Chamber seats, leaving it even farther from the two-thirds majority needed for constitutional reform. It duly failed to pass Congress in April even though 60 percent of the population supported it.

The military defied a June 1995 Supreme Court ruling that General Manuel Contreras, Pinochet's former secret police chief, be jailed for the 1976 murder of opposition leader Orlando Letelier in Washington, D.C. Contreras was finally jailed in October, but only after much saber-rattling by Pinochet, and after Frei's retreat from demanding full accountability for rights violations under military rule.

Political Rights and Civil Liberties: Citizens can change their government democratically. Democratic institutions are better established than in any other Latin American country outside of Costa Rica.

However, while reformed in some aspects, the 1980 constitution installed under Pinochet still limits civilian authority over the armed forces. The president cannot change armed forces commanders until 1997 or reduce the military budget. The constitution also allowed the former Pinochet regime to appoint eight senators to eight-year terms in 1989.

In 1990 a Truth and Reconciliation Commission was formed to investigate rights violations committed under military rule. The Commission's report implicated the highest level military and secret police in the deaths or disappearances of 2,279 people between September 1973 and March 1990. However, in 1978 the Pinochet regime had issued an amnesty for all political crimes, and the Supreme Court, packed by Pinochet before leaving office, has blocked all government efforts to lift it.

The amnesty has not stopped civilian governments from investigating rights cases. Hundreds of cases involving incidents after 1978 have been brought to civilian courts, resulting in a handful of convictions. In late 1995, however, the Supreme Court, possibly under pressure from the military, began dismissing dozens of cases with increasing speed, and without the depth of investigation it had exhibited previously.

In 1991 the Court made a dramatic turnaround in the special case of the 1976 murder in Washington of former Chilean ambassador to the U.S., Orlando Letelier. The Court ruled that the alleged authors of the crime---former secret police chief and retired General Manuel Contreras and Colonel Pedro Espinosa---be tried in civilian courts. Both were convicted in November 1993, the first time a civil court had convicted ranking officers for crimes committed under military rule. They were sentenced to seven and six years in prison, respectively.

The deaths of three teenage inmates in August during uprisings in jails in the south of the country drew attention to prison conditions. In addition, an opposition politician accused prison officials of infecting inmates with the HIV virus by using contaminated needles.

Most laws limiting political expression and civil liberties were eliminated by constitutional reforms in 1989. Media freedom was almost fully restored. Scores of publications represent all points of view. Radio is both private and public. The national television network is state-run, but open to all political voices. Universities run three non-commercial television stations.

However, a journalists' licensing law remains in place, and a number of restrictive laws remain in effect, including one granting military courts power to convict journalists or others for sedition or for libeling members of the military.

The draconian 1978 labor code has undergone significant reform. Strikes are legal, but organizational and collective bargaining provisions remain weak. The Frei administration has proposed reforms to strengthen labor rights guarantees, but in 1995 the right-wing bloc in Congress was still able to block the legislation.

Sporadic actions by remnants of the Manuel Rodriguez Patriotic Front (FPMR), the former armed wing of the Communist Party, continue. Human rights groups remain concerned about anti-terrorist legislation that broadened police powers. Reports of police abuses still are registered frequently, including those of torture and use of excessive force against political demonstrators, but there are also signs of greater accountability.

Implementation of a 1993 indigenous rights law has been slow because of lack of resources, according to the government.

China

Polity: Communist one-party
Economy: Mixed statist
Population: 1,213,026,000
PPP: $2,330
Life Expectancy: 68.6
Ethnic Groups: Han Chinese (93 percent), Azhuang, Hui, Uygur, Yi, Miao, Manchu, Tibetan, Mongolian, others
Capital: Beijing

Political Rights: 7
Civil Liberties: 7
Status: Not Free

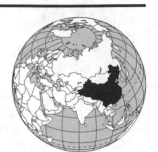

Overview: In 1996 the Chinese government continued to wield the full apparatus of state power against pro-democracy campaigners, ethnic separatists in predominantly Muslim Xinjiang province and independent religious groups.

Following decades of civil war, Chinese Communist Party (CCP) Chairman Mao Zedong proclaimed the People's Republic of China on October 1, 1949, upon victory over the Nationalist Kuomintang. The Great Leap Forward of 1958-60, Mao's attempt to accelerate industrialization and agricultural collectivization, created a rural famine that killed millions of peasants. In the Maoist Cultural Revolution (1966-76), which was a protracted intra-party struggle, up to one million people died and millions more were victimized. Following Mao's death in 1976 CCP general secretary Deng Xiaoping assumed control, and in late 1978 he began to introduce free market reforms.

Weeks of protests in Spring 1989 demanding democratic reforms and an end to runaway inflation ended with a bloody army assault on Tiananmen Square on June 3-4 in which hundreds, perhaps thousands, were killed. Hardliner Jiang Zemin replaced the relatively moderate Zhao Ziyang as CCP secretary general.

After a period of retrenchment in which hardliners appeared to control policy decisions, in 1992 Deng endeavored to make the economic reforms irreversible after his death, beginning with a highly-symbolic visit in January to two Special Economic Zones in the south. In October the CCP's fourteenth party congress formally adopted the goal of a "socialist market economy." The Chinese leadership's long-range strategy has been to promote economic growth through market reforms while maintaining its monopoly on political power by severely repressing dissent and appealing to nationalist impulses.

In March 1993 the rubber-stamp National People's Congress (NPC) elected CCP secretary general Jiang Zemin, Deng's handpicked successor as paramount leader, as state president. Jiang also holds a third position as chairman of the Central Military Commission, but lacks a support base in the military and is seen as a weak figure. The NPC also re-elected premier Li Peng to a second five-year term, and named as its chairman Qiao Shi, the CCP's former internal security chief. Qiao and Zhu Rongji, China's senior vice premier in charge of the economy, are widely expected to play leading roles in the post-Deng transition.

Dissent has been repressed ruthlessly. Most notably, in 1995 and 1996 courts sentenced Wei Jingsheng and Wang Dan to long prison terms for peacefully advocating democractic reforms.

Tensions continued in northwestern Xinjiang province, where Turkic-speaking Uighurs and other Muslim ethnic minorities accuse the central government of exploiting the region's rich mineral resources and altering the demographic balance by encouraging an influx of Han Chinese. During a crackdown that began in late April the authorities arrested more than 5,000 Muslims, and there were reports of assassinations of pro-government figures and deadly clashes between police and separatists.

In recent years hundreds of peasants have rioted in rural areas to protest illegal land seizures and arbitrary taxes levied by provincial officials. Income disparities between the booming coastal areas and the interior provinces, and agricultural reforms that have created 120 million surplus farm laborers, have contributed to a "floating population" of 80-100 million migrants seeking work in urban areas.

Political Rights and Civil Liberties:

Chinese citizens cannot change their government democratically. The regime has one of the worst human rights records in the world and the rule of law is nonexistent.

The National People's Congress (NPC), which under the 1982 constitution is nominally the highest organ of state authority, and whose delegates have shown some assertiveness in recent years by refusing to vote unamimously on certain issues, is subordinate in practice to the CCP.

Under the 1987 Village Committees Organic Law, more than 80 percent of the country's 900,000 village bodies are chosen through local elections. However, only CCP candidates and, in some places, non-party independents can compete. In many villages independents have won seats, but generally balloting is characterized by irregularities and unfair procedures.

The judiciary is an instrument of state control and rules of due process are ignored. Judges, nearly half of whom come from the armed forces, are generally selected on the basis of their standing within the CCP, and less than 20 percent have legal backgrounds. Suspects are routinely tortured to extract confessions.

In March 1996 the NPC revised the 1979 Criminal Procedure Law, effective 1997, to grant a greater role to defense lawyers and increase their access to defendants; to end the presumption of guilt (although not establishing a presumption of innocence); to bar judges from being part of the prosecution team, and to end a provision allowing judges to order quick trials and executions for crimes that allegedly "seriously endanger public order." While prospects that these changes will be respected in practice are dubious, the revised code reflects the influence of moderates such as NPC Chairman Qiao Shi, who seek to introduce the rule of law while maintaining tight CCP political control. Conversely, the changes also strengthen the role of party-controlled "adjudicative committees" (which are superior to the bench judges) in handling major cases, and introduce new summary trial procedures in certain situations.

Many criminal cases are, in any case, handled by the Public Security Bureau under administrative procedures which function outside of the judicial process. Two special types of punishment exist: the *laojiao*, or "re-education through labor" camps, and the *laogai*, or "reform through labor" camps. The laojiao system provides for administrative detention for up to four years without a hearing, completely bypassing the courts. By official count upwards of one million people each year are detained through a third process, "Shelter and Investigation," which permits detention without charge or trial for up to three months. Abuse of prisoners, particularly ordinary workers, is routine and widespread, and is often carried out by other inmates with the sanction of guards. In May 1995 a former police official reported that authorities sometimes sell organs of executed prisoners for transplant purposes, and at times schedule executions to meet organ demand.

In recent years the number of people executed during crackdowns on corruption and drug trafficking, often immediately following summary trials, has risen. Sixty-five crimes are punishable by death, and individuals have been executed for offenses as minor as hooliganism, stealing farm animals or rice, counterfeiting currency and forging tax invoices.

On April 28, 1996, the authorities launched the Strike Hard campaign, a mass crackdown on criminals as well as separatists in Xinjiang province that by early August had resulted in 162,000 arrests. Many of the more than 1,000 subsequent executions came within a week of the commission of the crime. The campaign allowed the younger generation of leaders to show a tough response to rising rates of murder, armed robbery, rape, kidnapping and drug trafficking, although many of the executions were for lesser offenses.

It is impossible to estimate accurately the number of political prisoners in China. In January 1995 the government said there were 2,679 people jailed for "counter-revolutionary" offenses. However, the authorities are increasingly charging dissidents with other crimes, such as "leaking state secrets." The June 1994 "Detailed Implementation Regulations" for the 1993 State Security Law criminalized peaceful acts, including working with foreign human rights organizations, and any articles or speech "which endanger state security." The official figure also does not include dissidents held without trial in re-education camps.

Although in recent years there has been a proliferation of non-political talk radio shows and tabloid magazines, the government still maintains tight control over the media, authors and film makers. In March the government announced that small newspapers run by private organizations would come under CCP control. All political coverage must conform to the strict guidelines set forth by the CCP's Propaganda Department. At least a dozen journalists are believed to be in prison, some merely for meeting with their Western counterparts. Foreign journalists are occasionally detained for questioning and barred from covering certain stories.

In January the government announced that foreign wire services would have to disseminate their business news in China through Xinhua, the state news agency. In February the government announced regulations to control Internet access and content that included forcing interactive computer networks to gain government approval and route all international connections through the Ministry of Posts and Telecommunications. The regulations broadly banned the spread through cyberspace of "information that may hinder public order." In September the government closed dozens of Internet web sites, including those of exiled dissidents, Hong Kong and Taiwanese newspapers, and Amnesty International and Human Rights Watch/Asia.

Civic organizations with strictly nonpolitical agendas are often tolerated but are closely monitored. Freedom of assembly is limited, and even nonpolitical gatherings are sometimes arbitrarily shut down. Public protests are occasionally tolerated if devoid of political content.

Religious practice is tightly controlled by the state, and the government has increased efforts to force underground Catholic and Protestant churches to register with authorities and join one of two officially sanctioned "Patriotic" movements. Scores of unofficial churches have been raided, closed or demolished, and hundreds of bishops, priests and ordinary worshippers have been detained for months and, in some cases, years. Students attending seminaries run by state-approved churches must pass exams on political as well as theological knowledge. The government regulates the publication and distribution of religious books and other materials. In January 1994 the government codified into law a longstanding ban against proselytizing by foreigners. In predominantly Muslim Xinjiang province restrictions exist on building mosques, and against underground Islamic study groups, religious publishing and the provision Islamic education to youths under 18.

China's family planning policy limits urban couples to one child; in rural areas, if the first child is a girl, the parents can petition the local authorities for permission to try to have a son. The policy is zealously enforced by some local officials through sanctions and even forced abortion and sterilization. Couples adhering to the policy receive preferential education, food and medical benefits, while those failing to comply face a loss of benefits and fines. Failure to pay the fines sometimes results in the seizure of livestock and other goods and the destruction of homes. Dissidents in Xinjiang province say the authorities often pressure Muslim women to marry Han Chinese.

Women face discrimination and sexual harassment in the workplace. In rural areas women are occasionally abducted or otherwise sold into prostitution or marriage. In 1996 Shanghai authorities allowed private donors to open the city's first shelter for battered women.

In January Human Rights Watch/Asia reported that thousands of children in Chinese orphanages died of starvation and medical neglect between 1988 and 1993. Many were intentionally starved under a policy of "summary resolution" designed to keep the population of orphanages stable.

Independent trade unions are illegal, and all unions must belong to the CCP-controlled All-China Federation of Trade Unions. No legal basis for strikes exists. In practice strikes are occasionally permitted to protest dangerous conditions and low wages, and occur most often in foreign-owned factories. Most prisoners are required to work, receiving little if any compensation.

The successes of both the Special Economic Zones in the south and the small-scale township and village enterprises in the countryside have helped remove millions of Chinese from dependence on the *danwei*, or state work unit. For most urban dwellers, however, the danwei controls everything from the right to change residence to permission to have a child. The system of *hakou*, or residence permit, has also been loosened to give workers more flexibility in filling jobs in areas of fast economic growth.

Colombia

Polity: Presidential-legislative democracy (insurgencies)
Economy: Capitalist-statist
Population: 37,999,000
PPP: $5,790
Life Expectancy: 69.4
Ethnic Groups: Mestizo (58 percent), European (20 percent), Mulatto (14 percent), Black, (4 percent), Indian (1 percent)
Capital: Bogota

Political Rights: 4
Civil Liberties: 4
Status: Partly Free

Overview:

In 1996 President Ernesto Samper avoided impeachment on charges of knowingly accepting drug money during his 1994 election campaign, but with foes continuing to call for his ouster and guerrilla violence increasing in the countryside, the second half of his term promised to be difficult.

Following independence from Spain in 1819, and after a long period of federal government with what are now Venezuela, Ecuador and Panama, the Republic of Colombia was established in 1886. Politics have since been dominated by the Liberal and Conservative parties. Under Liberal President Cesar Gaviria (1990-94) a new constitution was implemented that limits presidents to single four-year terms and provides for an elected bicameral Congress, with a 102-member Senate and a 161-member Chamber of Representatives.

Modern Colombia has been marked by the corrupt machine politics of the Liberals and Conservatives; left-wing guerrilla insurgencies; right-wing paramilitary violence; the emergence of giant drug cartels; and the gross violation of human rights.

Little changed under Gaviria, whose free-trade policies were applauded abroad while a rough estimate of three Colombian trade unionists were being killed per week. The Cali cartel emerged as the largest, most efficient cocaine- and heroin-trafficking operation in the hemisphere.

In the 1994 legislative elections the Liberals retained a majority in both houses of Congress. Samper, a former economic development minister, won the Liberal presidential primary. The Conservatives backed Andres Pastrana, a former mayor of Bogota, the capital. Both candidates vowed to continue Gaviria's free-market, free-trade reforms.

Samper won in a June 1994 runoff election, taking 50.4 percent of the vote to

Pastrana's 48.6 percent. Under U.S. pressure Samper went after the Cali cartel, and most of its top figures were captured in 1995. The arrests, however, netted overwhelming evidence that the cartel provided $6 million to the president's campaign and that Samper signed off on it.

In the second half of 1995 Samper twice imposed states of emergency that allowed him to govern virtually by decree. Meanwhile new traffickers stepped in to fill the shoes of the arrested Cali chiefs. In December a congressional commission dominated by Liberals cleared Samper of charges that he had authorized cartel contributions to his campaign. Opposition politicians and much of the media called it a whitewash.

In February 1996 the country's prosecutor general formally charged Samper with illegal enrichment, fraud, falsifying documents and cover-up regarding his campaign financing. As the crisis intensified, Samper's finance minister resigned in late April, citing the charges against the president. On June 13, the House, dominated by the president's Liberal Party, voted 111-43 to clear Samper on grounds of insuffcient evidence.

Over the summer, guerrillas and drug traffickers were partly behind occasionally violent protests by thousands of coca cultivators against government efforts to eradicate coca plantations. Soldiers killed several protesters. Meanwhile, in late summer, guerrilla violence surged in the countryside. On September 10 Vice President Umberto de la Calle resigned, citing the continuing controversy surrounding Samper.

Political Rights and Civil Liberties:

Citizens can change their government through elections. The 1991 constitution provides for broader participation in the system, including two reserved seats in the Congress for the country's small Indian minority.

But voter participation rarely exceeds 40 percent because of fear of political violence and a widespread belief that corruption renders elections meaningless.

During elections, candidates campaign under heavy security and tend to limit themselves to indoor appearances. In 1994 dozens of congressional and local candidates were killed, kidnapped or injured. Results indicated that left-wing guerrillas controlled up to 15 percent of the nation's 1,000-plus municipalities.

Strong evidence also suggests that the Cali cartel, through its lawyers, virtually dictated the 1993 penal code reform to Congress. It allows traffickers who turn themselves in as much as a two-thirds sentence reduction, and the dismissal of any pending charges to which they do not plead.

Constitutional rights regarding free expression and the freedom to organize political parties, civic groups and labor unions are severely restricted by political and drug-related violence and the government's inability to guarantee the security of its citizens. In April 1996, following a series of high-profile guerrilla attacks including an ambush killing of 31 soldiers, the government created "public order zones" which permit local military commanders, with the approval of elected officials, to impose curfews and restrict movement.

Political violence in Colombia continues to take more lives than in any other country in the hemisphere. The military and security forces are primarily responsible, but the right-wing paramilitary groups, left-wing guerrillas, drug-traffickers and hundreds, possibly thousands, of paid assassins all make their contributions.

Perpetrators of political violence operate with a high degree of impunity. According to Colombian human rights organizations, killings and disappearances carried out by security personnel have decreased somewhat in recent years, but the number carried out by paramilitary groups has increased.

Another category of killings is known as "social cleansing": the elimination of drug addicts, street children and other marginal citizens by vigilante groups often linked to the police. Overall, criminal violence results in dozens of murders per day. Homicide is the leading cause of death in Colombia. Kidnappings continued to occur regularly in 1996, about half being carried out by left-wing guerrillas.

Human rights organizations are numerous, but activists, as well as labor, peasant and student organizations, are consistently the targets of violence and intimidation. Murders of trade union activists continued as Colombia remained the most dangerous country in the world for organized labor.

Over the last decade the entire judicial system has been severely weakened by the onslaught of the drug cartels, and by generalized political violence. Much of the system has been compromised by corruption and extortion.

Under the 1991 constitution, the judiciary, headed by a Supreme Court, was revamped. A U.S.-style adversarial system was adopted, and government prosecutors are able to use government security services to investigate crimes. Previously, judges had investigated crimes without the help of major law enforcement agencies.

The judicial system remains overloaded and ill-equipped to handle high-profile drug and corruption cases. To protect the judiciary from drug traffickers, the Gaviria government instituted a system of 84 "faceless judges." This system, however, neither provides defendents with due process nor offers judges much security against the traffickers.

The military was untouched by constitutional reform. No demands were made on spending accountability, and mandatory military service was left intact. Cases involving police and military personnel accused of human rights violations are tried in military rather than civilian courts. In effect, the military and police remain accountable only to themselves, reinforcing the atmosphere of impunity that pervades the entire country. The states of emergency imposed by President Samper in the second half of 1995 and in effect through August 1996 caused widespread anxiety among the population.

Radio is both public and private. Television remains mostly a government monopoly and news programs tend to be slanted. Moreover, the "right to reply" provision of the new constitution has resulted in harsh judicial tutelage over all media. In December 1996 Samper signed a law tightening television licensing procedures, including mandatory reviews of news broadcasting licenses every six months, that is expected to constrain press freedom.

The press, including dozens of daily newspapers and weekly magazines, is privately owned. Dozens of journalists have been murdered in the last decade and many others have been kidnapped. While the situation has improved in recent years, impunity and the state of emergency in 1995-96 ensured that reporters continued to work in a climate of intimidation.

The new constitution expanded religious freedom by ending the privileges of the Catholic church, which had long enjoyed the advantages of an official religion.

Comoros

Polity: Dominant party
Economy: Capitalist
Population: 569,000
PPP: $1,130
Life Expectancy: 56.2
Ethnic Groups: Majority of mixed African-Arab descent,
East Indian minority
Capital: Moroni

Political Rights: 4
Civil Liberties: 4
Status: Partly Free

Overview:
The tiny Indian Ocean island nation of the Federal Islamic Republic of the Comoros was under pressures to become more federal and more Islamic in 1996. In March, Mohamed Taki, leader of the National Union for Democracy (UNDC), won the presidency in a second round run-off election. In October, a new constitution that increases the impact of Islamic law was adopted by an 85 percent vote in a referendum.

The Comoros have experienced 17 coups or coup attempts since gaining independence from France in 1975, including two mercenary invasions. In August, France re-established its military presence on the isles at the invitation of President Taki, whose conservative Islamic beliefs are not universally shared by his fellow Comorians. Divisive clan and personal rivalries persist, and residents of the country's two smaller islands, Moheli and Anjouan, are demanding either increased local powers or total separation from the central administration based on the largest island, Grand Comoros. Another island in the group, Mayotte, has remained under French rule since voting against independence in 1975, but is still claimed by the Comoros.

The Comoros' tumultuous history as an independent nation began with a coup shortly after independence that overthrew the Comoros' first president, Ahmed Abdallah Abderrahman. However, with the help of French mercenary Bob Denard, Abdallah launched a successful counter-coup in 1978. Abdallah was returned unopposed in 1978 and in 1984 one-party sham-elections, with Denard's backing as head of the army and presidential guard. Abdallah was assassinated in 1989, allegedly by his own troops on the orders of Denard, but the subsequent unrest drew French military intervention and Denard was forced to flee.

In 1990, Supreme Court Justice Said Mohamed Djohara won a six-year term as president, after succeeding Abdallah on an interim basis, in the country's first contested elections. A September 1995 coup attempt by elements of the Comoros security forces, aided by foreign mercenaries led by Bob Denard, was reversed by French soldiers. Nonetheless, President Djohar was effectively removed from office. He was flown to French-controlled Reunion Island, nominally for "medical treatment," but under de facto house arrest. Denard claims he acted in consultation with French security services.

Political Rights and Civil Liberties:
Comorians have the constitutional right to change their government democratically. The March 1996 elections, in which President Taki was declared victor with over 60 percent of the vote in a second round run-off, were reportedly the most honest and best-administered in Comoros' electoral history. Parlia-

mentary elections in November produced a strong ruling party victory, but also gave the conservative Islamic opposition party several seats in the national assembly. Yet a history of election fraud and irregularities, repression, continual coup attempts, foreign interference and political infighting give little confidence that representative government has really taken hold. Many constitutionally-mandated institutions thus far exist only on paper.

Two main political coalitions now exist. One is built around President Taki's Rally for Democracy and Renewal. An opposition alliance, the Front for National Reform, is headed by defeated presidential candidate Abbas Djoussouf.

A number of independent newspapers publish in the capital, Moroni, and some are highly critical of the government. In January, however, the government suspended the *Al-Watani* newspaper. The government-controlled Radio Comoros has been the only broadcaster permitted to operate since the country's sole independent station was ordered shuttered in 1995. Analysts cite the station's frequent criticism of the government and ties to opposition politicians as the reasons for its closure. However, transmissions from Mayotte are easily received, and many people have satellite dishes and access to international broadcasting. There are generally few restrictions on free expression, save during the numerous coup attempts, and foreign newspapers and other publications are easily available.

The Comorian legal system combines Islamic law and remnants of the French legal code. President Taki has pressed for increased Islamic influence on legal and social matters, and Islam is the official state religion. Non-Muslims are permitted to practice but not proselytize. In August, Taki authorized civil authorities to apply "Lex talionis" as punishment for various crimes. His use of decree power has been strongly criticized by the Comoros' few independent newspapers. The judiciary is largely independent, and headed by a Supreme Court. However, most minor disputes are settled by village elders or a civilian court of first instance. Prison conditions are reportedly very poor, with severe overcrowding compounded by an absence of proper sanitation, insufficient medical attention and poor diet.

Freedom of assembly is generally respected, but civilian relations with the security forces remain strained. Trade unions and strikes are permitted, but collective bargaining is weak in the small formal sector. Women possess constitutional protections despite the influence of Islamic law, but in reality enjoy little political or economic power, and have far fewer opportunities for education or employment in the formal sector.

The Comorian population is among the poorest in the world. Only about a tenth of its people are engaged in salaried work, and economic opportunity is limited. The government remains highly dependent on foreign aid for its administrative and development costs and for the reduction of its trade deficit.

Congo

Polity: Presidential-
parliamentary democracy
Economy: Mixed statist
Population: 2,528,000
PPP: $2,750
Life Expectancy: 51.2
Ethnic Groups: Kongo (48 percent), Sangha (20 percent),
Teke (17 percent), others
Capital: Brazzaville

Political Rights: 4
Civil Liberties: 4
Status: Partly Free

Overview: **S**ecurity and human rights conditions deteriorated amidst intense political maneuvering among Congo's several regional/ethnic-based parties ahead of the scheduled August 1997 elections, in which President Pascal Lissouba will seek a second five-year term. A brief army mutiny over pay in February, regional militia actions and the banning of private media slowed the trend toward increased security and respect for human rights.

A 1970 coup established a socialist state based on Marxist-Leninist principles a decade after gaining independence from France. In 1979, General Denis Sassou-Nguesso seized power and maintained one-party rule as head of the Congolese Workers' Party (PCT) until domestic and international pressure forced his acceptance of a transition to a multiparty system and open elections in 1992. Pascal Lissouba of the Pan-African Union for Social Democracy (Upads) party won a clear victory in the second round of presidential voting. The legislative elections produced no clear majority, and after an anti-Lissouba coalition formed, the president dissolved the assembly and called for another vote. New legislative polls in 1993 produced a presidential majority but were marred by numerous irregularities, and several parties boycotted the second round.

By late 1993, serious violence among the ethnic-based militias—with such names as Ninjas, Zulus and Cobra—wracked the capital, Brazzaville. A January 1994 peace accord brought power-sharing, decentralization and the integration of various party militias into the national army. The government has asserted increased, but not full, control over both militias and the army, which has been dominated by loyalists of former president Sassou-Nguesso. Private militias still loyal to the ex-president seized a town in northern Congo for several days in July.

While their country is rich in oil, most Congolese remain impoverished. The government continues to pursue free market economic reforms which have drawn strong international support, including a new three-year $100 million International Monetary Fund loan and the write-off of $1.5 billion dollars in debt.

**Political Rights
and Civil Liberties:**   **I**n 1992 and 1993, for the first time in their history, the Congolese people exercised their constitutional right to elect the president and the National Assembly deputies to five year terms of office through competitive multiparty elections. Local councils elect members of the less-powerful Senate to six year terms. President Lissouba's 1992

victory was widely considered free and fair, but 1993 legislative elections were disputed by the opposition. Most of these claims were rejected by an international commission, but armed clashes and intense political infighting came to an end only after a power-sharing agreement was reached.

Congo politics are marked by shifting alliances of ethnic-based parties. Members of President Lissouba's ethnic group from southern Congo hold most of the important cabinet posts. However, he has sought balance by including members of different groups, including a new prime minister from the north of the country, Charles David Ganao, appointed in August. The 1997 presidential and 1998 legislative contests will measure the maturity of the multiparty system.

In early August, the government banned all 15 private newspapers and magazines on the basis of a new press law adopted the previous month. Before the ban, independent newspapers circulated freely in Brazzaville. A 1995 law provides stronger penalties for defamation of senior officials, requires media to "show loyalty to the government" and permits seizure of private printing works during emergencies.

Freedom of assembly and association is constitutionally guaranteed, but public gatherings must be cleared with the Interior Ministry, and permission is occasionally denied. Freedom of religion is respected in law and in practice. Many nongovernmental organizations operate freely, including several devoted to human rights causes that publish reports highly critical of official practices as well as societal discrimination. In August, the Congolese Human Rights Watch (Observatoire Congolais des Droits de l'Homme) warned of "catastrophic" human rights violations, including unlawful executions, police torture and violence by private militias, that are unchallenged, or even assisted, by soldiers and police.

The formal judiciary consists of a three-tier system from local courts through courts of appeal to the Supreme Court, and is generally considered politically independent. Understaffing and a lack of resources create a backlog of cases that often mean long periods of pre-trial detention in extremely harsh prison conditions. Outside the cities, traditional courts retain broad jurisdiction, especially in civil matters.

Extensive discrimination against women continues despite constitutional protections. Discrimination includes limited access to education and poor employment opportunities, especially in the countryside. Civil codes regarding family and marriage formalize women's inferior status. Violence against women is reportedly widespread but not formally reported. Discrimination against pygmy groups is also prevalent.

Workers' rights to join trade unions and to strike are legally protected, and there are a half dozen labor confederations with various links to the government or political parties. Unions are legally required to accept non-binding arbitration before striking, but often do so without following this process.

The government's broad privatization program is drawing greater foreign investment and increasing local business opportunities. However, the process has cut jobs in both the civil service and the state-run enterprises, fueling local grievances which the government hopes a growing economy will ameliorate before the upcoming elections.

Costa Rica

Polity: Presidential-
legislative democracy
Economy: Capitalist-
statist
Population: 3,574,000
PPP: $5,680
Life Expectancy: 76.4
Ethnic Groups: Spanish, large mestizo minority
Capital: San Jose

Political Rights: 1
Civil Liberties: 2
Status: Free

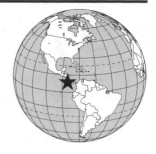

Overview: Worsening economic recession in Costa Rica produced record disapproval ratings for president Jose Maria Figueres in 1996. The country's economy contracted in each of the first seven months of the year as payments on the budget deficit swallowed over 30 percent of annual government spending.

The Republic of Costa Rica achieved independence from Spain in 1821 and became a republic in 1848. Democratic government was instituted in 1899 and briefly interrupted in 1917 and 1948. The 1949 constitution, which bans the formation of a national army, provides the framework for democratic governance.

The constitution provides for three independent branches of government. The president and the 57-member legislative assembly are elected for four years and are prohibited from seeking a second term. The assembly has co-equal power, including the ability to override presidential vetos.

Figueres's party, the social democratic National Liberation Party (PLN), has held power for 18 of the last 26 years. In the 1994 elections, Figueres defeated Miguel Angel Rodriguez of the Social Christian Unity Party (PUSC), the country's other principal political organization.

The 45-year-old Figueres, son of former President Jose "Pepe" Figueres, a national hero who led the fight to preserve democracy in the 1948 civil war, campaigned against the neo-liberal economic policies of outgoing President Rafael A. Calderon, Jr., of the PUSC. Rodriguez proposed to deepen structural reforms. The campaign was marked mostly by acrimonious personal attacks.

Figueres won with 49.7 percent of the vote, 2.2 points ahead of Rodriguez. The PLN won 28 seats in the assembly, one short of a majority, and the PUSC won 25. A handful of small parties divided the remaining four seats.

The country's economic woes result in part from a vast reduction in levels of foreign aid and international lending from governments that were eager to keep communists at bay. In an attempt to gain the confidence of Costa Ricans beset by economic hardship, Figueres asked his entire cabinet to resign in July. Such changes have not generated enthusiasm, however, and are seen as mainly cosmetic.

Political Rights and Civil Liberties: Costa Ricans can change their government democratically. The political landscape is dominated by the PLN and the PUSC, but numerous other parties run in elections.

Allegations implicating both major parties in drug-tainted campaign contributions have been made during recent elections. New campaign laws have been instituted to make party financing more transparent. But Costa Rica, with no army, navy or air force, remains an easy target for drug-traffickers, and there is great concern about increasing drug-related corruption and money laundering.

Constitutional guarantees regarding freedom of religion and the right to organize political parties and civic organizations are respected. In recent years, however, a reluctance to address restrictions on labor rights has been noticeable.

Solidarity, an employer-employee organization that private business uses as an instrument to prevent independent unions from organizing, remains strong and has generally been tolerated by successive governments. Solidarity organizations are entrenched in Costa Rica's free-trade zones, where labor abuses by multinational corporations are rife. Minimum wage and social security laws are often ignored and fines for noncompliance are minuscule. Women workers are often sexually harassed, made to work overtime without pay and fired when they become pregnant.

The judicial branch is independent, its members elected by the legislature. A Supreme Court with power to rule on the constitutionality of laws is in operation, as are four courts of appeal and a network of district courts. The members of the independent national election commission are elected by the Supreme Court.

The judicial system is marked by delays, creating a volatile situation in overcrowded, violence-prone prisons. The problem is linked to budget cuts affecting the judiciary and to the nation's economic difficulties, which have led to a rise in violent crime and clashes in the countryside between squatters and landowners.

Numerous charges still are made of human rights violations by police. Independent Costa Rican rights monitors report increases in allegations of arbitrary arrests and brutality, and instances of torture in secret jails have been reported.

An official ombudsman provides recourse for citizens or foreigners with human rights complaints. The ombudsman has the authority to issue recommendations for rectification, including sanctions against government bodies, for failure to respect rights.

The press, radio and television are generally free. A number of independent dailies serve a society that is 90 percent literate. Television and radio stations are both public and commercial, with at least six private television stations providing an influential forum for public debate. Though the Supreme Court ruled in 1995 that a decades-old law requiring the licensing of journalists was unconstitutional, inordinately restrictive libel laws remain in place.

Côte D'Ivoire

Polity: Dominant Party   **Political Rights:** 6
Economy: Capitalist   **Civil Liberties:** 5
Population: 14,733,000   **Status:** Not Free
PPP: $1,620
Life Expectancy: 50.9
Ethnic Groups: Baule (23 percent), Bete (18 percent),
Senoufou (15 percent), Malinke (11 percent), others
Capital: Yamoussoukro (official); Abidjan (de facto)

Overview:
Côte d'Ivoire maintained its position as one of sub-Saharan Africa's most prosperous countries with a strong economic recovery buoyed by two years of near-record cocoa crops. The country's relative wealth, however, seemed no closer to bringing either security or democratic rights to the Ivorian people. Rampant crime continued to plague Abidjan, particularly in sprawling shantytowns where two-thirds of the city's people reside, and harsh new anti-crime measures eroded civil rights. President Henri Konan Bédié, winner of a deeply flawed October 1995 election, moved to consolidate his personal power by sacking two generals and reviving a long-dormant law to create a new national security council. The National Assembly is dominated by his ruling Democratic Party of the Ivory Coast-African Democratic Rally (PDCI-RDA), which took 147 of the 175 National Assembly seats in November 1995 elections marred by serious irregularities. By-elections in December were conducted peacefully, and produced mixed results that raises opposition representation in the National Assembly but will not challenge the ruling party's dominance.

From independence in 1960 until his death in 1993, President Félix Houphouët-Boigny ruled Côte d'Ivoire through the only legal party, the PDCI. A multiparty system came into being in 1990.

Many people continued to be detained without charges since the opposition boycott of last year's presidential vote, and three journalists remained jailed for "insulting" the president. A new military district was also created to cover the country's remote frontier with Liberia; the violence of that country's long civil war has occasionally spilled onto Ivorian territory in this area. The country receives strong backing from France, its former colonial power and main trading partner, which maintains a military garrison near Abidjan, and whose advisors serve with many units of the 14,000 strong armed forces. The United States changed its own military cooperation with Côte d'Ivoire in 1996 through a month-long training exercise with Ivorian forces.

Political Rights and Civil Liberties:
Côte d'Ivoire's citizens were not permitted to freely choose their government in the 1995 presidential and legislative elections. President Henri Konan Bédié was declared president with 95 percent of the vote in a victory so thoroughly devalued by government manipulation as to be meaningless as a measure of the country's popular will. Alassane Ouattara, the most formidable opposition candidate, was barred from running. Ouatarra's exclusion could also become a serious

grievance for the 40 percent of Ivorians who share his Muslim faith.

The gravely flawed election was boycotted by the major opposition parties. It also raised religious tensions and sparked the first large-scale ethnic violence in Côte d'Ivoire in many years, leaving at least 23 people dead. The vote tallying was accurate, according to some international observers, but a ban on opposition demonstrations, ruling party profligacy in use of state resources, and media intimidation of the opposition prevented a fair election. National Assembly elections in November, which produced another big victory for the ruling PDCI-RDA, were conducted in relative calm but voters' lists problems, bans on opposition demonstrations and further harassment of oppositionists seriously reduced their credibility.

Only a handful of the 43 officially registered political parties in Côte d'Ivoire are active. The Ivorian Popular Front (FPI) and the Rally for a Democratic Republic (RDR) are the principal opposition parties, but are hampered by a lack of unity and by official harassment. The government requires all private associations to register, although it is not clear whether this is constitutional and has not generally been used to ban groups. Several human rights organizations are active, notable among them the Ivorian Human Rights League (LIDHO). While there is no systematic or official discrimination, Muslims complain of second-class treatment. It is clearly a sensitive topic; two journalists who reported on Muslim grievances were sentenced to one year's imprisonment in March 1995.

State-run broadcasting services are unabashedly pro-government; state-owned newspapers only slightly less so. The vigorous private print media continued to play the role of watchdog and advocate, but remained under threat of governmental repression. Crimes including "insulting the president," "threatening public order," and "defaming or undermining the reputation of the state" are interpreted broadly as tools to silence unwanted criticism. In September, a court denied application for bail by three journalists serving two-year jail terms for "insulting" President Bédié. Emmanuel Kore, Freedom Neruda and Abou Drahamane Sangare of *La Voie,* published by the opposition FPI, rejected a presidential offer of pardon in August that would have required them to apologize for an article that said Bédié's presence at a soccer match had brought the national team bad luck.

Côte d'Ivoire's judiciary is not independent. Judges are political appointees who are without tenure and are highly susceptible to external interference. Legal provisions regarding search warrants, rules of evidence and pre-trial detention are often ignored. A new law adopted in August providing the police with sweeping new search powers was denounced by human rights groups. Traditional courts still prevail in many rural areas, especially in handling minor matters and family law.

Prison conditions are reportedly extremely difficult, and are only ameliorated for prisoners with money to buy special treatment. Disease, aggravated by a poor diet and inadequate or non-existent medical attention, ensures a high death-rate. In October, the death of a detainee held without charges for participating in the 1995 election boycott was reported.

Women's rights are constitutionally protected and encouraged by government policy, but social custom makes for discrimination. Equal pay for equal work is offered in the small formal sector, but women have few chances to obtain or advance in wage employment. Education and job opportunities for women are even scarcer in rural areas that rely on subsistence agriculture.

Union formation and membership are legally protected. For three decades, however, the General Union of Workers of Côte d'Ivoire (UGTCI) was closely aligned to the sole legal party. The Federation of Autonomous Trade Unions of Côte d'Ivoire (FESCACI) represents several independent unions formed since 1991. Notification and conciliation requirements must be met before legal strikes. Collective bargaining agreements are often reached with the participation of government negotiators who influence wage settlements. Privatization plans for many of Côte d'Ivoire's state-run corporations are attracting renewed foreign investment, and debt rescheduling may give the economy a further boost. However, gross distortions in wealth distribution are a threat to both stability and long term growth.

⬇ Croatia

Polity: Presidential-par-
liamentary democracy
Economy: Mixed statist
Population: 4,420,000
PPP: na
Life Expectancy: na
Ethnic Groups: Pre-1995: Croat (77 percent),
Serb (12 percent), Muslim (1 percent), Hungarian, Slovene, Czech,
Albanian, Montenegrin, Ukrainian, others
Capital: Zagreb

Political Rights: 4
Civil Liberties: 4
Status: Partly Free

Overview: In 1996, Croatia's admittance to the Council of Europe was approved, then delayed, over such issues as press freedom, President Franjo Tudjman's refusal to recognize the election of an opposition-dominated Zagreb city council, the government's failure to fully cooperate with the Hague war crimes tribunal, and the reunification of the Bosnian city of Mostar, divided between Croats and Muslims. Another key issue was the status of the Croatian region of Eastern Slavonia, captured and ethnically-cleansed by Serbs and administered by the United Nations Transitional Administration for Eastern Slavonia (UNTAES), whose mandate expires in January 1997.

Hungary ruled most of what is Croatia from the twelfth century until World War I. In 1918, it became part of the Kingdom of Serbs, Croats and Slovenes, renamed Yugoslavia in 1929. A short-lived independent state was proclaimed in 1941 by the pro-fascist *Ustasa* movement. In 1945, Croatia joined the People's Republic of Yugoslavia under Communist leader Josip Broz (Tito). On June 25, 1991, Croatia and Slovenia declared independence. The Serb-dominated Yugoslav People's Army (YPA), backed by Serb militias, seized parts of Croatia, ultimately controlling one-third of the country and establishing the Krajina Serbian Republic (RSK). In December, all sides agreed to the deployment of U.N. peacekeepers (UNPROFOR). In 1993-94, Croatia supported the Croatian Defense Council (HVO) in Bosnia in a war with Muslims. But in March 1994, President Tudjman endorsed a Washington-engineered peace accord signed by Bosnia's Muslims and Croats, leading to the formation of a federated state in loose confederation with Croatia.

In the summer of 1995, Croat forces recaptured Western Slavonia and Krajina. Afterward, a September offensive by Bosnian Croat and Muslim forces recaptured 20 percent of the 70 percent of Bosnia under Serb control. A cease-fire took effect on October 12 as a prelude to November negotiations that resulted in the Dayton Accords.

In the October 1995 parliamentary elections, Tudjman's ruling Croatian Democratic Union (HDZ) won 44.8 percent of the vote. The joint list of the Croatian Peasants Party (HS), the Istrian Democratic Assembly (IDS), the Croatian Peoples Party (HNS), the Christian Democratic Union (HKDU) and the Croatian Party of Slavonia and Baranja (SBHS) won 18.2 percent. The opposition Croatian Social-Liberal Party won 11.5, and the Social Democratic Party of Croatia (SDP), 8.9 percent. International observers criticized the government for allowing 300,000 Bosnian Croats to vote, despite plans to return them to Bosnia.

In April 1996, the Council of Europe's parliamentary assembly voted to approve Croatia's application. But in an unprecedented move, on May 14 the foreign ministers of the 39-member Council voted to delay action, citing the government's failure to act on a 21-point program on democracy and human rights it had agreed to in April.

Throughout the year, Croatia sought to rectify the Council's concerns. In August, 16 Croat members of the Mostar city council elected in June agreed to end their boycott. The government reluctantly agreed to better cooperation with the war crimes tribunal, and in October parliament passed a media law which nominally protected journalists' rights. In October, the Council decided to admit Croatia, acknowledging the country's cooperation in the Dayton peace process, its improved human rights and a "satisfactory" record of cooperation with the Hague. On November 4, Croatia became the fortieth member of the Council.

In Zagreb, President Tudjman continued to defy the opposition-dominated city council elected in October 1995 by not allowing its mayoral candidates to run in four seperate elections. Despite the media law, pressure continued on the independent press. Serbs living in areas recaptured by Croatia continued to be subject to harassment, looting and violence.

Croatians displaced from Eastern Slavonia by Serb forces pressured the government to end the UNTAES mandate; the Serbian leadership called for a "special status" for the region with a high degree of autonomy for the Serbian population. In June, Croatian Foreign Minister Mate Granic said his government was prepared to guarantee all human and minority rights in the region, and UNTAES administrator General Jacques Paul Klein said that the international community did not support Slavonian territorial autonomy.

In August, Croatia and Yugoslavia signed an agreement on normalizing bilateral relations. Three commissions were established in September to deal with questions related to borders, assets of the former Yugoslavia, and refugee issues.

Political Rights and Civil Liberties: Citizens can change their government democratically, but presidential system tends toward authoritarianism. Irregularities in the 1995 parliamentary elections included voters "not always guaranteed" a secret ballot and numerous ballots " filled in publicly." Candidates in some districts were declared winners on the basis of incomplete results, and the opposition petitioned to nullify results in several districts. Changes in the election law increased the number of seats for the Croatian diaspora, and gave fewer seats to the Serb minority. Each party was allowed just one hour of air time on the state-owned television network, and could not criticize the HDZ.

The media came under government pressure throughout the year. More than 15 reporters were fired from the pro-government daily *Vjesnik;* the independent daily *Novi List* was fined a large amount of money for alleged customs violations; and broadcasting license applications from many independent radio and television stations were rejected. In November, authorities closed independent Radio 101, but re-opened it after domestic and international protests. Two editors of the investigative weekly *Feral Tribune* went on trial for defaming and insulting President Tudjman under March amendments to the penal code dealing with libel. They were ultimately acquitted in September. Several newspapers, including *Panorama*, were temporarily shut down. In August, a politically motivated purge of state-owned television personnel occurred. The October media law was designed in accordance with the conditions set down by the Council of Europe for Croatia's membership. The law protects journalists from revealing their sources and from prosecution in cases where they publish false information unintentionally; but provisions prescribing fines and imprisonment for reporters who insult top officials were retained. In November, authorities closed Independent Radio 101, but re-opened it after domestic and international protests.

Freedom of religion is nominally assured, but during Orthodox Serb control of Krajina and Western Slavonia, Roman Catholic Croats were expelled or persecuted and churches were destroyed. When the Croats returned, hundreds of thousands of Serbs fled. Only about 150,000 Serbs remain from a pre-1991 population of 580,000, and many face intimidation and violence. Laws from Zagreb also threatened Italian schools and cultural institutions in Istria, home to 30,000 ethnic Italians.

The judiciary is not wholly free from government interference. The power of judicial appointments and dismissals is firmly in the hands of an influential parliamentary committee dominated by a hard-line HDZ faction. Under an Amnesty Law which took effect on October 5, former Serb paramilitaries, except those charged with war crimes, were released from prisons.

There are several independent union federations, among them the Croatian Unified Trade Union (HUS), the Coordinating Committee of Croatian White-Collar Trade Unions and a coalition patched together from the Federation of Independent Trade Unions of Croatia and the Union of Trade Unions of Public Employees. Private business and nongovernmental organizations are allowed to function. Women are guaranteed equal rights under the law and are involved in politics, government and business.

Cuba

Polity: Communist one-party
Economy: Statist
Population: 11,007,000
PPP: $3,000
Life Expectancy: 75.4
Ethnic Groups: Creole (51 percent), European (37 percent), black (11 percent)
Capital: Havana

Political Rights: 7
Civil Liberties: 7
Status: Not Free

Overview:

In 1996 Fidel Castro cracked down on a tentative Cuban opposition coalition and ordered a strengthening of political orthodoxy in a continuing effort to maintain his absolute rule.

Cuba achieved independence from Spain in 1898 as a result of the Spanish-American War. The Republic of Cuba was established in 1902, but was under U.S. tutelage under the Platt Amendment until 1934. In 1959 Castro's July 26th Movement–named after an earlier, failed insurrection–overthrew the dictatorship of Fulgencio Batista, who had ruled for 18 of the previous 25 years.

Since then, Castro has dominated the Cuban political system, transforming it into a one-party Communist state. Communist structures were institutionalized by the 1976 constitution installed at the first congress of the Cuban Communist Party (PCC). The constitution provides for a National Assembly which, in theory, designates a Council of State which, in turn, appoints a Council of Ministers in consultation with its president, who serves as head of state and chief of government.

In reality, Castro is responsible for every appointment. As president of the Council of Ministers, chairman of the Council of State, commander-in-chief of the Revolutionary Armed Forces (FAR) and first secretary of the PCC, Castro controls every lever of power in Cuba. The PCC is the only authorized political party and it controls all governmental entities from the national to the municipal level.

Since the collapse of the Soviet Union, which sustained the Cuban economy, Castro has desperately sought Western foreign investment. With the U.S. embargo still in place, most investment has come from Europe and Latin America, but it has been a mere fraction of the former $5 billion in annual Soviet subsidies. The government claimed a return to economic growth in 1995 and 1996, but Cuba officially remained in a "special period," meaning a drastic austerity program involving severe cutbacks in energy consumption and tight rationing of food and consumer items. Economic reforms, including the legalization of the dollar since 1993, indicate Castro has opted for the oxymoronic "market Leninism" of China.

Dollarization has heightened social tensions, as the minority with access to dollars from abroad or through the tourist industry has emerged as a new moneyed class, and the majority without has become increasingly desperate as state-paid salaries dwindled to four dollars or less per month.

Since Castro began making economic reforms that threaten to unleash social forces he might not be able to control, cycles of repression have become more frequent. Authorities harassed and arrested dozens of dissidents to prevent a planned February 24-27, 1996, meeting of *Concilio Cubano* (Cuban Council), an opposition grouping formed in October 1995 and consisting of some 131 independent professional, religious and political organizations. During a late March meeting the PCC's Central Committee called for a harder line against dissent and a tightening of ideological orthodoxy. In another development, on February 24 Cuban fighter pilots shot down two unarmed American civilian aircraft in international airspace, killing four Cuban-Americans belonging to the Miami-based Brothers to the Rescue organization.

In October Hurricane Lili, the worst storm to hit the island in several years, severely damaged farm production and wrecked tens of thousands of homes.

Political Rights and Civil Liberties:

Cubans cannot change their government through democratic means. All political and civic organization outside the PCC is illegal. Political dissent, spoken or written, is a punishable offense.

With the possible exceptions of South Africa, Indonesia and China, Cuba under Castro has had more political prisoners per capita for longer periods than any other country. In 1996 there were an estimated 600-plus political prisoners, most locked in with common criminals, about half convicted on vague charges of "disseminating enemy propaganda" or "dangerousness." In 1995 a number of high-profile political prisoners were released in an effort to gain greater economic cooperation with the European Union.

Since 1991, the U.N. has voted annually to assign a special investigator on human rights to Cuba, but the Cuban government has refused to cooperate.

Although cultural life has thawed slightly, the educational system, the judicial system, labor unions, professional organizations and all media remain state-controlled. Outside of the Catholic church, whose scope remains limited by the government, and small, courageous groups of rights activists and dissident journalists, there is little semblance of independent civil society.

Groups that exist apart from the state are labeled "counterrevolutionary criminals" and are subjected to systematic repression, including arrests, beatings while in custody, confiscations and intimidation by uniformed or plainclothes state security. In 1996 courts sentenced four leading members of Concilio Cubano to prison sentences. Members of four small labor groups that have tried to organize independently remain subject to blacklisting and arbitrary arrest.

There is continued evidence of torture and killings in prisons and in psychiatric institutions, where a number of dissidents arrested in recent years have been incarcerated. Since 1990 the International Committee of the Red Cross has been denied access to prisoners. According to Cuban rights activists, more than 100 prisons and prison camps hold between 60,000 and 100,000 prisoners of all categories. In 1993 vandalism was decreed to be a form of sabotage, punishable by eight years in prison.

Freedom of movement and freedom to choose one's residence, education or job are severly restricted; attempting to leave the island without permission is a punishable offense.

Official discrimination against religious believers was lifted by constitutional revision in 1992. The measure was welcomed by the Catholic Church, which has seen an increase in membership in recent years.

As has been evident during the trials of human rights activists and other dissidents, due process is alien to the Cuban judicial system. The job of defense attorneys registered by the courts is to guide defendants in their confessions.

The government has continued restricting the ability of foreign media to operate in Cuba. Journalist visas are required, and reporters whom the government considers hostile are not allowed entry. Authorities expelled a Committee to Protect Journalists staff member in June and a representative of the Paris-based *Reporters Sans Frontieres* in July.

Cyprus (Greek)

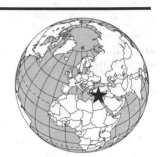

Polity: Presidential-legislative democracy
Economy: Capitalist
Population: Entire island: 735,000 Greeks: 602,000
PPP: $14,060
Life Expectancy: 78.7
Ethnic Groups: Greek majority, Turkish minority, and small Maronite, Armenian, and Latin communities
Capital: Nicosia

Political Rights: 1
Civil Liberties: 1
Status: Free

Overview: **D**emonstrations by Greek Cypriots against the Turkish occupation of Northern Cyprus led to some of the worst violence the island has seen since 1974. Four people were killed in clashes that began in August along the buffer zone separating Greek Cyprus from the Turkish-occupied north.

Efforts by the United Nations and the United States to settle the decades-old dispute over Cyprus have stalled in the face of violence, land disputes and unwillingness on the part of either side to agree on a basis for pre-talk discussions. However, France, Germany, and Britain are expected to present a new initiative, based on U.N. resolutions and focusing on the upcoming negotiations for Cyprus's accession to the European Union.

Annexed to Britain in 1914, Cyprus gained independence in 1960 after a 10-year guerrilla campaign demanding union with Greece. In July 1974, Greek Cypriot national guard members, backed by the military junta in power in Greece, staged an unsuccessful coup aimed at unification. Turkey invaded five days later, taking control of 37 percent of the island and expelling 200,000 Greeks from the north. Currently, the entire Turkish Cypriot community resides in the north, and property claims arising from the division and population exchange remain unsettled.

A buffer zone called the "Green Line" has partitioned Cyprus since 1974. The capital, Nicosia, remains the world's only divided city. The division of Cyprus has been a major point of contention in the longstanding rivalry between Greece and Turkey in the Aegean. Tensions and intermittent violence between the two populations have plagued the island since independence.

U.N. resolutions stipulate that Cyprus is a single country whose northern third is illegally occupied. In 1982 Turkish Cyprus made a unilateral declaration of independence that was condemned by the U.N. and remains unrecognized by every country but Turkey [See Turkish Cyprus under Related Territories].

Peace in Cyprus has been extremely precarious. Propaganda in schools and in the media has sustained hostility among Cypriot youth; blatant economic disparity exists between the prosperous south and the stagnating north; and even before a recent rearmament program by President Glafkos Clerides, Cyprus was among the most heavily-militarized countries in the world.

Escalated tensions surfaced in January, when Greek and Turkish warships faced off to enforce rival claims to sovereignty over Imia, a ten-acre uninhabited islet in the Aegean Sea. The dispute nearly erupted into war before U.S. President Clinton intervened.

An unarmed Greek Cypriot soldier was killed in June when he entered the buffer zone,for unknown reasons and approached the Turkish observation post. He was talking to a Turkish soldier when a second Turkish soldier from a nearby post shot him to death.

In mid-August, a Greek Cypriot demonstration pushed across the Green Line, setting off violent protest by Turkish Cypriots, who killed one Greek demonstrator. Violent clashes claimed the lives of four Greek Cypriots over the next few weeks, as Turkish soldiers fired upon Greek demonstrators and murdered one man who wandered into the North while collecting snails. A Turkish soldier was shot to death in September, though it is unclear who was responsible.

Cyprus is committed to joining the EU as soon as possible, and with its strong economy, stable currency, and fulfilment of all Maastricht Treaty convergence criteria, accession seems imminent. However, the Turkish Cypriot leader warned that war could ensue if the Greek Cypriots joined the EU without the north, and pushed to further negotiations on a settlement of the conflict. The government is adamant that the premise of a single Cyprus be recognized prior to the commencement of negotiations with Turkish Cypriots. However, it has not reassured the Turks that their rights or property will be secured in a unified Cyprus.

Political Rights and Civil Liberties:

Greek Cypriots can change their government democratically. Suffrage is universal and compulsory, and elections are free and fair. An ethnically representative system designed to protect the interests of both Greek and Turkish Cypriots was established by the 1960 constitution.

The independent judiciary operates according to the British tradition, upholding the presumption of innocence and the right to due process. Trial before a judge is standard, although requests for trial by jury are regularly granted.

Freedom of speech is respected and a vibrant independent press frequently criticizes authorities. Several private television and radio stations in the Greek Cypriot community compete effectively with government-controlled stations. In September, the government launched a Cyprus home page on the Internet. It contains data on the political situation and efforts to solve the island's protracted dispute, as well as on current developments and policy statements by Cypriot leaders.

Freedom of assembly and association as well as the right to strike are respected.

More than 90 percent of the labor force is unionized. High economic growth rates and a shortage of labor pushed the government to relax regulations on the issuance of work permits to foreigners, who work at lower wage levels than domestic workers.

Women in Cyprus generally have the same legal status as men. While legal provisions requiring equal pay for men and women performing the same job are effectively enforced, women disproportionately fill lower-paying jobs. Women are denied the right to transmit citizenship to their children if they marry foreign spouses. Under existing Cypriot law, only a Greek Cypriot male may transmit citizenship to his children automatically or obtain expeditious naturalization for his foreign spouse.

Greek Cypriots enjoy freedom of movement with the exception of travel to the north, which is impeded as it requires the traveler to fill out an entry card with the Turkish Republic of Northern Cyprus inscription. Freedom of worship is respected. The Greek Orthodox Church has the status of a state institution, and its property and activities are tax-exempt. Though the church influences public policy, it does not inhibit other religious groups from operating freely.

Czech Republic

Polity: Parliamentary democracy
Economy: Mixed capitalist
Population: 10,331,000
PPP: 8,430
Life Expectancy: 71.3
Ethnic Groups: Czech (94 percent), Slovak (3 percent), Roma (2 percent)
Capital: Prague

Political Rights: 1
Civil Liberties: 2
Status: Free

Overview: Parliamentary elections in June and Senate elections in November were the key political events in the Czech Republic in 1996. Meanwhile, despite some troubling false steps, the Czech economy remained among the strongest in Central and Eastern Europe.

Formed in 1918 after the Austro-Hungarian empire's collapse, Czechoslovakia's history mirrored the successive dramas of Central Europe in the twentieth century. Precariously free and dynamic between the world wars, it fell to totalitarian conquest on the eve of World War II. After a brief democratic interlude, communism replaced Nazism in the late 1940s. An attempt at reforms during the 1968 Prague Spring led to a Soviet-led invasion in August 1968.

Czechoslovakia regained its freedom in the "velvet revolution" of 1989. In 1993, the Czech Republic and Slovakia peacefully dissolved the 1918 union. Vaclav Klaus and his free-market Civic Democratic Party (ODS) led a coalition that won control of the Czech parliament in 1992.

The June 1996 parliamentary elections for the dominant Assembly heralded the end of the transitional phase in the Czech political scene, with the emergence of two strong parties on the left and the right in the West European mold. The ODS placed first in the election with nearly 30 percent of the vote, but only managed to get 99 of 200 seats with its coalition allies. The big winner on the opposition side were the Czech Social Democrats (CSSD) who, with 26 percent, quadrupled their vote since 1992 and now represent the major adversary to the ODS, which formed a minority government in July. The unreformed Communists and crypto-fascist Republicans remain marginal political forces.

The economy grew at an impressive rate of 5 percent in 1996, with low inflation (8.5 percent) and a balanced budget. Low unemployment (3 percent) and rising wages (9 percent real increase) are credited to the controversial labor market reforms initiated by Klaus in 1990 and pursued since. Mass privatization was essentially completed in 1996, with over two-thirds of the economy now in private hands. The Ministry of Privatization was closed in June. However, the collapse of *Kreditni banka* in August highlighted continuing problems in the financial sector, including low transparency, confused ownership, slow privatization and fraud. Problems also continue in the health insurance and pension programs, where an awkward mix of state and market manage to produce little security or efficiency.

Political Rights and Civil Liberties:

Czech citizens can change their government democratically. Numerous political parties exist, although only six have seats in the parliament. The June elections were free and fair.

Citizenship remains an unresolved issue in the Czech Republic. Between 10,000 and 24,000 people, mainly the minority Roma, are stateless. This is due to the cumbersome and overly bureaucratic naturalization procedures in Czech law. Roma have reported being denied citizenship when all necessary requirements have been met. However, fears of mass deportations have not been borne out.

The 1992 law on citizenship was amended in April. The Ministry of the Interior can now suspend the requirement that prospective citizens must have had a clean criminal record for five years, a controversial stipulation since the law does not discriminate between serious and trivial crimes.

There are scores of independent newspapers, an independent news agency, and private local and national television and radio stations (in fact, the private *Nova* television network dominates the market). The *Economist* evaluated the Czech press to be the fourth freest in the world, ahead of Germany and Britain.

An independent judiciary exists. The rule of law is upheld, and authorities observe the legal and constitutional rights of individuals. However, a still evolving legal code and a lack of experienced judges and lawyers hampers the judicial process. In 1995, a case took 222 days on average before it went to trial. There have been reports of neglect and even abuse, by police who are often slow to respond to calls for help by Roma who find themselves the targets of hate crimes, and by courts who mete out minor penalties after arrest.

There are signs of pressure for change from the center. In January, a special department was established to deal with extremist groups, and directives were issued to prosecutors to seek higher penalties in hate-crimes cases. In May, the Olomouc high court overruled a lower court in concluding that the 1995 murder of Tibor Berki, a Romany, was racially-motivated, which led to a harsher sentence.

Religious freedom is respected, and there is no official church. Restitution of Catholic Church and Jewish property nationalized by the Communists remains largely unresolved.

Workers exercise freely the right to organize and join trade unions. The government has eliminated the role of the Tripartite council, which negotiated national wage agreements between the state, labor and employers. Women enjoy the same legal rights as men.

The lustration law keeping Communist collaborators from certain positions continues to be enforced, although 75 percent of appeals against lustration decisions have succeeded. Freedom of assembly is respected, and political parties, professional organizations, cultural groups and other nongovernmental organizations can organize freely.

Denmark

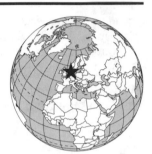

Polity: Parliamentary democracy
Economy: Mixed capitalist
Population: 5,245,000
PPP: $20,200
Life Expectancy: 75.3
Ethnic Groups: Overwhelmingly Danish, small German and immigrant groups
Capital: Copenhagen

Political Rights: 1
Civil Liberties: 1
Status: Free

Overview: Gang warfare between armed biker clubs, including the use of an anti-tank missile, resulted in at least eight deaths over the past year in Denmark, shocking this peaceful and law-abiding country with a strong civic tradition and comprehensive welfare state. Searching for a way to curb this violence, the government has proposed a range of measures giving police and courts greater power in their investigative and punitive efforts.

Prime Minister Poul Nyrup Rasmussen, head of the center-left Social Democratic Party (SDP), faced an unemployment rate of 10 percent. Denmark's future role in the European Union (EU) remains unresolved. The 1993 referendum decision to ratify the Maastricht Treaty occurred following the country's exemption from common defense and currency, EU citizenship and police cooperation.

Denmark is the oldest monarchy in Europe. Queen Margarethe II, whose reign began in 1972, appoints the premier and cabinet ministers, but only through consultation with parliamentary leaders. The 1953 constitution established a unicameral parliament (*Folketing*), in which 135 of 179 members are elected in 17 mainland districts. Two representatives from each of the autonomous regions of the Faeroe Islands and Greenland are also elected. The remaining seats are allocated on a proportional basis to parties receiving over 2 percent of the vote. An extensive system of local representation includes both regional and local councils, with mayors presiding over each.

Political Rights and Civil Liberties: **D**anes can change their government through democratic means. Representatives are elected to the Folketing at least once every four years by means of a modified system of proportional representation. The independent judiciary includes about 100 local courts, two high courts and a 15-member Supreme Court with judges appointed by the Queen, on recommendation from the government. There is freedom of association and assembly, and workers are free to organize and strike. The vast majority of wage earners belong to trade unions and their umbrella organization, the SDP-affiliated Danish Federation of Trade Unions.

Denmark's media reflect a wide variety of political opinions and are frequently critical of the government. The state finances radio and television broadcasting, though state-owned television companies have independent editorial boards. Independent radio stations are permitted by the state but are tightly-regulated and have occasionally been prohibited from broadcasting. In 1995, the Danish National Socialist Movement was banned from opening a radio station, as its campaign for a "racially clean" country was considered illegal incitement to racial hatred.

While freedom of worship is guaranteed to all, over 90 percent of the population belongs to the state-supported Evangelical Lutheran Church of Denmark. Discrimination on the basis of race, language and sex is illegal, and the media have taken a strong role in educating the public about non-Nordic immigrants and refugees to prevent the rise of racism. Women make up approximately 45 percent of the wage labor force and generally hold 20 to 30 percent of national legislature seats. The civil rights of homosexuals are protected, and same-sex marriages are legal.

Djibouti

Polity: Dominant party
Economy: Capitalist
Population: 589,000
PPP: $775
Life Expectancy: 48.4
Ethnic Groups: Somali (60 percent), Afar (35 percent), Arab
Capital: Djibouti

Political Rights: 5
Civil Liberties: 6
Status: Not Free

Overview: **E**thnic and clan rivalries over political control of this small but strategically-positioned Horn of Africa country led to the imprisonment of five politicians, and to rising tension over the succession to ailing octogenarian President Hassan Gouled Aptidon, whose term expires in April 1999.

Before receiving independence from France in 1977, Djibouti was known as the French Territory of the Afar and Issas, after the two largest ethnic groups. Most power remains concentrated with members of the Issa Mamassan sub-clan to which President Gouled belongs. The other largest ethnic group, the Afar, have fought against Issa dominance, although ethnic violence has receded since 1994, when Afar rebels of the Front for the Restoration of Unity and Democracy (FRUD) agreed to end their three year insurgency in exchange for inclusion in the government and electoral reforms before the next general election in December 1997. France remains highly influential in Djibouti's affairs. About 3,500 French troops are stationed there, along with thousands of civilian administrators.

With strong French support, Gouled ruled since independence under a one-party system, until a new constitution adopted by referendum in 1992 authorized four political parties. In 1993, Gouled won a fourth six-year term in Djibouti's first contested presidential elections with 60 percent of the popular vote. The poll, however, was considered fraudulent by both the opposition and international observers. The election was boycotted by the Afar-dominated FRUD and nearly all the candidates were members of the Issa ethnic group.

Djibouti's politics reflect the country's principal ethnic division between the Somalian Issa group, which comprises roughly half of the population and is concentrated in the south, and the Afar people, which comprises about 35 percent and occupies the northern and western regions. Somalians and Yemeni Arabs make up most of the remainder of the population. FRUD launched its rebellion in November 1991 with calls for the end to "tribal dictatorship" and the installation of a democratic, multiparty system. According to Amnesty International, the three-year struggle saw many gross human rights violations against the Afars by government security forces, including rape, torture and extrajudicial executions.

Ethnic and political tensions sparked violence several times in 1996.

Political Rights and Civil Liberties: Djiboutians have never been able to choose their government democratically. Legislative and presidential elections in 1992 and 1993, respectively, were reportedly fraudulent. The Popular Rally for Progress party (RPP) holds all 65 seats in the National Assembly, but is now riven by internal dissent. President Gouled has sought to achieve at least the appearance of ethnic balance in government by appointing Afars as prime ministers. FRUD leader Ali Mohammed Daoud, and its chairman and secretary general Ougoureh Kifleh, joined the cabinet as ministers of health and agriculture, respectively, as part of the December 1994 peace pact. Political power remains concentrated in the hands of the Issa majority, however.

In August, five politicians were sentenced to six months' imprisonment, loss of civic rights (including the right to hold public office) and heavy fines after being convicted of "offending the head of state." Amnesty International has declared them prisoners of conscience. A new coalition, the Coordination of Djiboutian Opposition (COD), was announced in May in efforts to solidify a fractious opposition.

Independent newspapers and other publications are allowed to circulate freely, but the government closely controls all electronic media. Freedom of assembly and association is protected under the constitution; however, the government has effectively banned political protest. Formation of opposition parties is also permitted by the constitution, but the ruling party determines which are to enjoy legality. Due to routine government interference, the judiciary is not independent. The constitution stipulates that arrests may not occur without a decree presented by a judicial magistrate, but security forces commonly arrest political demonstrators without proper authority. Despite a constitutional provision for freedom of speech, that right is severely curtailed. While Islam is the official state religion, freedom of worship is respected.

Women suffer serious discrimination under customary practices in inheritance and other property matters, divorce and the right to travel, despite equality under civil law. Women have few opportunities for education or in the formal economic sector. Female genital mutilation is almost universal among Djibouti's female population. Legislation forbidding mutilation of young girls is not enforced.

Workers may join unions and strike, but the government routinely obstructs the free operation of unions. The Djibouti General Workers' Union and the Djibouti Labor Union have denounced the "non-respect by the government of workers' union rights and brutality by the security forces." Wages are very low, with many workers earning less than $ 0.50 per hour.

Dominica

Polity: Parliamentary democracy
Economy: Capitalist
Population: 83,000
PPP: $3,810
Life Expectancy: 72.0

Political Rights: 1
Civil Liberties: 1
Status: Free

Ethnic Groups: Black and mulatto with a minority Carib enclave
Capital: Roseau

Overview:
In 1996 the United Workers' Party (UWP) gained an additional parliamentary seat through special elections, strengthening the shift away from rule by the Democratic Freedom Party (DFP).

Dominica has been an independent republic within the British Commonwealth since 1978. Internally self-governing since 1967, Dominica is a parliamentary democracy headed by a prime minister and a House of Assembly with 21 members elected to five-year terms. Nine senators are appointed, five by the prime minister and four by the opposition leader. The president is elected by the House for a five-year term.

In 1993 Prime Minister Eugenia Charles of the DFP announced her intention to retire in 1995 after 15 years in power. External Affairs Minister Brian Alleyne defeated three other candidates in a vote of DFP delegates to become the new party leader.

In June 1995 the UWP won a narrow majority, 11 of 21 seats, in parliamentary elections. UWP's Edison James, former head of the Banana Growers' Association, became prime minister. The UWP victory marked a significant shift in power from the traditional establishment to a new and younger business class.

The DFP and the Dominica Labor Party (DLP) won five seats each. The DFP's Alleyne and the DLP's Douglas reached an agreement to share the official opposition post by alternating each year. Alleyne assumed the post first. A High Court, however, ruled that one of the winning DFP candidates was not qualified to sit in parliament since he still held a public service position. The ruling reduced the DFP's representation in parliament to four seats. Special elections, held in 1996, resulted in an additional seat for the UWP, raising its share to 12 of the 21 seats. Douglas became the opposition leader.

In April 1996, Alleyne announced his resignation as DFP leader, citing personal and professional reasons. Former diplomat Charles Savarin replaced him.

Political Rights and Civil Liberties:

Citizens are able to change their government through free and fair elections. There are no restrictions on political, civic or labor organizations. Several civic groups have emerged in recent years calling for more accountability and transparency in government.

There is an independent judiciary and the rule of law is enhanced by the court's subordination to the inter-island Eastern Caribbean Supreme Court. But the judicial system is understaffed, which has led to a large backlog of cases. The only prison on Dominica continues to face overcrowding and sanitation problems.

The Dominica Defense Force (DDF) was disbanded in 1981 after being implicated in attempts by supporters of former prime minister Patrick John to overthrow the government. John was convicted in 1986 for his involvement and given a 12-year prison sentence. He was released by executive order in 1990, became active in the trade union movement and lost as a DLP candidate in the 1995 election. The Dominica Police is the only security force.

The press is generally free, varied and critical. Television and radio, both public and private, are open to a variety of views. Since 1990 television has been used as an effective campaign tool by all parties. The government respects academic freedom.

Freedom of religion is generally recognized. However, the small Rastafarian community has charged that their religious rights are violated by a policy of cutting off the "dreadlocks" of those who are imprisoned, and that Rastafarian women are harassed by immigration officials who single them out for drug searches.

Since 1990 the 3,000 indigenous Carib Indians, many of whom live on a 3,700-acre reserve on the northeast coast, have been represented in the House of Assembly by an elected Carib parliamentarian. In 1994 Hilary Frederick was elected chief of the Carib people for a five-year term, defeating Irvince Auguiste, the incumbent. A policeman was charged with the murder of a young man during the ensuing celebration.

Inheritance laws do not fully recognize women's rights. When a husband dies without a will, the wife cannot inherit the property, though she may continue to inhabit the home. There are no laws mandating equal pay for equal work for private sector workers. In the June 1995 elections, two women won parliamentary seats. Government welfare officials have expressed concern over the growing number of cases of child abuse.

There are no restrictions on forming local human rights organizations, but none exist. No international or regional human rights organizations requested permission to monitor or investigate human rights abuses in 1996.

Workers have the right to organize, strike and bargain collectively. Though unions are independent of the government and laws prohibit anti-union discrimination by employers, less than ten percent of the workforce are union members.

Dominican Republic

Polity: Presidential-legislative democracy
Economy: Capitalist-statist
Population: 8,089,000
PPP: $3,690
Life Expectancy: 69.7
Ethnic Groups: Mestizo and Creole (73 percent), European (16 percent), black (11 percent)
Capital: Santo Domingo

Political Rights: 3*
Civil Liberties: 3
Status: Partly Free

Ratings Change: The Dominican Republic's political rights rating changed from 4 to 3 because the 1996 national elections were freer than past elections.

Overview:

Leonel Fernandez won the 1996 presidential elections following a campaign marred by racist rhetoric. Former-President Balaguer's support of Fernandez raises the suspicion that he will continue to exert influence.

After achieving independence from Spain in 1821 and from Haiti in 1844, the Dominican Republic endured recurrent domestic conflict. The assassination of General Rafael Trujillo in 1961 ended 30 years of dictatorship, but a 1963 military coup led to civil war and U.S. intervention. In 1966, under a new constitution, civilian rule was restored with the election of the conservative Balaguer.

The constitution provides for a president and a Congress elected for four years. The Congress consists of a 120-member Chamber of Deputies and a 30-member Senate.

Balaguer was re-elected in 1970 and 1974, but was defeated in 1978 by Silvestre Antonio Guzman of the social-democratic Dominican Revolutionary Party (PRD). The PRD was triumphant again in 1982 with the election of Salvador Jorge Blanco, but Balaguer, heading the right-wing Social Christian Reformist Party (PRSC), returned to power in 1986 and was re-elected in 1990 in a vote marred by fraud.

In the May 1994 election the main contenders were Balaguer, fellow-octogenarian Juan Bosch of the Dominican Liberation Party (PLD) and the PRD's Jose Francisco Pena Gomez. Pena Gomez, black and charismatic, took a significant lead. The Balaguer machine responded by attacking Pena Gomez as a Haitian who secretly planned to unite the neighboring countries. Though ugly, the strategy appeared to narrow the gap.

Despite clear evidence of widespread fraud, Balaguer was declared the winner by a few thousand votes. Amid street protests and international pressure, Balaguer agreed to hold new presidential elections in 18 months. The legislative results stood. The PRD and allies took 57 seats in the Chamber and 15 in the Senate, the PRSC 50 and 14, and the PLD 13 and one.

When Congress convened, the PLD backed PRSC's plan to lengthen Balaguer's shortened term from 18 months to two years, with elections in May 1996. In exchange, Balaguer made a PLD legislator president of the Chamber. The PRD protested, but tacitly conceded by announcing that Pena Gomez would again be its candidate in 1996.

In 1995 Vice President Jacinto Peynado, head of a wealthy business family, won the PRSC primary.

When the PLD began spending lavishly, people suspected the money was coming from Balaguer. It was alleged that Balaguer, in the expectation of a defeat, wanted to ensure victory for Fernandez and not Pena Gomez, thereby avoiding any future corruption investigation. Meanwhile, the PLD took a page out of Balaguer's book and started to play the race card: placards showed Fernandez as a lion eating Pena Gomez, portrayed as a monkey.

On May 16, 1996, Pena Gomez won 45.9 percent of the vote; Fernandez 38.9 percent; and Peynado 15.0 percent. At the June 30 run-off, Fernandez won the presidency with 51.3 percent of the vote. Fernandez

Political Rights and Civil Liberties: Citizens can change their government through elections. Observers rated the 1995 elections as fair, but noted logistical and administrative problems

In 1995 a new, nominally more independent, electoral board was established and a revision of the electoral rolls was begun in preparation for the May 1996 vote.

Constitutional guarantees regarding free expression, freedom of religion and the right to organize political parties and civic groups are generally respected. However, the violent political campaigns, the frequent government-labor clashes, and the repressive measures taken by police and the military mean that free expression is somewhat circumscribed. Fifteen people died in clashes between rival supporters during the 1995 election campaign.

The judiciary, headed by a Supreme Court, is politicized and, like other government institutions, riddled with corruption. The courts offer little recourse to those without money or influence. Prisons are abysmal and violence routine. Nine out of ten prison inmates have not been convicted of a crime.

Independent rights groups continue to report widespread police brutality, including torture, and arbitrary arrests by the security forces. Criminal violence, much of it drug-related, and police corruption threaten the security of citizens. Poor women promised jobs in Europe for a fee often find themselves working as prostitutes in Germany and Spain.

Labor unions are well-organized. Although legally permitted to strike, they are often subject to government crackdowns. Peasant unions are occasionally targeted by armed groups working for large landowners. A new 1992 labor code established standards for workplace conditions and strengthened the right to bargain collectively. But companies in the 27 industrial "free zones," employing almost ten percent of the nation's workforce, remain reluctant to comply. Worker conditions in the zones remain below international standards, and discriminatory practices against women are prevalent.

Haitians, including children, continue to work in appalling conditions on state-run sugar plantations. The new labor code recognizes sugar workers' right to organize, but reports of abuses continue.

The media are mostly private. Newspapers are independent and diverse but subject to government pressure through denial of advertising revenues and taxes on imported newsprint. Dozens of radio stations and at least six commercial television stations broadcast. Journalists critical of the government are occasionally threatened. Narciso Gonzalez, a journalist and government critic, disappeared in May 1994, apparently after being arrested by state security forces.

Ecuador

Polity: Presidential-
legislative democracy
Economy: Capitalist-
statist
Population: 11,662,000
PPP: $4,400
Life Expectancy: 69.0
Political Rights: 2
Civil Liberties: 4*
Status: Free

Ethnic Groups: Mestizo (55 percent), Indian (25 percent),
European (10 percent), black (10 percent)
Capital: Quito
Ratings Change: Ecuador's civil liberties rating changed from 3 to 4 because of mounting evidence of systematic corruption in all branches of the government.

Overview:

In a stunning victory, Adbala Bucaram Ortiz, the former mayor of Guayaquil who twice went into exile under threat of prosecution on corruption charges, won the presidential election in a July 7 runoff. With 54 percent of the vote, he carried the vote in 20 of the country's 21 provinces. Considered by many to be unpredictable because of his populist demagogy, he has nonetheless turned to former Argentine Economy Minister Domingo Cavallo and members of his team to prepare a macroeconomic program that includes dollar convertibility for the local currency. Bucaram's energetic campaign in the countryside galvanized the poor, while his post-election appointments reassured the business sector.

Established in 1830 after achieving independence from Spain in 1822, the Republic of Ecuador has endured many interrupted presidencies and military governments. The last military regime gave way to civilian rule when a new constitution was approved by referendum in 1978.

The constitution provides for a president elected for four years, with a runoff between the two front runners if no candidate wins a majority in the first round. A 77-member unicameral National Chamber of Deputies is in place, with 65 members elected on a provincial basis every two years and 12 elected nationally every four years.

The main candidates in the 1992 election were Sixto Duran Ballen, who left the right-wing Social Christian Party (PSC) to form the Republican Union Party (PUR); Jaime Nebot of the PSC; Abdala Bucaram of the populist Ecuadorian Roldosist Party (PRE); and Raul Baca of the incumbent Democratic Left (ID). Duran Ballen won the first round with 31.9 percent of the vote. Nebot came second to make the runoff. Duran won with 57 percent of the vote but took office with a weak hand as his PUR had won only 13 of 77 legislative seats.

Duran Ballen's term was marked by general strikes against his economic austerity measures, indigenous protests against business-backed land reform and the impeachment of numerous cabinet ministers by an opposition-controlled legislature. Impeaching government officials on corruption charges has been a staple of the country's fragmented, gridlocked politics since the return to civilian rule. Both Duran Ballen and the vice president fell under suspicion before their terms ended.

Bucaram's apparent determination to follow in the footsteps of Argentine President Carlos Menem by carrying out extensive market-oriented economic reform is likely to be hampered by his PRE's weak position in Congress.

Tensions between Ecuador and Peru, which led to conflict from January to July 1995, subsided over the course of the year.

Political Rights and Civil Liberties:

Citizens can change their government through elections. Competition is fierce and violence usually mars election campaigns. Constitutional guarantees regarding freedom of expression, religion, and the right to organize political parties, labor unions and civic groups are generally respected.

The near-constant gridlock among executive, legislative and judicial branches has made the country practically ungovernable. Opinion polls and rising voter abstention indicate that the credibility of political institutions is declining.

Evidence suggests that drug traffickers have penetrated the political system through campaign funding, and sectors of the police and military through bribery. Ecuador is a transshipment point for cocaine passing from neighboring Colombia to the U.S. and a money-laundering haven.

The judiciary is headed by a legislatively-appointed Supreme Court. The Court is frequently caught in political tugs-of-war between the executive and the legislature, and its impartiality is often in doubt. The judiciary is generally undermined by the corruption afflicting the entire political system.

There are numerous human rights organizations. In this election, Luis Macas, the respected head of a new political movement of indigenous people, was elected to Congress, giving some hope that they will find a voice in the political system. Although activists are occasionally targets of intimidation, they continue to report arbitrary arrest and police brutality, including torture and rape of female detainees. Prisons are overcrowded, and conditions poor.

The military is responsible for a significant percentage of abuses, particularly when it is deployed under states of emergency during labor strikes, demonstrations and land disputes. Abuses are committed with relative impunity because police and military personnel are tried in military rather than civil courts.

The government and military have generally sided with landowners and multinational oil companies as they continue to infringe upon land rights granted to Indians in the eastern Amazon region by former administrations. Paramilitary units employed by landowners against indigenous organizations operate with a high level of impunity.

Labor unions are well-organized and have the right to strike. Strikes are often marked by violent clashes with police, and several labor activists have been killed. Unions have protested amendments to the labor code limiting public-sector strikes.

Newspapers are mostly private and outspoken. Radio and television stations are privately-owned, but the government controls radio frequencies. Broadcast media are supervised by two independent associations. Ecuador's numerous mostly-commercial television stations play a major role during political campaigns.

Egypt

Polity: Dominant party **Political Rights:** 6
(military-influenced) **Civil Liberties:** 6
Economy: Mixed statist **Status:** Not Free
Population: 63,693,000
PPP: $3,800
Life Expectancy: 63.9
Ethnic Groups: Eastern Hamitic (90 percent), Greek, Syro-Lebanese
Capital: Cairo

Overview: In 1996 Egypt's autocratic National Democratic Party (NDP) government amended a restrictive press law passed a year earlier, but failed to embrace the broad changes sought by journalists; and a new Islamic party, *Wasat* (Center), sought registration.

Egypt achieved independence from the British in 1922. Colonel Gamel Abdel Nasser, after leading a 1952 coup that overthrew the monarchy, ruled until his death in 1970. The 1971 constitution adopted under Nasser's successor, President Anwar al-Sadat, grants full executive powers to the president, who is nominated by the 454-member People's Assembly and elected for a six-year term in a national referendum. In October 1981 Islamic militants assassinated Sadat for making peace with Israel. Under Sadat's successor, Hosni Mubarak, the NDP continues to dominate a tightly-controlled political system. In October 1993 Mubarak won a third presidential term with 96.3 percent approval as the sole candidate in a national referendum.

In the spring of 1992 the militant Islamic Group, which has tapped into popular discontent with official corruption, high unemployment and widespread poverty, sharply escalated its attacks on the police, Coptic Christians and tourists in its drive to establish an Islamic republic by force. The authorities responded with crackdowns, and in early 1994 began arresting members of the non-violent Muslim Brotherhood, a grassroots movement dating from the 1920s which technically is outlawed but has been allowed to operate openly.

In the November 27, 1995, People's Assembly elections and the subsequent runoff on December 6, the NDP won 317 seats; pro-government "independents," who subsequently joined the NDP, 99; small opposition parties, 13; other independents, 5; with 10 seats by law appointed by the president.

On August 15, 1996, a military court acquitted three Muslim Brotherhood members of using their Wasat party–launched in January but still in the registration process–as a front for the banned Brotherhood. The surprising acquittals came after Wasat convincingly demonstrated its independence from the Brotherhood.

In another development, in early January, Mubarak appointed a new prime minister, Kamal al-Ganzoury, as part of a cabinet reshuffle designed to speed economic restructuring plans.

Political Rights and Civil Liberties: Egyptians cannot change their government democratically. The 1995 parliamentary elections were characterized by widespread fraud and irregularities. Political violence killed 51 people and wounded more than 850. The Muslim Brotherhood could not compete due to a ban on religious-based parties. While its members can run as independents, in 1995 the authorities arrested several of the Muslim Brothers planning to contest the November elections. Just before the vote a military court sentenced 54 members to jail terms of up to five years for non-violent activities.

The militant Islamic Group's battle against the secular government, now confined mainly to Assiut and Minya provinces, has resulted in the deaths of more than 1,000 security officers, militants and civilians since 1992. The security forces are accused of extrajudicial killings of militants.

The Emergency Law, in effect since Sadat's assassination in 1981, allows authorities to detain suspects without charge for up to 90 days. By some estimates more than 25,000 militants have been jailed or detained since 1992.

In May the United Nations Committee Against Torture accused the security forces of systematically torturing suspects to extract information or confessions. Women and children related to suspects at large are occasionally detained and tortured. Local police routinely abuse ordinary criminal suspects.

The judiciary is influenced by the government in sensitive cases. Since December 1992 the government has tried Islamic Group militants and Muslim Brotherhood activists in military courts, where due process rights are inadequate. In recent years, fundamentalist lawyers have filed numerous lawsuits against secular intellectuals under the Islamic doctrine of *hezba*, which allows any male Muslim to advocate against an issue considered offensive to Islam, regardless of whether he is directly involved. A January 1996 law permits only prosecuters to file such suits.

The controversial Press Law No. 93 of May 1995 increased prison penalties and fines for libel and slander, and provided for the detention of journalists for up to six months while being investigated on such charges. By May 1996 at least 20 journalists had been tried or were then being prosecuted under the law. On June 9 parliament passed a replacement law reducing the length of some prison sentences but maintaining the vague, broad language and heavy fines of its predecessor.

During the year the government banned numerous editions of newspapers and repeatedly ordered individual articles to be edited or deleted. The government also regulates the press through a licensing system. Most major newspapers are state-owned and offer some pluralistic views, but state-owned broadcast media rarely air opposition views. Extremists have physically attacked journalists and intellectuals.

Under the Emergency Law, the Interior Ministry sometimes denies approval for public demonstrations on political grounds. During the 1995 parliamentary election campaign police broke up several Muslim Brotherhood rallies. The Ministry of Social Affairs has broad powers to merge and dissolve nongovernmental organizations. The government refuses to license the Egyptian Organization for Human Rights and frequently harasses its members.

Women face official and informal discrimination in many legal and social matters. A 1996 Health Ministry ban on female genital mutilation is not expected to curb the practice in rural areas.

The government portrays itself as a staunch supporter of Islam, the state religion, while it cracks down on fundamentalist influences in academia, mosques and other institutions. The government frequently bans, confiscates or censors films, books and other artistic works for being anti-Islamic, while also routinely banning fundamentalist literature. In 1992 the government formally placed mosques under its control, although many unlicensed mosques still operate. In May 1996 the High Constitutional Court upheld a 1994 decree barring female university students from wearing the *niqab*, a face-concealing veil, and requiring girls to get parental permission to wear the *hijab*, a scarf covering the hair, to school.

Islamic militants have murdered, kidnapped or raped scores of Coptic Christians in recent years, and burned or vandalized Copt houses, shops and churches. The government has seized Coptic church-owned land, closed some churches, and frequently uses an 1856 Ottoman Empire-era law to deny permission to build or repair churches. Copts also face discrimination in employment and education opportunities.

The government-backed Egyptian Trade Union Federation is the only legal labor union federation. The 1976 law on labor unions sets numerous regulations on the formation and operation of unions and the conduct of elections. Child labor remains a serious problem.

↑ El Salvador

Polity: Presidential-legislative democracy (military-influenced)
Economy: Capitalist-statist
Population: 5,904,000
PPP: $2,360
Life Expectancy: 66.8
Ethnic Groups: Mestizo (94 percent), with small Indian and European minorities
Capital: San Salvador

Political Rights: 3
Civil Liberties: 3
Status: Partly Free

Overview:　　　　　In 1996, the government of President Armando Calderon Sol of the Nationalist Republican Alliance (ARENA) faced a continued increase in violent crime, the resurgence of far-right and leftist paramilitary groups, and corruption. With legislative and municipal elections due in 1997, there were also signs of increased political polarization and infighting within key parties.

Independence from the Captaincy General of Guatemala was declared in 1841, and the Republic of El Salvador was established in 1859. Over a century of civil strife and military rule followed.

Elected civilian rule was established in 1984. The 1983 constitution provides for a president elected for a five-year term and an 84-member, unicameral National Assembly elected for three years. Over a decade of civil war (which left more than 70,000 dead) ended with the United Nations-mediated peace accords signed in 1992 by the Farabundo Marti National Liberation Front (FMLN) and the conservative government of President Alfredo Cristiani.

The FMLN participated in the 1994 elections, backing former ally Ruben Zamora of the Democratic Convergence (CD) for president and running a slate of legislative candidates. The incumbent Nationalist Republican Alliance (ARENA) nominated San Salvador Mayor Armando Calderon Sol. The Christian Democrats (PDC) nominated Fidel Chavez Mena. The PDC had previously held power under President Jose Napoleon Duarte (1984-89).

ARENA, a well-oiled political machine, sounded populist themes and attacked the FMLN as Communists and terrorists. The FMLN-CD coalition offered a progressive but moderate platform and called for compliance with the peace accords.

In the March 1994 vote Calderon Sol won just under 50 percent, setting up a runoff against Zamora, who came in second with 25 percent. In the legislature ARENA won 39 seats, the FMLN 21, the PDC 18, the CD one, and the Unity Movement (MU), a small evangelical party, one. The right-wing National Conciliation Party (PCN) won four seats, giving ARENA an effective right-wing majority. In the runoff Calderon Sol defeated Zamora, 68 percent to 32 percent.

President Calderon Sol promised full compliance with the peace accords. As of December 1995, however, two months after implementation of the accords was to have been completed, the U.N. noted that major problems remained in regards to the program to transfer land to former FMLN and army combatants. Also reported were mounting human rights and corruption allegations involving the new National Civilian Police.

In 1996, violence by organized crime, some of it perpetrated by former death squad members and gangs made up of Salvadoran nationals forcibly returned from the U.S. after 1992, reached epidemic proportions, with killings, kidnappings and extortion. The escalating murder rate, driven by unemployment, a culture of violence and the availability of weapons, means that in the years since 1992, over 90,000 people are estimated to have been killed, more than in the civil war.

Paramilitary groups were also more visible in 1996, engaging in kidnappings, extortion and car bombings. At least six armed groups with extensive intelligence networks operate in the country. One paramilitary group is led by Hector Antonio Regalado, a co-founder of ARENA and former death squad leader who is a key suspect in the 1980 murder of Archbishop Oscar Romero.

In politics, the centrist PDC, which won national elections in 1984, was buffeted by infighting, while four key national figures resigned from the newly-formed socialist-oriented Democrat Party, which split from the FMLN in 1995 (taking seven of the FMLN's 21 parliamentary seats). In November, the FMLN announced it was seeking an alliance with democratic forces to weaken the power of the right in legislative and municipal elections due in 1997.

Political Rights and Civil Liberties: Citizens can change their government democratically. Still, the 1994 election was marred by right-wing violence, the ruling ARENA party's inordinate financial advantage, and registration irregularities that disenfranchised tens of thousands of eligible voters.

The opposition accepted the outcome of the election, having recognized that the results reflected the competing parties' relative electoral strength. The former FMLN guerrillas won a significant bloc of seats in the legislature, although the FMLN subsequently split, with one group leaving to form the social-democratic Democratic Party (PD).

The constitution guarantees free expression, freedom of religion and the right to organize political parties, civic groups and labor unions. Although the 1992 peace accords have led to a significant reduction in human rights violations, political expression and civil liberties are still circumscribed by sporadic political violence, repressive police measures, a mounting crime wave and right-wing death squads, including "social-cleansing" vigilante groups.

Although the country is overwhelmingly Roman Catholic, evangelical Protestantism has made substantial inroads, leading to friction. The Catholic church remained divided between activist leaders and conservatives led by Archbishop Fernando Saenz Lacalle who, shortly after assuming office in 1995, blasted "the poorly-named liberation theology" as a "re-reading of the Gospel with a Marxist view that leads to violence."

The underlying problem remains an ineffectual judicial system and a climate of impunity. A first step toward judicial reform came in 1994 with the naming by the new legislature of a more politically representative 15-member Supreme Court, which controls the entire Salvadoran judiciary. In late 1995, 14 judicial officials were removed and a number of judges placed under investigation. In 1996, judicial reforms stalled in the National Assembly, undermining the establishment of a rule of law.

Two amnesty laws have added to the sense of impunity. In 1992 the FMLN and the government agreed to the first of these, which covered most rights violations by both sides during the war. In 1993 the Cristiani government pushed a blanket amnesty through the legislature that immunized the military against charges subsequently recommended by a U.N.-sponsored Truth Commission, which also omitted most of those involved in death squad activities.

The peace accords mandated the creation of a new National Civilian Police (PNC), incorporating former FMLN guerrillas. But up to 500 former members of disbanded security forces were apparently integrated into the new force, and the PNC as a whole appeared in 1995 to be falling into corrupt practices and increasing rights violations. The U.N. and local rights groups were investigating reports of a tangled web of criminal operations within the new police. In August 1996, UN Secretary Boutros Boutros-Ghali warned of "increased signs" that the police were becoming "an instrument of authoritarianism that is not accountable to the public."

Prisons are overcrowded, conditions are wretched and up to three-quarters of the prisoners are waiting to be charged and tried. Dozens of inmates have been killed during prison riots in the last two years. In June 1996, inmates in the Santa Ana Prison, which was built for 350 but held 787, threatened to hold a "lottery of death" to alleviate overcrowding and appalling conditions. The protest was suspended after the government promised to ask the legislature to reduce sentences for non-violent crimes, to form a special commission and to build a new prison capable of holding 4,000 inmates.

Most media are privately owned. Election campaigns feature televised interviews and debates among candidates from across the political spectrum. The FMLN's formerly clandestine Radio Venceremos operates from San Salvador, and competes with nearly 70 other stations. Left-wing journalists and publications are occasionally targets of intimidation. At the end of 1995 the government was trying to push through a constitutional amendment that would severely restrict the media's access to and ability to report on judicial matters. In July 1996, the publisher of the tabloid *Colatino* was jailed for defaming a police official; the Association of Journalists of El Salvador called the arrest "an attack against the national press."

Labor, peasant and university organizations are well-organized. The archaic labor code was reformed in 1994, but the new code was enacted lacking the approval of most unions because it significantly limits the right to organize, in areas including in the export-processing zones known as *maquiladoras*. Unions that strike remain subject to intimidation and violent police crackdowns. In 1995 and 1996 hundreds of maquiladora workers were fired for organizing.

Equatorial Guinea

Polity: Dominant party (military-dominated)
Economy: Capitalist-statist
Population: 431,000
PPP: $1,800
Life Expectancy: 48.2
Ethnic Groups: Fang (75-80 percent), Bubi (15 percent), Puku, Seke and others (5-10 percent)
Capital: Malabo

Political Rights: 7
Civil Liberties: 7
Status: Not Free

Overview:

A February presidential election in Equatorial Guinea saw President Teodoro Obiang Nguema M'basogo declared victor of a contest that had little of the form and nearly none of the content of a free and fair election. The incumbent, who seized power in 1979 by deposing and executing his uncle, Francisco Macias Nguema, carried on the tradition of severe repression that has marked Equatorial Guinea as one of the world's least open and most repressed societies. Since independence in 1968, following 190 years of Spanish control, nearly all power has been concentrated in the hands of ethnic Fang people and, in recent years, the Esangui clansmen related to President Obiang. The president's renewed seven-year mandate, however flawed, may be encouraging a slight easing of the most overt signs of repression. New wealth from oilfields that came on line in August might also help ease the economic despair afflicting most of the country's 400,000 people.

As Equatorial Guinea's first president, Macias Nguema presided over a decade-long tyranny that saw the country's name become synonymous with state terror, as tens of thousands of people were murdered and many more were driven into exile. Few people lamented his overthrow and execution, but under Obiang repression continued.

In January 1992, bending to international pressure by donor countries demanding democratic reforms, Obiang proclaimed a new "era of pluralism." Political parties were legalized and multiparty elections announced; however, the three elections since then have offered little more than the trappings of a genuine democratic process. Opposition parties have been continually harassed and intimidated. Unlawful arrests, beatings and torture remain commonplace.

Political Rights and Civil Liberties:

Equatorial Guinea's citizens cannot change their government by peaceful and democratic means. The February 1996 presidential election was neither free nor fair, and was marred by official intimidation, a near-total boycott by the political opposition and very low voter turnout. The September 1995 municipal elections were widely believed to have been won overwhelmingly by the opposition, but the regime's official results released 11 days after balloting reported a large but unconvincing ruling party victory. Opposition parties had also disputed the November 1993 victory by President Obiang's Democratic Party of Equatorial Guinea (PDGE) in the country's first contested legislative elections since 1968. Intimidation and arrests of activists at voting centers, numerous electoral irregularities and the absence of international observers rendered ruling party victories meaningless.

President Obiang's regime effectively bars public participation in the policymaking process, and the president wields broad decree-making powers. The November 1991 constitution prohibits the impeachment of the head of state. Opposition parties, while legal, may not be organized on an ethnic, regional or provincial basis, although such is the obvious foundation of the ruling party. Each recognized party must pay a prohibitive deposit of CFA 30,000,000 (approximately $60,000). Opposition activists face harassment, arrest and torture, particularly outside the capital.

The judiciary is not independent, and, according to exiled groups, the regime has staged summary trials based on false charges to sideline political opponents. There are persistent allegations by human rights groups of torture by soldiers and police to extract confessions. Black Beach prison in Malabo, the capital, is described by survivors of incarceration there as one of the world's most hellish places.

All media are state-run and tightly-controlled. Independent or opposition publications are not tolerated, despite constitutional guarantees. However, underground pamphleteering appears to be lively, if judged by the regime's public denunciation of "the tons of paper used in clandestine printing presses."

Freedom of association is barred with partial exception for members of legalized political parties, as is freedom of assembly. Opposition demonstrations without prior authorization were banned in 1993. Any gathering of ten or more people for purposes the government deems political is illegal. There are no free trade unions. Freedom of movement is also restricted; citizens and residents must obtain permission for travel both within the country and abroad, and political activists are often stopped by security guards and forced to pay bribes.

Women enjoy constitutional and legal protections of equality that are honored only in name. Traditional practices discriminate against women and few receive education or participate in the formal economy of government. Violence against women is reportedly widespread.

Approximately 80 percent of the population is Roman Catholic and freedom of religion is generally respected, although President Obiang has warned the clergy against interfering in political affairs.

Eritrea

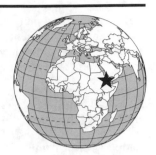

Polity: One-party (transitional)
Economy: Mixed statist
Population: 3,627,000
PPP: na
Life Expectancy: na
Ethnic Groups: Afar, Arab, Beja, Bilin, Jabarti, Kunama, Saho, Tigrawi
Capital: Asmara

Political Rights: 6
Civil Liberties: 4
Status: Partly Free

Overview: Eritrea's transition, from a war of independence lasting 30 years to popularly-mandated constitutional rule, continued through 1996, although President Isaias Afwerki again voiced his opinion that multiparty democracy is unsuitable for his country. The ruling Popular Front for Democracy and Justice (PFDJ) appeared to maintain broad support. After extensive public consultations, a new constitution is expected to win easy approval in a referendum early in 1997, to be followed by presidential and legislative elections by May. The Provisional Government of Eritrea and the country's political and economic life are dominated by the PFDJ, created in February 1994 as a successor to the wartime Eritrean Peoples Liberation Front (EPLF), and elections are not likely to change this any time soon.

Ethiopia was granted control over Eritrea in 1950 after nearly 50 years of Italian occupation. The Eritrean independence struggle began in 1962 as a nationalist and Marxist guerrilla war against the Ethiopian government of Emperor Haile Selassie. The war's ideological logic disappeared when a Marxist junta seized power in Ethiopia in 1974, and the EPLF's Marxist origins were discarded by the time it finally defeated Ethiopia's northern armies in 1991. Internationally-recognized independence was achieved in May 1993 after a U.N.-supervised referendum produced a landslide vote for statehood.

The PFDJ's austere and single-minded commitment to rebuilding Eritrea has won it many admirers, despite intolerance of criticism. The government seeks to balance senior governmental positions between the roughly equal Christian and Muslim populations. In response to guerrilla attacks by the Eritrean Islamic Jihad, believed to be backed by Sudan's fundamentalist regime, Eritrea has broken diplomatic ties with Sudan, and openly supports the armed Sudanese opposition. A simmering confrontation with Yemen over the potentially oil-rich Hanish islands in the Red Sea could flare into open conflict.

Political Rights and Civil Liberties: The Eritrean people have never exercised the right to elect their own leaders. The current national assembly is comprised of the PFDJ's 75 central committee members and three appointed representatives from each of Eritrea's administrative regions, which were cut from ten to six in 1995.

Presidential and legislative elections under the new constitution are planned by

May 1997. The new charter is expected to authorize independent political parties, but it is not clear from official statements whether new parties will in fact be registered; and parties based on ethnicity or religion will be pre-emptively prohibited. The government's desire to reduce ethnic identification has extended to the naming of the country's new regions, all of which will be geographical, not ethnic. The Eritrean government's administrative competence should make for well-run, but not necessarily fair (particularly with regard to media access), elections. The PFDJ's broad popularity will probably result in victory.

The PFDJ has sought to cultivate a broad public consensus, typified by the drafting of Eritrea's new constitution. Over half a million people attended seminars on the draft document, and these have been followed by an education campaign and further public debate, including consultation with overseas Eritreans in late 1996.

However, government control over all broadcasting and pressures against the small independent print media have constrained public debate. In November 1995, a Catholic-supported newspaper was closed after criticizing the government. While open discussion in public forums is tolerated, spreading dissenting views is not. A new press law adopted in June provides only qualified freedom of expression, subject to the government's interpretation of "the objective reality of Eritrea." Broadcast media will remain under state control, and external funding for independent print media barred.

An independent judiciary was formed by decree in 1993, and is apparently operating without executive interference. Lack of training and resources limit the courts' efficiency, however, and jurists have not been called on to handle the difficult cases that might challenge government policies.

Religious freedom is generally respected, although the activities of Islamist factions, most of which are believed to be externally-sponsored either by Sudan or Iran, could strain ties between religious communities. The government has denounced what it describes as political activities by the Roman Catholic Church, and a number of Jehovah's witnesses were stripped of citizenship and had property seized after refusing to serve in the armed forces or to take a national oath of allegiance.

The PFDJ government is actively involved in the economy, mostly in areas where private capital is not available, and has announced plans to privatize at least 23 state-owned companies. The task of reconstruction is complicated by severe environmental problems, especially as hundreds of thousands of Eritreans made refugees by the long war return home.

A small civil society sector is taking hold. The PFDJ has effectively shed several of the components of the EPLF, and newly-independent youth, women and labor organizations are struggling to find a new role. It remains too early to judge whether these groups will develop genuinely autonomous political voices.

During the independence struggle, women formed at least a third of the EPLF combat forces, and the government has strongly supported improvements in the status of women. Equal educational opportunity, equal pay for equal work, and penalties for domestic violence have been codified, yet traditional societal norms prevail for many women in a country that is largely rural and agricultural. Female genital mutilation is still widely practiced, even though it is discouraged by official education campaigns.

Promulgation of Eritrea's new constitution and elections promised for 1997 will measure the PFDJ leadership's commitment to an open and democratic society. Yet to emerge are key components for a free and fair election—pluralistic media and rights to political organization—that would reinforce the PFDJ's mandate in the eyes of both domestic opponents and the international community.

Estonia

Polity: Presidential- **Political Rights:** 1*
parliamentary democracy **Civil Liberties:** 2
Economy: Mixed   **Status:** Free
Capitalist
Population: 1,470,000
PPP: $3,610
Life Expectancy: 69.2
Ethnic Groups: Estonian (62 percent), Russian (30 percent),
Ukrainian, German, others
Capital: Tallinn
Ratings Change: Estonia's political rights rating changed from 2 to 1 because rapid naturalization of Russians enfranchised thousands of new citizens prior to the elections.

Overview: Continued sniping within the governing coalition, as well as during the September presidential elections and October local elections were the major political events of 1996.

Estonia became independent with the collapse of the Russian Empire in 1918. Soviet troops occupied the country during World War II as a result of the 1939 Hitler-Stalin pact, which forcibly incorporated Estonia into the Soviet Union. Russian immigration and deportation policy substantially changed the country's demography—ethnic Estonians made up 88 percent of the population before Soviet rule and just over 61 percent in 1989. Estonia regained independence with the disintegration of the Soviet Union in 1991.

The government, which consists of a fragile coalition of the Coalition Party, the left-leaning Rural Union and the center-right Reform Party, held despite strong tensions threatening to break it apart. In the first half of the year, the Rural Union continued to push for import tariffs for its agrarian constituency. This step was opposed by its coalition partners in support of Estonia's extraordinarily liberal trade regime, which incited the Rural Union's threat to leave the coalition over the issue. Despite continuing power struggles between the Coalition Party and the Reform Party, a government split was averted in October.

In a reprise of their 1992 contest, incumbent president Lennart Meri defeated Arnold Ruutel of the Country People's Party. Ruutel's allies made unproven allegations about Meri's collaboration with the KGB leading up to the election. The constitution establishes a figurehead presidency, but Meri's active role has been the source of much controversy.

Local elections were held in October, with a 52 percent turnout. In Tallinn, the winner was the Reform Party, which seems to be riding a wave of national popularity following the decline of the Center Party.

In 1996, the economy grew by 3 percent, a figure that does not take account of the large informal sector. Inflation remains problematic at 25 percent. The privatization of small- and medium-scale enterprises is over, but is continuing for large-scale firms. Seventy percent of the economy is now in private hands. A stock market began operating in May. Unemployment, at 2.3 percent, is extraordinarily low by European standards.

Political Rights and Civil Liberties:

Estonians are able to change their government democratically. The October local elections were free and fair. Political parties and groupings are allowed to organize freely, including several organizations representing the Russian minority. The Estonian citizenship law has been the source of some controversy, as Moscow accuses the government of effectively disenfranchising non-ethnic Estonians, particularly Russians. The law requires a basic colloquial understanding of the difficult non-Indo-European language and a knowledge of Estonian civics. Both the Finnish Helsinki Committee and the OSCE have concluded that the citizenship law conforms to international standards.

Nevertheless, a combination of cumbersome bureaucracy, a shortage of Estonian language teachers, and a lack of desire among many Soviet-era immigrants to learn the language has deprived many Russians of citizenship. Since 1992, 75,000 Russians have become naturalized, and 1,000 more become citizens every month. In June, 3,000 retired Russian military personnel were granted citizenship.

The judiciary is independent and free from government pressure. The OSCE mission in Estonia found no pattern of human rights violations in Estonia. Problems continue, however, in the area of the mistreatment of prisoners and the excessive use of force by police. Estonia ratified the European Convention against torture and inhuman or degrading punishment in 1996. The Council of Europe made the passage of this law a prerequisite to Estonia's membership. The law creates an international committee, composed of independent experts, which is authorized to investigate all official detention centers.

In October, the government adopted a minorities protection bill and sent it to the Riigikogu for ratification. Non-citizen residents have the right to vote in local elections. Non-citizens have the same property rights under Estonian law as do citizens, with the exception of land ownership.

Estonian language policy has continued to show flexibility. In local districts where a majority of the population speaks another language, citizens are entitled to information and local government services in their language. Parliament amended the language law to allow non-Estonian-speaking civil servants to serve until February 1997. In April, parliament passed a local electoral law that required candidates that graduated from non-Estonian language schools to pass a special exam to prove Estonian proficiency. After protests by the Minorities' Roundtable and ethnic Russians, Meri vetoed the bill and parliament backed down.

Estonians can freely express their views and an independent private press exists in both Estonian and Russian. There are private television and radio stations, and an independent news agency.

Freedom of religion is guaranteed by law and honored in practice. Estonians enjoy real freedom of assembly and association. There are few restrictions on the right to organize and run nongovernmental organizations. The "Russian Community in Estonia" organization, in operation since 1993, registered in September, allowing it to open its own bank accounts.

The constitution protects the right to strike, form and join unions. Unions are independent from the government and political parties. Women possess the same legal rights as men.

Ethiopia

Polity: Dominant party **Political Rights:** 4
Economy: Statist **Civil Liberties:** 5
Population: 57,172,000 **Status:** Partly Free
PPP: $420
Life Expectancy: 47.8
Ethnic Groups: Afar, Amhara, Harari, Oromo, Somali, Tigrean, others
Capital: Addis Ababa

Overview: Ethiopia's democratic transition remained hobbled in 1996 as the ruling Ethiopian People's Revolutionary Democratic Front (EPRDF) government continued to attack the independent media and harass political opponents. The repression further devalues the important step achieved in 1995, of holding an election that was described as generally free and fair despite an opposition boycott and other serious flaws. The new government is still dominated by ethnic Tigrayans from northern Ethiopia whose guerrilla armies defeated the Marxist military regime in 1991. The EPRDF faces political opposition from the traditionally-dominant Amhara people and low-intensity armed challenges by both Oromo and Somali peoples, whose demands for self-rule go beyond the federal decentralization the government is currently instituting. In August and again in December, Ethiopian troops crossed into Somalia to attack ethnic Somali rebel camps believed to be behind several border incidents and bombings in Ethiopian cities.

A transitional government was formed by the EPRDF after its 1991 victory over the 'Dergue' military junta headed by Colonel Mengistu Haile Mariam, which itself had overthrown Emperor Haile Selassie in 1974. It is reckoned that over 100,000 people were killed in efforts to quash ethnic rebellions, and during the waves of political terror that characterized the 17 years of Dergue rule. Extrajudicial executions, torture and detention without trial were widespread. Mengistu's downfall saw the abeyance of these practices, but the EPRDF's record in honoring fundamental freedoms is so far mixed.

The 1995 elections were conducted under a constitution adopted in December 1994 by a constituent assembly elected six months earlier. Opposition parties had also boycotted that election, claiming the government was giving unfair advantage to the ruling party. The subsequent parliamentary vote boycott allowed the EPRDF to take 483 out of 548 seats in the Council of People's Representatives.

Meles Zenawi was elected prime minister by the new Council of People's Representatives. Under the new constitutional arrangement, he retains much of the power he held as president of the 1991-95 transitional government. Prime Minister Meles's Tigray Peoples Liberation Front (TPLF), which led the military drive that toppled the Mengistu regime, is the most important political grouping and at the heart of the EPRDF. A president with only symbolic powers was also appointed.

Political Rights and Civil Liberties:

The people of Ethiopia chose their government through a relatively open electoral process for the first time in the May 1995 legislative elections. Most international observers judged the election as largely free and fair, despite substantial government manipulation. Inadequate protection of basic rights before the polls, which prompted an opposition boycott and a crackdown on the independent media in the months before the vote, caused European election observers to express fears that Ethiopia's "democratic evolution is not assured." The next elections are scheduled for 2000, and there are few signs indicate that a fairer procedure is in preparation.

The government has devolved some power to regional and local governments. The December 1994 constitution allows greatly-enhanced regional autonomy and even secession from the federation. In reality, as the EPRDF today controls all the elected regional councils directly or with coalition partners, there is little likelihood any region will soon exercise its right to secede.

Armed conflict and reports of human rights violations come from at least two areas. The ethnic Somali and Islamist-leaning *Al-Itihad Al-Islam* (Islamic Union) has claimed responsibility for the assassination of a senior general, and the wounding of a government minister, and for hotel bombings in three Ethiopian cities. Ethiopian forces retaliated in early August by launching an incursion, 50 kilometers into Somalia to raid Islamic Union base camps that reportedly caused several hundred rebel casualties. These latest battles are part of a centuries-old conflict between the Somali clans who inhabit the vast Ogaden Desert, over which Ethiopian rulers have long maintained at least nominal control. Ethiopia repulsed a Somali invasion aimed at annexing the territory in 1977. The fate of several alleged members of the Ogaden National Liberation Front (ONLF) who fled to Djibouti but were handed back to Ethiopian authorities in August is unknown.

Potentially more dangerous is an armed rebellion by the banned Oromo Liberation Front (OLF) and the Islamic Front for the Liberation of Oromia, which is simmering across southern Ethiopia. Oromos are Ethiopia's single largest ethnic group, comprising about 40 percent of the country's nearly 60 million people. Sporadic fighting in the countryside has produced numerous casualties and human rights abuses. Many OLF supporters are imprisoned. Oromo grievances include long periods of governmental neglect of their region, which remains desperately poor even by Ethiopian standards. Potential for unrest also remains high in the Afar areas of northeast Ethiopia.

Even opposition activists who eschew violence have been intimidated or harassed by security officials or detained without charges, and some have had their offices closed, international rights groups report. A nongovernmental organization, the Ethiopian Human Rights Council, has complained about the treatment of Dr.

Taye Woldesemayat, president of the Ethiopian Teachers' Association (ETA), who on May 30 was arrested on his return from a visit to Europe and charged, with five other men, with plotting against the government.

With broadcast media firmly under government control, independent print media are a special target of the authorities. According to an extensive report made in October by the New York-based Committee to Protect Journalists, the 31 journalists then jailed in Ethiopia exceeded the number of any other African country. Charges are often vague and court proceedings are little more than summary trials. In March, Solomon Lemma Gemechu, editor of the weekly *Wolafen*, was sentenced to 18 months imprisonment for publishing "false reports to incite war and unrest." Very high bail is set for journalists awaiting trial and severe fines can effectively close down publications.

The government remains highly sensitive to any criticism of current human rights problems, but it is acting to punish some human rights abuses committed by the previous regime. Citing Ethiopian law and the Nuremberg trials, a court in Addis Ababa has met intermittently for over a year to hear evidence of such crimes by 45 defendants, including eight members of the former ruling junta. Twenty-four defendants, including ex-President Mengistu, now in exile in Zimbabwe, are being tried in absentia.

Women face widespread social discrimination despite legal protections, and violence against women is reportedly common. Especially in rural areas, women are allowed few opportunities beyond agricultural labor, and traditionally have few land or property rights. In August, the government announced privatization plans for tobacco companies and garment factories, and the sale of hotels, other factories and retail businesses is being prepared. Trade unions are operating, though their freedom to bargain and to strike has not yet been fully tested. Religious freedom is respected.

Fiji

Polity: Parliamentary
democracy and
native chieftains
Economy: Capitalist
Population: 811,000
PPP: $5,530
Life Expectancy: 71.6
Ethnic Groups: Fijian (49 percent), Indian (46 percent), other
Pacific islander, Chinese
Capital: Suva

Political Rights: 4
Civil Liberties: 3
Status: Partly Free

Overview: Fiji's paramount chiefs ceded sovereignty over these South Pacific islands to the British in 1874 to end territorial conquests among rival kingdoms. In 1879 the British began bringing Indian laborers to the islands to work on plantations. At independence in 1970 the ethnic Fijian and Indo-Fijian communities were roughly equal in population.

The April 1987 elections brought to power a coalition of two predominantly Indo-Fijian parties, the National Federation Party (NFP) and the Fiji Labor Party (FLP), breaking the 17-year rule of the ethnic-Fijian Alliance Party. To thwart the emerging political influence of the Indo-Fijian community, (then) Lieutenant Colonel Sitiveni Rabuka took power in a pair of bloodless coups in May and September 1987.

In July 1990 an interim civilian government promulgated a controversial new constitution guaranteeing ethnic Fijians a perpetual parliamentary majority. Thirty-seven of the 70 seats in the House of Representatives are reserved for ethnic Fijians, with 27 for Indo-Fijians, five for "other races," mostly Chinese and Europeans, and one to the island dependency of Rotuma. Twenty-four of the 34 seats in the unelected Senate are reserved for ethnic Fijians. The prime minister must be an ethnic Fijian. The Great Council of Chiefs (GCC), a group of unelected, traditional rulers, selects the largely ceremonial president and appoints the ethnic Fijian Senate seats.

Following the May 1992 elections Rabuka took office as prime minister in a coalition government led by his Fijian Political Party (SVT). In November 1993 the president dissolved parliament following a stalemate over the 1994 budget.

At early elections in February 1994, in the ethnic Fijian polling the SVT won 31 seats; the Fijian Association Party, led by Joseveta Kamikamica, a Rabuka rival, 5; independents, 1. In the Indo-Fijian voting the NFP took 20 seats and the FLP 7. The General Voters Party (GVP) took four of the seats reserved for "other races" and an independent took one. On February 28 Rabuka began a five-year term as head of a coalition government of his SVT, the GVP and the two independents.

In September 1996 a three-member constitutional review commission recommended a new bicameral parliament with a lower house, with 12 seats reserved for ethnic Fijians, ten for Indo-Fijians, three for other races, and 45 open seats. The prime ministership would no longer be reserved for an ethnic Fijian, and the GCC's nomination for the presidency would have to be approved by this lower house. The recommendations are being reviewed by the GCC and parliament.

Political Rights and Civil Liberties: Fijians have voted twice under a constitution that ensures ethnic Fijians a parliamentary majority, and which was promulgated by an unelected, interim government without a referendum. The parliament's ethnic Fijian seats are weighted toward the rural areas, where voters support ethnic Fijian nationalist parties and traditional leaders in greater numbers.

Abuse of detainees and prisoners is a persistent problem. The judiciary is independent although subject to delays in hearing appeals. The magistrates' courts, which adjudicate 95 percent of the cases handled by the police, have delivered highly lenient judgments in some criminal cases.

The Public Order Act (POA) prohibits speech or actions likely to incite racial antagonism. The Press Correction Act (PCA) allows the Minister of Information to order a paper to print a "correcting statement" to an article, with a fine and/or imprisonment possible if the paper refuses. Under the PCA the government can also arrest individuals for publishing "malicious" material, including false news that can result in "detriment to the public." The POA and the PCA are rarely applied but their existence leads to some self-censorship. Further, the Rabuka government frequently criticizes editors and journalists for being "culturally insensitive." On May 20, 1996, the government banned controversial *Fiji Times* columnist Ronald Gatty from publishing, for claiming that Indo-Fijians do not speak freely for fear of reprisals by ethnic Fijians. The government lifted the ban three days later after a public outcry. The private Fiji One Television provides objective news coverage.

Rape and domestic violence are serious problems. In some rape cases the practice of *Bulubulu* (traditional reconciliation) is applied, allowing the offender to apologize to the victim's father or family (although ignoring the victim herself). If accepted, the felony charge is dropped. Child abuse is also a growing problem. Members of the Indo-Fijian community are occasionally subject to racially-motivated harassment, and are underrepresented at the highest levels of the civil service. Freedom of religion is respected.

Indo-Fijians are at the forefront of a vigorous independent trade union movement. Strikes are legal except in union recognition disputes. Working conditions, particularly in the garment and canning industries, are often poor, and enforcement of safety standards is weak.

Finland

Polity: Presidential-
parliamentary democracy
Economy: Mixed
capitalist
Population: 5,127,000
PPP: $16,320
Life Expectancy: 75.8
Ethnic Groups: Finn (94 percent), Swede, (Saami) Lapp, Gypsy
Capital: Helsinki

Political Rights: 1
Civil Liberties: 1
Status: Free

Overview:

Over a year after the Social Democratic Party won the March 1995 general elections, the government of Prime Minister Paavo Lipponen faced continued high unemployment rates and a rising national debt. The country fell into a severe four-year economic recession following the collapse of the Soviet Union and its subsequent loss as an important Finnish export market. Although the economy has stabilized to some degree as a result of the 1991 devaluation of the *markaa*, unemployment rates remained around 17 percent early in the year.

Finland declared independence in 1917, following eight centuries of foreign domination. Its current constitution, issued in July 1919, provides for a 200-seat parliament elected for a four-year term by universal suffrage. The directly-elected president holds considerable power, particularly because the multiparty, proportional representation system prevents any single party from gaining a parliamentary majority. The president can initiate and veto legislation, dissolve parliament at any time and call for elections; he also appoints the prime minister. The president currently holds primary responsibility for national security and foreign affairs, while the prime minister's mandate covers all other areas. However, the country's January 1995 accession to the European Union has led to a parliamentary debate over the evolving nature of these respective roles. The result may be a revised Finnish constitution. Eleven mainland provinces are headed by governors appointed by the president, while the Swedish-speaking island province of Aland enjoys autonomy.

Political Rights and Civil Liberties:

Finns can change their government by democratic means. In 1994 the country held its first direct presidential election since independence. Legislation passed in 1992 provides all Finnish citizens with the right to their own culture and equal protection under the law. However, Gypsies, who have lived in Finland for nearly 500 years and who outnumber the Saamis (or Lapps), often report being treated as outsiders by the largely homogeneous population. Discrimination on the basis of race, religion, sex, language or social status is illegal, and a recently-adopted law mandates that newspapers cannot identify people by race.

A wide selection of publications is available to the Finnish public. Newspapers are private, and the self-censorship that was traditionally practiced on issues relating to the Soviet Union is no longer in effect. Traditionally, many political parties owned or controlled newspapers, but several dailies have folded in recent years. The Finnish Broadcasting Company controls most radio and television programming; however, limited private broadcasting is available.

An overwhelming majority of Finnish workers, who have the right to organize, bargain and strike, belong to trade unions. The Central Organization of Finnish Trade Unions (SAK) dominates the labor movement.

Only 60,000 people in the country are foreign residents. While a strict refugee quota of 500 persons per year maintains the homogeneity of the population, those refugees who are granted admission receive free housing, medical care, monthly stipends and language lessons. In an effort to prevent "ethnic ghettos" from forming, some refugees are placed in small villages whose residents have never seen foreigners. The government has instituted educational programs to teach children about their new neighbors. Both the predominant Lutheran church and the smaller Orthodox church are financed through a special tax from which citizens may exempt themselves. Other faiths are permitted the freedom to worship.

France

Polity: Presidential-parliamentary democracy
Economy: Mixed capitalist
Population: 58,426,000
PPP: $19,140
Life Expectancy: 77.0
Ethnic Groups: French, regional minorities (Corsican, Alsatian, Basque, Breton), various Arab and African immigrant groups
Capital: Paris

Political Rights: 1
Civil Liberties: 2
Status: Free

Overview:　The conservative government of neo-Gaullist (RPR) Prime Minister Alain Juppe reached the historic low of 15 percent approval ratings in 1996, as it appeared to flounder on every issue from immigration to economic management. Facing a revolt within the RPR, President Jacques Chirac insisted on supporting his prime minister and said the government would stay on course.

This course was set by the Maastricht agreement for European Monetary Union (EMU), which commits member-states to an economic program with profoundly deflationary effects in France. Even members of Juppe's party have wondered aloud whether a unified Europe is worth the economic strain as unemployment soared to well over a record three million people.

Meanwhile, public frustration is vented on illegal immigrants, and the xenophobic National Front continues to gain in popularity, as indicated by its victory in an October by-election in a Marseilles suburb. The party's platform appeals to Frenchmen who fear job cuts under the Juppe plan and who blame immigration for the country's economic woes. More than a quarter of citizens polled in April said they agreed with the ideas of National Front leader Jean-Marie Le Pen, even though a majority said they saw him as a threat to democracy. A survey in January showed that 74 percent of the French were pessimistic about the economy, and nationwide opinion polls show public morale at its lowest point since 1987.

The government's apparent political strategy is to attack the National Front while reaching out to its voters. It responded in August to provocative comments by Le Pen asserting the "inequality of races" with legislation limiting "hate speech." The new law would impose mandatory jail sentences for comments like Le Pen's and could effectively outlaw his party. In addition to harsher immigration policy, Juppe has proposed changes in election laws to reinstate some form of proportional representation — a move that would guarantee the National Front representation in the legislature while preserving Chirac's majority for the 1998 elections.

The government announced in September its intention to propose even stronger laws limiting immigration to France. The number of deportations has shot up this year to over 7,600. After a two-month standoff, riot police stormed a church on August 23 and carried off 300 illegal African immigrants who were barricaded there to resist threatened expulsion from France. An unknown number of the immigrants was deported to Mali the next day by officials who said that granting them permission to stay and work in the country would set an unacceptable precedent at a time of 12.5 percent unemployment.

In an attempt to deal with escalating social and economic problems in France's urban areas, the government announced a plan in January to establish up to 30 tax-free zones, designed to aid existing business while attracting new enterprises and improving job prospects. Other proposals include loans to restore deteriorating housing and the creation of 100,000 jobs for local youth over five years. Many are skeptical about the new urban policy package, however, because it is only the latest of more than half a dozen similar initiatives in the last 15 years, and because of the current tight fiscal constraints on the government.

The struggle for autonomy in Corsica boiled over onto the French mainland when a bomb exploded at the Bordeaux city hall in early October. The FLNC, a militant separatist group in Corsica, claimed responsibility for the attack. Corsica has been shaken by almost nightly bombings since Juppe launched a crackdown on the separatists in response to the bombing.

President Chirac announced an early end to highly disputed French nuclear weapons tests in late January. A series of detonations began in the South Pacific last September, breaking a three-year international moratorium on nuclear testing and setting off angry protests worldwide.

Political Rights and Civil Liberties:

French citizens can change their government democratically. The constitution grants the president significant emergency powers, including rule by decree under certain circumstances. The president may call referenda and dissolve a hostile parliament, but may not veto its acts or routinely issue decrees. Decentralization has given mayors significant power over housing, transportation, schools, culture, welfare and law enforcement.

France has been charged repeatedly with poor treatment of immigrants. Children of immigrants are not granted citizenship at birth, but must apply when they are between 16 and 21 years of age or forfeit their right. Despite legal provisions authorizing refugee seekers to cross the border without visas or identity papers, border guards have occasionally used excessive force to discourage crossings.

The status of foreigners in France is confused by a succession of sometimes contradictory immigration laws. A parliamentary committee in April proposed a number of measures to toughen the laws, including a 45-day detention of illegal immigrants before deportation (as opposed to the current ten); fingerprinting for easier deportation; a national computer to keep tabs on anyone offering to harbor supposedly temporary visitors from abroad; and the deportation of delinquent minors, even those born in France, to their parents' country of origin. The National Front and other far-right groups have gained popularity by blaming immigrants for high unemployment. In fact, the jobless rate of immigrants is three times that of the native French.

The press in France is free, though the government's financial support of journalism and the registration of journalists has raised concerns about media independence. Publication of opinion poll results is prohibited in the week preceding any election. Officials perpetrated several violations against the media this year, including the arrest and interrogation of four journalists who covered a demonstration at the Chinese embassy in April; the seizure by air and border police of an Algerian newspaper; and the forcible appropriation of a local radio transmitter.

Incendiary racist remarks by Jean-Marie Le Pen led to the introduction of legislation to punish the publication of xenophobic and racist ideas with mandatory jail sentences. Current law only punishes acts that incite discrimination, hatred or violence. Human rights advocates express concern that the new law will open the door to repression of a wider range of ideas. Most publications banned in recent years have been neo-fascist or anti-Semitic in content.

Despite open suspicion toward Muslims and prohibitions against wearing religious garb or symbols in state schools, religious freedom is protected. Labor rights are respected in practice, and strikes are widely and effectively used to protest government economic policy.

Gabon

Polity: Dominant party
Economy: Capitalist
Population: 1,173,000
PPP: $3,861
Life Expectancy: 53.7
Ethnic Groups: Duma, Fang (25 percent), Mpongwe, Shogo, others
Capital: Libreville

Political Rights: 5
Civil Liberties: 4
Status: Partly Free

Overview: **A**s President Omar Bongo neared the end of his third decade as ruler of this small but oil-rich central African nation, some observers described the country's stalled transition from one-party rule as an "elastic democracy." Strongly backed by the army and by France, Bongo is ruling by decree despite the institution of the formal trappings of democracy. However, calm generally prevailed through 1996, as political rivalries were fought out within the ruling, fractious opposition coalitions rather than on the streets. An independent National Election Commission, created as part of a new constitution approved by a 1995 referendum, began work, but appeared to be neither entirely autonomous nor competent in its conduce of December's parliamentary elections, which were swept by the ruling party.

Straddling the equator on central Africa's west coast, this heavily forested country of about one million people gained independence from France in 1960. Moving from the army to the presidency with French support in 1967, Bongo continued his predecessor's consolidation of power by officially outlawing the opposition. Twenty-three years later, protests and economic duress forced Bongo to accept a broad-based national conference which oppositionists hoped would allow a peaceful transition to democratic rule. But in December 1993 Bongo retained his position in clearly fraudulent elections that sparked violent protests and repressive security measures. The country's only two independent radio stations were destroyed, the second in February 1994 by Bongo's Presidential Guard. In 1994 the government and opposition leaders signed an agreement, known as the Paris Accords, aimed at instituting true democratic reforms.

A July 1995 referendum approved several reforms, including limitation of presidential powers, restructuring the notoriously brutal Presidential Guard and creating an independent National Election Commission as prescribed by the Paris Accords. Yet opposition parties' hopes for a new transparency in governance and elections have not been realized. Legislative elections required by June 1996 were delayed until December as President Bongo ruled by decree. In October, troops and tanks were deployed in Libreville to avert violence as delayed local elections descended into chaos.

Political Rights and Civil Liberties:

Gabonese citizens' constitutional right to change their government democratically has never been realized in practice. Bongo's December 1993 election "victory" was declared before many votes were counted, and was marked by unabashed use of state resources and state media to support the incumbent. For nearly 30 years, Bongo has retained power by manipulating elections, co-opting opponents, and, occasionally, by using brute force. While opposition parties made some gains in October's municipal elections, December's vote for the National Assembly was marred by disorganization, irregularities and charges of outright fraud. French forces have intervened twice to preserve his regime. It is optimistic to believe that reforms agreed to in the Paris Accords and adopted by referendum in July may genuinely alter this situation.

Courts exercise some autonomy, but from the Constitutional Court downwards are subject to political interference. Constitutionally-guaranteed rights to legal counsel are generally respected. However, the law presumes one is guilty as charged and judges may deliver a verdict at an initial hearing if sufficient evidence is presented.

Torture remains a routine means for extracting confessions. Prison conditions are abysmal, with insufficient food and water, inadequate medical facilities and frequent beatings. In July, at least a dozen inmates died as a diarrhea epidemic swept through a Libreville prison. The government often detains illegal and legal refugees without charge, and there have been reports of forced labor by detainees.

Free speech is generally respected and print media can operate with little hindrance. There are over a dozen private weeklies, primarily controlled by opposition parties, in addition to a government daily. In a country of low literacy and few roads, however, broadcast media are the most crucial means of communication. Military destruction of private radio stations in 1994 was the de facto end of Gabon's private electronic media, except for cable entertainment channels. Foreign newspapers, magazines and broadcasts are usually widely available, but some editions containing criticisms of President Bongo have been seized.

The constitution does not restrict the rights of assembly and association, but permits are required for public gatherings. Freedom to form and join political parties is generally respected, although civil servants may face harassment because of their associations. Members of the Gabonese League of Human Rights have reported being harassed and threatened.

Although workers have the right to unionize and strike, unions must register with the government in order to be officially recognized. Nearly the entire formal sector work force is unionized. Despite legal protections, the government has taken action against numerous strikers and unions, and used force to suppress illegal demonstrations.

No legal restrictions on travel exist, but authorities routinely stop individuals to check their identification documents. Demands for bribes are common, particularly from non-Gabonese. Soldiers have several times physically prevented opposition leaders from leaving the country, and ordinary citizens have charged ethnic discrimination and year-long delays in the issuance of passports.

Religious freedom is constitutionally-guaranteed and respected. An official ban on Jehovah's Witnesses remains in effect, but the law is rarely enforced and permits are routinely issued to the group for large gatherings.

Legal protections exist for women, including equal-access laws for education, business and investment. In addition to owning property and businesses, women constitute over 50 percent of the salaried workforce in the health and trading sectors. They continue to face legal and cultural discrimination, however, particularly in rural areas. Domestic violence is reportedly widespread.

The Gambia

Polity: Military
Economy: Capitalist
Population: 1,155,000
PPP: $1,190
Life Expectancy: 45.2
Ethnic Groups: Mandinka (42 percent), Fulani (18 percent), Wolof (16 percent), Jola, Serahuli
Capital: Banjul

Political Rights: 7
Civil Liberties: 6
Status: Not Free

Overview:

In September, a little more than two years after seizing power in a military coup as an army lieutenant, Yahya A.J.J. Jammeh was proclaimed victor of deeply flawed presidential elections that barred the most formidable opposition candidates. The army employed violence and intimidation, and made heavy use of state resources to promote the recently retired Colonel Jammeh's candidacy. In the run-up to the polls, Jammeh's Armed Forces Provisional Ruling Council (AFPRC) banned several opposition parties and nearly monopolized the state media. Parlimentary polls set for November were postponed until January.

A new constitution, adopted by a closely-controlled referendum in August, paved the way for the 31-year-old Jammeh to transform his military dictatorship to a nominally civilian administration under his new Alliance for Patriotic Reorientation and Construction (APRC). Yet the army's intention to retain effective power was so blatant that even the Commonwealth and the Organization of African Unity, usually quite elastic in their election-observation standards, refused to send observers. The United States-funded National Democratic Institute for International Affairs had already withdrawn from the country in January.

For nearly three decades after receiving independence from Britain in 1965, the Gambia was a functioning electoral democracy under the rule of President Sir Dawda K. Jawara and his People's Progressive Party. The Gambia is a tiny and poor country of about one million people, which relied on foreign aid for more than three-quarters of its national budget and on European vacationers for most of its foreign exchange earnings. A 1981 coup by leftist military officers was foiled by armed intervention from Senegal, which surrounds the Gambia on three sides. The two countries agreed to create the Confederation of Senegambia a year later, an experiment that lasted seven years; then differences rising from disparate colonial legacies (Senegal was a French colony) and Gambians' fear of submersion into their far larger neighbor caused the Gambia to dissolve the arrangement. When Yahya Jammeh struck in 1994, Senegal made no move to rescue the Jawara government.

Condemned internationally, the AFPRC received a mixed domestic reception as it denounced the ousted government's alleged corruption and promised transparency, accountability and early elections. However, the junta quickly imposed several decrees curtailing civil and political rights, and has harassed the free media. A reported November 1994 counter-coup was crushed and several alleged plotters were summarily executed.

The Gambia's international standing is unlikely to improve after September's stage-managed elections. But losses from a sharp drop in tourism and Western aid are being partially compensated by Taiwanese and Libyan assistance. Some observers fear a Gambian—and Libyan—connection to the guerrilla struggle being waged in Senegal's southern Cassamance province by the ethnic Jola people, whose traditional lands straddle the two countries' frontier, and to which group President Jammeh himself belongs.

Political Rights and Civil Liberties: Despite the September presidential contest, Gambian citizens no longer have the right to choose or change their government by peaceful means. The electoral exercise was neither free nor fair, and President Jammeh cannot be considered a democratically-elected leader. The elected parliament was dismissed after the July 1994 coup and the AFPRC retains decree powers. The "Political Activities Resumption Decree" issued in August declared that anyone engaging in political activities before the official two-week campaign period would face a fine of $102,000 or life imprisonment.

Free expression has been severely limited since the July 1994 coup. According to the Committee to Protect Journalists, "the independent press has been a primary target of Jammeh's repression. Countless restrictive decrees, arbitrary detention, physical beatings, and deportations and expulsions are just a few of the weapons in Jammeh's arsenal." Independent newspapers continue to publish despite the pressure, but extensive self-censorship is common. AFPRC decrees allow arbitrary detention, and also prohibit the possession and distribution of anything deemed to be "political literature." State-run Radio Gambia broadcast only tightly-controlled news that was also relayed by the country's two private radio stations. No television station operates in Gambia, but broadcasts from Senegal are received throughout the country.

The assault on the press goes together with broader human rights abuses. The Gambia's legal system has been eviscerated since the coup. Arbitrary detention and a lack of due process is now standard. A number of extrajudicial killings and torture in jails and barracks are reported. Public assembly is now severely limited, and meetings of any kind without permission forbidden, except for religious observances. Three people were killed and dozens wounded when opposition presidential candidate Ousainou Darboe's last campaign rally was attacked by soldiers in September.

The Jammeh regime has extensive repressive powers. A 1995 decree gave the National Intelligence Agency power to "search, arrest or detain any person, or seize, impound or search any vessel, equipment, plant, property without a warrant when to obtain a warrant at the material time would cause or facilitate the commission of a crime or an act detrimental to state security." Another decree gave the interior minister the power to arrest anyone without warrant "in the interest of the security, peace and stability of the Gambia," adding that the right to seek a writ of habeas corpus would not apply in such cases.

Women suffer de facto discrimination in many areas despite legal protections. Education and wage employment opportunities for women are far fewer than those for men, especially in rural areas. Islamic *Shari'a* law provisions applied in family law and inheritance restrict women's rights. Female genital mutilation is widely practiced.

All workers but civil servants and security forces may unionize under the 1990 Labor Act, which also provides for the right to strike. The country's two labor federations, the Gambian Worker's Confederation and the Gambian Workers' Union, have not been banned, but their scope of action under the military regime is not clear. While the junta has not changed prevailing labor laws, trade union activities are not exempt from restrictions on political rights and civil liberties.

Georgia

Polity: Presidential-parliamentary democracy
Economy: Statist transitional
Population: 5,376,000
PPP: $1,750
Life Expectancy: 72.9
Ethnic Groups: Georgians (70 percent), Armenian (8 percent) Russian (6 percent), Abkhazian, Azeri, Ossetian, others
Capital: Tbilisi

Political Rights: 4
Civil Liberties: 4*
Status: Partly Free

Ratings Change: Georgia's civil liberties rating changed from 5 to 4 because civic institutions have grown and government repression has eased.

Overview: **P**arliamentary elections in the breakaway Abkhazia region and the status of Russian peacekeepers were the central issues facing President Eduard Shevardnadze in 1996. The economy continued to improve.

In the 1995 elections, Shevardnadze won over 75 percent of the vote as his Centrist Union won 150 of 235 seats in parliament. In an effort to stabilize the country, the president pushed through a new constitution, disbanded the paramilitary *Mkhedrioni*, and implemented an economic austerity program that improved the country's economic outlook.

Absorbed by Russia in the early nineteenth century, Georgia proclaimed independence in 1918, gaining Soviet recognition two years later. In 1921, it was overrun by the Red Army. In 1922, it entered the USSR as a component of the Transcaucasian Federated Soviet Republic, becoming a separate union republic in 1936. George declared independence from a crumbling Soviet Union after a referendum in April 1991. Nationalist leader and former dissident Zviad Gamsakhurdia was elected president, but his authoritarian and erratic behavior led to his violent ouster by opposition units that included the *Mkhedrioni.* In early 1992, former Soviet Foreign Minister Shevardnadze was asked by a temporary State Council to head a new government, and he was subsequently elected speaker of the parliament, making him acting head of state. In 1993, Georgia experienced the violent secession of the long-simmering Abkhazia region and armed insurrection by Gamsakhurdia loyalists. Though Shevardnadze blamed the Russians for arming and encouraging Abkhazian separatists, he legalized the presence of 19,000 Russian troops in five

Georgian bases in exchange for Russian support against Gamsakhurdia, who was defeated and reportedly committed suicide. In early 1994, Georgians and Abkhazians signed an agreement in Moscow that called for a ceasefire, the stationing of CIS troops under Russian command along the Abkhazian border, and the return of refugees under United Nations supervision.

In September 1996, Vladislav Ardzinba, president of Abkhazia, formally announced a referendum on independence for November 23. While questions of the referendum's legitimacy were raised due to the non-participation of 200,000 Georgians displaced by the fighting three years ago, Shevardnadze seemed inclined by year's end to accept the overwhelming vote for secession. Moreover, Abkhazia proceeded with scheduled parliamentary elections, which were judged free and fair by international observers, and which returned a pro-independence majority.

The Abkhaz election also raised the issue of the future of Russian peacekeepers. In the resolution condemning the vote, the Georgian parliament demanded that Russian troops leave Georgia if Moscow failed to help restore Georgian authority over Abkhazia. The resolution said that there was "no legal basis" for Russian armed forces or border guards to be in Georgia. Parliamentary Chairman Zurab Zhvania said that, in signing a 1995 accord to allow Russia to maintain military bases in Georgia, President Shevardnadze had made a "serious reservation" that the Georgian legislature would ratify the document only if his country's territorial integrity was restored. The resolution reflected frustration over the course of Russian-brokered mediation talks with Abkhazian officials and the failure of Russian troops to provide adequate security for Georgian refugees. While President Shevardnadze indicated that he supported the resolution, on October 30 the Chairman of the Committee for National Security and Defense Revaz Adamia proposed an amendment that allowed the use of foreign armed forces to ensure Georgia's security; the amendment was turned down. Throughout the year, reports were made of sporadic attacks on Russian peacekeepers along the Abkhazian border.

The 1995 austerity program, which freed prices, froze state spending, wiped out hyperinflation and launched large-scale privatization, paid dividends in 1996. During the second quarter, monthly inflation stood at just over 1 percent, and GDP increased by 14 percent. The public showed increased confidence in the currency (the lari). But problems remained, including widespread poverty, low tax revenues, a fragile banking system, and dependence on international financial institutions (IMF credits since 1994 total $190 million).

Political Rights and Civil Liberties: Georgians have the means to change their government democratically, but the government's loss of control over Abkhazia and South Ossetia affected the scope of the government's power and representation. The November 1995 elections were judged generally free and fair by international observers. However, voting in 10 of 85 districts, in Abkhazia and South Ossetia, was postponed indefinitely. The new constitution creates a federal state and gives the president the power to appoint and dismiss the prime minister; to dismiss the cabinet; and to appoint governors, heads of district administrations and city mayors. Parliament's role in the government's composition and policy is limited.

There are over 60 political parties registered; 52 contested the 1995 elections, but only three groupings met the 5 percent threshold for representation in parliament.

Under a 1991 press law, journalists are obliged to "respect the dignity and honor" of the president, and not to impugn the honor and dignity of citizens or undermine the regime. Publications could face legal action for "malevolently using freedom of the press, [and] spreading facts not corresponding to reality..." State-run radio and television generally reflect official views. Independent newspapers publish discerning and sophisticated political analysis, though their importance is being eclipsed by electronic media. There are some dozen local independent television stations which have faced varying degrees of government harassment. In July 1996, Rustavi-2, the most professional private TV station, was taken off the air on the grounds that its license was invalid. Ibervision, another independent TV station, has faced government pressure. Self-censorship is a problem, particularly in state-run media. Journalists founded an independent press club in 1996.

There are restrictions, often arbitrary, on freedom of assembly. Freedom of religion is generally respected in this predominantly Christian Orthodox country. Ethnic and minority rights remain under pressure. While some Georgian refugees have returned to Abkhazia, repatriation plans were halted in the face of violence against ethnic Georgians and stalled negotiations. The government has also claimed that Iran is fanning Islamic fundamentalism among the 200,000 ethnic Azeris to foment social discord for political and economic reasons.

The legal system remains a hybrid of laws from Georgia's brief period of pre-Soviet independence, the Soviet era, the Gamsakhurdia presidency and the State Council period. A nine-member Constitutional Court represents the three main branches of government and arbitrates constitutional questions, treaties, referendums, elections and jurisdictional disputes. Many "political" crimes remain on the books as the means to prosecute and deter opponents, and the system is plagued by documented cases of illegal arrests, arbitrary dismissal of defense attorneys and related problems. Members of the judiciary have engaged in corrupt practices, including bribery and bending to the influence of political leaders and gangsters. Nongovernmental Georgian human rights groups report that prisoners are subjected to poor prison conditions, torture, beatings and other abuses, as well as to violations of due process.

The Georgian Confederation of Trade Unions, the successor to the official Communist-era structure, includes about 30 different sectoral unions. There is a legal right to strike. Government concern about the status of and discrimination against women is minimal. Women are found mostly in traditional, low-paying occupations.

Germany

Polity: Federal par-
liamentary democracy
Economy: Mixed
capitalist
Population: 81,694,000
PPP: $18,840
Life Expectancy: 76.1
Ethnic Groups: German (95 percent), numerous immigrant groups
Capital: Berlin

Political Rights: 1
Civil Liberties: 2
Status: Free

Overview:

Chancellor Helmut Kohl's Christian Democrats and their coalition partners, the Free Democrats, fared unexpectedly well in provincial elections in March. The ruling coalition took 50.9 percent of the vote in Baden Wurttemberg, 47.6 percent in Rhineland-Palatinate, and 42.9 percent in Schleswig-Holstein, while the opposition Social Democrats lost ground in each contest, slipping, on the average; five percentage points. Election results were seen by analysts as less an endorsement of the ruling coalition than a rejection of the Social Democrats' weak, ineffectual policy.

Germany was divided into Soviet, U.S., British, and French occupation zones following World War II. Four years later, the Allies helped establish a democratic Federal Republic of Germany, while the Soviets oversaw the formation of the communist German Democratic Republic (GDR). The division of Berlin was reinforced by the 1961 construction of the Berlin Wall. After the collapse of Erich Honecker's hardline GDR regime in 1989 and the destruction of the wall in 1990, citizens voted in the country's first free parliamentary election, backing parties that supported rapid reunification.

Along with a new mandate to govern comes increased pressure on Kohl's government to solve the country's economic problems. Attempts to tackle record high unemployment, stalled growth and a budget deficit well above the limit for EMU have split the ruling coalition in the past and contributed to a near-paralysis of government. Proposed solutions such as a wage freeze, cuts in public spending and cuts in welfare entitlements have provoked mass protests by trade unionists and public sector workers. However, Kohl may take the March election results as a vote of confidence and gain the courage to enact a series of reforms before the 1998 general election.

**Political Rights
and Civil Liberties:**

German citizens can change their government democratically. The federal system allows a considerable amount of self-government among the 16 states. Individuals are free to form political parties, and to receive federal funding as long as the parties are democratic in nature.

The Basic Law (Constitution) provides for unrestricted citizenship and legal residence immediately upon application for ethnic Germans entering the country. Individuals not of German ethnicity may acquire citizenship if they meet certain requirements, including legal residence for ten years (five if married to a German) and renunciation of all other citizenships.

Germany has no anti-discrimination law to protect immigrants, and even ethnic German immigrants increasingly face hostility from citizens who attribute the country's economic woes to immigration. Leading up to the March state elections, the head of the left-wing Social Democrats called for a reduction in the number of ethnic Germans allowed into the country.

A court ruling in March barring Kurdish demonstrators from holding a rally to celebrate Kurdish New Year touched off violent clashes that resulted in hundreds of detentions and injuries. Legislation was proposed to toughen deportation laws as Chancellor Kohl criticized Kurdish protest as "an unacceptable abuse" of German hospitality.

The German press and broadcast media are free and independent. They offer pluralistic viewpoints, though Nazi propaganda and statements endorsing Nazism are illegal. In January, the press reported that an Internet provider had been pressured by authorities to block access to a neo-Nazi World Wide Web site.

Freedom of religion is provided for by the Basic Law. State governments subsidize church-affiliated schools and provide religious instruction in schools and universities for those of Protestant, Catholic or Jewish faith.

The Church of Scientology has been at the center of recent heated debate about its legal status as a religious organization. Major political parties exclude Scientologists from membership, arguing that Scientology is not a religion but a for-profit organization based on anti-democratic principles. The governing Christian Democrats approved a resolution this summer which would effectively ban Scientologists from public service employment. Bavaria began screening civil service applicants for Church membership, and refused to fund artistic activities involving Scientologists. Scientologists have taken complaints of government-condoned and societal harassment to the courts, with mixed results.

Labor, business, and farming groups are free, highly organized, and influential. Trade union federation membership has dropped sharply since 1991 due to the collapse of industry in the East and layoffs in the West.

Ghana

Polity: Presidential-
parliamentary democracy
Economy: Capitalist-
statist
Population: 17,974,000
PPP: $2,000
Life Expectancy: 56.2

Political Rights: 3*
Civil Liberties: 4
Status: Partly Free

Ethnic Groups: Akan (including Fanti) (44 percent),
Mossi-Dagomba (16 percent), Ewe (13 percent), Ga (8 percent), Ashanti, some fifty
others
Capital: Accra
Ratings Change: Ghana's political rights rating changed from 4 to 3 because
despite some irregularities, most observers rated Ghana's December 1996 elections
reasonably free and fair.

Overview: Ghana's December 1996 presidential and legislative elections returned President Jerry Rawlings and his National
Democratic Congress (NDC) party to another four years in
power. The elections included an extensive civic education campaign and international assistance with registration and other electoral procedures. They were judged
free and fair by international observers, even though the ruling party made extensive use of state media and patronage to support the incumbents. The opposition's
failure to forge a strong alliance also contributed to Rawlings's victory, which extended his 16-year rule since seizing power in a military's coup. In April, Ghana's
High Court ruled 57-year-old economist Kwame Pianim ineligible to run for president under a clause in Ghana's constitution barring the candidacy of anyone convicted of crimes involving state security. Pianim, considered the most credible
challenger to Rawlings, had served a ten-year jail term for his part in a failed coup
attempt in 1983. Rawlings's two successful coups apparently were not considered
transgressions sufficient to merit disqualification.

Long known as the Gold Coast and once a major slaving center, the former
British colony became black Africa's first independent state. The country was
wracked by a succession of military coups for 15 years after the 1966 overthrow of
its charismatic independence leader, Kwame Nkrumah, and by military and civilian governments that vied with each other in both incompetence and mendacity. In
1979, then-Flight-Lieutenant Rawlings led a coup against the ruling military junta
and, as promised, returned power to a civilian government after a "housecleaning"
of corrupt senior army officers. The new civilian administration did not live up to
Rawlings' expectations, however, and he seized power again in December 1981,
setting up the Provisional National Defense Council (PNDC). The PNDC junta was
initially radically socialist and populist, and brutally suppressed any dissent, banning political parties and free expression. A crumbling economy worsened by severe drought in the early 1980s convinced Rawlings that only massive international
aid could help Ghana revive its fortunes. Turning his back on socialism, Rawlings

transformed Ghana into an early model for structural adjustment programs urged by international lenders.

Political parties were legalized after the adoption of a new constitution in April 1992. Rawlings was declared president after elections held in November 1992. Extensive irregularities in the presidential poll convinced opposition parties to boycott legislative elections a month later, and the NDC, successor to the PNDC, swept into parliament unopposed, effectively continuing one-party rule. Inflation has eroded living standards over the past several years and revelations of governmental corruption in the newly-vigorous media forced inquiries that led to the resignations of several senior government figures in 1996.

Rawlings's re-election victory may mark the genuine renewal of representative rule in Ghana, following a progressive liberalization since the severe repression and failed socialism abandoned over a decade ago. Ghana's democratic transition, however, is still tempered by Rawlings's lingering authoritarian tendencies, and by corruption that has increasingly blemished his rule. It is far from certain whether Rawlings' new mandate or the significant opposition presence in parliament will help create greater transparency and accountability in governance.

Political Rights and Civil Liberties:

Ghanaians were able to elect their president and parliamentary representatives in generally free and fair elections in December. Ghana's 1992 constitution provides its people with the right to elect freely their representatives but multiparty elections that year were not free and fair. Ghana's 140-member legislature is elected on a single-member district system. The new parliament remains controlled by the NDC. The campaign was marred by occasional irregularities and the ruling party's reliance on state media and state resources in its campaign.

Ghana is characterized by vigorous and sometimes vociferous political debate. Constitutionally guaranteed freedom of expression is seen in over twenty opposition and independent newspapers of varying quality and political persuasion. Private media is constrained, however, by financial problems and government pressure. Criminal libel laws that make reporting false information a felony have been used to intimidate the media. In February, Eben Quarcoo and Tommy Thompson, editor and publisher of the weekly *Free Press*, and Nana Kofi Coomson, editor-in-chief of the *Ghanaian Chronicle*, were charged with libeling the state after publishing articles alleging government complicity in drug trafficking. They were arrested under a 1964 law invoked only once before, which makes anyone publishing a report "likely to injure the reputation of Ghana or its government and which he knows or has reason to believe is false" subject to felony charges.

The power of state media also creates serious imbalances. The government controls most broadcasting and the two daily newspapers and allows little expression of opposition views. Private radio stations have begun operating, but first licenses went to government supporters and the stations report little news. Broadcast media openness and accessibility are still restricted.

The right to peaceful assembly and association is constitutionally guaranteed, and permits are not required for meetings or demonstrations. Many nongovernmental organizations operate openly and freely, including human rights groups. Religious freedom is respected, but tensions are in evidence between Christian and Muslim communities and within the Muslim community itself.

Ghanaian courts are still subject to considerable governmental influence, but have acted with increased autonomy under the 1992 constitution. Traditional courts in rural areas often handle minor cases according to local customs that do not meet constitutional standards. Lack of resources also means that large numbers of people are held in pre-trial detention for long periods under harsh conditions.

Ghanaian women enjoy equal rights under the law but suffer societal discrimination that is particularly serious in rural areas, where opportunities for education and wage employment are limited. Domestic violence against women is reportedly common, but often unreported. The *tro-kosi* system of young girls being forced into indefinite servitude to traditional religious priests is still practiced in parts of northern Ghana. Several NGOs, including the National Council on Women and Development (NCWD), are campaigning against the practice.

Civil servants may not join unions. Other unions must officially register under the Trades Union Ordinance, but this requirement is not currently used to block union formation. The Industrial Relations Act requires mediation and arbitration before strikes are authorized. The umbrella Trade Union Congress is the only labor confederation. It has shown signs of autonomy, but is still aligned with the ruling party.

Ghana's privatization program proceeded in 1996, and strong mining profits help buoy the economy. Corruption is a continuing obstacle to growth. Media exposés forced an investigation of high level malfeasance, and two cabinet ministers and a top presidential aide resigned late in the year.

Greece

Polity: Parliamentary democracy
Economy: Mixed capitalist
Population: 10,492,000
PPP: $8,950
Life Expectancy: 77.7
Ethnic Groups: Greek (98 percent), Macedonian, Turk
Capital: Athens

Political Rights: 1
Civil Liberties: 3
Status: Free

Overview: On January 15, 1996, Prime Minister Andreas Papandreou retired and was succeeded by Costas Simitis, a former industry minister and leader of the pro-European faction of the Panhellenic Socialist Movement (Pasok). Disputes with Turkey concerning the sovereignty of dozens of small Aegean islands which have been considered Greek since the dissolution of the Ottoman empire led to naval standoffs that almost resulted in war. Greece's economic development continues to suffer from chronic state deficits and high inflation.

In February several hundred thousand workers protested the government's decision to hold pay increases below the year's projected inflation rate of six percent.

State banks and public utilities were closed, public transport in Athens and Thessaloniki was halted, and flights by Olympic Airways, the state carrier, were delayed. Strikes have also been sparked in the past several years following the introduction of new taxes and the enforced collection of those already in existence.

Simitis's election as Pasok party chairman after Papandreou's death in June was followed by triumph in the September parliamentary elections. This ended the intra-party power struggle between the Papandreou "old-guard" loyalists who support populist and sometimes anti-Western policies and Simitis's reformist wing, which seeks to lead Greece into the Economic and Monetary Union (EMU) through strict economic management, public sector reform and a less confrontational foreign policy. The prime minister further secured his authority in late September, when he named a cabinet which includes former rivals as well as close associates in key positions. Simitis's moderate views, his pledge to govern through consensus (as opposed to continuing his predecessor's autocratic style), and his plans to cut state spending and collect more taxes has won him the support of many overseas investors and Greek businessmen, many of whom have traditionally supported the conservative New Democracy Party.

Despite U.S. diplomatic efforts, Greek-Turkish relations deteriorated during 1996 due to unresolved minority issues and geographical boundaries in the Aegean, and the continuing conflict over Cyprus.

Greece gained independence from the Ottoman Empire in 1830. The ensuing century brought continued struggle between royalist and republican forces. Occupation by the Axis powers in 1941 was followed by civil war between noncommunist and communist forces until 1949. Following a 1967 coup that brought a military junta to power, a failed attempt by the Navy to restore the king led to the formal deposition of the monarch and the proclamation of a republic. The current constitution, adopted in 1975, provides for a parliamentary system with a presidency which is now largely ceremonial.

Political Rights and Civil Liberties: Greeks can change their government democratically. As voting is compulsory for those between the ages of 18 and 70, and change of voting address is not permitted, nearly 650,000 people are forced to travel to prior residences to take part in elections. The International Helsinki Federation for Human Rights (IHF) reported that during the first direct elections for local prefects and prefecture councils in 1994, two primarily Turkish districts were joined to adjacent districts to avoid the election of ethnic Turks.

Apart from politically related restrictions, the media have substantial freedom. The public prosecutor may press charges against publishers and can seize publications deemed offensive to the president or to religious beliefs. A controversial law bans "unwarranted" publicity for terrorists from the media, including terrorists' proclamations following explosions.

Greece has freedom of association, and all workers (except military personnel and the police) have the right to form and join unions–linked to political parties but independent of party and government control.

In September, the European parliament released a human rights report critical of Greece's imprisonment of conscientious objectors, as well as its restrictions on religious freedom, minority rights and freedom of expression. Greek Orthodoxy is the state religion and claims 98 percent of the population, at least nominally. Orthodox bishops have the privilege of granting or denying permission to other faiths to build houses of worship in their jurisdictions. This practice was condemned by the European Court of Human Rights in September 1996. Members of non-Orthodox communities have been barred from entering occupations such as primary school teaching, the military and the police.

The Turkish Muslim minority in Western Thrace, whose religious rights were guaranteed under the 1923 Treaty of Lausanne, objects to its classification as a "Turkish" rather than "Muslim" minority, as well as the Greek government's ability to choose its *mufti*, or leader of its Muslim community. Human Rights Watch has reported that a major instrument used against ethnic Turks and other minorities in 1996 was Article 19 of the Citizenship Law, which allows the state to revoke the citizenship of non-ethnic Greeks who travel abroad without the intent to return. The Macedonian minority in Greece also faces systematic cultural and political discrimination. Some 7,000 Albanian refugees were arrested in August during the third nationwide sweep in recent years.

Despite objections from Catholics, Jews, Muslims and other minorities, national identity cards, required since 1992, list one's religious affiliation. The constitution prohibits proselytizing, and Jehovah's Witnesses have been a target of political and legal persecution. The Greek parliament abolished capital punishment in 1993.

Grenada

Polity: Parliamentary democracy
Economy: Capitalist-statist
Population: 95,000
PPP: $3,118
Life Expectancy: 71.0
Ethnic Groups: Mostly black
Capital: St. George's

Political Rights: 1
Civil Liberties: 2
Status: Free

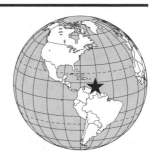

Overview:
In 1996 Prime Minister Keith Mitchell, head of the ruling New National Party (NNP), continued to face allegations of having made politically-motivated personnel changes in state institutions.

Grenada, a member of the British Commonwealth, is a parliamentary democracy. The British monarchy is represented by a governor-general. Grenada gained independence in 1974 and includes the islands of Carriacou and Petite Martinique. The bicameral parliament consists of a 15-seat House of Representatives and a 13-seat Senate, to which the prime minister appoints ten senators and the opposition leader three.

Maurice Bishop's Marxist New Jewel Movement seized power in 1979. In 1983

Bishop was murdered by New Jewel hardliners Bernard Coard and Hudson Austin, who took control of the country. A joint U.S.-Caribbean military intervention removed Coard and Austin, and in the 1984 elections, the NNP, now a coalition of three parties, won the majority of seats. Herbert Blaize became prime minister until his death in 1989, when Deputy Prime Minister Ben Jones replaced him.

In the 1990 elections the NNP coalition had unraveled and there were five principal contenders: The National Party (TNP) headed by Jones; the centrist National Democratic Congress (NDC) led by Nicholas Braithwaite, former head of the 1983-84 interim government; the NNP headed by Keith Mitchell; the leftist Maurice Bishop Patriotic Movement (MBPM), led by Terry Marryshow; and Eric Gairy's rightist Grenada United Labour Party (GULP). The NDC won seven seats and took in a defector from the GULP, and Braithwaite became prime minister with a one-seat majority. After implementing unpopular economic reforms, the aging Braithwaite stepped down in early 1995 in favor of agricultural minister George Brizan.

The 1995 campaign was a raucous affair. Brizan sought to retain power by pointing to the improved economy. The other candidates accused the ruling NDC of corruption and harped on high unemployment.

The NNP startled local observers by winning eight of 15 seats. The NDC won five seats and the GULP, two. Mitchell became prime minister. Afterwards, NDC deputy leader Francis Alexis split off to form the Democratic Labour Party (DLP), underscoring the fractious nature of Grenadian politics.

In his first months in office, Mitchell was accused by opposition leader Brizan and others of censoring news unfavorable to the government in state-run television and radio broadcasts, and of purging civil servants appointed during the NDC administration. Mitchell denied the allegations. In 1996 Mitchell's reorganization of the state-owned Grenada Broadcasting Corporation (GBC) was viewed by some as another attempt to fill political positions with NNP supporters and to control the dissemination of information at GBC.

Political Rights and Civil Liberties: Citizens are able to change their government through democratic elections. Many political parties exist, and few obstacles face those establishing new parties. But there has been a decline in turnout, as young people, in particular, appear to have lost confidence in a system riddled with fragmented politics and allegations of corruption.

The independent, nondiscriminatory judiciary has authority generally respected by the police. In 1991 Grenada rejoined the Organization of Eastern Caribbean States court system, with the right of appeal to the Privy Council in London. Detainees and defendants are guaranteed a range of legal rights which the government respects in practice. Like many Caribbean island nations, Grenada has suffered from a rise in violent drug-related crime, particularly among increasingly disaffected youth. Prison conditions are poor, though they meet minimum international standards and the government allows human rights monitors to visit.

Constitutional guarantees regarding the right to organize political, labor or civic groups are respected. The exercise of religion and the right of free expression are generally respected. Newspapers, including four weekly political party organs, are independent, and freely criticize the government. Television is both private and public, and radio is operated by the government. Since the 1995 elections, five new radio stations and one television station, not one of which is aligned with the NNP, were issued licenses to operate.

Numerous independent labor unions include an estimated 20 to 25 percent of the workforce. A 1993 law gives the government the right to establish tribunals empowered to make "binding and final" rulings when a labor dispute is considered of vital interest to the state. The national trade union federation claimed the law was an infringement on the right to strike. Workers have the right to organize and to bargain collectively.

Women are represented in the government, though in greater numbers in the ministries than in parliament. No official discrimination takes place, but women generally earn less than men for equal work.

Guatemala

Polity: Presidential-leg- **Political Rights:** 3*
islative democracy **Civil Liberties:** 4*
(military-dominated) **Status:** Partly Free
Economy: Capitalist-statist
Population: 9,858,000
PPP: $3,400
Life Expectancy: 65.1
Ethnic Groups: Mayan and other Indian (over 60 percent), mestizo
Capital: Guatemala City
Ratings Change: Guatamala's political rights and civil liberties ratings changed because a peace process appears to be ending decades of civil conflict.

Overview: On December 29, 1996, the government of President Alvaro Arzu and leaders of the insurgent Guatemalan National Revolutionary Unity (URNG) signed a United Nations-mediated accord that ended 36 years of armed struggle. The agreement was the culmination of six years of often contentious negotiations, and encompassed earlier accords signed in Mexico City, Stockholm, Oslo and Madrid on incorporating the URNG into Guatemalan society. URNG commander Pablo Monsanto pledged his group would seek the presidency in the year 2000.

In another significant development, the National Congress, over opposition protests, approved a controversial amnesty law in December which freed government officials, military members and rebels of any responsibility for political and other crimes commited during the conflict. The URNG opposed the measure because amnesty had been used previously to cover up human rights violations, massacres and political murders. The same month, the Archbishop's Human Rights Office reported over 1,400 human rights violations in 1996, the victims being public organizations, the media and members of the clergy. According to the report, despite the military's efforts to clean up its ranks and the demobilization of the Civilian Defense Patrols (PACs), many human rights violators continue in state employment.

Alvaro Arzu, a 49-year-old moderate conservative, finished first in the November 12, 1995 presidential election and won a January 1996 runoff. He promised to carry out a purge of the military and to end human rights abuses.

The Republic of Guatemala was established in 1839, 18 years after independence from Spain. The nation has endured a history of dictatorship, coups d'état and guerrilla insurgency, with only intermittent democratic government. It has had elected civilian rule since 1985. Amended in 1994, the 1985 constitution provides for a four-year presidential term and prohibits re-election. An 80-member unicameral Congress is elected for four years.

Right-wing businessman Jorge Serrano became president in 1991 after winning a runoff election. In 1993 Serrano attempted to dissolve the legislature. After initially supporting him, the military changed its mind as a result of mass protests and international pressure. Serrano was sent to Panama. The Congress, under pressure from an alliance of unions, moderate businessmen and civic groups, chose as president Ramiro de Leon Carpio, the government's human rights ombudsman.

De Leon Carpio, however, was practically powerless to halt human rights violations by the military or to curb its power as final arbiter in national affairs. U.N.-mediated talks were launched, however, between the government and URNG left-wing guerrillas. The URNG called a unilateral truce for the 1995 election and backed the left-wing New Guatemala Democratic Front (FDNG). The top presidential contenders were former Guatemala City mayor Arzu, of the National Advancement Party (PAN), and Alfonso Portillo Cabrera of the hard-right Guatemalan Republican Front (FRG). FRG founder and former dictator Efrain Rios Montt was constitutionally barred from running but remained a power in the party.

Arzu won 36.6 percent of the vote and Portillo Cabrera 22.0 percent. A handful of candidates split the rest. In the runoff on January 7, 1996, Arzu defeated Portillo, 51.2 to 48.8 percent. The PAN won 43 seats in Congress, the FRG 21, the centrist National Alliance nine and the URNG-backed FDNG six. But a turnout of only 36.9 percent (of 3.5 million registered voters) suggested growing disenchantment in the political process.

Soon after taking office, President Arzu reshuffled the military, forcing the early retirement of generals linked to drug-trafficking, car-theft rings and human rights abuses. Two colonels linked to killings involving Americans were also dismissed. The purge had the backing of a small but influential group of reformist officers who dominate the military high command. General Julio Balconi, a presumed moderate, was named defense minister. Many of the officers stripped of their titles continued to draw their pay, however, and dismissed policemen went to court to sue for reinstatement.

The shake-up in the army and police instigated a wave of kidnappings by former military men in an attempt to destabilize the government. By June, kidnappings, car-jackings and street crime had soared. Corrupt police officials were accused in the press of releasing prisoners on condition that they bring them a percentage of proceeds from robberies and muggings.

In March, President Arzu made a surprise visit to URNG headquarters in Mexico City, leading to an historic, open-ended cease-fire by the guerrillas as a gesture of goodwill. In May, the government and the guerrillas signed a social reform accord that addressed issues aimed at attacking poverty and called for the creation of a land bank to provide soft loans for peasants to buy property, the introduction of a land tax and the establishment of a registry to define land ownership. After a brief suspension of talks in October because of a rebel kidnapping, subsequent agreements on the return of rebel forces to civilian life and a permanent cease-fire led to the December accords.

In August 1996, President Arzu formally moved against the PACs, created in 1982 as civilian anti-insurgency groups, which had been responsible for numerous human rights violations and criminal activities. Demobilization of the estimated 200,000 PAC members, however, did not eliminate their power in rural areas because many refused to disarm, and persistent reports were made of PAC members carrying out rapes and other crimes against civilians. The decree establishing the PACs was abolished by the Congress on December 10.

Political Rights and Civil Liberties: Citizens can change governments through elections. But people are increasingly disillusioned with the process; turnout in the 1995 elections was only 46.8 percent, and just 36.9 percent voted in the January 1996 presidential runoff. In 1996, the president reshuffled the armed forces to reduce their ability to restrict constitutional powers granted to civilian administrations. The rule of law is undermined further by the endemic corruption that afflicts all public institutions, particularly the legislature and the courts.

The constitution guarantees religious freedom and the right to organize political parties, civic organizations and labor unions. However, political and civic expression is severely restricted by a climate of violence, lawlessness and military repression. Political and criminal violence, including murders, disappearances, bombings and death threats, continue unabated. Politicians, student organizations, street children, peasant groups, labor unions, Indian organizations, refugees returning from Mexico, human rights groups, and the media are all targeted.

The principal human rights offenders are the 40,000-member military, especially its intelligence unit; the rural network of paramilitary Self-Defense Patrols (PACs), an extension of the army; the police (under military authority); a network of killers-for-hire linked to the armed forces and right-wing political groups; and vigilante "social-cleansing" groups.

Despite penal code reforms in 1994 the judicial system remains little more than a black hole for most legal or human rights complaints. Reforms included trying soldiers accused of common crimes in civilian rather than military courts, but most civil courts remained corrupt. Drug-trafficking is a serious problem. In 1996, police seized $90 million worth of cocaine, but the country remains a warehousing and transit point for South American drugs going to the U.S.

The Runejel Junam Council of Ethnic Communities (CERJ) represents the interests of the country's Indians, a majority of the population who have faced severe repression and violence by the army and PACs. In 1996, Indians showed signs of flexing some political muscle. Indian candidates won control of an estimated 40 urban areas—including Guatemala's second largest city—and 10 percent of congressional seats. Under a new law, Mayan descendants are allowed to seek office as independents, and not as representatives of the national political parties that have ignored their needs. Many of the candidates, however, received death threats and were the subject of racial attacks in handbills. With 23 tribes and many Indian officials still beholden to national parties, Indian political power is still in a nascent stage. In 1996, Mayan political and cultural organizations were formed, and flurry of books, newspapers and radio programs executed in the Mayan language.

Workers are frequently denied the right to organize and subjected to mass firings and blacklisting, particularly in export-processing zones where a majority of workers are women. Existing unions are targets of systematic intimidation, physical attacks and assassination, particularly in rural areas during land disputes. Guatemala is among the most dangerous countries in the world for trade unionists. Child labor is a growing problem in the agricultural industry.

The press and most of the broadcast media are privately-owned, with several independent newspapers and dozens of radio stations, most of them commercial. Five of six television stations are commercially-operated. However, journalists are at great risk. In February 1996, a radio reporter was abducted, tortured and warned to discontinue coverage of drug-trafficking and car theft. On May 16, grenades were thrown at an editor of a major daily that had run articles critical of the military. In 1994 at least two journalists were murdered, numerous others suffered physical attacks and a number of media outlets were subjected to various attacks, including bombings. Many others received threats. In recent years, over a dozen Guatemalan journalists have been forced into exile. The 1993 murder of newspaper publisher Jorge Carpio Nicolle remains unresolved.

Guinea

Polity: Dominant party (military-influenced)
Political Rights: 6
Civil Liberties: 5
Status: Not Free
Economy: Capitalist
Population: 7,412,000
PPP: $1,800
Life Expectancy: 44.7
Ethnic Groups: Fulani (40 percent), Malinké (30 percent), Susu (20 percent), others
Capital: Conakry

Overview: Guinea is still feeling the aftereffects of a February army mutiny that nearly ousted long-serving President Lansana Conté. The rebellion was accompanied by widespread looting and destruction in the capital, Conakry. But Conté, who himself seized power in a 1984 coup and who was declared victor in a highly flawed December 1993 election, rallied loyal troops and reasserted control. Conté pledged to consult opposition parties and to address severe corruption and other problems; several reforms proposals put forth by the National Assembly are being adopted. But a new government formed in July included no opposition members, who complain of continued detentions and harassment of their activists. Guinea remains far from achieving the complete democratic transition President Conté has claimed.

Guinea declared independence in 1958 under Ahmed Sékou Touré and his Guinea Democratic Party. Alone among France's many African colonies it rejected continued close ties with its former colonial master. Guinea paid a heavy price for this stand; France removed or destroyed all colonial property and imposed an unofficial but devastating economic boycott. After an early effort to introduce egalitarian laws, Sékou Touré's one-party rule grew repressive, and Guinea became increasingly impoverished under his disastrous Soviet-style economic policies. The country today ranks last or near last on international social development indicators.

Guinea's politics are largely ethnic-based. President Conté's ruling Progress and Unity Party (PUP) is strongly Susu, the Rally of the Guinean People (RPG) party is mostly Malinké, and both the Party for Renewal and Progress (PRP) and the Union for the New Republic (UNR) party are Fulani-dominated. Issues of ethnicity and patronage dominate almost every political debate.

Political Rights and Civil Liberties: Guinea is no longer a simple one-party dictatorship, but the right of the people to change their government is not yet respected. The multiparty democratic election for Guinea's presidency guaranteed by the country's constitution was denied, by electoral manipulation and fraud of the 1993 polls that "elected" Lansana Conté to his current five-year term. The political process in Guinea opened marginally during 1995 with June elections for the country's national assembly that produced a large victory for President Conté's ruling PUP, along with significant opposition representation.

International observers described these results as generally free and fair, even in the face of vociferous opposition complaints of serious irregularities. Government influence over state institutions clearly affected the campaign. The electoral system allocates two-thirds of seats according to proportional representation. The polls were contested by 21 parties, nine of which won at least one seat in the new parliament, allowing a strong platform for opposition voices in the national assembly, but offering them no real role in national decision-making. The president retains decree powers that could eviscerate the parliamentary process.

War and near-anarchy in neighboring Liberia and Sierra Leone raised fears of ethnic war and national disintegration in Guinea. The country today hosts about a half million refugees from those two countries. It has sent troops to battle rebels in Sierra Leone, and in June shelled Liberian militia factions after incursions into Guinean territory.

A small but energetic, and often strongly partisan, private print media that operates in the capital, Conakry, came under serious pressure this year. Several journalists were arrested on charges of false reporting. A resident correspondent for Radio France International was expelled in July. However vigorous, print media have little impact in rural areas where incomes are low and illiteracy high. A restrictive press law allows the government to censor or shut down publications on broad and ill-defined grounds. Broadcast media and the country's largest newspaper are both state-controlled, and offer scant coverage of the opposition to or criticisms of government policies.

Despite constitutional guarantees, freedom of association is restricted in practice. The government has banned many demonstrations and sometimes arrested organizers of unlicensed opposition meetings. Registration requirements do not present inseperable obstacles to political party formation, and at least 46 have been recognized. Human rights groups such as the Guinean Organization for the Defense of Human Rights (OGDH), and many nongovernmental groups, operate openly. Constitutionally-protected religious rights are also respected in practice.

The judicial system remains weak, despite its nominally independent status. Corruption, nepotism, ethnic identity and political interference, as well as a lack of resources and training, affect the course of justice. Traditional courts formed along ethnic lines often handle minor civil cases. Security forces continue to act with impunity. Arbitrary arrests and detention are common and occasional serious mal-treatment and torture of detainees is reported. On New Year's Day 1996, 16 prison-ers were killed under suspicious circumstances in Conakry's central jail.

Women's rights, protected by the constitution, are often not realized in prac-tice. Women have far fewer educational and employment opportunities than men, and many societal customs discriminate against women. Female genital mutilation as a traditional rite is widely practiced. Spousal abuse and other violence against women is said to be prevalent.

The right to form and join unions is found in the constitution, although the country's preponderantly subsistence farming economy leaves a very small formal sector and only about one-twentieth of the work force is unionized. Several labor confederations compete in this small market and have the right to bargain collec-tively. A labor court in the capital and civil courts elsewhere regularly hear labor grievances.

Privatization plans and some civil service reforms continued in 1996, and were given greater urgency after the February mutiny. However, corruption and harass-ment remain a serious obstacle to business growth, and to the exploitation of the rich gold and bauxite deposits in the country.

Guinea-Bissau

Polity: Presidential-par-liamentary democracy
Economy: Mixed statist transitional
Population: 1,096,000
PPP: $860
Life Expectancy: 43.7
Political Rights: 3
Civil Liberties: 4
Status: Partly Free

Ethnic Groups: Balanta (30 percent), Fulani (20 percent), Mandjague (14 percent), Mandinka (13 percent), mulatto, Moor, Lebanese and Portuguese minorities
Capital: Bissau

Overview:

Guinea-Bissau's first openly-elected government faced in-creasing criticism and opposition calls for early elections over its handling of the country's economy. The ruling Af-rican Party for the Independence of Guinea-Bissau and Cape Verde (PAIGC), which held power for 13 years under one-party rule, does not yet appear entirely comfort-able with democratic processes. Human rights demonstrations have been banned, the free press faces difficulties and Prime Minister Manuel Saturnino da Costa has personally and publicly assaulted citizens on the streets of the capital, Bissau. Faced with a wave of public sector strikes, President Joao Bernardo Vieira, who also won office in the June 1994 elections, launched an anti-corruption commission in April. Budgetary reforms won release of blocked International Monetary Fund loans, but the country remains one of the world's poorest.

Guinea-Bissau achieved independence from Portugal in 1975 after a fierce twelve-year guerrilla war. The PAIGC ran a repressive one-party state until 1991 when constitutional revisions ended the PAIGC's status as the "leading force in society." Political parties were legalized and direct elections for both the president and members of parliament were introduced. Thirteen parties registered for national elections in 1994. The PAIGC won a majority in parliament and President Vieira retained his post in a runoff vote, in elections accepted as free and fair by both the opposition and a U.N. observer mission.

Guinea-Bissau's low life expectancy, high infant mortality and declining living standards are consequences both of Portuguese colonial neglect and misrule since independence. Economic reforms encouraged by international donors include sharply cutting the civil service and reducing imports.

Political Rights and Civil Liberties: In 1994, Guinea-Bissau's citizens voted in democratic elections for the first time. The PAIGC retained the presidency and a parliamentary majority, but six opposition parties are represented in the national assembly.

Freedom of assembly and expression is constitutionally guaranteed and generally respected. However, the Guinean Human Rights League was barred in June from holding a march to protest Prime Minster da Costa's attacks on people in Conakry. The group has also raised allegations of torture and other mistreatment by security forces.

Only a few private newspapers publish, and two of these did not appear for long periods in 1996, allegedly because the state-run printing press would not produce their newspapers. State media practice broad self-censorship and rarely question or criticize government policies. The mainly rural population is 60 percent illiterate, and radio remains the most important medium for reaching the people. Four private radio stations are now broadcasting, and providing more balanced coverage than government services.

The judiciary is part of the executive branch. The government has power to detain individuals suspected of "subversive" activities, but there are reports of illegal detention without resort to any statute. Political interference and poor training result in highly uneven judicial performance. Traditional law prevails in rural areas.

Religious freedom is respected. While official registration is required, no religious group has been denied registration since 1982. Most people follow traditional religions, but proselytizing is permitted and there is a significant Muslim population and a small Christian minority.

Women face some legal and significant traditional and societal discrimination. They generally do not receive equal pay for equal work and enjoy fewer opportunities for education and jobs in the small formal sector. Female genital mutilation is widespread.

Citizens may generally travel freely within the country, and no legal restrictions oppose foreign travel. The vast majority of Guineans survive on subsistence agriculture. Eleven labor unions operate in the formal sector. Workers have the right to organize and to strike with prior notice.

Guyana

Polity: Parliamentary democracy
Political Rights: 2
Civil Liberties: 2
Economy: Mixed statist
Status: Free
Population: 722,000
PPP: $2,140
Life Expectancy: 65.4
Ethnic Groups: East Indian (51 percent), black (36 percent), mixed (5 percent), Indian (4 percent), European
Capital: Georgetown

Overview: The issue of police brutality captured public attention, as citizens protested a number of incidents of excessive use of force in 1996.

Guyana is a member of the British Commonwealth. From independence in 1966 until 1992 it was ruled by the autocratic, predominantly Afro-Guyanese, People's National Congress (PNC). The 1980 constitution provides for a strong president and a 65-seat National Assembly elected every five years. Twelve seats are occupied by elected local officials. The leader of the party winning the plurality of parliamentary seats becomes president for a five-year term. The president appoints the prime minister and cabinet.

The first free and fair elections were held in 1992, and 80 percent of the eligible population voted. The PNC lost to the predominantly Indo-Guyanese People's Progressive Party (PPP) Civic alliance. PPP leader Cheddi Jagan, having moderated his Marxism since the collapse of communism, became president.

Indo-Guyanese outnumber Afro-Guyanese, 52 percent to 36 percent. Jagan won 52 percent of the vote; PNC leader Desmond Hoyte took 41 percent. A third candidate from the Working People's Alliance (WPA), the only mixed-race party in the country, won less than two percent. In the legislature, the PPP won 36 of 65 seats, the PNC 26; the WPA, which campaigned on a platform of multiracial cooperation, won two seats, and the centrist United Force (UF) took one.

Fear and distrust of the Indo-Guyanese ruling party continues among Afro-Guyanese, despite Jagan's record of governing in a relatively evenhanded manner. He was slow to move on promised constitutional and electoral reforms, but in 1995 got to work with an eye towards the next elections, due in 1997.

Political Rights and Civil Liberties: Citizens can change their government through direct, multiparty elections. The rights of free expression, freedom of religion and freedom to organize political parties, civic organizations and labor unions are generally respected. Nonetheless, without more explicit constitutional guarantees, political rights and civil liberties rest more on government tolerance than institutional protection.

The judicial system is independent; however, due process is undermined by the shortage of staff and funds. Prisons are overcrowded, and conditions poor.

The police force remains vulnerable to corruption, particularly given the penetration by the hemispheric drug trade. In 1996 the Guyana Human Rights Association (GHRA) charged the police force with excessive use of force, causing 20 deaths. The GHRA cited dozens of additional cases of brutality. Three incidents during the year in which individuals were allegedly either crippled or killed by police gave rise to the formation of community organizations aimed at protesting police conduct. The GHRA is independent, effective and backed by independent civic and religious groups.

Several independent newspapers operate freely, including the *Stabroek News* and the *Catholic Standard*, a Church weekly. Only two radio stations operate; both are government-owned. The government owns one television station. Fifteen privately-owned television stations freely criticize the government.

Labor unions are well-organized. In 1995 the government sought to dilute the right to strike among some public sector unions. Companies are not obligated to recognize unions in former state enterprises sold off by the government.

Racial clashes have diminished since the 1992 election, but long-standing animosity between Afro- and Indo-Guyanese remains a concern. The government has taken steps to form a multiparty race relations committee to promote tolerance.

A cabinet ministry of indigenous affairs exists, and the government has moved on a development plan to address the problems of 40,000 Amerindians living in the interior. The three main Amerindian organizations, however, continued to demand more land and local control.

Domestic violence against women is troubling, as is the government's reluctance to address the issue.

Haiti

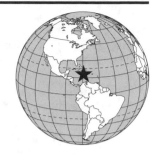

Polity: Presidential-parliamentary democracy
Economy: Capitalist-statist
Population: 7,269,000
PPP: $1,050
Life Expectancy: 56.8
Ethnic Groups: Black (95 percent), mulatto
Capital: Port-au-Prince

Political Rights: 4*
Civil Liberties: 5
Status: Partly Free

Ratings Change: Haiti's political rights rating changed from 5 to 4 because of improved citizen participation in the political process.

| **Overview:** | In February 1996 Rene Preval succeeded Jean-Bertrand Aristide in Haiti's first peaceful transition of presidential power since independence. But the deterioration of law and |

order, as well as an unemployment rate of more than 50 percent, seriously undermined the country's already weak, underdeveloped institutions.

Since gaining independence from France in 1804 following a slave revolt, the Republic of Haiti has endured a history of poverty, violence, instability and dictatorship. A 1986 military coup ended 29 years of rule by the Duvalier family, and the army ruled for most of the next eight years.

Under international pressure, the military permitted the implementation of a French-style constitution in 1987. It provides for a president elected for five years, an elected parliament composed of a 27-member Senate and an 83-member House of Representatives, and a presidentially-appointed prime minister.

In the 1990 elections Aristide, a charismatic left-wing priest, won in a landslide over conservative Marc Bazin. Aristide sought to establish civilian authority over the military; he also tried to end corruption. Haiti's mostly mulatto elites and the military then conspired to overthrow him. In response, he overstepped the constitution by calling on supporters to defend the government by violent means.

Aristide was overthrown in September 1991. Haiti came under the ruthless control of the military triumvirate of General Raoul Cedras, General Philippe Biamby and Colonel Michel Francois.

When the U.S. and the U.N. imposed a trade and oil embargo, the military agreed to negotiate with Aristide, but reneged on an accord for his return when they unleashed tens of thousands of armed civilian thugs. The military then built itself a political base by creating an armed group called the Front for the Advancement and Progress of Haiti (FRAPH).

In September 1994, facing an imminent U.S. invasion, Cedras and Biamby agreed to step down. U.S. troops took control of the country and Aristide was reinstated. His security, as well as that of average Haitians, now depended on the U.S. and U.N. forces.

Aristide dismantled the military before the June 1995 parliamentary elections got underway. International observers questioned the legitimacy of the June election and Aristide's supporters fell out among themselves. The more militant Lavalas movement remained firmly behind him. But the National Front for Change and Democracy (FNCD), a leftist coalition that had backed him in 1990, claimed fraud and boycotted the runoff elections. In the end, Lavalas won an overwhelming majority in parliament.

In the fall Lavalas nominated Preval, Aristide's prime minister in 1991, as its presidential candidate. With Aristide backing him and the FNCD and most other major opposition parties boycotting, the election's outcome was a foregone conclusion. Less than one-third of the electorate turned out on December 17, with about 89 percent of the vote going to Preval.

Preval took office on February 7, 1996. The U.N. had planned to withdraw its troops by the end of the month. The new Haitian National Police force, however, was clearly not ready to carry out its duties. At Preval's urging, the U.N. extended its stay, but cut its force size from 6,000 to 1,900 troops (and to 1,300 in late June). In late April the final American combat unit withdrew.

By early summer, the government was coming under increasing pressure from former soldiers who had not been paid back wages and pensions. On August 16 authorities arrested 20 persons, most of them former soldiers affiliated with the right-wing Mobilization for National Development (MDN) party, who, Preval claimed, had been planning to attack the National Assembly and assassinate political leaders. Two days later, an attack that killed one person was made against the national police headquarters and the Legislative Palace in Port-au-Prince. The perpetrators were believed to be former soldiers.

In September, parliament approved a much-delayed privatization program along with modest civil service reforms. This freed up more than $100 million in international assistance. Preval, at U.S. urging, purged much of his personal security detail which, according to American officials, was involved in the August murders of two MDN politicians.

Political Rights and Civil Liberties: During the 1995 parliamentary elections, the government was accused of serious irregularities and fraud. This led most major opposition parties to boycott the 1995 presidential vote, which, along with a very low turnout (less than one-third), called into question the legitimacy of the presidential transition.

The constitution guarantees a full range of political rights and civil liberties. The protection of such rights remained precarious in 1996, however, given the absence of any rule of law, not to mention the security vacuum that the hundreds of U.N. troops only partially filled. The international force was under orders not to disarm the population despite evidence that thousands of former military personnel and backers had stowed away caches of weaponry.

The new, 5,200-member Haitian National Police, hampered by a lack of adequate training and resources, frequently used excessive force and mistreated detainees. Police officers shot several civilians to death. A U.N. report released in August noted progress in efforts to increase the force's professionalism, but also cited, among other abuses, evidence of summary executions. In July authorities arrested three police officers on murder charges in the first crackdown on law enforcers. The police chief also fired at least 15 officers and detained others pending prosecution. Most abuses by police went unpunished, however.

In 1996 gunmen shot several off-duty police officers. The killings are believed to have been politically-motivated. Mob violence and armed gangs posed severe security threats in urban areas. The government claimed that former soldiers or others with links to the ousted military regime were responsible for the violence. However, many neutral observers attributed much of it to the random work of criminal gangs, some of which included former soldiers. A continuing crime wave in 1996 led to more than 100 vigilante killings as crowds attacked suspected criminals. The mayors of Port-au-Prince and other cities responded to the tense situation by forming private security forces, which carried out unauthorized searches and arrests.

In 1995 and 1996 more than two dozen political killings occurred. Most victims were linked either to current opposition groups or to the former military regime. Few, if any, of these cases had been resolved by the end of 1996. The government also arbitrarily detained members of the political opposition, former soldiers and others on vague charges such as "threatening national security".

The judicial system remains corrupt, inefficient and essentially dysfunctional, particularly in rural areas. Confidence in the judicial system dropped further in July after a jury acquitted two men accused of the 1993 killing of former Justice Minister Francois Guy Malary, who had attempted to reform the judiciary. Irregularities marred the trial.

Prison conditions remain grim. A severe backlog of cases result in lengthy pre-trial detention periods. Many reports are made of beatings, even of minors.

A number of independent newspapers and radio stations exist. Outlets critical of the government continue to be targets of intimidation, including violent mob attacks. Television is state-run and strongly biased toward the government.

Labor rights, as with all other legally-sanctioned guarantees, are essentially unenforced. Unions are generally too weak to engage in collective bargaining, and their organizing efforts are undermined by the high unemployment rate.

Honduras

Polity: Presidential-leg-
islative democracy
(military-influenced)
Economy: Capitalist-statist
Population: 5,605,000
PPP: $2,100
Life Expectancy: 67.9
Ethnic Groups: Mestizo (90 percent), Indian (7 percent)
Capital: Tegucigalpa

Political Rights: 3
Civil Liberties: 3
Status: Partly Free

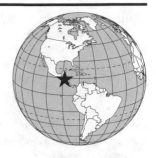

Overview: President Carlos Roberto Reina continued the process of reducing military influence in government, limiting its economic reach and pushing for accountability for the "dirty war" of the 1980s.

The Republic of Honduras was established in 1839, 18 years after independence from Spain. It has endured decades of military rule and intermittent elected government. The last military regime gave way to elected civilian rule in 1982. The constitution provides for a president and a 130-member, unicameral Congress elected for four years.

The two main political parties are the center-left Liberal Party (PL) and the conservative National Party (PN). In the 1993 elections, the PN nominated Oswaldo Ramos Soto, an outspoken right-winger. The PL, which had held power during most of the 1980s, nominated Reina, a 67-year-old progressive and former president of the Inter-American Court of Human Rights. The campaign was marked by vicious personal attacks. Reina won with 52 percent of the vote. The PL won 70 seats in the congress, the PN 56. Two small left-wing parties took the remaining four.

Reina promised a "moral revolution" and greater civilian control over the military. In his first three years results were mixed. Military spending is still kept secret, and officers suspected of rights violations continue to be protected. But positive developments include the abolition of compulsory military service; the separation of the police from the military; and the Supreme Court's reversal of the military amnesty for the nine officers accused of the detention, torture and attempted murder of six students in 1982. In December, Congress approved the final reading of a constitutional amendment to place the police under civilian control.

Reina's drive to end impunity has bred discontent among officers who feel their influence abating. The result has been a wave of bombings at the president's home, the courts, Congress, and at government ministries. Most of the bomb attacks appeared to be designed to frighten judges, prosecutors and members of government.

**Political Rights
and Civil Liberties:** Citizens are able to change their government through elections. In the1993 elections, however, 100,000 registered voters were incorrectly listed and thus unable to vote.

Constitutional guarantees regarding free expression, freedom of religion and the right to form political parties and civic organizations are generally respected.

But repressive measures coming in the face of peaceful protests and mounting crime have limited political rights and civil liberties.

The military exerts inordinate influence over the government. By law, legislators elect the armed forces commander for a three-year term from a list of nominees provided by the military. Inevitably, the military imposes its favored candidate. A constellation of military-owned businesses makes the armed forces one of Honduras' ten largest corporations.

The military remains the principal human rights violator. A government human rights office was established in 1993, but the military has generally refused to cooperate with it. In late 1995 the government challenged military impunity, taking the unprecedented step of indicting eight officers for kidnappings in 1982. The military, however, defied the arrest warrants and threatened prosecutors. It was unclear whether a trial would go forward.

Many violent crimes are now as much a product of greed as of politics, as the military and drug traffickers compete for profit and leverage. Targets include businessmen, trade unionists and peasant leaders. Arbitrary detention and torture by police continue despite steps to put the police under civilian authority. Human rights organizations claim that vigilante groups are responsible for dozens of extrajudicial killings of alleged criminals.

In July 1996, almost 2,000 soldiers were deployed in the capital and in the city of San Pedro Sula in response to dramatic increases in crime. The understaffed police forces estimated that in the first half of the year, over 2,000 people were murdered, 20 banks and 30 gas stations were robbed, and auto thefts averaged ten per day.

The judicial system, headed by a Supreme Court, is weak and rife with corruption. Judges who have asserted themselves in human rights cases face death threats and violent attacks. Most criminal cases against the military remain in the purview of military courts and usually result in the dismissal of charges. Prison conditions are deplorable and over 90 percent of those jailed have not been convicted of a crime.

Labor unions are well organized and can strike. Strikes frequently lead to violent clashes with security forces. Trade union membership subjects workers to the risk of losing their jobs, of being blacklisted among employers, or of being attacked by vigilantes. Labor leaders, religious groups and indigenous-based peasant unions pressing for land rights remain vulnerable to repression. Unions have achieved collective bargaining agreements in some export processing activities. Women workers, a majority in the zones, are subject to sexual harassment, forced overtime without pay and physical abuse.

Most press and broadcast media are private. Several newspapers represent various political viewpoints, but a licensing law restricts the practice of journalism. Some of the media have become targets of intimidation the moment they started to cover human rights cases and corruption.

Hungary

Polity: Parliamentary
democracy
Economy: Mixed
capitalist
Population: 10,197,000
PPP: $6,059
Life Expectancy: 69.0
Ethnic Groups: Hungarian (90 percent), Roma (4 percent),
German (3 percent), Slovak, Romanian
Capital: Budapest

Political Rights: 1
Civil Liberties: 2
Status: Free

Overview:
In 1996, a corruption scandal stemming from the government's privatization program and the resignation of Finance Minister Lajos Bokros undermined the credibility of the ruling coalition led by Socialist Prime Minister Gyula Horn.

With the collapse of the Austro-Hungarian empire after World War I, Hungary lost two-thirds of its territory under the 1920 Trianon Treaty, leaving 3.5 million Hungarians as minorities in neighboring Romania, Slovakia, Serbia, Croatia and Ukraine. After World War II, Soviet forces installed a Communist regime. In 1956, Soviet tanks quashed an armed uprising in Budapest. Under the politically-repressive regime of Janos Kadar, Hungary enjoyed relative economic well-being under consumer-oriented "goulash communism." The ouster of Kadar in 1988 led the way to political reform and to the introduction of a multiparty system in 1989.

In the 1994 parliamentary elections, the Hungarian Socialist Party (MSzDP), a successor to the (Communist) Hungarian Socialist Workers Party (MSzMP) made up largely of "reform" Communists, unseated the conservative Hungarian Democratic Forum (MDF), which had won control of the 386-member parliament in 1990. The MSzDP won 209 seats, the pro-market Alliance of Free Democrats (SzDSz) captured 70; the MDF, 37; the pre-war rightist Smallholders Party, 26; the Christian Democrats; 22, and the Young Democrats (FiDeSz), 20. The Socialists agreed to share power with the SzDSz, and former Foreign Minister Horn was named prime minister.

In early 1995, under new Finance Minister Bokros, the government announced radical spending cuts and devalued the forint by 9 percent. The unpopular reform package met strong opposition from unions, and led to the resignations of the welfare and national security affairs ministers. The government moved to make 19,000 civil servants redundant and stepped up privatization. While the Constitutional Court overruled some of the planned budget cuts, the program had a positive impact on the economy. Balance of payments and public finances improved, and the economy recovered, spurred by exports (made competitive by higher productivity and the devalued forint) and investment.

In February 1996, Finance Minister Bokros resigned after the second austerity package aimed at reforming the country's huge public sector, including its health and welfare systems, met stiff resistance from the Socialist-led cabinet. Bokros was replaced by Peter Medgyessy, a banker and former Communist, who pledged to take a more conciliatory approach to reforming the indebted social security fund which ran the country's state health and pension plans. In March, parliament accepted a much-delayed social security budget for 1996, paving the way for a critical loan from the International Monetary Fund (IMF) and membership in the Organization for Economic Cooperation and Development (OECD).

In October, the government fired the entire 11-member board of the state privatization agency (APV) after allegations that it had illegally hired a consultant and made a record amount of unjustified payments to her. The scandal further shook public confidence in the government's ability to manage the economy. The opposition, led by FIDESZ and the Smallholders, called on the government to halt privatization. Allegations of other shady dealings in various government projects began to surface.

In another important development, in September, Romania and Hungary signed a basic treaty that ended five years of often rancorous negotiations over the treatment of the Hungarian minority in Romania.

Political Rights and Civil Liberties:

Hungarians can change their government democratically under a multiparty system enshrined in an amended Communist-era constitution. Close to 200 parties have been registered since 1989, but most are small or inactive. The 1994 elections were free and fair.

After a six year "media war" over control of electronic media, parliament passed a media law in December 1995. It provides for the privatization of TV-2 and Radio Danubis, and the operation of public service television and radio (including satellite Duna TV) as joint-stock companies run by public foundations. Each of these media organizations would be directed and supervised by a board comprised of members nominated by political bodies and interest groups. In the eight-member presidency of each board, the political parties would have equal representation. The other 21 members would be drawn from prominent media experts, academics, religious and social groups, ethnic minorities and human rights organizations. Some foreign experts criticized the new statute as overly complex and susceptible to political pressure. Journalists criticized the complicated decision-making mechanism of the boards, and argued that since the heads of the boards would be exclusively political people, the influence of television and radio representatives would be diminished. By year's end, privatization of electronic media was slow, partly due to fears of the financial collapse of state broadcasters. In October, the government presented a draft law to parliament relinquishing control of MTI, the national news agency. A broad range of independent, private newspapers and periodicals offer varied commentary and opinions. Some newspapers publish masked advertisements===favorable articles printed in exchange for money. Hungarian companies have charged that several papers threatened to run unfavorable articles if not paid.

Freedom of assembly and association is respected. Freedom of conscience and religion is viewed as a fundamental liberty not granted by the state. Budapest's Great Synagogue was refurbished, with the government paying 80 percent of the cost, and dedicated in September 1996. In July, the government agreed to set aside about $27 million worth of compensation coupons, which could be used to buy state assets for those who suffered during the Holocaust. The country's estimated 500,000 Roma (Gypsies) continue to suffer de facto discrimination in employment and housing. In April, parliament established the Roma Commission to consider ways to improve the situation of the Gypsies in collaboration with the National Gypsy Autonomous Government. An amendment to the law on the rights of national and ethnic minorities approved funding for minority-langauge schools and institutes that foster minority cultures and traditions.

The judiciary is independent and the Constitutional Court has ruled against the government on several occasions, notably nullifying aspects of the 1995 austerity economic program. In 1993, the Court lifted the statute of limitations on the prosecution of former Communist officials who suppressed the 1956 uprising. In August, a draft law proposed by the Justice Ministry recommended the establishment of three courts of appeal and advocated higher standards and pay for judges. In 1996, the Association for Human Rights submitted petitions to the Constitutional Court, charging that the police law that came into force in 1994 granted too much leeway to investigating authorities to enter homes without a warrant, to use weapons and to cut deals with criminals to reduce charges.

In October, the vetting of parliamentary deputies began, with judges examining whether lawmakers held important positions in the secret service, interior ministry or the police during the 1956 anti-Communist uprising. The chairman of the vetting judges said that in addition to the 385 parliamentary deputies, judges would examine the pasts of the president, members of government, and the leaders of most important state institutions.

An estimated 2.5 million Hungarian workers belong to independent trade unions, the largest being the Confederation of Hungarian Trade Unions. In 1995, a national railway strike was called to protest the government's austerity program. Women enjoy the same legal rights as men and are represented in government and business.

Iceland

Polity: Parliamentary democracy
Economy: Capitalist
Population: 270,000
PPP: $18,640
Life Expectancy: 78.2
Ethnic Groups: Icelander
Capital: Reykjavik

Political Rights: 1
Civil Liberties: 1
Status: Free

Overview:

In the summer of 1996, Icelanders elected a new president, Olafur Ragnar Grimsson, thus ending the fourth four-year term of Vigdis Finnbogadottir, the world's first popularly-elected woman president. The April 1995 *Althing* (parliament) elections produced a new center-right ruling coalition.

Iceland achieved full independence in 1944. Multiparty governments have been in power since then. The center-left coalition formed in 1991 between the Independence Party and the Social Democratic Party (SDP) succeeded in stabilizing the faltering economy to a degree. In 1995, after attempting to appeal to younger voters and non-fish industry interests by advocating EU membership, the SDP lost three seats and more than four percent of the popular vote. The Independence Party opted to join forces with the anti-EU Progressive Party, pledging to continue economic stabilization efforts and to eliminate the country's budget deficit.

EU membership remains an unresolved issue. In 1996 Iceland, along with four other Nordic countries, joined Europe's Schengen Convention as an observer state. Iceland will participate in the abolition of systematic internal border controls, a common visa policy and close cooperation in police matters. This step, taken to preserve the Nordic countries "passport union," suggests that despite Iceland's reluctance to join the EU, it cannot avoid participation in EU policies. Though Iceland has strong historical, cultural and economic ties with Europe, Icelanders are hesitant to agree to the EU common fisheries policy that they believe would threaten its fish industry. This industry accounts for eighty percent of Iceland's exported goods and half of its export revenues.

Political Rights and Civil Liberties:

Icelanders can change their government democratically. The constitution, adopted by referendum in 1944, provides for a popularly-elected, primarily ceremonial, president ,responsible for appointing a prime minister from the largest party in the parliament (Althing) elected on the basis of a mixed system of proportional and direct representation. Elections are held every four years. Six political parties currently exist; one, Awakening of the Nation, broke away from the SDP just four months before the 1995 elections and managed to secure four Althing seats.

There is an independent judiciary. Juries are not used, but many trials, especially during the appeals process, use panels comprised of several judges. All judges serve for life. The Ministry of Justice administers the lower courts; the Supreme Court ensures that the judicial process is fair. Defendants are presumed innocent and are entitled to legal counsel. Two special courts handle cases of impeachment of government officials and disputes between employers and workers.

The constitution provides for freedom of speech, freedom of peaceful assembly and association, and freedom of the press. These freedoms are respected in practice. Constitutional bans on censorship are respected. A wide range of publications includes both independent and party affiliated newspapers. An autonomous board of directors oversees the Icelandic State Broadcasting Service, which operates a number of transmitting and relay stations. Over 95 percent of eligible workers belong to free labor unions, and all enjoy the right to strike. Citizens have the right to hold private property. Disabled persons enjoy extensive rights in employment and education.

Virtually the entire country holds at least nominal membership in the state-supported Lutheran Church. Nonetheless, legal protections against discrimination are respected: freedom of worship is upheld and discrimination on the basis of race, language, social class and gender is outlawed.

No legal barriers oppose women's political participation. There is an active women's party, the Women's List, holds 3 of the 63 seats in the Althing. However, women are paid 20 to 40 percent less than their male counterparts for comparable work. Labor union leadership is primarily male. The police and court systems are hostile to, or unsupportive of, victims of sexual abuse. Police conduct humiliating interrogations; convicted rapists often serve one to two years in prison.

India

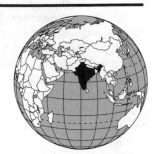

Polity: Parliamentary democracy (insurgencies)
Economy: Capitalist-statist
Population: 941,871,000
PPP: $1,240
Life Expectancy: 60.7
Ethnic Groups: Indo-Aryan (72 percent), Dravidian (25 percent), others
Capital: New Delhi

Political Rights: 2*
Civil Liberties: 4
Status: Partly Free

Ratings change: India's political rights rating changed from 4 to 2 because an activitist judiciary reduced political corruption.

Overview: India's April-May 1996 elections gave regional and lower-caste-based parties the balance of power for the first time, in a hung parliament. The Congress party, widely viewed as corrupt and indifferent to the poor, was abandoned by many low-caste Hindus and Muslims who had formed its core support since independence. After the swift collapse of a government dominated by the right-wing, Hindu nationalist Indian People's Party (BJP), a United Front coalition of 13 leftist, regional and caste-based parties took power under H.D. Deve Gowda. During the year an increasingly activist judiciary prosecuted key political corruption and human rights cases.

In August 1947 India achieved independence from Britain with the partition of the subcontinent into predominantly Hindu India, under Jawaharlal Nehru, and Muslim Pakistan. Independence was accompanied by widespread inter-communal violence, culminating in the murder of Mohatmas Gandhi by a Hindu upper-caste extremist. The 1950 constitution provides for a lower *Lok Sabha* (House of the People), and an upper *Rajya Sabha* (Council of States). Executive power is vested in a prime minister and cabinet.

The centrist, secular Congress party ruled continuously except for periods of opposition in 1977-80 and 1989-91. The 1991 elections were marred by the assassination of former premier Rajiv Gandhi, heir to the political dynasty of Nehru and his daughter Indira Gandhi. P.V. Narasimha Rao subsequently formed a minority Congress government. Faced with a balance of payments crisis, Rao began reforms aimed at transforming an autarkic, command economy into a market-based system that encourages foreign investment.

In early December 1992, 150,000 Hindu fundamentalists, incited by the BJP and militant Hindu organizations, destroyed a sixteenth-century mosque in Ayodhya, in the northern state of Uttar Pradesh. Two weeks of communal violence killed at least 1,700 people nationwide. In December 1992 and January 1993 communal violence in Bombay and Ahmedabad killed more than 1,000 people, the majority of them Muslims, as police participated in anti-Muslim attacks.

Between 1993 and late 1995 the Congress party lost 11 state elections amidst a string of corruption scandals, a backlash against economic reforms by poor and lower-caste voters, and Muslim anger over the government's failure to prevent communal violence. Regional parties in southern India, lower-caste-based parties and the BJP in Hindi-speaking northern states made considerable gains.

In January 1996 the Supreme Court ordered an investigation into $18.3 million in *hawala* (black money) payoffs made to politicians and bureaucrats by a prominent business family between 1988-91. By late February more than 25 politicians from most major parties had been charged with corruption.

During the election campaign opinion polls showed voters mainly concerned with unemployment, inflation and other regional matters. Voting over six days between April 27 and May 30 gave the BJP (161) and four allies 196 seats; the Congress party, 140; the seven-party, center-left National Front-Left Front (NF-LF) coalition headed by the Janata Dal party, 119; eight regional, lower-caste- and Muslim-based parties, 51; three regional-based Congress splinter groups, 24; four others, 4; and independents, 9.

Despite its plurality, the BJP failed to expand its support beyond urban, middle class Hindus and its stronghold in five northern and western states. Most voters rejected its appeal to *Hindutva* (Hindu ethos) and its anti-Muslim sentiments. The biggest swing went to 14 regional, lower-caste- and Muslim-based parties, including BJP allies and Congress splinters, which won 103 seats. In May a BJP-led minority government resigned 13 days after failing to attract secular allies. On June 1 the NF-LF, reconstituted as the 178-seat United Front, formed a government with the support of the Congress Party.

In the Fall, courts charged Rao in three separate criminal corruption cases. In December Sitaram Kesri became Congress president.

Political Rights and Civil Liberties: Indian citizens can change their government democratically. However, a weak rule of law, social and communal tensions, and traditional norms inimical to women's welfare contribute to civil liberties violations.

The April-May 1996 elections were the fairest in the country's history. Authorities monitored compliance with campaign spending limits and restricted use of state resources for campaigning. Photo identity cards helped prevent fraud. "Booth capturing," intimidation, violence and other irregularities were most prevalent in the northern state of Bihar.

Under the constitution, the central government can dissolve state governments following a breakdown in normal administration. The Congress Party frequently misused this power to gain control of states under opposition administration. More recently, in September, President Shankar Dayal Sharma dismissed a BJP government in Gujarat. He lifted the order in October; in addition, he imposed central rule in Uttar Pradesh after the BJP won a plurality of seats in state elections. Corruption is widespread at all levels of government. An official 1993 report, partially released in August 1995, concluded that organized criminals have penetrated politics, particularly in Bihar.

Police, army and paramilitary forces are occasionally responsible for rape and torture. They also are responsible for arbitrary detentions, "disappearances," staged "encounter killings" and destruction of homes, particularly in Kashmir and Punjab, and in Assam and other northeastern states. *(A separate report on Kashmir appears in the Related Territories section)*. The 1983 Armed Forces (Punjab and Chandigarh) Special Powers Act grants security forces wide latitude to use lethal force in Punjab. Maoist Naxalite guerrillas kill numerous police, politicians and landlords each year in Andhra Pradesh, Bihar and Orissa, and run parallel courts in parts of Bihar. Police are accused of extrajudicial executions of suspected Naxalites.

The security situation is tenuous in the seven northeastern states, where in recent decades the population has been swelled by settlers from other parts of India and from Bangladesh. Indigenous groups are demanding greater autonomy and more secure land tenure. More than 40 indigenous-based rebel armies operate in the region. The 1958 Armed Forces Special Powers Act grants security forces broad powers to use lethal force and to detain suspects in Assam and four nearby states. Security forces frequently rape, torture and kill civilians during counterinsurgency operations, particularly in Assam. The militant armies commit hundreds of killings and abductions each year. Since 1993 fighting between Naga and Kuki tribesmen in Manipur has killed some 950 people. In spring 1996 Bodo rebels massacred at least 75 Santhal tribesmen and burned 60 villages in Assam, leaving tens of thousands homeless.

The broadly-drawn 1980 National Security Act allows police to detain suspects for up to one year (two in Punjab) without charges. Police torture of suspects and abuse of ordinary prisoners, particularly low-caste members, as well as rape of female convicts is routine.

The judiciary is independent and in 1996 exercised unprecedented activism. In addition to the *hawala* scandal, the Supreme Court ordered investigations into a host of smaller corruption cases, and ordered parties to file audits for regular and election-related expenditures. In September and October lower courts handed down the first convictions for murders during anti-Sikh riots in 1984, although to date there have been no prosecutions of police who participated in the violence. In December the Supreme Court ordered the National Human Rights Commission to probe the cremations of 984 Sikh victims of police crackdowns in Punjab in the 1980s. The judicial system, however, is severely backlogged, subject to corruption and manipulation at the lower levels, and often inaccessible to poor people.

The private press is vigorous. The Official Secrets Act empowers authorities to censor security-related articles; in practice this is occasionally used to limit criticism of the government. Journalists are occasionally pressured and harassed by government officials and militant Hindu groups.

The government has monopolies on broadcast media, and political coverage favors the ruling party. In August 1996 the government affirmed a 1955 ban on the printing of foreign-owned periodicals (although publications printed abroad may be sold), and on the establishment of broadcast operations by foreign television networks.

Human rights organizations generally operate freely, but face harassment in rural areas from landlords and other powerful interests. Police and militants occasionally harass, torture or kill activists. On May 7, 1996, Parag Kumar Das, the general secretary of the Manab Adhikar Sangram Samiti human rights organization in Assam, was killed in Guwahati, apparently by a militant group backed by security forces.

Section 144 of the criminal procedure code empowers state authorities to declare a state of emergency, restrict free assembly and impose curfews. Authorities in West Bengal detained and, in some cases, beat hundreds of Bhutanese refugees during their several attempts to march peacefully from southeastern Nepal through Indian territory to Bhutan. On June 19 police violently dispersed Bhutanese refugees marching near Siliguri. In early May police made thousands of temporary arrests in Andhra Pradesh, Bihar and Maharashtra prior to voting. In November police detained 1,500 protesters in Bangalore in advance of the Miss World beauty pageant.

Several thousand women are burnt to death, driven to suicide or otherwise killed, and countless others are harassed, beaten, or deserted by husbands in dowry disputes each year. Convictions in dowry deaths are rare. Rape and other violence against women is prevalent. Many of the hundreds of thousands of women and children in Indian brothels have been trafficked across international borders, generally with the complicity of local officials. Many trafficking victims, including tens of thousands of Nepalese, are held in debt servitude and are subject to rape, beatings and other torture. Hindu women are often denied inheritances, and under *Shari'a* (Islamic law) Muslim daughters generally receive half the inheritance a son receives. Tribal land systems, particularly in Bihar, deny tribal women the right to own land.

The constitution bars discrimination based on caste, but in practice caste frequently determines an individual's occupation and marriage options. Members of lower castes are occasionally subjected to random beatings, rape and arson, and scores of people are killed each year in caste-related violence.

Freedom of religion is respected, although communal violence has been a notable feature of Indian life since independence. In January 1996 the Maharashtra government dropped 24 cases of incitement and other charges against Bal Thackeray, the leader of the extremist Shiv Sena party, relating to anti-Muslim violence in the Bombay riots of 1992-93.

Major cities have tens of thousands of street children, many of whom work as porters, vendors and in other informal sector jobs. A November 1996 Human Rights Watch/Asia report detailed illegal detentions, beatings and torture of street children by police. Child marriage, although banned, is relatively common.

The International Labor Organization estimates that anywhere from 44 million to 100 million child laborers, mostly from lower castes and ethnic minorities, are employed in agriculture, carpet and glass factories and in other areas. Several million of these children are bonded laborers. In December the Supreme Court ordered the government to fine businesses illegally employing an estimated six million children in "hazardous" industries, but notoriously corrupt inspectors make the ruling's implementation unlikely. Workers can join independent unions and bargain collectively. The central government occasionally uses its power to ban strikes in "essential" industries.

The 120,000 Chakma refugees from ex-East Pakistan (Bangladesh) in four northeastern states are frequently victims of beatings, burnings of homes and other abuses. Eighty-thousand Tamil refugees from Sri Lanka reside in Tamil Nadu.

Indonesia

Polity: Dominant party
(military-dominated)
Economy: Capitalist-
statist
Population: 198,947,000
PPP: $3,270
Life Expectancy: 62.0

Political Rights: 7
Civil Liberties: 5*
Status: Not Free

Ethnic Groups: Javanese (45 percent), Sundanese (14 percent), Madurese (8 percent),
Coastal Malay (8 percent), others
Capital: Jakarta
Ratings Change: Indonesia's civil liberties rating changed from 6 to 5 because of
continued growth in the number of nongovernmental organizations and civic
institutions.

Overview:
The Indonesian government's July 1996 crackdown on supporters of opposition leader Megawati Sukarnoputri sparked
rioting that rocked Jakarta. The unrest highlighted discon-
tent over widening income inequalities, official corruption and political repression
under President Suharto's authoritarian rule.

In August 1945 President Sukarno proclaimed Indonesia's independence from
the Dutch. Following an October 1965 coup attempt by the Indonesian Communist
Party (PKI), the Army Strategic Reserve, led by General Suharto, led a slaughter of
some 500,000 suspected Communists. In March 1968, two years after assuming
key political and military powers, Suharto formally became president.

Three political parties are legally-recognized: the ruling Golkar; the Indonesian Democratic Party (PDI), an amalgam of nationalist and Christian groups; and
the United Development Party (PPP), a coalition of Islamic groups. The 500-mem-
ber parliament has 400 elected legislators and 100 seats reserved for the military
(75 after 1997). The 1,000-member People's Consultative Assembly consists of
the parliament plus 500 appointed members. The Assembly elects the president and
vice president every five years, although Suharto has never faced opposition.

At the June 1992 parliamentary elections Golkar took 282 of the 400 contested
seats; the PPP, 62; the PDI, 56. In March 1993 the People's Consultative Assembly
formally gave Suharto a sixth five-year term.

In April 1994 a strike in the northwestern city of Medan exploded into anti-
Chinese riots. The government, which many accused of covertly instigating the riots, manipulated the unrest to discredit the independent labor movement.

In 1996 the government further limited the political space available to dissidents. On June 20-22 a rebel PDI faction held a government-backed meeting in
Medan and ousted Megawati Sukarnoputri, the daughter of the first president and
the leading opposition figure, as party leader.

On July 27 police and state-sponsored thugs forcibly evicted 150 Megawati
supporters from the PDI headquarters in Jakarta, touching off the worst rioting in
the capital since the mid-1970s. Troops killed at least five people and arrested 249
others. In August the government accused the tiny, unregistered People's Demo-

cratic Party of being a Communist front and fomenting the unrest, and arrested leader Budiman Sudjatmiko and more than 20 other members. On November 19 the Supreme Court, reversing its 1995 ruling, sentenced labor activist Mochtar Pakpahan to four years imprisonment for organizing the 1994 Medan strike.

Political Rights and Civil Liberties:

Indonesians lack the democratic means to change their government due to tight restrictions on political activity and free expression. The armed forces hold 20 percent of seats in national, provincial and district legislatures. Political parties, the media, nongovernmental organizations NGO's and individuals must conform to the official, consensus-oriented Pancasila philosophy, thus sharply limiting political discourse.

The most severe rights violations occur in Aceh, East Timor and Irian Jaya (*Separate reports on East Timor and Irian Jaya appear in the Related Territories section*). In Aceh province the army has killed some 2,000 civilians and *Aceh Merdeka* (Free Aceh) guerrillas since 1989, and security forces arbitrarily detain and torture suspects.

The judiciary is not independent. The executive branch appoints and can dismiss or reassign judges. Police frequently torture suspects and prisoners, and security forces are rarely punished for rights violations. In October six soldiers convicted in the deaths of at least three students during demonstrations in Ujung Pandang, South Sulawesi, in late April, received light sentences of up to three years in prison.

The Agency for Coordination of Assistance for the Consolidation of National Security (BAKORSTANAS) has wide latitude in curbing alleged security threats. Several hundred people are imprisoned under the 1963 Antisubversion Law, while scores or even hundreds of others, many of them political dissidents, are jailed under sedition or hate-sowing statutes. In April 1996 the government restored the voting rights of 1,157,820 alleged PKI members, although such individuals and their families still face discrimination in employment and public services. The government frequently invokes the banned PKI to restrict free expression and justify crackdowns on political and social activists.

The government often pressures newspaper editors to censor sensitive articles, and journalists practice self-censorship. Journalists must be licensed by the official Indonesian Journalists Association (PWI). In the summer of 1995 courts jailed two leaders of the unofficial Alliance of Independent Journalists. In June 1996 the Supreme Court upheld a June 1994 government ban on the weekly *Tempo* magazine which, along with two other weeklies banned at the same time, had criticized government policies. In October the government arrested four men connected with the underground *Voice of Independence* newspaper. The government owns and controls national broadcast media, and private companies face restrictions on news coverage.

In January 1996 the government ended permit requirements for seminars and political meetings. Public assemblies and demonstrations require permits, which are frequently denied, and police often forcibly break up unsanctioned peaceful demonstrations.

NGO activists face imprisonment, police raids on offices, restrictions on public speaking and other harassment. The official National Commission on Human Rights has been critical, and in October 1996 blamed the government for instigating the July riots.

In October Muslims in east Java burned 25 churches, killing five people, after a Muslim who defaced a Koran allegedly took refuge in a church. Ethnic Chinese face cultural, educational and business restrictions. Domestic violence and rape are fairly widespread. Female genital mutilation is widely practiced. Thousands of street children live in Jakarta and other cities.

Strict numerical requirements for trade union registration perpetuate a de facto single union system. The government-controlled All-Indonesian Workers Union is the sole recognized union. The independent Prosperous Workers Union of Indonesia is considered illegal. Civil servants and most state enterprise workers cannot join unions.

Factory owners frequently ignore minimum wage laws, dismiss labor activists and strike leaders, and physically abuse workers. The military often intervenes on behalf of factory owners in labor disputes. Since May 1993 at least three labor activists have died under mysterious circumstances, and others have been arrested.

Iran

Polity: Presidential-parliamentary (clergy-dominated)
Political Rights: 6
Civil Liberties: 7
Status: Not Free
Economy: Capitalist-statist
Population: 63,101,000
PPP: $5,380
Life Expectancy: 67.7
Ethnic Groups: Persian (51 percent), Azeri (24 percent), Kurd (7 percent), Turkic, Arab, others
Capital: Teheran

Overview:

On March 8, 1996, Iranians elected 270 members to the *majlis* (parliament). The government-appointed Council of Guardians severely restricted citizen participation by imposing bans on 44 percent of the more than 5,000 candidates. Candidates have begun preparations for the 1997 presidential elections.

In 1979, Mohammad Reza Pahlavi, the hereditary monarch who ruled for decades in a corrupt, authoritarian manner, fled Iran amid widespread unrest. Fundamentalists led by Ayatollah Ruhollah Khomeini established the world's first Islamic republic. The 1979 constitution provides for a directly-elected president and a 12-member Council of Guardians, which certifies that all bills passed by the directly-elected 270-member majlis accord with Islamic law. The Council of Guardians must approve all presidential and parliamentary candidates, effectively maintaining the political dominance of a core of Shiite Muslim clerics and their allies. In 1981 Khomeini usurped power from elected officials and unleashed a period of mass executions of political opponents.

Following Khomeini's death in June 1989, Ayatollah Ali Khamenei assumed the role of supreme religious leader and chief of state. In July a constitutional referendum approved a stronger presidency, and in August Ali Akbar Hashemi Rafsanjani, a cleric, took office after running unopposed and winning nearly 95 percent of the vote. During his first term Rafsanjani introduced limited free-market reforms, overcoming opposition from more radical clerics favoring statist economic policies.

In 1993, Rafsanjani, again running unopposed, won a second term, capturing a relatively low 63 percent of the votes. The results reflected widespread disillusionment resulting from declining living standards due largely to the economic devastation caused by the eight year war with Iraq.

In April 1995 economic riots broke out after food prices doubled and the value of the currency dropped sharply. Security forces responded by shooting and killing at least ten people.

Political Rights and Civil Liberties:

Iranians cannot change their government democratically. All presidential and legislative candidates must support the ruling theocracy, effectively barring any meaningful opposition. The country is run by a Shiite clerical elite. There is no separation of religion and state. Ninety percent of the population are Shiite Muslim. Political parties are strongly discouraged, and the few that exist are barred from participating in elections.

State control is maintained through terror—arbitrary detention, torture, disappearances, summary trials and executions. Several hundred people are executed annually for political reasons, often on false drug or other criminal charges. Neither avenues of appeal nor legal limits on the length of detention exist. Prison conditions are harsh.

The judiciary is not independent. Judges, like all officials, must meet strict political and religious qualifications. Bribery is common. Civil courts feature some procedural safeguards, although since 1995 judges may serve simultaneously as prosecutors during trials. Revolutionary courts try political and religious cases, but are often arbitrarily assigned cases normally falling under civil courts' jurisdiction. Defendants are often charged with vague crimes; the revolutionary courts have no due process rights; some trials last less than five minutes.

The Intelligence and Interior Ministries operate informant networks. Security forces enter homes and offices, open mail, and monitor telephone conversations without court authorization. In 1994 the Islamic Revolutionary Councils, which monitor government employees' religious fervor, purged dozens of civil servants. The government obstructs human rights monitors' activities.

Women face discrimination in legal, educational and employment matters. After 1979, women were expelled from the courts and removed from political positions. In 1994, however, women were allowed to be legal advisers in the courts. The government encourages fundamentalist groups to enforce strict Islamic dress guidelines for women, regardless of their faith. The penal code permits the flogging or stoning of women for moral offenses. In 1996 the majlis created a special subcommittee to address women's issues, though the effect of this remains unclear. Women need permission from a male relative to obtain a passport.

Some public criticism of government policy is allowed. Several relatively outspoken newspapers and cultural journals exist. However, tolerance is arbitrary and crackdowns occur frequently. In 1995 authorities closed at least four outspoken publications. Promoting the rights of ethnic minorities and criticizing the notion of an Islamic government is prohibited. The Ministry of Islamic Culture and Guidance censors all printed material and reviews imported publications.

All radio and television is state-owned, and broadcasts promote government views. The parameters for permissible creative work (written, film and music) shift quickly and unpredictably. Those whose work or ideas fall outside the parameters face punishment and censorship. Satellite dishes were banned in 1995, and the government authorized certain police units to raid homes to remove dishes.

The government has weakened or eliminated most independent civic institutions. Demonstrations not sponsored by the government are rare but occasionally tolerated.

Religious freedom is limited. Proselytizing Muslims is illegal. In 1994 three Protestant leaders accused of proselytizing were found murdered. The 1979 constitution recognizes Zoroastrians, Jews and Christians as religious minorities. Authorities rarely grant the necessary approval for publication of Christian texts, and church services are routinely monitored. Christians and Jews face restrictions on operating schools, and discrimination in areas such as education, employment and property-ownership. Demonstrating knowledge of Islam is required for university admission and civil service jobs. Jewish families cannot travel abroad together.

The Baha'i faith is not recognized as a religion. The 300,000 Iranian Baha'is face significant official discrimination, including confiscation of property, arbitrary detention, a ban on university admission, heavy employment restrictions, and prohibitions on teaching their faith and on practicing their religion communally. Amnesty International estimates that since 1979 over 200 Baha'is have been executed for reasons related to their religious beliefs.

Authorities have also placed cultural restrictions on the Kurdish community. In Kurdish regions security forces have razed villages, and frequently clash with opposition groups. The government has announced that the estimated 1.6 million Afghan refugees remaining in Iran must leave by March 1997. Some Afghans have reportedly been forcibly repatriated.

There are no independent labor unions. The government-controlled Worker's House is the only authorized federation. Collective bargaining is nonexistent. Private-sector strikes are infrequent and risk being disbanded by the militant Revolutionary Guards.

Iraq

Polity: One-party   **Political Rights:** 7
Economy: Statist   **Civil Liberties**: 7
Population: 17,422,000 **Status:** Not Free
PPP: $3,413
Life Expectancy: 66.1
Ethnic Groups: Arab (75 percent), Kurd (15 percent),
Turk, others
Capital: Baghdad

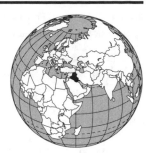

Overview: Iraqi strongman Saddam Hussein weathered at least two attempted coups in 1996 and appeared to maintain his absolute and repressive rule over the country. Yet significantly, those involved in the coup attempt included officers of the elite Republican Guards, officials from Saddam's hometown of Tikrit and members of the Sunni Muslim minority, traditionally three key pillars of his regime.

Iraq was established as an independent state in 1932. Since then, the minority Sunni Muslims have ruled under successive governments. A July 1958 military coup overthrew the Hashemite monarchy. A 1968 coup brought the Arab Ba'ath (Renaissance) Socialist Party to power. The frequently amended 1968 provisional constitution establishes a Revolutionary Command Council (RCC) with virtually unlimited and unchecked authority. In 1979 Saddam Hussein, considered the strongman of the regime since 1973, formally assumed the titles of State President and RCC Chairman.

In September 1980 Iraq attacked Iran, touching off an eight-year war of attrition during which the economy suffered extensively and at least 150,000 Iraqis died. In August 1990 Iraq invaded Kuwait. A 22-nation coalition liberated Kuwait in February 1991. At least 100,000 Iraqi troops died in the war. Immediately following its defeat, the Iraqi army ruthlessly crushed a nascent Shiite uprising in the south. In April the U.N. Security Council passed Resolution 687, ordering Iraq to destroy its weapons of mass destruction, accept long-range monitoring of its weapons facilities and recognize Kuwait's sovereignty before it can sell oil internationally. Iraq has not yet fully complied.

In May 1995 Doulaymi tribesmen in Anbar Province staged bloody anti-government riots, and in June predominantly Doulaymi army units launched a failed rebellion. In the aftermath the army reportedly executed at least 120-150 Doulaymi soldiers and officers. In August two sons-in-law of Saddam, who had been senior members in the regime, defected to Jordan.

In October 1995 Saddam ran as the sole candidate in a sham presidential election aimed at demonstrating his absolute authority. Voters were required to identify themselves on the ballots, and Saddam received 99.96 percent of the vote.

In February 1996 Saddam's two sons-in-law who had defected to Jordan were granted amnesty and returned to Iraq, only to be murdered shortly afterwards. In July Saddam foiled a coup attempt. Authorities reportedly immediately executed some 120 Sunni Muslim officers, including ten senior Republican Guards two of whom were from Tikrit. By August an estimated 800 military officers had been executed; the fate of many others remains unknown.

Political Rights and Civil Liberties: Iraqi citizens cannot change their government democratically. Saddam holds supreme power in one of the most repressive regimes in the world. Relatives and close friends from Tikrit hold most important positions. A 1991 law outlaws opposition parties, and the rubber-stamp, 250-seat National Assembly holds no independent power. All media, print and broadcast, are owned and operated by the Ba'ath Party.

Citizens are denied freedom of speech, assembly and religion. The rule of law is nonexistent. State control is maintained through extensive use of intimidation, including arbitrary detentions, torture and summary executions. The U.N. has documented the disappearance of over 16,000 Iraqi citizens in recent years. The security services routinely search homes without warrants, monitor personal communications, and maintain a large network of informers.

Defendants in ordinary cases receive some judicial safeguards. Political and "economic" cases are tried in separate security courts, where confessions extracted through torture are admissible as evidence and where no procedural safeguards are in evidence. Saddam can override any judicial decision. In both regular and security courts, punishments are often proportionally larger than the crime committed.

The death penalty is frequently used for any expression of dissent, such as insulting the president or the Ba'ath Party. In 1995 the government announced that those convicted of possession of stolen goods, and agricultural workers refusing to supply food for government distribution, would receive the death penalty. Theft, corruption and currency speculation are punished by amputation, branding and execution. Desertion from the army is punished by amputation of the ear and branding of the forehead. Several doctors reportedly have been executed for refusing to carry out these punishments, or for attempting reconstructive surgery.

The Shiite Muslim majority (over 60 percent of the population) faces severe persecution. The army has arrested thousands of Shiites and executed an undetermined number of these detainees. Security forces have desecrated Shiite mosques and holy sites. Bans on some Shiite public ceremonies and on the publication of Shiite books and television programs remain in effect. The army has indiscriminately targeted civilian Shiite Marsh Arab villagers, razed homes and drained the southern Amara and Hammar marshes in order to flush out Shiite guerrillas. Tens of thousands of Shiite civilians have been forcibly relocated, driven out of the country, or killed.

Other restrictions on religion apply to both the Shiite and Sunni communities. A 1981 law gives the government control over mosques, the appointment of clergy, and the publication of religious literature. The government harasses the tiny Turcoman and Christian Assyrian communities, and Jewish citizens face restrictions on traveling abroad and against contacting Jewish groups outside the country.

In 1988 the Government conducted the Anfal Campaign, an effort to exterminate the Kurdish population within its borders. An estimated 50,000 to 100,000 Kurds were killed during six months in a genocide plot which incorporated prison camps, firing squads and chemical attacks. Since 1991, the government had been blocking shipment of food, medicine and other goods to the Kurdish population in the north.

In September 1996, however, Saddam opened up the internal borders, allowing freer exchange of goods and travel.

Resources are frequently diverted to the army and other privileged groups. As a result, food shortages, exacerbated by the oil embargo, have caused particular hardship for children. 1996 saw an estimated 20,000 cases per month of malnutrition. Nearly half the rural population has no access to drinking water. The U.N. has authorized Iraq to sell a limited quantity of oil in order to purchase food and medicine. In the past, Saddam scorned similar offers, but in 1996, facing a worsening economic crisis, Saddam accepted the opportunity to sell oil to purchase food and medicine.

The state-backed General Federation of Trade Unions is the only legal labor federation. Independent unions do not exist. The right to collective bargaining is not recognized by law and is not practiced. The right to strike is limited by law; strikes do not occur.

Human rights monitors and other observers are restricted from investigating human rights abuses. The government and security forces has harassed, intimidated and reportedly offered rewards for killing international relief personnel.

Men are granted immunity for killing their daughters or wives caught committing "immoral deeds." Women are not permitted to travel abroad unescorted by a male relative. Numerous areas are off-limits for travel inside the country; for all, foreign travel is tightly restricted.

Ireland

Polity: Parliamentary democracy
Economy: Capitalist
Population: 3,588,000
PPP: $15,120
Life Expectancy: 75.4
Ethnic Groups: Irish (Celtic), English
Capital: Dublin

Political Rights: 1
Civil Liberties: 1
Status: Free

Overview: Ireland took over the six-month presidency of the European Union (EU) in July, with an agenda which focused special attention on unemployment and drug policy. With 18 million Europeans unemployed and drug-related crime on the rise, Irish foreign minister Dick Spring expressed the hope that Ireland would preside over a concerted European effort to find effective remedies for these perceived threats to the Union's well-being.

Unemployment and drug-related crime are significant problems at home as well as in Europe. While Ireland's economy is booming (the country saw a growth rate of at least 6 percent in 1996), unemployment, at 12.5 percent, is high even by European standards.

The drug problem in Ireland is arguably no worse than in the rest of Europe. It has, however, been allowed to flourish in a climate of lawlessness perceived by many to be a spillover from the North's 25 years of paramilitary violence. In recent years, the emergence of a drug culture has paved the way for "crime bosses" to set up shop. Organized crime in Ireland is at unprecedented levels; a series of murders in the last two years has been linked to gangland violence. The proliferation of drug-related crime has provoked public outrage, which came to a head in June when a popular journalist, Veronica Guerin, was murdered after her extensive investigation and reporting of gangland crime.

The 26 counties of Ireland enjoyed Dominion status within the British Commonwealth from 1921 until 1948, when Ireland became a fully independent state. The six counties of Northern Ireland remained part of the United Kingdom at the insistence of its Protestant majority [see *Northern Ireland* under United Kingdom, Related Territories]. Despite Articles 2 and 3 of the Irish constitution, which lay claim to the Northern territory, the republic plays only a consultative role in Northern affairs, as set out by the 1985 Anglo-Irish accord.

In November, *Taoiseach* (Prime Minister) John Bruton faced a threat to the survival of his coalition government as a result of the release of 17 prisoners, mostly IRA suspects, through an administrative mistake centering on the qualifications of a judge who heard their cases despite having been removed from the court involved. Though all of the prisoners were subsequently re-arrested, their detention is to be contested. Opposition parties tabled a motion of no-confidence in Bruton, but his three-party coalition retained its overall majority and survived.

Cooperation between British Security Services, the Royal Ulster Constabulary and Irish police resulted in numerous raids and seizures of suspected IRA arms in the republic late in 1996. After a massive explosives seizure in London in September, officials made several discoveries of alleged IRA arms dumps and bomb factories along the border with the North. At least 11 suspects have been remanded into custody for alleged terrorist activities.

A foreign policy paper released by the government in March ignited a heated political debate because of its proposal to modify Ireland's long-standing policy of military neutrality. The paper raised the issue of Ireland's joining NATO's Partnership for Peace, a system of defense coordination and cooperation, but avoiding full military involvement. Ireland has remained steadfastly neutral since its independence from Britain, viewing its position as a refusal to fight in British wars.

Meat and dairy farming, still the country's leading economic activity, is expected to be hard hit by the "Mad Cow" epidemic which devastated the British beef industry. Forty-one cases of Bovine Spongiform Encephalopathy (commonly called "Mad Cow" disease) have been reported in Ireland this year, and steadily increasing numbers are seen as potentially disastrous for Irish beef exports to Russia and the Middle East.

After years of highly emotional debate, a constitutional amendment was passed in November after voters decided in favor of lifting Ireland's 60-year-old ban on divorce. The first divorce was granted to a Dublin couple less than two months later.

Political Rights and Civil Liberties: Irish citizens can change their government democratically. The Northern Irish are considered citizens and may run for office in the republic. Currently, only diplomatic families and security forces living abroad may vote by absentee ballot.

The Irish media are free, with an injunction against publishing or broadcasting anything likely to undermine state authority or promote violence. In addition to international cable broadcasts, international newspapers, particularly from Britain, are gaining a growing share of the Irish market. The government has been accused of placing Irish newspapers at a disadvantage by levying on them the highest value-added tax in the EU. Concentrated ownership and harsh libel laws also restrict freedom of the press.

The question of journalistic privilege arose in November when Barry O'Kelly of the *Star* newspaper was threatened with imprisonment for refusing to reveal his source of confidential information in a court case in which he was a witness. The judge presiding over the case declined to jail O'Kelly, however, because his refusal did not prevent the conclusion of the case. The National Union of Journalists continues to challenge the laws which fail to allow journalists to protect sources; this case was expected to go to the High Court in early 1997.

In December, the government published a long-awaited Freedom of Information Bill. The Irish state currently operates on the basis that all official information is presumed secret unless otherwise stated. If enacted, the bill would compel officials to presume in favor of openness unless divulging information would injure public interest. The bill would also put the burden of proof on the body or individual denying access, and would create an Information Commissioner to head an appeals process for those denied access to information. Critics cite the bill's long list of exemptions, which includes information relating to security, international relations and law enforcement. Critics also note that ministers would be able to issue secrecy certificates which could not be effectively challenged in court. Concerns have been raised about possible abuse of this provision.

In 1995, the government lifted the 56-year-old state of emergency, but stopped short of revoking all special powers associated with emergency law. Among these provisions are special search, arrest, and detention powers of the police, and the juryless Special Criminal Court for suspected terrorists. The regular judiciary is independent.

In response to public outcry over the murder of Veronica Guerin, the government proposed anti-crime measures which have been criticized by civil liberties activists as draconian. They include a curtailment of the right to silence, use of the Special Criminal Court, and seven-day detention without trial for those accused of drug-related offenses. In a November referendum, voters backed changes in bail laws which would allow courts to refuse bail to suspected criminals likely to commit further crimes while out on bail.

Israel

Polity: Parliamentary
democracy
Economy: Mixed
capitalist
Population: 5,819,000
PPP: $15,130
Life Expectancy: 76.6

Political Rights: 1
Civil Liberties: 3
Status: Free

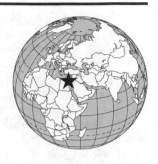

Ethnic Groups: Jewish (83 percent), Arab (17 percent)
Capital: Jerusalem (most countries maintain their embassies in Tel Aviv)

Overview: The May 1996 elections brought a coalition of right-wing, religious, and pro-immigrant parties to power under the leadership of Likud's Benjamin Netanyahu, who pledged neither to compromise Israeli security nor make further concessions to Palestinian autonomy in the West Bank.

Israel was formed in 1948 out of less than one-fifth of the original British Palestine Mandate. Its neighbors, having rejected a United Nations partition plan that would have also created a Palestinian state, attacked immediately following independence in the first of several Arab-Israeli conflicts.

Israel has functioned as a parliamentary democracy since independence. Since 1977 the conservative Likud and the center-left Labor party have shared or alternated power. Following the June 1992 *Knesset* (parliament) elections, Yitzhak Rabin formed a Labor-led coalition government. Through a series of secret negotiations Israel and the Palestinian Liberation Organization (PLO) reached a breakthrough agreement in August 1993, providing for gradual Palestinian autonomy in the Israeli-occupied West Bank and Gaza Strip. (*Separate reports on the Israeli-administered and Palestinian National Council-administered territories appear in the Related Territories section*).

On November 4, 1995, a right-wing Jewish extremist, opposed to the peace process on grounds that it would lead to a Palestinian state in the West Bank, assassinated Rabin in Tel Aviv. Foreign Minister Shimon Peres became acting prime minister.

With elections called for late May, the militant Islamic Hamas movement, beginning on February 25 carried out four suicide attacks within eight days in Jerusalem, Ashkelon and Tel Aviv killing 59 people. The bombings appeared to be aimed at derailing the peace process by boosting the Likud's electoral prospects. During the campaign the party criticized transferring West Bank territory to Palestinian authority as harmful to Israeli security interests, and opposed any future return of the northern Golan Heights to Syria as well as the division of Jerusalem.

In Israel's first direct elections for prime minister on May 29, the Likud's Benjamin Netanyahu defeated Peres with 50.5 percent of the vote. In concurrent Knesset balloting Labor won 34 seats; a coalition of Likud and two right-wing parties, 32; three ultrareligious parties, 23; the leftist Meretz, 9; two Arab parties, 9; the Russian-immigrant based Yisrael Ba-Alliya, 7; and two minor right-wing parties, 6.

Netanyahu formed a 66-seat governing coalition consisting of the Likud coalition, the religious bloc and two smaller parties.

By the Fall Netanyahu was experiencing increasing opposition pressure to show progress on Israeli military redeployments and the expansion of Palestinian territorial autonomy called for in the treaty agreements. Critics warned that failure to respect obligations would have severe consequences for Israel's economic and diplomatic normalization drive. In late September authorities opened a second entrance to an ancient tunnel in the old city of Jerusalem, triggering Israeli-Palestinian confrontations in Gaza and the West Bank that killed 78 people.

Political Rights and Civil Liberties: Israeli citizens can change their government democratically. Although Israel has no formal constitution, a series of Basic Laws have the force of constitutional principles.

Since the September 1993 Israeli-PLO peace accord, suicide bombings by Islamic militants have killed more than 100 Israelis. The *Shin Bet* (General Security Service) is accused of torturing Palestinian detainees. In November 1996 two border policemen were videotaped beating six Palestinian laborers caught illegally crossing into Israel. Internal security regulations from 1987 allow security forces to apply "moderate physical pressure" to suspects during interrogation. A November 1994 government order, confirmed by a November 1996 court ruling, further eased restrictions on the use of physical force against suspects who might have knowledge of imminent terrorist attacks.

The judiciary is independent and procedural safeguards are respected. Security trials can be closed to the public only on limited grounds. A 1979 law provides for administrative detention without charge for renewable six-month periods, subject to automatic review every three months. Most administrative detainees are Palestinians. Detention facilities run by the Israeli Defense Forces holding male Palestinian security prisoners do not meet international norms.

Freedom of assembly and association is respected. Newspaper and magazine articles dealing with security matters must be submitted to a military censor, although the limits on permissible reporting are expanding. Editors can appeal a censorship decision to a three-member tribunal which includes two civilians. Arabic-language publications are censored more frequently than are Hebrew-language ones. Newspapers are privately-owned and vigorously criticize government policies. Authorities barred several Palestinian journalists from entering Israel to cover the May elections.

Women face discrimination in employment. Domestic violence is a problem. In Druze and Bedouin communities, women are sometimes victims of traditional "family honor" killings.

Freedom of religion is respected. Each community has jurisdiction over its members in questions of marriage and divorce. Orthodox Jewish authorities have jurisdiction over marriage, divorce and burial affairs for the entire Jewish community. In July and August police and ultraorthodox Jews clashed in Jerusalem after the Supreme Court suspended a government ban on vehicular traffic on a busy thoroughfare during the Jewish Sabbath. The clashes underscored the concerns of ultraorthodox Jews that the Court will erode religious authority in areas where religious and civil laws conflict.

The 900,000 Arab citizens receive inferior education, housing, and social services relative to the Jewish population, although under the outgoing Labor government the gap had been decreasing. Apart from the Druze and Circassian communities, which serve at their own initiative, Israeli Arabs are not subject to the draft (although they may serve voluntarily). This places them at a disadvantage in obtaining housing subsidies and certain other economic benefits for which army veterans receive preferential access.

Workers can join unions of their choice and enjoy the right to strike and bargain collectively. Three-quarters of the workforce either belong to unions affiliated with *Histadrut* (General Federation of Labor) or are covered under its social programs and collective bargaining agreements. Workers from developing countries are reportedly often mistreated by employers.

Italy

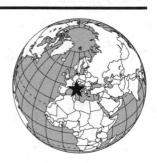

Polity: Parliamentary democracy
Economy: Capitalist-statist
Population: 57,339,000
PPP: $17,160
Life Expectancy: 77.6
Ethnic Groups: Italian, small German, Slovene, Albanian and Roma minorities
Capital: Rome

Political Rights: 1
Civil Liberties: 2
Status: Free

Overview:
On April 21, Italians elected their first left-of-center government in 50 years, though left-of-center parties had belonged to coalition governments. Prime Minister Romano Prodi took office in May promising to make Italy "a normal European country;" that is, one with an accountable government which lasts years instead of months and is committed to a political program. After only a month in office, he began to implement government austerity measures, a top priority of his administration. Undeterred by numerous investigations of corruption, Silvio Berlusconi's Forza Italia party, aligned with the National Alliance—a party which evolved out of the pro-fascist MSI—garnered 39 percent of the vote.

Northern League leader Umberto Bossi declared the independence of Padania, the League's proposed separate northern state, at a secessionist march and rally along the Po river in mid-September. Though state and religious leaders decry Bossi's separatism as absurd, they have felt obliged to assert the unity of Italy by mounting their own rallies throughout the country. Northern League headquarters in Venice and Milan were the targets of firebombs and police searches during the march, and Bossi and his secessionist movement have been placed under investigation by authorities in Mantua, following death threats made against the city's chief public prosecutor by a man claiming to be part of the Padanian National Guard.

Modern Italian history dates from the nineteenth-century movement for national unification. Most of Italy had merged into one kingdom by 1870. Italy was allied with Germany and Austria-Hungary at the outset of World War I, but switched to side with the Allied Powers. From 1922-43, the country was ruled by fascist dictator Benito Mussolini. As the Allies advanced, the Germans established a puppet state in the north called the "Republic of Salo." At the end of World War II a republican constitution replaced the monarchy.

The president, whose role is largely ceremonial, is elected for a seven-year term by an assembly of parliamentarians and delegates from the Regional Councils. The president chooses the prime minister, who is often, but not always, a member of the largest party in the Chamber of Deputies, the lower house of parliament. Members of the upper house, the Senate, represent the regions.

Forza Italia won the March 1994 elections on a platform of reform, but the Berlusconi government fell less than a year later, when the Northern League withdrew its support. President Oscar Luigi Scalfaro appointed Lamberto Dini to head a technocratic interim government that would overcome political deadlock and tackle Italy's deteriorating public finances. At the end of 1995, Dini resigned. Failing to assemble another workable interim government, Scalfaro called elections for April.

An aggressive anti-corruption campaign led by magistrates has led to thousands of indictments of politicians and businessmen since 1992. Former Prime Minister Bettino Craxi—beyond reach in Tunisia—was sentenced to prison in November in a high-profile bribery trial. Just when it seemed that Italy's political establishment was cleaning up, a new scandal broke in mid-September as the head of Italy's railways was arrested on an array of corruption charges. This second scandal is expected to claim a number of public figures; it is already being called *tangentopoli due* (Bribesville-2), recalling the enormity of the first scandal.

By August, Prodi's government had produced more than 100 draft laws to deal with his two high-priority policy areas, the economy and constitutional reform. The austerity program was forced through parliament in early August. Efforts to qualify for European Monetary Union (EMU) membership were applauded by the European Commission president, who said that if the lira returns to the EMS this year, Italy will have complied with Maastricht exchange rate stability criteria. The goal of reducing the deficit to three percent, as mandated by the treaty, has been approved by parliament.

In November, the government unveiled plans for far-reaching reforms of public administration and federalization. Such plans involve trimming the state and delegating powers to regional governments and local bodies. The Senate has approved reforms which will abolish six ministries and 25,000 public agencies.

Political Rights and Civil Liberties: Italians can change their government democratically. Electoral reforms implemented in 1993 allowed voters to choose individual candidates rather than party lists and converted 75 percent of parliamentary seats to a British-style "first-past-the-post" system. The new system has helped bring Italian politics towards a bipolar structure with broad alliances on the right and left.

Italian citizens are free to form political organizations, with the exception of reorganizing the constitutionally forbidden prewar fascist party. Attempting to guarantee the end of authoritarian rule, the postwar constitution established an elaborate system of checks and balances in which the Senate and the Chamber of Deputies hold equal power. The result has been a heavy reliance on the popular referendum as a tool for breaking political deadlock (more than 30 have been held since 1974), which arguably diminishes the power of parliament to legislate efficiently.

Italy's judiciary is independent but notoriously slow. A 1995 law states that preventive detention can be imposed only as a last resort, or if there is convincing evidence of a serious offense, such as crimes involving the Mafia or those related to drugs, arms, and subversion. A maximum of two years of preliminary investigation is permitted. Preventive custody can be imposed only for crimes punishable by a maximum sentence of four or more years. Despite these measures, as of mid-1995, over 40 percent of inmates were in prison because they were awaiting trial or the outcome of an appeal. The average waiting period for trials is about 18 months, but can exceed two years.

The press in Italy is free and competitive, with restrictions on obscenity and defamation. Although most of the 80 dailies are independently-owned, editorial opinion is highly influenced by the church and tends to lean to the right.

The main state-owned television network, and the three main channels of Radio Audizioni Italiane, or RAI, provide Italians with most of their news; their boards of directors are entirely parliament-appointed. The August board appointments for the top posts at the channels drew criticism from Prodi supporters, who were disappointed when members of his Olive Tree coalition took most of those jobs for themselves. Umberto Bossi threatened to blow up RAI's transmitters when Northern League politicians were effectively shut out of the race for positions.

Freedom of speech is guaranteed in the constitution, as is freedom of assembly and association, with the exception of fascist and racist groups. Unions are active, though in 1995 were weakened by a voter referendum and government legislation aimed at restricting their power.

Religious freedom is guaranteed in this overwhelmingly Roman Catholic country. Italy's first grand mosque opened in 1995. North African migrants comprise many of the estimated 650,000 Muslims currently residing in Italy. Immigrants and other foreigners face discrimination and physical attack. Romani people, estimated at 65,000, encounter difficulties finding places for their groups to live.

Women generally receive lower salaries than men for comparable work. They are underrepresented in many fields, such as management and the professions, and are laid off more frequently than men. Their participation in government remains at an estimated 10 percent. Numerous organizations exist to tackle these problems, but they often lack the financial resources to effect significant improvement.

Jamaica

Polity: Parliamentary democracy
Economy: Capitalist
Population: 2,594,000
PPP: $3,180
Life Expectancy: 73.7
Ethnic Groups: Black (76 percent), Creole (15 percent), European, Chinese, East Indian
Capital: Kingston

Political Rights: 2
Civil Liberties: 3
Status: Free

Overview: The formation of the National Democratic Movement (NDM) in late 1995 indicated a possible end to Jamaica's traditional two-party system. In the short term, however, it led to rising political violence in 1996.

Jamaica, a member of the British Commonwealth, achieved independence in 1962. It is a parliamentary democracy, with the British monarchy represented by a governor-general. The bicameral parliament consists of a 60-member House of Representatives elected for five years and a 21-member Senate, with 13 senators appointed by the prime minister and eight by the leader of the parliamentary opposition. Executive authority is vested in the prime minister, who leads the political party commanding a majority in the House.

Since independence, power has alternated between the social-democratic People's National Party (PNP), currently in power, and the conservative Jamaica Labor Party (JLP). The PNP's Michael Manley was prime minister from 1972 to 1980, and again from 1989 until his resignation for health reasons in 1992. JLP leader Edward Seaga held the post from 1980 until 1989.

In 1992 the PNP elected P.J. Patterson to replace Manley as party leader and prime minister. In the 1993 elections, the PNP won 52 parliamentary seats, and the JLP eight. The parties differed little on continuing the structural adjustment begun in the 1980s, but the JLP was hurt by longstanding internal rifts.

Irregularities and violence marred the vote. The PNP agreed to address subsequent JLP demands for electoral reform. Meanwhile, the Patterson government continued to confront labor unrest and an unrelenting crime wave.

In October 1995 Bruce Golding, a well-respected economist and businessman and former chairman of the JLP, left the party to launch the NDM, one of the most significant political developments since independence. Golding brought with him a number of key JLP figures, including one other member of parliament, cutting the JLP's seats to six.

Politically-motivated fighting between supporters of the JLP and the NDM broke out in January 1996, fueled in part by belligerent statements coming from JLP leadership. The violence claimed at least ten lives during the year.

Political Rights and Civil Liberties: Citizens are able to change their government through elections. However, the 1993 elections were marked by thuggery on both sides, police intimidation, large-scale confusion, scattered fraud and a voter turnout of only 59 percent (the lowest since the pre-independence 1962 elections). Progress on electoral reform has been slow.

Constitutional guarantees regarding the right to free expression, freedom of religion and the right to organize political parties, civic organizations and labor unions are generally respected.

Labor unions are politically influential and have the right to strike. An Industrial Disputes Tribunal mediates labor conflicts.

Violence is now the major cause of death in Jamaica, and the murder rate continues to rise. Much of the violence is the result of warfare between drug gangs known as posses. Mobs have been responsible for numerous vigilante killings of suspected criminals. The police have been responsible for over 2,100 deaths in the past nine years, as well as for numerous cases of physical abuse of detainees. But domestic violence (particularly against women), common criminal activity and vigilante actions in rural areas continue. The work of the Jamaica Council for Human Rights has led to successful prosecution in a number of cases, with victims receiving court-ordered, monetary reparations. But officers found guilty of abuses usually go unpunished and many cases remained unresolved.

The judicial system is headed by a Supreme Court and includes several magistrate courts and a Court of Appeal, with final recourse to the Privy Council in London. The system is slow and inefficient, particularly in addressing police abuses and the deplorable, violent conditions of prisons. Despite government efforts to improve penal conditions, a mounting backlog of cases and a shortage of court staff at all levels continue to undermine the judicial system.

A mounting crime rate led the government to take the controversial steps of restoring capital punishment and flogging. Rights groups protested both measures. Critics charged that flogging was unconstitutional because it could be characterized as "inhuman or degrading punishment."

Newspapers are independent and free of government control. Journalists are occasionally intimidated during election campaigns. Broadcast media are largely public but are open to pluralistic points of view. Public opinion polls play a key role in the political process, and election campaigns feature debates on state-run television.

Japan

Polity: Parliamentary democracy
Economy: Capitalist
Population: 125,792,000
PPP: $20,660
Life Expectancy: 79.6
Ethnic Groups: Japanese (98 percent), Korean, Ainu
Capital: Tokyo

Political Rights: 1
Civil Liberties: 2
Status: Free

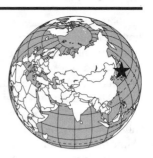

Overview: **V**oters ushered in another LDP-dominated coalition government in the October lower-house elections. Reform-oriented parties had swept the conservative Liberal Democratic Party (LDP) out of office in 1993 after 38 years of continuous rule. Japanese voters sensed little had changed. Shifts in the economy as well as changes in Japan's international position led voters to choose stable conservatism on issues of foreign policy and the economy.

Following its defeat in World War II, in 1947 Japan adopted an American-drafted constitution that invested legislative authority in the two-house Diet (parliament) and ended the emperor's divine status. In October 1955 the two wings of the opposition Japan Socialist Party (JSP) united and, in November, the two main conservative parties merged to form the ruling LDP. This "1955 system" remained in place throughout the Cold War as the LDP won successive elections and the leftist JSP served as an institutional opposition.

By the early 1990s a series of corruption scandals in which the LDP was involved had led to calls for political reform. Ordinary Japanese increasingly began to question the LDP's favoritism towards big business, farmers and other special interests, as well as the burdensome regulations imposed by the country's powerful bureaucracy. The LDP lost its lower-house majority for the first time in 38 years in the July 1993 elections. In August the JSP, renamed the Social Democratic Party (SDP), and six smaller conservative and centrist parties formed a governing coalition, sending the LDP into the opposition for the first time.

In June 1994 the LDP returned to power in coalition with the SDP, its longtime rival, and the smaller, newly-formed New Harbinger Party (NHP). The SDP's Tomiichi Murayama took office as prime minister, allowing the faction-ridden LDP to avoid the internally divisive process of choosing one of its own for the post. Voter disillusionment quickly increased over this opportunistic left-right alliance. In early December nine conservative opposition parties joined to form the New Frontier Party (NFP). Its platform included economic deregulation and a more assertive Japanese foreign policy.

In the July 1995 elections for 126 of the 252 seats in the upper house of parliament, the governing coalition lost 10 seats to finish with 65, while the NFP, in its first national poll test, scored well with 39 seats. Smaller parties and independents split the remainder. International trade and industry minister Ryutaro Hashimoto was elected LDP president in September, and Ichiro Ozawa, a reformer who spent years as an LDP back-room fixer, won the top NFP spot in December.

The LDP won 239 of the 500 lower-house seats in the October 1996 lower-house elections. Falling short of an overall majority, it was forced to form a coalition with the NFP and the Democratic party (formed a month before the elections, as a hybrid of several parties with a majority of former SDP members). This is a more coherent alliance than the fractious three-party team of the last government. The SDP had a poor showing, losing more than half its seats. The New Harbinger party garnered only 2 seats and the Japanese Communist Party 26; ten seats went to independent parties. In November, Hashimoto was re-elected for a second term as prime minister and appointed a cabinet consisting entirely of LDP members for the first time in three-and-a-half years. Hashimoto proposed to streamline government and to deregulate the economy. Of some concern was the low voter turnout of only 60 percent, down 8 percent from the previous record low.

Political Rights and Civil Liberties:

Japanese citizens can change their government democratically. Reform legislation passed in 1994 reduced the permissible disparity in population between urban and rural districts. Additionally, campaign finance laws were tightened. Multiple-seat constituencies were scrapped in favor of a 500-seat lower house with 300 single-seat districts and 200 seats chosen on a proportional basis; and an upper house with 152 single-seat districts and 100 seats chosen on a proportional basis. The July 1995 upper-house elections were the first to be held under the new laws.

The treatment accorded to the 700,000 Korean permanent residents in Japan continues to be troubling. Koreans regularly face discrimination in housing, education and employment opportunities; they are not granted automatic Japanese citizenship at birth, and must submit to an official background check and adopt Japanese names to become naturalized. Both the Burakumin, who are descendants of feudal-era outcasts, and the indigenous Ainu minority also face unofficial discrimination and social ostracism.

The judiciary is independent. The criminal procedure code allows authorities to restrict a suspect's right to counsel during an investigation. Local human rights groups have criticized the frequent practice of using police cells to hold the accused between arrest and sentencing, and report that police sometimes physically abuse suspects to extract confessions. Local groups have also criticized prison conditions for their rigid emphasis on discipline. In addition, immigration officers are accused of beating detainees.

Civic institutions are strong and freedom of expression, assembly and association is respected in practice. Exclusive private press clubs provide journalists with access to top politicians and major ministries, and in return journalists often practice self-censorship of sensitive stories. Foreign news services must negotiate with each club directly, and entry is occasionally denied.

For decades the Education Ministry has censored passages in history textbooks describing Japan's military aggression in the 1930s and 1940s. In March 1993 the Supreme Court ruled that the Ministry has the right to censor textbooks on "reasonable grounds."

Women face significant discrimination in employment and are frequently steered into clerical careers. The 1986 Equal Employment Opportunity Law discourages discrimination in the workplace but does not make it illegal. According to a May survey by the Japanese Trade Union Confederation (RENGO), 40 percent of working women have experienced sexual harassment in the workplace. Thousands of women from the Philippines and Thailand have been trafficked to Japan for prostitution. Full freedom of religion is in place; Buddhism and Shintoism predominate. Workers, with the exception of police and firefighters, are free to join independent unions of their choice and to hold strikes.

Jordan

Polity: Monarchy and elected parliament
Economy: Capitalist
Population: 4,232,000
PPP: $4,380
Life Expectancy: 68.1
Ethnic Groups: Palestinian and Bedouin Arab (98 percent), Circassian, Armenian, Kurd
Capital: Amman

Political Rights: 4
Civil Liberties: 4
Status: Partly Free

Overview:
Rioting in August 1996 over reduced wheat subsidies reflected a deeper frustration, that Jordan's 1994 peace treaty with Israel has failed to revive a stagnant economy.

The British installed the Hashemite monarchy in 1921 and granted it full independence in 1946. The current monarch, King Hussein, came to the throne in 1952. The 1952 constitution vests executive power in the king, who appoints the prime minister and can dissolve the National Assembly. The Assembly currently consists of a 40-member Senate appointed by the king, and an 80-member, directly-elected Chamber of Deputies.

In 1989, after rioting erupted in southern cities over fuel price increases, Hussein eased tensions by lifting restrictions on freedom of expression and ending a 32-year ban on party activity. In November of that year the country held its first elections since 1956, albeit on a non-party basis.

In November 1993 multiparty elections resumed, with the key issue being the recent Israel-Palestine Liberation Organization peace treaty. Bedouins and "East Bank" Jordanians, who form the king's bedrock support base, feared the treaty would empower and eventually allow the "West Bank" Palestinians, a 60 percent majority in Jordan, to overthrow the Hashemite monarchy. Pro-government independents and Bedouin tribal leaders won 54 seats; the fundamentalist Muslim Brotherhood's political party, the Palestinian-based Islamic Action Front (IAF), 16; and minor parties, 10.

In October 1994 Jordan and Israel formally ended a 46-year state of war. At the July 1995 municipal elections, pro-government candidates scored heavy victories over IAF candidates opposed to the peace accord.

On August 16-17, 1996, Bedouins and "East Bank" Jordanians rioted in Kerak and other poor southern towns after the government sharply reduced wheat subsidies, doubling the price of bread, under a structural adjustment program. Hussein suspended the summer session of parliament to protect the prime minister from further criticism. Security forces arrested at least 190 people; most of them were released, although several members of pro-Iraqi groups remained in detention at year's end.

Political Rights and Civil Liberties: Jordanians cannot change their government democratically. King Hussein holds broad executive powers, can dissolve parliament and must approve all laws. The electoral districts favor the king's rural stronghold. Constitutional changes are highly unlikely, since a two-thirds majority of the 120 seats is required and the king appoints the entire 40-member Senate.

The authorities frequently arbitrarily arrest Islamic fundamentalists, and police abuse detainees to extract confessions. The judiciary is not independent in sensitive cases. Defendants in state security courts often lack sufficient access to lawyers prior to trial.

Jordanians freely criticize the government's policies, although direct criticism of King Hussein is rare. In February a state security court sentenced the spokesman of the banned militant Islamic Liberation Party to three years in jail for criticizing the King's ties to Israel, and in September a student received eight months in prison for slandering him during a poetry recital. The penal code criminalizes defamation of public officials and foreign heads of state. The authorities have suppressed opposition to closer relations with Israel by suspending certain preachers from sermonizing and purging some public school teachers, and, in May 1995, by banning a conference by groups opposed to the agreement.

The 1993 Press and Publications Law restricts coverage of the royal family, the armed forces, monetary policy and other sensitive issues. Several journalists have been fined and jailed under the law. Newspaper coverage of the August riots led to a series of arrests and pending charges against journalists under the press law and penal code. Journalists generally practice self-censorship. The broadcast media are state-owned and provide some criticism of government policies.

The government routinely grants permits for demonstrations. Nongovernmental organizations generally operate freely. In October 1996 the local Arab Organization for Human Rights published a report accusing the security forces of torture and arbitrary arrests despite the press law's ban on publishing information about the security forces.

Islam is the state religion. The government does not permit the Baha'i faith to run schools, and Baha'i family legal matters are handled in the Islamic *Shari'a* courts.

Males average 30 to 60 "honor killings" of female relatives each year for alleged moral offenses. The penal code sharply limits the sentences for such killings. Women must receive permission from a male guardian to travel abroad and are discriminated against in inheritance and divorce matters. The population of street children continues to grow.

Private sector workers can join independent unions. The government can prohibit private sector strikes by referring a dispute to an arbitration committee. Some government employees can form unions; but none can strike. The International Confederation of Trade Unions has called for greater protection against anti-union discrimination.

Kazakhstan

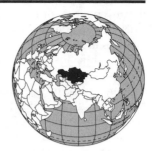

Polity: Dominant party
(presidential-dominated)
Economy: Statist
transitional
Population: 16,460,000
PPP: $3,710
Life Expectancy: 69.7
Ethnic Groups: Kazakh (43 percent), Russian (35 percent),
Ukrainian (6 percent), others
Capital: Almaty

Political Rights: 6
Civil Liberties: 5
Status: Not Free

Overview: In 1996, bolstering cooperation with regional neighbors, particularly Russia and China, enacting agreement over a multinational oil pipeline construction project and maintaining political stability were key issues facing President Nursultan Nazarbayev, who has tightened his grip since his election in 1991.

This sparsely populated, multi-ethnic land the size of India, stretching from the Caspian Sea east to the Chinese border, was controlled by Russia from 1730 to 1840. After a brief period of independence in 1917, it became an autonomous Soviet republic in 1929 and a union republic in 1936. Kazakhstan formally declared independence from a crumbling Soviet Union in December 1991. President Nazarbayev, former first-secretary of the Kazakhstan Communist Party and head of the Kazakhstan National Unity Party (PNEK), was directly elected in 1991. In March 1995, faced with continuing opposition charges that the parliament elected in 1994 was illegitimate because of wide-scale irregularities and a challenge from the Constitutional Court, Nazarbayev dissolved parliament and ruled by decree, scheduling elections for a new bicameral parliament—a 47-member Senate (upper house) and a 135-member *Majilis*—for December. Forty senators were to be directly elected, and seven chosen by the president. Nazarbayev ordered a referendum extending his rule to the year 2000 (his term expired in 1996), and on April 29 a reported 95 percent supported the measure. On August 30, voters overwhelmingly approved a new constitution, which gave the president the right to dissolve parliament if it approves a no-confidence vote in the government or twice rejects his nominee for prime minister. It also codified periods of presidential rule by decree. The December 5 Senate elections were largely uncontested, with Nazarbayev supporters taking all the seats. The PNEK dominated the vote for the Majilis. Akezhan Kazhegeldin is the prime minister.

In March 1996, the presidents of Kazakhstan, Russia, Belarus and Kyrgyzstan signed a series of quadripartite agreements that formalized a Customs Union and coordinated information systems. President Nazarbayev and Russian President Boris Yeltsin signed a series of bilateral economic accords giving Russian interests 44 percent control of Caspian Sea oil. Kazakhstan also approved "confidence-building" measures with neighboring China.

In November, a three-year deadlock was broken when ten oil companies and the governments of Kazakhstan, Russia and Oman settled remaining differences over construction of an export pipeline for at least $30 billion worth of Western oil ventures in Kazakhstan.

In political issues, President Nazarbayev continued to use his constitutional powers to dictate the agenda and dominate parliament. In June, parliament averted a political crisis by supporting a controversial bill that raised the retirement age by three years. If parliament had voted against the bill a second time, President Nazarbayev would have been constitutionally mandated either to accept the resignation of the government or to dissolve parliament for the third time in as many years. The president had blamed previous parliaments for blocking his reforms. As one Western diplomat observed: "It was a game. The parliamentarians just wanted to show that they existed."

In April, a group of leading intellectuals and public figures launched a new opposition movement, *Azamat* (Citizen), to address the "deep social crisis" and to work for "a government of honest and competent people, based on people's trust." A month earlier, 74 members of the intelligentsia had signed an open letter published in the independent press that expressed concern over the "near catastrophic social climate" in the country. Among the founders of Azamat were Petr Sovik of the Socialist Party of Kazakhstan, a moderate offshoot of the Communist Party, who advocated strategic cooperation with reform forces within the government.

The only possible threat to President Nazarbayev's almost complete authority is Prime Minister Kazhegeldin, who helped to improve the economy, pushed the president's allies from the cabinet and built a power base among the country's emerging economic elite.

Another source of tension has been the large Russian minority in the north. Leaders of Russian and Cossack movements have complained of intimidation and violence at the hands of the Kazakh militia.

The Taliban movement's capture of Kabul in Afghanistan forced the leaders of Kazakhstan, Kyrgyzstan, Tajikistan Uzbekistan and Russian Prime Minister Viktor Chernomyrdin to formulate a joint response to possible destabilization of the region.

In economic matters, the government announced in March that small-scale privatization had been completed. A new tax code and the July abolition of export tariffs encouraged continued foreign investment in the oil, gas and gold industries.

Political Rights and Civil Liberties:

Citizens have the power to change their government, but a new constitution has enshrined de facto power centered in the hands of President Nazarbayev, whose regime has cracked down on the opposition, controls the media and monitors political opponents. The 1995 parliamentary elections failed to meet international standards. International observers cited such irregularities as one individual voting for an entire family. The Communist Party complained that only nine of 28 candidates received registration, while 38 candidates were registered for the PNEK. Most opposition parties boycotted the vote, while a few opposition candidates ran as independents.

Opposition parties include the Socialists (former Communists), the nationalist *Azat* (Freedom) Party, the ethnic-Russian Unity Party and the Rightist Republican Party, as well as smaller groups. Opposition parties have complained of harassment, surveillance, denial of access to the state-run media and arbitrarily being banned from registering candidates. A new group, *Azamat*, was established in April. A draft law passed in April to regulate relations between public organizations and the government maintained some restrictions on the rights of nongovernmental groups.

Obstacles to press freedom include economic factors as well as government interference. In January, President Nazarbayev signed a decree establishing a reorganized National Agency for the Media, responsible to the President and not the government, with the president having the power to appoint and dismiss the chairman. Journalists have warned that the new agency gives the president control of all newspapers and magazines financed through the state budget. There are provisions in the criminal code which proscribe insulting the honor of the president. Independent local radio stations have to petition the Ministry of Communications because broadcast towers are state-owned. The main cities have at least one local independent or quasi-independent television station. Stations with national range are state-controlled. Independent newspapers face financial difficulties, as do party and union publications, particularly outside the capital, Almaty. The Kazakhstan-American Bureau on Human Rights alleged on April 9 that independent journalists were being increasingly persecuted by the state, and that a new censorship regime had been introduced by the State Radio and Television Committee. The report accused the committee of banning a number of programs that criticized the government, and of persecuting Erik Nurshin, editor of the independent paper *Dozhivem do ponedelnika*. The Russian-language news analysis program *Nedelya* was taken off the air on June 16 for broadcasting an appeal by Russian presidential candidate Aleksandr Lebed.

Freedom of assembly is restricted. In March, unsanctioned rallies took place in the north calling for restoration of the Soviet Union; organizers, mostly Russians, were taken into custody and fined. In November, authorities banned a mass rally in Almaty protesting deteriorating social and economic conditions organized by the opposition, citing concerns for public order and safety.

The constitution guarantees freedom of religion, but religious associations may not pursue political goals. Christians, Muslims and Jews can worship freely. Minority and ethnic rights remained an issue. Russian, Germans and other non-Kazakhs have charged discrimination in favor of ethnic Kazakhs in state-run businesses, government, housing and education. Ethnic Russians have left in droves, particularly from the northern industrial cities such as Karaganda. Some 65 percent of ethnic Germans left the country since 1990, leaving 370,000. Russian-,German- and Korean-language newspapers publish. The government has sought to staunch the Russian "brain drain" by making Russian the language of intra-ethnic communication and by simplifying citizenship procedures. The government has also cracked down on the Uigur minority that supports the Uigur independence movement in northern China. A new language law introduced in September would guarantee equal treatment and respect for all languages.

The judiciary is not wholly free of government interference. Judges are subject to bribery and display political bias. Judges are appointed by the Ministry of Justice with little or no parliamentary oversight. Supreme Court and lower court judges are now required to take exams attesting to their professional qualifications. A special committee consisting of well known scholars, lawyers and parliamentary deputies will review the exams. In August, Amnesty International issued a report on the grim conditions in the country's prisons. In June, the government granted amnesty to

20,000 prisoners convicted of non-violent crimes.

The largest trade union remains the successor to the Soviet-era General Council of Trade Unions, which is practically a government organ. The Independent Trade Union Center, with 12 unions, includes the important coal miner's union in Karaganda. A new labor law places restriction on the right to strike. In October, independent and state labor unions staged rallies demanding wage arrears, a minimum wage and protection of pensions. In a televised interview in November, President Nazarbayev singled out trade unions as "destabilizing." Several independent women's groups exist to address issues of discrimination in hiring and education, as well as those of domestic violence.

Kenya

Polity: Dominant-party **Political Rights:** 7
Economy: Capitalist **Civil Liberties:** 6
Population: 28,176,000 **Status:** Not Free
PPP: $1,400
Life Expectancy: 55.5
Ethnic Groups: Kikuyu (21 percent), Luhya (14 percent),
Luo (13 percent), Kalenjin (12 percent), Kamba (11 percent),
Somali (2 percent), others
Capital: Nairobi

Overview:
President Daniel arap Moi continued to rule through a combination of state patronage, media control and repression as he prepared for the December 1997 presidential and legislative elections that he and his Kenya African National Union are expected to dominate. Moi's already formidable prospects are raised by a limited economic revival, but more importantly by a divided opposition. A wide range of political parties and civil society groups have called for constitutional and other reforms before the coming elections, and have denounced widespread corruption, condemning Moi's repression and human rights abuses. But there are few signs of their uniting behind a credible challenger.

Kenya was conquered by British imperial forces in the late eighteenth century to open a route to control the River Nile headwaters in Uganda. Kenya remained under British control until its 1963 independence under President Jomo Kenyatta's Kenya African National Union (KANU) party. Kenyatta was a leader of the 1952-58 Mau-Mau rebellion, dominated by people of his Kikuyu ethnicity. The Kikuyu remained pre-eminent in Kenya's politics until Kenyatta's death in 1978. Vice-President Moi's succession kept KANU in power but eventually reduced Kikuyu influence. Opposition parties were banned in 1982, and ethnic tensions between Moi's Kalenjin ethnic group and others—widely believed to have been provoked by the government itself—took thousands of lives from 1989-93.

Moi lifted the ban on opposition parties and permitted multiparty elections in December 1992 after pressure from international aid donors. Moi was proclaimed victor with 36 percent of the vote in polls marked by both opposition discord and highly-suspect procedure. Absent constitutional and other reforms, Moi may face an opposition boycott to his bid for another five-year term that will further devalue his already dubious claim to electoral legitimacy.

Political Rights and Civil Liberties: Kenyans' right to freely choose their government is severely limited. Since Moi's tainted 1992 re-election, his regime has increasingly used police powers and executive decrees to muzzle opposition. He is helped by a generally compliant judiciary that backs repressive actions.

The government has refused to register new political parties since 1992, including the new opposition party, *Safina* (Swahili for "Noah's Ark"), whose leader is prominent white Kenyan, Richard Leakey.

The regime has ruled out constitutional changes such as the creation of an independent election commission, demanded by the National Convention Facilitating Committee (NCFC), an alliance of opposition parties, and the Citizens' Coalition for Constitutional Change (Four Cs). The NCFC has also demanded that laws directly limiting freedom of association and the political organization itself be changed, including the Public Order Act, the Public Security Act and the Chief's Authority Act. Without such reform, the existence of a multiparty system in Kenya remains little more than window-dressing for KANU's tight grip on power.

Freedom of expression is severely limited. The regime or the ruling KANU party retains nearly complete control over broadcast media, and transmits endless paeans to President Moi. The first private radio license was issued in January to a businessman close to the ruling party. The state-run Kenya Broadcasting Corporation censors news about Kenya received from BBC World Television. Private print media are vibrant but journalists have been assaulted, and independent magazines are subject to harassment in their business operations. In August, the printer of an independent newspaper was firebombed. The government has threatened to expel foreign correspondents for their reporting on increasing crime, corruption and the ongoing political crisis. President Moi has decreed it a crime to "insult" him; and sedition laws are being used to silence any criticism. In September, the ruling party set up a press committee to counter what it calls negative publicity about Kenya. Efforts to pass a highly restrictive new press law were abandoned in the face of strong local and international criticism, however.

The Moi regime is increasingly adept at using the law as a tool of repression rather than as a means for justice. More direct violence is also recorded. Opposition gatherings have been attacked. In April, Karimi Nduthu, Secretary-General of Release Political Prisoners (RPP), a group founded in 1992 by ex-detainees, was murdered in his Nairobi home. Twenty-one other RPP members were arrested in July for holding a public meeting to commemorate Nduthu. The nongovernmental Kenyan Human Rights Commission (KHRC) charged in September that killings and torture by police are mounting. Human rights advocates and environmentalists also report attacks and threats. The Law Society of Kenya, Legal Advice Center and KHRC have faced intimidation for publicizing abuses and demanding respect for human rights.

Safina leader Richard Leakey has evoked racist responses from the Moi regime, which is also accused of fanning ethnic unrest for its own political ends. Kenyans of Somali ethnicity have been subjected to numerous abuses, and must carry special identification. Kenyan Asians, who are heavily represented in the country's commercial class, have also been the object of racist propaganda, some of it from opposition politicians.

In October 1995, leading oppositionist Koigi wa Wamwere was sentenced to four years' imprisonment and six lashes on armed robbery charges. Independent observers described the court proceedings as a farce. Wamwere's lawyers and journalists seeking information on the case were harassed and detained. Wamwere is reportedly in ill health, suffering from ailments for which he has not received proper treatment while imprisoned.

Women face legal discrimination in inheritance and property rights as well as restrictions on obtaining credit and passports. Females have less educational opportunity, especially at higher levels. Violence against women is reportedly widespread, and female genital mutilation is still common.

While unions are active, the right to strike has been superseded by a 1993 Ministry of Labor decree forbidding all strikes. Central government civil servants and university academic staff may join only government-designated unions. Nepotism and corruption inhibit economic opportunity. Women's groups such as the International Federation of Women Lawyers (FIDA)-Kenya and Kitua cha Sheria (Legal Advice Center) offer legal aid and advocate on behalf of domestic violence victims.

Kiribati

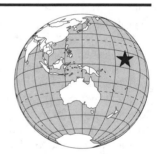

Polity: Parliamentary democracy
Economy: Capitalist-statist
Population: 81,000
PPP: na
Life Expectancy: na
Ethnic Groups: Micronesian (84 percent), Polynesian (14 percent), others
Capital: Tarawa

Political Rights: 1
Civil Liberties: 1
Status: Free

Overview: The Republic of Kiribati consists of 33 islands of the Gilbert, Line and Phoenix groups scattered over two-million square miles of the Pacific Ocean. The country, with a Micronesian majority and a Polynesian minority, became an independent member of the British Commonwealth on July 12, 1979.

The 1979 constitution established a unicameral *Maneaba ni Maungatabu* (House of Assembly) with 39 directly-elected members who serve four-year terms, one representative from Banaba Island elected by the Banaban Rabi Council of Leaders, and the attorney general, if he is not already an elected member. The president is directly elected from a list of three to four candidates nominated by the parliament from among its members, and is limited to three four-year terms. In July 1991 founding President Ieremia Tabai served out his third term and threw his support in the presidential election behind Teatao Teannaki, who beat out his main competitor, Roniti Teiwaki.

In May 1994 parliament voted to set up a select committee to investigate misuse of public funds by a cabinet minister. Reading this as a vote of no-confidence in the administration, the speaker dissolved parliament, and President Teannaki resigned from office. Acting according to the constitution, a three-man caretaker administration took power consisting of the speaker of parliament, the chief justice and the chairman of the Public Service Commission (PSC). A bizarre but ultimately inconsequential constitutional crisis emerged on June 1, when police forcibly removed acting head of state, Tekire Tameura, on the grounds that his tenure as chairman of the PSC had expired three days earlier.

On July 21-22 the country held early elections for a new parliament, with 206 candidates competing. Following runoff balloting on July 29-30, the newly-formed opposition Christian Democratic Party (MTM) won 19 seats, with the remainder split between the ruling National Progressive Party and smaller, less formal groupings. In September voters elected the MTM's Teburoro Tito as president.

A five-man select committee, established in late 1994, is reviewing the 1979 constitution. The 1994 constitutional crisis, albeit minor, highlighted the fact that many clauses are vague and ill-defined.

Political Rights and Civil Liberties:

Citizens of Kiribati can change their government democratically. In addition to the directly-elected parliament, local island councils serve all inhabited islands. Politics are generally conducted on a personal and issue-oriented basis rather than on a partisan level. Several parties exist but lack true platforms and business offices.

Freedom of speech, press, assembly, religion and association is respected. The legal system is modeled on English common law, and provides adequate due process rights. The judiciary is independent. Traditional customs permit corporal punishment, and island councils on some outer islands occasionally order such punishment for petty theft and other minor offenses. The government-run Kiribati Broadcasting Service's radio station and the country's one newspaper, a state-owned weekly, offer pluralistic viewpoints. Church newsletters are also an important source of information.

Women are entering the workforce in growing numbers but still face social discrimination in this male-dominated society. Citizens are free to travel internally and abroad. Workers are free to organize unions, bargain collectively and strike. Although more than 90 percent of the workforce is in subsistence agriculture and fishing and operates outside the wage structure, the well-organized Kiribati Trade Union Congress includes seven trade unions with approximately 2,500 members.

Korea, North

Polity: Communist
one-party
Economy: Statist
Population: 23,904,000
PPP: $3.000
Life Expectancy: 71.2
Ethnic Groups: Korean
Capital: Pyongyang

Political Rights: 7
Civil Liberties: 7
Status: Not Free

Overview:

In 1996 Kim Jong Il appeared to be firmly in control of the totalitarian state that he inherited from his father, Kim Il Sung, two years earlier. As North Korea's economy continues to implode the country's future looks increasingly bleak.

The Democratic People's Republic of Korea was formally established in September 1948, three years after the partition of the Korean Peninsula. Marshall Kim Il Sung, installed with Soviet backing, created a Stalinist personality cult based largely on his supposed leading role in fighting the Japanese in the 1930s. For decades Kim used an all-encompassing "ideology," *Juche* (I Myself), stressing national self-reliance and independence, to justify the country's isolation from the rest of the world. Meanwhile the government nurtured a slavish devotion to the "Great Leader" Kim and his son, "Dear Leader" Kim Jong Il, by indoctrinating citizens through the media, the workplace, the military, mass spectacles and cultural events.

In December 1991 the younger Kim replaced his father as supreme commander of the armed forces in what appeared to herald the world's first Communist dynastic succession. Kim Il Sung died suddenly of a heart attack on July 8, 1994. Kim Jong Il announced that he would wait a year before taking the positions of state president and general secretary of the Korean Workers' Party, formerly held by his father. This is in observance of the traditional two-year Confucian mourning period; however, the inappropriateness of having a coronation during a famine is a more likely reason for the delay. Nevertheless, South Korean intelligence analysts say Kim is firmly in charge of the country.

The disintegrating economy and widespread famine forced desperate measures on Pyongyang. Trade dropped to $2.05 billion in 1995 (equivalent to about a week of exports in South Korea), and hunger has been widespread. In a breach of the Military Armistice Agreement to establish a limit of 35 soldiers and five officials from each side in the Demilitarized Zone, the North Koreans moved upwards of 300 troops there in April 1996. Pyongyang expressed "deep regret" over last September's attempt to infiltrate a submarine into South Korea, that resulted in the deaths of soldiers and civilians. This expression of remorse eased tensions, and paved the way for four-way talks with the United States, China and South Korea some time in 1997. The possibility of the North gaining much needed foreign assistance is now likely.

The perilous state of the economy, which has contracted since 1990, has forced North Korea to open up somewhat to the outside world. In October 1994 the U.S. and North Korea signed a complex, three-stage deal under which North Korea agreed to a ten-year timetable for dismantling its clandestine nuclear program. In exchange, the U.S., South Korea and Japan would provide emergency oil supplies and build two light-water reactors.

Political Rights and Civil Liberties:

North Koreans live in the most tightly-controlled country in the world and cannot change their government democratically. The Supreme People's Assembly holds no independent power. Elections are held on a regular basis but all candidates are state-sponsored, either by the ruling Workers' Party or by smaller, state-organized parties. Opposition parties are illegal, and because of the regime's repressive, isolationist policies, as well as the severe economic hardship, little organized dissent of any sort appears to exist. The government denies citizens all fundamental freedoms and rights. The rule of law is nonexistent and there is no civil society.

Under the criminal code citizens are subject to arbitrary arrest, detention and execution for "counterrevolutionary crimes" and other broadly defined political offenses. In practice, these offenses can include nonviolent acts such as attempted defection, criticism of the Kim family or listening to the BBC or other foreign broadcasts.

The judiciary is government-controlled. Defense lawyers urge defendants to plead guilty rather than seek justice for them. Prison conditions are brutal. Prisoners are severely mistreated and, according to some reports, summary executions occur frequently. Entire families are sometimes imprisoned together. The regime operates "re-education through labor" camps where forced labor is practiced. Tens of thousands of political prisoners and their family members are reportedly held in these remote camps. Defectors say some political prisoners are "re-educated" and released after a few years, while others are held indefinitely.

Authorities conduct monthly checks of residences, and electronic surveillance of homes is common. Children are encouraged at school to report on their parents' activities. The government assigns a security rating to each individual that, to a somewhat lesser extent than in the past, still plays a role in determining access to education, employment and health services. North Koreans face a steady onslaught of propaganda from radio and television.

Religious practice is restricted to state-sponsored Buddhist and Christian services. Permission to travel outside one's town is generally granted only for state business, weddings or funerals. The disintegrating economy and the growing hunger problem has led to an increase in defections, an offense punishable by execution. One Russian official said that he decided against turning in two refugees when a third was executed on the spot by border guards. The government reportedly forcibly resettles politically suspect citizens, and access to the capital, Pyongyang, is tightly controlled. Few citizens are permitted to travel abroad.

All jobs are assigned by the state. The General Federation of Trade Unions of Korea is the sole legal trade union federation, and its affiliates function as tools of state control. There is no right to strike, and strikes do not occur.

Korea, South

Polity: Presidential-
parliamentary democracy
Economy: Capitalist-
statist
Population: 45,253,000
PPP: $9,710
Life Expectancy: 71.3
Ethnic Groups: Korean
Capital: Seoul

Political Rights: 2
Civil Liberties: 2
Status: Free

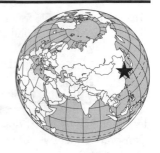

Overview:

South Korean President Kim Young Sam's popularity plummeted in 1996 because of allegations of connections to huge political slush funds, unilateral legislative decisions and a downturn in the economy.

The Republic of Korea was established in August 1948. General Park Chung Hee took power in a 1961 military coup. He led the country until his assassination in 1979, when General Chun Doo Hwan assumed power through another coup. In May 1980 the army killed several hundred anti-government protesters in the southern city of Kwangju. In June 1987, violent student-led protests rocked the country after Chun picked another army general, Roh Tae Woo, as his successor. Roh responded by submitting to direct presidential elections in December 1987, in which he beat the country's best known dissidents, Kim Young Sam and Kim Dae Jung.

The February 1988 constitution limits the president to a single five-year term, and revoked his power to dissolve the 299-seat National Assembly. In January 1990 Kim Young Sam and another opposition leader, Kim Jong Pil, merged their parties with the ruling party to form the governing Democratic Liberal Party (DLP).

In the December 1992 presidential vote, the cleanest in the country's history, the DLP's Kim Young Sam took 42 percent of the vote to beat Kim Dae Jung and billionaire businessman Chung Ju Yung. Kim took office in February 1993 as the first civilian president since 1961. In its first two years in office the Kim administration reduced the security services' internal surveillance powers, sacked several top generals, and ended the practice of allowing individuals to maintain bank accounts under false names.

Nevertheless, Kim's popularity was eroded by a string of industrial and construction accidents and by a perception that his reforms have not gone deep enough. In the April 1996 legislative elections, the New Korea Party (NKP) narrowly lost its majority, winning 139 of the 299 seats in the National Assembly. The opposition vote was deeply divided between the center-left National Congress for New Politics and the conservative United Liberal Democrats.

In December, President Kim's attempt to reform South Korea's labor laws initiated the largest work stoppage in South Korean history. The legislation was passed in a clandestine pre-dawn session without the opposition being present. An earlier government-drafted bill had called for the authorization of multiple national labor groups starting in 1997. The final NKP bill, however, put this off until the year 2000 but enacted pro-employer legislation allowing companies to lay off workers, increasing employer flexibility in setting work schedules and maintaining restrictions on "third party" involvement in labor disputes. Some 1.4 million workers (one tenth of the total workforce), from car makers to subway locomotive engineers, walked out or declared to walk out on partial or general strike in protest.

In another key issue in 1996, a court sentenced former presidents Chun and Roh to death and to 22 years' imprisonment, respectively, on charges of corruption, and treason arising from their roles in the 1979 coup and the Kwangju massacre. Chun's and Roh's sentences were later reduced to 17 years. The trials were both praised for instituting accountability and criticized as politically motivated.

Political Rights and Civil Liberties:

South Koreans can change their government democratically. The judiciary is independent.

The continued application of the broadly-drawn National Security Law (NSL) remains the country's key human rights issue. Since President Kim took office scores of people have been arrested under the NSL for allegedly expressing pro-North Korean views. NSL and ordinary detainees are frequently beaten to extract confessions, and suspects are generally not allowed access to attorneys during interrogation.

Three years after reducing the operations of the Agency for National Security Planning, parliament passed, along with the new labor laws, legislation restoring the agency's power to spy on its citizens and resume some of its old interrogative practices, on the grounds of a heightened security threat posed by North Korea.

The broadcast media are state-supported but generally offer pluralistic views, while the largely private print media practice some self-censorship. Authorities reportedly pressure editors not to report critical and unflattering stories of the government. Two major foreign newspapers were threatened with libel suits after reporting on alleged bribery, and a foreign correspondent was expelled for the first time since the transition to democratic rule for articles critical of President Kim. Civic institutions are strong and local human rights groups operate openly.

Under the Kim administration the authorities have been generally lenient in granting permits for peaceful demonstrations. Women face social and workplace discrimination, and domestic violence is fairly widespread. Religious freedom is respected. Travel to North Korea is tightly restricted.

The Trade Union Law prevents the establishment of alternative unions or confederations in industries or fields where a union already exists. In practice this maintains the dominance of the Federation of Korean Trade Unions (FKTU), formed during military rule, and its affiliated unions. Civil servants and public and private school teachers may not form unions or bargain collectively. Strikes are not permitted in government agencies, state-run industries and defense industries. Laws against "third-party" intervention prevent outside experts and unrecognized unions from helping workers.

Two officials from the Korean Federation of Metalworkers Unions were arrested and tried for their role as "third party" instigators in disputes at the Korea Textile Company. The Chairman and Vice President of the dissident Korean Confederation of Trade Unions (KCTU) were tried for their involvement in the 1994 subway and railroad strikes, and for allegedly organizing illegal and violent strikes in the public sector. The International Confederation of Free Trade Unions(ICFTU) allege that over 40 trade unionists were imprisoned for prolonged periods.

Kuwait

Polity: Traditional mon-
archy and limited
parliament
Economy: Mixed
capitalist-statist
Population: 1,764,000
PPP: $21,630
Life Expectancy: 75.0

Political Rights: 5
Civil Liberties: 5
Status: Partly Free

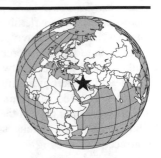

Ethnic Groups: Kuwaiti (45 percent), other Arab (35 percent), Iranian,
various foreign workers
Capital: Kuwait City

Overview: On October 7, 1996, Kuwait held National Assembly elections, the second parliamentary elections since the 1990-
1991 Iraqi invasion. Sixteen of the 50 National Assembly
members were unseated. Pro-government candidates won 30 seats, Islamists won
16 and liberals won 4. Political parties are banned; therefore, only non-partisan candidates were allowed to run. Kuwait is the only Gulf state to hold legislative elections.

The al-Sabah family has ruled Kuwait since 1756. Britain handled the emerate's
foreign affairs and defense from 1899 until 1961. The 1962 constitution vests broad
executive powers in an emir, the state leader, from the al-Sabah family. The emir
appoints the Council of Ministers and the prime minister, who is traditionally the
Crown Prince.

In 1976 the emir suspended the National Assembly. The current emir, Sheik
Jabir al-Ahmad al-Sabah, reopened the Assembly in 1981 but suspended it again in
1986. In October 1990, while in exile following the Iraqi invasion two months earlier, the emir agreed to hold parliamentary elections in 1992. In February 1991 a
32-nation, U.S.-led coalition liberated Kuwait.

In the October 1992 elections opposition candidates, comprised of liberals, Islamists and independents, took 31 of the 50 seats. The emir minimized the
opposition's gains by giving key cabinet posts to the al-Sabah family.

**Political Rights
and Civil Liberties:**   Kuwaiti citizens cannot change their government democratically. The hereditary emir holds executive powers and
under the constitution can declare martial law and suspend
both the parliament and specific articles of the constitution. In 1996, the eligible
voting pool expanded from men over 21 who can trace their Kuwaiti ancestry back
to 1920 (13 percent of the nationals in 1992), to include men who have been citizens for over 20 years. In 1996, 107,000 men of the 720,000 Kuwaitis were eligible
voters. Women are denied suffrage. Political parties are banned under a 1986 decree but operate informally. The parliament cannot overrule the emir.

Following Kuwait's liberation in February 1991, the Kuwaiti government declared a period of martial law. Those suspected of Iraqi collaboration, primarily
Palestinians, Iraqis, Jordanians and *bidoon* (stateless Arabs), were subject to extra-

judicial executions, arbitrary arrests, torture and "disappearances." Hundreds of alleged collaborators were tried in court proceedings not meeting international norms. Some State Security Court cases relied on confessions obtained through torture. An estimated 160 people convicted in unfair proceedings of Iraqi collaboration are believed to still be serving sentences. Most of the killings, as well as over 62 cases of "disappeared" individuals, remain unresolved.

No military court trials have taken place since 1991. In 1995, the State Security Courts were dissolved. Prison conditions have improved in recent years. However, police reportedly abuse detained prisoners to extract confessions. The executive branch controls the judicial branch. Foreign judges serve under one-year renewable contracts; Kuwaiti judges are given lifetime appointments. Several hundred Palestinians, Iraqis and bidoon are detained under administrative deportation orders not subject to review.

Citizens freely criticize the government but not the al-Sabah family. The press law prevents publication of articles critical of the royal family, as well as articles that might "create hatred, or spread dissension among the people." There are seven privately-owned newspapers, two in English. Broadcast media are state-owned and coverage favors the government. It is possible to access international media through satellite dishes and radio. Foreign periodicals are sold freely. In March 1995, the government used a 1986 decree to suspend the daily *al-Anba* for five days.

The government occasionally denies permits for political gatherings. In 1996 women organized a series of protests, including a one-day work stoppage, in a campaign to obtain the vote.

Since 1985 the government has only licensed two new NGOs. Both have ties to the royal family. In 1993 the government shut down all unlicensed NGOs, curtailing the activities of several human rights NGOs formed since 1991.

The 150,000 bidoon remaining in Kuwait have been declared illegal residents. They are barred from employment, restricted in their movement and denied education and social services. Many are detained and threatened with deportation. As many as 160,000 fled Kuwait during the 1990 invasion and are not permitted to return, despite claims that their families remain behind.

Kuwaiti women are restricted from working in certain professions, though they do receive equal pay for equal work. Women must receive permission from their husbands to travel abroad.

Islam is the state religion; both Sunnis and Shiites practice freely. Christians are allowed to worship and build churches. Proselytizing Muslims is prohibited. Only Muslims can become citizens. People of religions not recognized by the *Shari'a* (Islamic law) are banned from holding public gatherings. Thus, Hindus, Sikhs and Buddhists may not build places of worship, but may practice their religion at home.

The government maintains financial control over unions through subsidies that account for 90 percent of union budgets. Only one union is allowed per industry or profession, and only one labor federation, the pro-government Kuwaiti Trade Union Federation, is permitted. Strikes are legal and do occur. One 1995 strike resulted in improved conditions for workers, yet four Bangladeshi organizers were detained and subsequently deported.

Foreign workers face discrimination in legal proceedings. They cannot join labor unions before residing in Kuwait for five years. These restrictions are criticized by the International Labor Organization (ILO). Roughly 100,000 foreign-born domestic servants are not covered by the labor law and are subject to rape, beatings and other abuse.

Kyrgyz Republic

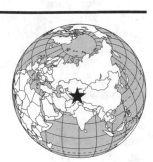

Polity: Presidential-par-
liamentary democracy
Economy: Statist
(transitional)
Population: 4,579,000
PPP: $2,320
Life Expectancy: 69.2
Ethnic Groups: Kirghiz (52 percent), Russian (22 percent),
Uzbek (13 percent), German, others
Capital: Bishkek

Political Rights: 4
Civil Liberties: 4
Status: Partly Free

Overview: In 1996, a referendum amending the constitution strengthened the powers of President Askar Akayev, who pledged to weed out corruption and accelerate economic reforms in this impoverished Central Asian Republic.

The Kyrgyz Republic declared independence from the Soviet Union in 1991. In what was called the "Silk Revolution," President Akayev, a respected physicist, led the country to multiparty democracy and market reforms. In the face of resistance from a Communist-dominated, 350-member parliament elected in 1990, however, Akayev in 1994 dissolved the legislature (after the government resigned to strengthen the president's hand) and decreed a national referendum for changes in the constitution and for the creation of a bicameral, 105-member body (*Jogorku Kenesh*) with a 35-seat lower chamber as a permanent legislature and a 70-member upper chamber that meets only occasionally to approve the budget and confirm presidential appointees. Nearly 75 percent of voters approved the proposal.

In the 1995 parliamentary elections, 82 seats went to a mix of governing officials, businessmen, intellectuals and clan leaders, with the Communists winning a handful of races. In the presidential election, Akayev was re-elected with over 60 percent of the vote.

In February 1996, voters approved by referendum more constitutional changes that further enhanced presidential power. The new document gives the president the power to appoint all top officials except the prime minister, who requires parliamentary approval. However, if parliament rejects three of the president's nominees, he can dissolve the body.

After the vote, the government of Prime Minister Apas Dzhumagulov resigned. In March, a new government was formed, with the prime minister and numerous cabinet members keeping their previous posts.

Key issues during the year were corruption and drug-trafficking. In September, the president issued a decree dismissing several high-ranking officials for financial improprieties on the recommendation of the Kyrgyz Security Council. Over 100 officials had been arrested on suspicion of taking bribes in the first seven months of the year. Speaker of the Legislative Assembly of the Supreme Council Mukar Cholponbayev barely survived a vote to oust him for alleged abuses of his post.

In June, United Nations officials urged priority assistance to the country in fighting drug traffic. In September, the government reported that not only was the country a major transit route for drugs from Southeast Asia, but that underground heroin processing plants had sprung up and 50,000 citizens were drug addicts.

In economic matters, the parliament's main objectives were to pass civil and land codes and to develop a tax code by 1997. Presidential decrees sought to interest foreign investors in the ongoing privatization. The president also reorganized local administrations, giving *oblast* governors more power to implement reforms, improve infrastructure and facilitate privatization. In September, the government launched a new joint venture between a Canadian oil firm and the state-owned oil company.

In February, the government signed a Customs Union with Russia, Kazakhstan and Belarus. President Akayev also signed a series of agreements with Kazakhstan and Uzbekistan dealing with regional economic and military cooperation.

Political Rights and Civil Liberties:

Citizens can change their government under a multiparty system. Parliamentary and presidential elections in 1995 included instances of violations such as ballot-stuffing, inflation of voter turnout, media restrictions and intimidation.

There are several political parties, from the Communists on the left to the nationalist Asaba on the right. In between are the Social Democrats, the Republicans, the Agrarians and *Erkin* (Freedom). The largest political movement is the pro-government Democratic Movement of Kyrgyzstan. In August, the Party of Protection was founded by members of the Union of Industrialists and Entrepreneurs. Most parties are small and weak, with vague platforms and little financial support.

The press laws place some restrictions on journalists, forbidding the publication of state secrets, materials that advocate war, violence or intolerance of ethnic groups. In 1995, two journalists from *Res Publica*, an independent paper, were sentenced to 18 months' imprisonment (with a year suspended) for libelous publications insulting the honor and dignity of the president. Akayev had sued the Russian-language paper for claiming he had a villa in Switzerland. Although the sentences were later commuted, both have been banned from writing until January 1997. No private local radio or television stations exist. Only one private radio station— Radio Almaz—and one private television station, Pyramid, operate nationally. Most media, while not ignoring social problems, unemployment, drug abuse or economic conditions, stop short of criticizing government policies or officials. In March, President Akayev appointed Amanbek Karypkulov, a hard-line former Communist ideological secretary, the head of Kyrgyz State Radio and Television, and dismissed several editors of state-run papers, raising concerns by the Moscow-based Glasnost Defense Fund and the Kyrgyz-American Bureau.

In 1995, constitutional revisions called for greater oversight of the judicial branch by the executive. Judges' lack of experience with the rule of law and low salaries produced incentives for corruption. The government stated that it hoped presidential nomination of judges at all levels would increase the degree to which laws are consistently applied and enforced. Under Kyrgyz traditions, the *Aksaqal* (elders' court) continue to pass judgment on criminals in their villages, but in some cases have exceeded their authority. The Aksaqal are backed by their own police, the *Choro*, which often carry out arbitrary arrests, detention and punishment such as whipping or stoning. Amnesty International has reported several cases of torture and ill-treatment of prisoners. In January, Topchubek Turgunaliev, head of the Erkin party, went on a hunger strike to protest his arrest several days before the December 1995 presidential elections for allegedly inflaming ethnic hatred between Kyrgyz and Kazakhs.

Freedoms of assembly and movement are generally respected. Freedom of religion is guaranteed in this predominantly Islamic country, and Christians and Jews can worship freely and openly. In November, the president ordered religious groups to register with the proper authorities, noting that only 47 of 200 religious organizations were registered. The State Commission on Religious Affairs said registration would allow the commission to "compare the tasks and aims of the religious organizations not registered so far with Kyrgyz laws as well as the principles of state security."

Although the constitution guarantees minority rights and the government has shown sensitivity to the Russian minority (in 1995, Russian was elevated to an official language), an exodus of educated and skilled Russians and Germans has occurred. In April, the government suspended the Uigur organization *Ittipak* (Unity) from campaigning in the media and from holding public meetings for three months to curb its "separatist activities." The move was to placate neighboring China, where Uigur attempts at greater sovereignty have been repressed. The president declared 1996 "the year of women," and many women serve in government posts. The Democratic Women's Party was registered in October 1994. In October 1996, parliamentary hearings on the situation of women in the country recommended emphasis on training, and the creation of new jobs for them in the state and private sectors by offering tax breaks to enterprises where women make up over 30 percent of the workforce. Cultural traditions include bride-stealing. Though illegal, the practice of abducting women for marriage is common.

Although a 1992 law permits the formation of independent unions, the overwhelming majority of workers belong to the Federation of Independent Trade Unions of Kyrgyzstan (FITUK), the successor to the Soviet-era labor federation. Over 450 non-governmental organizations are registered, ranging from business groups to sports and charitable associations.

Laos

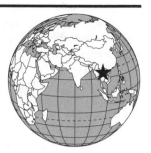

Polity: Communist one-party
Economy: Mixed-statist
Population: 4,976,000
PPP: $1,458
Life Expectancy: 51.3
Ethnic Groups: Lao (50 percent), Thai (20 percent), Phoutheung (15 percent), Miao (Hmong), Yao, others
Capital: Vientiane

Political Rights: 7
Civil Liberties: 6
Status: Not Free

Overview:　　　This landlocked Southeast Asian country became a French protectorate in 1893. Following the Japanese occupation during World War II, Laos won independence from the French in October 1953. Royalist, Communist and conservative factions turned on each other in 1964. In May 1975 the Pathet Lao captured the capital, Vientiane, from the royalist government, and seven months later established a one-party state under the Lao People's Revolutionary Party (LPRP).

In August 1991, the rubber-stamp National Assembly approved the country's first constitution, which codifies the LPRP's leading political role. The constitution also expanded the powers of the president, who serves as head of the armed forces and has the ability to remove the prime minister. Prime Minister Kaysone Phomvihane subsequently took over as president, while veteran revolutionary Khamtay Siphandone succeeded him as prime minister. In March 1996, General Khamtay Siphandone succeeded the retiring Nouhak Phoumsavan as president.

Although Laos' rich natural resources and accessibility to the rest of the South East Asian region has attracted foreign investment, the economy remains very poor and 85 percent of the population are subsistence farmers. The LPRP introduced market reforms in 1986 to revive an economy decimated by a decade of central planning. The authorities have privatized farms and some state-owned enterprises, removed price control, and encouraged foreign investment. In May 1995, the Lao government approved a United Nations Development Programme (UNDP) aid project. The three-year project is to assist Lao officials in drafting a new framework of legislation that will cover areas of environmental protection and judicial reform, with the aim of establishing a legal structure for a market economy based on the rule of law by 2000.

The government permitted pre-approved independents to compete for the first time in the December 1992 elections for the 85-seat National Assembly. Several independents are believed to have won seats, although the government has not provided a breakdown.

Political Rights and Civil Liberties:　　　Laos is a one-party state controlled by the Lao People's Revolutionary Party (LPRP), and citizens cannot change their government democratically. Opposition parties are not expressly banned, but in practice are not tolerated by the government.

Some elements of state control, including the widespread monitoring of civilians by police, have been relaxed in recent years. However, the security services still search homes without warrants, monitor some personal communications, and maintain neighborhood and workplace committees that inform on the population.

The Hmong, the largest of several hill tribes that collectively comprise half the population, have conducted a small-scale insurgency since the Communist takeover. Both the Hmong guerrillas and the government are accused of occasional human rights violations relating to the insurgency, including extrajudicial killings.

The rule of law is nonexistent. The judiciary is subservient to the government and trials lack adequate procedural safeguards. Mistreatment of detainees and prisoners is apparently rare, although prison conditions are harsh.

The government has released nearly all of the tens of thousands of people who were sent to "re-education camps" following the 1975 Communist victory. The regime is holding at least three members of the former royalist government, however, and may be holding several hundred political prisoners overall, including three LPRP officials who have been held since 1990 for denouncing official corruption and calling for a multiparty system. In 1992, the three received 14-year prison sentences.

Freedom of speech and of the press is nonexistent. Newspapers and electronic media are controlled by the government and promote its views. Although the constitution provides citizens with the right to organize and join associations, these are party-controlled and defined by party policies. The government does not cooperate with domestic or international human rights organizations. However, U.N. human rights observers have been permitted to monitor the treatment of refugees. The government's record on religious freedom is mixed. Buddhists can generally worship freely, but the Catholic Church is unable to operate in the north and, in recent years, some Christian clergy members have reportedly been detained. Christian seminaries have been closed since the Communist takeover.

Members of minority groups are underrepresented in the government, and these hill tribes are largely unable to influence official policy regarding their lands. Thousands of Laotians who fled after the Communist takeover have been voluntarily repatriated, and the government has apparently not targeted them for specific harassment. Since 1994, the government has eased restrictions on internal travel, and Laotians are also increasingly freer to travel abroad.

Under the 1990 labor code all unions must belong to the LPRP-dominated Federation of Lao Trade Unions. There is no legal right to bargain collectively or to strike, and in practice such activities do not occur.

Latvia

Polity: Presidential-
parliamentary democracy
(ethnic limits)

Economy: Mixed cap-
italist transitional

Population: 2,476,000

PPP: $5,010

Life Expectancy: 69.0

Ethnic Groups: Latvian (52 percent), Russian (34 percent),
Ukrainian, Pole, Belarusian, Lithuanian

Capital: Riga

Political Rights: 2
Civil Liberties: 2
Status: Free

Overview:

A presidential election and divisions within the government
coalition highlighted political events in Latvia this year.

An independent republic from 1918 to 1940, Latvia was
forcibly incorporated into the Soviet Union after the Hitler-Stalin pact. More than
50 years of Soviet occupation saw a massive influx of Russians accompanied by
the deportation of Latvians; the proportion of Latvians fell from 77 percent in 1940
to 52 percent in 1991, the year the country declared independence from a crumbling Soviet Union. In the October 1995 elections for the 100-member parliament
(*Saeima*), a fragmented vote necessitated the formation of a six-party coalition covering a huge ideological spectrum. Andris Skele, a young businessman with no party
affiliation, was chosen to hold the government together.

In June, Guntis Ulmanis was re-elected president by the Saeima with 53 votes
in the first round. He defeated Saeima speaker Ilga Kreituse. Although the constitution establishes a weak president, Ulmanis successfully created the current ruling
coalition and has helped maintain it.

Nevertheless, Skele's government teetered on the edge of collapse in 1996. In
May, the Latvian Unity Party (LVP) reversed its previous decision to quit the coalition following the sacking of its chairman and Agriculture Minister, Albert Kauls.
Kauls had been advocating increasing agricultural protectionism. In October, Cevers
resigned as deputy prime minister, claiming that Skele was attempting to establish
"authoritarian" rule.

The Democratic Party Saeimnieks (DPS), headed by Ziedonis Cevers, absorbed
several smaller parties in 1996 and increased its parliamentary representation, and
consequently, its leverage in the governing coalition. The DPS merged with the
Latvian Democratic Party in February, and with the LVP and the Republican Party
in July. Also in July, the Popular Concord Party split following its decision not to
merge with the DPS, and two of its deputies joined the latter. The party is a rather
eclectic mix of free marketeers, centrists and technocratic ex-communists, and it
commands new force with 27 deputies in the Saeima.

Volatility extended to the rest of the parliament. In August, the Saeima voted to
expel Jiachim Siegerist for not attending its sessions. He had done very well in the
previous elections despite not knowing Latvian and allegedly holding anti-Semitic
views. September was a bad month for the Kreituse family, as allegations of finan-

cial improprieties caused Ilga Kreituse to be dismissed as Saeimas speaker following her husband's expulsion as finance minister.

The economy, while robust by the standards of the former Soviet Union, has not emerged from a post-transition slump and the recurrent bank crises. It grew by 0.6 percent in 1996, while inflation increased at a 20 percent rate. With tax evasion commonplace, the informal economy is the biggest in the Baltics, estimated at 14 percent of GDP. In July, Skele dissolved several ministries and replaced several ministers in order to hasten the pace of economic reform. However, Latvia managed to impose a blanket ban on all non-EU agricultural imports.

Political Rights and Civil Liberties: Latvians can change their government democratically. The parliamentary elections held in October 1995 were free and fair. In April, the Saeima rejected a proposal to give noncitizens the vote in local elections.

While there are no ethnic restrictions on citizens' political participation, the majority of the non-ethnic Latvian population (mostly Russian) remain without Latvian citizenship. Despite the July 1994 amendments in the citizenship law which made the naturalization process easier, only about 1,000 people were naturalized in 1996, which is slower than even the 1995 rate. The agency in charge of these issues, the Department of Citizenship and Immigration (CID), often violated the law by improperly denying citizenship to eligible residents. In fact, while CID decisions are theoretically subject to judicial review, it has sometimes refused to comply with court rulings to overturn its decisions.

An independent press publishes in both Latvian and Russian. The state-controlled Latvian radio broadcasts nationally on three channels in Russian and Latvian. A large number of private radio and television broadcasters operate, including cable companies. Media are editorially independent.

The judiciary is generally free from government interference. After the presidential election, the Saeima finally instituted a true Constitutional Court with power to examine the constitutionality of legislation. Prior to this law, the Latvian Supreme Court did not have clear authority in deciding issues of constitutionality.

Serious problems exist, however. The courts are forced to rely on administrative support from the Ministry of Justice. Moreover, outside Riga, conditions are comparatively poor. Judges often lack a strong legal education.; courts are sometimes too weak to enforce their decisions; much of the court system is reputed to be corrupt. Reports of inmate beatings by police and prison officials are common. Some feeble attempts have been made to punish these abuses.

In January, the government agreed to establish a National Human Rights Office to inform people of their rights and to receive complaints. In June, the Saeima approved legislation allowing noncitizens the right to own land in Latvia. In November, the draft requirement was reduced from 18 months to 12.

The right of association is respected. Business, cultural and other nongovernmental institutions are allowed to exist, among them the League of Non-Citizens. Religious rights are respected in this largely Lutheran country. Freedom of assembly is guaranteed, but some interference with this right has occurred in Riga, where permission was denied to some lawful demonstrations by noncitizens.

The law establishes the right of Latvians to join unions and to strike. While unions are generally independent, some of their leaders became candidates in the

1995 elections. Russian-dominated, Communist-era unions are not truly independent because of their known affiliation with the Russian army and the KGB. Women
enjoy the same legal rights as men.

Lebanon

Polity: Presidential-   **Political Rights:** 6
parliamentary (military- **Civil Liberties**: 5
and foreign-influenced, **Status:** Not Free
partly foreign-occupied)
Economy: Mixed statist
Population: 3,776,000
PPP: $2,500
Life Expectancy: 68.7
Ethnic Groups: Arab (90 percent), Armenian (4 percent) Greek, Syro-Lebanese
Capital: Beirut

Overview: While Lebanon's second post-war election in August-September 1996 was marred by controversy, the reelection of
Prime Minister Rafiq Hariri, architect of Lebanon's esti-
mated $60 billion reconstruction plan, is a positive sign for the country's economy
and for foreign investors. However, the severe government clampdown on the
country's free press has raised concern.

With some 35,000 troops in Lebanon, Syria continues to dominate the country
politically and militarily. The new 128-member parliament is expected to continue
the policy of its predecessor in following the Syrian line on internal and regional
policies. In April 1996 escalating hostilities between Israeli Defense Forces (IDF)
and Hezbollah, Lebanon's only remaining armed militia, led to the death of over
100 refugees seeking shelter in a United Nations compound in Qana.

Lebanon gained full sovereignty from France in 1946. The genesis of the
country's 1975-90 civil war lay in the unwritten 1943 National Pact, which gave
Christians political dominance over the Muslim population through a perpetual 6:5
ratio of parliamentary seats. Following three decades in which non-Christian groups
tried to end this system, a civil war that ultimately claimed the lives of over 150,000
people broke out in 1975 between numerous Muslim, Christian and Druze militias.
An added factor was the presence of the Palestine Liberation Organization (PLO),
which had been expelled from Jordan and whose militias behaved like an occupying force. In 1976 Syria sent troops into the country to support the government. The
Syrians, who consider Lebanon part of Greater Syria, stayed.

A reconciliation process began at Taif, Saudi Arabia, in November 1989, with
an Arab League-sponsored accord that provided for a new power-sharing constitution. The Taif accord continued the tradition of a Maronite Christian president chosen by the parliament for a six-year term, but it transferred many executive powers
to the prime minister, by agreement a Sunni Muslim. A Shi'ite Muslim serves as
speaker of parliament, which is now evenly split between Muslims and Christians.

A 1991 treaty signed by Syria and Lebanon linked the country's economic and security policies and officially sanctioned the continued presence of Syrian troops on Lebanese soil. To date, the Lebanese government lacks full control of the country. While Syria maintains its significant military presence, the South Lebanon Army (SLA) administers Israel's 440-square mile security zone, the Hezbollah militia is still active in many southern towns and Palestinian factions control several southern refugee areas. These extra-governmental groups detain suspects and administer justice, generally without due process, in areas under their control. Hezbollah is backed by both Syria and Iran, and draws its internal support from the poor among the country's 1.3 million Shi'ites, and from others suffering the effects of the Israeli occupation in the south.

Political Rights and Civil Liberties: In 1996 Lebanese citizens changed their government for the second time in two decades, in elections that were not free and fair. A 1996 election law split the Mount Lebanon region into smaller constituencies both to reduce the showing of anti-Syrian Christians, who boycotted the 1992 elections protesting Syrian dominance, and to ensure victory for the key pro-Syrian Druze leader allied with Hariri. A Syrian-imposed coalition between Hezbollah and the rival Shia faction Amal in the final two rounds of elections assured Hezbollah a comeback after initial losses in the first three rounds.

In October 1995 the parliament arbitrarily amended the constitution to extend President Elias Hrawi's term by three years. This move angered Lebanon's Christian community, which has become increasingly marginalized as a result of the government's pro-Syrian policies. Voter lists included names of deceased persons and in some districts voters were forced to cast their ballot under the watchful eye of local officials.

Thousands of disappearances during the 1975-90 civil war remain unsolved. While politically-motivated killings have decreased, Palestinian factions, Syrian troops and the SLA act with impunity. Opponents of the government and of Syria's role in Lebanon face arbitrary arrest. Security forces are accused of using excessive force against detainees and prisons are severely overcrowded. An independent judiciary exists; however, influential politicians intervene in some cases. Corruption is common.

In contrast to Lebanon's tradition of press freedom, this year the government announced it would block the operation of more than 30 television stations and 130 radio stations by the end of November. In September only four privately owned television stations and 11 radio stations, all of which are linked to pro-Syrian government officials, were granted licenses to broadcast. Although the state-owned Lebanon Television has a legal monopoly on television until 2012, private stations had been tolerated in great measure. Criticism of the president and foreign leaders is legally restricted, and the 1991 Syria-Lebanon agreement broadly prohibited publication of security-related information. Police must approve all leaflets and other non-periodical materials, and citizens have been imprisoned for unauthorized pamphleteering.

Public assemblies require government permits, which are frequently denied to Christian groups. In March, the army imposed an 11-hour curfew in response to a worker's protest called by the General Labor Confederation. Unsanctioned demonstrations are often blocked by security forces. Several human rights groups operate openly.

Legal and social discrimination limit opportunities for women. The government does not extend normal legal rights to some 180,000 undocumented stateless persons, many of whom live in disputed border areas. Many of the 350,000-500,000 Palestinian refugees in Lebanon live in camps and are not allowed to conduct normal commercial affairs outside the camps.

Freedom of religion is respected. Citizens can travel abroad freely; however, internal travel is restricted in certain areas under Israeli or Hezbollah control. Government workers do not have the right to join trade unions or hold strikes, although in practice brief strikes by such employees have been permitted.

Lesotho

Polity: Parliamentary democracy (military- and royal-influenced)
Economy: Capitalist
Population: 2,105,000
PPP: $980
Life Expectancy: 60.8
Ethnic Groups: Sotho
Capital: Maseru

Political Rights: 4
Civil Liberties: 4
Status: Partly Free

Overview:

Lesotho's fragile democracy survived the accidental death of 59-year old King Moshoeshoe II in January, an apparent coup attempt in February, continued political infighting, and increasing unrest among workers throughout 1996. Rivalries among the security forces, within the royal family and between traditional chiefs complicated the democratic transition begun in 1993. Some form of union with South Africa is debated openly and is a realistic possibility.

A landlocked country of roughly 1.8 million people, Lesotho is entirely surrounded by South Africa. Its status as a British protectorate saved it from the apartheid system. After independence in 1966, King Moshoeshoe II reigned until a 1990 military coup installed his son as King Letsie III. In 1993, democratic elections produced a government under the Basotho Congress Party (BCP), led by Prime Minister Ntsu Mokhehele. But after bloody military infighting, assassinations and a suspension of constitutional rule in 1994, King Letsie III abdicated to allow his father's reinstatement in January 1995.

Moshoeshoe II's death in an automobile crash returned King Letsie III to the throne in January. On February 29, three men forced their way into a radio station in the capital and broadcast claims that a new government had taken power. It is not clear whether the transmission was part of a larger conspiracy. The security forces operate outside parliamentary control under the Defense Commission, and the civil service shows little respect for the elected BCP government, weakened by Prime Minister Mokhehele's illness.

South African President Nelson Mandela visited Lesotho in July 1995. About half of Lesotho's workforce is employed in South Africa, and the two countries have a currency and customs union. The end of apartheid in South Africa has prompted some Sothos on both sides of the border to suggest that it makes economic sense to unite the two countries. This proposal, however, is sharply condemned by Sotho nationalists who believe an independent state will better protect their cultural heritage.

Political Rights and Civil Liberties: Lesotho's citizens freely chose their government in 1993 in open elections under a democratic constitution. Although it won a landslide victory, the BCP government is severely constrained in the real exercise of its constitutional authority. The military and the royal family remain autonomous and outside effective control of the elected representatives. The August 1995 local elections broadened the possibilities of political participation, though the new local council's relations with traditional clan and chieftancy structures remains unclear.

All Lesotho's broadcast media are state-run. However, extensive radio and television broadcasts reach Lesotho from South Africa. Vigorous independent print media operate in the capital, Maseru. Local journalists have expressed concern over proposals to create an official press council, whose role and powers have not been clearly defined.

Constitutional rights to assembly and expression are generally respected, as is religious freedom. Yet there are continuing reports of arbitrary detention and mistreatment of civilians by security forces, who enjoy apparent impunity from prosecution. The Lesotho Human Rights Alert Group (LHRAG) continues to operate openly, but under fear of harassment or actual assault.

While higher courts are still subject to outside influence, local courts generally operate independently. Laws inconsistent with the 1993 constitution are still on the books, including the 1984 Internal Security Act, which provides for up to 42 days of detention without charges in political cases.

Labor rights are guaranteed by the constitution, but the number of workers in the formal sector is small. Strikes by civil servants, police and teachers occurred in 1996. In September, police killed five striking workers at the site of a controversial dam project in the country's east. The right to collective bargaining is also recognized by law, but is sometimes rejected by government negotiators. Legal requirements for union registration have not been enforced against unregistered unions.

Women's rights are not fully respected. The 1993 constitution prohibits discrimination based on sex, but customary practice and law still restrict women's rights in several areas, including contracts, property rights and inheritance. If her husband is alive, a woman is considered a legal minor. Although not officially quantified, domestic violence is reportedly widespread.

Lesotho relies almost entirely on South Africa for its economic viability. The 1995 Privatization Act calls for extensive divestiture of state-run enterprises, which comprise nearly all of the modern economic sector. Land is the property of the kingdom, and its distribution is generally controlled by local chiefs.

Liberia

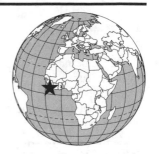

Polity: Monrovia: interim
civilian goverment
(foreign military- and
foreign-influenced); else-
where: rival ethnic-based militias
Economy: Capitalist
Population: 2,100,000
PPP: $843
Life Expectancy: 55.6
Ethnic Groups: Krahn, Mandinka, Gio, Mano, other indigenous groups
(95 percent), Americo-Liberian (5 percent)
Capital: Monrovia

Political Rights: 7
Civil Liberties: 6
Status: Not Free

Overview:

An August 1996 statement by the Catholic bishops of Liberia, condemning the various factions responsible for prolonging the seven-year civil war, declared: "Violence as a way of life has been and continues to be institutionalized. There is no respect for human life nor for private or public property. Morality seems to be something of the past."

Fighting in the capital, Monrovia, for seven weeks in April and May, left much of the city in ruins after a paroxysm of pillage and murder that killed at least 1,500 people. Refugees fled into the bush or onto the high seas in overcrowded ships that were repeatedly refused safe haven in neighboring countries.

More than 160,000 people have died since 1989 in a vicious conflict fed by ethnic rivalries and outside intervention. Several peace plans brokered by West African leaders and involving multinational peacekeeping forces have been abandoned. U.N. observers and aid workers worked in conditions of near-anarchy in the countryside, often suspending operations despite the desperate needs of the civilian population.

The war's fourteenth peace accord was reached at the end of May, and held firm through the rest of the year. It calls for demobilization of at least 60,000 fighters from nine rival ethnic militias, this time with a deadline of January 31, 1997. Elections are set for the end of May 1997. More than 10,000 West African peacekeepers, who have been reported to be looting instead of protecting people, remain in Liberia. With pledges of $30 million in new American aid, their leaders have pledged to make a final effort to enforce the newest peace pact. It is far from certain that they, or the Liberian factions, possess the political will to succeed.

Settled by freed American slaves in 1847, Liberia was for more than a century dominated by their "Americo-Liberian" descendants. In 1980, army sergeant Samuel Doe led a bloody coup. His regime concentrated power among members of his Kranh ethnic group and suppressed others. In the last days of 1989, the National Patriotic Front of Liberia (NPFL), led by ex-government minister Charles Taylor and backed by the Gia and Mano ethnic groups, launched a guerrilla war against the Doe regime. A joint armed intervention by several West African countries (ECOMOG) set up an interim government in 1990, preventing Taylor from consummating his victory against the Armed Forces of Liberia (AFL). In 1991, the United Liberation Movement (ULIMO), another rebel group dominated by Kranh and Mandingoe people, entered the war. ULIMO has since split, but is still a major force, along with the Liberia Peace Council (LPC).

With scant funding for its implementation, and without serious commitment by the several factions, the 1996 peace plan may well fall like those before it. If so, international peacekeepers will likely quit Liberia and abandon its people to "institutionalized violence."

Political Rights and Civil Liberties: Liberians do not enjoy the right to elect their representatives or change their government through democratic means. Elections were last held in 1986 under the Doe dictatorship and were neither free nor fair. The current peace accord calls for presidential and legislative elections by the end of May 1997—an improbable, though not impossible timetable. Most Liberians have been displaced from their homes over the years of war. A third of the country's 2.5 million people have fled the country. Their repatriation, the compilation of voters lists and the creation of electoral infrastructure are enormous tasks. Peacekeeping and election administration alone will cost over $200 million.

The rule of law is almost entirely absent from Liberia. The independent media have been harassed, which has led to a large degree of self-censorship. Indiscriminate arson and looting in Monrovia in April and May destroyed news offices, presses and broadcasting stations. Radio stations run by various factions broadcast partisan propaganda and incitements to violence.

Religious groups, relief organizations and human rights organizations, including the Center for Law and Human Rights Education, were badly affected by looting, but sought to resume operations in Monrovia and to reach people isolated by fighting in the countryside. This year's peace agreement has allowed renewed relief operations, but optimism must be muted after the breakdown of several earlier agreements. Rebuilding the country and, perhaps most dauntingly, the lives of more than 10,000 child-soldiers recruited as fighters will be enormous undertakings.

Famine threatens several regions of Liberia. Normal economic life does not exist. Food production is at historically low levels.

Libya

Polity: Military
Economy: Mixed statist
Population: 5,445,000
PPP: $6,125
Life Expectancy: 63.4
Ethnic Groups: Arab and Berber (97 percent), Tuareg
Capital: Tripoli

Political Rights: 7
Civil Liberties: 7
Status: Not Free

Overview:
Islamist groups and other foes of Colonel Mu'ammar al-Qadhafi stepped up attacks on security forces as the mercurial 54-year old leader faced the most serious threat to his rule since seizing power in a 1969 coup. Qadhafi handed more power to the military and ordered "purges" against black market traders. Tightening his dictatorial and secular rule, Qadhafi repaired his strained ties with other regimes in the region facing similar fundamentalist challenges. The U.S. sought to tighten sanctions against Libya, imposed by the United Nations in April 1992 because of Libya's refusal to extradite two suspects in the 1988 bombing of Pan American Flight 103 over Scotland.

Moral and material support for radical revolutionary and terrorist groups around the world have earned Libya the opprobrium of civilized nations, but petroleum wealth keeps its economic links with most countries very strong. The regime reportedly received weapons from both Ukraine and Yugoslavia. The sanctions' effects are serious but ultimately limited by their exclusion of oil exports, which earn Libya 90 percent of its foreign exchange. Further, concern over the security situation in several Maghreb states could also soften support for sanctions in the region and in Europe.

Colonized by Italy in 1912, Libya became independent in 1952 after a short period of joint Anglo-French administration. The country was aligned with the West under King Idriss and hosted a large American military presence until Qadhafi took over in 1969. The dictator's personalized and highly idiosyncratic rule has led Libya to clashes with its neighbors (with Egypt in 1977, and with Chad over several years) and to adventures further afield, such as an ill-fated Libyan expeditionary force that vainly sought to bolster Idi Amin's crumbling army in Uganda in 1979. In both foreign and domestic policy, Qadhafi has run Libya by decree, with a nearly total absence of accountability and transparency.

Domestically, Colonel Qadhafi has also become increasingly isolated, even from his own Qadhadhifa clan, and relies on close family members as his closest advisors. Rivalries among senior junta officials remained a potential threat to his 28-year rule. It is unclear whether the growing Islamist threat, especially in mountainous areas around Derna in eastern Libya, will exacerbate or at least temporarily alleviate the regime's internal discord. Numerous clashes were reported throughout the year, with responsibility claimed by the "Islamic Fighting Group," among others. Qadhafi's efforts to placate fundamentalist sentiments, including broadening *Shari'a* law provisions in 1994, appear to have had little effect. High unemployment and perceptions of corruption have also eroded support for the regime.

Yet the Islamist threat could make Qadhafi appear as the more palatable of two evils, especially to neighbors facing similar unrest. Signs that Qadhafi's regional rehabilitation continued in 1996 were evident, as Libya reportedly repatriated to an uncertain fate 500 Algerian militants to whom it had provided refuge. Libya is still far from being welcomed back entirely into the international fold however, and U.S. opposition to any easing of sanctions will at least slow the process.

Political Rights and Civil Liberties: Libyans have never been able to select their representatives through democratic means. No formal constitution exists. Qadhafi rules primarily by decree. His *Green Book*—a mélange of Islamic belief and socialist theory—provides principles and structures of governance, but has no legal status. Libya is officially known as a *jamahiriya* (state of the masses), as described by the Green Book's "Third Universal Theory." Formal elections take place, and include mandatory voting, but real power rests with Qadhafi and a small coterie who appoint civil and military officials at every level. An elaborate structure of Revolutionary Committees and People's Committees serve more as a tool of repression than consultation.

Neither free expression nor free media exist in Libya. There is very limited public debate within the nominally-elected bodies. Rare criticisms of the government or its actions usually presage purges or policy shifts. State-run media offer only propaganda. Official controls are so rigid that little formal censorship is required.

All political parties or any other types of associations not sanctioned by the regime are barred. Torture and mistreatment of detainees is reportedly routine, and brutality is said to be increasing in response to Islamist guerrilla activities and other dissidence. In January 1996, Amnesty International reported that at least two dozen high school students were being tortured after refusing to attend a public meeting in support of the regime. It is very difficult to garner accurate information regarding events within Libya. The regime's security apparatus is pervasive, and contacts with foreigners or the world are closely monitored.

Berber and Tuareg peoples outside the Libyan mainstream have suffered discrimination under policies intended to "Arabize" them. Women's access to education and employment has improved, yet cultural norms that relegate women to an inferior role still prevail, and may regain strength as Qadhafi seeks to placate fundamentalist opinion by stricter imposition of *Shari'a* law, which among other matters affects marriage, divorce and inheritance rights.

Religion is subject to the state. Islamic practice is tailored to Qadhafi's interpretations, and mosques are closely monitored for incipient political opposition. A small Christian community is permitted to worship quietly in two churches.

There is no freedom to form or join unions, nor are there rights to strike or to collectively bargain. Although Libya is economically statist, foreign investment is welcomed .

Liechtenstein

Polity: Prince and parliamentary democracy
Economy: Capitalist-statist
Population: 31,000
PPP: na
Life Expectancy: na
Ethnic Groups: Alemannic German (95 percent), Italian, other European
Capital: Vaduz

Political Rights: 1
Civil Liberties: 1
Status: Free

Overview:

Negotiations are currently underway to modify the principality's 74-year-old customs union with Switzerland. While Liechtenstein's voters approved accession to the European Economic Area (EEA)—a free trade agreement between the European Free Trade Association and the European Union—Swiss voters rejected it. Liechtenstein seeks to maintain its open border with Switzerland while participating in the EEA.

Domestically, the debate about constitutional reform continues, aimed at clearly defining the roles of the prince, the government and parliament. Prince Hans Adam, the current head of state, caused a stir two years ago when he asserted that the monarch should remain head of state only at the behest of the people. He suggested that the constitution be amended to allow for a possible vote of no-confidence in the monarchy, and even for its abolition.

The Principality of Liechtenstein was established in its present form in 1719, having been purchased by the Austrian Liechtenstein family. The royal family lived mainly in Moravia (once part of the Austro-Hungarian empire, now a Czech territory) until 1938, when Nazism forced it to flee to Liechtenstein. Native residents of the state are primarily descended from the Germanic Alemanni tribe, and the official language is a German dialect.

In 1923, Liechtenstein entered into a customs union with Switzerland, which continues to administer the principality's customs and provide for its defense and diplomatic representation. The government since 1938 has been a coalition of the Progressive Citizens' Party (FBP) and the Fatherland Union (VU). The FBP has been the senior partner for most of this period.

The prince exercises legislative powers jointly with the 25-member *Landtag* (legislature). He appoints the prime minister from the majority party or coalition in the Landtag, and the deputy chief of government from the minority. Prince Hans Adam has effectively ruled Liechtenstein since 1984 although he did not assume his father's title until the elder sovereign's death in 1989.

Political Rights and Civil Liberties:

Liechtensteiners can change their government democratically. Parties with at least eight percent of the vote receive representation in the Landtag, which is directly elected every four years. The sovereign possesses the power to veto legislation and to dissolve the Landtag. Prime Minister Mario Frick of the VU has headed a coalition with the FBP since 1993. The Free List environmentalist party holds one seat.

The independent judiciary is headed by a Supreme Court and includes both civil and criminal courts, as well as an administrative Court of Appeal and a state court to address questions of constitutionality. Due to the small size of the state, regional disparities are minimal and modern social problems are few. However, a strict policy keeps significant numbers of second- and third-generation residents from acquiring citizenship. The native population decides by local vote whether to grant citizenship to those who have five years' residence. Prime Minister Frick has advocated liberalization of the citizenship law in order to reduce the "immigrant" population to about half its present size.

Liechtenstein has one state-owned television station, as well as two radio stations, one state-owned and one private. Residents receive radio and television freely from neighboring countries. Both major parties publish newspapers five times per week.

Although Roman Catholicism is the state religion, other faiths practice freely. Roman Catholic or Protestant religious education is compulsory in all schools, but exemptions are routinely granted.

Liechtenstein is too small to have numerous organizations, but freedom of association and one small trade union exist. Workers have the right to strike but have not done so in over 25 years. The prosperous economy includes private and state enterprises. An ongoing labor shortage coupled with high wage rates is beginning to drive some companies to set up factories in Switzerland and Austria, where labor costs are lower.

The enfranchisement of women at the national level was unanimously approved in the legislature (though only narrowly endorsed by male voters) in 1984 after defeat in referenda in 1971 and 1973. By 1986, universal adult suffrage at the local level had passed in all 11 communes. General elections in 1989 awarded a seat in the Landtag to a woman for the first time. Three years later, a constitutional amendment guaranteed legal equality.

Lithuania

Polity: Presidential-
parliamentary democracy
Economy: Statist
transitional
Population: 3,708,000
PPP: $3,110
Life Expectancy: 70.3
Ethnic Groups: Lithuanian (80 percent), Russian (9 percent), Polish (8 percent),
Ukrainian, Belarusian, others
Capital: Vilnius

Political Rights: 1
Civil Liberties: 2
Status: Free

Overview: **A** corruption scandal that brought down the prime minister
and parliamentary elections which overthrew the ruling ex-
communists were the most significant Lithuanian political
developments in 1996.

An independent state from 1918 to 1940, Lithuania was forcibly annexed by
the Soviet Union under provisions of the 1939 Hitler-Stalin Pact; it regained independence from a disintegrating Soviet Union in 1991. The 1992 parliamentary elections, in which the Lithuanian Democratic Labor Party (LDDP), the renamed ex-
Communists, took political control from anti-Communists, set a trend in Eastern
Europe of voters voluntarily handing power back to former Communists.

The LDDP government began unraveling in January, as prominent ministers
resigned in protest over new revelations of a financial scandal involving Prime
Minister Adolfas Slezevicius. Just before the 1995 "Christmas banking crisis"
Slezevicius removed his money from a failing bank. The bank also paid him twice
the going interest rate on his deposits. Under pressure from President Algirdas
Brazauskas and the opposition over this scandal, Slezevicius resigned in February.
A new government was formed with Mindauas Stankevicius as the prime minister.
Slezevicius was indicted in October and charged with abuse of power in connection
with the banking scandal.

Parliamentary elections for the *Seimas* were held in two rounds in October and
November. The rightist Homeland Union-Conservatives of Lithuania [TS(LK)] won
a decisive victory by winning 70 seats in all, while their allies, the Christian Democratic Party (LKDP), won 16. The LDDP won only 12 seats compared with 75 in
1992.

The new coalition government headed by the TS(LK) was inaugurated in November, with its leader, independence hero Vytautas Landsbergis, as prime minister.

November also saw the beginning of the trial of the Lithuanian Communist
leaders involved in the 1991 attack by Soviet troops on an unarmed crowd that left
13 dead. Two of the six on trial may face the death penalty.

The Lithuanian economy did not grow at all in 1996. Inflation was 26 percent.
Unemployment is 7.4 percent. The bank crises in 1995 have been "solved" with
massive government bailouts. Sixteen of 27 banks in Lithuania are either under suspension or facing bankruptcy. The LDDP's commendable liberalization efforts suf-

fered a setback when massive new tariffs were imposed in April on non-EU agricultural imports. Some of TS(LK)'s populist stances, if implemented, could slow liberalization further.

Political Rights and Civil Liberties: Lithuanians can change their government democratically. The October-November parliamentary elections were free and fair, according to international observers. However, voting in secret was difficult in many polling stations. President Brazauskas submitted a request to the Constitutional Court to investigate possible miscounts, and one allegation of misconduct in the Tesiai district.

In June, a new electoral law raised the minimum share of votes necessary to join the Seimas in party-list voting from 4 to 5 percent. The law also abolished a lower 2 percent barrier for national minority parties. Despite criticism from ethnic Poles, internal division and low turnout in Polish-dominated districts (like Salcininkai) actually doomed the two minority parties, the Electoral Action of Poles in Lithuania and the Alliance of National Minorities.

Unlike its two Baltic neighbors, Lithuania extended citizenship in 1992 to all those born within its borders. This meant that over 90 percent of non-Lithuanians received citizenship. Naturalization requirements are tough: a ten-year residency, a permanent job and knowledge of laws and the Lithuanian language.

Press freedom is protected. In April, the Seimas amended media law by allowing information about the private lives of politicians to be made public. However, an electoral law requires that the media organization that publishes "harmful" material discrediting campaigning candidates allows them opportunity for a rebuttal. Journalists have complained of pressure to avoid criticism of government policies. Several independent newspapers operate, as do private radio and television broadcasters, as well as a significant non-Lithuanian language press.

The right of assembly and association is respected. Freedom of religion is guaranteed in this predominantly Roman Catholic country.

The judiciary is independent, and a nine-member Constitutional Court reviews laws or decrees that might conflict with the constitution. In 1993, a new anti-organized crime law was "temporarily" adopted, allowing the police to detain suspects without charge for up to two months. Local press reports show that police beatings of detainees are commonplace. A shortage of qualified lawyers makes the constitutional right to counsel difficult to implement in practice. In May, a change in the criminal code took away the power to issue warrants for arrest from prosecutors and gave it solely to the courts.

Intraethnic problems remain. In June, Poles demonstrated in Vilnius to complain about a government decision to expand the administrative borders of the capital. They pointed out that restitution claims for the land surrounding Vilnius, owned by Poles before the Communist takeover, had not yet been resolved. Indeed, the processing of such claims appears to be moving slowly in Polish-dominated areas.

The constitution protects unions' right to strike. Wage decisions are increasingly made on the enterprise level. Nongovernmental organizations are thriving. Women possess the same legal rights as men. Recently, since enrollment of women in universities has exceeded that of men, some university faculties have introduced preferential admission for men.

Luxembourg

Polity: Parliamentary democracy
Economy: Capitalist
Population: 415,000
PPP: $25,390
Life Expectancy: 75.8
Ethnic Groups: Luxembourger (70 percent), other European (30 percent)
Capital: Luxembourg

Political Rights: 1
Civil Liberties: 1
Status: Free

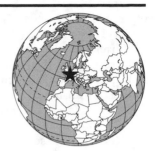

Overview: In accordance with its continued commitment to the cause of European unity, Luxembourg remained on course for European Monetary Union (EMU), and is one of the first countries to fulfill the criteria for participation set out by the 1992 Maastricht Treaty. A positive GDP growth rate and the lowest rate of unemployment in the European Union mean that Luxembourg fares significantly better economically than its neighbors. The traditionally strong industrial sector, however, has felt the adverse effects of continuing recession in Luxembourg's main trading partners.

After centuries of domination and occupation by foreign powers, the small, landlocked Grand Duchy of Luxembourg was recognized as an autonomous, neutral state in 1867, and came under the present ruling house of Nassau-Weilbourg in 1890. An economic union with Belgium was established in 1922, though Luxembourg retains independent political institutions through its 1868 constitution. After having been occupied by Germany during both world wars, Luxembourg abandoned its neutrality and became a vocal proponent of European integration.

Luxembourg has a multiparty electoral system based on proportional representation. In recent years, the country has been ruled by coalition governments headed by the Christian Social People's Party or the Democratic Party, allied either with each other or with the Socialist Workers' Party. Executive authority is exercised on behalf of the Grand Duke by the prime minister and the cabinet, who are appointed by the sovereign but are responsible to the legislature.

Political Rights and Civil Liberties: Luxembourgers can change their government democratically. Voting is compulsory for citizens, and foreigners may register after five years of residence. The prime minister is the leader of the dominant party in the popularly-elected Chamber of Deputies. The Council of State, whose members are appointed by the Grand Duke, serves as an advisory body to the Chamber.

The independent judiciary is headed by the Superior Court of Justice and includes a Court of Assizes for serious criminal offenses, two district courts and three justices of the peace. Judges are appointed for life by the Grand Duke. In response to a 1995 decision by the European Court of Human Rights, the government passed legislation establishing an administrative court system. The European Court had held that Luxembourg's Council of State could no longer serve as both a legislative advisory body and as an administrative court. This dual role was seen as a violation of the right to a fair trial. The new administrative courts are to begin operating on January1, 1997.

Luxembourg enjoys a vibrant, free press. All news media are privately-owned and free of censorship. While there is no domestic news agency, a number of foreign bureaus operate. Radio and television broadcasts from neighboring countries are freely available.

Religious freedom is respected in this predominantly Roman Catholic country. There is no state religion, but the state pays the salaries of Catholic, Protestant, and Jewish clergy, and several local governments subsidize sectarian religious facilities.

Although foreigners make up over 30 percent of the population, anti-foreigner incidents are infrequent. Citizens of the EU who reside in Luxembourg were granted the right to vote and run in municipal elections. Minimum residency requirements are six years for voters and 12 years for candidates. The government granted asylum to three persons in 1996; it also continued to allow about 1,800 persons from the former Yugoslavia to remain in protected status on humanitarian grounds.

Freedom of association is respected, and unions operate without governmental interference. About 65 percent of the labor force is unionized. Workers are organized in two competing labor federations affiliated with the Socialist and Christian Social parties. The right to strike is constitutionally guaranteed.

Macedonia

Polity: Presidential-
parliamentary democracy
Economy: Mixed statist
Population: 2,102,000
PPP: na
Life Expectancy: na
Ethnic Groups: Macedonian (65 percent), Albanian
(22 percent), Turk (5 percent), Macedonian Muslim (3 percent),
Roma (2 percent), Serb (2 percent)
Capital: Skopje

Political Rights: 4
Civil Liberties: 3
Status: Partly Free

Overview:	In 1996, the fragile ruling coalition of Social Democrats and the Liberal Party unraveled with the ouster of the Liberals in February, despite appeals for dialogue from President Kiro Gligorov, who escaped an assassin's bomb in 1995. He has defused tensions with the large Albanian minority and alleviated historic rivalries with neighboring Greece, Serbia, Albania and Bulgaria. Prime Minister Branko Crvenkovski's new government included five ministers from the Albanian-dominated Party for Democratic Prosperity (PDPA).

In the first round of local elections on November 17, the Social Democratic Union (SDSM) captured a majority of municipal council seats, with strong showings by the nationalist opposition Internal Macedonian Revolutionary Organization-Democratic party for Macedonian National Unity (VMRO-DPMNE), and by the Socialists, the SDSM's coalition partner. The PDPA won in Albanian strong-holds such as Tetovo, Gostivar and Kumanove. Elections on December 1 gave the ruling SDSM 500 of the 1,903 council seats at stake.

Macedonia was ruled by the Ottoman Turks for 500 years prior to the Balkan Wars in 1912-13, after which its territory was divided among Greece, Serbia and Bulgaria. After World War II, Communist partisan and subsequent Yugoslav leader Josip Broz (Tito) launched military campaigns to unite Macedonian territories in Greece with Yugoslavia during the Communist-incited Greek civil war in 1946, further fueling Greek distrust of Macedonian motives. Several of Macedonia's neighbors dispute that there is a distinct ethnic Macedonian identity.

Gligorov, a former Communist leader and head of the Social-Democratic Alliance for Macedonia, was appointed interim president in 1992 and directly elected in 1994. The country's first parliamentary elections since independence from Yugoslavia, held in October 1994, were marred by fraud and irregularities, and run-offs were boycotted by the VMRO-DPMNE, the free-market nationalist Democratic Party and others. The Alliance, composed of the SDSM, the Liberals, the Socialists and the PDPA, won 95 of 120 seats.

In early 1996, tensions between the SDSM, a successor to the Communists, and the free-market Liberal Party, established in 1990, came to a head. In the past, the Liberals had accused the SDSM of slowing down democratization and exerting control over the media. The Liberals were accused of profiting from the sale of the country's most lucrative enterprises. The crisis was intensified by VMRO-DPMNE's calls for early parliamentary elections after a four-day petition drive, which gathered 162,000 votes.

On February 10, Prime Minister Crvenkovski fired four Liberal Party cabinet ministers. A new coalition government included the SDSM, the PDPA, and the Socialists. Parliamentary Chairman Stojan Andov, leader of the Liberals, resigned, and was replaced by Tito Petkovski of the SDSM. On March 28, parliament passed a law governing citizens' petition drives for parliamentary elections. It invalidated the VMRO-DPMNE four-day petition drive, and appeared to guarantee that the seated parliament will conclude its term in 1998.

As a prelude to November's local elections, in August parliament passed a local election law under which municipal councils would be elected by a proportional system, and mayors by majority vote. Parliament also approved a law dividing the country into 123 municipalities and communities. The pre-election campaign saw incidents of violence. On November 9, VMRO-DPMNE supporters clashed with backers of an independent candidate for mayor of Skopje, Roma (Gypsy) politician Amdi Bajrami, in a predominantly Roma, Turkish and Albanian neighborhood. Council of Europe monitors said that in some areas 25 percent of eligible voters could not vote, but that the local vote was "essentially fair and orderly." The Organization for Security and Cooperation in Europe (OSCE) found no proof of any problems which could have affected the outcome of the elections. President Gligorov said that the elections finalized the process of establishing a state based on the rule of law.

Ethnic tensions escalated in July as thousands of Albanians protested the imprisonment of Fadil Sulejmani, dean of the outlawed Tetovo University, funded privately by ethnic Albanians. He was sentenced to 18 months in prison for inciting demonstrators in May 1995. Demonstrators demanded the legalization of the school and its integration into the Macedonian education system.

In other issues, Greek-Macedonian talks continued in the fall over Macedonia's formal name and related issues. In 1995, after U.S. mediation, Greece lifted a 19-month trade embargo imposed when Macedonia took the name of a Greek region and used a cherished Greek symbol—a 16-point star—in its flag. In April, Macedonia and Yugoslavia signed a mutual recognition agreement. In November, U.N. Secretary General Boutros Boutros-Ghali recommended that the mandate of the U.N. Preventive Deployment Force (UNPREDEP) be extended by six months at a reduced strength, to scale down from 1,100 troops to 800 by April 1, 1997. Earlier, parliament ratified an agreement with the United States providing for the presence of U.S. troops if the UNPREDEP is scaled back. There are some 500 U.S. troops in the country. Macedonia signed agreements of cooperation with the European Union (EU) and NATO.

Political Rights and Civil Liberties: Macedonians can change their government through elections, though the October 1994 vote was plagued by irregularities and the run-off was boycotted by several leading opposition groups. The 1996 local elections saw some irregularities and opposition protests, but were called "fair" by international monitors.

Numerous political parties, including those representing the interests of Albanians and Serbs, run the gamut from leftist to extreme nationalist.

The political crisis affected the media. After Saso Ordanoski, director of Macedonian Television (MTV) and a SDSM appointee, read an editorial criticizing the Liberal Party and demanding that it be excluded from any new government, Macedonian Radio and Television (MRTV) Director-General Melpomeni Korneti, a member of the Liberal Party and a political appointee, demoted Ordanoski to commentator. Several journalists and officials resigned in protest. Six months later, Korneti was fired, ostensibly for poor job performance, including failure to give ethnic Albanians enough airtime. 29 state-owned radio stations and five state television stations operate in the country. In all, 24 private TV stations and 912 combined radio and television stations share the airwaves, airing mostly top-40 music, video clips and pirated movies, with most operating on shoe-string budgets. News coverage is weak. Albanian-language TV is limited to only one hour a day, and the Albanian-language newspaper is distributed only three days a week. Most major newspapers receive state subsidies. Small independent newspapers have been launched.

Some restrictions on freedom of assembly and association are in place, particularly if they are seen to endanger public safety. Freedom of religion is respected; the dominant faiths are Macedonian Orthodox and Muslim (Albanians and the Turks).

The judiciary is not yet free from political or government interference. In the area of minority rights, the constitution refers specifically to Macedonians, Albanians, Turks, Roma (Gypsies) and Vlachs, but makes no reference to Serbs. In July, Macedonia signed the Council of Europe's framework convention for the protection of national minorities. Albanians have consistently criticized discrimination in citizenship, government employment and education, underrepresentation in the military and police forces, and police brutality and violations of due process. In June, the Democratic Party of Serbs charged police harassment, illegal searches and intimidation, particularly after the assassination attempt against President Gligorov in October 1995.

The Union of Independent and Autonomous Trade Unions confederation was formed in 1992. The Council of Trade Unions of Macedonia is the successor to the Communist labor federation. The constitution and laws guarantee men and women equal rights, but women face discrimination in employment and education, particularly in rural and Albanian areas.

Madagascar

Polity: Presidential-parliamentary democracy
Economy: Mixed statist
Population: 15,236,000
PPP: $700
Life Expectancy: 56.8
Ethnic Groups: Malayan-Indonesian highlanders, black and mixed coastal peoples, European, Asian and Creole minorities
Capital: Antananarivo

Political Rights: 2
Civil Liberties: 4
Status: Partly Free

Overview: **A**dmiral Didier Ratsiraka's narrow victory in a second round presidential run-off election against impeached President Albert Zafy capped a year of political turbulence in Madagascar. Zafy was impeached by parliament on corruption charges in July, after more than three years of tension between the president and the national assembly, aggravated by a September 1995 constitutional referendum that gave the president authority to appoint the prime minister.

Madagascar—the world's fourth largest island, 220 miles off Africa's southeastern coast—gained independence in 1960 after 70 years of French colonial rule, which was maintained, after World War II, by murderous repression. The regime of President Philbert Tsiranana was toppled by a military coup in 1972, and a leftist junta took power. Admiral Didier Ratsiraka emerged as leader in 1975, keeping power until his increasingly authoritarian regime bowed to social unrest and nonviolent mass demonstrations in 1991. In one instance, troops killed at least 40 protesters when they fired on crowds in front of the presidential palace. A new government was formed, which included opposition political parties that had been legalized by a High Constitutional Court decree the previous year. Voters approved a new constitution in 1992 and elected Zafy, leader of the Active Forces opposition coalition, to the presidency with over 65 percent of the vote in a February 1993 run-off election. The opposition consolidated this victory four months later by winning 70 of 138 National Assembly seats. Divisions prevented it from gaining the premiership.

Race and ethnicity are important factors in Madagascar's politics. Its 14 million, mostly very poor people are divided between Merina people of Malay origin who occupy highland areas and coastal peoples, mostly of black Africa origin.

Political Rights and Civil Liberties: Madagascar's voters exercised their right to choose their government in free and fair elections in 1993. The presidential election of 1996 was free and fair. The bicameral parliament consists of a Senate and a National Assembly of deputies elected to four-year terms on the basis of proportional representation. A new three-tiered local government structure established in 1995 has not been fully implemented.

An independent judiciary functions with little government interference, although a lack of training and resources impairs the courts' effectiveness. Magistrates have been on strike sporadically since 1995 to demand judicial reforms. Prison conditions are extremely harsh, and a majority of the prison population, which numbers more than 20,000, are awaiting trial due to court backlogs. Traditional *dina* courts that follow neither due process nor standardized judicial practice are used in many rural areas, and often hand down a severe and summary form of justice.

Women account for over 40 percent of the formal labor force, concentrated in subsistence activities. They hold significantly more government and managerial positions than women in continental African countries, but still face societal discrimination, and have fewer opportunities than men for higher education and official positions.

There is freedom of religion. Over half the population adhere to traditional Malagasy religions and coexist with Christians as well as Muslims. The right to free association is respected, and hundreds of NGOs are active, including lawyers' groups and others working on human rights issues. A vibrant free press includes several dailies and weekly newspapers which publish reports highly critical of the government and various politicians. Television is state-controlled and, while favoring the government in its reporting, presents a wide range of views. At least ten private radio stations are now broadcasting.

Several free labor organizations exist, many with political affiliations. Workers have the right to join unions and to strike. Transport workers, judges and civil servants each conducted strikes in 1996. More than 80 percent of the labor force is employed in agriculture, fishing and forestry at subsistence wages. The state socialism practiced from 1972-92 severely limited Madagascar's economic growth.

Malawi

Polity: Presidential-par-
liamentary democracy
Economy: Capitalist
Population: 9,453,000
PPP: $710
Life Expectancy: 45.5
Ethnic Groups: Chewa, Nyanja, Tumbuku, other Bantu
Capital: Lilongwe

Political Rights: 2
Civil Liberties: 3
Status: Free

Overview:

The ethnic and regional restrictiveness of Malawi's three main parties raises concerns for the long-term stability of the country's four-year old multiparty democracy. The for-mal coalition between President Bakili Muluzi's southern-based United Democratic Front (UDF) party and its parliamentary partner, the northern-based Alliance for Democracy (AFORD), was dissolved in June. The Malawi Congress Party (MCP), with its strong base in central Malawi, showed signs of resurgence. With presidential and legislative elections not scheduled until 1999, much more political maneuvering is anticipated. President Muluzi's UDF may benefit from economic improvements aided by an end to a regional drought, and from a popular anti-crime drive. The government's human rights record continues to be good.

The UDF and AFORD parties' formal coalition dissolved this year. AFORD leader Chakufwa Chihana resigned as second vice president, but five AFORD cabinet ministers kept their posts and enabled the government to enjoy a working majority in the National Assembly. The government has sought to balance cabinet posts and other appointments to prevent perceptions of regional bias. Several opposition parties exist, but only the MCP, with 55 seats, is represented in parliament.

For nearly three decades after gaining independence from Britain in 1963, Malawi was ruled by President (later President-for-Life) Hastings Kamuzu Banda. Banda exercised dictatorial and often eccentric rule through the Malawi Congress Party (MCP) and its paramilitary youth wing, the Malawi Young Pioneers. Facing a domestic economic crisis and strong international pressure, Banda accepted a referendum approving multiparty rule in June 1993.

Both Banda and the MCP were soundly defeated in presidential and legislative elections in May 1994. Muluzi was victorious with 42 percent of the vote. The election was free and fair. Chances for a free election were helped by the army's dispersal of the Young Pioneers in December 1993. As many as 2,000 Banda loyalists fled to neighboring Mozambique. It is believed that former Young Pioneers may be behind the Malawi Movement for the Restoration of Democracy, which has threatened attacks against the government.

In December 1995, ex-president Banda and his closest advisor, John Tembo, were found not guilty of ordering the murder of several senior politicians in 1983, and little legal redress has been made for widespread abuses during the Banda dictatorship. Several new court cases have been brought against opposition politicians and journalists, however, raising concerns that the judiciary may revert to being a tool for the restriction of rights.

Political Rights and Civil Liberties: Malawi's people chose their government in free and fair elections on May 17, 1994, in the country's first multi-party elections. The president and members of the 177-seat National Assembly were elected for five-year terms. Suffrage was universal for citizens over 18. Serving members of the military were barred from voting to protect the army from politicization. Parliamentary by-elections since 1994 have been marred by vote-buying and other frauds.

Malawi's reputation of having the freest media in Africa was damaged by governmental interference with state-run broadcasting and prosecution of independent journalists. Legislation enacted in 1995 can compel journalists to reveal their sources or face up to two years' imprisonment and $1,300 in fines.

In 1994, the state-owned Malawi Broadcasting Corporation (MBC) introduced television for the first time, but is more important for its radio service, especially to rural areas with high rates of illiteracy. Malawian journalists have reported pressures not to report stories critical of the government. A popular musician's songs lamenting social conditions have been banned. In August, President Muluzi sued the newspaper *Tribune* for defamation after it published allegations of improprieties in a presidential land deal. Muluzi's wife, Anne, also obtained an injunction barring another newspaper, *The Statesman*, from publishing a satirical column titled "Dear Anne."

Free expression and free assembly is otherwise generally respected. A constitution adopted in May 1995 provides strong protection for fundamental freedoms, although critics argue that it allows for excessive presidential power and does not sufficiently protect women's and children's rights. Many nongovernmental organizations operate openly and without interference, including groups focusing on human rights and civil liberties. Religious practice is free, and the country's roughly 12 percent Muslim minority suffers no discrimination.

There are no reported political prisoners or detainees in Malawi. Instances of police brutality are still said to be common, as retraining of the country's 5,000-strong police force continues with international assistance. Prison conditions are reportedly terrible, and in April, 16 prisoners died after being crammed into a tiny cell with 60 other people. Human rights organizations have suggested several actions to improve conditions, but the government has taken no initiatives.

The judicial system suffers from lack of resources and training, and due process is not always respected. The courts have shown independence from the current government in several rulings favoring ex-dictator Banda. The September arrest of Banda's long-time companion Cecilia Kadzamira and his heir-apparent John Tembo on charges of involvement in the shooting of an Asian shopowner, as well as a corruption probe aimed at AFORD president Chihana, may further test the courts' autonomy.

Women receive full and equal protection of the law under the 1995 constitution, but traditional practices maintain de facto discrimination in educational, employment and business opportunities. Few women serve in parliament. Customary practices in rural areas deny women inheritance and property rights. Violence against women is described as routine.

The right to form unions is constitutionally guaranteed. Unions must register with the Ministry of Labor, but this has not been an impediment to union formation since the end of the Banda regime. The right to strike is legally protected, with notice and mediation requirements for workers in essential services. Collective bargaining is widely practiced but not specifically protected by law. Malawi's labor movement has been testing its strength under the democratic system.

Economic liberalization has also continued. The government relaxed price controls long imposed by parastatals to allow free market prices for agricultural commodities, and announced plans to privatize several state enterprises. However, serious levels of corruption are threatening the country's economic revival, as well as its government's political legitimacy.

Malaysia

Polity: Dominant party   **Political Rights:** 4
Economy: Capitalist   **Civil Liberties:** 5
Population: 20,581,000   **Status:** Partly Free
PPP: $8,360
Life Expectancy: 70.9
Ethnic Groups: Malay (46 percent), other indigenous
(9 percent), Chinese (32 percent), Indian (13 percent)
Capital: Kuala Lumpur

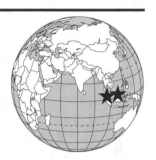

Overview: In October 1996, Malaysian premier Mahathir Mohamad won party approval for an additional three years in office, while a key opposition party defected to the ruling National Front coalition.

Malaysia was established in 1963 through a merger of independent, ex-British Malaya with the then-British colonies of Sarawak, Sabah and Singapore (Singapore withdrew in 1965). Executive power is vested in the prime minister and cabinet. The parliament consists of a 58-member Senate and a 192-member, directly-elected House of Representatives. The King, as head of state, can delay legislation for 30 days.

The economic success of the ethnic Chinese minority triggered race riots in 1969. In 1971 the government responded with the New Economic Policy (NEP), which established quotas for Malays in education, the civil service and business affairs. The 1991 National Development Policy has similar goals.

The 14-party, ruling National Front coalition has captured at least two-thirds of lower house seats in nine straight general elections since 1957. The coalition is dominated by the conservative, ethnic-Malay-based United Malays National Organization (UMNO). Prime Minister Mahathir Mohamad, in office since 1981, has disparaged democracy as a Western concept that inhibits development, and champions "Asian values" to justify his authoritarian rule.

In 1988, following internal UNMO disputes, ex-Trade Minister Razaleigh Hamzah formed Semangat '46 (Spirit of '46, the year UMNO formed). In 1989 Semangat '46 joined a four-party, Malay-based coalition that failed to gain power in the 1990 national elections. In the April 1995 parliamentary elections the National Front took 162 seats; Democratic Action Party, 9; United Sabah Party, 8; Pas, 7; and Semangat '46, 6.

At UNMO's triennial elections in early October 1996, neither Mahathir nor deputy premier Anwar Ibrahim faced challenges to their posts as party president and deputy president, respectively. This guaranteed Mahathir another three years as premier and apparently confirmed Anwar as heir apparent. The same month Semangat '46 members, frustrated with being in opposition, dissolved the party and began joining UMNO.

Political Rights and Civil Liberties: Malaysians have a limited ability to change their government democratically. The government exercises significant control over the media, uses security laws to restrict freedom of expression and chill political activity, and dissuades foreign investment and reduces development funds to opposition-held states.

The government detains former Communists, religious extremists and others under the broadly-drawn 1960 Internal Security Act (ISA) and the 1969 Emergency (Public Order and Prevention of Crime) Ordinance, both of which permit detention of suspects for up to two years. In April 1996, the government reported that 692 people had been held under the ISA between 1986 and 1996.

Police occasionally abuse suspects to extract confessions. The judiciary is subject to government influence in sensitive political and commercial cases. Premier Mahathir, as Home Affairs minister, controls all important judicial appointments. In a landmark ruling, a federal court's July 27, 1996 acquittal of a man appealing a death sentence for drug-trafficking raised the burden of proof for conviction in criminal cases to "beyond reasonable doubt."

Freedom of speech is restricted by the 1970 Sedition Act Amendments, which prohibit discussion of the privileges granted to ethnic Malays and other sensitive issues. In January 1996, DAP deputy chief Lim Guan Eng went on trial for criticizing the government's handling of rape charges against a former state chief minister. In March, Irene Fernandez, head of the Tenaganita women's rights group, went on trial on charges of falsely reporting that at least ten illegal immigrant workers had died of disease in detention centers between January and May 1995.

A 1987 amendment to the 1984 Printing Presses and Publications Act bars the publication of "malicious" news, expands the government's power to ban or restrict publications and prohibits publications from challenging such actions in court. The government occasionally uses these powers to shut down newspapers, and journalists practice self-censorship.

During the 1995 election campaign, the opposition received limited coverage on the broadcast media and in the major newspapers, all of which are owned by individuals and companies close to the ruling National Front. In Kelantan, the only opposition-held state, the federal government reportedly restricts the circulation of pro-opposition newspapers, and has refused to allow the state to establish its own television and radio stations.

The 1967 Police Act requires permits for all public assemblies. Since 1969, political rallies have been banned, although indoor "discussion sessions" are permitted. Under the 1966 Societies Act any association of more than six members (including political parties) must register with the government, and the authorities have deregistered some opposition organizations. The independent National Human Rights Association and several smaller groups generally function without harassment. On November 9, 1996, 200 members of UMNO's youth wing forcibly broke up a conference on East Timor held in Kuala Lumpur, the capital. Police temporarily detained 94 conference participants and ten journalists.

In April, 317 Vietnamese became the first of some 4,000 Vietnamese refugees expected to be forcibly repatriated. Conditions in detention centers for illegal immigrants are grim, and in August 1995 the government admitted that 40 detainees had died in the past eighteen months in a center near Kuala Lumpur.

Official policy discriminates against Chinese, Indians and other minorities in education, employment and business affairs. Islam is the official religion in this secular country. Between May and July 1996, police arrested 18 former leaders of the messianic Islamic *al-Arqam* sect, which was banned in 1994. Muslims are required to take family disputes to *Shari'a* (Islamic law) courts, where women generally have little recourse in rape or domestic violence cases. Non-Muslim minorities worship freely.

Each trade union and labor federation can cover only one particular trade or occupation, and the government must approve of and can deregister all unions. In the electronics industry the government permits only "in-house" unions rather than a nationwide union. The right to strike is legally restricted.

Maldives

Polity: Nonparty, presidential-legislative (elite-clan dominated)
Political Rights: 6
Civil Liberties: 6
Status: Not Free
Economy: Capitalist
Population: 270,000
PPP: $2,200
Life Expectancy: 62.4
Ethnic Groups: Mixed Sinhalese, Dravidian, Arab, and black
Capital: Male

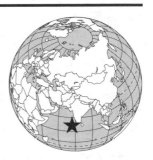

Overview:
The Republic of Maldives, a 500-mile string of 26 atolls in the Indian Ocean, achieved independence from the British in 1965. A 1968 referendum ended the ad-Din sultanate's 815-year rule. The 1968 constitution grants the president broad executive powers including the right to appoint top officials. The *majlis* (parliament) has 40 directly-elected seats and eight seats appointed by the president, serves a five year term, and must approve legislation. Every five years the majlis elects a sole presidential candidate who is voted on by citizens in yes-or-no referendum.

Several coup attempts have been made since independence. Most recently, in 1988 President Maumoon Abdul Gayoom called in Indian troops to crush a coup attempt by Sri Lankan mercenaries. In the aftermath, Gayoom strengthened the National Security Service and named several relatives to top government posts. In early 1990 a brief period of press freedom occurred as the Maldives prepared to host the South Asian Association for Regional Cooperation summit. By June authorities had banned outspoken publications, and several journalists were arrested later in the year.

Gayoom won the August 1993 parliamentary nomination for the presidential referendum, beating out Illyas Ibrahim, a minister who had fled the country after Gayoom accused him of using witchcraft to win the nomination, and another minister. In October, Gayoom won a fifth term in a yes-or-no referendum.

A court subsequently convicted Ibrahim in absentia of actively campaigning for the presidential nomination, which is illegal under Maldivian law. The December 1994 majlis elections were generally free though not fair, largely due to heavy restrictions on political parties and campaigning (see below).

Political Rights and Civil Liberties: Maldivians cannot change their government democratically. The indirectly elected president, who under the constitution must be a male Sunni Muslim, holds broad powers, and exerts influence over the majlis by appointing one-sixth of its members. Individuals may not campaign for the parliamentary nomination for president. Political parties are not expressly banned but are discouraged by the government, and none exists. Nevertheless, in recent years the majlis has increasingly become a forum for critical debate.

The penal code prohibits speech or actions that could "arouse people against the government," although a 1990 amendment decriminalized factual newspaper reports about government errors. A 1968 law prohibits speech considered inimical to Islam, a threat to national security, or libelous.

The government can shut down newspapers and sanction journalists for articles allegedly containing unfounded criticism. Regulations make editors responsible for the content of the material they publish. Two outspoken publications, that had their licenses revoked in 1990, *Sangu* and *Hukuru*, remain closed. Journalists practice self-censorship, but the mainly private press carries some criticism of the government. The sole television and radio stations are state-owned but carry some pluralistic views.

On April 3, 1996, a court sentenced journalist Mohamed Nasheed to two years in prison on sedition and defamation charges over an October 1994 article criticizing electoral procedures in the 1994 general election. In September 1996, the High Court reduced the sentence on appeal to six months, although in October the Court set Nasheed's release for December 26.

The president strongly influences the judiciary through his powers to appoint and remove judges, although the latter power is rarely exercised, and to review High Court decisions. The legal system, based on both *Shari'a* (Islamic law) and civil law, does not always provide adequate due process protection. Persons suspected of terrorism, sedition or drug offenses can be detained without trial indefinitely.

The constitution guarantees freedom of assembly, but the government restricts political gatherings during campaigns to small meetings on private premises. Civic associations are permitted, but no local human rights groups have organized and civil society is underdeveloped. Traditional norms relegate women to largely subservient roles in society. Under Shari'a, woman receives half the inheritance accorded to a man.

Under the constitution Islam is the official religion and all citizens must be Muslims. Practice of other religions is prohibited, although private worship by non-Muslims is tolerated. There are no legal rights to form trade unions, stage strikes and bargain collectively, and in practice such activity does not occur.

Mali

Polity: Presidential-parliamentary democracy
Economy: Mixed statist
Population: 9,653,000
PPP: $530
Life Expectancy: 46.2
Ethnic Groups: Mande (Bambara, Malinke, Sara Kole)
(50 percent), Peul (17 percent), Voltaic (12 percent),
Songhai (6 percent), Tuareg and Moor (10 percent), others
Capital: Bamako

Political Rights: 2
Civil Liberties: 2*
Status: Free

Ratings Change: Mali's civil liberties rating changed from 3 to 2 because the continued growth of civil society contributed to consolidation of democracy.

Overview: **P**olitical maneuvering intensified in anticipation of presidential and legislative elections expected in 1997, although opposition parties have little chance of unseating President Alpha Oumar Konaré, or wresting control of the national assembly from his ruling Alliance for Democracy in Mali (ADEMA). Mali's apparent stability and democratic progress, especially since a five-year rebellion by Tuareg people in the country's north ended in 1995, was threatened by allegations of a coup plot in October. At the end of the same month, the constitutional court declared unconstitutional numerous provisions of a new electoral code that was strongly criticized by opposition parties.

For over three decades after achieving independence from France in 1960, Mali was ruled by military or one-party dictators. President Moussa Traoré was overthrown by his own military in March 1991, after over 100 protesters were killed as demonstrations demanding a multiparty system were brutally crushed.

A national conference followed the coup, and in elections that most observers rated free and fair, Alpha Oumar Konaré won the presidency in April 1992. Democratic consolidation has followed, with increasing respect for fundamental freedoms. The country remains desperately poor, however, and hundreds of thousands of Malians are economic migrants throughout Africa and Europe.

The 1995 peace pact that ended a five-year conflict among Tuareg guerrillas, black ethnic militias and government forces continued to hold through 1996 over a vast swath of northern Mali. Longer-term efforts to accommodate the Arab Tuareg people in the increasingly open and democratic system dominated by the country's black African majority may prove difficult. Human rights abuses are much fewer since the end of armed conflict.

Political Rights   **T**he current government was elected by universal suffrage
and Civil Liberties: in free and fair elections in 1992. President Konaré's
ADEMA party controls 76 of 116 National Assembly seats.
Domestic debate is open and extensive, including a nationally broadcast annual "open forum" with top leaders each December. Over 50 political parties are registered, and a number of them offer scathing criticism of government policies. The various

opposition parties are deeply divided, however, with no strong leader and are un-likely to mount a unified challenge in the 1997 presidential and legislative elec-tions. Opposition parties boycotted the September parliamentary vote on a new electoral code, which included some proportional representation and an indepen-dent election commission, both of which, they complained, favored the ruling party. The constitutional court struck down these and 28 more of the new law's 196 pro-visions in October. It is not clear whether the law's invalidation might delay the electoral schedule.

A variety of independent newspapers and radio stations operate freely, and the media are among Africa's most open. Even state-run television, radio and print me-dia offer a diversity of views, although this policy may be tested during the 1997 electoral campaign. Local radio stations broadcast in regional languages in several parts of the country, especially important for a largely rural country with a 75 per-cent rate of illiteracy. Legislation enacted in 1993 provides harsh penalties for slan-der or "public injury" to public officials, and is a potential threat to press freedom. So far, it has apparently only been used against an opposition national assembly deputy, Youssouf Traoré. In August, his parliamentary immunity was lifted and he was arrested on defamation charges after accusing local officials of corruption.

Mali's human rights record has improved since the1995 peace pact which pro-vides for development assistance and local autonomy. Furthermore, three languages spoken by Tuareg people have received recognition as national languages and will be used in local schools in Tuareg areas. Disputes over land tenure and water rights could lead to a revival of conflict. An alleged plot to assassinate President Konaré and other senior officials was reportedly foiled in October with the arrest of at least six soldiers and several civilians. Armed Forces chief General Amadou Toumani Touré, who launched Mali's democratic transition after briefly seizing power in 1991, remains supportive of the electoral process.

Labor unions remain a strong force after playing a leading role in the pro-de-mocracy movement. Although predominantly Muslim, Mali is a secular state, and minority and religious rights are protected by law. Legal advances in the protection of women's rights have yet to be realized in practice, especially in rural areas. Fe-male genital mutilation is common, and while no law yet prohibits it, the govern-ment has undertaken an educational campaign to reduce its prevalence.

Mali is exceedingly poor, and decades of one-party rule has left an entrenched and corrupt bureaucracy that still stifles economic development and opportunity. Fears remain that unemployment and economic hardship could help fuel local vari-ants of Islamic fundamentalism. World Bank and International Monetary Fund-im-posed structural adjustment programs have caused at least a temporary decline in living standards, but are helping draw increased international investment. Foreign aid makes up about a fifth of the national budget.

Malta

Polity: Parliamentary
democracy
Economy: Mixed cap-
italist-statist
Population: 374,000
PPP: $11,570
Life Expectancy: 76.2
Ethnic Groups: Maltese (mixed Arab, Sicilian, Norman,
Spanish, Italian, and English)
Capital: Valletta

Political Rights: 1
Civil Liberties: 1
Status: Free

| **Overview:** | A general election on October 26 brought to power the first Labor Party government in nine years. Under Prime Minister Alfred Sant, Labor took 51 percent of the vote in the par- |

liamentary elections.

The new government announced it would not seek full European Union membership and would withdraw from the NATO Partnership for Peace Program. EU requirements such as a VAT and the full opening of its markets were domestically unpopular. The Labor Party views membership in the EU and the Partnership for Peace as incompatible with Malta's constitutional provisions for neutrality. The government did decide to focus on cultivating close political and economic relations with the U.S.

Great Britain was, in the nineteenth century, the last of a long succession of foreign powers to occupy this strategically-located Mediterranean island. Malta became independent within the British Commonwealth in 1964 and opted for republican status in 1974. In 1979 the country lost its British military installations and accompanying expenditures at the expiration of an Anglo-Maltese defense agreement. The Labor Party government turned to Libya's Mu'ammar al-Qadhafi, who promised financial support. Italy later pledged to protect Malta's neutrality and to provide loans and subsidies. Both agreements had lapsed by 1987, but political and economic cooperation with Libya were reaffirmed the following year.

Parliamentary leadership has alternated between the two main parties, the Malta Labor Party and the Nationalist Party. The constitution was amended in 1987 to allow the award of extra seats so that the party winning a majority of the popular vote might secure a legislative majority in the House of Representatives.

Malta's new government inherited a healthy $2.9 billion economy with a growth rate of 7 percent, with tourism revenue that doubled in the past decade and unemployment at only 3 percent.

| **Political Rights and Civil Liberties:** | Citizens of Malta can change their government democratically. Members of the House of Representatives are elected on the basis of proportional representation every five years. |

The party winning a majority of the popular vote is awarded additional House seats if needed to secure a legislative majority. Parliament elects a president to a five-year term. Although the role is largely ceremonial, the president is charged with appointing a prime minister and the cabinet from the parliament.

The judiciary is independent of the executive and legislative branches. The Chief Justice and nine judges are appointed by the president on the advice of the prime minister. The constitution requires a fair public trial before an impartial court. Defendants have the right to counsel of their choice, or if they cannot pay the cost to court-appointed counsel at public expense. Defendants enjoy a presumption of innocence.

Since 1992, the government has sponsored media diversification. Two English-language weeklies publish in addition to several Maltese newspapers. Both public and private domestic broadcasting are available, as are international radio broadcasts in several languages and Italian television programming. The only exception to freedom of speech and press is a 1987 law prohibiting foreign involvement in Maltese election campaigns.

Roman Catholicism is the state religion, but freedom of worship for religious minorities is respected. All groups enjoy freedom of association. There are independent labor unions as well as a federation, the General Union of Workers. A constitutional amendment banning gender discrimination took effect in July 1993, but divorce is still not legal.

Marshall Islands

Polity: Parliamentary democracy
Economy: Capitalist-statist
Population: 58,000
PPP: na
Life Expectancy: na
Ethnic Groups: Marshallese (Micronesian)
Capital: Majuro

Political Rights: 1
Civil Liberties: 1
Status: Free

Overview:

The Marshalls, independent since 1986 and consisting of 33 Micronesian islands in the Pacific Ocean, came under German control in 1885. Japan governed the islands from 1920, under a League of Nations mandate, until the United States Navy occupied them in 1945. The U.S. administered the islands under a United Nations trusteeship after 1947.

The 1979 constitution provides for a bicameral parliament with a directly-elected, 33 seat *Nitijela* (House of Representatives) that serves a four-year term. The lower house chooses a president, who holds executive powers as head of state and head of government, from among its members. The upper *Iroji* (Council of Chiefs) has 12 traditional leaders who offer advice on customary law.

In 1979 parliament elected Amata Kabua as the country's first president. In 1983 the Marshall Islands signed a Compact of Free Association with the United States, which entered into force in October 1986. Under the Compact the country is fully sovereign, but defense remains the responsibility of the United States until at least 2001. In 1990, the U.N. recognized the dissolution of the trusteeship, and in 1991 the country received full membership in the world body.

Parliament re-elected Kabua in 1984, 1988 and 1991. At the November 1991 balloting for parliament a newly-formed, informal Our Islands party, chaired by Kabua, defeated a Democratic Party headed by Tony DeBrum, a former Kabua associate. The November 20, 1995, parliamentary elections were conducted largely on non-party lines. In January 1996, parliament re-elected Kabua to a fifth four-year term. Kabua's political longevity owes largely to personal loyalties within parliament and a limited pool of viable alternative candidates.

A key issue facing the country is the Kabua government's controversial August 1994 proposal to rent remote, uninhabited islands as nuclear waste dumps. The issue is particularly sensitive in light of the 67 atmospheric nuclear tests the United States conducted over the islands in the 1940s and 1950s. Data released in 1994 indicated that the extent of the radioactive fallout from the tests was greater than previously disclosed. The proposal is on hold pending an environmental impact study, which could take eight or more years to complete. With a 15-year, $700 million U.S. aid package set to end in 2001, the government is also examining ways to diversify the economy by developing tourism and other industries.

Political Rights and Civil Liberties:

Citizens of the Marshall Islands can change their government democratically. Politics are based mainly on personal loyalties rather than party affiliations.

The constitution contains a bill of rights. The rule of law is well established. The judiciary is independent, and trials are conducted with adequate due process safeguards. The sole newspaper, the weekly *Marshall Islands Journal*, is privately-owned. The paper carries diverse views and criticizes the government, although its journalists occasionally practice self-censorship on sensitive political issues. The official monthly *Marshall Islands Gazette* contains general notices and avoids political coverage. Three of the four radio stations are privately-owned, and all stations offer pluralistic views. Opposition members own the local cable television station.

Freedom of assembly is respected in practice. Civil society is underdeveloped, although several women's groups, including the umbrella Women United Together for the Marshall Islands organization, conduct civic education and advocacy programs. Inheritance of property and traditional rank is matrilineal, and in most matters women hold a social status equal to men. However, women are underrepresented in politics and government. Women's groups say domestic violence is not widespread but is nevertheless under-reported.

There are no restrictions on religious observance in this predominantly Christian country. Freedom of internal movement is unrestricted except on Kwajalein Atoll, the site of a major U.S. military installation.

The government broadly interprets the constitution's guarantee of free association to extend to trade unions, although in practice none exists. There is no formal right to strike or to engage in collective bargaining, although in practice no restraints bar such activities.

Mauritania

Polity: Dominant party (military-dominated)
Economy: Capitalist-statist
Population: 2,333,000
PPP: $1,610
Life Expectancy: 51.7
Ethnic Groups: Black Maur (40 percent), white Maur (30 percent), Tuculor, Hal-Pulaar, Soninke, Wolof, others
Capital: Nouakchott

Political Rights: 6
Civil Liberties: 6
Status: Not Free

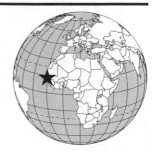

Overview:

Mauritania came under continued criticism in 1996 over reports of discrimination against the country's black African minority and the persistence of de facto slavery affecting tens of thousands of people. Mauritania's basic political divisions run deeply along racial and ethnic lines. The gradual liberalization of recent years stalled in 1996. The flawed October elections saw the military-backed ruling Social Democratic Republican Party (PRDS) take all but one of 79 National Assembly seats against a divided opposition. Media censorship also continues. Yet political activity, open discussion and criticism of the government were generally tolerated, even if President Maaouya Ould Sid Ahmed Taya seemed little inclined to allow any real challenge to his expected 1998 re-election bid.

After nearly six decades of French colonial rule, Mauritania's borders as an independent state were formalized in 1960. Among its 2.2 million people are the dominant "white Maurs" of Arab extraction and Arabic-speaking Muslim black Africans known as "black Maurs." Other black Africans mainly inhabit the country's southern frontiers along the Senegal River valley, and comprise about one-third of the population. Mauritania's politics have long revolved around racial and ethnic rivalries. For centuries, black Africans were subjugated and taken as slaves by both white and black Maurs. Slavery has been officially outlawed—several times—but remnants of servitude clearly linger, and credible allegations of actual chattel slavery persist. In 1989-90, tens of thousands of black Mauritanians fled into exile in Senegal and Mali as Arab militants and soldiers drove them from their lands. Several thousand blacks were detained during this period and as many as 600 may have been executed.

The country was ruled as a civilian one-party state until a 1978 military coup. Economic collapse hastened by the burden of enforcing Mauritania's decision to share in Morocco's seizure of the Spanish Sahara (now known as Western Sahara) helped prompt the coup. The new junta pulled out of Western Sahara and renounced Mauritania's claim. An internal purge installed Colonel Ould Taya as junta chairman in 1984. In January 1992, Ould Taya was declared winner of a six-year presidential term in the country's first, and problematic, multiparty election. The main opposition parties boycotted National Assembly elections two months later, and the ruling PRDS swept into power and continued a de facto one-party state.

Mauritania is clearly less repressive than it was a decade or even five years ago.

Some tolerance of free expression and association now exists. Yet progress towards democratization and respect for human rights is fitful, at best.

Political Rights and Civil Liberties: Mauritanians have not been able to change their government democratically. The country's 1991 French-style constitution provides for democratic rule that has not been respected in reality. The 1992 presidential poll was marred by severe fraud. Manipulation and fraud were reported in the October 1996 National Assembly elections that were all but swept by the ruling party. The Action for Change party took one seat, won by an ex-slave in what some observers claim was a purposeful concession engineered by the ruling party. Protesting alleged irregularities, the opposition Union of Democratic Forces-New Era party boycotted the second round. The PRDS had already taken 17 of 18 Senate seats contested in April.

Pre-publication censorship and state monopoly over broadcast media and ownership of two daily newspapers devalues constitutional guarantees of free expression. Opposition viewpoints are rare in government media, and some topics, like allegations of continued slavery or reports criticizing Islam, are taboo. "Promoting national disharmony" and "insulting the president" are criminal offenses. Private newspapers are often openly critical of the government and some are affiliated with various political parties, but all publications must be officially registered. The weekly *Mauritanie Nouvelle* newspaper was suspended for three months, and several individual issues were seized after it criticized French policies in Africa.

Political parties and nongovernmental organizations must register with the government, although for most groups this has been a formality. Some black African activist groups are banned, as are Islamist parties, including the Oumma party. Several NGOs working specifically on human rights, including the Mauritanian Human Rights Association (AMDH), operated openly despite not being registered. Black Africans reportedly are barred from holding meetings or harassed when they attempt to do so without permission. The El Hor (Free Man) Movement has fought for black rights and is seeking to transform itself into a political party. Widespread discrimination against blacks continues, and despite the formal end of slavery, up to 100,000 blacks still live in conditions of servitude. In October, the U.S. Congress passed legislation suspending all non-humanitarian aid to Mauritania until anti-slavery laws are properly enforced.

Senegal-based banned black resistance groups, including the Mauritanian Forces of African Liberation (FLAM) and the United Front for Armed Resistance in Mauritania (FURAM), still call for armed struggle. Over 66,000 black Wolof and Peul peoples who fled the 1989-90 ethnic cleansing are still in refugee camps in Senegal.

Freedom of religion does not exist. Mauritania is an Islamic state, and by statute all Mauritanians are Sunni Muslims who may not possess other religious texts or enter non-Muslim households. Non-Mauritanian Shi'a Muslims and Christians are allowed to worship privately.

Mauritania's legal system is heavily influenced by the government and many decisions are shaped by *Shari'a* law, especially regarding family and civil matters. A woman's testimony is weighted as only half that of a man's. A number of legal protections regarding property and pay equality exist, but are often only respected in urban areas among the educated elite. Prison conditions are reportedly severe.

Any government will face severe economic difficulties in the vast and mostly arid desert country. The country's foreign debt is virtually unpayable, but a new fishing rights pact with the European Union is expected to bring significant income. While only about a quarter of Mauritania's workers are in the formal sector, nearly all the wage-earners are unionized. The 1993 labor code ended the monopoly of the Union of Mauritanian Workers (UTM) on trade union activities. The UTM is closely aligned with the government and remains the dominant labor organization. However, the government has officially recognized a new independent confederation, the General Confederation of Mauritanian Workers (CGTM). The government takes an important role in negotiating all labor agreements, and can imposing binding tripartite arbitration.

Mauritius

Polity: Parliamentary democracy
Economy: Capitalist
Population: 1,129,000
PPP: $12,510
Life Expectancy: 70.4
Ethnic Groups: Indo-Mauritian (68 percent), Creole (27 percent), Sino-Mauritian, and Franco-Mauritian
Capital: Port Louis

Political Rights: 1
Civil Liberties: 2
Status: Free

Overview: After a sweeping victory in the December 1995 elections, the coalition government of the Labour Party (LP) and the Mouvement Militant Mauricien (MMM) faltered in 1996. Ministerial inefficiency, allegations of corruption and unpopular proposals for tax hikes ended the new government's honeymoon period. Opposition parties posted a commanding win in October's local elections, winning 100 of 111 seats contested. Yet the LP-MMM government, which took all 60 national assembly seats in 1995, was in no danger of falling. LP leader Navin Ramgoolam, son of the island's revered first premier, will probably concede more power to Paul Berenger, chief of MMM, the junior partner in the coalition.

Despite the unsettled political scene, the economy, which had grown by an annual average of about 6 percent since 1970, continued to expand. Often cited as one of post-colonial Africa's few success stories, Mauritius boasts a rapidly increasing per capita income and low unemployment. The country's assets include a well integrated multinational population, political stability, and preferential European and U.S. market access for its principal exports, sugar and garments. The Mauritian standard of living has improved markedly and the island's infrastructure has been overhauled since the mid-1980s. However, rapid growth and economic prosperity have led to destruction of nearly all the country's native forest and fauna as well as to the decay of its Creole culture.

Mauritius has no indigenous people; its ethnically mixed population, mostly descended from immigrants from the Indian sub-continent, were brought to the island as laborers during 360 years of Dutch, French and then British colonial administration. Since gaining independence from Britain in 1968, Mauritius has maintained one of Africa's most successful democracies. The island became a republic within the British Commonwealth in 1993, with a largely ceremonial president as head of state. The National Assembly consists of a speaker, 62-directly elected members and an attorney general, if he is not already an elected member. Additionally, as many as eight "best loser" seats are awarded according to party or ethnic underrepresentation, although only four are currently assigned.

Political Rights and Civil Liberties:

Mauritians can choose their government in free, fair and competitive elections. Decentralized structures govern its island dependencies, the largest of which, Rodrigues Island, has its own government and local councils, as well as two elected deputies in the National Assembly. Ethnic and religious minorities are guaranteed legislative representation through the "best loser" system. The independent judiciary is headed by a Supreme Court and the legal system is based on both French and British traditions.

There are no known political prisoners and no reports of political or extrajudicial killings. Civil rights are respected, although excessive use of force by police is reported. Freedom of religion is respected and both domestic and international travel are unrestricted.

Freedom of expression and of the press is constitutionally-protected. Numerous private daily and weekly publications are often highly critical of both government and opposition politicians and their policies. All broadcast media are state-owned, however, and usually reflect government viewpoints. Freedom of assembly and association is respected. Numerous nongovernmental organizations operate and nine labor federations comprise 300 unions.

The government has attempted to improve the status of women by removing legal barriers to advancement; however, women still occupy a subordinate role in society and make up just over 20 percent of the paid labor force. No laws exist mandating equal pay for equal work or prohibiting sexual harassment in the workplace. Women represent only about one-third of the student population at the University of Mauritius. Domestic violence against women is common. While no laws specifically address family violence, governmental and nongovernmental agencies have launched educational initiatives on domestic violence issues and begun assistance programs for abuse victims.

The constitutional prohibition of discrimination on the basis of race or religion is generally respected, but tensions between the Hindu majority and Muslim and Creole minorities persist, marking one of the country's only potential political dangers.

Mexico

Polity: Dominant party
Economy: Capitalist-
statist
Population: 94,843,000
PPP: $7,010
Life Expectancy: 71.0
Ethnic Groups: Mestizo (70 percent), Indian (20 percent),
European (9 percent), others
Capital: Mexico City

Political Rights: 4
Civil Liberties: 3*
Status: Partly Free

Ratings Change: Mexico's civil liberties rating changed from 4 to 3 because of
a cessation of violence in Chiapas.

Overview:

In 1996, a year before scheduled elections to the 500-member Chamber of Deputies, President Ernesto Zedillo and the ruling Institutional Revolutionary Party (PRI) faced continuing economic crisis, charges of corruption, increased political and criminal violence, and drug-trafficking scandals. Promises of meaningful electoral reform were diminished in the fall when the PRI, which has ruled Mexico since 1929, backed out of an earlier commitment to accept campaign spending limits and new rules governing coalitions, which would have made the political system fairer to opposition parties.

Mexico achieved independence from Spain in 1810 and established itself as a republic in 1822. Seven years after the Revolution of 1910, a new constitution was promulgated under which the United Mexican States became a federal republic consisting of 31 states and a Federal District (Mexico City). Each state has elected governors and legislatures. The president is elected to a six-year term. A bicameral Congress consists of a 128-member Senate elected for six years with at least one minority senator from each state, and a 500-member Chamber of Deputies elected for three years—300 directly and 200 through proportional representation.

Since its founding in 1929, the PRI has dominated the country by means of its corporatist, authoritarian structure maintained through co-optation, patronage, corruption and repression. The formal business of government takes place mostly in secret and with little legal foundation.

Carlos Salinas won the 1988 presidential election through massive and systematic fraud. Most Mexicans believe Salinas actually lost to Cuauhtemoc Cardenas, who headed a coalition of leftist parties that later became the Party of the Democratic Revolution (PRD).

Wielding the enormous power of the presidency, Salinas overhauled the economy and joined the North American Free Trade Agreement with the U.S. and Canada. Political reforms were minimal and the basic structures of the state-party system remained. Under Salinas, corruption reached unparalleled proportions. The wife of his brother, Raul, was detained by Swiss officials in connection with drug-trafficking and money-laundering after she and her brother attempted to withdraw $84 million from Swiss bank accounts. Under Salinas, the number of billionaires in

Mexico increased from one in 1987 to 24 in 1994. Meanwhile, Mexico's income inequality, already among the world's most striking, grew even worse.

Salinas conceded a few gubernatorial election victories to the right-wing National Action Party (PAN), which had supported his economic policies. In return PAN dropped its demands for political reform and abandoned plans to establish a pro-democracy coalition with the PRD.

Until the outbreak of the Zapatista rebellion in the southern state of Chiapas on New Year's Day 1994, it was assumed that Salinas's hand-picked successor, Luis Donaldo Colosio, would defeat Cardenas and PAN congressman Diego Fernandez de Cevallos in the 1994 presidential election. The Zapatistas' demands for democracy and clean elections resonated throughout Mexico. Colosio, who infuriated PRI hardliners by advocating greater democratization, was assassinated on March 23, 1994. As theories abounded about whether PRI hardliners or drug traffickers were responsible, Salinas substituted Zedillo, a 42-year-old U.S.-trained economist with little political experience.

PRI hardliners put aside their animosity for the party technocrats, and placed the government machinery firmly behind Zedillo. The PRI put to use the enormous resources of the state, not to mention the broadcast media and their supporters among the elite.

On August 21, 1994, Zedillo won with nearly 50 percent of the valid vote. The PRI won 95 Senate seats, the PAN 25 and the PRD eight. In the Chamber the PRI won 300 seats, the PAN 118 and the PRD 70. Both opposition parties disputed the elections' legitimacy. Only PRI legislators in the Chamber voted to sanction the results.

Francisco Ruiz Massieu, the PRI secretary general who had been an advocate of reform, was assassinated on September 28, 1994, his murder evidently ordered from somewhere within the PRI.

Weeks after Zedillo took office on December 1, 1994, the Mexican peso collapsed. Despite a massive U.S. bailout, the economy fell into a deep, year-long recession. Zedillo's promises to reform politics and establish the rule of law were lost on most Mexicans, who struggled to survive amid massive job losses and with a currency worth less than half its previous value.

In early 1995, the now-reviled Salinas went into self-imposed exile and Raul Salinas was accused of involvement in the Ruiz Massieu murder, along with a major corruption scandal. By year's end, however, and despite Zedillo's appointment of an attorney general from the PAN, none of the assassinations had been cleared up and no PRI leader had been held accountable for corruption.

Under Zedillo an IMF-directed austerity program left most Mexicans in dire economic straits. Wages, employment and consumption remained far below 1994 levels, raising the crime rate as well as social tensions throughout 1996. On April 1, the government boosted the minimum wage by 12 percent, but the price of food staples and other commodities rose 30 percent. Meanwhile, Mexico became the leading supplier of illegal drugs to the U.S., accounting for two-thirds of the cocaine and 20 to 30 percent of the heroin entering the country. Many state-owned companies privatized under Salinas were bought by drug traffickers, further exacerbating the well-entrenched corruption.

The slumping economy had a severe impact on an already hard-pressed middle-class, which lost substantial purchasing power. With a foreign debt approaching

$200 billion, Mexico was poised for a serious decline, and millions of Mexicans continued to enter the United States illegally.

In 1996, opposition parties of the left and the right won important municipal elections in three states—Mexico State, Coahuila and Hidalgo. Post-electoral conflicts took place in several regions. In the southern states of Guerrero, Oaxaca, Tabasco and Chiapas, political violence continued to be a fact of life. But the elections left the PRI governing just two of Mexico's 12 largest cities.

A 1994 cease-fire with the Zapatistas held, but even after 30 months of negotiations no resolution of the war was in sight by year's end. A new guerrilla group, the Popular Revolutionary Army, was responsible for several violent raids in a seven-state area wounding and killing dozens of police and army personnel.

In April, the main political parties, with the exception of the PAN, agreed on reforms aimed at bringing about fairer elections. The reforms introduced direct elections for the mayoralty of Mexico City and abolished government control of the Federal Electoral Commission. The government pledged to increase public financing of political parties and to guarantee them fairer access to television during elections. But unilateral changes by the president and PRI limited the scope of the law and the main opposition parties voted against it in November.

In September, with Zedillo weakened by political infighting and a poor economy, the PRI's raucous national convention resolved that the party would not be committed to free-market "social liberalism" but to "revolutionary nationalism," vowed to oppose privatization of the petrochemical industry, and placed restrictions on the eligibility of its candidates for president and governor. The decisions marked a victory of PRI hardliners over the party technocrats. Analysts concluded that the changes, which would make it almost impossible for certain cabinet members and businessmen to stand as PRI candidates, made the party more insular and regressive.

Political Rights and Civil Liberties: The 1994 elections were freer than those of the past, but still decidedly unfair because of the ruling party's domination of state resources and broadcast media. Despite reforms, PRI continues to exercise substantial control over the electoral system. Irregularities, however, did not prevent the opposition from winning municipal and state races in 1996. Since the second half of 1994, the PAN has won a few gubernatorial races in elections much freer than in the past.

Constitutional guarantees regarding political and civic organizations are generally respected in the urban north and central parts of the country. However, political and civic expression is restricted throughout rural Mexico, in poor urban areas and in poor southern states where the government frequently takes repressive measures against the left-wing PRD and peasant and indigenous groups. The nearly feudal conditions in southern states were at the root of the New Year's Indian rebellion in Chiapas.

Civil society has grown in recent years: human rights, pro-democracy, women's and environmental groups are active. However, anyone critical of the government remains subject to numerous forms of sophisticated intimidation that rights activists refer to as "cloaked repression"—from gentle warnings by government officials and anonymous death threats, to unwarranted detention and jailings on dubious charges.

An official human rights commission was created in 1990. But only minimal progress has been made in curtailing the widespread violation of human rights—false arrests, torture, disappearances, murder and extortion—perpetrated by the Federal Judicial Police and by the national and state police forces. The rights commission is barred from examining political and labor rights violations, and is unable to enforce its recommendations.

The government persecutes political and labor figures, journalists, human rights activists and criminal detainees. Corruption and rights violations are a matter of routine for the Federal Judicial Police, which often makes political arrests under the pretext of drug enforcement. The same goes for Mexico's other law enforcement agencies. In 1996, Attorney General Antonio Lozano Gracia fired more than 1,200 members of the judicial police for corruption, connections to the drug trade, and theft. Many police dismissed for poor conduct have subsequently been implicated in kidnappings for ransom.

During the outbreak of the Chiapas rebellion the military was responsible for widespread human rights violations, including the deaths of dozens of civilians, mass arbitrary arrests, torture of detainees and summary executions of at least five Zapatista fighters. To this day, the military has never been held accountable. During a military crackdown against the Zapatistas in early 1995, numerous reports were made of arbitrary detentions, torture and coerced confessions. Ranchers and landowners, sometimes aided by police, stepped up attacks by their own private police against indigenous and left-wing groups. In April 1996, five peasants in Chiapas were killed during a campaign to evacuate squatters. Human rights groups blamed the police.

Supreme Court judges are appointed by the executive and rubber-stamped by the Senate. The court is prohibited from enforcing political and labor rights, and from reviewing the constitutionality of laws. In April, the Supreme Court ruled that Ruben Figueroa Alcocer, former PRI governor of Guerrero, and seven other officials tried to cover up a police massacre near Acapulco in 1995 in which 17 leftist protesters were killed. He had earlier been cleared by his own prosecutor. But the court failed to identify who ordered the killings, and left open what agency would pursue criminal charges. Overall, the judicial system is weak, politicized and riddled with the corruption infecting all official bodies. In most rural areas, respect for laws by official agencies is nearly nonexistent. Lower courts and law enforcement in general are undermined by widespread bribery. The exposure of endemic government corruption rarely results in legal proceedings. Drug-related corruption is evident in the military, police and security forces, and increasingly in government at both the local and national levels.

The media, while mostly private and nominally independent, depend on the government for advertising revenue. A handful of daily newspapers and weeklies are the exceptions.

The ruling party's domination of television, by far the country's most influential medium, was evident in the blanket, uncritical coverage of the PRI during the 1994 election campaign. Not only did Televisa, the dominant PRI-allied network, systematically support PRI candidates, but opposition parties were offered only limited airtime. In 1996, Televisia, the country's dominant media group, reported losses. Two newly-privatized stations, Azteca, have shown little inclination to buck the government line, and their owner in 1996 admitted receiving a "loan" of $29 million from Raul Salinas to buy the stations in 1993.

In 1992 the constitution was amended to restore the legal status of the Catholic Church and other religious institutions. Priests and nuns were allowed to vote for the first time in nearly 80 years. Nonetheless, activist priests promoting the rights of Indians and the poor, particularly in southern states, remain subject to threats and intimidation by conservative landowners and local PRI bosses. Protestant evangelism is making inroads among Mexico's indigenous peoples, which has resulted in conflict with the Catholic Church.

Officially-recognized labor unions operate as political instruments of the PRI. In 1996, the Confederation of Mexican Workers (CTM), which has been a pro-government and pro-PRI group for 60 years, saw tens of thousands of rebel trade unionists take to the streets on May 1 to protest the economic crisis and ineffective union leadership. They marched despite assurances by 96-year-old CTM leader Fidel Velazquez that the confederation would not participate. The Forum for a New Trade Unionism comprising electricians, pilots, teachers, transport workers, bank employees and some car industry unions demanded a new labor code to free Mexico's labor movement from its subordination to PRI. The government does not recognize independent unions, denying them collective-bargaining rights and the right to strike. Independent unions and peasant organizations are subject to intimidation, blacklisting and violent crackdowns. Dozens of labor and peasant leaders have been killed in recent years in ongoing land disputes, particularly in the southern states where Indians comprise close to half the population. Exploitation of teenage women is increasing in the manufacturing-for-export sector, as the government consistently fails to enforce child-labor laws.

Micronesia

Polity: Federal parliamentary democracy
Economy: Capitalist
Population: 107,000
PPP: na
Life Expectancy: na
Ethnic Groups: Micronesian majority, Polynesian minority
Capital: Palikir

Political Rights: 1
Civil Liberties: 1
Status: Free

Overview: The Federated States of Micronesia occupy the Caroline Islands archipelago in the Pacific Ocean. The 607 islands have a Micronesian majority and Polynesian minority. In 1899, Germany purchased the Carolines from Spain, and in 1914 Japan seized the islands, ruling them from 1920 under a League of Nations mandate. The United States Navy occupied the islands during World War II, and in 1947 the Caroline Islands became part of the U.S. Trust Territory of the Pacific.

In July 1978, four districts of the Trust Territory–Yap, Chuuk, Pohnpei and Kosrae–approved a constitution grouping themselves into the Federated States of Micronesia. The constitution, which went into effect in May 1979, provides for a unicameral, 14-Senator Congress. One Senator is elected at-large from each of the four states for a four-year term, with the remaining ten Senators elected for two-year terms from single member districts. The president and vice president are selected by Congress from among its four at-large members.

In 1982, the territory concluded a Compact of Free Association with the United States, which entered into effect in November 1986. Under the Compact the country is fully sovereign, although the U.S. is responsible for defense until at least 2001. In December 1990 the U.N. formally recognized the end of the trusteeship, and in September 1991 admitted the country to the world body.

At the March 1991 parliamentary elections, John Haglelgam, the country's second president, failed to win his seat and thus could not stand for a second presidential term. In May, the Congress elected Bailey Olter of Pohnpei state, a former vice president, to succeed Haglelgam. At the March 3, 1995, parliamentary elections, Olter retained his seat in balloting which, as in the past, was conducted on an individual rather than party basis. In the subsequent parliamentary balloting for the presidency Olter defeated Senator Jacob Nena of Kosrae state, the vice president, to hold on to the top office.

The economy is heavily dependent on fishing, subsistence agriculture, tourism and U.S. aid. In early 1995 the Micronesian Maritime Authority warned that excessive commercial fishing by fleets from Japan, South Korea and other nations may be depleting the country's stock.

Political Rights and Civil Liberties:

Citizens of the Federated States of Micronesia can change their government democratically. There are freely-elected governments at the federal, state and municipal levels. Politics tend to be based on individual and clan loyalties, and while parties are permitted none has formed.

The rule of law is strong and basic freedoms are respected in practice. The judiciary is independent of the government, and trials are open and fair. No private newspapers exist, although the federal government publishes a twice-monthly information bulletin, *The National Union*, and the four state governments publish newsletters. Each of the four state governments operates a radio station, and religious groups also own stations. Some states also operate television services.

Freedom of association is respected but there are few nongovernmental organizations. There are no restrictions on freedom of assembly. During the 1995 parliamentary campaign, candidates frequently held public question-and-answer sessions. Citizens enjoy full freedom of religion.

The country's main human rights issue is the condition of women. Domestic violence, often alcohol-influenced, is common. Although assault of women by spouses or male relatives is a criminal offense, the authorities, influenced by traditional norms, often view domestic violence as a family issue. The government formed a National Women's Advisory Council in 1992 to educate women about their rights, although so far its activities have been limited. Women also face discrimination in employment that generally limits them to entry-level jobs.

Workers have the constitutional right to form "associations," although owing to the small size of the wage economy no associations or trade unions have thus far been formed. There is no legislation regarding collective bargaining, and its practice appears limited.

Moldova

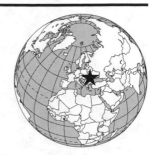

Polity: Presidential-par-
liamentary democracy
Economy: Statist
(transitional)
Population: 3,629,000
PPP: $2,370
Life Expectancy: 67.6
Ethnic Groups: Romanian (65 percent), Ukrainian
(14 percent), Russian (13 percent), others
Capital: Chisinau

Political Rights: 3*
Civil Liberties: 4
Status: Partly Free

Ratings Change: Moldova's political rights rating changed from 4 to 3 because free and fair presidential elections took place in November.

Overview: Petru Lucinschi defeated incumbent president Mircea Snegur in the November presidential election. A constitutional crisis over the attempted dismissal of the defense minister was the other main event in this year's political events in Moldova.

The predominantly Romanian-speaking former Soviet republic, bordering Ukraine and Romania, declared independence from the Soviet Union in 1991. In 1990, Slavs in the Transdniester region, a sliver of land that was part of Ukraine until 1940 and joined to Moldova after Soviet annexation, proclaimed the Dniester Moldovan Republic. Fighting in the Transdniester ended with a ceasefire in 1992.

The bitter feud between Snegur and the Agrarian Democratic Party-dominated (PDAM) government headed by Prime Minister Andrei Sangheli continued this year. Snegur continually threatened to dismiss the government and things took an ugly turn in March. Snegur accused Defense Minister Pavel Creanga of corruption and demanded his resignation. However, under Moldovan law, only the prime minister has the authority to dismiss ministers. After Creanga refused to resign, Snegur dispatched troops which surrounded the building for several hours before an emergency parliamentary session ended the impasse. In April the Constitutional Court ruled the dismissal illegal. Snegur then assumed direct control of the military, a move which the Constitutional Court ruled in December was constitutional given the president's powers as commander-in-chief.

Events seem to have stabilized as of the November presidential election. In the first round, Snegur led the field, with parliament chairman Petru Lucinschi close behind and Sangheli, Communist Vladimir Voronin, and reformist Metei all equally far away. In the second round run-off, Lucinschi comfortably defeated Snegur with 54 percent of the vote. Lucinschi, a former Soviet Communist official who favors closer ties to Russia and the CIS, was backed by the leftist parties, including PDAM, the Socialists and the Communists. Snegur was supported by the pro-Romanian Christian Democratic Popular Front and the Alliance of Democratic Forces, in addition to his Party of Revival and Conciliation of Moldova (PRCM).

Lucinschi forced Sangheli's government to resign in December. However,

Sangheli remained acting prime minister through the end of the year.

The Moldovan economy performed rather well in 1996—growing 3 percent with 21 percent inflation—as a result of reforms initiated by Snegur. However, the shadow economy remains large at 20 percent of GDP, and rural privatization in this predominantly agricultural nation has not yet begun.

Political Rights and Civil Liberties: Moldovan citizens can change their government democratically. According to Organization for Security and Cooperation in Europe (OSCE) observers, the November presidential elections were free and fair. Despite irregularities, such as the intrusive presence of local police and politicians at polls, no systematic problems occurred.

State-owned media are little more than government mouthpieces. However, the largest newspapers are published by political parties, and they frequently criticize government policies. Only about one in four newspapers can be considered independent. A 1994 press law sets out criminal sanctions against "contesting or defaming the state or the people." Several independent local radio stations exist, but no private national radio does. The state-owned Teleradio-Moldova dominates national broadcasting. The private CTV—now a little over a year old—can broadcast only 40 km outside of Chisinau, and has declared its intention to stay out of politics.

Still, five men in police uniforms kidnapped Ion Frunza, the deputy head of CTV. The state has issued conflicting statements on the matter, and Frunza has yet to be located. Three journalists for *Mesagerul*, the party newspaper of the opposition Alliance of Democratic Forces, were beaten up in January; two were threatened with death if they continued to write about police involvement in a racketeering ring. Valeriu Saharneanu, the chairman of the Moldovan Journalists Union, estimated this year that "our state continues to control and censor more than half of the country's publications and audiovisual media."

Corruption remains a major system-wide problem in Moldova. This was ironically underlined when the Moldovan Justice Minister was stopped in Austria driving a stolen car. Privatization not based on the voucher method is very corrupt. In March, top officials resigned as a result of debates on new anti-corruption legislation. The government this year ordered the Interior Ministry to form a department to fight crime and corruption. By mid-year, all civil servants were required to declare revenues, bank accounts and other assets.

A law passed last year bans rallies seen as slandering the state or subverting the constitutional system. In March, a proposed law legalizing the sale of farm land was heatedly debated in parliament, and ultimately rejected.

Freedom of religion is generally respected. Following fierce debates over what constituted an "ethnic minority," Moldova ratified in October the Council of Europe's Convention on the Protection of Ethnic Minorities.

The Soviet code on penal procedure remains largely in place, along with the old Soviet mindset. Police beat suspects and inmates. While prosecutors issue warrants, warrantless searches are not discouraged. The judiciary is still not independent, and the appellate court system is not fully implemented. Obtaining a fair trial in Moldova is frequently difficult. The state often impedes suspects' access to qualified public defenders and hired attorneys. Prosecutors' recommendations carry great weight in trials. Local prosecutors have occasionally brought unjustified charges against those who accuse them of corruption.

Another major problem is that the intelligence services and police continue to monitor Moldovans (especially government opponents) electronically. A major scandal erupted in the run-up to the presidential election this year when national television broadcast an illegally-recorded conversation between two of Snegur's top aides in an attempt to embarrass the president. The prosecutor's office, which is supposed to authorize wiretaps, is unable to exert any real check on the activities of these agencies.

The main trade union organization is the successor to the Soviet-era official organization. Generally, workers are free to strike, except for those in government or strategic sectors like health and energy. Wages are set collectively through national tripartite negotiations between labor, employers and government. Women face no legal obstacles to participating in society.

Monaco

Polity: Prince and
legislative democracy
Economy: Capitalist-statist
Population: 32,000
PPP: na
Life Expectancy: na
Ethnic Groups: French (47 percent), Italian (16 percent),
Monegasque (16 percent), others
Capital: Monaco

Political Rights: 2
Civil Liberties: 1
Status: Free

Overview: January 8, 1997, will mark the 700th anniversary of Monaco's royal family. As the principality prepares to celebrate this milestone, it faces serious economic challenges which will require decisive action if its tradition of prosperity is to be maintained.

Since he came to power in 1949, Prince Rainier III has been responsible for Monaco's impressive economic growth. Under him the economy diversified, ending its exclusive dependence on gambling revenue. He also implemented urban redevelopment programs and built important sports and cultural facilities.

Nevertheless, Monaco's economy is suffering due to increasing competition from other European tourist spots. The property boom of the 1980s has stalled, pushing down prices; the government is racked with deficits unprecedented in recent history; and the state-controlled Societe des Bains de Mer, operator of Monaco's casinos, luxury hotels, and restaurants, has been in the red for three years. Many are wondering whether the measures taken to diversify the economy have been sufficient.

The Principality of Monaco is a full member of the United Nations, recognized internationally as independent and sovereign. During the first six centuries of rule under the Grimaldi family, Monaco was intermittently controlled by European powers until it achieved independence from France in 1861. Under a treaty ratified in 1919, France pledged to protect the territorial integrity, sovereignty, and independence of the principality in return for a guarantee that Monegasque policy would conform to French interests.

Out of a total of 30,000 residents, Monaco is home to only 5000 Monegasques. Only they may participate in the election of the 18-member National Council. The head of state, currently Prince Rainier III, holds executive authority, formally appointing the four-member cabinet and proposing all legislation on which the Council votes. Laws initiated by the prince are drafted in his name by the cabinet and then debated for passage in the National Council. The prince holds veto power over the Council.

Political Rights and Civil Liberties: Citizens of Monaco may change the National Council and their municipal Communal Councils democratically. The prince delegates judicial authority to the courts and tribunals, which adjudicate independently but in his name. Though Monaco does not have a Minister of Justice, it does have a Supreme Court which deals with constitutional claims and jurisdictional conflicts.

Freedom of expression and association is guaranteed by the 1962 constitution. Denunciations of the Grimaldi family are prohibited, however, by an official Monegasque penal code. The Tibetan flag is banned in Monaco, and four pro-Tibetan activists were arrested three years ago for wearing T-shirts that read "Olympics 2000-Not In China" while protesting near the International Olympic Community meeting.

Press freedom is respected. Aside from the weekly government journal and the monthly *Gazette Monaco-Cote d'Azur*, French newspapers publish editions widely available in Monaco. Radio and television are government-operated, and sell time to commercial sponsors. All French broadcasts are freely transmitted to the principality. France maintains a controlling interest in Radio Monte Carlo, which broadcasts in several languages.

Although Monaco experiences chronic labor shortages and relies heavily on migrant and cross-border labor, nationals are given legal preference in employment. Citizenship laws and cultural preservation are issues much discussed, as indigenous Monegasques constitute only about 15 percent of the population. A 1992 law stipulates that foreign women marrying male Monegasque citizens are no longer accorded automatic citizenship. Instead, a provision was introduced which requires women to remain with their spouses for five years to acquire eligibility. Also in 1992, women citizens were granted the right to pass their nationality on to their children.

Freedom of association is respected, including the right of workers to organize. Trade unions are independent of the government. Religious freedom is constitutionally guaranteed; the state religion is Roman Catholic.

Mongolia

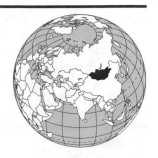

Polity: Presidential-parliamentary democracy
Economy: Statist transitional
Population: 2,323,000
PPP: $2,090
Life Expectancy: 63.9
Ethnic Groups: Khalkha Mongol (75 percent), other Mongol (8 percent), Kazakh (5 percent), others
Capital: Ulaanbaatar

Political Rights: 2
Civil Liberties: 3
Status: Free

Overview: In 1996 Mongolia's democratic transition continued as an opposition coalition swept the ex-Communist Mongolian People's Revolutionary Party (MPRP) out of office after 72 years in power.

China controlled this vast Central Asian region for two centuries until 1911, and again in 1919 until Soviet-backed Marxists seized power in 1921. The MPRP formed a Communist state in 1924 following three years of nominal rule by aging Buddhist lamas. For the next 65 years the country existed as a virtual republic of the Soviet Union.

The country's one-party system began to crack in December 1989 with the formation of the opposition Mongolian Democratic Union. In May 1990 the government scrapped the MPRP's monopoly on power, and in July the country held its first multiparty elections. The MPRP took 357 of 430 seats in the Great Hural (parliament) against an unprepared opposition. In September the Hural named the MPRP's Punsalmaagiyn Ochirbat as president.

In January 1992, parliament approved a new constitution providing for an executive president directly elected for a four-year term. The president names the prime minister and can veto legislation, subject to a two-thirds parliamentary override. The constitution also established a 76-seat, unicameral Great Hural, or parliament.

At the June 1992 Great Hural elections the MPRP--- split into factions ranging from orthodox Communists to free-market reformers---took 71 seats. Two opposition parties, the Mongolian United Party (MUP) and the Social Democratic Party (SDP), took four seats and one seat, respectively. The MPRP formed a new government under Prime Minister Jasrai.

In April 1993, MPRP hardliners combined forces to dump Ochirbat as the party's candidate for the June presidential election, choosing instead Lodongiyn Tudev, editor of the party paper, *Unen* (Truth). Two days later, the opposition Mongolian National Democratic Party, formed in October 1992 through a merger of the MUP and three other opposition parties, and the SDP jointly named Ochirbat as their candidate. Ochirbat won the June 7 election with 57.8 percent of the vote, compared to Tudev's 38.7 percent.

In April 1994, opposition activists demonstrated against official corruption. The strike ended with a government promise to look into the matter; however, little has happened since then.

In the June 1996 legislative elections, the opposition Democratic Union Coalition won 50 out of 76 seats in an upset. The oppositionists' well-planned campaign (with an emphasis on policy as opposed to ideology) and popular frustration with the ongoing economic restructuring to a free-market system contributed to the victory. In the October local elections, the MPRP captured 14 out of 21 provincial assemblies. A Presidential election is scheduled for July 1997.

Political Rights and Civil Liberties:

Mongolians can change their government democratically. The judiciary is independent. A key concern is that many of the civil liberties guaranteed by the constitution have yet to be codified into law. The law does not guarantee a criminal defendant the right to see an attorney. Police and prison officials often beat or otherwise abuse detainees and prisoners. Mongolian law requires prisoners to work for food, clothing, electricity and heat. In April 1995 Amnesty International reported that between autumn 1993 and autumn 1994 more than 90 prisoners had died, many from starvation and related illnesses. The group also reported that prisoners had been deliberately starved prior to trial.

The key constraint on the press is a lack of resources. Most newspapers are printed on a single, aging, government-owned printing press. The government no longer controls the allocation of newsprint, but it is still sometimes in short supply. There are several radio stations and one television station, all owned by the government but offering pluralistic views. Freedom of assembly is respected.

A local human rights group functions without hindrance and freedom of association is respected, although civil society is still rudimentary. Economic and societal changes have caused personal hardship, thereby fueling domestic violence and child abuse. The government has established shelters to assist a growing population of street children, although it has been slow in recognizing the extent of the problem. Freedom of religion is respected in practice, and since the 1990 revolution Buddhist activity has blossomed throughout the country.

All workers can join independent unions. However, civil servants and "essential workers" cannot strike, and the law allows the government to punish union leaders for calling a strike in an essential industry, or where there is "insufficient cause."

Morocco

Polity: Monarchy and limited parliament
Economy: Capitalist-statist
Population: 27,563,000
PPP: $3,270
Life Expectancy: 63.6
Ethnic Groups: Arab and Berber (99 percent), black
Capital: Rabat

Political Rights: 5
Civil Liberties: 5
Status: Partly Free

Overview: **K**ing Hassan II continued to implement his vision of guided democracy in Morocco as a September referendum approved decentralization and a new bicameral legislature. The country's human rights performance showed gradual improvement, but serious problems remained, notably in Western Sahara, where Morocco continued to obstruct a United Nations referendum on independence. Yet international pressure on the issue is weakening, as King Hassan and his heir-apparent, Prince Sidi Mohamed, firmed ties with France, which views Morocco as a crucial ally against rising Islamist power in the Maghreb. Union unrest led to a June general strike as a new labor code was considered, but robust economic growth may reduce the appeal of Islamist radicals among Morocco's poorer classes.

Morocco became independent in 1956 after 44 years of French rule. Hassan II assumed the throne in 1961. Although he is basically a traditional autocrat, Hassan II has allowed democratic institutions to evolve. Real power still rests in the palace; the king appoints the prime minister and dissolves the legislature, which has very limited authority, when he chooses. The opposition "Democratic Bloc" took 119 seats in the 1993 parliamentary elections, despite many credible reports of irregularities. Demanding reforms, opposition parties have refused to join a national unity cabinet; topping their list is a revision of the electoral code.

Hassan II claims direct lineage from the prophet Mohammed and carries the title of "Commander of the Faithful," but this only serves to infuriate Islamist radicals.

Political Rights and Civil Liberties: **M**oroccans cannot change their government by democratic means. The King is head of state and must approve any constitutional changes. A new constitution approved in a September referendum, with virtually no dissent, will lead to the creation of a bicameral legislature with a directly-elected Chamber of Representatives and an upper house selected by an electoral college of trade union, employer, professional groups and local council representatives. The current unicameral legislature serves as a useful forum for political debate, with 16 political parties represented and oppositionists holding over one-third of the seats. But it does not govern, and it is not clear that the new parliament will possess any powers. Provincial and local officials are appointed, with only less-powerful municipal councils elected. A trend continues towards more openness, but governance remains neither transparent nor accountable.

Constitutional guarantees of free expression are not binding. Increased liberalization has produced independent and pluralistic print media, but serious constraints remain. Broadcast media are still mostly in government hands. Political control is exercised through publication licensing requirements. The press code empowers the Interior Ministry to seize or censor publications. Criticizing the King or his family can bring five to 20 years' imprisonment. Other issues are beyond criticism, including the validity of Morocco's claim to Western Sahara and the sanctity of Islam. At least 16 books, magazines and newspapers have been banned, and numerous issues of foreign publications seized, over the last decade. In September, the Interior Ministry banned a performance by popular satirist Ahmed Sanoussi, who has regularly lampooned government censorship. In November, one of the country's best-read political newspapers, the independent weekly *al-Oussbou Assahafi Assiassi*, was banned.

Freedom of assembly is constitutionally protected but limited by the requirement that public gatherings receive permits from the Interior Ministry. Religious freedom is limited to Islam, Christianity and Judaism, although proselytizing is barred. Many nongovernmental organizations operate, including three officially-recognized human rights groups. In recent years, they have issued reports detailing torture, harsh prison conditions and the harassment of former political prisoners. At least 300 Western Saharan activists have disappeared over the last decade.

The courts are subject to political control. Civil code provisions discriminate against women, and societal discrimination is acute. Women enjoy no entitlements or support after a divorce, and much domestic violence is unreported and unpunished. An active women's lobby, led by the Moroccan Association for Human Rights for Women (AMDF), is campaigning for legal reforms to protect women's rights.

Morocco's formal labor sector is strongly unionized. About five million workers are members of 17 umbrella federations, some of which are aligned with various political parties. The government generally respects labor rights, including the right to bargain collectively and to strike. A general strike demanding improved pay paralyzed the country in June, and in April security forces wounded at least seven unionists protesting provisions of a new labor code. Talks between union leaders and government officials in October brought agreement on the disposition of $350 million in social benefits.

Mozambique

Polity: Presidential-
legislative democracy
Economy: Mixed statist
Population: 16,537,000
PPP: $640
Life Expectancy: 46.4
Ethnic Groups: Lomwe, Makonde, Makua, Ndau,
Shangaan, Thonga, Yao, others
Capital: Maputo

Political Rights: 3
Civil Liberties: 4
Status: Partly Free

Overview:
Mozambique's abandonment of decades of repressive rule,
first of the Portuguese colonial and then of the Marxist one-
party variety, continued in 1996. Economic reconstruction
gave hope that Mozambique would soon cease to be the poorest country in the world.
Tensions between the ruling National Front for the Liberation of Mozambique
(Frelimo) and its long-time guerrilla foe, the Mozambique National Resistance
(Renamo) remain, but seem increasingly likely to be resolved peacefully. Widespread banditry and endemic corruption threatened stability, however, as did incipient tensions between the country's Christians and Muslims.

A protracted and costly guerrilla war preceded Portugal's 1975 surrender of
power to the then-Marxist Frelimo party. Renamo rebels were organized and armed,
first by the white-minority Rhodesian regime, and then by South Africa's secret
services. The bush war was one of Africa's most deadly and devastating. The end
of the Cold War led to a negotiated peace and the 1992 Rome Accords. Both sides
accepted multiparty elections and largely disarmed. Frelimo discarded socialist
economics along with one-party rule, and its leader, President Joaquim Chissano,
won a clear victory in October 1994 elections that also gave Frelimo 129 seats in
the 250-seat parliament. Renamo took the balance save for nine seats won by the
Democratic Union party. The UN had paid for the elections, and despite initial protests, Renamo accepted the results along with promises of further international funding.

Full integration of Renamo's wartime parallel administration in Mozambique's
central provinces, which are the party's stronghold, is still contentious. Renamo
leader Afonso Dhlakama pressed for greater representation in government as Frelimo
continued to reject the idea of a power-sharing coalition.

**Political Rights
and Civil Liberties:**
In a massive turnout, Mozambique's people freely chose
their government in the country's first genuine open elections in October 1994. The UN spent over $60 million to
run the polls, and declared them free and fair. Consolidation of the democratic process is far from certain. Funding for scheduled presidential and legislative elections
in 1999 may not be available. Local polls set for 1996 have been postponed until at
least May 1997 for lack of international aid. Frelimo enjoys an absolute parliamentary majority, and Renamo's strong showing in winning 38 percent has not translated into a serious voice in national policy.

Eighteen political parties contested the 1994 legislative elections, although some suffered intermittent harassment. Nongovernmental organizations are increasingly able to work openly and some, like the Mozambican Human Rights League, issue reports critical of official conduct, including appalling prison conditions that lead to many prisoner deaths. Police brutality is also widely reported, compounded by a lack of accountability throughout the government and a weak judiciary. In November, criticism of police performance led to the dismissal of the interior minister.

The constitution and the peace pact that ended the long bush war protect media freedom. The state controls most media and owns or influences several of the most important newspapers. Direct criticism of the president or reporting on widespread corruption is rare, and self-censorship is widely practiced. Criminal libel laws are an important deterrent to open expression, as is harassment and intimidation of independent journalists. The opposition is covered very little in government media, which remain largely Frelimo propaganda tools. Independent newspapers and fax newsletters published in Maputo have scant influence outside the capital.

Free religious practice suffers no reported interference. Mozambique's legal structures are antiquated relics of the Portuguese colonial era, and often conflict with new statutes or the constitution. Women suffer both legal and societal discrimination. Inheritance laws limit widow's rights, and women have less access to education and formal sector jobs, particularly in rural areas where 80 percent of the population lives. Wife-beating is said to be common.

Mozambique's labor unions were long under Frelimo control. The major trade confederation, the Organization of Mozambican Workers, is now nominally independent. In 1994, a second and independent group, the Organization of Free and Independent Unions, was formed. Other than employees of essential services, workers have the right to strike, and the right to bargain collectively is legally protected.

The government has continued a broad program of privatization, and has attracted some major Western investors, including many from the ex-colonial power, Portugal. Some Frelimo elements appear not to be committed to market reforms, however, and severe corruption deters some investors. Among the more intrepid arrivals were a group of 13 white South African farmers to whom the government granted land in October in hopes of spurring the growth of agribusiness. Good rains had raised expectations for a larger harvest, although threatened by an infestation of red locusts late in the year.

Namibia

Polity: Presidential-
legislative democracy
Economy: Capitalist-statist
Population: 1,580,000
PPP: $3,710
Life Expectancy: 59.1
Ethnic Groups: Ovambo (47 percent), Kavango (9 percent),
Herero, Damara, Baster and Colored, European, Nama/Hottentot,
Bushman, others
Capital: Windhoek

Political Rights: 2
Civil Liberties: 3
Status: Free

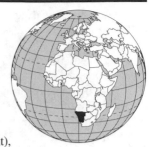

Overview:

Namibia faced a severe drought that threatened steady economic growth, amidst concerns that increasing income disparities are leaving most Namibians with few material benefits after nearly seven years of independence. The country faces growing demands on limited resources by ethnic minorities and the many poor and unemployed. Unease over a military buildup in neighboring Botswana could divert funds desperately needed for development to arms spending. The government, dominated since 1990 by President Sam Nujoma's South West Africa People's Organization (SWAPO), continued to respect civil and political rights, and Namibia remains one of Africa's most open and democratic societies.

Namibia was conquered by German colonialists in the nineteenth century, but awarded to South Africa as a protectorate after German forces were driven out during World War I. It was administered by South Africa from 1948 until independence in 1990, following 13 years of bitter guerrilla war. The U.N.-supervised democratic transition included free and fair elections. The country's first post-independence elections took place in November 1994, and saw a sweeping SWAPO victory and President Nujoma's re-election with over 70 percent of the vote. Respect for the rule of law has been consolidated since independence, and legislation expanding constitutional guarantees has been enacted.

SWAPO's first term in power saw broad support for national reconciliation and a willingness by all groups to defer expectations of quick economic progress. Increasing militancy has appeared among several groups, including ex-guerrilla fighters and workers. Minority ethnic groups charge that the predominant Ovambo ethnic group, which makes up about half the population and is a bedrock of SWAPO support, receives a disproportionate share of development funds.

**Political Rights
and Civil Liberties:**

Namibians are able to choose their president and legislative representatives through free and fair elections, and in November 1994 citizens exercised their constitutional right for the second time. President Sam Nujoma was re-elected in a landslide and SWAPO captured 53 of 72 National Assembly seats. Some observers fear SWAPO might use this huge majority to make constitutional changes inimical to multiparty democracy. SWAPO dominance might also raise ethnic tensions in a diverse country where the ruling party's main support comes from the country's single largest ethnic group, the Ovambo.

Namibia's human rights record ranks among Africa's best. Political discussion is open and uninhibited. Political parties can organize and operate freely. The greatest constraint on political activity is financial, especially with Namibia's 1.6 million people spread over such a vast country. Opposition parties accuse SWAPO of using government transport and employees for party work. Legislation enacted in 1996 will provide state financing for political parties, but the formula adopted, according to which grants are awarded in direct proportion to votes received in the last general election, will reinforce only established parties and bolster SWAPO above all.

In general, the media are free. The state dominates electronic media, although the government has generally respected the editorial independence of the Namibia Broadcasting Corporation, which has regularly presented views critical of the government. Private radio stations operate, and independent newspapers, some strongly partisan, operate without official interference. Yet the independent press watchdog group, the Media Institute of Southern Africa, warned that continued vigilance is necessary. It led a successful campaign to scrap proposed legislation in 1996 that would have introduced restrictions on the reporting of parliamentary activities.

Local human rights groups target specific areas where respect for human rights could be improved. Improper arrests and police mistreatment of suspects remains common, according to the Legal Assistance Centre and the National Society for Human Rights. Especially in rural areas, local chiefs with power over traditional courts often ignore constitutional procedures in arresting and trying suspects, although usually involving minor offenses.

The country's smaller ethnic groups, including Herero and Damara people, are demanding larger government allocations for development in their home areas. Increasingly vocal criticism is being made of the large disparity in incomes between the country's economic elite made up of the 6 percent white minority and an increasing, but still relatively small, number of blacks, and the vast majority of Namibians, who earn an average monthly wage of less than $20. The gap was highlighted this year as members of parliament voted a large salary increase for themselves and for a broad range of civil servants. Land reform programs are slowly being implemented, and may help the country's poor rural majority, but the country's priorities were questioned again in May when a bilateral defense treaty with Russia provided for huge weapons purchases. The move is justified as response to a string of arms acquisitions by neighboring Botswana, with which Namibia contests demarcation of their riverine border, a dispute now being considered by the International Court of Justice.

Women continue to face serious discrimination despite constitutional guarantees. Legislation adopted in 1996 removed the legal definition of married women as minors without economic rights. Obstacles in customary law and other traditional societal practices persist, such as unequal rights to property. In some areas, widows can be divested of all property by their late spouse's family. Rape and other violence against women is reported to be widespread.

Trade union rights are constitutionally guaranteed and the government has not interfered with union formation or operation. The right to strike for all but essential public sector workers is similarly protected, and the 1992 Labor Act broadened that right to include government employees and farm and domestic workers. Trade unions registration is required but treated as a formality. Some domestic and farm workers remain heavily exploited, union organizers say, because many are illiterate and do not understand their rights. The National Union of Namibian Workers and the Namibia People's Social Movement are the two main union federations.

Economic development is based on the extractive industries which reguire large amounts of capital. Medium-size businesses are still largely dominated by the white minority. The state has encouraged private investment but a small domestic market has limited economic opportunity for small-scale entrepreneurs. The government plans to create major export-process zones. The Namibian government's greatest challenge over the next year will be to maintain its generally exemplary human rights record while trying to improve the country's economic performance.

Nauru

Polity: Parliamentary democracy
Economy: Mixed capitalist-statist
Population: 11,000
PPP: na
Life Expectancy: na

Political Rights: 1
Civil Liberties: 3
Status: Free

Ethnic Groups: Nauruan (58 percent), other Pacific islander (26 percent), Chinese (8 percent), European (8 percent)
Capital: Yaren

Overview: Nauru, a tiny island located 1,600 miles northeast of New Zealand, became a German protectorate in 1888. Following World War I Australia administered the island under mandates from the League of Nations and, later, from the United Nations. The country achieved independence on January 31, 1968.

Following the November 1995 general elections, parliament elected Lagumot Harris as president over three-term incumbent Bernard Dowiyogo. On November 12, 1996, parliament replaced Harris with Dowiyogo. No explanation was given for the change.

Phosphate mining has given Nauru one of the highest per capita incomes in the world. Decades of mining have left 80 percent of the island uninhabitable, however. After independence the Nauruan government sought additional compensation from Australia for mining done during the trusteeship period. Nauru claimed that the royalties it received during the trusteeship period were inadequate since Australia had sold the phosphates domestically at below world-market prices.

In 1989 Nauru sued Australia in the International Court of Justice for additional royalties as well as for compensation for the physical damages done to the eight-square-mile island. In July 1993 the two sides reached an out-of-court settlement under which Australia agreed to pay $70.4 million in compensation over 20 years. The government is currently examining plans for a 23-year program to rehabilitate mined-out areas.

The government's $700 million Nauru Phosphate Royalties Trust (NPRT) will provide income for future generations after the phosphate supply is depleted. In recent years several government agencies have borrowed from the fund, leaving it dangerously overloaded with high-risk property investments. Moreover, the NPRT has lost millions of dollars in imprudent investments.

Political Rights and Civil Liberties:

Citizens of Nauru can change their government democratically. The 1968 constitution provides for an 18-member parliament, representing 14 constituencies, that is directly elected for a three-year term. Parliament elects the president, who serves as head of state and head of government, from among its members. The elected Nauru Local Government Council provides public services. Political parties are legal although none has formed. Instead, parliamentary blocs coalesce according to specific issues.

The judiciary is independent of the government, and the accused enjoy full procedural safeguards. Many cases are settled out of court through traditional mediation procedures. The government-owned Radio Nauru carries Radio Australia and BBC broadcasts, but not local news. A private fortnightly newspaper, the *Central Star News* publishes, as does a weekly government information bulletin. A private television service broadcasts from New Zealand. Several foreign publications are available.

A key problem is the treatment of women in this male-dominated society. The Dowiyogo government emphasized the child-bearing role of women, and reportedly revoked the scholarships of some Nauruan women studying abroad in order to discourage them from joining the workforce. The Dowiyogo government also failed to address the problem of domestic violence.

Freedom of assembly is generally respected. There are no restrictions on freedom of association, although in practice few formal elements of civil society are present. All religious faiths worship freely.

The constitution guarantees workers the right of association, although successive governments have generally discouraged labor organizing and no trade unions have formed. Workers do not have formal rights to bargain collectively or to hold strikes. Foreign workers are generally housed in inadequate facilities and claim that they do not receive the same level of police protection as do Nauruan citizens. By law, any foreign worker who is fired must leave the country within 60 days.

Nepal

Polity: Parliamentary democracy
Economy: Capitalist
Population: 23,226,000
PPP: $1,000
Life Expectancy: 53.8
Ethnic Groups: Newar, Indian, Tibetan, Gurung, Magar, Tamang, Bhotia, others
Capital: Kathmandu

Political Rights: 3
Civil Liberties: 4
Status: Partly Free

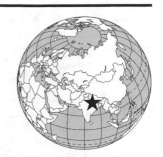

Overview:

Nepalese prime minister Sher Bahadur Deuba held his year-old ruling coalition together in 1996 but faced a potential leadership challenge from within his Nepali Congress (NC) party.

King Prithvi Narayan Shah unified this Himalayan land in 1769. Following two centuries of palace rule, in 1959 the center-left NC won the country's first elections. A year later, after the NC had initiated land reforms, King Mahendra dissolved parliament and banned political parties.

Pro-democracy demonstrations beginning in early 1990 climaxed violently in April when police fired on demonstrators in Kathmandu. King Birendra acceded to a constitution, promulgated in November, that established a multiparty parliamentary system with an elected 205-seat House of Representatives and an appointed 60-member National Council.

Nepal's first multiparty elections in 32 years, in May 1991, brought the NC to power under premier Giraja Prasid Koirala. Koirala's tenure was marked by opposition protests over the 1991 Tanakpur hydroelectric agreement with India and internal NC wrangling. In June 1994, after losing a budget vote, Koirala resigned and persuaded the King to call early elections.

Key issues in the November 5, 1994, elections included rising prices and the NC's factionalism and corruption. The Communist Party of Nepal (United Marxist-Leninist) (CPN-UML) won 88 seats; NC, 83; the pro-monarchist National Democratic Party (RPP), 20; minor parties and independents, 14. In late November the CPN-UML's Man Mohan Adhikary formed Nepal's first Communist government.

The minority Adhikary government initiated land reforms and other populist measures. In June 1995 Adhikari, facing a no-confidence motion, convinced the King to call fresh elections. In late August the Supreme Court ruled the request unconstitutional, and on September 10 the NC, RPP and the tiny Nepal Goodwill Party voted down the government. The three parties formed a coalition government under the NC's Sher Bahadur Deuba.

The May 1996 election of former premier Koirala as NC president set up a potential challenge to Deuba's leadership prior to the next general elections, due in 1999. In September parliament ratified the controversial Mahakali River Treaty with India, which critics say affords greater electricity and irrigation benefits to New Delhi. In December Deuba's coalition narrowly won a vote of confidence.

In another development, on February 12 the radical Communist Party of Nepal

(Maoist) (CPN-Maoist) launched a "people's war" in several midwestern hill districts. By mid-November terrorist attacks and police shootouts had killed 62 people and wounded dozens of others.

Political Rights and Civil Liberties:

Nepalese can change their government democratically. The 1994 elections were free but were marred by vote selling, ballot box tampering and other irregularities. Low-caste Hindus and ethnic minority groups are politically marginalized. The country's location between China and India has led successive governments to limit discussion of numerous sensitive issues.

In 1996 the Deuba government further politicized an already partisan bureaucracy by placing some 60 "advisors" in key positions and creating 24 new top civil service posts. Corruption is entrenched in politics.

The rule of law is weak and police impunity continues to be a key human rights issue. Officers frequently use excessive force in routine situations, beat suspects to extract confessions and abuse prisoners. Several custodial deaths have occurred in recent years. The government rarely prosecutes offending officers. In 1996 human rights activists accused authorities of using excessive force in countering the CPN-Maoist insurgency in midwestern Nepal. In the past three years police have shown greater discipline during public demonstrations.

The Public Security Act (PSA), as amended in 1991, allows the government to detain suspects for up to12 months without charge. The 1970 Public Offenses Act grants the 75 Chief District Officers broad powers to detain suspects. By law ordinary detainees must be brought before a court within 24 hours of arrest, but this is frequently ignored. The Supreme Court is independent but lower courts are susceptible to political influence. Procedural safeguards during trials are adequate.

The constitution restricts speech or writing that could jeopardize national security, promote communal discord or do harm in other broadly-defined areas. The Press and Publications Act places restrictions on articles regarding the monarchy, national security and other sensitive issues, and requires journalists to be licensed. Nevertheless, private newspapers and magazines vigorously criticize government policies. The government owns the main Nepali-language paper and the sole television and radio stations, which do not adequately cover opposition viewpoints.

Successive governments have been wary of offending India or China. On March 18, authorities arrested some 200 human rights activists beginning a march to the Chinese embassy, and in June police arrested 15 activists protesting a recent Chinese nuclear test. The government similarly restricts discussion of Indian rights abuses in Kashmir. Nongovernmental organizations are active and operate freely.

Religious freedom is respected. Caste discrimination is prevalent in rural areas. More than 100,000 ethnic Thaurus, a lower-caste group, are bonded laborers in southwestern Nepal. Women face legal discrimination in property and divorce matters, and rarely receive the same educational opportunities as men. Domestic violence is common. Tens of thousands of Nepalese women and girls, many from the Tamang, Gurung and other ethnic minority groups, have been trafficked to Indian brothels with the complicity of border police. Those who manage to return to Nepal are often ostracized by their relatives and communities.

Nepal hosts some 90,000 Bhutanese refugees (see Bhutan report) and has assimilated more than 20,000 Tibetan asylum-seekers. However, police occasionally use excessive force against Tibetans crossing the border, and in recent years authorities have forcibly deported, turned back or turned over to Chinese authorities scores of asylum seekers.

An estimated three million children are laborers, many of them bonded laborers. Many of the hundreds of street children in Kathmandu and other cities work as ragpickers or street vendors. Enforcement of labor laws protecting children is nearly nonexistent. Workers are free to join independent unions. Strikes are prohibited in certain "essential services," and the government can suspend a strike or a trade union on "national interest" grounds.

Netherlands

Polity: Parliamentary democracy
Economy: Mixed capitalist
Population: 15,545,000
PPP: $17,340
Life Expectancy: 77.5
Ethnic Groups: Dutch (97 percent), Indonesian, others
Capital: Amsterdam

Political Rights: 1
Civil Liberties: 1
Status: Free

Overview: As the Netherlands prepares to assume the presidency of the European Union (EU) in January 1997, its September budget indicates that the guilder will be among the founding members of the European Monetary Union in 1999. With low inflation and a deficit well within the Maastricht treaty criteria, the country's only remaining problem is its debt. At 76.2 percent of GDP, government debt is higher than the 60 percent allowed by the Maastricht Treaty.

The Dutch won independence from Spain in the sixteenth century, whereupon the governors of the House of Orange assumed rule of the United Provinces of the Netherlands. A constitutional monarchy based on representative government emerged at the close of the Napoleonic period. Queen Beatrix appoints the arbiters of executive authority, the Council of Ministers and the governor of each province on the recommendation of the majority in parliament, which she cannot refuse. The bicameral States General (parliament) consists of an indirectly-elected First Chamber and a larger and more powerful directly-elected Second Chamber.

From the end of World War II until December 1958, the Netherlands was governed by coalitions in which the Labor and Catholic parties predominated. From 1958 to 1994, governments were formed from center-right coalitions of Christian Democrats and Liberals, with the social democratic-oriented Labor party usually in opposition.

The current government, formed in August 1994, is a three-way "Purple Coalition" of the Labor, Liberal, and Democrats '66 parties, headed by Prime Minister Kok of the Labor Party. The coalition parties hold 92 of the 150 seats in the Second Chamber, the Christian Democratic Appeal constituting the main opposition with 34 seats. Eight minor parties hold the remaining 24 seats.

The Netherlands' tolerant drug policy met growing opposition in the EU, most notably from France. Drugs are not legal in the Netherlands, but they are commonly bought and sold in urban coffee shops. Dutch policy treats domestic drug use as a health issue rather than as a legal issue, stressing prevention and treatment.

France and the Netherlands put aside their dispute in November when France agreed to amend the EU's joint action on drug policy. A passage in the agreement which could be interpreted as a mandate to close Dutch coffee shops was scrapped.

Political Rights and Civil Liberties:

The Dutch can change their government democratically. A series of amendments to the original constitution has provided for welfare and democratic reform. Local voting rights are accorded to foreigners after five years in residence.

A 24-member Supreme Court heads an independent judiciary which includes five courts of appeal, 19 district courts and 62 lower courts. All judicial appointments are made by the crown on the basis of nominations by the parliament. Judges are nominally appointed for life but actually retire at age 70.

The press in the Netherlands is free and independent, though journalists practice self-censorship when reporting on the royal family. All Dutch newspapers cooperate in the administration of the independent Netherlands News Agency. Radio and television broadcasting operate autonomously under the supervision and regulation of the state, and offer pluralistic views. Free speech is guaranteed, with the exceptions of promulgation of racism and incitement to racism.

The Kurdish station MED-TV is fighting to keep its right to broadcast in the Netherlands, after having lost that right in Portugal, France and Poland. The Turkish ambassador has been pressing the Netherlands to take action against the station, which Turkey regards as a "propaganda instrument." The Dutch Media Commission, Foreign Ministry, and Education and Culture Ministry are examining the extent to which MED-TV needs a permit to produce programs in the Netherlands.

Integration of racial and ethnic minorities into the social and cultural mainstream remains a difficult domestic issue. Discrimination on the basis of race or nationality is prohibited by law, and those who believe that they have been discriminated against may take the offender to court under civil law. According to the Criminal Investigation Service, the number of incidents of violence against foreigners and ethnic minorities had increased in recent years.

Immigrant groups face some de facto discrimination in housing and employment. Concentrated in the larger cities, immigrants suffer from a high rate of unemployment. The government has been working for several years with employers' groups and unions to reduce minority unemployment levels to the national average. As a result of these efforts in recent years, the rate of job creation among ethnic minorities has been higher than among the general population.

Membership in labor unions is open to all workers including military, police and civil service employees. People are entitled to form or join unions of their own choosing without previous government authorization, and unions are free to affiliate with national trade union federations.

Freedom of religion is respected. The population is over 50 percent Protestant, and roughly 35 percent Catholic. The state continues to subsidize church-affiliated schools based on the number of registered students.

New Zealand

Polity: Parliamentary democracy
Economy: Capitalist
Population: 3,602,000
PPP: $16,720
Life Expectancy: 75.6
Ethnic Groups: European (79 percent), Maori (12 percent), Pacific islander (3 percent), others
Capital: Wellington

Political Rights: 1
Civil Liberties: 1
Status: Free

Overview:

New Zealand achieved full self-government prior to World War II, and gained formal independence from Great Britain in 1947. Since 1935, political power in this parliamentary democracy has alternated between the mildly conservative National Party and the center-left Labor Party, both of which helped develop one of the world's most progressive welfare states. In response to an increasingly competitive global trade regime, in 1984 the incoming Labor government began an economic deregulation program that included cutting farm subsidies, slashing tariffs and privatizing many industries.

The harsh effects of the economic reforms and a deep recession contributed to a National Party landslide at the October 1990 parliamentary elections. Rather than slow the reforms, however, new Prime Minister Jim Bolger's government continued them by slashing welfare payments, restructuring the labor law to discourage collective bargaining, and ending universal free hospital care.

The October 1996 parliamentary elections were based on a new electoral system. Voters had chosen to replace the first-past-the-post electoral system with a mixed-member proportional system (MMP). Each citizen got two votes for an expanded parliament: the first was cast for the 65 geographical constituency seats, and the second for the 55 seats decided by party-preference proportional representation. The results left neither the National Party nor the Labor Party with a majority, and Winston Peter's New Zealand First held the balance of power. After two months of negotiations the latter formed a coalition with the National Party, giving Prime Minister Jim Bolger a third term in office. Most noteworthy in this election, 15 Maori politicians entered the new parliament, proportionate to the 13 percent Maori population. A record 80 percent of the Maoris turned out to vote.

Resolution of land claims by the Maori minority remains a key issue. Winston Peter had persuaded the National Party to drop the limit of $1 billion as compensation for land confiscation. Under the 1840 Treaty of Waitangi, the Maori ceded sovereignty to the British in return for guarantees on land rights. However, by 1890 the Maori had lost all but 4.4 million of the country's 26.8 million hectares, and that figure has since shrunk to 1.2 million hectares. In late 1994, the government established a $633 million fund to settle all outstanding Maori land claims within ten years. In December 1994, the government reached a settlement with the Waikato tribe that included a $41.6 million cash payment and an award of public land valued at $66.5 million. However, many Maori leaders rejected the fund as being too small and refused to negotiate.

In 1995 Maori activists waged a civil disobedience campaign that included symbolic occupations of parks and other tracts they claimed as ancestral lands. In May the Tainui tribe signed a cash-and-land package worth $112 million, putting pressure on other Maori groups to negotiate or go empty-handed.

Political Rights and Civil Liberties:

New Zealanders can change their government democratically. Four parliamentary seats are reserved for representatives of the Maori minority. Several new parties have formed to contest the vote.

New Zealand has no written constitution, but all fundamental freedoms are respected in practice. The judiciary is independent and trials are free and open. The country has a vigorous private press. The broadcast media are both privately and publicly held, and express a variety of viewpoints. In January 1995, Maori activists disrupted a news broadcast at the central studio of the TVNZ television network to protest what it called insufficient Maori-language programming. The network promised to review the grievances. Civil society is well developed. Freedom of religion is respected. The authorities are responsive to complaints of rape and domestic violence. The Domestic Violence Act came into effect in July.

The indigenous Maori minority and the tiny Pacific Islander population face unofficial discrimination in employment and education opportunities. The 1983 Equal Employment Opportunities Policy, designed to bring more minorities into the public sector, has been only marginally successful. Maori leaders are also pressing for more equitable returns on their so-called reserved land. An agreement reached in the nineteenth century, and codified in 1955, leases Maori land in perpetuity to the "settlers." Today, the rents received by the Maori on some 2,500 leases average far lower than those received by commercial landowners.

Workers can join independent trade unions, and collective bargaining is legal. However, the 1991 Employment Contracts Act (ECA) has weakened the power of unions by banning compulsory membership and other practices that had made unions the sole, mandatory negotiators on behalf of employees. Contracts are now generally drawn up at the factory or even at the individual level, and wages and union membership rolls have fallen. In 1994, the ILO criticized a provision of the ECA that prohibits strikes designed to force an employer to sign an industry-wide contract.

Nicaragua

Polity: Presidential-leg-
islative democracy
(military-influenced)
Economy: Capitalist-statist
Population: 4,584,000
PPP: $2,280
Life Expectancy: 67.1
Ethnic Groups: Mestizo (69 percent), European (17 percent),
black (9 percent), Indian (5 percent)
Capital: Managua

Political Rights: 3*
Civil Liberties: 3*
Status: Partly Free

Ratings Change: Nicaragua's political rights and civil liberties ratings changed
from 4 to 3 because the election of President Aleman was an important move
toward the stabilization of the country.

Overview:

In October 1996, conservative businessman and former
Managua mayor Arnoldo Aleman, leader of the Liberal
Alliance (AL), was elected president; he defeated ex-presi-
dent Daniel Ortega of the Sandinista National Liberation Front (FSLN), 51 to 38
percent. Though the European Union and others among the 3,000 international observers deemed the election free and fair, irregularities and registration problems.
The country remains politically polarized by such issues as land ownership, poverty, and criminal activities by ex-Contras and ex-Sandinistas.

The Republic of Nicaragua was established in 1838, 17 years after independence from Spain. Its history has been marked by internal strife and dictatorship.
The authoritarian rule of the Somoza regime was overthown in 1979 by the
Sandinistas. Subsequently, the Sandinista National Liberation Front (FSLN) attempted to impose a Marxist dictatorship, which led to a civil war and indirect U.S.
intervention of behalf of the Contras. The FSLN finally conceded in 1987 to a new
constitution that provides for a president and a 96-member National Assembly elected
every six years. Under the dictatorial Sandinista regime, the economy came close
to collapse and inflation ran at 3,000 percent. Shortly before the 1990 elections,
hundreds of thousands of acres of farmland were turned over to peasant cooperatives under a land reform program while Sandinistan leaders confiscated the best
luxury properties and businesses for themselves.

In 1990, newspaper publisher Violeta Chamorro easily defeated incumbent
President Ortega. Her 14-party National Opposition Union (UNO) won a legislative majority in the National Assembly. Chamorro gave substantial authority to her
son-in-law and presidency minister Antonio Lacayo. Lacayo reached an agreement
with Ortega's brother Humberto, allowing him to remain head of the military.
Lacayo's action caused allegations within the UNO of a co-government. UNO soon
unraveled into a number of factions. Later, the FSLN split, with moderates following former vice-president Sergio Ramirez to found the social-democratic Sandinista
Renewal Movement (MRS), while hardliners remained with Daniel Ortega in a rump-
FSLN.

In 1994, the MRS and the anti-Lacayo UNO factions proposed constitutional reforms to limit the powers of the president and end nepotism in presidential succession. Lacayo and Daniel Ortega opposed the measure. In February 1995, after passage of a law ensuring the military's autonomy, Humberto Ortega turned over command of the military to General Joaquin Cuadra. The army was reduced from 90,000 to 15,000 troops. Despite the apparent "de-politicization" of the army, including the integration of former Contras, the leadership remained essentially the same. The armed forces continued to own a profitable network of business and property amassed under the Sandinista regime.

Mrs. Chamorro was forbidden by law to seek a second term. The 1996 elections were held under the auspices of the five-member Supreme Election Council (CSE), an independent branch of government. The CSE was burdened with issuing national identification cards and voting documents, and delays and confusion ensued over registration. Much of the confusion was due to a fraudulent 1995 census that grossly undercounted the population, thus disenfranchising 400,000 voters likely to vote Liberal. About 352,000 "lost" peasants were "found" among 600,000 "missed" Nicaraguans, adding 15 percent back to the electorate.

During the 1996 campaign, Ortega tried to portray himself as a moderate committed to national unity and reconciliation. He dismissed the hardline former head of security, Tomas Borge, and his running mate was non-Sandinista Juan Manuel Calderal, a prominent cattle rancher. In September, Ortega signed a pact with several one-time Contra leaders, promising them three cabinet posts. He also promised not to reinstate the military draft and to honor land-dispute resolutions reached under President Chamorro. The CSE banned five candidates, including Alvaro Robelo, a banker believed to have been involved in international money-laundering; Antonio Lacayo, because he was president Chamorro's son-in-law (he was also accused of diverting $30 million in Venezuelan aid to finance his campaign); and Eden Pastora, the ex-Sandinista known as "Commandante Zero," who was disqualified because he had become a citizen of Costa Rica.

In all, 24 candidates vied for the presidency. Aleman ran on a platform that promised economic reforms, dismantling the Sandinista-era bureaucracy, cleaning up the army and returning property confiscated by the Sandinistas to its original owners. Unlike President Chamorro, who sought negotiation and compromise with the Sandinistas, Aleman took a hard line against the FSLN. He defeated Ortega 51 to 38 percent, avoiding a run-off.

In elections to the National Assembly, the Liberal Alliance won 42 seats; the FSLN, 36; the Party of the Nicaraguan Christian Road (PCCN), 4; the National Project (Pronal), 2; Conservative Party of Nicaragua (PCN), 2; the MRS, 1; the Nicaraguan Resistance Party (PRN), 1; the Unity Alliance (Unidad), 1; the Independent Liberal party (PLI),1; and the UNO 96, 1. Twenty deputies were chosen from nationwide lists, 70 from lists presented in each of the 15 departments and 2 autonomous regions, and three defeated presidential candidates added another three. In November, Ortega was chosen FSLN legislative bloc leader.

President-elect Aleman's top priority was to reform the army and the police. President Chamorro had served as nominal Minister of Defense, with real power exercised by General Humberto Ortega as military commander. President-elect Aleman named civilian Jaime Cuadra Somarriba as head of a civilian-led Defense Ministry. While the Army General Staff continues to be dominated by the Sandinistas the new military code will secure greater power for the defense minister. The size of the national police has been reduced from 16,000 to 6,800, but its leadership is still made up of old Sandinista cadres. For changes in the military code to pass the national assembly, Aleman and the AL would have to cobble together a coalition, probably with the PCCN, Pronal and the PCN. The substantial Sandinista bloc in the Assembly suggests that any attempt to pass property and constitutional reform legislation will lead to dangerous polarization.

Political Rights and Civil Liberties: Nicaraguans can change their government democratically. Though the FSLN and other parties claimed that the elections were illegitimate they were deemed free and fair by international observers. The 1996 elections were plagued by irregularities such as armed groups disrupting registration in rural areas. In general, the military remains a powerful political force through substantial property and monetary holdings.

Political parties are allowed to organize; over 20 candidates ran for president and nine parties or blocs are represented in the National Assembly. But political and civic activities continue to be restricted by intermittent political violence, corruption and drug-related crime.

Numerous bands of former Contras continue to operate in the north, competing in criminal activities with groups of former Sandinista soldiers. The cash-strapped government has been unable to guarantee land grants or credits to former Contras, the core of the 1990 Contra demobilization agreement. The army and the Sandinistas control the mountains from Matagalpa eastward and the Organization of American States (OAS) estimates that more than 300 former Contras have been murdered (some analysts put the number at 700). A Tripartite Commission, set up by President Chamorro in 1992, looked into the unresolved deaths of former Contras. The commission concluded its review in October 1996 and recommended action in 83 human rights cases which involve the deaths of 164 ex-combatants. As of the end of the year, however, no action had been taken.

Violence and lack of government control over large parts of the country place de facto restrictions on freedom of movement.

Faced by more than 5,000 claims to property confiscated by the Sandinista regime, the government in 1995 passed a law providing some compensation in the most egregious cases. Cash-starved peasants who received land during the Sandinista reforms have been selling it to wealthy estate owners.

Nicaragua's human rights groups have reported continuing intimidation, kidnappings (a USAID official was seized in June), false arrest, arbitrary detention and torture. The judicial system is weak and often corrupt, and prison conditions are very poor. The Supreme Court removed a judge from office in August 1996 for taking bribes and sexually abusing female inmates; he was found dead after two hours in detention.

Print media are varied and partisan, representing hardline and moderate Sandinista, as well as pro- and anti-government positions. Before leaving office, the Sandinistas "privatized" the national radio system, mostly to Sandinista loyalists. There are five television stations, three of which carry news programming with partisan political content. A September 1996 law established a professional journalists' guild requiring journalists in the Managua area to have a bachelors' degree in journalism or five years of journalistic experience; opposition forces claimed the law was a blow to freedom of expression. Government attempts to block the publication of pro-Sandinista papers, such as *Barricada*, on account of their outstanding debts, have met with protest.

Freedom of religion in this overwhelmingly Roman Catholic country is generally respected, but sporadic bombings of Catholic churches continued in 1996. Church officials characterized the attacks as the work of extremists determined to stop the church's civic education campaigns.

Labor rights are complicated by the Sandinistas' use of unions as violent instruments to influence government economic policy. By means of the public sector unions, the Sandinistas have managed to gain ownership of over three dozen privatized state enterprises. The legal rights of non-Sandinista unions are not fully guaranteed. Citizens have no effective recourse when labor laws are violated either by the government or by violent Sandinista actions.

Women's rights are primarily violated by domestic and sexual violence. One study reported that 1 of 2 women has been a victim of abuse. Abused women's aid groups grew from 62 to 90 between 1993 and 1995.

Indigenous peoples, about 6 percent of the population, live in two autonomous regions, the Northern Autonomous Atlantic Regions (RAAN) and the Southern Autonomous Atlantic Region (RAAS). These are primarily Miskito, Sumo, Rama and Garifuna peoples. Despite some efforts by the government to include indigenous peoples in the political process, they have been left out of the debate on land use and expropriation.

Niger

Polity: Military rule   **Political Rights**: 7*
Economy: Capitalist   **Civil Liberties:** 5
Population: 9,465,000   **Status:** Not Free
PPP: $790
Life Expectancy: 46.7
Ethnic Groups: Hausa (56 percent), Djerma (22 percent), Fulani (9 percent), Tuareg (8 percent), Arab, Dhaza, others
Capital: Niamey
Ratings Change: Niger's political rights rating changed from 3 to 7 because a January coup toppled the democratic government.

Overview: **A** military coup toppled Niger's democratically-elected government in January, ousting President Mahamane Ousmane and shattering the country's fragile transition to representative rule. In July, coup leader Colonel Barre Mainassara Ibrahim was proclaimed victor of an election plagued by gross irregularities. The November parliamentary elections, boycotted by opposition parties, completed Barre's destruction of any semblance of representative government in Niger.

Niger achieved independence from France in 1960. For the next three decades, the country experienced one-party and military rule dominated by leaders of Hausa and Djerma ethnicity. In 1987, 13 years of direct army control was transformed into a one-party rule under the leadership of General Ali Seibou, who became head of state and leader of the National Movement for a Development Society (MNSD). In 1990, Niger joined the Africa-wide trend towards democratization. The country's trade union umbrella organization, the Niger Union of Trade Union Workers (USTN), led massive pro-democracy demonstrations, and international pressures amplified domestic demands for change.

A 1991 all-party national conference agreed on a transitional High Council of State that prepared a new multiparty constitution, which was overwhelmingly approved by a national referendum at the end of 1992. The February 1993 legislative elections, deemed free and fair by international observers, returned a majority for the Alliance of Forces for Change (AFC) party led by Ousmane Mahamane. Ousmane won a five-year term as the country's first democratically-elected president a month later and Niger's democratic transition appeared to be going smoothly.

The process faltered in 1994 and 1995 amidst political infighting and open rebellion. Defections cost the AFC its parliamentary majority, and new elections were called for January 1995. The elections were called free and fair by observers and gave the former sole legal party, the MNSD, 43 of 80 National Assembly seats. Its leader, Hama Amadou, was named prime minister. From mid-1995, the rivalry between president and prime minister threatened to paralyze the government, as each issued decrees and counter-decrees provoking confrontations between the presidential guard and the regular army. The inability of elected leaders to work effectively together was cited by Colonel Mainassara as a prime reason for his coup.

The April 24, 1995, peace pact with the country's Tuareg nomads that ended four years of war in northern Niger held through 1996. The agreement granted Tuareg demands for autonomy and development in their vast desert homelands. Violence over four years had claimed hundreds of lives. While peace reigned in Tuareg areas, however, occasional ethnic violence continued in the country's far east. Guerrilla fighters of the Democratic Renewal Front (FDR), made up of ethnic Kanuri and Toubou people, engaged in sporadic actions to call attention to alleged discrimination against their groups.

Political Rights and Civil Liberties: The January 1996 military coup usurped the Nigerien people's right to elect their representatives. Presidential elections conducted in July were deemed neither free nor fair by independent observers. Nigerians had elected their legislative representatives and president in open, democratic elections for the first time in 1993. The January 1995 parliamentary elections were again conducted in a generally free and fair manner, and resulted in a change in the parliamentary majority and the naming of a new prime minister. Coup leader Colonel Barre has returned Niger to military rule barely disguised by a veneer of democratic institutions.

The 1992 constitution guarantees many basic rights and provides for universal suffrage by secret ballot for all citizens over 18 years of age. The system distributes power between the president, parliament and an independent judiciary, and the national assembly includes special districts to represent ethnic minorities. However, it is not clear how the new military-dominated government will conduct itself, and the formal allocation of constitutional powers today means little in Niger.

Freedom of expression is guaranteed by the constitution but its exercise under the new military-dominated government is uncertain. The Superior Council of Communication (CSC), mandated by the 1992 constitution, is charged with protecting free and fair media. Licenses to operate private radio stations have been granted, but the government still controls most broadcasting and publishes a daily newspaper. More than a dozen private newspapers, some strongly partisan, publish regularly, and carry critiques of politicians and policies of all parties.

Freedom of assembly and association is guaranteed by the constitution, but these rights were not respected after the coup or during the election period. Authorities can prohibit gatherings by claiming that they will lead to violence. Freedom of religion is respected, although political parties formed on religious, ethnic or regional bases are barred. Many nongovernmental organizations operate openly and actively, including several devoted to human rights research and advocacy. These include the National League for Defense of Human Rights and the Nigerian Association for the Defense of Human Rights Democracy, Liberty, and Development.

The judicial system is by law independent. The Supreme Court has on occasion demonstrated some real autonomy, but lower courts are more subject to local external influences and are constrained by lack of training and resources. Traditional courts handle some civil matters.

Women suffer extensive societal discrimination, and some laws appear to contradict constitutional guarantees. Family law, especially, gives women inferior status in inheritance rights and divorce. Islamic conservatives have opposed efforts to revise the most discriminatory provisions. Domestic violence against women is reportedly widespread. Members of the country's ethnic minority groups have long asserted second-class treatment in regional development and educational and employment opportunities, and some have turned their grievances into armed rebellion.

The rights of Niger's strong labor movement were formalized in the 1992 constitution. Although only about 5 percent of the country's workforce is employed in the formal sector, unionized civil servants and other wage earners have exercised formidable political power. A 1993 law stipulates that notice of intent be given and negotiations attempted before a strike is called, and that workers can be legally required to provide essential services. Collective bargaining agreements are negotiated, but all under the framework of a tripartite agreement among government, employers and unions that defines work categories and wage guidelines. Working conditions and other labor issues could become increasingly contentious as the government applies structural adjustment programs that cut the civil service and privatize state-run enterprises.

Nigeria

Polity: Military rule **Political Rights**: 7
Economy: Capitalist **Civil Liberties:** 6*
Population: 103,912,000 **Status:** Not Free
PPP: $1,540
Life Expectancy: 50.6
Ethnic Groups: Hausa (21 percent), Yoruba (20 percent),
Ibo (17 percent), Fulani (9 percent), Kanuri, others
Capital: Abuja
Ratings Change: Nigeria's civil liberties rating changed from 7 to 6 because several independent newspapers and nongovernmental organizations continue to operate despite adverse conditions.

Overview: **N**igeria's military junta proclaimed its intention to return Africa's most populous country to at least a semblance of civilian rule by late 1998. The only effective tool to pressure the generals to respect human rights and restore democracy— an embargo on petroleum exports— was rejected by Western governments whose companies earn immense profits from pumping Nigeria's oil. The daylight assassination in June of the wife of the imprisoned victor of 1993's democratic presidential election, Moshood Abiola, coming on top of other political murders and continuing severe repression, was not enough to convince the United States, Britain, Holland, France and other countries to endanger corporate profits by angering the military regime.

Reports by the United Nations, Amnesty International and other human rights groups described a country where the judicial system is mocked by military tribunals and decrees, where arbitrary arrest, torture and summary executions are commonplace, and where free expression and free media are muzzled. Striking unions have been banned and new political parties allowed to register only under stringent conditions. Rampant lawlessness, corruption and drug trafficking continued to mark the rule of General Sani Abacha, who seized power in a palace coup in November 1993. The US Justice Department also reported that thousands of Americans have fallen prey to swindles that sometimes involve Nigerian government officials. A multi-million dollar public relations campaign, mounted by American lobbying firms hired by Abacha, evidently helped avert imposition of effective sanctions.

Since independence from British rule in 1960, Nigeria has known only ten years under elected governments. A succession of military dictatorships dominated by officers from the mainly Muslim north of the country have ruled the country for the past 11 years, and retained firm control over the far wealthier southern regions. The June 1993 presidential polls were meant to mark Nigeria's full and final transition to civilian rule, but the military coup entrenched authoritarianism while exacerbating the country's profound ethnic divisions. The military's new plan includes several sets of elections leading to a new national government in October 1998. The first non-party polls for local councils held in March gave good reason to suspect the generals' intentions; the polls were immediately followed by an army decree giving General Abacha power to dismiss any elected official.

Political Rights and Civil Liberties: **N**igerians cannot today choose their government freely. The 1993 elections, won by a southerner, Chief Moshood K.O. Abiola, were quickly annulled by the military regime of General Ibrahim Babangida. It named an interim government nominally charged with holding new elections. As massive strikes against the regime wracked the country, the high court returned a surprise ruling declaring the interim government illegal. In November 1993, General Abacha, a principal architect of previous coups, moved to take power for himself. All democratic structures were dissolved and political parties banned. A predominantly military Provisional Ruling Council (PRC) was appointed.

In June, 1994, Chief Abiola was arrested after declaring himself Nigeria's rightful president. General Abacha's pledge of an eventual return to civilian government is hardly reassuring. A compliant "constitutional convention" in 1995 effectively confirmed Abacha's open-ended term of office. Reshuffles within the ruling clique and a series of dismissals of senior military officers in 1996 have apparently cemented his power for now. The blatant rejection of the June 1993 poll results offer little hope the army will ever accept an election result that displeases it.

Various military decrees from the current and former military juntas severely restrict civil liberties. Authorities may detain without charges persons suspected of undefined acts "prejudicial to state security or harmful to the economic well-being of the country." A 1994 decree authorizes the PRC vice chairman or the police commissioner to detain persons for up to 3 months. Decree 14 of 1994 effectively suspends the right of habeas corpus by barring courts to order the government to produce prisoners in court.

The military dictatorship has kept a tight rein on all opposition. All writings of Ken Saro-Wiwa, executed last November after a show-trial on murder charges, remain banned. Saro-Wiwa provoked the army's wrath by exposing military brutality against southeastern Nigeria's Ogoni people. Oil drilling has usurped and despoiled the Ogoni's traditional land. The regime's response to Saro-Wiwa's campaign was to arrest him on what most observers believe were trumped-up murder charges. He was convicted by a special court without appeal. Saro-Wiwa is just one of the best known of the regime's many victims. Over two-thirds of Nigeria's nearly 70,000 prison inmates are detained without trial, most under terrible and even life-threatening conditions.

During the year journalists were arrested and newspapers forced to suspend publication. The threat of renewed closure is forcing self-censorship upon every Nigerian journalist.

As repression continues, ethnic tensions are high, and Nigeria's 100 million people are closer to serious internal conflict than at any time since the horrific Biafra civil war of 1967-70. In July 1995, a secret military tribunal handed down 14 death sentences and several life terms against army officers and civilians accused of plotting a coup against Abacha. International media reports claim that dozens of other lower-ranking military men were summarily executed shortly after the alleged March 1995 coup attempt.

Most notable among those convicted were senior politicians and ex-generals Olusegun Obasanjo and Shehu Musa Yar'Adua, who received long prison sentences. Obasanjo had led a previous military regime from 1976-79, but handed power to a civilian government, and was pressing General Abacha to do the same. Yar'Adua was number two in the same military regime, and was seen in some quarters as compromised civilian successor to Abacha. Several prominent journalists were found guilty for allegedly concealing information about the plot. Charles Obi, editor of *Weekend Classique,* Ms. Chris Anyanwu, editor-in chief-of *The Sunday Magazine*, George Mba, assistant editor of *Tell* magazine, and reporter Kunle Ajibade were given life sentences by a secret military tribunal. The country's first private radio station marked its second year of operation in September, but has broadcast little other than light entertainment programming. Some pro-democratic pirate radio stations have transmitted sporadically.

Union activities are still tightly controlled. The university lecturers' union was banned in August as its strike closed university campuses throughout the country. Four oil workers' union leaders have been detained without trial since the army quashed industrial unrest in August and September 1994 and placed unions under surveillance.

Religious strife has also flared. Shiite fundamentalists in northern Nigeria have repeatedly rioted and are subject to severe military surveillance. The region's Christian minority has come under repeated attack.

Political instability is also hindering Nigeria's economic prospects. Corruption and crime in some areas discourage investment, fed in part by large-scale drug-trafficking. Some observers believe there is official participation in the trade, which includes massive trans-shipments of heroin from Asia. The U.S. government says that Nigeria is not acting in good faith to curb trafficking. The U.S. has "decertified" Nigeria, a status that makes the country ineligible for foreign assistance beyond basic humanitarian aid. Decertification also requires that the U.S. vote against any loans to Nigeria from major multilateral development banks. Development prospects are also hindered by pervasive government involvement in the economy through parastatals and a plethora of other regulatory disincentives.

In November, Abacha outlined long-term economic reforms in a document titled "Vision 2010," which also raised concerns among some observers that he intends to remain in office until at least that date. Revenues from oil and gas extracted by European companies such as Shell (Anglo-Dutch), Elf (French) and Agip (Italian), which are expected soon to begin a $4 billion dollar project, and by American companies like Chevron—which signed a $320 million investment deal with the Abacha regime in 1995—earn Nigeria 90 percent of its foreign exchange.

Norway

Polity: Parliamentary
democracy
Economy: Mixed
capitalist
Population: 4,384,000
PPP: $20,370
Life Expectancy: 77.0
Ethnic Groups: Norwegian, indigenous Finnish and
Lappic (Saami) minorities, immigrant groups
Capital: Oslo

Political Rights: 1
Civil Liberties: 1
Status: Free

Overview:

In October 1996 Prime Minister Gro Harlem Brundtland announced her resignation to give her Labor Party time to select a new leader well before the September 1997 *Storting* (parliament) elections. Thorbjoern Jagland will succeed her.

The Eisvold Convention, Norway's present constitution, was drawn up under a period of de facto independence just prior to the acceptance of the Swedish monarch as king of Norway in 1814. After the peaceful dissolution of its relationship with the Swedish crown, Norway chose a sovereign from the Danish royal house and began functioning as a constitutional monarchy with a multiparty parliamentary structure.

The present minority Labor government was formed following the 1993 general election, in which Labor carried 37 percent of the vote. Further disadvantaging Brundtland's government was the strong showing of the anti-EU Center Party at the expense of the pro-European Conservatives. In a 1994 referendum, Norwegians voted against EU membership which Labor supported. Norway enjoys nearly full access to the EU's single market through membership in the European Economic Area. The economy has been growing and unemployment has been falling.

EU membership remains an issue. The Labor Party has attempted to defer the issue until after the 2001 parliamentary elections, claiming the question cannot be adequately addressed any earlier. In 1996 Norway took an observer status in the European Schengen, accord which ends border controls, sets up a common visa policy and institutes close cooperation in police matters.

**Political Rights
and Civil Liberties:**

Norwegians can change their government democratically. The 165-member Storting is directly elected by universal suffrage and proportional representation for a four year term. Once elected, the Storting selects one quarter of its own members to serve as the upper chamber or *Lagting*. Neither body is subject to dissolution. A vote of no-confidence in the Storting results in the resignation of the cabinet, and the leader of the party holding the most seats is asked to form a new government.

Since 1989, the approximately 20,000-strong Lappic (Saamic) minority has elected an autonomous assembly that functions as an advisory body on such matters as regional control of natural resources and preservation of Saami culture.

The constitution guarantees freedom of peaceful assembly, association, and the right to strike. Sixty percent of the work force belong to unions, which are free from government control. Collective bargaining is customary for the purpose of work constraints.

An independent judicial system headed by a Supreme Court operates at the local and national levels. Judges are appointed by the king with advice from the ministry of justice. A special labor relations court handles disputes between both public and private sector employers and workers. Human rights monitors operate without government restrictions.

Women make up roughly 45 percent of the labor force, with half employed part-time. Women are concentrated in sales, clerical and social service jobs. Women hold over one third of the national legislature seats, and eight out of 19 cabinet positions. The Storting has more women than any other national assembly.

The state finances the Evangelical Lutheran Church, in which more than 90 percent of the population holds at least nominal membership. While other churches receive public funding if they register with the government, there are some restrictions on religious freedom. The law requires that the sovereign and at least half the cabinet are Lutheran. Potential employers are permitted to inquire about one's religious convictions and practices for certain teaching positions. The state religion is taught in school. Discrimination on the basis of race, gender, language and class, however, are prohibited by law.

Freedom of the press is constitutionally guaranteed, and many newspapers are subsidized by the state in order to promote political pluralism. The majority of newspapers are privately owned and openly partisan. Broadcasting is also state funded, but the government interferes with editorial content neither on radio nor television. Private radio stations were authorized in 1982, followed by the first licensed commercial television channel in 1991. The Film Control Board has the right to censor blasphemous, overly violent and pornographic films. The power to censor alleged blasphemy, however, has not been exercised in over 20 years.

Oman

Polity: Traditional monarchy
Economy: Capitalist-statist
Population: 2,281,000
PPP: $10,420
Life Expectancy: 69.8
Ethnic Groups: Arab (74 percent), Baluchi, Indian
Capital: Muscat

Political Rights: 6
Civil Liberties: 6
Status: Not Free

Overview:

In 1996 Oman continued its reform and modernization plan by implementing fiscal cutbacks and revenue raising efforts. In November, the sultan's minor legislative reform indicated an intention to gradually develop constitutional rule.

Oman, an absolute sultanate, received independence from Great Britain in 1951. In July 1970 the current sultan, Qabus ibn Sa'id al Sa'id, overthrew his father in a palace coup. Since a 1971-75 insurrection in the southern Dhofar Province, the sultan, who rules by decree with the assistance of a Council of Ministers, has faced little opposition.

In 1991, the sultan organized caucuses of prominent citizens in each of the country's 59 provinces to nominate three citizens per province for a new *majlis al-shura* (consultative council). The sultan selected one nominee per province to sit in this majlis. The majlis comments on legislation and voices citizens' concerns but has no legislative power. In 1994 the sultan named an expanded, 80-seat majlis that will sit through 1997.

In May, June and September 1994, police arrested at least 200 alleged Islamic fundamentalists and questioned dozens of others. The government charged 131 suspects with subverting national unity and using Islam for political purposes. The trials were held in secret in a special State Security Court that did not meet international standards. In November, the court sentenced two defendants to death, and the others to prison terms ranging from three to 15 years. The sultan subsequently commuted the death sentences, and granted amnesty to others.

Political Rights and Civil Liberties:

Omani citizens cannot change their government democratically. The sultan holds absolute power and rules by decree. Neither elections nor political parties are currently in vogue. The sultan limited participation in the nominating process for the majlis to prominent citizens. The sultan appoints provincial governors, and tribal leaders wield significant authority over local matters in rural areas. The only redress for ordinary citizens is through petitions to local governors, and through direct appeals to the sultan during his annual three-week tour of the country.

Calls for autonomy sporadically come from Shihayeen tribesmen in Rous al-Jibal Province on the Musandam Peninsula. Administered by Oman since 1970, the province is geographically separate from the rest of the country.

The rudimentary judicial system operates mainly according to tradition. Reports are made of arbitrary arrest, mistreatment of prisoners, detention without charge beyond the permitted 24-hour period, and denial of access to legal counsel. Warrants are not required for arrests. The rights of the accused are not codified, but in practice, defendants are presumed innocent and generally enjoy some procedural rights. Defendants are not guaranteed the right to legal counsel, and no jury trials take place.

Criticism of the sultan is prohibited, although citizens do criticize government policies. The government censors all publications, and foreign publications critical of Oman are banned. Omanis exercise significant self-censorship. Two of the four daily papers are owned by the government, and the other two rely heavily on government subsidies. Coverage in all four dailies supports government policies. The state-controlled television and radio broadcasts carry only official views. The government does not permit private broadcast media.

All public gatherings must be approved by the government, although this is not always strictly enforced. All associations must be registered, and the government permits only strictly non-political groups. International human rights organizations' activities are restricted by the government, which prohibits the establishment of local human rights organizations.

Islam is the state religion, and the majority of the population are Sunni Muslims. The authorities monitor mosque sermons. Christians and Hindus can worship freely, but only Muslims may publish religious books. No laws prohibit discrimination, and some Shiite, east Africans, and other minorities report instances of discrimination in employment and educational opportunities.

Despite noticeable gains in education and career opportunities, women face discrimination in the job market. Approximately half the students at Sultan Qabus University are women as are and nearly twenty percent of civil servants. Women must receive permission from their husband or male relative to travel abroad, and under Islamic law receive half the inheritance that men do. Female genital mutilation is practiced in some rural areas.

The labor law makes no provision for trade unions, and none exists. Employers of more than 50 workers must form a body of labor and management representatives to discuss working conditions. However, these committees cannot negotiate wages. Strikes are illegal, although brief strikes occasionally occur. Employers exercise significant leverage over foreign workers due to a requirement that employers provide them with letters of release before they can change jobs.

Pakistan

Polity: Presidential-par-
liamentary democracy
(military influenced)
Economy: Capitalist-statist
Population: 133,516,000
PPP: $2,160
Life Expectancy: 61.8

Political Rights: 4*
Civil Liberties: 5
Status: Partly Free

Ethnic Groups: Pujabi, Sindhi, Pathan, Urdu, Baluchi, Afghan, Mohajir, others
Capital: Islamabad
Ratings Change: Pakistan's political rights rating changed from 3 to 4 because
of the continued use of presidential powers to undermine elected governments.

Overview:

President Farooq Leghari used a controversial constitutional amendment to dismiss premier Benazir Bhutto's government in November 1996 on charges of corruption, undermining the judiciary and sanctioning extrajudicial killings in the southern city of Karachi.

Pakistan was formed in August 1947 with the partition of the subcontinent upon independence from Britain. In 1971 Bangladesh (ex-East Pakistan) achieved independence after a nine-month civil war. The 1973 constitution provides for a parliamentary system with a lower National Assembly, which currently has 217 directly-elected seats including 10 reserved for non-Muslims, and an 87-seat Senate appointed by the provincial assemblies. The president is chosen for a five-year term by an electoral college.

In 1977 General Zia ul-Haq overthrew populist premier Ali Bhutto. In 1985, with the country still under martial law, Zia secured parliamentary approval of the controversial Eighth Amendment, which empowers the president to dismiss the prime minister and dissolve parliament. Zia and his successor as president, Ghulam Ishaq Khan, used the Eighth Amendment to sack three successive elected governments between 1987 and 1993, including administrations headed by Bhutto's daughter, Benazir Bhutto, in 1990, and by Nawaz Sharif in 1993. The October 1993 elections brought Bhutto's Pakistan People's Party (PPP) to power over Sharif's conservative Pakistan Muslim League (PML).

In 1996 Bhutto largely ignored a March Supreme Court ruling aimed at tightening the requirements for appointing and transfering judges, as well as a June court order to dismiss 24 judges appointed under the old rules. In dismissing Bhutto's government and dissolving the National Assembly on November 5, Leghari almost certainly acted with the approval of the army. By year's end prime minister Meraj Khalid's interim government had been heavily criticized for failing to bring corruption charges against Bhutto, opposition leader Sharif or other senior politicians in advance of fresh elections called for February 3, 1997.

Political Rights and Civil Liberties:

Pakistanis can change their government through elections that are reasonably free, although not fair. Press freedom is restricted and the electoral system concentrates political power in a rural landowning elite. The electoral boundaries, drawn in 1984, are based on a 1981 census and thus do not reflect subsequent large demographic shifts from rural to urban areas. Consequently, according to the Bangkok-based *Asia Times,* wealthy landowners held nearly 135 seats in the ousted parliament. Democratic institutions and basic liberties are undermined by a weak rule of law and widespread corruption.

In 1996 presidential ordinances were increasingly used for lawmaking, bypassing the elected parliament. The more than one million residents of the Northern Areas are not represented in parliament, and according to the independent Human Rights Commission of Pakistan (HRCP), some 20 million bonded laborers and 1.5 nomads are ineligible to vote. In December the president granted citizens of the Federally Administered Tribal Areas (FATA) of the North-West Frontier Province (NWFP) the right to choose their parliamentary representatives; previously this had been done by tribal leaders. The PPP regained control of the legislative assembly in Pakistan-administered Azad Kashmir in June 30 elections that the local opposition Muslim Conference charged were marred by irregularities.

Police and army soldiers kill scores of suspects each year in staged "encounters." Police routinely torture detainees to extract confessions and rape female detainees and prisoners. In Karachi the death toll in 1996 from ethnic, factional and sectarian strife was lower than the 2,100 killed in 1995. However, both security forces and the Immigrants National Movement (MQM), an organization representing Urdu-speakers who migrated to Pakistan after Partition, continued to be responsible for widespread human rights abuses. Police and paramilitary units in Karachi conducted sweeping crackdowns that resulted in the detention of tens of thousands of Urdu-speaking males, several hundred of whom remained in jail at year's end. Security forces extrajudicially executed suspected MQM militants with impunity.

Sectarian violence between the Sunni-based Sipah-e-Sahaba (SSP) and the Shiite Sipah-e-Mohammed extremist groups continued throughout the year. An August 18 attack by masked gunmen on a Shiite procession in Punjab killed 18 people in one of the worst sectarian massacres in Pakistan's history. In September sectarian clashes near Parachinar, NWFP killed at least 100 people. In another development, a series of bomb attacks throughout the year in Punjab, including a April 14 blast at a cancer center in Lahore run by cricket star-turned-politician Imran Khan, killed more than 200 people.

Laws and constitutional provisions restricting freedom of expression cover broad subjects including the army and Islam. Journalists are occasionally detained, warned against covering sensitive stories or otherwise harassed by authorities, and attacked by members of the SSP and other groups. Nevertheless, Pakistan's English-language press is among the most outspoken in South Asia. The government owns nearly all electronic media, and news coverage favors the ruling party.

In late October authorities arrested hundreds of supporters of the fundamentalist Jamaat-e-Islami party during anti-government clashes with police in Islamabad and Rawalpindi. Authorities generally permit peaceful demonstrations and political rallies.

In 1996 the judiciary increasingly asserted itself against arbitrary executive power. A March 20 Supreme Court ruling requires the government to make senior judicial appointments in consultation with the chief justices and on the basis of seniority. A December ruling requires the president to accept the prime minister's advice on judicial appointments. Lower courts are subject to manipulation by powerful interests and to pressure from Islamic fundamentalists, and are severely backlogged.

The 1986 blasphemy law of the penal code mandates the death sentence for defiling the Prophet Mohammed. Thus far no lower court convictions for blasphemy have been upheld, and magistrates are now required to conduct investigations before filing charges; but spurious blasphemy charges against Ahmadis, Christians, Hindus and other religious minorities have made them targets for Islamic fundamentalists. A 1984 ordinance prohibits Ahmadis, who by law are considered non-Muslims, from performing certain religious acts. Asma Jahangir, HRCP chairperson, has received death threats from Islamists for defending religious minorities and women in sensitive cases.

The 1979 Hadood Ordinances introduced *Shari'a* (Islamic law) into the penal code. The most severe penalties, including death for adultery, have never been carried out, but their presence on the books has adverse consequences. Under the Hadood Ordinances a woman requires four male witnesses to prove she was raped. The accused can file a countercharge of adultery, which carries the death penalty and thus deters many women from reporting rape. On September 24 the Lahore High Court ruled that a Muslim women cannot enter into marriage without the consent of a male guardian, which places women at risk for being prosecuted under the Hadood Ordinances for extramarital sex if they seek to marry without obtaining such consent. Violence against women, including rape, domestic violence, beatings and killings in dowry disputes and for alleged adultery, remains a serious problem.

The Karachi-based Lawyers for Human Rights and Legal Aid estimates that some 200,000 Bangladeshi women have been trafficked to Pakistan, often with the complicity of local officials. Many are sold into prostitution or as domestic servants and are physically abused. Some 2,000 trafficking victims are detained under criminal charges, mainly for entering Pakistan illegally, or for extramarital sex under the Hadood Ordinaces.

The revelation that souvenir balls for the Euro 96 soccer championship had been produced by child workers in the northeastern town of Sialkot brought increased attention to the problem of child labor in Pakistan. The HRCP estimates that 10 million children, many of them bonded laborers, work in brick kilns, carpet factories, farms and other workplaces. Workers in agriculture, hospitals, radio and television and export-processing zones cannot form unions. The 1952 Essential Services Maintenance Act restricts union activity and strikes in numerous sectors.

Palau

Polity: Presidential-leg-
islative democracy
Economy: Capitalist
Population: 17,000
PPP: na
Life Expectancy: na
Ethnic Groups: Palauan (Micronesian, Malayan
and Melanesian), mixed Palauan-European-Asian, Filipino
Capital: Koror

Political Rights: 1
Civil Liberties: 2
Status: Free

Overview:

These 200-odd Micronesian islands of the Carolines chain in the western Pacific were transferred from Spanish to German control in 1899. The Japanese seized the islands in 1914, and began a formal administration under a League of Nations mandate in 1920. The United States Navy administered the islands from 1944, and in 1947 the possessions became part of the U.S. Trust Territory of the Pacific under a United Nations mandate.

The constitution, which was adopted by a popular referendum in 1979 and took effect in 1981, vests executive powers in a directly-elected president who serves a four-year term. The directly-elected, bicameral *Olbil Era Kelulau* (parliament) has a 14-member Senate and a 16-seat House of Delegates, with one member coming from each of the states.

In November 1992 Vice President Kuniwo Nakamura defeated challenger Johnson Toribiong in a presidential election.

In November 1993 voters finally approved the Compact of Free Association with the United States. Under the Compact, Palau is a sovereign country, but the U.S. remains responsible for defense. The U.S. is providing $442 million in aid over 15 years in exchange for the right to maintain military facilities. In December 1994 Palau became the 185th member of the U.N.

**Political Rights
and Civil Liberties:**

Citizens of Palau can change their government democratically. Elections are competitive and tend to focus on personalities and issues rather than on party affiliations. The judiciary is independent of the government. The rule of law is well-established, although Palau is increasingly being used as a transshipment point for illegal drugs going from Southeast Asia to the U.S.

A 16-member Council of Chiefs advises the government on matters of tribal laws and customs. The chiefs wield considerable authority, and tensions often materialized between the chiefs and political leaders. Inheritance of property and traditional rank is matrilineal, giving women a high status in society. In addition, each of the two traditional high chiefs is chosen by one of the two Councils of Women Chiefs. Women's groups say domestic violence is an underreported problem.

Freedom of association is respected, although few institutions of civil society are in place. The constitution guarantees the right to organize and bargain collectively, even if few exercise it in practice. There is no legal right to strike, and legislation protecting worker's rights is inadequate. Foreign workers comprise nearly half of the labor force and 20 percent of the population, and face discrimination in employment, education and other areas, as well as random violence. Employers occasionally coerce foreign workers, particularly domestics and unskilled laborers, into remaining in their present jobs by withholding passports, and by other means.

Panama

Polity: Presidential-leg- **Political Rights:** 2
islative democracy **Civil Liberties:** 3
Economy: Capitalist-statist **Status:** Free
Population: 2,655,000
PPP: $5,890
Life Expectancy: 72.9
Ethnic Groups: Mestizo (70 percent), West Indian (14 percent),
European (10 percent), Indian (6 percent)
Capital: Panama City

Overview: **S**ix years after the end of General Manuel Noriega's dictatorship, the ruling Democratic Revolutionary Party (PRD) was accused of involvement in drug-trafficking. This was brought to light by the collapse of the Agricultural, Industrial, and Commercial Bank of Panama (BANAICO) in January. An investigation by the Banking Commission found accounts empty and $50 million unaccounted for, as well as evidence that the bank was a central money-laundering facility. BANAICO was named in several American drug investigations, including one into Jose Castrillon Henao, a Colombian who was arrested in April as the reputed organizer of the Cali cartel's seagoing cocaine shipments to the U.S.

Panama was part of Colombia until 1903, when a U.S.-supported revolt resulted in the proclamation of an independent Republic of Panama. A period of weak civilian rule ended with a military coup that brought General Omar Torrijos to power.

After the signing of the 1977 canal treaties with the U.S., Torrijos promised democratization. The 1972 constitution was revised, providing for the direct election of a president and a legislative assembly for five years. After Torrijos's death in 1981, Noriega emerged as Panamanian Defense Force (PDF) chief and rigged the 1984 election that brought to power the PRD, then the political arm of the PDF.

The Democratic Alliance of Civic Opposition (ADOC) won the 1989 election, but Noriega annulled the vote and declared himself head of state. He was removed during a U.S. military invasion, and ADOC's Guillermo Endara became president.

Endara's prestige plummeted and ADOC unraveled amid charges of corruption and poverty-fueled social unrest. In the 1994 election, the three main presidential candidates were the PRD's Ernesto Perez Balladares, singer-actor Ruben Blades, and Ruben Carles, a former official in the Endara government. Perez Balladares, a 47-year-old millionaire and former banker, won with 33.3 percent of the vote. The PRD won 32 of 71 seats in the Legislative Assembly and, with the support of allied parties that won six seats, achieved an effective majority.

Perez Balladares kept a campaign promise by choosing for his cabinet technocrats and politicians from across the ideological spectrum. But economic reforms, rising unemployment, and a doubling of ministerial salaries led to widespread protests in 1995 by labor unions and students. The president's popularity declined when the government met protests with harsh crackdowns.

During the 1994 campaign, Perez Balladares pledged to rid the country of drug influence. He claims to have been successful. Mayor Alfredo Aleman, a board member of BANAICO, is also a friend and top advisor to Perez Balladares, and was a major financial contributor to the party's 1994 campaign. Fighting off allegations of drug connections, Perez Balladares himself confessed in June that his electoral campaign unknowingly accepted a contribution from Jose Castrillon Henao.

The Perez Balladares administration further damaged its popularity when it restored government jobs and awarded a reported $35 million in back pay to former members of the Dignity Battalions who had been Noriega's paramilitary enforcers. They were notable human rights abusers who lost their jobs after the U.S. invasion. The PRD was also set to offer amnesty to nearly 1,000 human rights violators from the Noriega regime until violent student protest and intense opposition in the Legislative Assembly forced its retreat in June.

Political Rights and Civil Liberties:

Panama's citizens can change their government democratically. The constitution guarantees freedom of political and civic organization. More than a dozen parties from across the political spectrum participated in the 1994 elections.

The judicial system, headed by a Supreme Court, was revamped in 1990. It remains overworked, however, and its administration is inefficient, politicized, and undermined by the corruption endemic to all public and governmental bodies. The disarray is compounded by an unwieldy criminal code and a surge in cases, many involving grievances against former soldiers and officials which have accumulated over two decades of military rule.

The penal system is marked by violent disturbances in decrepit facilities packed with up to eight times their intended capacity. About two-thirds of prisoners face delays of about 18 months in having their cases heard, and less than 15 percent of the nation's inmates in 1995 had been tried and convicted.

Labor unions are well organized. However, labor rights were diluted in 1995 when Perez Balladares pushed labor code revisions through Congress. When 49 unions initiated peaceful protests, the government cracked down in a series of violent clashes that resulted in four deaths and hundreds of arrests. According to UNICEF, the workforce includes over 60,000 children earning less than the monthly minimum wage of $150.

The media are a raucous assortment of radio and television stations, daily newspapers and weekly publications. Restrictive media laws dating back to the Noriega regime remain on the books, however. The law permits officials to jail without trial anyone who defames the government. Perez Balladares began to apply the laws against media critical of his government in 1995.

The Panamanian Defense Forces were dismantled after 1989, and the military was formally abolished in 1994. But the civilian-run Public Force (national police) that replaced the PDF is poorly disciplined, corrupt and practices physical abuse. It includes former lower-ranking military officers whose loyalty to democracy is questionable. It has been ineffectual against the drug trade, as Panama remains a major transshipment point for both cocaine and illicit arms, as well as a money-laundering hub.

Since 1993, indigenous groups have protested the encroachment of illegal settlers on Indian lands and delays by the government in formally demarcating the boundaries of those lands.

Papua New Guinea

Polity: Parliamentary
democracy (insurgency)
Economy: Capitalist
Population: 4,313,000
PPP: $2,530
Life Expectancy: 56.0
Ethnic Groups: Papuan, Melanesian, some
1,000 indigenous tribes
Capital: Port Moresby

Political Rights: 2
Civil Liberties: 4
Status: Partly Free

Overview: Papua New Guinea Premier Julius Chan's March 1996 decision to resume military operations on Bougainville Island, and the October assassination of the island's provincial premier, threatened to escalate a secessionist conflict that since 1989 has caused hundreds of civilian deaths.

This South Pacific country, consisting of the eastern part of New Guinea and some 600 smaller islands, has functioned as a parliamentary democracy since achieving independence from Australia in 1975. The 1975 constitution vests executive power in a National Executive Council consisting of a largely ceremonial governor general and a prime minister and cabinet. The parliament, which serves a five-year term, has 89 nationally-elected seats, and 20 seats elected one apiece from the 19 provinces plus the capital, Port Moresby.

At the 1992 parliamentary elections the ruling, urban-based Papua New Guinea United Party (Pangu Pati) won a plurality with 22 seats; the People's Democratic Movement (PDM), 15; six smaller parties, 40; independents, 31; with 1 seat vacant. In July parliament elected PDM leader Paias Wingti as prime minister over the incumbent, the Pangu Pati's Rabbie Namaliu.

In September 1993 Wingti pulled a "political coup" by resigning and immediately getting re-elected by parliament, thus winning the fresh 18 months of immunity from no-confidence motions constitutionally granted to an incoming premier. In August 1994 the Supreme Court invalidated Wingti's "re-election." Parliament subsequently elected People's Progress Party leader Sir Julius Chan, a former premier, to the top spot.

The country's most severe crisis since independence has been the continuing insurgency on the island of Bougainville, 560 miles northeast of the capital. Beginning in late 1988 miners and local landowners organized guerrilla attacks on an Australian-owned mine to demand compensation and a 50 percent share of the profits, forcing the mine's closure in 1989. The movement's leaders subsequently formed the Bougainville Revolutionary Army (BRA) and declared an independent Republic of Bougainville. In September 1994 the government and the BRA signed a ceasefire, and in April 1995 the government swore in a Bougainville Transitional Government (BTG).

On March 21, 1996, after the BRA had killed 12 policemen and soldiers on Bougainville since January, Chan unilaterally ended the ceasefire, which had been honored mainly in the breach. On October 12, unknown gunmen assassinated Theodore Miriung, the Bougainville provincial premier and head of the BTG.

Political Rights and Civil Liberties: Citizens of Papua New Guinea can change their government democratically, although national and provincial balloting is generally marred by violence and irregularities. Parliamentary elections are due in mid-1997. The government's attempt in 1995 to reform the corruption-ridden provincial governments by naming an MP as governor of each province, while recasting the former provincial premiers as deputy premiers, has had the collateral effect of consolidating central power.

The country's democratic and civic institutions generally operate freely but are under fiscal pressures. The extreme cultural differences between the cities and highlands as well as the presence of some 1,000 tribes are causing problems. The judiciary is independent. The press reports openly on the widespread official corruption and the Bougainville crisis, although authorities restrict journalists' access to Bougainville. Authorities generally respect the state-run National Broadcasting Commission's independence in its news coverage. Police approval for demonstrations is frequently denied for public safety reasons, although not on political grounds. Nongovernmental human rights organizations are outspoken and active.

The army, two army-backed militias called "Resistance and Spear," and the BRA have been responsible for torture, disappearances, arbitrary detentions and extrajudicial executions against combatants and civilians on Bougainville. A May 1996 United Nations report documented at least 64 alleged extrajudicial killings by the army on Bougainville in the three years prior to October 1995, some of them of civilians fleeing to the Solomon Islands. On December 5 Radio Australia quoted a BRA spokesman as saying that army soldiers and army-backed militias had killed more than 20 civilians in three incidents between November 26 and December 1. Overall, hundreds of civilians on Bougainville and nearby Buka Island have died in the conflict, many due to a lack of medical treatment and supplies during periods when the islands are under military blockade. Some 70,000 of Bougainville's 168,000 residents live, many under duress, in army-run "care centers" on the island, where there are reports of torture, rape and restrictions on movement.

The 1993 Internal Security Act gives police expanded powers to conduct searches without warrants. Police frequently use excessive or disproportionate force against suspects and ordinary civilians, and are responsible for several deaths in recent years. Police also continue to abuse detainees and prisoners. In the highlands police occasionally burn homes to punish communities suspected of harboring criminals or of participating in tribal warfare, which has killed dozens of people in recent years, or to punish crimes committed by individuals. In urban areas violent gangs known as "Rascals" have contributed to a severe law and order crisis.

In rural areas foreign logging companies frequently swindle villagers and generally renege on promises to build local schools and hospitals. Private security guards hired by the companies are suspected in occasional physical attacks on forestry officials. Women face significant social discrimination, and rape and domestic violence are serious problems.

Workers are free to join independent unions, bargain collectively and stage strikes. The International Labor Organization has criticized a law allowing the government to invalidate arbitration agreements or wage awards not considered in the national interest.

Paraguay

Polity: Presidential-legislative democracy (military-influenced)
Political Rights: 4
Civil Liberties: 3
Status: Partly Free
Economy: Capitalist-statist
Population: 4,955,000
PPP: $3,340
Life Expectancy: 70.1
Ethnic Groups: Mestizo (95 percent), Indian, European, black
Capital: Asuncion

Overview:
In what has been called Paraguay's worst political crisis since General Alfredo Stroessner's dictatorship was toppled in 1989, President Juan Carlos Wasmosy averted a military coup staged by army commander General Lino Oviedo in April. This confrontation between the military and Wasmosy's fledgling democracy effectively ended a three-year power struggle between the two. Wasmosy emerged as the heroic champion of democracy.

After the 1989 coup that ended the 35-year dictatorship, General Andres Rodriguez took over Stroessner's Colorado Party and engineered his own election to finish Stroessner's last presidential term.

The Colorados won a majority in a vote for a constituent assembly, which produced the 1992 constitution. It provides for a president, a vice-president and a bicameral Congress consisting of a 45-member Senate and an 80-member Chamber of Deputies elected for five-year terms. The president is elected by a simple majority and reelection is prohibited. The constitution bars the military from engaging in politics.

In the 1992 Colorado primary election, Luis Maria Argana, an old-style machine politician, defeated construction tycoon Wasmosy. Rodriguez and Oviedo engineered a highly dubious re-count that made Wasmosy the winner.

The 1993 candidates were Wasmosy, Domingo Laino of the center-left Authentic Radical Liberal Party (PLRA), and Guillermo Caballero Vargas, a wealthy businessman. Wasmosy promised to modernize the economy. Laino played on his decades of resistance to Stroessner. Caballero Vargas campaigned as a centrist, free of the politics of the past.

Every poll showed Wasmosy trailing until three weeks before the election, when

Oviedo threatened a coup if the Colorado Party lost. He declared that the military "would govern together with the glorious Colorado Party forever and ever." Fear of a coup proved decisive, as Wasmosy won with 40.3 percent of the vote. Laino took 32 percent and Caballero Vargas 23.5. The Colorados won a plurality of seats in each house of Congress.

Oviedo was then appointed army commander, becoming the most powerful officer in the armed forces. Wasmosy has since allowed Oviedo to eliminate rivals from within the military by retiring them. However, a political tug-of-war persisted, with Wasmosy trying to reduce military influence in government. Oviedo, backed by a hardline Colorado faction, appears to have been using Wasmosy as a stepping-stone for achieving the presidency himself.

In what appeared to be a sudden move, Wasmosy ordered the General to step down on the morning of April 22. Oviedo refused, demanding the president's resignation and threatening to topple the government. As word of troop movements was broadcast just hours later, Wasmosy prepared to resign. He was dissuaded by a diplomatic contingent including ambassadors from the U.S. and Mercosur. Paraguayans took to the streets in mass pro-democracy rallies. The diplomatic effort produced an offer to appoint Oviedo to the post of Defense Minister in return for his resignation. The offer, which Oviedo accepted, proved unpopular with the public, whose protests grew in fervor. Bolstered by public and diplomatic support, Wasmosy rescinded the offer. Oviedo, a civilian and without loyal troops, was forced to go quietly. He did vow to seek the presidency through elections scheduled for 1998.

Political Rights and Civil Liberties: The 1992 constitution provides for regular elections. But elections are neither free nor fair because of military pressures, serious irregularities and fraud. Overall, the inordinate influence of the military greatly weakens the authority of the civilian government.

Overcrowding, unsanitary living conditions and mistreatment are serious problems in Paraguayan prisons. Over 95 percent of prisoners are being held pending trial, many for months or years after arrest. The constitution permits detention without trial until the accused completes the minimum sentence for the alleged crime.

The constitution guarantees free political and civic organization and religious expression. However, political rights and civil liberties are undermined by the government's resort to repressive tactics when faced with demonstrations and protests. During the April coup attempt, people in the streets were beaten back by police truncheons. At least two opposition protestors were hospitalized. The police were also accused of using excessive force during a general strike in May, when 130 people were injured.

Peasant and Indian organizations demanding land often meet with police crackdowns, detentions, and forced evictions by vigilante groups in the employ of large landowners. Over a dozen peasants have been killed in the ongoing disputes. Activist priests who support land reform are frequent targets of intimidation. The government's promise of land reform remains largely unfulfilled, as nearly 90 percent of agricultural land remains in the hands of foreign companies and a few hundred Paraguayan families.

There are numerous trade unions and two major union federations. Strikes are often broken up violently by the police and the military, and labor activists are detained. The 1992 constitution gives public-sector workers the rights to organize, bargain collectively and strike, but these rights are often not respected in practice. A new labor code designed to protect worker rights was passed in October 1993, but enforcement has been weak.

The judiciary remains under the influence of the ruling party and the military, susceptible to the corruption pervading all public and governmental institutions. It is mostly unresponsive to human rights groups that present cases of rights violations committed either before or after the overthrow of Stroessner. Allegations include illegal detention by police and torture during incarceration, particularly in rural areas. Colombian drug-traffickers continue to expand operations in Paraguay, and accusations of high official involvement in drugs date back to the 1980s.

The media are both public and private. State-run broadcast media present pluralistic points of view and a number of independent newspapers publish. However, journalists investigating corruption or covering strikes and protests are often the victims of intimidation and violent attacks by security forces. Free expression is also threatened by vague, potentially restrictive laws that mandate "reponsible" behavior by journalists and media owners.

Peru

Polity: Presidential-military (insurgencies)
Economy: Capitalist-statist
Population: 24,041,000
PPP: $3,320
Life Expectancy: 66.3
Ethnic Groups: Indian (45 percent), mestizo (37 percent), European (15 percent), black, Asian
Capital: Lima

Political Rights: 4*
Civil Liberties: 3*
Status: Partly Free

Ratings Change: Peru's political rights and civil liberties changed because of modest improvement in the security situation.

Overview:

President Alberto Fujimori's approval rating dropped from 75 percent to 48 percent in 1996 due to an economic slowdown and discontent over authoritarian rule. In December, leftist guerrillas seized the Japanese embassy and held the guests hostage. This incident belied Fujimor's claim of having crushed the country's insurgents.

Since independence in 1821, Peru has seen alternating periods of civilian and military rule. Civilian rule was restored in 1980 after 12 years of dictatorship. That same year the Maoist Shining Path terrorist group launched a guerrilla war that killed 30,000 people over the next 13 years.

Fujimori, a university rector and engineer, defeated novelist Mario Vargas Llosa in the 1990 election. In 1992 Fujimori, backed by the military, suspended the constitution and dissolved Congress. The move was popular because of people's disdain for Peru's corrupt, elitist political establishment and fear of the Shining Path.

Fujimori held a state-controlled election for an 80-member constituent assembly to replace the Congress. The assembly drafted a constitution that established a unicameral Congress more closely under presidential control. The constitution was approved in a state-controlled referendum following Shining Path leader Abimael Guzman's capture.

Fujimori's principal opponent in the 1995 elections was former U.N. Secretary General Javier Perez de Cuellar, who vowed to end Fujimori's "dictatorship" and initially looked strong in opinion polls. Fujimori countered with a massive public-spending and propaganda campaign that utilized state resources. The National Intelligence Service (SIN), under de facto head Vladimiro Montesinos, a Fujimori ally, was employed to spy on and discredit Perez de Cuellar and other opposition candidates.

On April 9, Fujimori won an easy victory, outpolling Perez de Cuellar by about three to one, while his loose coalition of allies won a majority in the new 120-seat Congress.

Prior to the 1995 presidential election the government had increased spending; by early 1996 subsequent spending cuts had led to an economic slowdown. In April Fujimori appointed a revamped cabinet, headed by premier Alberto Pandolfi, that was more supportive of the president's privatization program and free market reforms.

In August Congress passed a law allowing Fujimori to run for a third term, despite a constitutional provision limiting the president to two terms. The law evaded this by defining Fujimori's current term as his first under the 1993 constitution.

In November Rodolfo Robles, a retired general who had accused the military of orchestrating the October bombing of a television transmitter, was abducted and placed in a military prison. Following a public outcry authorities released Robles in December.

On December 17, rebels of the Tupac Amaru Revolutionary Movement (MRTA), which had largely been confined to the Upper Huallaga Valley since the arrest of its leader in 1992, stormed a reception at the Japanese ambassador's residence in Lima and seized more than 600 hostages. The group demanded that the government free roughly 450 of its imprisoned members and reverse some free market reforms. By year's end the rebels still held 83 hostages.

Political Rights and Civil Liberties:

The Fujimori government is a presidential-military regime with the trappings of formal democracy. Although Fujimori had considerable popular support, the 1995 election was not fair by international standards due to the massive use of state resources and military and state intelligence during the campaign. Electoral laws require any party that failed to obtain 5 percent of the popular vote in 1995 to obtain 400,000 signatures to re-register; few parties have managed to do so. Given the marginalization of political parties, the lack of an independent judiciary, and the relative weakness of trade unions and other elements of civil society, few independent power centers exist outside of the president and his allies in the military high command.

Under the December 1993 constitution, the president can rule virtually by decree. Fujimori can dissolve Congress in the event of a "grave conflict" between the executive and legislature, as he did in 1992. The constitution overturned Peru's tradition of no re-election.

In 1994 a new, nominally independent election commission was named. The Congress, dominated by the government, blocked the commission's attempts to limit the regime's overwhelming advantages in the 1994-95 campaign. However, in a development that indicated a degree of autonomy, in 1996 the commission ruled that a new law tightening the requirements to hold a popular referendum could not be applied retroactively. This gave momentum to an ongoing petition drive to hold a referendum on whether Fujimori can run for a third term.

In 1994, there were judicial reforms and a new Supreme Court was named. But judicial independence remains suspect. In August 1996 Congress installed a Tribunal of Constitutional Guarantees, as called for under the 1993 constitution, with powers of judicial review. However parliament also passed a law requiring the votes of six of the seven members of the Tribunal to declare a law or government action unconstitutional. This virtually assures that a court challenge to the law permitting Fujimori to run for a third term will fail.

A draconian 1992 antiterrorist decree practically eliminates judicial guarantees in a system of military tribunals with anonymous judges installed to try alleged subversives. The defense lawyers may not call witnesses or cross-examine government witnesses, who are unidentified. Sentences are pronounced within hours. In August 1996 the government set up a congressionally mandated ad hoc commission to review cases of detainees believed to be wrongly imprisoned or accused of terrorism or treason. By year's end Fujimori had granted more than 100 pardons.

The government justifies the faceless court system, which Congress extended in October 1996 for another year, as necessary to counter the Shining Path's policy of assassinating judges. In 1996 nearly half the population remained under a militarized state of emergency. The January 1996 sentencing of an American woman to life imprisonment on charges of treason over her involvement with the MRTA further highlighted the use of faceless courts.

In 1995 the regime implemented an amnesty law absolving everyone implicated in human rights violations during the counterinsurgency against the Shining Path, thus reprieving hundreds of police and soldiers responsible for extrajudicial killings, rapes, disappearances and torture. The regime imposed a law dictating that the judiciary could not dispute the amnesty's constitutionality. In July 1996 the U.N. Human Rights Committee criticized the amnesty law.

Torture remains routine in police detention centers, and conditions remain deplorable in prisons for common criminals. In April 1996 the head of the National Prison Institute conceded that 75 percent of the nation's prisoners were awaiting trial or sentence. Following the MRTA's seizure of hostages the government suspended an agreement that had allowed the International Committee of the Red Cross to visit some 4,000 accused or convicted terrorists.

In the summer of 1996 the Shining Path launched a series of coordinated terrorist attacks in the countryside, demonstrating that the group, while greatly weakened, has reorganized somewhat after its collapse in the wake of Guzman's arrest. During the year the group killed more than 100 civilians.

The labor code authorizes the government to disband any strike it deems to be endangering a company, an industry, or the public sector. In June 1996 the International Labor Organization criticized the labor code for failing to protect workers from anti-union discrimination, and for restricting collective bargaining rights.

Forced labor, including child labor, is prevalent in the gold-mining regions of the Amazon.

The press is largely privately-owned. Radio and television are both privately- and publicly-owned. State-owned media are blatantly pro-government. Since 1992, many media, especially television and print journalists, have been pressured into self-censorship or exile by a broad government campaign of intimidation—death threats, libel suits, withholding of advertising, police harassment, arbitrary detentions and physical mistreatment. Since 1993, between ten and 30 journalists have been in jail at any one time. Most were charged with "apology for terrorism" and several were convicted in the faceless courts.

Philippines

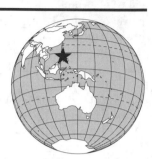

Polity: Presidential-legislative democracy
Economy: Capitalist-statist
Population: 71,974,000
PPP: $2,590
Life Expectancy: 66.5
Ethnic Groups: Christian Malay (92 percent), Muslim Malay (4 percent), Chinese (2 percent)

Political Rights: 2
Civil Liberties: 3*
Status: Free

Ratings Change: The Philippines's civil liberties rating changed from 4 to 3 because of the signing of a peace pact in August with a Muslim insurgent group, and because of a continuing reduction in the traditional ruling families' influences.

Overview: In 1996 Philippines President Fidel Ramos continued to insist he would stand down at the end of his term in 1998, even as supporters laid the groundwork for a referendum on scrapping term limits to allow for his re-election. A September accord ended the Muslim-based Moro National Liberation Front's (MNLF) 24-year campaign for autonomy on southern Mindanao island.

The Philippines achieved independence in 1946 after 43 years of colonial rule by the United States and occupation by Japan during World War II. President Ferdinand Marcos ruled for 21 years until being swept out of office in the February 1986 "People Power" revolution protesting massively rigged elections. His opponent, Corazon Aquino, subsequently took office. The 1987 constitution provides for a directly-elected president who is limited to a single six-year term, and a bicameral Congress consisting of a 24-member Senate and a House of Representatives with 201 directly-elected members and up to 50 more appointed by the president.

Former army chief-of-staff Fidel Ramos won the 1992 presidential election with just 23.5 percent of the vote. The Ramos administration's economic reforms have raised GDP growth rates and ended chronic power shortages, but have brought only marginal benefits to poorer Filipinos. At the May 1995 congressional elections a coalition of the president's National Union of Christian Democrats (Lakas-NUCD) party and the Democratic Filipino Struggle (LDP) took nine of the 12 seats being contested in the Senate; and 170 seats in the House, with the National People's Coalition taking the remaining 31 House seats.

In early 1996 Ramos's popularity waned as critics charged that the broad anti-terrorism bill backed by the president, which ultimately failed to gain congressional approval, was reminiscent of Marcos-era martial law. On May 31 LDP formally ended its coalition with the Lakas-NUCD to better position itself to field a presidential candidate in 1998. Meanwhile, Ramos's supporters are working to get the required public signatures to hold a referendum in 1997 on scrapping term limits to allow the president to run for re-election.

In a key development, on September 2, 1996 Ramos and Nur Misuari, the leader of the MNLF, signed a peace agreement establishing Misuari as head of a transitional body to oversee development projects in 14 provinces on Mindanao. The accord calls for a plebescite in these provinces in 1999 to determine the size of a future autonomous political region. However, the pact has not been recognized by the Moro Islamic Liberation Front (MILF), the Abu Sayyaf movement and other radical groups seeking an independent Islamic state. Further, several local Christian leaders claim the accord gives Muslims too much control in a region that is 65 percent Christian. Tensions heightened with reports that militant Christians were forming vigilante groups.

Political Rights and Civil Liberties:

Filipinos can change their government democratically, although elections continue to be marred by irregularities. Economic reforms have diminished somewhat the disproportionate political power wielded by economic oligarchies, wealthy landowners and political elites. Official corruption is rampant.

In recent years human rights violations by the army and the Citizens Armed Forces Geographical Units (CAFGU), a poorly trained paramilitary force, have declined along with a decrease in insurgency activity by the Communist Party of the Philippines, which is engaged in peace negotiations. However, the armed forces continue to commit human rights abuses against civilians in counterinsurgency operations in Mindanao. Succesive post-War governments have encouraged Christians to settle on Mindanao, creating economic and social grievances among the Muslims and the indigenous tribal people. In 1996 the extremist Abu Sayyaf group carried out bombings and arson attacks on churches and other targets on Mindanao and nearby Basilan Island, as well as kidnappings and killings of civilians, while skirmishes continued between the army and the MILF on Mindanao and Basilan.

Police frequently use excessive force against suspects during interrogations. Private armies kept by politicians and wealthy landowners are responsible for extrajudicial killings. Private security forces hired by logging operations have killed and arbitrarily detained members of indigenous groups in forest areas. Kidnappings, particularly of ethnic Chinese, continued in 1996.

The judiciary is independent of the government, but corruption is rife and the system is heavily backlogged. The private press is vigorous, although journalists face intimidation outside Manila from illegal logging outfits, drug smugglers and others. The government frequently restricts free assembly in the interest of not antagonizing fellow-members of the Association of Southeast Asian Nations. In November police forcibly broke up several protests prior to the Asia Pacific Economic Cooperation (APEC) forum summit in Manila. Authorities denied a visa to Jose Ramos-Horta, East Timor resistance movement spokesman and co-winner of the 1996 Nobel Peace Prize, during the summit.

The well-developed civil society includes numerous nongovernmental human rights organizations. However, security forces frequently falsely link human rights activists to the Communist insurgency, thus creating a climate that leads to human rights abuses against activists.

Freedom of religion is respected. Trafficking of Filipino women abroad is a serious problem, and domestic prostitution, including child prostitution, is rampant. Rape and domestic violence are widespread. Cities have large numbers of street children. The government has forcibly resettled tenant farmers and urban squatters to make way for development projects, and in 1996 authorities razed several thousand shanties in Manila prior to the APEC summit.

Workers are free to join independent unions. The International Labor Organization has criticized several provisions of the labor code restricting the right to strike, including a 1989 law allowing the government to order compulsory arbitration of disputes in "essential" industries. Police continue to harass striking workers, and several labor activists have been killed in recent years. Anti-union discrimination has prevented workers from organizing in most of the country's export processing zones (EPZ). In the Rosario EPZ south of Manila the provincial government has colluded with businesses to supress trade union activity, and workers frequently receive less than the minimum wage.

Poland

Polity: Presidential-parliamentary democracy
Economy: Mixed capitalist
Population: 38,639,000
PPP: $4,702
Life Expectancy: 71.1
Ethnic Groups: Polish (98 percent), German, Ukrainian, Belarusian
Capital: Warsaw

Political Rights: 1
Civil Liberties: 2
Status: Free

Overview:

Allegations of collaboration with Soviet, and subsequently Russian, intelligence led to the resignation of Prime Minister Jozef Oleksy in January 1996. He was replaced by Wlodzimierz Cimoszewicz, speaker of the *Sejm* (parliament) and a member of the ruling Democratic Left Alliance (SLD) headed by President Alexander Kwasniewski.

Other key issues were government reform, debate over a new constitution, preparations for 1997 parliamentary elections and a referendum on privatization. A strong economy paved the way for Poland's admittance to the Organization for Economic Cooperation and Development (OECD).

Partitioned by Prussia, Russia and Austria in the eighteenth century, Poland re-emerged as an independent republic after World War I. In 1939, it was invaded and divided by Nazi Germany and Stalinist Russia, coming under full German control after the Nazi invasion of Russia in 1941. After the war, its eastern territories became part of Ukraine. Poland was reimbursed for this loss by large tracts of eastern Prussia. The Communists gained control after fraudulent elections in 1947.

In 1980, the Solidarity free trade union was established by striking workers in the Gdansk shipyards. In December 1981, General Wojciech Jaruzelski declared martial law, banned the union and detained most senior activists.

In 1989, round-table discussions between the opposition and the ruling Communists ended post-war Communist dominance. In 1992, a so-called "Little Constitution" gave considerable power to Walesa, who had been directly elected in 1990. A fragmented parliament, with some 30 parties, and a powerful president led to a series of failed governments while so-called "shock therapy" market reforms steadily improved economic conditions.

In 1993, Poles swept the former Communists back into power under a new electoral law designed to reduce the number of parties in parliament. The SLD won 171 seats in the 460-seat Sejm (lower house), followed by the Peasant Party (PSL), an allied party in the Communist era, with 131 seats. The Democratic Union (UD), the mainstream Solidarity party, won 74 seats. The year-old leftist Union of Labor (UP) won 41 seats. Walesa's Non-Party Bloc to Support Reform (BBWR) gained 20 seats, while the nationalist Confederation for An Independent Poland (KPN) took 24. Waldemar Pawlak of the PSL was named prime minister.

In March 1995, Pawlak was replaced as prime minister by Oleksy after a three-month crisis during which opposition groups called for a caretaker non-party government of national unity. In November 1995, Kwasniewski defeated President Walesa in a run-off, winning 51.7 percent of the vote.

After months of charges that he had held regular meetings with Soviet and Russian intelligence since 1983, Oleksy stepped down in January 1996 and was replaced by Cimoszewicz. The new government was made up chiefly of SLD and PSL members.

In February, a referendum called by Walesa to change the method of privatization attracted a turnout of under 50 percent, too low for the vote to be binding. Of the 32 percent of voters who took part, 94 percent approved the proposal to distribute among the population assets that were still in state hands. The Solidarity union and the Catholic Church backed the referendum, charging that the current privatization policies favored a takeover of the economy by former Communists.

Privatization and government restructuring became a source of conflict between the SLD and the PSL a year before national parliamentary elections. In October, a government reshuffle left Finance Minister Grzegorz Kolodko in overall charge of the economy but turned responsibility for the sale of state sector companies over to Miroslaw Pietrewicz of the PSL, who once headed the defunct central planning office. The appointment was part of a political compromise to ensure survival of the ruling coalition. The privatization ministry, run by Wieslaw Kaczmarek (SLD), was eliminated. The PSL had criticized Kaczmarek for his zeal over privatization. The reforms created a new ministry of the economy which subsumed the former trade and industry and foreign trade ministry functions. This new ministry remained in the hands of the SLD, which got the powerful joint ministry of public administration and the interior. But further privatization was put in limbo.

In December, the PSL threatened to leave the government coalition if the SLD persisted with the idea of introducing a district (*powiat*) level of local government administration. Leszek Miller, head of the Office of the Council of Ministers (URM) said he supported a single, three-tier model of territorial self-government.

In 1996, the politicians were getting ready for the 1997 vote. Local self-government will clearly be an issue. Former Prime Minster Jan Olszewski, leader of the Movement for the Restoration of Poland (ROP), met Marian Krzaklewski, leader of the Solidarity union, in March to discuss the possibility of a common electoral front. In June, Solidarity and a group of smaller rightist parties established the Solidarity Electoral Action (AWS). In all, some 30 parties united to oust the SLD, and in July, polls showed that the AWS enjoyed 23 percent support, compared to 19 for the SLD. The ROP rejected invitations to join the AWS, which itself declined an offer to field a joint list of candidates for the Senate with the Freedom Union (UW), the largest opposition in parliament. The nationalist KPN and Walesa's Non-Party Bloc in Support of Reforms (BBWR), which have parties in parliament, are key members of the AWS.

Solidarity and other opposition groups want a constitution to be adopted after the 1997 elections. Unlike the "Little Constitution" of 1992, the new draft diminishes presidential powers, widens the prerogatives of the constitutional tribunal and allows citizens a greater say in legislative matters. While a preamble was adopted in November, the PSL and the Union of Labor Party held up parliamentary ratification by opposing the three-tier territorial administration and arguing that the constitution did not guarantee basic social rights, such as free medical care and free public schools.

Poland's economic recovery continued in 1996. Production and real wages grew, while unemployment and inflation fell. The IMF and the World Bank cited slow privatization, household debt and the lack of appropriate laws as hampering further economic development.

Political Rights and Civil Liberties: Poles can change their government democratically under a multiparty system. In 1992, President Walesa signed into law the so-called "Little Constitution." A new constitution has been drafted and should be adopted by parliament before being voted on by popular referendum in 1997.

Poland has over 200 political parties. But most are small or exist mainly on paper. The 1993 parliamentary elections were free and fair, as was the 1995 presidential vote.

There is a bustling free and independent press, and 85 percent of the media are privatized. Article 270 of the penal code prohibits anyone from deriding the Polish nation, its political system, or its principal organs. Article 273 imposes a prison term of up to ten years for anyone who violates Article 270 in print or through the mass media. The law has been enforced on several occasions. Foreign ownership of newspapers and magazines is limited to no more than 45 percent.

Personnel changes at Polish Public Television (TVP) led to the cancellation of programs too critical of the communist era. Tomasz Siemoniak, director of the most popular television station, Channel 1, was fired by a TVP board of directors dominated by the ruling coalition. In March Wieslaw Walendziak resigned as TVP president after his decisions were overruled. Polsat remains the most popular commercial television network. A license for central Poland was granted to TVN, which is owned by the Polish company ITI and the Central European Media Enterprises Group.

Freedom of discussion, assembly and association is respected. Religious freedom is accepted though critics have charged that the Roman Catholic Church exercises too much influence on public life, particularly in the drafting of a new constitution. Jewish cemeteries and synagogues have been restored, and cultural centers and schools are open, many supported by U.S.-based foundations.

The judiciary is not wholly free of interference from government, and financial and personnel problems continue to plague the justice ministry, the prosecutor's office and the courts. Most judges are holdovers from the Communist era. Political parties, parliamentary commissions, the State Security Office (under the jurisdiction of the minister of internal affairs), the government and the president's office continue to exert political pressure on the justice minister and prosecutors.

Four national interbranch industrial unions operate along with 17 other major independent industrial branch unions and three agricultural unions. The Independent Self-Governing Trade Union (NSZZ) Solidarity has a membership of 2 million. Spin-offs from mainstream Solidarity include the Christian Trade Union Solidarity and Solidarity '80. The National Alliance of Trade Unions (OPZZ), the successor of its Communist-era namesake, has about 3 million members and 61 parliamentary deputies. Other unions include the Free Miners' Union, which claims more than 300,000 members, and the National Teachers' Union. Several strikes took place in 1996, including actions by coal miners and doctors.

While the existing constitution guarantees equality of the sexes, women face discrimination in the job market. Anecdotal evidence suggests that there is a significant level of domestic violence, particularly in rural areas, often involving alcoholism and spousal abuse. As many as 20,000 nongovernmental organizations may be operating in the country, including political, professional, cultural, ecological, and single-issue groups and associations, as well as polling groups, think tanks, student and women's organizations.

Portugal

Polity: Presidential-
parliamentary democracy
Economy: Mixed
capitalist
Population: 9,942,000
PPP: $10,720
Life Expectancy: 74.7
Ethnic Groups: Portuguese, African minority
Capital: Lisbon

Political Rights: 1
Civil Liberties: 1
Status: Free

Overview:

Socialist candidate Jorge Sampaio won a decisive victory in January's presidential election over his conservative opponent, former Prime Minister Anibal Cavaco Silva. Just four months after the election of a Socialist government under Antonio Guterres, Sampaio's win estabished the Socialists as the dominant political force in Portugal.

In parliament, however, the Socialists are four seats short of an overall majority, and so risk defeat by a combined vote of opposition parties of the right and left. This government will need considerable support as it prepares to make spending cuts to meet European Monetary Union criteria.

Once a great maritime and colonial empire, Portugal's monarchy ended in a bloodless revolution in 1910. The subsequent republic, plagued by chronic instability and violence, ended in a military revolt in 1926, followed by a fascist dictatorship under Antonio Salazar from 1932 to 1968. In 1968, the dying Salazar was replaced by his lieutenant, Marcello Caetano. During what is now termed the "Marcello Spring," repression and censorship were relaxed somewhat, and a liberal wing developed inside the one-party National Assembly. Caetano was overthrown in a bloodless coup in 1974 by the Armed Forces Movement, tired of an endless colonial war in Mozambique and Angola. The following year, a transition to democracy began with the election of a constitutional assembly that adopted a democratic constitution.

Sampaio's election marks the end of a conservative era which advanced Portugal economically but failed to satisfy voters' eagerness for social change. In his ten years as prime minister, Cavaco Silva led the country into the European Union (EU), launched an ambitious privatization program, and channelled massive funding into Portugal's infrastructure. Sampaio has vowed to continue economic reforms, but he won popularity by adding a social dimension to his agenda. Issues like education, health, housing and the environment have taken on greater importance in the minds of constituents than the materialism which dominated over ten years of conservative rule.

Despite opposition from small groups on the left and right to the Maastricht criteria for European Monetary Union (EMU), Prime Minister Guterres has promised to forge ahead. His government in October proposed a budget designed to bring the country's fiscal deficit below the target of three percent of GDP in 1997. By the end of the year, opinion surveys favored Guterres, the government was more stable than expected, and Portugal was within sight of meeting EMU criteria to join the first group of single currency countries in 1999.

Political Rights and Civil Liberties: Portuguese can change their government democratically. In direct, competitive elections, voters, including a large number of Portuguese living abroad, select both the president and members of parliament. Political association is unrestricted with the exception of fascist organizations. However, members of small extreme-right groups have run candidates for public office without interference.

Portuguese courts are autonomous, bound only to established law and the demands of the constitution. They are generally noted for adherence to traditional principles of independent jurisprudence, but inefficient bureaucratic organization has created a tremendous backlog of cases in the system.

Freedom of speech and assembly is respected with few exceptions. Though the law forbids insults directed at the government or the armed forces with intent to undermine the rule of law, the state has never prosecuted under this provision.

The print media are owned by political parties and private publishers. They are free and competitive. Until 1990, television and radio were state-owned with the exception of the Catholic radio station, Radio Renascenca. Although television broadcasting remains dominated by the state-owned Radiotelevisao Portuguesa, by mid-1994 two independent stations had begun to operate.

Workers have the right to strike and are represented by competing Communist and non-Communist organizations. In recent years the two principal labor federations, the General Union of Workers and the General Confederation of Portuguese Workers Intersindical, have charged "clandestine" companies with exploiting child labor in the impoverished north. The minimum employment age will be raised from 15 to 16 in January 1997, when the period of compulsory schooling is to be extended.

The status of women has improved with economic modernization. Concentrated in agriculture and domestic service, women workers now comprise 37 percent of the official labor force. Despite a few prominent exceptions, female representation in government and politics averages less than ten percent.

Qatar

Polity: Traditional monarchy
Economy: Capitalist-statist
Population: 667,000
PPP: $22,910
Life Expectancy: 70.6
Ethnic Groups: Arab (40 percent), Pakistani (18 percent), Indian (18 percent), Iranian
Capital: Doha

Political Rights: 7
Civil Liberties: 6
Status: Not Free

Overview:

On February 20 the emir, Shaikh Hamad bin Khalifa Al-Thani, arrested 100 soldiers and police for plotting to depose him in favor of his father, who denied any complicity in the alleged conspiracy. By October, an agreement enabled the father to return to Qatar and accept his son's leadership position.

Qatar became a British protectorate in 1916 and gained independence in 1971. Under the 1970 Basic Law, an emir is chosen from adult males of the Al-Thani family. The Basic Law also provides for a Council of Ministers and a partially elected *Majlis al-Shura* (Advisory Council). However, no elections have ever been held, and the Majlis is appointed. In 1972 Sheik Khalifa ibn Hamad Al-Thani deposed his cousin, Emir Ahmad ibn 'Ali ibn 'Abdallah Al-Thani, in a palace coup.

In December 1991, 50 prominent citizens signed a petition calling for democratic reforms. The government interrogated several signers and prevented three from attending a pro-democracy conference in Kuwait.

On June 27, 1995, Crown Prince Hamad, long recognized as the real power in the country, deposed his father in a palace coup while the emir was in Switzerland. In November, the new emir announced he would hold municipal elections in the future. In May 1996 elections were set for mid-1997.

Political Rights and Civil Liberties:

Citizens of Qatar cannot change their government democratically. Political parties are illegal, and there have never been elections. The emir holds absolute power and appoints the cabinet. While the emir consults with leading members of society on policy issues and works to reach a consensus with the appointed Majlis, the only recourse for ordinary citizens is to submit appeals to the emir.

The security apparatus includes the Interior Ministry's Mubahathat (Investigatory Police), which handles sedition and espionage cases, and the military's Mukhabarat (Intelligence Service), which monitors political dissidents. Both services can detain suspects indefinitely without charge while conducting an investigation, although long-term detention occurs infrequently. These two units, together with the Interior Ministry's regular police and General Administration of Public Security unit, mostly monitor foreigners, who outnumber Qataris four to one.

The judiciary is not independent. Most judges are foreign nationals whose residence permits can be revoked at any time. Civil courts have jurisdiction in civil and commercial disputes, while Islamic *Shari'a* courts handle criminal and family cases. Shari'a court trials are not open to the general public, although family members are permitted. Lawyers help participants prepare cases but are not permitted in the courtroom. Non-Muslims cannot bring suits to the Shari'a courts.

Freedom of speech, expression and press is severely restricted. Public criticism of the ruling family or of Islam is forbidden. In October 1995 Sheik Hamad ended official censorship of the privately owned press, though significant self-censorship is practiced; and on June 26, 1996, the daily *As Sharq* was suspended for three months for publishing a Saudi poem. Moreover, the Ministry of Endowments and Islamic Affairs, in protecting public morality and religious values, censors cable television, imported videos, and "offensive" photos and stories from international publications.

The electronic media are state-owned and promote official views. A government censorship board screens all locally published books and cultural items. Academic freedom is not protected and university professors reportedly practice self-censorship. Civil society is limited to professional associations and other strictly non-political organizations which are monitored by the government.

Foreign nationals employed as domestic workers face sexual harassment and physical abuse. Although the authorities have investigated and punished several employers, most women apparently do not report abuse for fear of losing their residence permits. Women face social and legal discrimination in divorce and inheritance matters. Men may prevent wives or female relatives from traveling abroad. Women need permission from male relatives to obtain a driver's license. Children trafficked from South Asia and Africa are used as jockeys in camel races, in which they are often injured, sometimes fatally.

The Wahabbi branch of Sunni Islam is the state religion. Non-Muslims may not worship publicly and face discrimination in employment.

Workers cannot form labor unions or bargain collectively. Workers can belong to "joint consultative committees" composed of worker and management representatives that discuss issues, including working conditions and work schedules, but not wages. The government's Labor Conciliation Board is charged with mediating disputes. Except for government employees and domestic help, workers can hold strikes if mediation fails. Strikes rarely occur in practice, in part because employers may dismiss employees after the Board has heard a case. Employers sometimes exercise leverage over foreign workers by refusing to grant mandatory exit permits.

Romania

Polity: Presidential-par-
liamentary democracy
Economy: Mixed statist
transitional
Population: 22,644,000
PPP: $3,727
Life Expectancy: 69.9

Political Rights: 2*
Civil Liberties: 3
Status: Free

Ethnic Groups: Romanian (88 percent), Hungarian (9 percent),
German, Roma (Gypsy)
Capital: Bucharest
Ratings Change: Romania's political rights rating changed from 4 to 2 because a
competitive multiparty system was affirmed in free and fair elections that saw
opposition non-Communist forces come to power.

Overview:

The local and national elections that ended the rule of President Ion Iliescu and the ex-communist Party of Social Democracy of Romania (PSDR) were the most significant Romanian political developments in 1996.

Romania became independent following the 1878 Berlin Congress. Soviet troops entered the country in 1944, whereupon King Michael dismissed the pro-German regime and backed the Allies. In 1945, he was forced to accept a Communist-led coalition government. Nicole Ceausescu's autarkic economics and bizarre personality devastated Romania during his rule from 1965-89. A popular uprising and palace coup by disgruntled Communists toppled Ceausescu, who was tried and executed on Christmas 1989. A provisional government was formed under President Ion Iliescu, a high-ranking Communist.

The governing coalition under Prime Minister Nicolae Vacaroiu underwent severe tension as the year went by and elections drew close. In March, the neo-communist Social Labor Party quit the government; at the same time, that the PSDR decided to break with the ultranationalist Party of Romanian National Unity (PUNR). When this tactic failed in local elections, the PSDR finally decided to abandon the PUNR in September in the hopes of burnishing its image for the national elections. PUNR itself appeared to be disintegrating as several prominent members left.

Local elections for mayoralties and local councils in 3000 constituencies were held in June. The opposition, led by the Democratic Convention of Romania (CDR) and the Social Democratic Union (USD), made important gains, especially in urban areas. The PSDR continued to control rural areas. In Bucharest, the CDR's Victor Ciorbea beat PSDR candidate and former tennis star Ilie Nastase for mayor.

Early opinion polls for the presidential and the parliamentary elections showed Iliescu and the PSDR comfortably in the lead. Emil Constantinescu, the CDR standard-bearer, promised a "Contract with Romania" styled after the slogan of the U.S. Republican Party, with faster economic and political reform, a campaign against corruption, the removal of barriers to private enterprise, welfare reform, and tax cuts. The campaign was a bitter one, and filled with anti-Hungarian and anti-Semitic overtones, as well as mysterious incidents such as break-ins to opposition party headquarters.

In the first round of the presidential election in early November, Iliescu held a 4 percent lead over Constantinescu, with Roman close behind. In the parliamentary elections, the CDR pulled off an upset, winning 30 percent of the vote. The PSDR won 22 percent, while the the the USD and the Hungarian Democratic Fedaration of Romania (UDMR) received 13 percent and 7 percent, respectively. The extremist Greater Romania Party (5 percent) and PUNR (4 percent) continued their slide into marginality.

The CDR, USD and the UDMR inked a coalition pact in which the latter two threw their support behind Constantinescu in the presidential run-off election. Constantinescu defeated the incumbent, 54 to 46 percent. In December, a coalition accord was finalized between the three parties, which control 287 of 486 seats in parliament. The CDR, the main party in the coalition, nominated Ciorbea as prime minister.

The economy grew less quickly in 1996. Both structural and macroeconomic reforms slowed down tremendously this year as electoral politics intruded on economic policy and the PSDR turned toward populism. Huge strikes were held this year by coal, auto, steel, refinery and mass transit workers. A paper mill strike turned violent.

Political Rights and Civil Liberties:

Citizens can change governments democratically. While the June local elections were generally regarded as free and fair, they were not without problems. In Bucharest, for example, 100,000 dead Romanians were mysteriously registered to vote at the same time that entire neighborhoods were dropped off the electoral rolls. 20 percent of ballots were ruled invalid. The opposition charged that the government set up bureaucratic hurdles to prevent opposition candidates from registering. Council of Europe and OSCE observers judged the November elections as "free and generally fair," though there were some irregularities. Two million invalid ballots were cast, 5 percent of the total.

Despite harsh opposition from left and right extremist organizations the Political Parties Law was passed in March, allowing for ethnic parties to form. In April, a new law was passed on local administration. Prefects are no longer able to dismiss mayors without prior judicial approval, a practice which had largely been a tool to get rid of opposition mayors.

While the Romanian press remains vigorous, some disturbing events this year on both the local and national level have marred its progress. Local administrators in small towns have tried to control the press by bringing charges of slander against local journalists. In July, two journalists from the daily newspaper, *Telegraf,* were sentenced to seven months in prison for libel and fined 25 million lei ($8200). These journalists reported on local corruption, which had resulted in the dismissal of a deputy mayor. Following a firestorm of criticism, the chief prosecutor suspended their sentences. In August, journalists protested the replacement of the editor-in-chief at the state RADOR news agency with a former activist in the Communist Party's Central Committee. In October, an editor and a journalist from the daily *Ziua* were forbidden to work in the press again and sentenced to one year and 14 months, respectively for "offending the authorities." This offense consisted of suggestions that Iliescu had been recruited by the KGB in his youth.

State-run television, the only truly nationwide broadcaster, is the primary source of news for 75 percent of Romanians. Private television, led by the one-year old Ronald Lauder's PRO-TV, is growing rapidly, but still reaches less than half of Romanians. Private FM stations reach small audiences. Adrian Nastase, chairman of the PSDR, formally asked the National Council for Media to prevent local radio stations from broadcasting BBC reports on Romania because of their alleged bias against his party.

Ethnic relations with the Hungarian minority are strained. Evidence shows state discrimination against Hungarians, especially in administrative posts. Restitution has been quite slow to Hungarian churches. While religious freedom is generally respected, reports have been made that several Protestant denominations have been subject to harassment and bureaucratic interference by low-level officials. Religious broadcasting is also subject to restrictions.

The judiciary is only partly independent. The military prosecutor's office oversees police conduct. Under a 1992 judiciary reorganization, the Justice Ministry controls judges' selection and advancement. Substantial evidence suggests that the judiciary is strongly influenced by the executive branch. Constitutional court decisions may be overruled by a two-thirds vote in parliament. However, a draft law making it even easier to overturn court decisions was voted down in June. In addition, the importance of the judiciary grew this year as a means of settling electoral disputes. As in previous years, 1996 witnessed an inconsistent and often arbitrary application of due process, especially for Hungarians and Roma. Suspects and prisoners were frequently abused at the hands of the police, and often were uninformed as to their legal rights.

Corruption is pervasive in Romanian government as a whole and has led to widespread cynicism in society about the state. The Romanian police chief, Ion Pitulescu, resigned in protest in February over rank corruption in the judiciary which allegedly had led to early release of felons.

The right to strike and join trade unions is guaranteed; however, trade unions face difficulties in state-owned enterprises. While women face no legal obstacles to participating in society, the authorities are lax in the enforcement of equal rights.

Russia

Polity: Presidential-par- **Political Rights:** 3
liamentary democracy **Civil Liberties:** 4
Economy: Mixed statist **Status:** Partly Free
transitional
Population: 147,700,000
PPP: $4,760
Life Expectancy: 67.4
Ethnic Groups: Russian (82 percent), over 100 ethnic groups
Capital: Moscow

| **Overview:** | In 1996, Boris Yeltsin was re-elected president, but persistent heart problems, subsequent surgery and long convalesce emboldened the opposition to raise the issue of his ability |

to govern. But power remained in the hands of Yeltsin's close advisers, Chief of
Staff Anatoly Chubais and Prime Minister Viktor Chernomyrdin. Alexander Lebed,
who challenged Yeltsin in the presidential election, was made head of the Security
Council and point man on negotiating a settlement to the crisis in the breakaway
republic of Chechnya, before being suddenly dismissed by Yeltsin in October. In
June, Yeltsin replaced Defense Minister Pavel Grachev with hardline General Igor
Rodionov.

With the USSR's collapse in December 1991, Russia—the only constituent
republic not to declare sovereignty —gained de facto independence under President Yeltsin, directly elected in June 1991. In 1992, Yeltsin was repeatedly challenged by a hostile anti-reform legislature. Parliament replaced acting Prime Minister Yegor Gaidar, a principal architect of reforms, with Viktor Chernomyrdin, a
Soviet-era manager.

In 1993, the struggle between Yeltsin and parliment intensified over presidential powers and a new constitution. In September, Yeltsin suspended hardline Vice
President Rutskoi, dissolved parliament and set parliamentary elections for December. Opposition deputies barricaded themselves in the parliamentary complex. In
early October, after riots by extremists supporting the protesters, troops crushed
the uprising, arresting Khasbulatov and Rutskoi.

In December 1993, Russians approved Yeltsin's constitution which established
a bicameral Federal Assembly: a Federation Council (Upper House) consisting of
two representatives from the country's 89 regions and territories, and a 450-member State Duma. Communists and nationalist blocs dominated the elections.

In parliamentary elections in December 1995 communists and nationalists again
scored an impressive victory. Nearly 70 million of 107 million eligible voters went
to the polls. Each voter cast two votes, one for a single candidate and one for a
party. Half of the 450 members were elected in single-seat constituencies; the other
225 were elected according to party lists. The Communist Party took 157 seats; Our
Home is Russia, 55; the Liberal Democrats, 51; Yabloko, 45; the Agrarians, 20;
Democratic Choice, 9; Power to the People, 9; the Russian Communities, 5; and
Women of Russia, 3. Independents accounted for 77 seats, and the rest went to smaller
parties.

In the 1996 presidential campaign, the Communists led by Gennady Zyuganov sought to capitalize on their parliamentary gains. But Zyuganov's lack of a coherent program other than a return to socialism did not strike a responsive chord among voters. Despite poor health, Yeltsin campaigned vigorously and was openly supported by Russia's most influential media and business elite. Grigory Yavlinsky, author of the radical "500 Day" economic reform measures under Gorbachev, the buffoonish Zhirinovsky and the populist General Lebed rounded out the field. The first round on June 16 was close, with Yeltsin edging out Zyuganov 35 to 32 percent, with Lebed getting 14 percent, Yavlinsky 8, and Zhirinovsky 6. Yeltsin handily won July's runoff, 53.9 percent to 40.3 percent.

In August, Yeltsin formed a government committed to pressing ahead with economic reform but with a greater emphasis on social welfare. Lebed was named national security chief, and Chubais the liberal economic reformer who had been ousted as first deputy prime minister in January but who had directed Yeltsin's successful presidential campaign was named chief of staff. Vladimir Potanin, a pro-market banker, was appointed deputy prime minister in charge of the economy. Alexander Livshits, chief presidential economic aide, was named head of a strengthened finance ministry with a brief to raise more tax revenue and close a widening budget deficit.

General Lebed, among the country's most popular politicians, was ousted by Yeltsin in the fall after his bitter rival, Interior Minister Anatoly Kulikov, accused him of planning a coup. Charges of corruption added to the political uncertainty, which held up foreign investment and economic revival. Oleg Soskovets, who stepped down in June as the second most senior government minister, was accused of profiting from deals in the metal industry. Persistent rumors alleged that his arch-rival Chubais had avoided paying income taxes.

In 1996, 48 governors appointed by the president faced elections for the first time; 20 incumbents held on to their jobs and 24 were defeated. At the end of the year, three held their jobs pending repeat elections and one run-off was scheduled for January 1997. Members of the government and presidential administration voiced concern about the state of federalism in Russia. On October 29, Chief of Staff Chubais promised to crack down on what he called "legal separatism," whereby regional and local governments adopt laws and sign economic agreements that are not in accordance with federal legislation. Central government authorities also expressed fears that the direct election of governors provided a power base independent of Moscow that could accelerate the trend toward decentralization.

In economic affairs, reforms moved haltingly along. Yeltsin dismissed fears that state control would be re-introduced over some privatized industries. Private share of GDP rose to over 60 percent, but overall economic output fell by 3 percent. Privatization of large state-run enterprises lagged; state monopolies still controlled the railways, natural gas and electricity. The banking sector remained in urgent need of reform as several commercial banks closed down or were in financial trouble. Tax evasion was rampant. The 1997 budget included greater outlays for social spending and welfare.

Political Rights and Civil Liberties: Russians can change their government democratically. The 1993 constitution established a strong presidency, but decentralization and institutional checks put limits on executive authority. The 1995 parliamentary elections were generally free and fair, though over 1 million votes were invalidated, and the presidential race in 1996 was also free and fair.

Forty-three parties contested the 1995 parliamentary elections, and more than 50 parties and groups are registered. There are several "unregistered" groups, mainly extremists on the left and right of the political spectrum. In December 1996, the State Duma passed a law to limit so-called "divan parties," in which all members could fit on a single sofa. The law stipulates that only a group of at least 100 people can found a political party. Parties that seek to violently change the constitutional order or to violate the territorial integrity of the Russian Federation would be prohibited, as would the creation of armed groups or parties that promote racial, ethnic and religious hatred.

More than 150 independent TV and radio companies operate in Russia, as well as foreign cable broadcasters and satellite dishes in large cities. In mid-1995, the State Press Committee announced that 10,500 newspapers were published in the country, most with print runs of less than 10,000 copies. Ostankino and Russian State Television (ORT)—of which the government owns 51 percent of shares—transmit nationwide and to most of the Commonwealth of Independent States. Independent companies include NTV, TV-6, and "2X2". The government has attempted greater control, and shows have been suspended or canceled. Television studios on local levels operate more or less independently. They function as affiliates, opting to use programs from the national company and producing local news shows independently. Local authorities sometimes subject these affiliates to pressure. In 1996, the Glasnost Defense Foundation, which monitors press freedom, reported that in some regions, not a single regional newspaper or broadcaster was independent; and during the 1996 gubernatorial races, regional journalists in many areas faced harassment and intimidation by authorities. News agencies include the Russian Information Telegraph-Telegraphic Agency of the Sovereign Countries (ITAR-TASS), the Russian Information Agency-Novosti, as well as several independent agencies, the most influential of which is Interfax. While censorship is proscribed by the constitution and the Law on Mass Media, court decisions have substantially limited journalists' freedom to criticize public figures. Libel cases are tried in court on the basis of the Law on the Mass Media and the Law on the Protection of the Honor, Dignity, and Business Reputation of Citizens (1991). Penalties are normally financial in nature. The President's Judicial Chamber on Information Disputes has ruled that journalists and editors are responsible for disseminating false information, even if an article contains disclaimers such as " it is rumored," "it is said," or "according to unverified information."

Freedom of assembly is generally respected. Freedom of religion also exists in this primarily Russian Orthodox country. Reports were made of violence and intimidation directed at Evangelical Christians, especially in Muslim regions and southern Russia. Incidents of anti-Semitism were also reported.

The process of reforming the legal and judicial systems has been progressing slowly. In July 1993, parliament passed a law authorizing the phased introduction of a jury system. The constitution provides for the presumption of innocence, but prosecutors enjoy numerous built-in procedural advantages. In 1991, the death penalty was abolished for foreign currency speculation and bribery, as was the law banning private enterprise. A 1992 draft criminal code gave priority to the defense of the individual, the interests of property owners and private enterprise. Additional reforms were made in 1995-96. The Constitutional Court ruled that Article 220 of the criminal code, which restricts the legal right to contest arrests, was unconstitutional. In February 1995, the Duma passed a bill reducing the period in which suspects can be held in custody without indictment from 30 to 10 days. President Yeltsin signed into law reforms to criminal procedure that gave certain privileges to prisoners held in isolation. Moreover, it provided for prisoners to serve their sentences in their own regions, and separated first-time offenders from recidivists. A new criminal code, adopted in May 1996 and meant to go into force on January 1, 1997, replaced the RSFSR's criminal code of 1960. Although it retains the death penalty (albeit for five rather than 18 crimes) and increases the maximum sentences for banditry and murder, it significantly reduces sentences for non-violent crimes.

A new law to improve the independence and qualifications of judges went into effect on June 27, 1995. Judges will be required to have at least five years of experience in the legal profession. In addition, the law raised judges' salaries and changed retirement rules in order to attract the best jurists to the profession. Some regions and republics had demanded the right to appoint their own judges to higher courts. A spate of resignations among judges and procurators in August 1996 was triggered by austerity measures introduced by presidential decree. Financial and legislative constraints upon the judiciary means that it is not fully independent of other branches of government. In December 1996, the Federation Council passed a law on the judicial system which stipulated that judges will be appointed by the Russian president, and all courts would be funded entirely by the federal budget.

The Federal Security Service, a successor to the KGB, still enjoys extra-judicial powers, including the right to search premises without a court order. Pretrial detention centers are generally deplorable, and prisoners presumed innocent often languish for months in filthy, overcrowded cells before coming to trial.

An independent commission reported serious, widespread human rights violations, citing ethnic and religious discrimination; labor exploitation; attacks on the media and prisoners' rights. Abuses by Russian forces were rampant in Chechnya; Sergei Kovalev, head of the government's human rights commission, resigned in protest.

The Federation of Independent Unions of Russia, a successor to the Soviet-era federation, has a membership estimated at 39 million. Newer, independent unions represent between 500,000 and 1 million workers, including seafarers, dockworkers, air traffic controllers, pilots and some coal miners. Several major strikes took place in 1996, including a national strike of miners. A multitude of nongovernmental civic, human rights, social, youth, cultural and women's organizations operate freely. Certain extremist groups were banned after the October 1993 crisis.

Women are entitled to the same legal rights as men, and are well represented at many levels of the general economy. However, women face discrimination in such areas as equal pay and promotions. Women's groups have raised such issues as domestic violence and women's role in society.

Rwanda

Polity: Dominant party **Political Rights:** 7
(military-dominated) **Civil Liberties:** 6
Economy: Mixed statist **Status:** Not Free
Population: 6,853,000
PPP: $740
Life Expectancy: 47.2
Ethnic Groups: Hutu (84 percent), Tutsi (15 percent), Twa (1 percent)
Capital: Kigali

Overview: **G**uerrilla attacks and assassinations by Hutu extremist, and murderous reprisals by Rwanda's Tutsi-dominated army, marked a violent year in Rwanda even as local and inter-national efforts to bring to trial perpetrators of the country's 1994 genocide picked up speed. In October, threats of ethnic cleansing against ethnic Tutsi long resident in eastern Zaire prompted a rebellion aided by Rwanda, and precipitated a new hu-manitarian crisis. About 60,000 soldiers and militia loyal to the former regime, re-trained and armed with foreign assistance, had for two-and-one-half years kept a firm hold on more than a million Hutu refugees along the country's frontiers, and used their camps as bases for attacks into Rwanda. Most of the camps were broken up in the October-November fighting, and over a half million refugees have now returned to an uncertain future in their homeland.

This tragedy is just the latest in the region's terrible modern history. In April-June 1994, a half million people or more, mostly ethnic Tutsis but also many politi-cally-moderate Hutus, were massacred in a swift and savage genocide. The ethnic rivalries have long roots. Belgian colonists drew boundaries that forced the two groups to vie for power in a modern state. Traditional Tutsi dominance ended with a Hutu rebellion in 1959 and independence in 1962. Hundreds of thousands of Tutsi were killed or fled the country over the next decades in recurring paroxysms of violence. In October, 1990, the Tutsi-led Rwanda Patriotic Front (RPF) launched a guerrilla war to force the Hutu regime, then led by General Juvenal Habyarimana, to accept power-sharing and resettlement of Tutsi refugees. Hutu chauvinists of-fered a simple resolution of claims to land and power by Rwanda's Tutsi minority (roughly 15 percent of the 8 million pre-genocide population): their physical elimi-nation as a people.

The immediate cause of the slaughter was the suspicious crash that killed Presi-dent Habyarimana, along with Burundian President Cyprien Ntaryamira, as their plane approached the airport at Rwanda's capital, Kigali. But the massacres had already been well-plotted; piles of machetes had been imported and death-lists were read out over the radio. As the killings spread, the small UN force in Rwanda with-drew, and Tutsi rebels advanced. The only intervention came in late 1994 when French troops arrived not to halt the genocide, but to preserve some territory for the crumbling government army.

International relief efforts eased suffering among more than two million Hutu refugees along Rwanda's frontiers. But with them in Zaire were large numbers of ex-government troops. Credible reports say French advisors and weapons, with the cooperation of Zairian authorities, have helped to rearm and retrain the defeated force, which is still commanded by the architects of the genocide. A UN commission investigating arms shipments to these killers has reportedly discovered the complicity of several governments.

Political Rights and Civil Liberties:

Rwandans have never exercised the right to change their government by peaceful and democratic means. Elections were last held in 1988 under a one-party state. A power-sharing pact was negotiated in 1992 between the then-government and rebel RPF, but never came into force. The current government is self-appointed and dominated by the RPF. A 70-member multiparty national assembly was appointed in November 1994. No date for elections has been set, and the RPF is highly unlikely to allow voting on a one-person, one-vote basis, which would inevitably return power to the majority Hutu. The national constitution, known as the Fundamental Law, is an amalgam of the 1991 constitution, two agreements among various parties and groups and the RPF's own 1994 declaration on governance.

Several political parties are operating, although ethnic or religious-based parties are prohibited. Two political parties closely identified with the 1994 massacres are banned. The RPF has made well-publicized efforts to include Hutu representatives in the government, including the appointment of President Pasteur Bizimungu, but it has also been hit by Hutu defections.

Broadcast media are still controlled by the state, and the several independent newspapers publishing in Kigali reportedly exercise considerable self-censorship. The immediate future will test the freedom and responsibility of the media. During the genocide, 50 journalists were among those murdered, while some of their colleagues, in particular radio journalists, broadcast incitements to slaughter. At least three Hutu radio journalists were detained in 1996 on charges of participation in the 1994 genocide. Suggestions of how best to combat such "hate media" range from bombing and jamming radio stations to setting up rival "pro-peace" media outlets.

The guerilla war in Rwanda's countryside through most of 1996, especially along the Zaire frontier, was facilitated by cross-border incursions from Hutu extremists among refugees in Zaire. Genocide survivors and local officials were particular targets for the militia. Human rights monitors also reported numerous extrajudicial executions by government forces.

About 80,000 people—many surely genocide participants but others likely falsely accused—were held under abysmal conditions in prisons meant for a small fraction of that number, and arrests continued through 1996. The virtual paralysis of the Rwanda justice system ensures little effective investigation. However, new legislation covering genocide crimes was approved in August and the appointment of 280 new judges in September raised hope for faster processing of cases. Meanwhile, constitutional and legal safeguards regarding arrest procedures and detention are widely ignored.

Religious freedom is generally respected, although many clerics were among both the victims and perpetrators of the genocide. Local nongovernmental organizations, including the Collective Rwandan Leagues and Associations for the Defense of Human Rights (CLADHO), operate openly. International human rights groups and relief organizations have been very active, although the government suspended operations of some in late 1995.

Women's rights also receive legal protection, but serious de facto discrimination continues. Rape by Hutu soldiers and militias was widespread in 1994. Constitutional provisions provide for labor rights, including the right to form trade unions, to engage in collective bargaining and to strike. As long as Rwanda and the region remain at war, however, respect for human rights and fundamental freedoms are likely to improve little. The first genocide trial opened in late December.

St. Kitts-Nevis

Polity: Parliamentary democracy
Economy: Capitalist
Population: 41,000
PPP: $9,340
Life Expectancy: 70.0
Ethnic Groups: Black (95 percent), mulatto
Capital: Basseterre

Political Rights: 1
Civil Liberties: 2
Status: Free

Overview: In 1996 Nevis nearly seceded from this two-island country until Nevis Reformation Party (NRP) leaders decided to reexamine the economic implications of such action.

The national government is comprised of the prime minister, the cabinet and the bicameral legislative assembly. Elected assembly members, eight from St. Kitts and three from Nevis, serve five-year terms. Senators, not to exceed two-thirds of the elected members, are appointed, one by the leader of the parliamentary opposition for every two by the prime minister. The British monarch is represented by a governor-general who appoints as prime minister the leader of the party or coalition with at least a plurality of seats in the legislature. Nevis has a local assembly comprised of five elected and three appointed members. St. Kitts has no similar body. Nevis is accorded the constitutional right to secede if two-thirds of the elected legislators approve and two-thirds of voters endorse it through a referendum.

The center-right People's Action Movement (PAM) gained power in 1980 with NRP support. In 1983 the country achieved independence. The PAM-NRP coalition won majorities in the 1984 and 1989 elections.

In the 1993 elections the St. Kitts Labour Party (SKLP) and the PAM each won four seats, though the former won the popular vote. The Concerned Citizens Movement (CCM) took two Nevis seats and the NRP one. The CCM opted not to join the coalition, leaving a PAM-NRP to rule with a five-seat plurality.

SKLP leader Denzil Douglas protested the new government, calling for a government shutdown. Violence erupted, leading to a two-week state of emergency. The SKLP boycotted parliament in 1994.

In late 1994, the PAM government was shaken by a drugs-and-murder scandal that involved the deputy prime minister and two of his sons, and the killing of a police official who had been investigating a third son's murder. The weakened government agreed to hold early elections.

The July 1995 elections ended 15 years of PAM rule. The SKLP won seven of eight St. Kitts seats and 60 percent of the popular vote. The PAM took the eight St.

Kitts seats, and 40 percent of the popular vote. On Nevis, the CCM retained its two seats and the NRP held on to the third. Since the elections, PAM alleges that the SKLP is dismissing or demoting PAM supporters and filling positions with SKLP supporters.

In July 1996 Nevis premier Vance Amory, reacting to St. Kitts' unwelcome move to open a government office in Nevis, announced his intention to break the 100-year political link between the two islands. Initially, all five elected Nevis assembly members offered their support. Shortly after, the two NRP members had a change of heart.

The amount of cocaine passing through the Caribbean en route to the U.S. has reportedly doubled in the past five years. St. Kitts is one of more than ten Caribbean islands to sign drug-enforcement pacts with the United States.

Political Rights and Civil Liberties: Citizens are able to change their government democratically. Constitutional guarantees regarding free expression, the free exercise of religion and the right to organize political parties, labor unions and civic organizations are generally respected.

However, drugs and money-laundering have corrupted the political system. Apart from the 1995 drug-and-murder scandal questions also regard business relations between SKLP leaders and known drug trafficker Noel "Zambo" Heath.

The judiciary is generally independent. However, in March 1996 when the drug-and-murder scandal came to trial, the Public Prosecutions Office failed to send a representative to present the case. The charges were dropped, raising suspicions of a government conspiracy. The highest court is the West Indies Supreme Court in St. Lucia, which includes a Court of Appeal and a High Court. Under certain circumstances there is a right of appeal to the Privy Council in London.

The traditionally strong rule of law has been tested by the increase in drug-related crime and corruption. In 1995, it appeared that the police had become divided along political lines between the two main political parties. The national prison is overcrowded and conditions are terrible.

The main labor union, the St. Kitts Trades and Labour Union, is associated with the ruling SKLP. The right to strike, while not specified by law, is recognized and generally respected in practice.

Television and radio on St. Kitts are government-owned and opposition parties habitually claim the ruling party takes unfair advantage. In 1996 Prime Minister Douglas confirmed he would keep his campaign promise to privatize St. Kitts television and radio. Each major political party publishes a weekly or fortnightly newspaper. Opposition publications freely criticize the government and international media are widely available. Nevis has a religious television station and a privately-owned radio station.

Though women have been elected to parliament in the past, none ran in the 1995 elections. Women do hold high-ranking public positions and are active in political parties. Though they face no restrictions, human rights groups have not been established on St. Kitts-Nevis.

St. Lucia

Polity: Parliamentary democracy
Economy: Capitalist
Population: 145,000
PPP: $3,795
Life Expectancy: 72.0
Ethnic Groups: Black (90 percent), mulatto
Capital: Castries

Political Rights: 1
Civil Liberties: 2
Status: Free

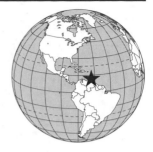

Overview: In January 1996 Prime Minister John Compton, leader of the center-right United Workers Party (UWP), announced his decision to retire, triggering a series of changes throughout the government.

St. Lucia, a member of the British Commonwealth, achieved independence in 1979. The British monarchy is represented by a governor-general.

Under the 1979 constitution, a bicameral parliament consisting of a 17-member House of Assembly is elected for five years, and an 11-member Senate, six of whom are appointed by the prime minister, three by the leader of the parliamentary opposition, and two by consultation with civic and religious organizations. The island is divided into eight regions, each with its own elected council and administrative services.

Compton's decision to retire was apparently linked to a number of scandals over the past few years which included an alleged affair with a teenager. He had also been accused of knowing about the misappropriation of UN funds. Soon after his announcement, his deputy both as prime minister and party leader, 72-year-old George Mallet, announced his decision to retire, clearing the way for Compton's handpicked successor, former director-general of the Organization of Eastern Caribbean States (OECS), Vaughan Lewis. Lewis won Mallet's vacated seat in February's by-elections.

Now holding a seat, Lewis was qualified to assume the party leadership. In April, since his party won the most seats, he automatically became the prime minister. Compton had been prime minister for all but three of the past 32 years and had served in parliament for 40 years. He is expected to remain a powerful figure behind the scenes.

In June, upon the retirement of Governor-General Sir Stanislaus James, Mallet was sworn in as the country's fourth governor-general over protests that the post be reserved for those outside the sphere of party politics.

Opposition leader Julian Hunte also stepped down after taking third place in the February by-elections. Former Education Minister Kenny Anthony replaced him as leader of the St. Lucia Labor Party (SLP). By the end of 1996 the SLP had merged with smaller opposition parties and was expected to present a formidable challenge to the UWP's hold on power in elections scheduled for the first half of 1997.

In 1996, strikes and disruptions continued to plague the banana industry, which employs over 30 percent of the workforce. Farmers remain disgruntled claiming they lack control over management and administrative decisions. The U.S.-based

Chiquita banana company hotly contested the preferential treatment that several islands, including St. Lucia, receive in the European market.

Political Rights and Civil Liberties: Citizens are able to change their government through democratic elections. Constitutional guarantees regarding the right to organize political parties, labor unions and civic groups are generally respected, as is the free exercise of religion.

The competition among political parties and allied civic organizations is heated, particularly during election campaigns when one side invariably accuses the other of occasional violence and harassment. Opposition parties have complained intermittently of difficulties in obtaining police permission for demonstrations, charging the government with interference.

Newspapers are mostly private or sponsored by political parties. The government has been charged with trying to influence the press by withholding government advertising. Television is privately owned. Radio is both public and private. In November 1995 the government refused to reissue a license for Radyo Koulibwi, a small FM station critical of the ruling party.

Civic groups are well organized and politically active, as are labor unions, which represent a majority of wage earners. However, legislation passed in 1995 restricts the right to strike. The measure provides for a fine of about $2,000 (U.S) or two years in prison for inciting any person to cease performing...any lawful activity on his property or on the property of another person. The government said the measure was aimed at curtailing strikes in the banana industry. Nonetheless, in October 1996, a 14-day strike took place in which banana industry workers demanded a greater role in management decisions. The strike resulted in violence and the police used tear gas and rubber bullets to disperse crowds, seriously injuring several people.

The judicial system is independent and includes a High Court under the West Indies Supreme Court (based in St. Lucia), with ultimate appeal under certain circumstances to the Privy Council in London. Traditionally, citizens have enjoyed a high degree of personal security. However, an escalating crime wave, much of it drug-related, violent clashes during banana farmers' strikes and increased violence in schools have sparked concern among citizens. Prisons are greatly overcrowded.

Though there are no official barriers to the participation of women and minorities in government, these groups are underrepresented. A growing awareness of the seriousness of violence against women has led the government and advocacy groups to take steps to offer better protection for victims of domestic violence.

St. Vincent and the Grenadines

Polity: Parliamentary democracy
Economy: Capitalist
Population: 118,000
PPP: $3,552
Life Expectancy: 71.0
Ethnic Groups: Black, mulatto
Capital: Kingstown

Political Rights: 2
Civil Liberties: 1
Status: Free

Overview:

In 1996 the opposition parties, now united into the Unity Labour Party (ULP), continued to contest the 1994 election results, charging that voter registration irregularitieshad occurred. The government had failed to comply with a constitutional provision requiring a review of constituency lines prior to elections after a national census.

St. Vincent and the Grenadines is a member of the British Commonwealth, with the British monarchy represented by a governor-general. St. Vincent achieved independence in 1979, with jurisdiction over the northern Grenadine islets of Beguia, Canouan, Mayreau, Mustique, Prune Island, Petit St. Vincent and Union Island.

The constitution provides for a 15-member unicameral House of Assembly elected for five years. Six senators are appointed, four by the government and two by the opposition. The prime minister is the leader of the party or coalition commanding a majority in the House.

In 1994, Sir James F. Mitchell won a third term when his center-right New Democratic Party (NDP) won 12 seats. The center-left alliance comprising the St. Vincent Labour Party (SVLP), which had held power in 1979-84, and the Movement for National Unity (MNU), won the remaining three seats.

In 1995, Deputy Prime Minister Parnel Campbell faced charges of financial impropriety when, disregarding government regulations, he took a loan from an offshore bank. With the ULP pressing for a no-confidence vote in parliament, Campbell resigned. Mitchell, prime minister since 1984, then announced he would postpone plans to retire at the next general election.

Political Rights and Civil Liberties:

Citizens can change their government through elections. However, the legitimacy of the 1994 elections was tainted by apparent registration irregularities. It remains unclear to what extent irregularities caused some eligible voters to be disenfranchised, though they were not so extensive as to alter the overall outcome of the vote. But the lack of a boundaries' review meant that voters may have been disproportionately distributed in some existing constituencies, which could have affected the result in those constituencies.

Constitutional guarantees regarding free expression, freedom of religion and the right to organize political parties, labor unions and civic organizations are generally respected. Labor unions are active and permitted to strike.

Political campaigns are hotly contested, with occasional charges from all quarters of harassment and violence, including police brutality, as well as allegations of funding from drug traffickers. The 1994 campaign saw an ugly rock-throwing clash between supporters of the main parties that left one NDP supporter dead.

The press is independent, with two privately owned independent weeklies, the *Vincentian* and the *News*, and several smaller, partisan papers. The opposition has charged the *Vincentian* with government favoritism. The only television station is privately-owned and free from government interference. Satellite dishes and cable are available to those who can afford them. The radio station is government-owned and call-in programs are prohibited. Equal access to radio is mandated during electoral campaigns, but the ruling party takes inordinate advantage of state control over programming.

A local human rights organization has accused police of using excessive force and illegal search and seizure, and of improperly informing detainees of their rights in order to extract confessions. The regional human rights organization, Caribbean Rights, estimates that 90 percent of convictions in St. Vincent are based on confessions. In April, a 12-year-old boy was the victim of police brutality which resulted in the dismissal of two officers and the demotion of a third.

The judicial system is independent. The highest court is the West Indies Supreme Court (based in St. Lucia), which includes a Court of Appeal and a High Court. A right of ultimate appeal reports under certain circumstances to the Privy Council in London. In 1996 Human Rights Watch criticized St. Vincent and the Grenadines for carrying out three death sentences.

The independent St. Vincent Human Rights Association has criticized long judicial delays and the large backlog of cases caused by personnel shortages in the local judiciary. It has also charged that the executive at times exerts inordinate influence over the courts. Prison conditions remain poor and there are allegations of mistreatment.

Penetration by the hemispheric drug trade is increasingly causing concern. Allegations have been made of drug-related corruption within the government and police force, and of money-laundering in St. Vincent banks. The drug trade has also caused an increase in street crime. In 1995 the U.S. government described St. Vincent as becoming a drug-trafficking center, and alleged that high level government officials are involved in drug-related corruption. Since then, St. Vincent has taken steps to cooperate with U.S. anti-drug trade efforts, such as signing an extradition treaty in 1996 with the United States.

Women are underrepresented in the government, holding just two of the 15 assembly seats. Nearly 40 percent of all households are headed by women, but the trend has yet to have an impact in the political or civic arenas.

San Marino

Polity: Parliamentary democracy
Economy: Capitalist
Population: 25,000
PPP: na
Life Expectancy: 76.0
Ethnic Groups: Sammarinese (78 percent), Italian (21 percent)
Capital: San Marino

Political Rights: 1
Civil Liberties: 1
Status: Free

Overview:

The oldest and second smallest republic in the world, San Marino was reputedly founded by a stonemason in the fourth century. Though the Sanmarinese are ethnically and culturally Italian, their long history of independence dates from Papal recognition in 1631. An 1862 customs union with Italy began an enduring relationship of political, economic and security cooperation. Despite substantial reliance on Italian assistance ranging from budget subsidies to news media, San Marino maintains its own political institutions and became a full member of the United Nations in 1992.

The Grand and General Council has served as the legislature since 1600. Its 60 members are directly elected by proportional representation every five years. The council chooses the ten-member State Congress, which functions as a cabinet. The Secretary of State for Foreign Affairs has come to assume many of the prerogatives of a prime minister. Directly elected Auxiliary Councils serving two-year terms and led by an elective captain are the arbiters of local government in each of the country's nine "castles." The legislature appoints two captains-regent—one representing the city of San Marino and one the countryside—to exercise executive authority for six-month terms.

The government extends official recognition to 17 communities of the more than 10,000 Sanmarinese living abroad. The state funds summer education and travel programs to bring Sanmarinese students living abroad to the republic.

Political Rights and Civil Liberties:

San Marino's citizens can change their government democratically. In a September referendum, they voted to abrogate Article 5 of the electoral law, under which the state provides transport costs for emigrants to return to the republic and vote.

San Marino carries on a long tradition of multiparty politics, with six parties represented in the current Council. Although the ruling center-left coalition maintained a substantial majority in the 1993 elections, three smaller parties emerged, including a hardline splinter group from the recently reconstituted Communist Party. Women were permitted to stand as candidates for seats in the Grand and General Council for the first time in 1974.

An independent judiciary, based on Italian law, includes justices of the peace, a law commissioner and an assistant law commissioner, a criminal judge of the Primary Court of Claims and two Appeals Court judges. A Supreme Court of Appeal acts as a final court of appeal in civil cases. The judicial system delegates some of its authority to Italian magistrates, in both criminal and civil cases.

All workers (except the military, but including police) are free to form and join unions under a 1961 law. Unions may freely form domestic federations or join international labor federations. Union members constitute about half of the country's workforce (which numbers about 10,000 Sanmarinese plus 2,000 Italians, from the country's total population of about 24,000). Trade unions are independent of the government and the political parties, but they have close informal ties with the parties, which exercise strong influence on them. The right to strike is guaranteed, though no strikes have occurred in the last seven years. Freedom of association is respected.

San Marino boasts a free press, and Italian newspapers and broadcasts are readily available. The government, some political parties, and the trade unions publish periodicals, bulletins and newspapers, though there are no dailies. Radio Titano is privately operated and remains the country's only broadcasting service. An information bulletin called *Notizie di San Marino* is broadcast daily over Radio Televisione Italiano.

The republic has a vibrant, primarily private-enterprise economy. In addition to agriculture, principal economic activities include livestock raising, light manufacturing and tourism, which is the leading source of foreign exchange. Trade is dominated by Italy through a customs union agreement stipulating that the larger country will contribute to its smaller partner's budget in exchange for a monopoly of its markets.

Immigrants and refugees are eligible for citizenship only after 30 years' residence. Another citizenship law grants automatic citizenship to the foreign spouses and children of male Sanmarinese, but not those of their female counterparts.

Sao Tome and Príncipe

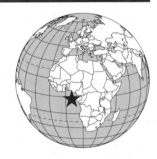

Polity: Presidential-parliamentary democracy
Economy: Mixed statist (transitional)
Population: 144,000
PPP: $600
Life Expectancy: 67.0
Ethnic Groups: Mulatto majority; Portuguese minority
Capital: Sao Tome

Political Rights: 1
Civil Liberties: 2
Status: Free

Overview:

President Miguel dos Anjos Trovoada was re-elected to a second five-year term after winning 52.7 percent of the vote in a second round run-off on July 21 against rival and former leader Manuel Pinto da Costa. Eighty percent of the 50,000 eligible voters cast ballots, and international observers declared the results free and fair, despite numerous allegations of vote-buying and other irregularities. President Trovoada faces an opposition-controlled parliament that will serve until October 1998, and social unrest stoked by the country's extreme poverty, which flared into strikes and violence this year. In September, the National Assembly brought down the government through a vote of censure, and President Trovoada began talks to form a national unity government.

São Tomé and Principe are two islands about 125 miles off the coast of Gabon in the Gulf of Guinea. They were seized by Portugal in 1522 and 1523, and became a Portuguese Overseas Province in 1951. The Portuguese government granted local autonomy in 1973, and independence talks began the following year with the Movement for the Liberation of São Tomé and Principe (MLSTP). The MLSTP, formed in 1960 as the Committee for the Liberation of São Tomé and Principe, took power upon independence in 1975. The MLSTP remained the only legal party until an August 1990 referendum established multiparty democracy. In March 1991 Trovoada, an independent candidate backed by the opposition Democratic Convergence Party, became the first democratically elected president.

For one week in 1995, an abortive, bloodless coup threatened this tiny island-state's elected government. On August 15, 40 junior army officers seized President Trovoada in a pre-dawn raid on the presidential palace, dissolved parliament, suspended the four-year-old constitution and placed the prime minister under house arrest. The rebels announced they were protesting governmental corruption which they described as a leading cause of São Tomé's endemic poverty, as well as army pay arrears. International condemnation and threats of aid cut-offs prompted negotiations. With promises of amnesty, the soldiers returned to their barracks and the democratic government reasserted its rule.

Political Rights and Civil Liberties: The right of citizens of São Tomé and Principe to elect their leaders democratically was exercised in free and fair presidential elections in 1991 and 1996, and in October 1994 legislative elections that marked the first time in Africa that a former ruling party achieved a parliamentary majority through peaceful, democratic elections.

The August 1990 referendum on multiparty rule established an independent judiciary headed by a Supreme Court whose members are designated by and responsible to the national assembly. The system, however, remains overburdened, understaffed and underfunded.

Freedom of the press and freedom of expression are constitutionally protected and respected in practice. However, the state owns most print and broadcast media. Pamphlets criticizing the government circulate freely. A 1994 law allows the opposition access to state-owned media

Citizens have the constitutional right to assemble and demonstrate with 48 hours' advance notice to the authorities. They may also travel freely within the country, although exit permits are required for foreign travel. Roman Catholicism is the dominant religion, but freedom of religion is respected. Women hold few leadership positions, and most occupy domestic roles in the subsistence economy.

Most islanders are impoverished as São Tomé's cocoa-based economy continues a long decline, especially in the face of explosive population growth. A surge in cocoa production has brought better growth in the last two years, but the country is saddled with an unpayable $600 million foreign debt and about 40 percent unemployment. The country faces increasing social unrest, which flared again into violent strikes in August. A scheme to create a free trade zone on Principe may generate some income.

Saudi Arabia

Polity: Traditional
monarchy
Economy: Capitalist-
statist
Population: 19,354,000
PPP: $12,600
Life Expectancy: 69.9
Ethnic Groups: Arab (90 percent), Afro-Asian (10 percent)
Capital: Riyadh

Political Rights: 7
Civil Liberties: 7
Status: Not Free

Overview:

On June 25, 1996, a truck bomb destroyed an American military housing complex near the eastern city of Dhahran, killing 19 Americans and wounding more than 270. The blast occurred less than a month after the Saudi government beheaded four Muslim militants allegedly responsible for a November 1995 bombing that killed five Americans and two Indians in Riyadh. American officials, including Attorney General Janet Reno, expressed their displeasure at the lack of Saudi cooperation in the investigation. The Americans were also concerned with the deepening unrest in Saudi society, and the inability of the royal family to maintain order. The Saudis in turn blamed Iran for the terrorism and bombings.

The government's fiscal austerity program, introduced in 1994 in order to cope with shrinking oil revenues and a population boom, has shredded a social contract in which Saudis had largely tolerated the regime in exchange for lavish social spending. Oil revenues in Saudi Arabia, home to the world's largest oil reserves, have decreased from $116 billion in 1981 to $33 billion by 1995, and per capita income was down from $17,000 in 1981 to $7,000 in 1993.

King Ibn al-Saud consolidated the Nejd and Hejaz regions of the Arabian Peninsula into the Kingdom of Saudi Arabia in 1932, and incorporated the Asir region the following year. The king rules by decree and serves as prime minister, appointing all other ministers.

As a result of a stroke he suffered late last year, King Fahd temporarily handed power to his more conservative half-brother Crown Prince Abdullah, the deputy prime minister, for several months. The king's brother, Prince Sultan, serves as defense minister.

During the Persian Gulf War, the kingdom allowed some 500,000 Western troops to be stationed on its soil, despite the shock this caused among many conservative Saudis. The presence of 5,000 US troops is viewed as a profanation of Muslim land.

In May 1993, several Islamic fundamentalist leaders announced the creation of the Committee for the Defense of Legitimate Rights (CDLR), headed by Muhammad al-Masaari, a radical cleric, to press for a more rigorous application of Islamic laws. The highest government-appointed religious body, the *Ulema* (Muslim scholars) Council, promptly banned the CDLR, and al-Masaari fled to London.

Political Rights and Civil Liberties: Saudi citizens cannot change their government democratically. Political parties are illegal, the king rules by decree, and there are no elections at any level. In response to increasing popular discontent, King Fahd inaugurated a 60-man appointed *Majlis al Shura* (Consultative Council) in December 1993. However, the council lacks real authority and its membership is not representative of the population.

The judiciary is not independent of the monarchy. The legal system is based on *Shari'a* (Islamic law). Under the law, persons convicted of rape, murder, armed robbery, adultery, apostasy and drug trafficking face beheading (192 people in 1995). Police routinely torture detainees, particularly Islamic fundamentalists and non-Western foreigners, in order to obtain confessions. Defense lawyers are not permitted in the courtroom and trials are generally closed and conducted without procedural safeguards. In some cases foreigners are not provided translators. Suspects arrested by the Interior Ministry's General Directorate of Intelligence may be held, incommunicado, for months without being charged. Since 1993 hundreds of Islamic fundamentalist activists, Shi'ite Muslims and Christians have been arbitrarily detained or forced into exile.

Freedom of expression is severely restricted. Criticism of the government, Islam or the ruling family is forbidden. A 1965 national security law and a 1982 media policy statement prohibit the dissemination of any literature critical of the government. The Interior Minister must approve and can remove all editors-in-chief, and this power has been utilized on numerous occasions. The privately-held press practices substantial self-censorship, while the reporting of the government-owned radio and television media is limited to official views.

In March 1994 the government outlawed private ownership of satellite dishes. In 1996 the Saudi regime, along with four other Gulf monarchies that make up a censorship board which reviews foreign publications before they can be sold in their respective countries, confiscated and destroyed more than 9,000 copies of the June issue of *Reader's Digest* because of an article accusing the royal family of corruption, waste and repression. In early April a Saudi-owned company terminated its contract with the BBC and canceled an Arabic television service because of news broadcasts on the health of King Fahd and the activities of dissidents.

Professional groups and associations cannot form without government permission and must be non-political. Islam is the only religion allowed; worship by non-Muslims is prohibited and conversion is punishable by death. The Shi'ite minority, concentrated in the Eastern province, faces considerable discrimination in employment opportunities and religious affairs and has been the target of a government crackdown in recent months. Christians are arrested, flogged and otherwise harassed.

Women are segregated in workplaces, schools and restaurants, and must wear the *abaya*, a black garment covering the entire head, body and face. The official Committee for the Promotion of Virtue and Prevention of Vices, *Mutawwa'in*, harasses women for violating conservative dress codes and for appearing in public with an unrelated male. Occasionally, Mutawwa'in enter homes without obtaining a warrant. Also, Islamic vigilante groups patrol neighborhoods.

Women must obtain permission from close male relatives to travel, cannot drive cars and are informally prevented from working in certain fields. They also face legal discrimination in divorce and inheritance matters. Domestic violence is reportedly common. African nationals practice female genital mutilation in some areas.

Foreign-born domestic workers are subject to abuse, work long hours and are sometimes denied wages. The court system discriminates against African and Asian workers, and employers generally hold the passports of foreign employees. Employers use these means as leverage in resolving business disputes, or as a means of forcing employees to do extra work.

The government prohibits trade unions, and collective bargaining and strikes are illegal. In accordance with a five-year development plan, aimed at creating more than 65,000 jobs for Saudis by the end of the century, the Minister of Labor gave private companies a November 11 deadline to increase the number of Saudi nationals by five percent or face penalties. About five million foreigners (out of a total population of 17 million) work in the country, and it is estimated that less than seven percent of private sector employees are citizens.

Senegal

Polity: Dominant party   **Political Rights:** 4
Economy: Mixed   **Civil Liberties:** 4*
capitalist   **Status:** Partly Free
Population: 8,532,000
PPP: $1,710
Life Expectancy: 49.5
Ethnic Groups: Wolof (36 percent), Mende (30 percent), Fulani (17 percent), Serer (16 percent), others
Capital: Dakar
Ratings Change: Senegal's civil liberties rating changed from 5 to 4 because civil society continues to expand in the face of adversity.

Overview: **S**enegal's national unity government came under strain as its component parties waged a strong campaign for control of local councils in the November elections that could influence the scheduled May 1998 National Assembly contest. President Abdou Diouf and his dominant ruling Socialist Party (PS) had dampened opposition criticisms by bringing the Senegal Democratic Party (PDS) into the government in 1994. But opposition parties expressed concerns about the honesty of new voters' lists and renewed calls for an independent election commission in the run-up to the November 24 local elections which produced an overwhelming victory for the ruling party but were conducted amidst administrative chaos. President Diouf pledged to continue decentralization plans that may help bring peace to the southern Casamance region, where sporadic attacks by secessionist rebels and government reprisals have caused continued human rights abuses.

Since its independence from France in 1960, Senegal has avoided military or dictatorial rule. President Léopold Senghor exercised de facto one-party rule under the PS for over a decade after independence, but the country gradually liberalized, with three additional parties permitted between 1974-81 and most restrictions lifted after that. The PS has continued to dominate the nation's political life through patronage and electoral manipulation. President Diouf succeeded Senghor in 1981 and won lopsided re-election contests in 1988 and 1993 marked by confusion and irregularities that oppositionists denounced as fraudulent. Unemployment and diminished earning power that have been grist for mainstream opposition politicians are also drawing cards for Islamist groups in a country that is about 90 percent Muslim.

An uneasy cease-fire has held since July 1993 with rebels in the southern Casamance Province. Almost entirely cut off from the rest of Senegal by the Gambia, Casamance produces almost all its rice, has most of the country's remaining forests and boasts popular tourist beaches. Yet little of the earnings from the region's resources have been allocated for local development. The Movement of Democratic Forces of Casamance (MFDC), led by ex-Catholic priest Diamacoune Senghor, launched a separatist campaign in 1982. Senghor is now under house arrest in Casamance's regional capital, Ziguinchor, as desultory negotiations for a lasting peace continue. However, control of the MFDC's armed wing may have passed to younger and more radical leaders.

Numerous human rights violations have been ascribed to both sides in the conflict. Long-term military operations in Casamance could deter tourism, disrupt rice production and deflate hopes for steady improvement in Senegal's economy.

Political Rights and Civil Liberties:

Senegal's citizens possess the constitutional right to choose their president and legislative representatives in multiparty elections. Periodic elections have occurred, but the Socialist Party's overwhelming dominance has blocked the rise of a genuine opposition. For the first three decades of independence, voting regulations strongly favored the ruling party. The 1992 Electoral Code lowered the voting age to 18, introduced the secret ballot and, on paper, created a fairer framework. Election administration remains largely under the PS-controlled government, which has used state patronage and state media to protect its position. The PS won 84 of 120 seats in the May 1993 National Assembly elections, while the main opposition PDS took 27 seats and four smaller opposition parties shared the other nine.

Freedom of expression is generally respected, although a strong element of self-censorship is instilled by the existence of laws against "discrediting the state" and disseminating "false news." Independent media, often highly critical of the government and political parties, operate freely despite the legal threat. Registration of publications is required, but this is now a formality. The government does not practice censorship and allows unrestricted circulation of foreign periodicals. Concerns for the future of the independent media were raised in June, however, when the respected daily *Sud* was convicted of libel. Five of its journalists were sentenced to a month in jail and a drastic fine was imposed on the newspaper. The case received wide attention due to suggestions it was politically motivated, and brought because the articles alleged fraud by a French-affiliated company with close ties to the government.

Freedom of assembly is restricted by permit requirements, but except for some activities by Islamist groups, legal groups are rarely hindered. Religious freedom is respected. Many nongovernmental organizations are registered, including several that work locally and regionally on human rights issues.

While the judiciary is by statute independent, poor pay and lack of long-term tenure opens it to considerable external influence. Administration of justice is generally hindered by scarce resources. Detainees are kept for long periods without charge and without access to legal representation as police fail to comply with already lengthy periods of detention permitted by law.

Rights constitutionally guaranteed to women are often unrealized in practice, especially in the countryside. Women's opportunities for education and formal-sector employment are much less than men's. Spousal abuse and other domestic violence against women is reportedly common. Many elements of Islamic and local customary law are discriminatory to women, particularly regarding inheritance and marital relations.

Union rights to organize and to strike are legally protected. The main union group, the National Confederation of Senegalese Workers (CNTS), is intertwined with and an important base for the ruling party. Its smaller rival, National Union of Autonomous Labor Unions of Senegal (UNSAS), is more independent.

Privatizations of 22 parastatal companies and liquidation of 11 others required as part of international loan and debt rescheduling packages are slowly dismantling the still extensive network of state-run corporations. Political connections remain very important to business opportunity in Senegal, and are an obstruction to independent business development.

Seychelles

Polity: Presidential-legislative democracy
Economy: Mixed-statist
Population: 75,000
PPP: $4,960
Life Expectancy: 71.0
Ethnic Groups: Seychellois (mixed African, South Asian, European)
Capital: Victoria

Political Rights: 3
Civil Liberties: 3
Status: Partly Free

Overview: Three years after multiparty elections, President France Albert René's government amended the constitution to strengthen the ruling Seychelles People's Progressive Front (SPPF) party's already formidable hold on power. A new national flag and national anthem were adopted, but allegations of corruption by senior officials were unresolved, and President René, who has held power for twenty years since leading a 1977 coup, still rules with little effective opposition. The government scrapped the controversial Economic Development Act (EDA), passed by parliament last year but never enacted, which would have offered broad legal immunities, including protection against extradition, for people investing at least $10 million dollars in the country. Critics had warned that the law could make the Seychelles a haven for money-laundering, drug-trafficking and other illicit operations.

René, designated prime minister at independence in 1976, took power the following year by ousting then President Sir James Richard Mancham. After René declared his SPPF the sole legal party, Mancham and other opposition leaders operated parties and human rights groups in exile. President René won single-party elections in 1979, 1984 and 1989. By 1992, the SPPF had passed a constitutional amendment legalizing opposition parties, and many exiled leaders returned to participate in a constitutional commission and multiparty elections. In the 1993 multiparty general election, René won his first legitimate mandate. Ex-president Mancham's opposition Democratic Party has proposed formation of a national unity government, an idea so far rejected by President René.

Political Rights and Civil Liberties:

Seychellois chose their government democratically in open elections for the first time in 1993. Both the president and the National Assembly are elected by universal adult suffrage. The 1993 constitution provided for a 33-seat National Assembly, with 22 members directly elected and eleven allocated on a proportional basis to parties with at least eight percent of the vote. As amended in 1996, ten seats will be allocated based on proportional representation with a party threshold of ten percent, and three directly-elected additional seats will be added in Mahé. The combined effect of these changes will reduce an already feeble opposition voice in national politics. Local governments comprised of district councils, abolished in 1971, were reinstated in 1991.

Media freedom is limited. The government monopolizes nearly all media outlets, including the only daily newspaper. At least two other newspapers are published by, or support, the SPPF. During the last general election campaign, however, the government-controlled Seychelles Broadcasting Corporation provided substantial coverage of both government and opposition candidates. Opposition parties publish several newsletters and other publications, but the only independent weekly, *Regar*, has been sued repeatedly for libel. Freedom of speech has improved since 1993, although some self-censorship remains.

The judiciary includes a Supreme Court, a Court of Appeal, an Industrial Court and magistrates' courts. Judges generally decide cases fairly, but still face some government pressure. Although they are largely engaged in subsistence agriculture, almost 98 percent of all adult women are classified as "economically active." They are also more likely than men to be literate. Four ministers in the present cabinet are women. There is de facto discrimination against islanders of Creole extraction. Nearly all the Seychelles' political and economic life is dominated by people of European and Asian origin.

Workers formally possess the right to strike under the 1993 Industrial Relations Act, but regulations inhibit its free exercise. The National Workers' Union is associated with the SPPF, but no longer holds a monopoly on union activity. The government may deny passports for reasons of "national interest," but does not restrict domestic travel. Religious freedom is respected in this overwhelmingly Roman Catholic country.

The now-discarded investment law demonstrates the government's pressing need to revive the depressed economy. Nearly one-third of the Seychelles' population has emigrated, and there is little formal development. The islands have few natural resources and little industry. Tourism has provided about a fifth of the islands' gross domestic product, but high prices are reducing the islands' appeal. The private sector has been pressing for economic liberalization and the loosening of restrictions on foreign exchange transactions. The government has announced plans to privatize several loss-making parastatal companies. Relaxation of currency regulations could lead to considerable political dangers for the government, as factory closures and layoffs would be the likely results.

Sierra Leone

Polity: Presidential-parliamentary democracy (transitional)
Economy: Capitalist
Population: 4,617,000
PPP: $860
Life Expectancy: 39.2
Ethnic Groups: Temme (30 percent), Mende (30 percent), Krio (2 percent), others
Capital: Freetown

Political Rights: 4*
Civil Liberties: 5*
Status: Partly Free

Ratings Changes: Sierra Leone's political rights rating changed from 7 to 4 and its civil liberties rating changed from 6 to 5 because of civil war cease-fire and successful national elections.

Overview:

Sierra Leone's March election to replace an army junta and the end of a six-year guerrilla war raised hopes for peaceful democratic development in a country that only a year ago was viewed by pessimists as a complete failure. The voting was the country's first open multiparty election in two decades.

The war had taken about 10,000 lives and displaced over a million people. Sporadic unrest continued in the countryside through most of 1996, mostly ascribed to banditry and lingering indiscipline among armed factions. A September army coup, whose initial action was to have been the assassination of newly elected President Ahmed Tejan Kabbah, was averted at the last moment. Despite the new government's electoral legitimacy, media repression has heightened and the country's democratic transition appears to be very fragile.

Sierra Leone was founded by Britain in 1787 as a haven for liberated slaves. It became independent in 1961. Its nearly five million people have suffered greatly during six years of civil war, since the rebel RUF launched a guerrilla campaign from neighboring Liberia in 1992 aimed at ending 23 years of increasingly corrupt one-party rule by the All Peoples Congress (APC) party. Junior army officers led by Captain Valentine Strasser seized power in 1992 protesting poor pay and conditions. Political parties were banned, and sporadic harassment of the media and other independent voices ensued. Strasser in turn was quietly deposed as head of the National Provisional Ruling Council (NPRC) by Brigadier Julius Maa Bio in January 1996, amid fears that he intended to clothe his military dictatorship in civilian guise by running for president. Elections went ahead, despite military and rebel intimidation, and 60 percent of Sierra Leone's 1.6 million eligible voters cast ballots.

Battle deaths, starvation and disease have claimed thousands of lives since 1992, and both government and rebel forces are accused of massive human rights violations. The November peace plan is but the first step in re-establishing rule of law, which has all but disappeared from the countryside and maintains only a tenuous hold even in the main cities. Amnesty International has strongly criticized a plan to give indemnity to all combatants as part of a peace plan.

Political Rights and Civil Liberties:

Sierra Leoneans voted for their president and legislative representatives in February and March in elections that were clearly far from ideal. Interim National Electoral Commission (INEC) chairman, James Jonah, a widely respected former senior United Nations diplomat (and now the newly-elected government's U.N. ambassador), was instrumental in convincing the military to accept honest polls. In a second round runoff on March 18, Ahmed Tejan Kabbah of the Sierra Leone People's Party (SLPP), defeated John Karefa-Smart of United National People's Party (UNPP).

Attacks by the rebel RUF continued until the November peace treaty was signed. Fighting severely wracked the east and south, Sierra Leone's largest grain-producing region, and tens of thousands of farms were abandoned.

The capital, Freetown, was hit by violence during the election period, and again in July as soldiers rampaged through parts of the city. A purge of senior commissioned and non-commissioned officers in early September, including former dictator Strasser, may have prompted the abortive coup plot. Combat troops from Guinea and Nigeria and South African mercenaries strengthened the army. They are required to withdraw under the peace agreement. The RUF has received assistance from factions in the Liberian civil war and from Libya. Civilians bore the brunt of the violence. The RUF, led by former army corporal Foday Sankoh, has exhibited a savagery that was nearly matched by that of the ill-disciplined government forces. Thousands of children were recruited to fight on both sides, and their rehabilitation will be an urgent task. Traditional hunters, hired as anti-rebel auxiliaries, clashed with soldiers and disrupted relief operations around the city of Bo in September.

Many new independent newspapers were set up during and since the election period, but journalists experienced increasing harassment. Several editors and reporters have been charged with seditious libel for reporting on corruption allegations. In October, Sheka Tawaralli, editor of *Torchlight* newspaper, was jailed for a month by a parliamentary committee after publishing reports of parliamentarians being bribed. Ex-BBC broadcaster Hilton Fyle was charged for reporting on allegedly corrupt business deals in his weekly *123* newspaper.

Courts have shown some independence, but low pay, lack of training and intimidation reduces their impartiality. Prison conditions are harsh, and abuses against detainees, especially suspected rebels, are reported.

Women are guaranteed equal rights under the constitution, but face extensive legal and de facto discrimination and have limited access to education and jobs in the formal sector. Especially in rural areas, where customary law prevails, married women have few property rights. Female genital mutilation is widespread, and reports have been made of ritual killings of children by animist cults.

The war has crippled Sierra Leone's economy. The country is rated by the U.N. as the world's second-poorest. Most people are subsistence farmers, and the war has cut food production severely. International mining interests appear keen to resume exploitation of diamond, bauxite and rutile reserves once security conditions permit.

Singapore

Polity: Dominant party
Economy: Mixed capitalist
Population: 3,045,000
PPP: $19,350
Life Expectancy: 74.9
Ethnic Groups: Chinese (77 percent), Malay (15 percent), Pakistani and Indian (7 percent)
Capital: Singapore

Political Rights: 4*
Civil Liberties: 5
Status: Partly Free

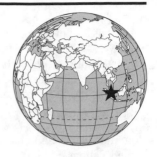

Ratings change: Singapore's political rights rating changed from 5 to 4 for methodological reasons.

Overview:

On December 16, 1996, the parliament was dissolved, clearing the way for general elections which the government had been required to hold before April 1997. Elections were scheduled for January 2, 1997. Forty-seven People's Action Party (PAP)-held parliament seats are uncontested; most of the remaining 36 seats are expected to remain in PAP hands.

Singapore came under British control in 1867. The colony became self-governing in 1959, entered the Malaysian Federation in 1963 and became fully independent in 1965 under Prime Minister Lee Kuan Yew. The authoritarian PAP swept all elections from 1968 to 1980 before losing a by-election in 1981.

In October 1990, Lee stepped down in favor of his hand-picked successor, Goh Chok Tong, although the former premier still exerts considerable influence as senior minister. In the snap elections of August 1991, the PAP had its worst showing ever, but still won 77 of the 81 seats.

In August 1993 Singapore held elections for an expanded presidency with the power to approve budgets and political appointments. The strict requirements for holding office meant that only about 400 citizens could qualify as potential candidates. A three-member Presidential Election Committee rejected two of the opposition's candidates for lack of proper character and financial experience. In a clear rebuff to the PAP, deputy prime minister Ong Teng Cheong won with only 58.7 percent of the vote against a retired civil servant who barely campaigned.

Political Rights and Civil Liberties:

Citizens of Singapore nominally can change their government through elections, although the PAP is politically dominant. Security laws and media regulations are used to protect political interests, opposition figures are often dismissed from public-sector jobs, and the judiciary weakens, intimidates and bankrupts politicians who oppose the PAP.

In 1996 Democratic Party leader Chee Soon Juan was charged with "contempt of parliament" after using incorrect figures in a public debate. Though he claims he made an error, this incident could result in a prison sentence or fines. In 1993 he had been dismissed from the National University for alleged petty financial irregularities and was later fined $200,000 in damages plus legal costs over a subsequent defamation suit.

The government brought Worker's Party leader J.B. Jeyaretnam close to financial ruin through a series of controversial court cases, including a 1986 fraud conviction that was criticized by the Privy Council in London.

Under the Internal Security Act (ISA), authorities can detain suspects without trial for an unlimited number of two-year periods. The government continues to restrict the travel, residence, speech and publishing rights of two former detainees, both political dissidents. Under the Criminal Law (Temporary Provisions) Act, the government can detain without trial and search without warrants those suspected of drug-trafficking or secret society-related offenses. Currently over 500 such suspects are being detained. A 1989 constitutional amendment limits judicial review of detentions under these two acts to procedural grounds, and bars the judiciary from reviewing the constitutionality of any anti-subversion law.

Police reportedly abuse detainees to extract confessions. In March 1996, three officers pled guilty to manslaughter after a prisoner died in August 1995.

The death penalty is mandatory for certain drug offenses. In March 1995, the government executed a Filipino maid for murder even after new evidence came to light suggesting her innocence. Caning, which was introduced under the 1966 Vandalism Act, is now used as punishment for approximately 30 other offenses. Women, children and the elderly are exempt from caning. Prison conditions generally meet international standards; however, human rights monitors are denied access.

The judicial system is efficient, though not independent of the central government. There is no right to public trial under the ISA or the Misuse of Drugs Act (MDA). The Legal Service Commission determines the term of judicial appointments, and judges, especially in the Supreme Court, have close ties to PAP leaders. No trials by jury are conducted.

Broad restrictions on freedom of expression exist in Singapore. The government does not tolerate discussions of government corruption, nepotism or a compliant judiciary in the media. In 1996 Christopher Lingle was assessed additional fines for his 1994 articles published in the *International Herald Tribune* (*IHT*). In 1995 Lingle, the *IHT* and several other defendants lost two lawsuits arising from articles allegedly critical of the government and were fined. The *IHT* was ordered to pay over $600,000.

All general circulation newspapers and 20 percent of Singapore Cablevision are owned by Singapore Press Holdings (SPH), which has close ties to the government. Hence, editorials and domestic news coverage strongly favor the ruling party. Though international newspapers and magazines are not censored, the number of copies allowed in the country may be restricted. This happens regularly to the *Far Eastern Economic Review*, *Asiaweek* and the *Asian Wall Street Journal*. Foreign journalists must renew their work permits annually. The government can and has banned certain domestic and foreign publications.

The government-linked Singapore International Media PTE, Ltd. operates all four free television channels and ten of the 15 radio stations. Of the remaining five radio stations, only the British Broadcasting Corporation (BBC) is free from government control. Movies, television, videos, music and, beginning in July 1996, the Internet are subject to censorship.

The unauthorized release of government data to the media is prohibited. In March 1994 a court found the editor of the *Business Times*, a journalist and three economists guilty of publishing advance GDP figures.

Organizations of more than ten people must register with the government, and political activity is restricted to political parties. However, the PAP wields strong influence over ostensibly nonpolitical associations such as neighborhood groups, while the opposition is not permitted to form similar groups. Overall, few truly independent elements of civil society can be found in Singapore. Approval is required for individual speakers at public functions, and the authorities occasionally deny permits to opposition party members seeking to address dinners and banquets. Any public assembly of more than five people must be authorized by the government.

Freedom of religion is generally respected, although the Jehovah's Witnesses and the Unification Church are banned, and religious groups must register with the government.

While ethnic Malays face unofficial employment discrimination, the law ensures a degree of ethnic minority representation in parliament. Women, on the other hand, are underrepresented in the government. Though they enjoy the same legal rights as men in many areas, they continue to hold the majority of low-paying positions.

Workers can form independent unions, but most unions are affiliated with the pro-government National Trade Unions Congress. Workers, other than those in essential industries, are permitted to strike, though there has not been a strike since 1986.

Slovakia

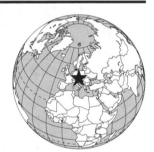

Polity: Parliamentary democracy
Economy: Mixed-capitalist transitional
Population: 5,386,000
PPP: $5,620
Life Expectancy: 70.9
Ethnic Groups: Slovak (82 percent), Hungarian (11 percent), Roma (5 percent), Czech (1 percent)
Capital: Bratislava

Political Rights: 2
Civil Liberties: 4*
Status: Partly Free

Ratings Change: Slovakia's civil liberties rating changed from 3 to 4 because of government pressure on freedom of expression and minority rights.

Overview:

In 1996, bitterness between populist Prime Minister Vladimir Meciar and President Michal Kovac continued to be the key political story. A draft media bill raised concerns in the West about restrictions on press freedom, and a controversial penal code amendment passed by parliament in December was criticized for placing restrictions on freedom of assembly and free speech. Meanwhile, Slovakia's economy continued its impressive growth, while also possessing one of the lowest inflation rates in East-Central Europe.

Slovakia was established on January 1, 1993, following Czechoslovakia's formal dissolution, which ended a 74-year-old federation. Slovakians trace their ancestry to the short-lived Great Moravian Empire of the ninth century. By the tenth century Hungarians had seized control of the region and ruled there until 1918. Interwar Czechoslovak unity ended with Nazi Germany's dismemberment of Czechoslovakia, providing an opportunity for militant Slovak nationalists to seize power. The Nazi puppet state under Father Josef Tiso was tainted by its role in the deportation of Jews and Roma (Gypsies). Communists ruled reunited Czechoslovakia from 1948 to 1989.

Meciar and his Movement for a Democratic Slovakia (HZDS) won elections in 1992, but in 1994 his government was forced to resign amid political bickering and accusations by President Kovac that the government was undemocratic and manipulating privatization and the state media. Former Foreign Minister Jozef Moravcik headed a caretaker government and stepped up economic reform and privatization. But the HZDS's popularity, reinforced by Meciar's anti-reform and anti-Hungarian rhetoric, among pensioners, the unemployed and peasants saw the party win 61 of 150 seats in the parliamentary elections in September-October 1994. The leftist Common Cause coalition led by the Party of the Democratic Left (SDL), made up of former Communists, got 18 seats; a coalition of Hungarian parties won 17 seats; the Democratic Union, 15; the left-wing Workers Association (ZRS), 13; and the ultra-nationalist Slovak National party (SNS), 9. A coalition government was announced in December consisting of the HZDS, the ZRS and the SNS.

In 1995, Meciar pushed through a series of parliamentary measures aimed at reducing the president's powers and slashing the presidential budget and staff. The ruling coalition also passed a no-confidence vote against Kovac, a symbolic move without constitutional validity. Meciar tried in vain to secure the three-fifths majority needed to oust the president. In September, after the bizarre kidnapping of Kovac's son, allegedly by security forces, the government demanded the president "abdicate" because he was "betraying our nation."

In March 1996, under pressure from the United States and the European Union, President Kovac vetoed legislation approved by parliament and backed by Meciar which would have affected freedom of expression and other democratic rights by banning rallies deemed to subvert the country's constitutional system, territorial integrity or defenses. Groups protesting the legislation included the Roman Catholic bishops, judges, civic associations, and the 1.2 million-member confederation of trade unions. Parliament approved a modified version of the bill after the veto. A new media law limiting press freedom and putting undue financial strain on the independent press was passed in March, but amended the following month after domestic and international criticism. The new law incorporated provisions on the protection of information sources, but the government in May filed a lawsuit against *Sme* editor Peter Toth, charging him with "intolerance and gross and ungrounded attacks against the cabinet."

Throughout the year, the prime minister used heavy-handed tactics against the opposition. He tried to use the constitution to expel an opposition party from parliament and sought to curb registration of charities for fear that they would be too independent. In July, the government passed a law that redrew the boundaries of Slovakia's administrative regions and districts in a way that diluted the influence of the Hungarian minority, estimated at 570,000. The prime minister also moved to change the country's electoral system from one based on proportional representation to one that includes a first-past-the-post system. Under the new system, the

HZDS would not need coalition partners. In August, Prime Minister Meciar sacked the three most senior members of his cabinet, in a move which appeared to strengthen his position while deflecting opposition attacks on government policy.

In November, opposition parties—the Christian Democratic Movement (KDH), Democratic Union (DU), Democratic Party and the Hungarian coalition—organized a series of "save Slovakia" rallies around the country to protest government policies. The Party of the Democratic Left also opposed the government. The same month, parliament passed a law allowing the government "to intervene in matters belonging to the jurisdiction of universities and faculties, deans and academic senates." Earlier, the minister of culture had purged many museum directors and fired the director of Slovakia's National Theater, leading to a three-day strike by actors. On December 17, parliament passed another version of the penal code "on the protection of the republic" that was submitted by the rightist Slovak National Party. The new proposal replaced the phrase "organize public rallies" with "call for mass riots" which, its authors said, conformed to European standards. It also omitted a clause about spreading false information. The opposition still claimed the law threatened civic freedoms because of vague wording. A spokesman for the Christian Democratic Movement said the law "retains the previous catch-all articles which can be interpreted almost at will and can be easily abused." Other groups said the bill would "disqualify" Slovakia from joining NATO and the EU.

The amendment came 13 days after parliament stripped a dissident HZDS deputy of his mandate, a move that led to considerable criticism from the West.

In economic issues, the Constitutional Court annulled a law allowing continued government involvement in important privatized companies, after ruling that the state's "golden share" in strategic companies was unconstitutional. Close ties between the political and industrial establishments, and the difficulty in many cases of discovering details of individual privatization agreements, have bred public cynicism about direct sales. Overall, the economy continued to expand and inflation and unemployment dropped. Domestic demand fueled growth in 1996, supported by several ambitious infrastructure programs. Two-thirds of the GDP is generated by the private sector thanks to the rapid growth in the number of small and medium-sized enterprises, although state influence prevailed in several sectors of heavy industry and banking.

Political Rights and Civil Liberties:

Citizens have the means to change the government democratically under a 1992 constitution; the 1994 elections were deemed "free and fair."

About 50 parties emerged since 1989, and 20 parties registered for the 1994 elections. Opposition parties have charged intimidation by government security forces. Several new parties were formed in 1995.

The media have come under pressure from the government. The government controls state-run television and radio through appointments to oversight commissions and editorial boards. By the summer, the government had gained indirect control over several national and regional newspapers bought by companies connected to Alexander Rezes, the communications minister, and Vladimir Lexa, a former top Communist official and the father of Slovakia's intelligence chief. In 1996, the opening of the first national, privately owned terrestrial TV station challenged the stranglehold of state-owned channels. TV Markiza, co-owned by the

Central European Media Enterprises (CME), had larger market-share in areas it covered than the state channels, STV1 and STV2. But TV Markiza stayed away from hard news programs. VSZ, a steel manufacturer and the country's largest company, emerged as the dominant owner of the national daily, *Narodna Obroda*. Entrepreneur Jozef Majsky gained major control of Radio Twist and *Sme*, which have become bastions of the anti-government media in Slovakia and took the lead in investigating allegations that the security service was involved in the 1995 kidnapping of President Kovac's son.

Freedom of expression has been eroded, and the language law curtails the use of minority languages. Freedom of religion in this overwhelmingly Roman Catholic country is respected, though the SNS and other nationalist parties have been openly anti-Semitic.

The judiciary is not wholly free from political interference, and the government has strained the constitution by eroding presidential power. The Hungarian minority has faced discrimination and laws aimed at undermining Hungarian culture. Roma (Gypsies) have been the targets of discrimination and of violence that is often ignored by the courts and police.

Workers have the right to form unions and strike. The Slovak Confederation of Trade Unions is the main labor confederation, claiming 1.2 million members. The unions have openly opposed government laws curtailing rights and have demanded better wages. Women nominally have the same rights as men, but are underrepresented in managerial posts. Close to 10,000 nongovernmental organizations are registered in such areas as culture, health-care, social services, humanities and environmental protection.

Slovenia

Polity: Presidential-parliamentary democracy
Economy: Mixed-statist (transitional)
Population: 1,994,000
PPP: na
Life Expectancy: na
Ethnic Groups: Slovene (91 percent), Croat, Serb, Muslim, Hungarian, Italian
Capital: Ljubljana

Political Rights: 1
Civil Liberties: 2
Status: Free

Overview: At the end of 1996, the ruling Liberal Democratic Party (LDS) of Prime Minister Janez Drnovsek was unable to form a new government following the defection of one of its main coalition partners, the former-communist United List of Social Democrats (ZLSD). The November 10 elections saw the LDS and its allies lose seats in the 90-member National Assembly.

Consultations by President Milan Kucan and parliamentary leaders remained deadlocked, as Marjan Podobnik's rightist Slovenian People's Party (SLS), which won 19 seats (second overall to the LDS's 25) balked at forming a coalition with the LDS and pushed for a government of rightist parties that ran under the "Slovenian Spring" banner. Other issues included tensions with Italy over the Italian minority in Slovene-controlled Istria and Rome's demands that Italian citizens, or their descendants, be able to recover property. The issue clouded Slovenia's future admission to the European Union (EU).

Slovenia was for centuries part of the Hapsburg empire before being incorporated into the newly created Yugoslavia after World War I. After World War II, Yugoslav forces fought their way to the Italian city of Trieste, pushing the Yugoslav-Italian frontier 50 kilometers west of its pre-war position. A series of treaties, culminating in the 1975 Treaty of Osimo, eventually allotted part of the Istrian territory to Italy and part of it to Yugoslavia (it is currently split between Slovenia and Croatia). After declaring independence from a fraying Yugoslavia in June 1991, Slovenia beat back an invasion by the Yugoslav People's Army.

In January 1996, the LDS coalition lost its absolute majority in parliament when the ZLSD, with its 14 seats, went into opposition, leaving the two remaining partners, the LDS and the Slovenian Christian Democrats (SKD), with 45 seats. Strains over economic policy and the need for tighter budget restraint and for urgent reform of the country's under funded pension system led to the ZLSD split.

In the November parliamentary vote, the LDS won with a plurality of 27.1 percent of the popular vote and 25 seats, five fewer than before. The SKD won 9 seats, six fewer than in 1992. The rightist SLS won 19 seats and the ultraconservative Social Democrats (SDSS), led by controversial former defense minister Janez Jansa, took 16 seats. Other parties that cleared the 3 percent threshold were the United List of Social Democrats, the Democratic Party of Retirees and the National Party. Janez Podobnik of the SLS (Marian's brother) was elected parliamentary speaker. Negotiations over a new government stalled by year's end.

Slovenia's economy continued to be among the strongest in the post-Communist world, with an average net monthly wage of $620, single-digit inflation, positive economic growth since 1993, budget deficits of less than 1 percent of GDP, low public debt, foreign trade oriented toward the EU and a manageable foreign debt. Privatization has moved slowly, with only 666 of 1,500 enterprises slated for privatization.

Relations with Italy remain a problem. President Kucan met with Italian Prime Minister Romano Prodi in December. Though an association agreement with the EU was reached in June, the issue of land restitution and ownership by foreigners remained contentious. Italy was also concerned about a Slovene Supreme Court decision declaring the program of the Istrian Democratic Congress-Dieta Italiana (IDZ-DDI) as unconstitutional, thereby barring its registration as a political party. The group supported the return of land to Italian citizens or their descendants who left Istria. Slovenia charged that a crisis in the Trieste Credit bank undermined trust in Italian banking and financial institutions which played a role in the life of Italy's Slovene minority.

Political Rights and Civil Liberties: Slovenes can change their government democratically. The 1996 parliamentary elections were contested but were judged "free and fair."

Slovenia is a multiparty democracy, at last 30 political parties from the far-left to the far-right, and over a dozen represented in parliament. Of the 40 members of the upper house, 22 are directly elected and 18 are designated by electoral colleges of professional and other interest groups. In the 90-member lower house, 40 members are elected by constituency-based majority voting and 50 by proportional representation with one seat each reserved for Hungarian and Italian ethnic minorities.

Slovenia has lively broadcast and print media. Newspapers, several affiliated with political parties, print diverse views. Though the state controls most radio and television, private stations do operate, among them Kanal A in Ljubljana, the capital. Journalists have faced limited suspension for commentary on statements by government officials, and self-censorship remains an issue. Article 169 of the penal code bars defamation, and in May 1996 a journalist from *Mladina* was given a one-month jail term for libeling the mayor of Ljubljana.

Freedom of assembly is guaranteed and respected.; faces no restrictions on freedom of religion.

Minority rights are guaranteed by law, but the Supreme Court banned an Italian group in Istria from becoming a political party. The judiciary is independent. Judges are elected by the National Assembly on the recommendation of an 11-member Judicial Council, five of whose members are selected by parliament on the nomination of the president, and six of whom are sitting judges selected by their peers.

There are three main labor federations and most workers are free to join unions that are formally independent from government and political parties, though members may and do hold positions in the legislature. The year saw strikes by rail workers, journalists, and medical professionals. Women are guaranteed equality under the law. Numerous business, charitable, cultural and professional associations operate.

Solomon Islands

Polity: Parliamentary democracy
Economy: Capitalist
Population: 382,000
PPP: $2,266
Life Expectancy: 70.5
Ethnic Groups: Melanesian (93 percent), Polynesian (4 percent), Micronesian, European minorities
Capital: Honiara

Political Rights: 1
Civil Liberties: 2
Status: Free

Overview: In 1996 the Papua New Guinea Defense Forces (PNGDF) and allied militias launched a series of cross-border raids into the Solomon Islands over claims that the government and local residents support the Bougainville Revolutionary Army (BRA). Since 1989 the BRA has been fighting the PNG government, with the aim of gaining an independent Bougainville Island.

The Solomon Islands, a predominantly Melanesian country in the western Pacific Ocean, achieved independence from the British in 1978. Under the 1977 constitution the unicameral parliament (which currently has 47 seats) is directly elected to a four-year term. Executive power is vested in a prime minister and cabinet. The largely ceremonial governor-general serves as head of state and represents the British crown in this parliamentary democracy.

Key issues in the May 1993 elections, the country's fourth since independence, were the poor state of the economy, official corruption and the lack of adequate secondary schools. The Group for National Unity and Reconciliation, formed prior to the election by Prime Minister Solomon Mamaloni, took 21 seats; the People's Alliance Party, 7; five smaller parties, 14 and independents, 5.

In June 1993 parliament elected Francis Billy Hilly, a businessman who ran as an independent, as prime minister over Mamaloni. One of the Hilly government's major policy decisions was to place a moratorium on logging, the country's main source of export earnings. It cited rampant corruption in the awarding of contracts to foreign companies, and concern for environmental degradation.

Governor-General Moses Pitakaka's October 1994 decision to sack Hilly after the premier lost his parliamentary majority touched off a brief constitutional crisis that was resolved after the High Court ruled that a governor-general lacked the authority for such a move. Hilly then resigned of his own accord, and in November parliament elected Mamaloni as prime minister.

The Mamaloni government, which created a controversy shortly after taking office by ending the logging moratorium, now looks set to complete its term prior to elections due in spring 1997. But the government seems powerless to prevent alleged BRA operations in the Solomon Islands territory, and consequently must contend with the PNGDF's cross-border raids on Shortland and Choiseul islands in the northern Solomon Islands.

Political Rights and Civil Liberties: Citizens of the Solomon Islands can change their government democratically. Party affiliations are weak and tend to be based on personal loyalties rather than ideology or policy goals. Power is decentralized through elected provincial and local councils.

A key civil liberties issue has been the spillover from the Bougainville Island secessionist conflict in Papua New Guinea (see above). In June 1996, following several cross-border raids by the PNGDF, correspondents reported that local residents on Choiseul Island were fleeing inland and that authorities had imposed a dawn-to-dusk curfew in coastal areas. In one of the most serious incidents, in May a suspected pro-PNG militia group raided Moli village in south Choiseul and opened fire on seven Bougainvilleans seeking medical treatment. In June *Agence-France Presse* reported that suspected PNGDF soldiers were threatening residents on Gizo Island.

Police occasionally abuse suspects, although courts generally discipline officers involved in such incidents. The independent judiciary provides adequate procedural safeguards for the accused.

The country's three regular private newspapers vigorously criticize government policies. A semi-weekly in the Pidgin vernacular began publishing in late 1996. The state-owned Solomon Islands Broadcasting Corporation's (SIBC) radio service generally offers diverse viewpoints in its news coverage. However, in April 1996, Mamaloni banned SIBC from broadcasting statements by the locally based spokesman of the BRA. In a separate development, following the broadcast of an allegedly false news item in May the SIBC governing board ordered all news shows to be vetted by management prior to broadcast. A privately-owned FM station also broadcasts.

Permits are required for demonstrations but are not denied on political grounds. In an unusual departure from normal practice, in spring 1995 police on tiny Pavuvu Island arrested 56 landowners protesting the award to a local company of a timber concession that will involve the resettlement of several thousand affected islanders. Freedom of association is respected. There are several active nongovernmental organizations working mainly on women's and environmental issues.

Religious freedom is respected in this predominantly Christian country. Women suffer de facto discrimination in education and employment opportunities in what is a traditional male-dominated society. Domestic violence reportedly occurs frequently, and social norms generally mitigate against the enforcement of existing legal protections.

Although less than 15 percent of the population works in the formal economic sector, trade unions are vigorous and regularly engage in collective bargaining. The law only recognizes the right of private sector workers to strike, although a 1989 walkout by public school teachers established a de facto right to strike in the public sector.

Somalia

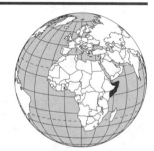

Polity: Rival ethnic-based militias; unrecognized de facto state in north
Economy: Mixed-statist
Population: 9,484,000
PPP: $712
Life Expectancy: 47.2
Ethnic Groups: Somali (Hawiye, Darod, Isaq, Isa, others), Gosha, Bajun
Capital: Mogadishu

Political Rights: 7
Civil Liberties: 7
Status: Not Free

Overview: The August death in battle of Somalia's leading warlord, Mohammed Farah Aideed, raised hopes for a lasting peace in the war-ravaged country, but a cease-fire negotiated in October almost immediately disintegrated amidst fierce clashes in the divided capital, Mogadishu. Clan-based factions fought over territory and control of the country's banana trade. In some areas, harsh Islamic law brought a semblance of order. Somalia's chances to be a unified country continued to diminish.

The $4 billion United Nations 1993-95 peacekeeping effort seems to have had no lasting effect. The last international forces withdrew in March 1995; casualties reached 100, including 20 Americans. The international community has, in effect, abandoned Somalia. Even international aid agencies are able to operate only sporadically in the volatile situation, and have repeatedly suspended operations to protest assaults on aid workers.

The massive intervention was prompted by famine and civil strife that since 1991 has taken as many as 300,000 lives. Civil war, starvation and widespread banditry and brutality have wracked Somalia since the struggle to topple military dictator Siad Barre began in the late 1980s. Barre, who had seized power in a 1969 coup, increasingly relied on divisive clan politics to maintain his grip on power. By the time he was toppled in January 1991, Somalia was awash with heavily-armed guerrilla movements and militias based on ethnic, clan or sub-clan loyalties. Fierce fighting among the various contestants—mostly over economic assets like ports, airfields and banana plantations—led to anarchy and famine.

Over 20,000 American troops landed in December 1992, to be eventually replaced by an 18,000-strong multinational force under U.N. command. The humanitarian mission succeeded in quelling clan combat long enough to end the famine, but slowly turned into battles with Somali militias.

Somalia is an excellent example of a "failed state." No central authority exists, and many of the powers of the modern state, including administration of justice, are devolving back to traditional clan authorities. A permanent division of the country may have already occurred, as northern clans consolidated their declared Somaliland Republic in what had been the colonial British Somaliland. The British colony had merged with Italian-controlled territory to the south to form a single independent country in July 1960.

Political Rights and Civil Liberties: Somalis cannot choose their government. Rival warlords rule by force alone. One faction of the United Somali Congress/Somalia National Alliance (USC/NSA) is now led by its late leader's son, Hussein Mohamed Aideed. His main rivals are leader of another USC/NSA faction, Osman Hassan Ali "Ato," and Ali Madhi Mohamed of the Somalia Salvation Alliance. Other armed factions, including the Rahawyayn Resistance Army, are also in the fray.

External meddling in the form of money or guns to various factions is alleged, from as far afield as Libya and Afghanistan. In August, Ethiopian troops struck into Somali territory to destroy bases of ethnic Somali rebels who had mounted cross-border raids into Ethiopia. Fierce fighting has repeatedly occurred over Somalia's banana trade, which reportedly earns the Aideed faction several million dollars per year. Banana plantation workers have complained of virtual slave labor conditions as men, women and children are forced to work long hours for paltry pay under guard by armed militiamen.

No real political entities exist beyond the ascriptive ties clan loyalties provide. Autonomous civic or political groups cannot organize or operate safely. Widespread lawlessness has spread in some areas in the vacuum of central authority. In parts of Mogadishu, a backlash of severe Islamic justice has taken hold. Islamic courts are imposing sentences that include executions and amputations according to *shari'a* law. Rights to free expression and association are simply ignored. Few independent journalists work in the country, and international correspondents visit only at great risk. There are no free domestic media. A few photocopied newsletters circulate; various factions operate some radio stations.

Children are forcibly recruited into various armed factions. Women suffer intense societal discrimination, and infibulation, the most severe form of female genital mutilation, is routine.

In northern Somalia, where resistance to the Siad Barre dictatorship in the 1980s was most intense, a de facto but internationally unrecognized state already exists on the ground. The Republic of Somaliland, with its capital in Hargeisa, which declared its independence in May 1991, also faces internal clan divisions and reports of human rights abuses, but is far more cohesive than the rest of the country. President Mohammed Ibrahim Egal, whose term expires in 1997, has stated he will not seek re-election. The government earns most of its income from livestock exports to the Gulf states. Relief agencies are able to operate more effectively and safely in the Somaliland Republic than the rest of Somalia. If the de facto republic's leader Egal can achieve accord among rival clans, the international community may be hard-pressed not to accept a new country emerging from the failed state of Somalia.

South Africa

Polity: Presidential-legis-   **Political Rights:** 1
lative democracy   **Civil Liberties:** 2
Economy: Capitalist-statist   **Status:** Free
Population: 44,485,000
PPP: $3,127
Life Expectancy: 63.2
Ethnic Groups: Black (Zulu, Xhosa, Swazi, Sotho,
others) (75 percent), European (Afrikaner, English) (14 percent),
Coloured (9 percent), Indian (12 percent)
Capital: Cape Town (legislative), Pretoria (executive), Bloemfontien (judicial)

Overview: **S**outh Africa sought to assure itself a democratic future in 1996 while struggling to confront its violent past. A new constitution initially rejected by the Constitutional Court was finally approved after being amended by the Constitutional Assembly (CA) consisting of all 490 members of the National Assembly and Senate. The new constitution replaces the interim charter in place during the transition from apartheid, and includes extensive and strong provisions to protect human rights. Freedom of expression and assembly are guaranteed, as is the right to form and join trade unions. Detention without trial and any form of torture or "cruel, inhuman or degrading treatment or punishment," all too familiar in South Africans' recent memory, are explicitly banned. A strongly-independent judiciary is in place, and free expression is respected.

The question of justice in dealing with the excesses of the apartheid era, however, is causing new tensions. Former defense minister General Magnus Malan was acquitted of murder charges relating to apartheid-era killings, but some former security officials have been convicted, and other trials are in the works. Nobel peace laureate and recently-retired Archbishop Desmond Tutu has been conducting public hearings of the official Truth and Reconciliation Commission. Numerous officials of the former white minority regime have appeared before the panel, admitted wrongdoings and requested amnesty. Bishop Tutu has threatened to resign unless members of the African National Congress (ANC) who undertook terrorist acts or committed extrajudicial killings during the liberation struggle do the same.

Efforts to open South Africa's mostly white-controlled economy and media continued. Burgeoning urban population has led to increasingly violent crime. President Nelson Mandela's personal popularity remained higher than his party's. The ANC is still struggling to transform itself from a coalition against apartheid to a political party with a constituency based on issues; meanwhile, corruption is eroding its legitimacy. Thirteen small parties that garnered scant support during the 1994 general election have formed the Justice and Freedom Alliance (JAFA), in advance of 1999 presidential and parliamentary elections. However, the main contenders will be the Afrikaner-dominated National Party, which this year withdrew from the Government of National Unity formed after the 1994 polls, and the Zulu Inkatha Freedom Party (IFP), which controls the provincial government of KwaZulu/Natal. These racial and ethnic divisions represent the most dangerous divide of South African politics, one that many people fear Nelson Mandela's successors will not be able to bridge.

Political Rights and Civil Liberties:

The process of extending electoral rights to the country's non-white majority on the basis of one person-one vote began with presidential and parliamentary elections in April 1994, and was completed with local elections in nearly all parts of the country in October 1995. South Africans of all races now can choose their national and local government representatives through democratic elections, although charges of vote-rigging have marred electoral credibility in KwaZulu/Natal.

Constitutional compliance is adjudicated by an 11-member Constitutional Court, which has repeatedly demonstrated its strong independence. A constitutionally-mandated Human Rights Commission is appointed by parliament "to promote the observance of, respect for and the protection of fundamental rights...and develop an awareness of fundamental rights among all people of the republic."

A Gender Commission, also constitutionally-mandated, has been formed "to promote gender equality and to advise and make recommendations to parliament [regarding] any laws or proposed legislation which affects gender equality and the status of women." Several women have recently been appointed to judgeships, but women overall make up less than five percent of sitting judges. Nearly a third of National Assembly members are women, but only three serve in the 28-member cabinet. Violence against women in townships and rural areas is reportedly common, and a sharp rise in rape cases has been reported. Discriminatory practices in customary law remain prevalent. Violence against children is also reported to be widespread.

Putting constitutional provisions into meaningful action in a country still divided by race and ethnicity will be at least as challenging as was negotiating the new charter. South African whites, being much more prosperous than blacks, enjoy better education and social services. Most economic power remains solidly with the white minority. Over three-quarters of South Africa's 44 million people are black, but share only 29 percent of total incomes. The country's 5.3 million whites take almost 60 percent. Eighteen million people, nearly half of the country's population, live in rural areas, where most eke out a barely subsistence existence. The government's Reconstruction and Development Plan (RDP) is seeking major improvements in rural areas and townships where South Africa's poorest reside, but without alienating the economically crucial white elite. Large-scale child healthcare and nutrition programs, as well as housing, water supply and electrification projects have been undertaken, but it is difficult for any government to meet popular expectations that socio-economic change will match the enormous shift in political power.

Demands for greater autonomy by the mainly Zulu IFP represent a potentially serious ethnic flashpoint. The IFP controls KwaZulu/Natal province after emerging as the strongest party in 1994 elections marked by numerous irregularities, and occasional violence still flares between IFP and ANC supporters. The often obstreperous and occasionally belligerent IFP leader Mangosuthu Buthelezi remains in the national cabinet. White concerns center on the growing "reverse discrimination" and the rampant crime. Vigilante groups have sprung up in several areas, most visibly in Cape Town, where they have attacked and killed suspected drug dealers.

The media are generally free, although most are either state-run or controlled by a few major corporations. *The Sowetan* and the *New Nation* are the only two of South Africa's 33 dailies and weeklies that are black-owned. A government commission launched an inquiry into press-ownership issues in 1996. The state-run South African Broadcasting Corporation is today far more independent than during its days as a propaganda organ for the apartheid regime, but suffers from self-censorship and a complacency borne from lack of competition.

Freedom of association and assembly is constitutionally-guaranteed and respected. Labor rights were codified under the 1995 Labor Relations Act (LRA), which protects the right to strike after reconciliation efforts, which can be assisted by the official Commission for Conciliation, Mediation, and Arbitration (CCMA). However, the law also allows employers to hire replacement workers. There are over 250 trade unions. The country's largest union federation, the Congress of South African Trade Unions (COSATU), is formally linked to both the ANC and the South African Communist Party, and took a leading above-ground role in the anti-apartheid struggle. Its ties to the government are fraying and increasingly ambivalent, however, as the ANC makes political compromises and economic decisions that do not satisfy workers' demands.

South Africa's economy is still dominated by a handful of large interlocking corporations which were protected from foreign competition both by sanctions and by government-design during the apartheid era. Economic liberalization is slowly taking hold, and South Africa is finding new export markets in the region and across Africa. Several major international corporations that pulled out of South Africa in the 1980s have now returned, but high labor costs compared to other developing economies and concerns over political stability are making many investors wary.

Spain

Polity: Parliamentary democracy
Economy: Capitalist
Population: 39,250,000
PPP: $13,660
Life Expectancy: 77.7
Ethnic Groups: Spanish (72 percent), Catalan (16 percent), Galician (8 percent), Basque (2 percent), others
Capital: Madrid

Political Rights: 1
Civil Liberties: 2
Status: Free

Overview: The conservative People's Party (PP), led by the popular young Jose Maria Aznar, narrowly defeated the PSOE, (Spanish Socialist Workers Party), which had been in power for 13 years with its charismatic leader, Felipe Gonzalez, serving as prime minister. The socialists had warned voters that the PP's ideological genisis was on the extreme nationalist right. But as prime minister, Aznar immediately made it clear, through his moderate policies and prudent governing style, that there was no danger of Franco-style nationalism.

Foremost in the minds of voters this year was the economy; with unemployment at 23 percent, voters were receptive to Aznar's promises to cut taxes and reduce unemployment without sacrificing pensions and other benefits. Realistically, however, if Spain is to meet the criteria for participation in the European Monetary Union, the prime minister must halve the budget deficit, reduce inflation, reform the country's labor laws, and terminate or sell off a number of state industries.

Rampant corruption among Socialist officials led even once-adamant supporters to vote for the People's Party in this election. In recent years, 39 people have been implicated in illegal financing of the Socialist party; the former governor of the Bank of Spain was charged with tax fraud and the manipulation of share prices; the chief of the paramilitary Civil Guard was arrested on charges of embezzlement and bribery; and 14 former police and government officials were indicted for involvement in an anti terrorist operation whose "death squads" killed 27 people in a campaign against the independence movement, the Basque Homeland and Freedom Group (ETA). Seven of the victims had no connection with the terrorists. Former Prime Minister Gonzalez was investigated for suspected links to the undercover war. Though cleared of any wrongdoing in April, his role may still be at issue as new information is uncovered.

Those who predicted a landslide victory for Aznar were disappointed when he garnered only 37 percent of the popular vote and 156 seats in parliament – 20 short of an absolute majority. Over two months of bargaining for support from the Catalan Convergence and Unity Party and the Basque National Party brought him the 181 votes needed for a working majority. Aznar was able to win an investiture vote in May, though concern remains that his government will lack stability and will postponeeconomic reforms will be postponed.

Accompanying the election campaign was a resurgence of Basque violence, which included the assassinations of two close allies of Gonzalez. Basques have expressed concern over aspects of PP policy, and they are wary of the Spanish right's tendency to concentrate power at the Castilian center.

Political Rights and Civil Liberties: Spanish citizens can change their government democratically. Spain has been governed democratically since 1977, following nearly 40 years of dictatorship under Francisco Franco and a brief transitional government under Adolfo Suarez.

The country is divided into 17 autonomous regions with limited powers, including control over such areas as health, tourism, local police agencies and instruction in regional languages. The bicameral federal legislature includes a territorially-elected Senate and a Congress of Deputies elected on the basis of proportional representation and universal suffrage. Although the Socialist party has ruled that women must occupy 25 percent of senior party posts and a feminist party has been officially registered since 1981, female participation in government remains minimal.

A Supreme Tribunal heads the judiciary, which includes territorial, provincial, regional and municipal courts. The post-Franco constitution and subsequent parliamentary legislation established the right to trial by jury. The legislation took effect in 1996.

Freedom of speech and a free press are guaranteed. The press has been particularly influential in setting the political agenda in recent years, with national dailies such as *El Mundo, ABC* and *El Pais* covering corruption and prompting the re-opening of the investigation into the "death squad" killings. An investigation instigated by *Diario-16* led to the arrest of Luis Roldan, chief of the Civil Guard police. In addition to the state-controlled station, which has been accused of pro-government bias, three independent commercial television stations broadcast.

In January, Contrabanda FM, an independent, alternative, five-year-old radio station in Barcelona had its signal drowned out by a new municipal station run by the Barcelona City Council. The new station, which has no legally-assigned frequency, began to broadcast on Contrabanda's frequency, effectively silencing the independent station.

The rights to freedom of association and collective bargaining are constitutionally-guaranteed. However, Spain has one of the lowest levels of trade union membership in the European Union, and unions have failed to prevent passage of new labor laws facilitating dismissals and encouraging short-term contracting.

In 1978, the constitution disestablished Roman Catholicism as the state religion, while directing Spanish authorities to "keep in mind the religious beliefs of Spanish society." Freedom of worship and the separation of church and state are respected in practice.

Spain is home to many cultural and linguistic groups, some with strong regional identities. Although popular support for the ETA separatist movement and its political wing, Herri Batasuna, has significantly declined, ETA remains the most active terrorist group in Western Europe, having claimed some 800 lives over 25 years.

Spain lacks anti-discrimination laws, and ethnic minorities, particularly immigrants, continue to report bias and mistreatment. In particular, North African immigrants report physical abuse and discrimination by authorities.

Sri Lanka

Polity: Presidential-
parliamentary democracy
(insurgency)
Economy: Mixed
capitalist-statist
Population: 18,396,000
PPP: $3,030

Political Rights: 3*
Civil Liberties: 5
Status: Partly Free

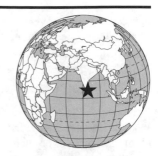

Life Expectancy: 72.0
Ethnic Groups: Sinhalese (74 percent), Tamil (18 percent), Moor (7 percent), others
Capital: Colombo
Ratings Change: Sri Lanka's political rights rating changed from 4 to 3 because
although civil conflict continues, the government is slowly consolidating areas under
its control.

Overview: More than two years after campaigning on a platform of
respecting press freedom, abolishing the country's powerful presidency and ending the civil war, Sri Lankan Presi-
dent Chandrika Bandaranaike had by late 1996 largely failed to deliver on her
pledges.

Sri Lanka achieved independence from Britain in 1948. Political power has
alternated between the centrist United National Party (UNP) and the nationalist,
leftist Sri Lanka Freedom Party (SLFP).

Colonial-era language policies favoring Tamils and other minorities contributed to communal tensions that continued after independence. Legislation in 1956
making Sinhala, the language of the majority Sinhalese, the official language of
government provoked the first of several anti-Tamil riots since independence.

The 1978 constitution established a directly-elected president with broad executive powers who can serve two six-year terms and dissolve parliament. The 225-
member parliament serves for up to six years. Under President Junius Jayewardene
(1977-88) of the UNP, Sri Lanka adopted market-oriented economic policies.

Escalating communal unrest led to the outbreak of civil war in 1983. Tamil
guerrillas claimed discrimination in education and employment opportunities. By
1986 the Liberation Tigers of Tamil Eelam (LTTE), which called for an independent Tamil homeland in northern and eastern Sri Lanka, controlled the northern
Jaffna Peninisula. An Indian peacekeeping force in the north between 1987-90 failed
to end the fighting. Its presence triggered an anti-government insurgency in the south
by the left-wing, Sinhalese-based People's Liberation Front (JVP). By 1990 the
government had crushed the JVP with the help of military-backed death squads;
insurgency-related deaths totaled 30,000.

Political violence peaked in spring 1993 with the assassinations of opposition
leader Lalith Athulathmudali and President Ranasinghe Premadasa within days of
each other, the latter by a suspected LTTE suicide bomber. During the August 1994
parliamentary election campaign, the People's Alliance (PA), an SLFP-dominated
coalition led by Chandrika Kumaratunga, promised to end the civil war and introduce greater government accountability. The PA won 105 seats to oust the UNP

(94 seats) after 17 years, with four minor parties winning 16 seats and independents, ten.

Kumaratunga entered the 1994 presidential race against UNP candidate Gamini Dissanayake. In October a suicide bomber killed Dissanayake, and in the November 9 election Kumaratunga won 62 percent of the vote to defeat Dissanayake's widow.

In August 1995 Kumaratunga unveiled a devolution proposal aimed at ending the civil war by granting ethnic minorities greater autonomy through new regional councils. In December the army captured the LTTE's stronghold of Jaffna city. The fighting displaced some 350,000 civilians.

A spring 1996 army offensive placed the Jaffna Peninsula under government control for the first time in a decade. In late September the army captured the LTTE's new stronghold at Kilinochchi. Some 200,000 civilians fled the fighting. Kumaratunga's presidency faces a key test as she plans to begin the constitutional amendment process for devolution.

Political Rights and Civil Liberties:

Sri Lankans can change their government democratically. The 1994 parliamentary elections were generally free, although the civil war caused voting irregularities. Only 19,000 of some 600-800,000 displaced persons were declared eligible to vote. No polling took place in LTTE-controlled areas.

In spring 1996 the government used the Emergency Regulations (see below) to postpone local elections due by June, citing security conditions. Voting is scheduled for spring 1997. There have been no local elections in the war-torn north and east for 13 years. In December the government again postponed voting in these areas.

Since 1983 the country has been under a near-continuous state of emergency which Kumaratunga largely withdrew in 1994. In April 1996 the government reimposed emergency rule throughout the country. The Emergency Regulations (ER) allow authorities to detain suspects for up to one year without charge and to ban political meetings. Under the separate Prevention of Terrorism Act (PTA), authorities can detain suspects for eighteen months without charge.

The judiciary is independent. A controversy in late 1996 surrounding the appointment of a law professor with no judicial experience to the Supreme Court underscored a long-standing concern that the constitution grants the president sole authority to appoint judges. Security personnel routinely torture detainees. Few police officers or soldiers have been prosecuted for these and other abuses, creating a climate of impunity.

A Human Rights Task Force, established by the Kumaratunga government in 1994, monitors arrests and detentions under the ER and the PTA. Three commissions established in 1995 to investigate "disappearances" since 1988 are scheduled to disband in spring 1997 despite a backlog of unfinished business. In December the government formed a military commission to look into alleged human rights abuses by security forces; critics called for a civilian body.

Government security forces, the LTTE, and state-backed Sinhalese, Muslim and anti-LTTE Tamil "home guards" are responsible for considerable human rights abuses related to the civil war, which has killed some 50,000 people. Police and army soldiers continued to commit extrajudicial killings in the north and east, mainly against LTTE guerrillas but also against civilians in reprisal for LTTE attacks on security forces; On February 11 troops killed 24 civilians in the eastern Kumarapuram village in retaliation for an LTTE ambush that killed two soldiers. In 1996 security forces were implicated in several hundred disappearances, particularly of suspected LTTE guerrillas.

The armed forces have also indiscriminately bombed and shelled populated areas of Jaffna Peninsula. The Colombo *Sunday Observer* reported that a March 16 air force bombing in the northern town of Nachchikudah killed 15 civilians.

The LTTE continues to kill Sinhalese and Muslim villagers in the north and east, indiscriminately shell civilian areas, commit abductions and forcibly conscript children. The LTTE rules its territory in an arbitrary, brutal manner and denies basic rights to civilians.

The LTTE is suspected in several major urban terrorism attacks in 1996, which include the January 31 bombing of the Central Bank in Colombo that killed 91 people. Authorities responded by detaining and sometimes torturing thousands of young Tamil civilians, mainly in the north and east and in Colombo. Some spent months in prison.

Authorities are reestablishing civilian administration on the Jaffna Peninsula and resettling internally displaced civilians. Some 46,000 Muslims, forcibly expelled by the LTTE from northern towns in 1990, remain in refugee camps.

The desertion of at least 15,000 army soldiers in the past two years has swelled the ranks of criminal gangs. Partisan violence escalated in 1996, particularly in southern Sri Lanka, with PA supporters linked to many attacks.

The government controls a sizable share of the media, including the Lake House group, the largest media chain. The Kumaratunga government has filed at least three criminal defamation suits against editors of leading private papers, and in December 1996 authorities arrested the news director of an independent broadcast company under the PTA for broadcasting false news.

The government imposed censorship on all domestic media coverage of the civil war for three months from September 1995, and again between April 19 and October 8, 1996. The government has also limited journalists' access to the conflict. In August Kumaratunga warned that newspapers "publishing irresponsible and false material" related to the war effort could be shut down.

Sri Lanka's vibrant civil society includes active human rights, nongovernmental and social welfare organizations. Religious freedom is respected.

Rape and domestic violence remain serious problems. Many of the thousands of children working as domestic servants are physically and sexually abused. Enforcement of laws against child prostitution is weak and Sri Lanka has become a major destination for foreign pedophiles. In October local human rights groups reported that orphanages are increasingly supplying children for sex with foreigners. High populations of street children live in major cities.

Trade unions are independent and collective bargaining is practiced. State workers are prohibited from striking. The 1989 Essential Services Act allows the president to declare a strike in any industry illegal. On May 31 Kumaratunga invoked the Act to end a three-day strike by electricity workers. In December authorities arrested several trade union activists during a dispute with management at a South Korean-owned steel factory.

Sudan

Polity: Military
Economy: Mixed
capitalist
Population: 28,855,000
PPP: $1,350
Life Expectancy: 53.2
Ethnic Groups: Sudanese Arab (40 percent), Dinka (11 percent), Nuba (8 percent), Neur, Shilluk, Fur, some 600 other groups
Capital: Khartoum (executive), Omdurman (legislative)

Political Rights: 7
Civil Liberties: 7
Status: Not Free

Overview: **C**ivil war and massive human rights abuses continued to wrack Africa's largest country through 1996. Widespread slavery persisted in parts of the country, as genocidal campaigns against minorities continued. Sudan has been ravaged by Africa's longest and bloodiest war, and new fighting flared along the Eritrean frontier. Sudan's ruling dictatorship, dominated by Arab Islamic fundamentalists, seeks to subjugate the country's black African minority and secular and democratic forces. Sudanese President and Prime Minister, Lieutenant-General Omar Hassan Ahmed al-Bashir, sought to clothe himself in the mantle of electoral legitimacy in heavily-manipulated March elections. Elections were also held for 264 members of the National Parliament, whose remaining 136 seats are filled by presidential appointment.

Repression against the media, other elements of civil society and women intensified. Riots over deteriorating economic conditions flared in several cities. The regime quashed at least two reported coup attempts from within the military. Sudan also faces incremental UN sanctions in response to official Sudanese involvement in the June 1995 assassination attempt against Egyptian President Hosni Mubarak in Addis Ababa.

Sudan has been embroiled in civil war for 20 of its 30 years as a modern state since regaining independence in 1956 after nearly eight decades of British rule. From 1956-72, separatists of the Anya Nya movement, representing mainly Christian and animist Black Africans in southern Sudan, battled government forces. A 1972 agreement gave the south extensive autonomy, and an uneasy peace prevailed for a decade. In 1983, General Jafar Numeiri, who had toppled a parliamentary government in 1969, sought to dilute southern autonomy and to introduce *shari'a* law. These moves, as well as pervasive racial and religious discrimination and fears of economic exploitation by the government as it plans to pipe oil discovered in the south to northern Sudan, sparked renewed civil war. Although Numeiri was overthrown in 1985 and civilian rule was restored in 1986, the war went on. General al-Bashir toppled the freely-elected government in 1989, and has ruled through a military-civilian regime with strong backing of senior Muslim clerics. Sudan is unlikely to know peace as long as the Islamist regime continues its efforts to impose fundamentalist values on a diverse and multicultural society.

Political Rights and Civil Liberties: Sudan's people cannot choose or change their government democratically. The March 1996 presidential and parliamentary elections were neither free nor fair, and cannot be said to reflect the will of the Sudanese people.

The 1989 military coup that deposed a democratically-elected government installed hardline Islamist-backed military rulers who have not sought peaceful resolution of the country's civil war. Sudan is now officially an Islamic state. All political parties were banned and the imposition of shari'a was accelerated. Few independent voices in media or civil society are tolerated, and officials act with impunity. President and Prime Minister General al-Bashir is official head of state and government, although Hasan Al-Turabi, leader of the fundamentalist National Islamic Front (NIF), is highly influential and often deemed the country's de facto leader. The entire judiciary and the security apparatus are controlled by the NIF.

Devastation caused by fighting has been compounded by famine among the displaced populace, and over half a million people have died in the last dozen years of conflict. The war in southern Sudan is exacerbated by ethnic divisions within rebel ranks. In 1991, the Sudan People's Liberation Army (SPLA), led by Colonel John Garang, was split when ethnic Nuer troops joined dissident Riak Machar in the Southern Sudan Independence Movement in protest over alleged ethnic Dinka domination. Machar defected to the government in April, although some of his commanders refused and have rejoined the SPLA.

Abuses by nearly every faction involved in the war have been reported. Accounts of particularly terrible excesses by government forces against Nuba people in western Sudan continued this year, in what has been described as a genocidal "war of annihilation" against 1.5 million Nuba people. In the mostly Arab north of the country, repression continued. Torture is reportedly routine at secret police "ghost houses" in many cities. Among detainees are at least 100 soldiers who were reportedly involved in coup attempts in March and August. A secret trial of 31 alleged plotters was underway late in the year, amidst reports that some of the accused had confessed under torture. In September, several people were reported killed in Khartoum when protests against bread shortages flared into violence. Sporadic demonstrations in other cities were also reportedly harshly suppressed.

Massive relocation drives backed by armed force are also driving squatters, nearly all of them blacks from southern Sudan, away from Khartoum. Black children have reportedly been seized–perhaps 100,000 or more have been placed in Islamic schools. Others have been enslaved, along with black villagers seized in raids by Arab militia. Relief agencies make regular forays into rural areas to purchase slaves' freedom. The Sudan government has officially denounced slavery, but has taken no action to end it.

The once-vigorous print media are being strangled as several more publications were closed in 1996, including the last independent newspaper, *Rahi al Akhar* (Alternative View). A new press law, passed in November, erects new legal impediments to independent media. The regime has maintained restrictions on international contacts and domestic communication, by confiscating fax and telex machines, typewriters and copiers. Broadcast media are entirely state-controlled.

In June, most of the women journalists working for two state-owned media houses were fired, and in September unmarried women employed in state broadcasting were advised to marry within three months or face unspecified consequences.

Women also face extensive societal discrimination. Female genital mutilation is routine, despite laws forbidding it.

Christians are frequently harassed for practicing their religion. They are not permitted to worship or build new churchs. The government has been involved in church closings and the burning of church structures.

Resistance to the Islamic regime is being supported by neighboring Eritrea, where the National Democratic Alliance (NDA), a broad coalition of secular and religious groups from both northern and southern Sudan, is headquartered. Attacks on the main roads in the north and east of the country threaten access to Sudan's only link to the sea at Port Sudan.

The NDA enjoys strong Eritrean and Ethiopian support, and receives American assistance. Sudan is accused of supporting Christian millennialist rebels operating in northern Uganda, and the entire frontier zone has become a quilt of warring factions with different benefactors and sometimes indeterminate loyalties.

Suriname

Polity: Presidential-parliamentary democracy
Economy: Capitalist-statist
Population: 428,000
PPP: $3,670
Life Expectancy: 70.5
Ethnic Groups: East Indian (37 percent), Creole (31 percent), Javanese (15 percent), Bush Negro, Indian, Chinese, European
Capital: Paramaribo

Political Rights: 3
Civil Liberties: 3
Status: Partly Free

Overview: The election of Jules Wijdenbosch, the candidate of former military strongman Desi Bourterse's National Democratic Party (NDP), as Suriname's president in September 1996 raised fears that Bourterse had effectively regained control of power.

The Republic of Suriname achieved independence from the Netherlands in 1975. A 1980 military coup brought strongman Desi Bourterse to power as head of a regime that bruatally suppressed civic and political opposition. In 1987 Bourtese permitted elections under a constitution providing for a directly-elected, 51-seat National Assembly, which serves a five year term and selects the state president. If the Assembly is unable to select a president with the required two-thirds vote, a People's Assembly, comprised of parliament and regional and local officials, chooses the president. The Front for Democracy and Development, a three-party coalition, easily won the 1987 elections. The military-organized NDP won just three seats. The Assembly elected Ramsewak Shankar president.

In 1990 the army ousted Shankar, and Bourterse again took power. Under international pressure the army allowed elections in 1991. The New Front, a coalition of mainly East Indian, Creole and Javanese parties that had been ousted in 1990, won 30 seats, the NDP, 12, and the urban-based Democratic Alternative 91, nine.

The Assembly subsequently selected the Front's candidate, Ronald Venetiaan, as president.

In 1992 Bourterse quit the army to lead the NDP. During its tenure the Venetiaan government took some constititutional measures to limit the power of the military. In late 1995 and early 1996 the government purged several high-ranking, pro-Bourterse military officials. But the government's economic structural adjustment program led to social and labor unrest amidst an inflationary spiral and a collapse of the Surinamese guilder.

During the campaign for the May 23, 1996, parliamentary elections the NDP pledged to reverse many of the government's economic reforms. The voting resulted in a fragmented parliament. The four-party New Front won a plurality of 24 seats, down from 30. The Front entered into a coalition with the smaller Central Bloc, consisting of two opposition groups, but still could not muster the necessary two-thirds majority in parliamentary balloting to return Venetiaan to office.

Bourterse's NDP (16 seats) subsequently gained the support of the Javanese-based Party of National Unity and Solidarity and of dissident members of the East Indian-based United Reform Party. In September an 869-member People's Assembly of MPs and local officials, convened as required under the constitution, broke the deadlock by electing Jules Wijdenbosch, the NDP's candidate, as president.

Political Rights and Civil Liberties: Citizens of Suriname can change their government democratically. The May 1996 elections, which marked the first transfer of power from one elected government to another since independence, were generally free and fair, although former military strongman and current NDP head Bourterse claimed there were irregularities. Parties are organized mostly along ethnic lines, which contributes to parliamentary gridlock in Suriname's ethnically-complex society. Civic institutions are weak and Bourterse continues to exert considerable influence on the political process.

The government generally respects freedom of expression. Radio is both public and private, with a number of small commercial radio stations competing with the government-owned radio and television broadcasting system. State broadcast media generally offer pluralistic viewpoints. The private press practices some self-censorship, particularly regarding the activities of Bourterse.

Indigenous groups, which comprise 15 percent of the population, face social discrimination and alleged dislocation by the operations of foreign mining companies. Their geographic isolation mitigates against greater participation in the political process. Under a 1992 peace accord between the government and two rebel groups, the Bush Negro-based Jungle Commando and the indigenous-based, military-linked Tucuyana Amazonas, the insurgents agreed to disarm in return for economic assistance to indigenous communities. However, the government has largely been unable to provide more resources to these communities and some rebels have reorganized as bandits.

The judiciary is weak and reluctant to handle cases involving human rights issues, the military and supporters of Bourterse. In 1996 a lower court rejected a challenge to a 1992 law that grants amnesty to former rebels and soldiers for rights violations committed between 1985 and mid-1992. Despite pressure from human rights groups the government has not actively investigated "disappearances" dating from periods of military rule. Police abuse of detainees is a problem and prisons are dangerously overcrowded.

Human rights organizations function relatively freely. Several organizations specifically address violence against women, reports of trafficking of Brazilian women, and related issues.

Workers can join independent trade unions, and the labor movement is active in politics. Collective bargaining is legal and practiced fairly widely. Civil servants have no legal right to strike but in practice do so.

Swaziland

Polity: Traditional monarchy
Economy: Capitalist
Population: 999,000
PPP: $2,940
Life Expectancy: 57.8
Ethnic Groups: Swazi, Zulu, European
Capital: Mbabane

Political Rights: 6
Civil Liberties: 5
Status: Not Free

Overview:

After strikes and demonstrations had led to violence early in the year, Swazi King Mswati III acceded to demands by trade unionists and advocates for democracy for constitutional revisions. For decades, Swaziland was a regional oasis of calm as war and turmoil raged in neighboring Mozambique and South Africa. Now, the tiny kingdom of less than one million people has southern Africa's only unelected government. In July, the king named a 29-member constitutional review panel, but traditional chiefs are unlikely to accept reform quickly. Political activity has been officially banned since 1973.

Swaziland was a British protectorate that achieved independence with an elected parliament in 1968. Mswati III is the latest monarch to rule in the 240-year-old Dlamini dynasty. His predecessor, Sobhuza II, who died in 1983, scrapped the multiparty system in favor of *tinkhundla* (regional councils) in 1973, and no representative elections have taken place since.

The ban on all political activity is only sporadically enforced. Trade unionists and banned political groups have united in the Swaziland Democratic Alliance (SDA) to press for democratization. A series of *vusela* (consultations) were held among Swaziland's people from 1991-95, ostensibly to determine popular opinion regarding political and economic changes. Mswati's promise to create a constitution to replace the suspended 1968 charter is regarded with deep cynicism. Yet even opposition activists recognize the strong unifying role of the monarchy in Swazi society and seek limitations on its power, not its abolition, although disputes within the royal family could contribute to its demise.

Political Rights and Civil Liberties:

Swaziland's people cannot freely elect their representatives or change their government through democratic means. All Swazis are subjects of absolute monarch Mswati III. A report recommending multiparty elections was rejected by the king in 1993, and local chiefs voted through the *tinkhundla* system for 55 of 65 members of the House of Assembly. Ten more members are appointed by the King, who also names 20 of 30 members of the Senate, whose other ten members are selected by the House of Assembly.

The King can issue decrees with the full force of law, and the bicameral legislature of indirectly-elected and appointed members do little more than affirm his decisions. Swaziland's new prime minister, Dr. Sibusiso Barnabas Dlamini, a respected former World Bank official appointed to the post in July, said in October that a new constitution will be in place before elections scheduled for 1998.

With the King and conservative chiefs still wielding power, it is unclear what sort of document will emerge. The constitutional committee is expected to conduct wide public consultations through the *vusela* system of open meetings, an exercise that is more an effort to defuse public opinion than to heed it. A leading opposition figure withdrew from the committee in October, charging its chairman with obstructing its transparency.

The new constitutional committee has been assigned broad authority to prosecute people who "belittle" or "insult" it, including the power to impose fines of $1500, up to five years' imprisonment, or both. On other political issues or matters regarding the royal family, free expression remains limited. Self-censorship long prevailed in the kingdom, although the early 1990s saw increased openness. Legislation banning publication of any criticism of the monarchy was introduced in 1995 after a private newspaper criticized what it deemed King Mswati's extravagance. Only one independent newspaper publishes, and its journalists, as well as the staff of the government newspaper, are routinely harassed. State-run television and radio stations are the country's most important media, and remain closely controlled by the government. However, a wide range of broadcast and print media from South Africa are received in the country.

Freedom of religion is respected, and a variety of Christian sects operate freely. Nongovernmental organizations not involved in politics are also permitted. Several political groupings, including the People's United Democratic Movement (PUDEMO) and the Swaziland Youth Congress (SWAYOCO) operate openly, but members are routinely harassed and detained, usually for brief periods, by security forces.

Prisons are increasingly crowded with people detained without trial under the 1993 Non-Bailable Offences Order. The decree covers serious crimes, including murder, robbery, rape, weapons offenses and poaching, but requires only charges and not evidence for indefinite detention. The Swazi Law Society and international groups contend that the decree serves effectively to convict people without trial and denies the presumption of innocence.

Swazi women are unequal in both formal and customary law. Married women are considered minors, and require spousal permission to enter into almost any form of economic activity, from borrowing money to opening a bank account. They also enjoy limited inheritance rights. Employment regulations requiring equal pay for equal work are not always observed. Wife-beating and other violence against women is common, and traditional values still carry weight even in modernized settings.

Union rights are recognized in the 1980 Industrial Relations Act, and unions are able to operate independently. The Swaziland Federation of Trade Unions (SFTU) led a week-long general strike that paralyzed the country in January, and has been a leader in demands for democratization. Teachers and civil servants struck again for nearly a month in June and July. Wage agreements are often reached by collective bargaining, and 75 percent of the private workforce are unionized. In May, a new forum comprising of unions and the country's main employers' association announced plans to support economic reform and democratization.

Swaziland's free market sector operates with little government interference; but most Swazis continue to engage in subsistence agriculture. Government plans to privatize parastatal concerns are proceeding slowly. Significant foreign investment will not come until greater transparency in governance is achieved, and until an end to the misuse of public funds and royal excesses is visible.

Sweden

Polity: Parliamentary democracy
Economy: Mixed capitalist
Population: 8,842,000
PPP: $17,900
Life Expectancy: 78.3
Ethnic Groups: Swede (88 percent), Finn (2 percent), Lappic (Saami), immigrant groups
Capital: Stockholm

Political Rights: 1
Civil Liberties: 1
Status: Free

Overview:

In March 1996 Finance Minister Goeran Persson became prime minister upon Ingvar Carlsson's retirement. The Deputy Prime Minister, Mona Sahlin, had been expected to take the post. However, a credit card and bill-payment scandal made the planned succession impossible. General elections are scheduled for September 1998.

Sweden is a constitutional monarchy led by King Carl Gustaf XVI and a multiparty parliament. The Social Democratic Party (SDP) won 45 percent of the votes in the 1994 election. An informal agreement with the Left Party, which won six percent of the votes, enabled the SDP to form a one-party minority government. Seven parties ran candidates and won seats in the 1994 elections.

In the November 1994 national referendum Swedes voted to join the European Union. In 1996 opinion polls showed Swedes to be reluctant to join the European Monetary Union, an event slated for 1999. However, initial reluctance at the outset will not bar Sweden's membership later.

Political Rights and Civil Liberties:

Swedes can change their government democratically. Every three years, 310 members are directly elected to the *Riksdag* (parliament) through universal suffrage. To ensure absolute proportionality to all parties securing over four percent of the vote, another 39 representatives are selected from a national pool. Citizens abroad are entitled to absentee votes in national elections, and non-nationals in residence for three years can vote in local elections. The Sami (Lappic) community elects its own local parliament with significant powers over education and culture. It serves as an advisory body to the government.

The King's role is ceremonial. The prime minister is appointed by the speaker of the house and confirmed by the Riksdag. The independent judiciary includes six Courts of Appeal, 100 district courts, a Supreme Court and a parallel system of administrative courts.

Freedom of assembly and association is guaranteed, as are the rights to unionize and strike. In April 1996 over 2,000 newspaper journalists struck over pay negotiations. Strong and well-organized trade union federations represent 90 percent of the labor force. Despite historic ties with the SDP, the labor movement has become increasingly independent in recent years.

The media are independent. Most newspapers and periodicals are privately owned, and the government subsidizes daily newspapers regardless of political affiliation. The government's monopoly over broadcasting has ended as a number of satellite and ground-based commercial television channels and radio stations have appeared in recent years.

Citizens can freely express their ideas and criticize their government. The government can prevent publication of national security information. A quasi-governmental body censors extremely graphic violence from film, video and television.

Religious freedom is constitutionally guaranteed. Nearly 90 percent of the population is Lutheran. In 1995 the government and the church agreed to disestablish the state religion. By the year 2000 baptism will be required for membership and only baptized members will be required to pay the three percent income tax or "church tax." Catholics, Muslims, Buddhists, Hindus and Jews are represented among the population, and compulsory religion classes in schools now include surveys of various religious beliefs.

A 1996 Human Rights Watch report cites Sweden for its increasingly strict immigration policies, which resulted in a sharp decline in the number of refugees admitted annually. Sweden does not systematically provide asylum-seekers legal counsel or an adequate appeals process. Asylum seekers are sometimes detained together with criminals despite criticism from European human rights organizations.

In the summer of 1996 Sweden permitted a neo-Nazi rally to take place with participants from Sweden, Denmark, Germany and Norway. Dozens of violent incidents with anti-immigrant or racist overtones have been reported annually in recent years, several resulting in death. The government supports volunteer groups working against racism. Human rights monitors operate without government restrictions.

Though the 17,000 strong Sami population currently enjoy some political autonomy, Sweden was the last of the Nordic countries to allow the formation of the Sami Parliament. In 1994 the government removed the Sami right to control hunting and fishing on their village lands. Reports of discrimination against Sami in housing and employment continue.

In 1994, in an effort to foster gender equality, the Riksdag passed a law requiring fathers to take at least one month of state-subsidized child care leave or lose a month of benefits. Women constitute roughly 45 percent of the labor force. Women are well represented in government, due in part to an SDP pledge to appoint an equal number of men and women to cabinet positions.

Switzerland

Polity: Federal parliamentary democracy
Economy: Capitalist
Population: 7,101,000
PPP: $22,720
Life Expectancy: 78.1
Ethnic Groups: German, French, Italian, Romansch
Capital: Bern (administrative), Lausanne (judicial)

Political Rights: 1
Civil Liberties: 1
Status: Free

Overview: Though the Swiss remain divided on the issue of EU membership, negotiations on the unresolved issues of freedom of movement of persons and overland traffic proceeded in 1996. In December, Switzerland joined NATO's Partnership for Peace program, thus opening the door for participation in non-military humanitarian and training missions.

With the exception of a brief period of centralized power under Napoleonic rule, Switzerland has remained a confederation of local communities as established in the Pact of 1291. Most responsibility for public affairs rests at the local and cantonal levels. The 1815 Congress of Vienna formalized the country's borders and recognized its perpetual neutrality.

Switzerland is often cited as a rare example of peaceful coexistence in a multi-ethnic state. Encompassing German, French, Romansch and Italian communities, the republic is divided into 20 cantons and six half-cantons.

In a 1992 referendum, a narrow majority of voters rejected joining the European Economic Area, thus rejecting a move towards EU membership. With over 20 percent of the population comprised of foreigners, a fear of a mass influx of EU immigrants influenced the vote.

In the 1995 elections, the biggest victors were the left-wing, pro-EU, pro-welfare Social Democrats, who won 54 seats, up from 42 in 1991, displacing the centrist Radical Democratic Party as the coalition's strongest member. The right-wing, anti-EU People's Party gained five seats, four seats behind the Christian Democrats.

Political Rights and Civil Liberties: The Swiss can change their government democratically; free and fair elections are held at regular intervals. Initiatives and referenda give citizens an additional degree of involvement in the legislative process. The cantonal system allows considerable local autonomy. Localities' linguistic and cultural heritages are zealously preserved.

At the national level, both houses of the Federal Assembly have equal authority. Once legislation has been passed in both the directly-elected, 200-member National Council and the Council of States, comprised of two members from each canton, it cannot be vetoed by the executive or reviewed by the judiciary. Seven members of the Federal Council, or *Bundesrat*—chosen from the Federal Assembly according to a "magic formula" ensuring representation for each party, region and language group—exercise executive authority. Each year, one member serves as president. The judicial system functions primarily at the cantonal level, with the exception of a federal Supreme Court that reviews cantonal court decisions involving federal law. Switzerland's judiciary is independent.

The government's postal ministry operates broadcasting services and the broadcast media enjoy editorial autonomy. Foreign broadcast media are readily accessible. In addition, many private television and radio stations exist. A myriad of privately-owned daily, weekly and monthly publications are available in each of the most common languages, and are free from government interference.

Freedom of speech, assembly, association and religion is observed. No single state church exists, however; many cantons support one or several churches. Taxpayers may opt out of contributing to church funds, yet, in many instances, companies cannot. Switzerland's anti-racist law prohibits racist or anti-Semitic speech and actions, and is strictly enforced by the government. The government allows human rights monitors to operate freely. Academic freedom is respected. The government respects the right to privacy.

A 1994 Amnesty International report cited excessive police force used against persons in custody, particularly foreigners. The report was issued shortly after the National Council increased police powers of search and detention of foreigners lacking identification, in an effort to curb the drug trade.

In February 1995, federal laws aimed at dissuading drug traffickers from entering Switzerland authorized pretrial detention of illegal residents for as long as nine months. With 33,000 drug addicts in a population of 7 million, use of hard drugs has become one of the country's most pernicious social ailments.

Though the law on gender equality came into force this year, women still face some barriers to political and social advancement. Some studies estimate women's earnings to be 15 percent lower than men's for equal work. Some charge that the army, from which women are excluded, creates networking opportunities for men, thus producing an economic disadvantage for women. Women were not granted federal suffrage until 1971, and not until 1990 did the half canton, Appenzell-Innerrhoden, give up its status as the last bastion of all-male suffrage in Europe. Until the mid-1980s, women were prohibited from participating in the Federal Council.

Workers may unionize, strike and bargain collectively. Unions are independent of the government and political parties. Approximately one third of the workforce is unionized.

Syria

Polity: Dominant party (military-dominated)
Economy: Mixed statist
Population: 15,609,000
PPP: $4,196
Life Expectancy: 67.3
Ethnic Groups: Arab (90 percent), Kurd, Armenian, others
Capital: Damascus

Political Rights: 7
Civil Liberties: 7
Status: Not Free

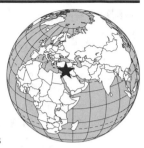

Overview:

In 1996 Syrian president Hafez al-Assad appeared to be firmly entrenched as head of what is one of the world's most repressive regimes.

Following four centuries of rule under the Ottoman Empire, Syria came under French control after World War I and gained independence in 1944. A 1963 military coup brought the pan-Arab, socialist *Ba'ath* party to power. In 1970 General Hafez al-Assad, head of the *Ba'ath* Party's military wing, took power in a coup. Assad, who formally became president of this secular, repressive regime in 1971, has given most key military and intelligence positions to members of his Alawite minority, which constitutes 12 percent of the population.

The 1973 constitution vests executive power in the president, who must be a Muslim, and who is nominated by the Ba'ath party and elected through a popular referendum. The directly-elected People's Assembly, which serves a four-year term and presently consists of 250 members, holds little independent power.

In the late 1970s the fundamentalist Muslim Brotherhood, drawn from the Sunni majority, carried out anti-government attacks in several northern and central towns. In 1982 the army crushed a Muslim Brotherhood rebellion in Hama, killing 15-20,000 militants and civilians.

Assad last won re-election in December 1991, running unopposed in a tightly-controlled vote. The death of Major Basil al-Assad, the son of the president and the heir apparent, in a January 1994 auto accident left the question of Assad's successor unclear. However, the president's firm grip on the political apparatus was evident at the August 1994 parliamentary elections, where the ruling National Progressive Front, dominated by the Ba'ath Party, took all 167 seats it contested, with pro-regime "independents" winning the remaining 83 seats.

In May 1996 a series of yet-unexplained bomb explosions rocked Damascus. In the aftermath, security forces arrested at least 600 people, mostly members of the Kurdish minority. On December 31 a bomb on a bus in Damascus killed 11 people.

With his domestic credibility based largely on his hard line against Israel, Assad is in no rush to negotiate a peace treaty leading to the return of the Israeli-controlled Golan Heights, since this would likely require establishing full diplomatic relations with Jerusalem. Prior to losing the Golan in 1967, Syria had used the territory to shell northern Israeli towns.

Political Rights and Civil Liberties: Syrians cannot change their government democratically. President Hafez al-Assad maintains absolute authority in this military-backed regime. The security forces use arbitrary arrests, torture, "disappearances" and other forms of intimidation to create a climate of fear and to suppress political dissent. Opposition parties are not permitted.

The Emergency Law, in effect since 1963 (except during 1973-74), allows the authorities to carry out "preventive" arrests and supercedes due process safeguards during searches, arrests, detentions and interrogations, and in trials in the military-controlled State Security Courts, which handle political and security cases. There are several internal security services, and all operate independently of each other and without any judicial oversight. The authorities monitor personal communications and conduct surveillance of suspected security threats.

Since late 1991 the government has freed several thousand political prisoners, although many have faced harassment after their release. Many of the 1,200 prisoners freed in late 1995 were members or supporters of the Muslim Brotherhood. The regime reportedly still holds several thousand other dissidents, many of whom are held incommunicado for lengthy periods without charge or trial. Political prisoners are often pressured to sign statements supporting the government as a condition for release. According to Amnesty International 21 prisoners who refused to sign such statements have been transferred to Tadmor military prison, a facility known for the particularly brutal treatment meted out to civilian inmates.

The judiciary is subservient to the government. Defendants in ordinary civil and criminal cases receive some due process rights, although there are no jury trials. In the State Security Courts confessions obtained through torture are generally admitted as evidence and no due process rights exist. Nevertheless, in recent years some acquittals have been granted in political cases. Trials in the Economic Security Court, which hears cases involving currency violations and other financial offenses, are likewise conducted without procedural safeguards.

Authorities sharply restrict freedom of expression. The government and the Ba'ath party own and operate all media, which are mouthpieces for the regime. By law citizens may not own satellite dishes. Freedom of assembly is denied, and freedom of association is limited to a few strictly non-political organizations.

The state forbids both Jehovah's Witnesses and Seventh-Day Adventists from worshipping as a community or owning church property. The security apparatus closely monitors the Jewish community, bars Jews from most state jobs, and requires Jews to have their religion stamped on their passports and identity cards. Since 1992 the government has permitted Jews greater freedom to emigrate.

The government places linguistic and cultural restrictions on the Kurdish minority, and suspected Kurdish activists are routinely dismissed from schools and jobs. According to Human Rights Watch, some 200,000 Syrian-born Kurds are arbitrarily denied the right to Syrian nationality and are stateless. Stateless Kurds fall into two main groups: those classified as "foreigners," who face severe restrictions on property ownership, employment, access to social services and the right to leave the country; and a smaller group of *maktoumeen* (unregistered), who are not issued identity cards or entered into population registers and face even greater hardships, including difficulties in sending children to school. Some 360,000 Palestinian refugees, many of whom were born in the country, face some restrictions in traveling abroad. Traditional norms place Syrian women in a subordinate position in marriage, divorce and inheritance matters. Women face legal restrictions on passing citizenship to children.

All unions must belong to the government-controlled General Federation of Trade Unions. By law the government can nullify any private sector collective bargaining agreement. Strikes are strongly discouraged and rarely occur.

Taiwan (Rep. of China)

Polity: Presidential-legislative democracy
Economy: Mixed capitalist
Population: 21,421,000
PPP: na
Life Expectancy: 74.5
Ethnic Groups: Taiwanese (84 percent), mainland Chinese (14 percent), aboriginal (2 percent)
Capital: Taipei

Political Rights: 2*
Civil Liberties: 2*
Status: Free

Ratings Change: Taiwan's political rights and civil liberties ratings changed from 3 to 2 because the country completed its democratic transition to a competitive multiparty system with a free presidential election.

Overview: Taiwan completed its democratic transition in March 1996 by holding its first direct presidential election in which the incumbent, Lee Teng-hui, took 54 percent of the vote against three challengers.

The island, located 100 miles off the Chinese coast, came under control of China's Nationalist government after World War II. Following the Communist victory on the mainland in 1949, Nationalist leader Chiang Kai-shek established a government-in-exile on Taiwan. For the next four decades the Kuomintang Party (KMT) ruled Taiwan in an authoritarian manner. Both Taiwan and China still officially consider Taiwan to be a province of China. Today native Taiwanese make up 84 percent of the population.

The 1947 Nationalist constitution provides for a National Assembly that can amend it. Until 1994, the Assembly also had the power to elect the president and vice-president. The president is now directly elected by the people, serves a four-year term and holds executive powers. The government has five specialized *yuan* (branches), including a Legislative Yuan that enacts laws.

The country's democratic transition began with the lifting of martial law in 1987. In 1988 Lee Teng-hui became the first native-born Taiwanese president, and a year later the government formally legalized opposition parties. In 1990 the Assembly elected Lee to a full term. Since then Lee has alienated the once-dominant mainlander faction of the KMT by asserting native Taiwanese control of the party, and by largely abandoning the party's formal commitment to eventual reunification with China.

A new National Assembly was elected in 1991. At the time the Assembly consisted mostly of aging mainlanders elected in 1947 or 1969 whose terms had been frozen to maintain the KMT's political monopoly. The KMT won the majority of seats. In 1992 the country held its first full Legislative Yuan elections since the Nationalists fled the mainland; the KMT took 96 of the 161 seats.

In February 1993, the Legislative Yuan swore in Lien Chan as the first native Taiwanese prime minister. In August a group of disgruntled second-generation mainlanders led by Jaw Shau-kong left the KMT to form the New Party. In July 1994, the National Assembly amended the constitution to clear the way for direct presidential elections in March 1996.

In the December 1995 Legislative Yuan elections the ruling KMT won only 85 seats; the Democratic Progressive Party (DPP), which favors formal independence, 54; the New Party, 21; and independents, four (three seats were added to adjust for the larger population).

Political Rights and Civil Liberties: On March 23, 1996, Taiwan completed its transition to democracy, holding presidential elections in which Lee Teng-hui took 54 percent of the popular vote.

The KMT maintains significant advantages over the opposition through its control of the media and the government apparatus, and through its huge financial holdings. Elections at all levels are marred by vote-buying and campaign violence. However, in the past three years, hundreds of elected officials and civil servants (notably a number of politicians, judges and police officers) have been convicted of election fraud and other crimes in an unprecedented anti-corruption campaign. Several dozen businesspeople have been convicted of bid-rigging — public works project fraud reportedly provides organized crime with more income than drugs or prostitution.

Gang-related violence rose in 1996. Several politicians were attacked or threatened after criticizing the underworld and its penetration of business and politics. Violence climaxed on November 21, 1996, with the bloody assassination of Justice Minister Liao Cheng-hao and seven others in Liao's home.

The judiciary is not fully independent. In 1996 a number of judges were indicted on bribery charges. Judges rather than attorneys normally interrogate witnesses. Arrest warrants are not needed for certain crimes and search warrants are not required when searches are conducted in conjunction with an arrest. Prisons are overcrowded and conditions are harsh in detention camps holding illegal mainland Chinese immigrants and other foreign workers.

Police abuse of suspects in custody is a continuing problem. The "Anti-Hoodlum Law" allows police to detain alleged hoodlums on the basis of testimony by secret informers, and suspects can be sentenced to reformatory education through administrative procedure rather than trial.

Printed material is not censored, and the press express a wide range of views. Though the government asserts its right and intention to screen all material from mainland China, few publishing companies comply.

The KMT control over broadcast media has lessened in recent years. Though the ruling party retains significant control over the three television stations where political coverage strongly favors the government, over 70 percent of households receive cable television with access to international and privately-funded channels.

In 1993 and 1994 the government issued the first fully private radio licenses, but only for low-powered stations with limited ranges, minimizing their ability to counterbalance the KMT-dominated stations. Between August 1994 and January 1995 the government raided several pro-DPP pirate radio stations.

The Parade and Assembly Law (PAL) requires a permit for demonstrations, and prohibits the promotion of Communism or the advocacy of separation from mainland China. Some opposition leaders have been charged under a section of the PAL that holds organizers responsible for public order at demonstrations. Under the Civic Organizations Law all organizations must register with the government. Nongovernmental organizations are active and generally function without harassment. Freedom of religion is respected.

Women face workplace discrimination, including lower salaries and fewer promotion opportunities than men. Incidents of rape and domestic violence are widespread and child prostitution is a serious problem.

The 357,000 Aborigines, whose ancestors' presence on Taiwan predates the first Chinese settlers, suffer from social and economic alienation. They are not permitted to sell or develop land, and have only a limited say in policy decisions regarding their land and natural resources. More recent changes, however, include a 1996 law that now permits Aborigines to use non-Chinese names on legal documents; and primary schools now offer some Aboriginal-language classes.

The authorities have refused to certify new trade unions, claiming that competing unions in a given sector already exist. The law only permits one labor federation, and this grants a monopoly to the pro-KMT Chinese Federation of Labor. Civil servants, defense industry workers and teachers cannot unionize and may not bargain collectively. Several provisions of the labor code restrict the right to strike. The authorities can impose involuntary mediation of disputes; the majority of a union's members must approve a strike; and the authorities must approve the meetings that hold the strike votes. The lack of effective legislation against anti-union discrimination has facilitated the dismissal of scores of trade union activists in recent years.

Tajikistan

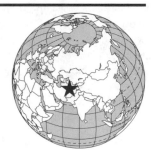

Polity: Dominant party (presidential-dominated)
Political Rights: 7
Civil Liberties: 7
Status: Not Free
Economy: Statist
Population: 5,935,000
PPP: $1,380
Life Expectancy: 70.4
Ethnic Groups: Tajik (65 percent), Uzbek (25 percent), Russian (4 percent), others
Capital: Dushanbe

Overview:

In 1996, the regime of President Emomali Rakhmonov and the United Tajik Opposition (UTO) led by Said Abdullo Nuri reached an accord in late December aimed at ending nearly five years of a bloody civil war that has killed tens of thousands and driven tens of thousands more into exile, primarily to Afghanistan and Kyrgyzstan. Despite an agreement, which came after a year-long series of negotiations, that called for the formation of a National Reconciliation Commission, the presence of renegade brigades, warlords and criminal gangs presaged a difficult transition to political stability.

Among the poorest of the former Soviet republics, Tajikistan was carved out of the Uzbek Soviet Republic on Stalin's orders in 1929. Leaving Samarkand and Bukhara, the two main centers of Tajik culture, inside Uzbekistan angered Tajiks, who trace their origins to Persia. The four leading regionally-based tribes are the Leninabad and Kulyab (the current ruling alliance), and the Gharm and the Badakhshan.

In December 1992, after months of ethnic and political conflict, a governing coalition of Muslim activists from the Islamic Renaissance Party (IRP), secular democrats and nationalists who had replaced the Communists, was overthrown by former Communist hardliners backed by the Russians. Rakhmonov, a Communist, was named head of state (he was directly elected in November 1994), and launched an ethnic war in the Gharm, Badakhshan and Pamiri regions from which support for the democratic-Islamic opposition was coming. The terror drove some 60,000 people across the Armu Daray River into Afghanistan, from which the opposition launched violent raids. Some 25,000 Russian troops were stationed along the Afghan border to discourage rebel incursions.

The February 1995 parliamentary vote was boycotted by the opposition, including the Party of Popular Unity led by former presidential candidate Abdumalik Abdulladjanov, who lost to Rakhmonov. Opponents blamed violations of election law and official pressure on their candidates. Of the handful of legal political parties, the Communists were the strongest, but even they fielded only 46 of 345 registered candidates; more than 40 percent of seats were uncontested. Most new deputies were not formally affiliated with any party but were firmly pro-Rakhmonov.

In early 1996, the government faced a serious political crisis when a renegade commander, Colonel Mahmud Khudaberdiyev, head of the elite First Brigade, moved on Dushanbe, the capital, from his base in Kurgan-Tyube. Also, Ibodullo Baimatov, the former mayor of Tursan Zade, site of Central Asia's largest aluminium plant, who had been in self-exile in Uzbekistan, returned to the city and launched an offensive against Dushanbe. Both leaders demanded wholesale changes in the government, which they claimed was incompetent and corrupt. The forces pulled back when the government dismissed Prime Minister Jamshed Karimov and others from their posts. Karimov was replaced by Yakhiye Azimov, a businessman.

Throughout the year, opposition forces took control of strategic cities and villages, among them Komsomolabad, and fighting was reported in the Tavil-Dara region in the foothills of the Pamir mountains. Baimatov's takeover of Turan Zade turned the city into a den of bandits with various armed groups fighting for control of the aluminum plant.

In politics, three former prime ministers, including former presidential candidate Abdumalik Abdulladjanov, established the National Rival Movement in the spring, which was courted by the government and the UTO. All three ex-prime ministers are from the Leninabad region in northern Tajikistan, home to 40 percent of Tajikistan's population and more than home to half of the republic's Tajiks live.

After months of negotiations, it was agreed that the composition of the National Reconciliation Commission would be 40 percent government, 40 percent UTO and 20 percent other groups, notably the National Revival Movement. The government and the opposition also agreed to a full exchange of prisoners under the supervision of the UN Observer Mission and the International Red Cross. Both sides promised to conclude peace talks by July 1, 1997.

Years of war left the economy in a state of collapse. Food shortages were a problem. In March, the IMF announced a $22 million loan to Tajikistan, contingent on tight budget discipline. The government also announced plans to boost privatization. North-south regional rivalries threatened economic revival, however. With the southern-based minority Kulyabis controlling the government, the Tajiks in the north, (largely unscathed by the civil war) accused the Kulyabis of taking over shops, houses and local governments. Thousands joined anti-Kulyabi demonstrations in northern cities in May. Squabbles erupted over resources such as cotton and the lucrative drug trade. Over three metric tons of raw opium and heroin were seized in the Gorno-Badakhshan region in 1996. President Rakhmanov accused the opposition of working with the militant Islamic Taliban movement in Afghanistan to smuggle drugs to finance the war against his government.

Political Rights and Civil Liberties:

Citizens cannot change their government democratically in what is a de facto one-party system controlled by President Rakhmonov. The constitution, adopted by referendum in 1994, provides for a strong executive, who serves as head of parliament and has broad powers to appoint and dismiss officials. Parliamentary elections were boycotted by the in-country quasi-opposition parties and were not "free and fair."

While political parties are nominally allowed, only five officially- recognized groups operate—the Communist Party, the Party of Political and Economic Revival, the Popular Party, the Party of Popular (People's) Unity and the National Revival Movement. The IRP, the Democratic Party and the Lali Badakhshan are banned, and most of their top leaders reside outside the country.

The government has total control of the Tajik media. All opposition media are closed. Under the press law, legal penalties exist for libeling officials, and Soviet-era restrictions on criticism of government bureaucrats apply.

Islam was revived after many decades, though the regime has intruded into religious life to preclude fundamentalism and anti-government activities.

Pervasive security forces and a Soviet-era judiciary subservient to the regime effectively curtail freedom of expression, assembly and association. Killings and assassinations are common, both by government forces and rebels. The government has been accused of "ethnic cleansing" in the southern Gharm and Pamir regions. External and internal refugees have returned to certain regions where the Kulyabis exercise less local control and where the UN High Commission on Refugees is present; in other areas, returning refugees have faced harassment, intimidation and murder. Inmates in the country's prisons faced starvation; 80 percent had no footwear; and harassment and beatings were common, according to former prisoners.

No independent trade unions operate. The rights of women are circumscribed in practice. The few nongovernmental organizations are monitored or repressed. Islamic groups are prevented from active participation in political life.

Tanzania

Polity: Dominant party
Economy: Statist
Population: 29,058,000
PPP: $630
Life Expectancy: 52.1
Ethnic Groups: African, Asian and Arab minorities
Capital: Dar-es-Salaam

Political Rights: 5
Civil Liberties: 5
Status: Partly Free

Overview: Tanzania's new president, Benjamin Mkapa, launched anti-corruption drives on several fronts which appeared to bolster public support for his long-ruling Cham Cha Mapinduzi (CCM, Party for the Revolution), which retained power in deeply-flawed October 1995 elections. President Mkapa's new broom has as yet hardly swept clean, but his reforms are gaining plaudits and new aid commitments from the international donor community, as well as growing increased domestic support.

Outside a few instances of military indiscipline, the Tanzanian mainland was calm in 1996. The country has so far escaped any serious repercussions from ongoing turmoil in neighboring Burundi and Rwanda, but the reported presence of Hutu militia among refugees raises fears for future unrest. However, Zanzibar and Pemba islands were hit by repression and violence after the CCM's fraudulent election victory there.

The CCM, under President Julius Nyerere, dominated Tanzania's political life after the county gained independence from Britain in 1961. Following a bloody 1964 revolution that deposed its Arab sultans, Zanzibar and Pemba Islands merged with then-Tanganyika to become Tanzania, under a power-sharing arrangement that guaranteed the islanders limited autonomy. The islanders number 700,000 and are 90 percent Muslim, compared to 28 million people, mostly Christian and animist, on the mainland. Nyerere's socialist policies gradually impoverished his country, and were accompanied by quiet but thorough repression that was barely noticed, the world being far more preoccupied with the long struggles against white minority rule in southern Africa.

Nyerere officially retired in 1985, but retained strong influence over Mwinyi's regime. Opposition parties were legalized in 1992, but the one-party parliament was allowed to complete its five-year life in October 1995. While the 1995 elections were not free and fair, they marked a step toward the opening of Tanzania's political system.

**Political Rights
and Civil Liberties:**   Tanzania squandered an opportunity to join the ranks of democratic states as the country's October 1995 legislative and presidential elections were marred by administrative chaos and irregularities and by outright fraud in Zanzibar. The ultimate result of the presidential contest might well represent the will of the people in a general sense, and President Mkapa can claim a tarnished mandate. The ruling CCM's landslide legislative victory is less credible. The ruling party's partisan use of state broad-

casting and other government resources during the campaign tilted the electoral playing field even before ballots were cast. The CCM took four-fifths of the 232 parliamentary seats, and opposition representation in the new National Assembly is weak. It is not clear whether the legislature can provide a meaningful forum for political debate, or if the ruling CCM will carry on its long tradition of authoritarian—and largely incompetent and corrupt—one-party rule.

Zanzibar's election results were fraudulent. On Zanzibar and Pemba, balloting went smoothly with a very high turnout. The election was apparently stolen during vote counting and reporting. The official Zanzibar Election Commission (ZEC) took four days to announce that the ruling CCM's candidate for the isles' presidency had won, with a lead of only about 1 percent of nearly 330,000 votes counted. Local legislative elections produced a similar narrow CCM victory over the opposition Civic United Front (CUF). Independent observers found the ZEC miscounted or reversed results in several constituencies to keep the CCM in power. Opposition parties' demands for fresh polls were summarily rejected by the High Court. The CUF boycotted the municipal elections in March.

In 1996, the CUF conducted a non-cooperation campaign on Zanzibar and Pemba. Hundreds of people have reportedly been arrested in a campaign of intimidation against CUF supporters.

Media freedom has expanded markedly since political opposition was legalized in 1992, but the government's dominance over broadcast media still severely limits free expression. The few private radio stations broadcast mostly non-political programming. Several dozen independent newspapers and magazines appear with various degrees of regularity, but their circulation is limited mostly to the major cities. In one of his first speeches as president, Mkapa, a former journalist, pledged to uphold press freedom, and direct harassment of the media seems to have abated, except on Zanzibar.

Despite some signs of autonomy, Tanzania's judiciary is still subject to considerable political influence. Constitutional protections for the right to free assembly are generally but not always respected in practice. Laws allow rallies only by officially-registered political parties, which may not be formed on religious, ethnic or regional bases and cannot oppose the union of Zanzibar and the mainland. Freedom of religion is respected. Fundamentalist groups on Zanzibar are pressing for a stricter application of *Shari'a* law there.

Laws regarding arrest and pre-trial detention are often ignored. Prison conditions in Tanzania are harsh, and beatings and other abuses by police are said to be common. Numerous nongovernmental organizations are active, but some concerned with human rights issues have had difficulty in receiving required official registration. The broad distribution of Tanzania's population among many ethnic groups has diffused potential ethnic rivalries that have wracked its neighbors, but resentment against the prosperous South Asian minority could become a serious flashpoint.

Women's rights exist on paper more than in fact. Women's opportunities for formal sector employment are restricted by both custom and statute. Especially in rural areas and in Zanzibar, traditional or Islamic customary law discriminatory to women prevails in family law. Domestic violence against women is common, and rarely prosecuted.

Workers do not have the right to organize freely and join trade unions. The Organization of Tanzania Trade Unions (OTTU) is the official and only labor federation, and remains loosely linked to the ruling CCM. The right to strike is restricted by complex notification and conciliation requirements, and collective bargaining effectively exists only in the small private sector.

A large-scale privatization program is being planned to revive the country's moribund economy. Deeply-embedded corruption and remnants of statist policies remain as obstacles. President Mkapa cut 30,000 state jobs in 1996, and sacked his finance minister on suspicion of improprieties. Other senior politicians are also under investigation. The clean-up and other reforms are prerequisites of the larger international loans, credit and aid the country desperately needs to reverse three decades of corrupt crypto-socialism. A renewal of East African cooperation with neighbors Kenya and Uganda, begun in 1996, could also help raise economic prospects.

Thailand

Polity: Parliamentary democracy (military-influenced)
Economy: Capitalist-statist
Population: 60,657,000
PPP: $6,350
Life Expectancy: 69.2
Ethnic Groups: Thai (75 percent), Chinese (14 percent), Malay, Indian, Khmer, Vietnamese
Capital: Bangkok

Political Rights: 3
Civil Liberties: 3*
Status: Partly Free

Ratings Change: Thailand's civil liberties rating changed from 4 to 3 because civic organizations are playing an increasingly important role in mobilizing support against child trafficking, prostitution and other human rights abuses.

Overview: In September 1996 the parliament held a three-day no-confidence debate. Prime Minister Banharn Silpa-archa agreed to resign in exchange for a vote of confidence in the existing government. A week later Banharn recanted his promise, dissolved parliament and called for elections. In the November 17 elections, the New Aspiration Party (NAP) won the most seats, by a two-seat margin, and formed a ruling coalition with five other parties, excluding Banharn's party. NAP leader General Chavalit Yongchaiyudh became prime minister.

Thailand is the only Southeast Asian nation never colonized by a European country. A 1932 bloodless coup, the first of 17 coups or attempted coups this century, led to a new constitution that limited the power of the monarchy. Today King Bhumibol Alduyadej's only formal political duty is to approve the prime minister, but he is widely revered and exerts informal political influence.

In December 1991, after a February 1991 coup, an interim National Assembly approved a controversial new constitution that allowed the military to appoint the entire 270-seat Senate and permitted the prime minister to come from outside the ranks of elected MPs.

At the March 1992 Assembly elections three pro-military parties won 190 seats, winning a slim majority in the 360-seat House of Representatives. The Assembly named coup leader Suchinda Kraprayoon, who had not stood in the elections, as prime minister, leading to widespread street demonstrations in Bangkok in May. Soldiers killed more than 50 protesters. Suchinda was forced to resign and the constitution was amended, requiring that future premiers come from among the elected MPs. In fresh elections in September the Democratic Party took 79 seats and formed a five-party, pro-democracy coalition under party leader Chuan Leekpai.

In May 1995 Chuan's coalition collapsed over a land reform scandal, ending Chuan's 32 months in office as Thailand's longest-serving elected premier. At the July parliamentary elections the rural-based Thai Nation party won the most seats and formed a seven-party governing coalition. Thai Nation leader Banharn became premier.

In April 1996, Banharn, in appointing the members of the Senate, substantially reduced the number of seats held by active-duty or retired military officers. The previous appointments to the Senate had been made by a military government.

Political Rights and Civil Liberties: Thai citizens can change their government democratically, although vote-buying is rampant, especially in rural areas. During the November 1996 election, politicians reportedly spent over $1 billion buying votes; off-duty police and soldiers were used to intimidate voters; and ballot stuffing occurred. Official corruption is widespread. Several high-level politicians have been implicated in drug-trafficking schemes, and law-enforcement is lax.

Credible reports divulge that police officers have committed extrajudicial killings and that detainees are frequently tortured and beaten. Of the 90 cases of killings by civil officials in 1995 and the 21 killings during the first half of 1996, all but one case were dismissed; one case is still under investigation. Hundreds of detainees have died in custody; many of them are reported as suicide. Prison conditions do not meet minimum international standards. Conditions at the Suan Phlu immigration detention center are harsh and female detainees are frequently raped. An amnesty protects soldiers responsible for more than 50 deaths in the May 1992 pro-democracy demonstrations.

The judiciary is independent of the government, but highly corrupt. Military court rulings cannot be appealed. No trials by jury are performed and the court may order a proceeding to be closed to the public.

Laws broadly restrict expression in several areas. People are prohibited from defaming the monarchy, advocating a Communist government and inciting disturbances. The press freely criticizes government policies but exercises self-censorship regarding the monarchy and national security. Journalists refrain from criticizing the judiciary to avoid unfair treatment during libel proceedings. A handful of newspapers and weeklies were fined for "disturbing the peace" when reporting on the May 1996 parliamentary debate on the government. In August 1995 package-bombs were sent to the editor and publisher of *Thai Nation*, a major newspaper that had criticized promotions in the police ranks. In October 1995 the government temporarily denied visas to Australian journalists after an unflattering cartoon of the monarch appeared in a Melbourne daily.

The government licenses and oversees radio and television stations. Radio stations must renew their license annually. Television and radio broadcasts are censored for pornographic or politically-sensitive material.

Nongovernmental organizations (NGOs) operate openly, but are often monitored and sometimes harassed by police. In March 1996 two Amnesty International representatives were detained in Bangkok just as they were about to release to the press documentation on human rights practices in China. Rural officials occasionally falsely charge peaceful demonstrators with inciting unrest and intent to commit violence.

NGOs estimate that at least 250,000 prostitutes work in Thailand; up to one-fifth are under 18 years of age. Many of the women come from hill tribes and from neighboring Burma. In some cases, families sell girls into prostitution, where they become bonded laborers. The government has taken steps to combat prostitution, such as extending compulsory education, expanding a public information campaign, and passing a September 1996 law that now criminalizes those involved in trafficking prostitutes, not just the prostitutes themselves. Efforts are undermined, however, by the complicity of police and local officials in prostitution schemes. Women face widespread domestic violence, are frequently not paid the minimum wage and are underrepresented in parliament.

Muslims face societal and employment discrimination. By some accounts have been several Muslim activists imprisoned on criminal charges for their political views. Roughly half of the 500-600,000 members of hill tribes are not registered as citizens, and thus cannot vote or own land and have difficulty obtaining social services. More than 100,000 ethnic minority Burmese reside in 34 camps in Thai territory along the Burmese border. These camps are subject to attack by the Burmese-government supported Democratic Karen Buddhist Army. Several refugees and Thai security forces have been killed or abducted. The Thai government has been criticized for offering inadequate protection of refugees.

The law grants only private sector workers the right to join independent unions. State enterprise workers may only join "associations," which by law may not negotiate wages or hold strikes. Workers in the process of establishing a union are not protected from anti-union discrimination. Child labor is widespread. Safety regulations are flouted at many factories and enforcement is lax.

Togo

Polity: Military
dominated
Economy: Mixed statist
Population: 4,571,000
PPP: $1,020
Life Expectancy: 55.2
Ethnic Groups: Aja, Ewe, Gurensi, Kabye, Krachi, Mina, Tem, others
Capital: Lome

Political Rights: 6
Civil Liberties: 5
Status: Not Free

Overview:

Africa's longest-serving leader, President Gnassingbé Eyadéma, reasserted nearly full control over the Togolese government after parliamentary by-elections and party defections gave him a working majority in the country's National Assembly. The main opposition party boycotted the elections, however, which were run by the interior ministry in violation of earlier agreements. Eyadéma also won a constitutional court case that favored the president in his dealings with the prime minister. All three constitutional court justices deciding the case were appointed by Eyadéma before the transition to multiparty rule.

Eyadéma has effectively regained the personalized rule he exercised since seizing power in a 1967 military coup. The security forces are still mostly comprised of members of Eyadéma's Kabye ethnic group, who with other northerners dominate Togo's government. The democratic transition's reversal has been sanctioned by Togo's main foreign backer, France, in the form of loans and high-level diplomatic visits. A French minister visiting Togo in June refused to meet with opposition leaders. Denial of democracy inevitably leads to increased ethnic and political violence. More than 100,000 Togolese are refugees, and reports have been made of nascent guerrilla activity.

Once part of the Togoland colony seized from Germany in 1914, Togo was held as French territory until its 1960 independence. Its first post-independence leader, Sylvannus Olympio, was assassinated in 1963, and his successor was deposed by Eyadéma's January 1967 coup. With the constitution suspended, Eyadéma extended his repressive rule through mock-elections and a puppet political party.

As French policy in 1990 briefly pressured many West and Central African autocrats to liberalize their political systems, Eyadéma was also faced with mounting internal unrest that forced him to make concessions to opponents demanding democratization. In 1991, free political parties were legalized and multiparty elections promised. The transition did not go smoothly, however, as soldiers and secret police harassed, attacked and killed opposition activists. Gilchrest Olympio, son of the country's slain founding president and the strongest opposition candidate, was himself the victim of an assassination attempt, and then was banned from contesting the August 1993 election. Other opposition candidates withdrew in protest against electoral conditions. The day before polling, American and German observers left the country stating that conditions for a free and fair election no longer existed.

Unsurprisingly, Eyadéma was victorious with a reported 96 percent of the vote.

The February 1994 legislative elections were marked by less, but still considerable, violence and intimidation. The opposition Action Committee for Renewal (CAR) party won 36 seats and its ally, the Togolese Union for Democracy (UTD) party took seven seats in the 81-seat national assembly. Post-election bickering gave Eyadéma the opportunity to split the opposition and co-opt the smaller UTD, whose leader, Edem Kodjo, was named prime minister. The 1996 by-elections allowed Eyadéma's Rally of the Togolese People (RPT) party to take control of the National Assembly. A new prime minister, Kwassi Klutse, was appointed in August.

Political Rights and Civil Liberties: The Togolese people's right to choose their government has been realized only partially in form, and even less so in substance. Eyadéma's 1993 re-election was blatantly fraudulent. Intimidation and irregularities in the 1994 legislative polls did not prevent an opposition victory, which would probably have been far larger in a genuinely open election. Manipulated by-elections in 1996 and the defection of several opposition deputies to the government effectively abrogated the will of the electorate, however. The overwhelming concentration of power in the hands of the president leaves few constraints on his behavior in any case. Even the opposition-controlled legislature found itself virtually impotent, especially with courts still heavily influenced by the president.

The government controls broadcast media to which the opposition has only very limited access. A variety of private newspapers publish in Lomé, but independent journalists are subject to harassment and the perpetual threat of criminal charges. In June, the newspaper *Les Tribune des démocrates* was closed for six months, and its editor Eric Lawson sentenced to five years' imprisonment in absentia on charges of disseminating false information.

Togo's criminal courts generally respect legal procedures, and traditional courts handle many minor matters. But the security forces are above the law and act with impunity in political repression. Human rights groups report that killings, arbitrary arrest and torture continued in Togo despite its multiparty facade.

Religious practice is constitutionally protected and generally respected, but similar protection of the right to assembly is ignored by the regime. Demonstrations are often banned or broken up. Political parties, legal since 1991, operate openly but face constant menace. Nongovernmental organizations can organize, but those involved in human rights work, including the Togolese League for Human Rights and the Association for the Promotion of the Rule of Law, experience close scrutiny from and sometimes harassment by government agents.

Ethnic discrimination is prevalent, and most political power is held by members of a few ethnic groups from northern Togo. Southerners dominate the country's commerce, and violence occasionally flares between the two groups. The historical ethnic divide is a constant potential flashpoint which is exacerbated by the competition for state power within the political boundaries of modern Togo.

Educational and employment opportunities for women are limited, despite constitutional guarantees. Discriminatory laws allow a husband to bar his wife from working or to receive her earnings. Customary law denies any rights to women in case of divorce or inheritance. Wife-beating and other violence against women is widespread. Female genital mutilation is practiced, especially among the country's northern ethnic groups. Togo received unusual attention in the United States in 1996 due to the well-publicized case of Fauziya Kasinga. The 19-year-old fled Togo to avoid being circumcised, and applied for American asylum. Only a large public outcry—and a law case—secured her release from detention by U.S. immigration authorities, and a court ruled that the threat of circumcision constituted persecution that qualified Kasinga for political asylum.

Essential workers are exempted from the constitutional right to form and join unions, and health care workers may not strike. The 15 percent of the labor force that is unionized are from the small formal sector; most people work in rural subsistence agriculture. Unions have the right to bargain collectively, but most labor agreements are actually brokered by the government in tripartite talks involving unions and management. Several labor federations are divided roughly along political lines.

Tonga

Polity: Monarchy and partly elected legislature
Political Rights: 5
Civil Liberties: 3
Economy: Capitalist
Status: Partly Free
Population: 106,000
PPP: na
Life Expectancy: 74.5
Ethnic Groups: Tongan (98 percent), other Pacific islander, European
Capital: Nuku'alofa

Overview: **P**ro-democratic candidates swept all nine directly-elected seats in Tonga's January 1996 Legislative Assembly elections, but the king and ruling elite continue to dominate politics through a constitutionally-granted monopoly on power.

This predominantly Polynesian, South Pacific Kingdom of 169 islands became an independent member of the British Commonwealth in 1970. King Taufa' Ahau Tupou IV has reigned since 1965.

Since the early 1990s growing calls have been made for a more representative government within the framework of the existing monarchy. In August 1992 a group of reform-oriented People's Representatives, led by 'Akilisi Pohiva, formed the Pro-Democracy Movement (PDM). The PDM favors direct elections for all 30 parliamentary seats, and for parliament rather than the king to select the Privy Council. In November 1992 the PDM organized a seminal conference on amending Tonga's constitution that was backed by the influential Roman Catholic and Free Wesleyan churches and attended by nearly 1,000 people, many of whom were members of the country's growing middle class.

At the February 1993 People's Representatives elections, pro-democracy candidates won six seats, a gain of one. In August 1994 the PDM organized the kingdom's first political party, the Tonga Democratic Party, subsequently renamed the People's Party.

Political Rights and Civil Liberties: Tongans cannot change their government democratically. The constitution grants the king and the hereditary nobles a perpetual supermajority in the Legislative Assembly with 21 of the 30 seats, allowing major policy decisions to be made without the assent of the popularly-elected People's Representatives, or commoners. Roughly 95 percent of the population is represented by the nine seats reserved for commoners. The king and the nobility also hold a pre-eminent position in society through substantial land holdings. The judiciary, which has expatriates as top judges, is independent.

A key civil liberties issue in recent years has been the official harassment of pro-democracy politicians and outspoken journalists. In January 1994 the king signed legislation increasing penalties under the Defamation Act, which has had a chilling effect on editors and journalists of the country's four private newspapers and sole private magazine.

On February 23, 1996, police raided the offices of the weekly *Times of Tonga*, the country's leading newspaper and a strong advocate of democratic reform, and detained three staff members and a man who had recently written a letter to the paper criticizing Clive Edwards, the police minister. Edwards had said in a January radio interview that "the law would come down hard" on pro-democracy activists after the upcoming elections. In July the government denied permission for an Agence-France Press correspondent, who had written several articles on Tongan politics, to attend the Pacific Island News Association (PINA) convention in August.

On September 20 the Legislative Assembly found Pohiva and the editor and deputy editor of the *Times of Tonga,* in contempt of parliament and sentenced them to 30 days in jail. The move came in response to the *Times*'s publication in early September of an impeachment notice, drafted by Pohiva against the Justice Minister (for having traveled to the Atlanta Olympics without proper authorization) that had not yet been tabled in parliament. On October 14 the Supreme Court ordered the three released on the grounds that the Legislative Assembly had acted unconstitutionally. In mid-November PINA reported that authorities had detained Pohiva and Teisina Fuko, another pro-democracy MP, overnight and warned them that they were being investigated for sedition and defamation of the King. The investigation related to an interview with Fuko in the *Times of Tonga* and opinion pieces in Pohiva's publication, *Kele'a* (Conch Shell).

Political coverage on the Tonga Broadcast Commission's Radio Tonga generally favors the government, particularly prior to elections. A government-owned weekly newspaper carries some opposition coverage.

Traditional practices continue to relegate women to a subordinate role in society. Several female-based nongovernmental organizations actively work on women's rights issues. Religious freedom is respected in this predominately Christian society. The 1964 Trade Union Act recognizes the right of workers to form independent unions, although none has formed.

Trinidad and Tobago

Polity: Parliamentary
democracy
Economy: Capitalist-statist
Population: 1,272,000
PPP: $8,670
Life Expectancy: 71.7
Ethnic Groups: Black (43 percent), East Indian (40 percent),
mixed (14 percent), European
Capital: Port-of-Spain

Political Rights: 1
Civil Liberties: 2
Status: Free

Overview: In its first full year in office Premier Basdeo Pandey's ruling coalition continued efforts to secure Trinidad and
Tobago's entry into the North American Free Trade Agreement (NAFTA).

Trinidad and Tobago, a member of the British Commonwealth, achieved independence in 1962. The 1976 constitution established the two-island nation as a republic with a president, elected by a majority of both houses of parliament, replacing the former governor-general. Executive authority remains vested in the prime
minister. The bicameral parliament consists of a 36-member House of Representatives elected for five years, and a 31-member Senate, with 25 senators appointed by
the prime minister and six by the opposition.

In the 1986 elections the National Alliance for Reconstruction (NAR), a coalition that bridges traditional political differences between the black and East Indian
communities, led by A.N.R. Robinson, soundly defeated the black-based People's
National Movement (PNM), which had ruled for 30 years. The coalition unraveled
when Basdeo Panday, the country's most prominent East Indian politician, was
expelled and then formed the East Indian-based United National Congress (UNC).

In July 1991 a radical Muslim group briefly seized parliament. In the aftermath,
tensions increased between the black and East Indian communities, each of which
comprises roughly 40 percent of the population. This eroded political support for
the NAR. In December Patrick Manning led the PNM to victory by taking 21 of 36
parliamentary seats. Manning's government deregulated the economy and floated
the currency, but the social costs of these economic reforms caused the PNM's popularity to decline. Hoping to revive his party's standing, Manning called snap elections for November 6.

The election campaign focused on unemployment and other effects of the structural adjustment program. In the event voting went largely on ethnic lines, with
East Indians voting overwhelmingly for the UNC and blacks for the PNM. Each
party won 17 seats on Trinidad. The NAR retained its two seats on Tobago. The
NAR entered into a coalition government with the UNC in exchange for a ministerial position for former premier Robinson and a promise of greater autonomy for
Tobago. UNC leader Panday became Trinidad's first prime minister of East Indian
descent.

The UNC's decision to pursue NAFTA membership is both a break with its
own traditional left-of-center ideology and a continuation of a process begun by the

previous PNM administration. However, the United States is likely to insist that Caribbean nations jointly apply for membership, which could delay Trinidad's bid indefinitely.

Political Rights and Civil Liberties: Citizens of Trinidad and Tobago can change their government democratically. Politics and party affiliations are largely polarized along ethnic lines.

High levels of drug-related violence and common crime continue to undermine the protection of civil liberties. The country's geographic location has made it an important transshipment point for cocaine. Successive governments have also failed to enforce certain criminal laws. For example, although parliament passed laws in the mid-1980s to deal with the problem of money-laundering, to date no prosecutions have occurred. In June 1996 the attorney general conceded that the problems of drugs and crime, which have received considerable media attention, are actually underestimated. Corruption in the police force, often drug-related, is endemic.

The judiciary is independent. A right to obtain ultimate appeal to the United Kingdom's Privy Council. Due to rising crime rates the court system is severely backlogged, in some cases up to five years. Prisons are seriously overcrowded. A 1994 law denies certain repeat criminal offenders the possibility of release on bail.

Local human rights organizations allege increasing police brutality, including some extrajudicial killings. There are also occasional charges of police harassment against the Muslim community, which comprises 6 percent of the population, although religious freedom is generally respected.

In 1994, the government resumed capital punishment, a move condemned by human rights groups. That year a convicted murderer was hanged while his lawyers were still arguing in the Appeals Court, and after the Privy Council in London had ruled to grant a stay of execution.

The press is privately owned, vigorous and offers pluralistic views. The broadcast media are both public and private. Freedom of association and assembly are respected.

Domestic violence and other violence against women remain a problem. The police and judicial officials generally assign a low priority to domestic violence complaints.

Labor unions are well organized, powerful and politically active. Strikes are legal and occur frequently. An independent industrial court plays a central role in labor arbitration.

Tunisia

Polity: Dominant party
Economy: Mixed capitalist
Population: 9,163,000
PPP: $4,950
Life Expectancy: 68.0
Ethnic Groups: Arab-Berber (98 percent)
Capital: Tunis

Political Rights: 6
Civil Liberties: 5
Status: Not Free

Overview: President Zine el-Abidine Ben Ali maintained a firm grip on power in 1996, stifling dissent and harshly suppressing Islamic fundamentalists. Tunisia continued to increase counter-Islamist security cooperation with Algeria and Libya. As many as 2,000 suspected Islamists remain in detention, and two leading oppositionists and a human rights activist were imprisoned. President Ben Ali has achieved a modicum of popular support through steady economic growth and continuation of past governments' promotion of social benefits and women's rights. The president's Constitutional Democratic Rally (RCD) party won all but six of 4,090 seats contested in May's municipal elections.

For three decades after Tunisia's independence from France in 1956, Tunisia was led by President Habib Bourguiba. In 1987, then-General Ben Ali ousted Bourguiba on grounds of senility. Ben-Ali introduced numerous reforms and promised an open, multiparty political system. Opposition parties were crippled by arrests and harassment or banned outright, as was the Islamist En-Nadha (Renaissance) party in 1992. In May 1994, Ben-Ali was re-elected to a second five year term with 99.9 percent of the vote in an election that barred all credible challengers and defied credibility.

Political Rights and Civil Liberties: The Tunisian people's constitutional right to change their government has never been respected in practice. The ruling RCD is successor to parties that have controlled Tunisia since it achieved independence. The 1994 presidential and legislative elections were neither open nor competitive. Opposition leaders were blocked from qualifying as candidates, and the RCD deployed sizable state resources in its campaign. The RCD won all 144 single member districts in the legislative polls. A facade of a multiparty system and a forum for protected debate was maintained by allotment of 19 seats to other parties on a proportional basis. Elections are due again before March 1999. Yet, sweeping changes in electoral administration will need to be implemented before any results could be said to represent the will of the Tunisian people.

Tunisia's already small democratic space shrank further in 1996. Social Democrats Movement (MDS) leader Mohammed Moada was sentenced to 11 years imprisonment in January on what many observers believe were trumped-up charges. His deputy, Khemais Chammari, was given a five-year prison sentence in July for allegedly revealing "secrets" about Moada's prosecution. MDS party headquarters were closed in August. In January, lawyer and human rights activist Najib Hasni received an eight-year jail sentence for alleged forgery after he had defended several suspected Islamists in court. Other human rights activists have been harassed and briefly detained.

Tunisians' constitutionally-protected right to free information and expression has never been respected. The government tightly controls domestic broadcast media, and has restricted the rebroadcasting of foreign programming. Severe new regulations and a stiff tax are limiting ownership of satellite receiving dishes. Considerable self-censorship constricts the independent print media, and the press code, as amended in 1993, includes vaguely-defined prohibitions against defamation and subversion. Official news guidelines shape coverage, and pre-publication submission requirements allow the government to seize without compensation any publication it decides is breaking its rules. Human rights groups usually cannot find printers willing to print their statements or reports for fear of government retribution. All foreign publications are censored.

Maintenance of independent nongovernmental organizations was made more difficult by complicated reporting requirements in the 1992 legislation. Some human rights organizations continue to operate, including notably the Tunisian Human Rights League. No political party based on religion or region is permitted, and all require licenses. Any party that could effectively challenge the RCD stands little chance of being allowed to register. The judiciary is controlled by the executive, and legal limits on detention without trial are flouted. There is little hope for redress in the courts, especially in political matters. Torture and other forms of ill-treatment by police are reportedly commonplace. A major problem is lack of accountability for security forces.

Islam is the official state religion. The practice of other religions (which cannot proselytize) is tolerated, with the except of Baha'i, whose adherents are sometimes harassed. The government keeps tights control over the Muslim clergy, appointing prayer leaders and paying their salaries .

While most rights are severely restricted, general equality for women has advanced more in Tunisia than elsewhere in the Arab world. Employment rights are legally protected and educational and employment opportunities have grown. An increasing role for women is seen both as a challenge to, and bulwark against, radical Islamists.

Tunisia's sole labor federation, the Tunisian General Federation of Labor, (UGTT) is nominally independent but operates under severe restrictions. The right to strike and bargain collectively are both protected, though labor settlements can be imposed by arbitration panels. By late 1996, nearly a quarter of 400 state enterprises had been sold in a broad privatization plan, and the government had agreed to faster liberalization. Tourism earnings were estimated to top $1 billion in 1996, and in October, Michael Jackson made his first African concert appearance in Tunis.

Turkey

Polity: Presidential-parliamentary democracy (military-influenced) (insurgency)
Economy: Capitalist-statist
Population: 63,898,000
PPP: $4,210
Life Expectancy: 66.7
Ethnic Groups: Turk (80 percent), Kurd, Armenian, Jewish
Capital: Ankara

Political Rights: 4*
Civil Liberties: 5
Status: Partly Free

Ratings Change: Turkey's political rights rating changed from 5 to 4 because despite continued human rights violations the political process has become more open.

Overview:

In June 1996 the Welfare Party's (Refah) Necmettin Erbakan formed modern Turkey's first Islamist-led government, ending six months of disarray during which secular parties failed to form a stable governing coalition.

The secular, nationalistic legacy of Mustafa Kemal Ataturk, who proclaimed Turkey a republic in 1923, has exerted a powerful influence on the country through most of the century, and notably in the post-World War II period. The military used the doctrine of "Kemalism" to justify three coups between 1960 and 1980. Under the 1982 constitution the Grand National Assembly (currently 550 seats) is directly elected for a five-year term. The Assembly elects the president for a seven-year term. Although the president can dismiss the prime minister, the office is considered largely ceremonial.

The country returned to civilian rule in 1983, with the conservative Motherland Party (Anap) winning a majority in November elections. In 1984 the Marxist Kurdistan Worker's Party (PKK) began an insurgency in southeastern Turkey, with the goal of establishing an independent Kurdish state. Brutally repressed by the army, the conflict's toll has reached an estimated 19,000 deaths, destroyed villages and created thousands of refugees.

At the 1991 parliamentary elections Suleyman Demirel led the conservative True Path Party (DYP) to a 178-seat plurality victory and subsequently headed a coalition government. Following the death in 1993 of Anap's Turgut Ozal, who had served as president since 1989, parliament elected Demirel as his successor. The DYP's Tansu Ciller became Turkey's first female prime minister.

In September 1995 the governing coalition collapsed after the small center-left Republican People's Party (CHP) withdrew its support over Ciller's refusal to increase public sector wages and sack the hardline police chief of Istanbul. In the mid-term elections on December 24, Refah, taking advantage of discontent over an 88 percent inflation rate and high unemployment, took 158 seats; DYP, 135; Anap, 132; Democratic Left, 76; CHP, 49.

After a shaky coalition between DYP and Anap collapsed in May, on June 28 Refah and the DYP formed a coalition government. Erbakan became prime minister with Ciller in charge of foreign affairs.

Political Rights and Civil Liberties: Turkish citizens can change their government democratically, but the country is beset by considerable human rights abuses.

Most human rights violations are related to the PKK insurgency. Security forces carry out extrajudicial killings of suspected PKK terrorists, and are believed to be responsible for dozens of unsolved killings and disappearances of journalists, Kurdish activists and suspected PKK members, either directly or through state-backed death squads.

Due to the PKK insurgency nine southeastern provinces continue to be under a state of emergency declared in 1984 (emergency rule was lifted in Mardin province in November 1996). Under emergency powers wielded by the regional governor, the army has forcibly depopulated more than half of the 5,000 villages and hamlets in the southeast, in some cases killing and torturing villagers. Government-sponsored Kurdish "village guards," or civil defense forces, have garrisoned the remaining villages. The regional governor also has powers of censorship and can ban strikes.

The PKK and other smaller Kurdish groups such as *Dev Sol* (Revolutionary Left) have carried out scores of abductions and extrajudicial killings of village guards, their families, local officials and other civilians. The PKK has also murdered dozens of teachers for teaching in Turkish rather than Kurdish.

The judiciary is independent of the government. However, in the 18 State Security Courts, which try defendants accused of terrorism and several other crimes, procedural safeguards are inadequate and the right to appeal is limited. The criminal code permits suspects to be held incommunicado for 15 days for alleged crimes of a political or conspiratorial nature (30 days in provinces under emergency rule). An August 1996 law amended several laws to strengthen police powers and extend them throughout the country. The few convictions of police and other members of security forces for human rights violations create a climate of impunity.

In March 1994 parliament lifted the legal immunity of the 13 MPs of the Kurdish-based Democratic Party (DEP), and in December a court sentenced seven of them, and an independent MP, to jail terms of up to 15 years on charges of supporting the PKK and its leader, Abdullah Ocalan. In 1995 courts upheld four of the sentences and overturned four on appeal; however in April 1996 a court convicted the latter four on similar charges.

On September 25, 1996, 41 members of the Kurdish-based People's Democracy Party (HADEP), a successor to the banned DEP, went on trial in a state security court for alleged ties with the PKK, following the tearing down of a Turkish flag at the party's June 1996 convention (an action which the HADEP leadership disavowed). More than a dozen HADEP members have been killed since the party's founding in May 1994, including three members who were murdered in Kayseri in central Anatolia following the June convention. In March the Constitutional Court used its powers to shut down the Kurdish-based Democracy and Transformation Party, and authorities are taking legal action against several other parties.

Police routinely abuse and torture detainees. A November 1996 Amnesty International report detailed increasing police brutality against children in custody, many of whom are detained on minor charges. A series of incidents in 1996 highlighted the abysmal conditions in the country's prisons, characterized by widespread torture, sexual abuse and denial of medical attention to inmates. Most notably, more than 2,100 mainly leftist prisoners in 43 jails across the country participated in a

69-day hunger strike that led to 12 deaths before ending on July 27. Authorities agreed to some demands but refused a request to stop transferring prisoners away from their trials in Istanbul, which denies them contact with lawyers.

According to the independent Human Rights Foundation of Turkey (HRFT), 154 Articles affect freedom of expression in various codes, including Article Eight of the 1991 Anti-Terror Law (ATL) regarding the dissemination of separatist propaganda, and Article 312 of the penal code, which forbids incitement to racial or ethnic hatred. An October 1995 parliamentary amendment to Article Eight of the ATL requires prosecutors to show a harmful motive or intent. Nevertheless, according to the Commission on Security and Cooperation in Europe (CSCE), dozens of writers, journalists and others have been jailed under the amended Article Eight, and hundreds more have been jailed under similarly restrictive statutes.

According to the Committee to Protect Journalists, Metin Goktepe, who died in custody in January 1996, was the 24th journalist killed in Turkey since 1989. Authorities arrested 11 journalists during the year.

In recent years numerous newspapers, mostly leftist, pro-Kurdish and Islamist publications, have been suspended or shut down permanently. A June 28 government decree severely restricts the promotional schemes used by newspapers to increase circulation.

Political coverage on the state-run broadcast media favors the government. However, in the early 1990s the government eased restrictions on private broadcast media and, according to the U.S. Department of State, by October 1996, 259 television stations and 1,202 radio stations were registered.

According to the CSCE 15 southeastern branches of the Human Rights Association (HRA) have been closed (although several have subsequently been reopened), and a number of top officials have been killed by state-backed death squads; hundreds of members also have been arrested and imprisoned. The government has initiated at least two court cases against staff at clinics run by the HRFT that treat torture victims; one trial ended in acquittal in November while a second continued at year's end.

Laws ban Kurdish-language broadcasts and the use of the Kurdish language at political gatherings. Authorities frequently use the ATL to seize publications on Kurdish culture and history.

Roughly 99 percent of the population is Muslim. Religious freedom is generally respected in this secular state. However, religious worship is restricted to designated sites, legal restrictions exist for certain minority religions on building new sites, and authorities monitor Armenian and Greek Orthodox churches. Female civil servants and university students face restrictions on wearing religious head scarves or veils. Domestic violence is reportedly widespread.

Workers, except for members of security forces, can join independent trade unions. The government must grant unions approval to hold meetings, and can send police to monitor and record the proceedings. There are legal restrictions on the right to bargain collectively and hold strikes.

Turkmenistan

Polity: Dominant party (presidential-dominated)
Economy: Statist
Population: 4,624,000
PPP: $3,128
Life Expectancy: 65.1
Ethnic Groups: Turkmen (73 percent), Russian (10 percent), Uzbek (9 percent), Kazakh (3 percent), others
Capital: Ashgabat

Political Rights: 7
Civil Liberties: 7
Status: Not Free

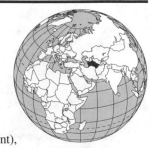

Overview:

The former Soviet Central Asian republic of Turkmenistan, bordering Afghanistan and Iran, remained under the one-man rule of President Saparmurad Niyazov, former first secretary of the Turkmen Communist Party. Niyazov renamed himself Turkmenbashi, or Head of the Turkmen, while building an elaborate cult of personality. The one-party regime continued to curtail political and civil rights while seeking foreign investment to exploit the country's vast natural gas and oil reserves and cotton-producing capacities.

Turkmenistan was ruled by various local leaders until the thirteenth century, when the Mongols conquered it. In the late nineteenth century, Tsarist Russia seized the country. In 1924, after the Bolsheviks ousted the Khan of Merv, the Turkmen Soviet Socialist Republic was declared.

Turkmenistan declared independence after a national referendum in October 1991; Niyazov won a one-man election in December. In 1992, after the adoption of a new constitution, Niyazov was re-elected, claiming 99.5 percent of the vote. The main opposition group, Agzybirlik, formed in 1989 by leading intellectuals, was banned and its leaders harassed. The country has two parliamentary bodies, the 50-member *Majlis* (Assembly)and the *Khalk Maslakhaty* (People's Council), which includes the members of the Assembly, 50 directly-elected members and leading executive and judicial officials. Niyazov is president of the People's Council.

In the December 1994 parliamentary elections, only Niyazov's Democratic Party of Turkmenistan (DPT) was permitted to field candidates. The president has extensive powers. He can prorogue the parliament if it has passed two no-confidence motions within an 18-month period. In addition, he issues edicts that have the force of law, appoints and removes all judges, and names the state prosecutor. He is also prime minister and commander-in-chief. Parliament extended his term to the year 2002.

Despite having an estimated at 700 million tons of oil and 8,000 billion cubic meters of natural gas, in 1996 Niyazov had yet to fulfill his prediction of transforming Turkmenistan into the Kuwait of Central Asia. His failure to implement economic reforms has led to abject poverty and shortages of basic foodstuffs. Cotton and grain harvests were disastrous in 1996, and desertification remained a serious environmental problem.

A key issue in 1996 was the opening of a strategic rail link between Turkmenistan and Iran. The Meshhed-Sarakhs-Tedzhen railway provides Central Asian states access to Iran's warm-water ports, making it a key hub for European and Middle East-bound trade. An Iranian-Turkmen gas pipeline is expected to be completed in 1997-98. Turkmenistan remained a major drug transit state; in September, Russian border guards seized large amounts of heroin from Afghanistan.

In October, the president reiterated the country's commitment to "permanent neutrality," eschewing participation in any military blocs or alliances or "inter-state coalitions with rigid obligations." The language would appear to preclude participation in the Commonwealth of Independent States (CIS). The text specified that the country would not host foreign military bases. The Turkmen border with Afghanistan is patrolled by Russian troops under contract.

Through the summer of 1996, President Niyazov reshuffled his cabinet, dismissing and reassigning several ministers and the chairman of the Supreme Court, ostensibly for corruption.

Political Rights and Civil Liberties:

Citizens of Turkmenistan do not have the means to change their government democratically. Power is concentrated in the hands of the president. The one-party, single party elections to a rubber-stamp parliament in 1994 were undemocratic. Candidates proposed as alternatives in some constituencies were all disqualified or withdrew on one pretext or another.

The DPT is the only legal party. Opposition parties have been banned, and most leaders of Agzybirlik have fled, many to Moscow. Those still in the country face harassment and detention from the Committee on National Security (KNB), the successor to the Soviet-era KGB. Most telephones are bugged.

The judiciary is subservient to the regime; the president appoints all judges for a term of five years without legislative review.

At least 20 political prisoners are still being held, including four men serving prison terms for an alleged plot to commit violent anti-state crimes. Seven people involved in a July 1995 protest against severe economic hardships are believed to be imprisoned. Political prisoners have reportedly been detained in a psychiatric hospital (in Geok-Tepe) and prison conditions are atrocious. In August, three prisoners were killed and seven wounded during a prison riot in Mary Vilayet. In August 1995, 27 mutinous prisoners were reportedly killed in a maximum security prison in Ashgabat.

In October 1996, President Niyazov announced the opening of the Democracy and Human Rights Institute to handle complaints from citizens about human rights and democratic freedoms. Its opening appeared a gesture to the international community's complaints about human rights abuses. Niyazov said the purpose of the institute was to protect the presidency "from the influence of other branches of power" and warned citizens not to take their complaints too far.

The government controls and funds all electronic and print media. According to a prominent staff member of the state-owned newspaper *Turkmenskaya Iskra*, the paper exercises self-censorship. Newspapers mostly adhere to the old Communist style of publishing verbatim legislative texts, congratulatory speeches, letters flattering the president and reports of successful harvests. In 1996, authorities issued an official statement declaring that President Niyazov was the founder of all local newspapers published in the country and that the mass media have been "essentially monopolized."

Local ordinances effectively ban freedom of assembly and public demonstrations. Although the population is overwhelmingly Sunni Muslim, the government has kept a rein on religion to avert the rise of Islamic Fundamentalism. Religious congregations are required to register with the government. Muslims have a free hand if they do not interfere in politics, and the government has built several mosques. In 1996, the country's first Islamic theological school was established by Turkey.

There are no independent trade unions, and Turkmen law does not provide for the right to collective bargaining. Although women's rights are mentioned in the constitution, discrimination in education and other social-religious limitations restrict women's freedom. Married women are not allowed to be students. The government continued to discourage the formation of nongovernmental organizations in 1995. Attempts to register political or unsanctioned cultural groups have met with severe repression.

Tuvalu

Polity: Parliamentary democracy
Economy: Capitalist
Population: 10,000
PPP: na
Life Expectancy: 61.0
Ethnic Groups: Polynesian (96 percent)
Capital: Fongafale

Political Rights: 1
Civil Liberties: 1
Status: Free

Overview: This tiny Polynesian country in the central South Pacific, formerly the Ellice Islands, achieved independence from the United Kingdom in October 1978. The 1978 constitution vests executive power in a prime minister and a cabinet of up to four ministers. The prime minister is elected by and from among the 12-member *Fale I Fono* (parliament). The fono is directly-elected for a four-year term in this parliamentary democracy. The governor general, a Tuvalu citizen appointed by the prime minister to represent the British monarch, can dissolve the fono if its members cannot agree on a premier, and appoint the cabinet members in its stead.

The country's fourth post-independence elections in September 1993 saw nine of the 12 sitting MPs returned to the fono. The new fono twice failed to elect a prime minister, with both the incumbent, Bikenibeu Paeniu, and challenger Dr. Tomasi Puapua, the opposition leader and a former premier, each receiving six votes. Then-Governor General Sir Toalipi Lauti used his constitutional powers to dissolve this new fono, and the country held fresh elections in November. In December parliament elected Kamuta Laatasi, a former general manager of BP Oil in Tuvalu, as prime minister. Laatasi had been a backbencher in the Paeniu government but, supported by his wife, also an MP, crossed over and received the support of five former opposition MPs.

In January 1994 prime minister Laatasi dismissed Governor General Toomu Sione, who had served for only seven months, and replaced him with Tulaga

Manuella. Laatasi argued that Sione had been a political appointee of the previous government and thus could be dismissed by the new government.

Tuvalu has a poor resource base and is dependent on food imports. The local economy is based on the cocoa palm, taro and fishing. Much of the country's revenue comes from remittances by some 1,500 countrymen living abroad, as well as from the sale of stamps and coins. Interest from the Tuvalu Trust Fund, established in 1987 by major aid donors, covers one-fourth of the annual budget.

Political Rights and Civil Liberties:

Citzens of Tuvalu can change their government democratically. Political parties are legal but only one loosely-organized group has formed, former Prime Minister Bikenibeu Paeniu's Tuvalu United Party. Most elections hinge on village-based allegiances rather than policy issues. Power is decentralized on the nine permanently-inhabited islands through directly-elected, six-person island councils. These councils are generally influenced by hereditary elders who wield considerable traditional authority.

The judiciary is independent, and citizens receive fair public trials. Freedom of speech and press is respected. State-run Radio Tuvalu and *Tuvalu Echoes*, a government-owned fortnightly, are the only media and offer pluralistic viewpoints. A monthly religious newsletter is also published. There are no restrictions on freedom of association, although few nongovernmental organizations have been formed. Freedom of assembly is respected.

All religious faiths can practice freely. Some 70 percent of the population belongs to the Protestant Church of Tuvalu. Women face traditional social discrimination but increasingly are securing positions in education and healthcare. The Paeniu government in particular brought women into the cabinet and other senior positions.

Workers are free to join independent unions, although only the Tuvalu Seamen's Union has been organized and registered. Strikes are legal but none has occurred, largely because much of the population is engaged outside the wage economy in subsistence agriculture. Similarly, collective bargaining is legal but rarely practiced.

Uganda

Polity: Dominant party (military-influenced)
Economy: Capitalist-statist
Population: 21,963,000
PPP: $910
Life Expectancy: 44.7
Ethnic Groups: Acholi, Baganda, Kakwa, Lango, Nkole, Soga, Teso, others
Capital: Kampala

Political Rights: 4*
Civil Liberties: 4
Status: Partly Free

Ratings Change: Uganda's political rights rating changed from 5 to 4 because recent elections are a positive step toward a true democratic transition after decades of dictatorial rule.

Overview:

Uganda's first elected government in nearly 15 years took office in 1996 in voting that restricted formal political party participation but was deemed by most observers generally free and fair. President Yoweri Museveni, after over a decade as Uganda's president, won an electoral mandate with 74 percent of the vote against his only serious rival, Democratic Party (DP) head Paul Ssemogerere. The May election was denounced by oppositionists as fraudulent, and most boycotted legislative elections the following month. Museveni's National Resistance Movement (NRM) clearly dominates the new parliament, despite the nominally non-party status of all candidates. His victory is believed to be responsible for the relative peace Uganda has enjoyed since he took power after a six-year guerrilla war in 1986, and for the strength of the country's economy. About 20 oppositionists took seats in the 276-seat parliament, most of them members of the Uganda People's Congress (UPC) party, still led from exile by Milton Obote, under whose rule hundreds of thousands of Ugandans were murdered in the early 1980s.

For Uganda, 15 years of national nightmare began with Idi Amin's coup against Milton Obote in 1971. Amin's buffoonery and brutality made world headlines, while hundreds of thousands of people were being killed during his reign. But only after he invaded Tanzania in 1978 did any country take action against him. Tanzanian forces and Ugandan exiles routed Amin's forces, and made way for Obote's return to power in December 1980 elections marred by fraud. Obote and his backers from northern Uganda repressed his critics, who were mainly from the ethnic groups of southern Uganda. Political opponents were tortured and murdered and soldiers terrorized the countryside. An army coup ousted Obote for a second time in July 1985, but conditions only worsened.

A quarter of a million people were probably killed, most massacred by government soldiers, before Museveni led his National Resistance Army (NRA) into the capital Kampala. Museveni formed a broad-based government under the NRM, with extensive local consultations with "Resistance Committees" first set up during the guerrilla war. The NRM government has been strongly influenced by the NRA (Museveni himself still carries the rank of Lieutenant-General and is Minister of Defense) and has faced a series of lingering guerrilla conflicts in the north and east of the country. Remnants of the defeated government army were crushed by 1988, amidst reports of NRA human rights abuses, but millennialist Christians of the Lord's Resistance Army (LRA) still raid along the Sudanese frontier. That conflict is entangled with Sudan's war of annihilation against southern Sudanese rebels and threatens to flare into a major confrontation between Uganda and Sudan. Other attacks were mounted in 1996 by rebels in the northwestern West Nile Province and along Uganda's southwestern border with Zaire.

Ethnic divisions remain the greatest threat to Uganda's long-term peace. The Baganda in the country's south demand more recognition of their traditional kingdom, and northern ethnic groups complain of government neglect. However, Uganda today is safer and more stable and has a stronger economy than at any time since the mid-1960s, although the country is still very poor and debilitated by the AIDS epidemic.

Political Rights and Civil Liberties:

Uganda's only competitive multiparty elections were the pre-independence elections in 1961. Uganda's 1995 constitution extended the formal ban on political party activities imposed by Museveni in 1986 for a further five years until 1999, when a referendum on multiparty politics is scheduled. Despite this legal prohibition, both the Democratic Party and the Uganda People's Congress party, main rivals for power since independence in 1962, maintain offices and unofficially field candidates.

In 1996, Ugandans voted for their president and parliamentarians in elections that were not truly open. Critics complained that the NRM mobilized state resources and state media to support Museveni's candidacy, and that the ban on formal party activities barred them from organizing effectively. Most observers believe Museveni would have won handily even with party participation, and poll watchers described the electoral process as transparent, despite minor irregularities.

Broad public debate takes place and the freedom of expression of the media is generally respected. Vigorous opposition print media, including over two dozen daily and weekly newspapers, are highly critical of the government and offer a full range of opposition viewpoints. Two private radio stations and one private TV station report openly on local political developments. However, the largest newspapers and broadcasting facilities that reach rural areas are state-owned. While governmental corruption is reported and opposition positions are presented, coverage is often not balanced. The Uganda Journalists Safety Committee has complained that the provisions of the 1995 and 1996 press laws restrict journalists from doing their jobs by imposing educational and training requirements.

A more serious threat to press freedom is the occasional use of sedition laws to arrest or intimidate journalists, which leads to actual imprisonment of some individuals and wide self-censorship.

While freedom of assembly for banned political parties is proscribed, many meetings have been held without interference. Scores of nongovernmental organizations are active, and registration requirements are not used to block any particular group. Many are directly involved with human rights issues, including the Uganda Human Rights Activists, the Uganda Law Society, and the Foundation for Human Rights Initiatives. Freedom of religion is constitutionally-protected. There is no state religion. Various Christian sects and the country's Muslim minority practice their creeds freely.

While increasing its autonomy, Uganda's judicial system remains hampered by inadequate resources and the army's failure to respect civilian court authority. Prison conditions are harsh. Human rights violations by the Uganda People's Defense Forces (UPDF) were reported in conflict zones, but far more egregious abuses were committed by Lord's Resistance Army (LRA) guerrillas. A November report by UNISEX said that at least 3,000 children had been abducted by the LRA, and many of them horribly mistreated.

Discrimination against women based on traditional law is prevalent, particularly in the countryside. Inheritance, divorce and citizenship laws all provide unequal standards for men and for women, who also must receive their husband's permission to obtain a passport. Domestic violence against women is widespread.

The country's largest labor federation, the National Organization of Trade Unions (NOTU), is independent of the government and political parties. An array of "essential workers" are barred from forming unions. Strikes are permitted only after a lengthy reconciliation process, but the most serious economic disruption in 1996 came with a two-week traders' and shopkeepers' strike in September to protest a new value added tax.

Uganda has one of Africa's most open economies. A massive public relations campaign was launched in 1996 to persuade the public to support the privatization of state enterprises. Since 1993, about 40 parastatals have been sold for over $100 million. The government is also preparing to sell the Uganda Commercial Bank, the country's largest, the Coffee Marketing Board, and Uganda Airlines. Liberalized exchange policies have also helped encourage strong growth over the last five years.

Ukraine

Polity: Presidential-parliamentary democracy
Economy: Statist-transitional
Population: 51,148,000
PPP: $3,250
Life Expectancy: 69.3
Ethnic Groups: Ukrainian (73 percent), Russian (22 percent), others
Capital: Kiev

Political Rights: 3
Civil Liberties: 4
Status: Partly Free

Overview:

In 1996, the political power struggle between President Leonid Kuchma and Prime Minister Yevhen Marchuk, the former KGB official he appointed in 1995, ended with the latter's dismissal in May. He was replaced by First Deputy Prime Minister Pavlo Lazarenko. In June, parliament adopted a new constitution that expanded presidential powers, called for a unicameral legislature and defined Crimea as an autonomous republic.

In other issues, Ukraine and Russia remained at loggerheads over the Black Sea Fleet and Russia's claim on the Crimean city of Sevastopol.

Ukraine, a major agricultural-industrial center, was the site of the medieval Kievan Rus' realm that reached its height in the tenth and eleventh centuries. Russia dominated the large eastern part of the country for over 300 years, while Poland and Austria-Hungary ruled the west. Ukraine enjoyed a brief period of independent statehood between 1917 and 1920, after which Soviet ruled was extended over most Ukrainian lands with the creation of the Ukrainian Soviet Socialist Republic. Western Ukraine was forcibly annexed from Poland in 1940 under the Hitler-Stalin Pact. Ukraine declared independence from a crumbling Soviet Union in 1991, and Leonid Kravchuk was elected president by direct vote.

Legislative elections in 1994 were conducted under a complex electoral law passed in November 1993. The law was entirely majoritarian and clearly biased against political parties (only 11 percent of candidates had party affiliations), making it difficult for them to register candidates while any "group of electors" (minimum membership of ten) or "worker collectives" (no minimum membership) could easily nominate whomever they wanted. The election law led to a series of run-offs, but by year's end some ten percent of seats had not been filled and parliament suspended further balloting. While 18 parties were represented in the new parliament, the 418 elected deputies coalesced around 11 major blocs.The leftist Communist, Socialist, Peasant and Agrarian parties accounted for 169 seats; the centrists, represented by Inter-Regional Bloc, Yednist (Unity), the Constitutional Center, Liberals and Independents, 173; the rightists, consisting of the Reform Bloc, Democratic National Rukh bloc, the Statehood bloc and non-faction members, 76.

In the 1994 presidential race, incumbent President Kravchuk beat Kuchma, an industrialist and former prime minister, 37.7 percent to 31.3 percent in the first round. Neither polled over 50 percent, forcing a run-off. Turnout was 68 percent. In the July 10 run-off, Kuchma won, 52 percent to 45 percent, with over 71 percent of eligible voters taking part. In 1995, Kuchma wrested new political power from the legislature, which amended the constitution, giving up its power to name Ukraine's cabinet and its claim to authority over provincial and local governments. In June, Kuchma and parliament agreed to a "constitutional treaty." In return for broader rights to issue decrees and appoint ministers, the president agreed to a one-year deadline for a new constitution.

In early 1996, Kuchma pressed a reluctant parliament to adopt a new national charter, with little support from the prime minister. The executive was factionalized between Kuchma supporters, many from the industrial city of Dnipropetrovsk, the president's political base, and Marchuk loyalists. In early May, the president threatened the cabinet with dismissal if it stood in the way of market reforms. On May 27, Kuchma signed a decree firing the pro-Russian Marchuk for failing to launch structural economic reforms and for not resolving the state's ongoing wage debt crisis. His replacement, 43-year-old Deputy Prime Minister Pavlo Lazarenko, was a member of the Yednist caucus from Dnipropetrovsk. In July, he was the victim of an assassination attempt when a bomb blew up his car on the way to Kiev's airport for a flight to Donetsk. It was widely suggested that the attempt was connected to the president's efforts to clean up the country's coal industry and the developing political rivalry between Dnipropetrovsk and other regional elites. In November, Yevhen Shcherban, a parliamentary deputy and one of the richest men in Ukraine, was murdered in Donetsk airport. He had been accused of involvement in the attempt on Lazarenko.

The constitutional debate pitted Kuchma against the Communists and Socialists, who opposed strong presidential authority, the provisions on the state language, and a free land market. The president warned that he would call for a popular referendum if parliament failed to pass the document. He also charged that the Communists were trying to delay approval until after the Russian presidential elections in June, pinning their own political aspirations on a victory by Communist Gennady Zyuganov. On June 28, parliament voted 315 to 36 in favor of the constitution after an all-night session. After the adoption the constitution, which called for a new government within three months, Prime Minister Lazarenko and his cabinet resigned on July 5, only to be renominated by Kuchma and re-appointed a few days later. The 16-member Constitutional Court, led by Chief Justice Ivan Tymchenko from Dnipropetrovsk, was sworn in by parliament on October 18.

In September, President Kuchma completed forming a new government with the appointment of pro-market economist Viktor Pynzenyk as deputy prime minister for the economy and Anatoly Minchenko as minister for industrial policy and the energy complex. In December, Kuchma dismissed presidential chief of staff Dmytro Tabachnyk and stripped him of his military ranks after he faced sharp criticism from parliament for alleged illegal dealings in real estate and abuse of his position.

In economic affairs, the National Bank introduced the hryvnya as the new official currency in August to replace the karbovanets. To avoid inflation in the period immediately after the announcement, the government slapped a 30-day freeze on retail prices, threatening to do the same to the karbaovanets; it also instituted the dollar exchange-rate, and vowed to prosecute vendors who refused to accept payment in karbovantsi. By the end of August, the price of the dollar had fallen back to the interbank level, thus averting a macroeconomic crisis.

Ukraine continued to face very serious economic problems. The GDP fell in 1996, and wage and payment arrears continued to choke the financial system. On October 15, Prime Minister Lazarenko presented the government's economic program to parliament. The 134-page program, approved by a 252-64 vote, aimed to reduce inflation through fiscal austerity while simultaneously promoting economic growth. Promises to pay off the state budget arrears in 1997 conflicted with reducing government spending and the budget deficit. The program also contained some 40 programs to support restructuring in the large state enterprises whose lobbying strength has strongly influenced Ukraine's economic policies since 1992 by pushing for state protection and subsidies for "key" sectors and firms. In August, the IMF granted the fourth *tranche* of a $867 million stand-by credit.

In September, the State Property Fund told parliament that Ukraine had completed its small-scale privatization program, except in Crimea. It said 80 percent of small enterprises were taken over via employee buyout lease options. In regard to large-scale privatization, 40 million residents had already picked up vouchers, but investment declined because many potentially profitable companies were barred from privatization.

In other issues, tensions with Russia continued over the Black Sea Fleet. On December 26, the Russian Federation Council called on President Boris Yeltsin to impose a moratorium on any agreement over the fleet until a special commission examines the status of the main base, Sevastopol. The following day, a presidential spokesman said that President Yeltsin had not changed his position that "Sevastopol and Crimea are part of Ukraine." Several pro-Russian Ukrainian deputies introduced a draft law demanding the withdrawal of Ukrainian "occupational forces" from Sevastopol. Several Russian leaders, including Aleksandr Lebed, claimed that Sevastopol was never legally given to Ukraine.

Political Rights and Civil Liberties:

Ukrainians can change their government democratically. Presidential and parliamentary elections in 1994 were deemed generally "free and fair" by international observers, though there were reports of irregularities and pre-election intimidation and violence directed at democratic organizations and activists. Democrats claimed the November 1993 electoral law was designed to hinder a multiparty system by weakening the role of political parties in the electoral process. In June 1995, a new electoral law was drawn up to eliminate the 50 percent turnout threshold.

The Ukrainian parliament adopted a new constitution in June, which replaced a 1991 charter that was a hybrid of the 1978 Constitution of the Ukrainian SSR, modified since independence. Citizens are free to organize in political groupings and associations and 47 national political parties (and 16 in the Crimea) represent the political spectrum from far-left to far-right. The Agrarian Party of Ukraine held its founding conference in December. The Justice Ministry refused to register the ultra-nationalist Ukrainian National Assembly (UNA), despite the group's efforts to temper its radicalism by disbanding its paramilitary wing. In November, the Crimean parliament suspended an order by the Ukrainian Justice Ministry disbanding local parties registered under Crimean law.

A 1991 press law purports to protect freedom of speech and press, but it only covers the print media. The constitution, the Law on Information (1992) and the Television and Radio Broadcasting Law (1994) protect freedom of speech, but laws banning attacks on the president's "honor and dignity." About 5,500 Ukrainian- and Russian-language newspapers, periodicals and journals are publishing. Many receive some state subsidies, a form of indirect control. The price and availability of newsprint and print facilities, as well as an inadequate state-owned distribution system, have hampered publications. Some independent newspapers are mailed through the post office and distributed by vendors or privately-owned kiosks. In 1994, President Kuchma signed the Law on State Support for the Press exempting state-owned media from paying high taxes, thus making it difficult for independent media to compete. The Ukrainian State Committee for Television and Radio broadcasts in Ukrainian and Russian. Several private local TV and radio stations operate throughout the country, broadcasting views and stories critical of the government. Satellite dishes are available. The state grants air time to commercial channels and access to the state cable system, thereby creating the possibility of arbitrary restrictions on certain types of programs. In May, parliament voted to dismiss state TV and radio's top officials for alleged corruption. In September, the government set up a committee to monitor the distribution of broadcast licenses in response to parliament's declaration of a moratorium on licensing by the National Broadcasting Council. Viktor Petrenko, chairman of the Council, said the decision was an illegal attempt by the legislature and government to regain control of the airwaves from his presidentially-appointed body. The Council had given Ukrainian State Television exclusive rights to Channel 1, the most powerful national channel. On

December 31, it was reported that a TV news show critical of President Kuchma, *Vikna*, would be taken off the air in the new year. The government granted a German-funded company, Studio 1+1, a license to transmit on the same wavelength. Several independent news agencies also operate.

Freedom of discussion and assembly is recognized and generally respected. Although the previously outlawed Ukrainian (Uniate) Catholic and Ukrainian Autocephalous Orthodox churches are legal, conflicts between the two churches and the old Russian Orthodox Church continue over property and churches. There are three Ukrainian Orthodox churches, two with allegiances to patriarchs in Kiev and one with allegiance to Moscow. The Orthodox schism has led to violent flare-ups. In October 1996, a conflict among hierarchs threatened to split the Orthodox Church into a fourth faction. Ukraine's estimated 500,000 Jews are organized and maintain schools and synagogues. In October, parliament adopted new citizenship law that abolished dual citizenship, which was allowed under a 1991 statute.

An independent judiciary and the rule of law remain in formative stages. There have been modifications of Soviet-era laws that have enhanced defendants' rights in such areas as pre-trial detention and appealing arrests. President Kuchma's tough anti-crime bill, signed in July 1994, permits police to hold suspected criminals for up to 30 days; suspected criminal locations may be raided without search warrants. In June 1995, Kuchma issued a decree dealing with legal reform that created a presidential committee on legislative initiatives and a committee to review Ukraine's legal and criminal codes. On December 3, Justice Minister Serhiy Holowaty revealed that Ukraine had violated its pledge to the Council of Europe to uphold a moratorium on the death penalty, with more than 100 executions.

Ukrainian workers are organized in several trade unions. The Federation of Trade Unions, a successor to the former official Soviet body, claims 21 million workers. In 1992, five independent unions united under the umbrella of the Consultative (Advisory) Council of Free Trade Unions, which interacts freely with international labor groups. Estimates of membership in independent unions range from 100,000-200,000; over 80 percent of the workforce are unionized. In October, two leaders of the Independent Miners' Union were sentenced in Luhansk to two-and-a-half years in prison for organizing an illegal strike in July to protest unpaid wages. Coal miners had gone on strike in Donbas and western Ukraine in July. On August 20, the Donetsk Court of Arbitration ruled to disband the Donetsk Worker's Committee for organizing illegal strikes, blocking roads and railroad cars.

Women have educational opportunities, and are represented among the professional classes. Independent women's organizations exist and have raised such issues as spousal abuse and alcoholism.

United Arab Emirates

Polity: Federation of
traditional monarchies
Economy: Capitalist-
statist
Population: 1,946,000
PPP: $20,940
Life Expectancy: 73.9
Ethnic Groups: Native and other Arab, Persian, Pakistani, Indian
Capital: Abu Dhabi

Political Rights: 6
Civil Liberties: 5
Status: Not Free

Overview: In 1996 the seven former Trucial States of the Lower Gulf—
Abu Dhabi, Dubai, Sharjah, Ajman, Umm al Qaiwain, Ras
al Khaimah and Fujiairah—marked 25 years as the United
Arab Emirates. Annual oil and gas export earnings (over $13 billion in 1995) have
enabled the country's economy to boast one of the highest per-capita incomes in
the world. The need for extensive construction to support the country's enormous
economic expansion created an influx of foreign workers in the past quarter of a
century. However, stiff new laws aimed at cracking down on unlawful foreign labor led to an exodus of up to 200,000 illegal workers in 1996.

Each emirate has been governed internally as an absolute monarchy since independence was attained from Britain in 1971. Under the provisional constitution of
1971, the monarchs collectively form a Federal Supreme Council, which elects a
state president (who appoints a prime minister and cabinet) and vice-president from
among its members for a five-year term. A 40-member consultative Federal National Council, composed of delegates appointed by the seven rulers, holds no legislative power. While there are separate consultative councils in several emirates,
neither popular elections nor political parties exist.

Sheikh Zayed ibn Sultan al Nuhayyan of Abu Dhabi, the largest emirate and
capital of the UAE, has served as president since independence and is considered
largely responsible for the country's unification and economic success.

Legislation passed in 1996 set a November 1 deadline for all illegal migrants,
between 15 and 20 percent of the workforce in the UAE, to leave the country or
face up to three years in prison and fines of up to $8,000. In the months leading up
to the deadline, approximately 200,000 illegal workers, mostly from the Indian subcontinent and South-East Asia, left the country. A subsequent labor vacuum has
resulted in a downturn in economic activity.

The UAE has maintained a pro-Western foreign policy since the Persian Gulf
War and military cooperation with the United States, France and Britain continues.
Iran holds three islands near the Strait of Hormuz claimed by the UAE. Although
the islands had been jointly ruled for two decades by Iran and the emirate of Sharjah,
the Iranian government expelled the emirate's citizens in March 1992. In response
to these and other Iranian threats (Iran has been carrying out large-scale naval ma-
neuvers in the Gulf), the UAE has spent an estimated $60 million on arms purchases
since the Gulf War. The government plans to acquire a fleet of strike aircraft in
coming months.

Political Rights and Civil Liberties: Citizens of the United Arab Emirates cannot change their government democratically. Political parties and demonstrations are illegal, no popular elections take place and all power is held by the seven emirs and their families. Male citizens can express grievances at *majlises* (gatherings) held by the rulers of each emirate, while women can attend majlises presided over by the wives of the seven rulers.

The judiciary is generally independent of the government. The dual court system includes *Shari'a* (Islamic) courts, located in each emirate, and civil courts, most of which (excluding Dubai and Ras al-Khaimah) are responsible to the Federal Supreme Court in Abu Dhabi. While incommunicado detention is permitted under the law, the accused receive adequate procedural safeguards in the court system.

The media are largely privately held Journalists practice considerable self-censorship on matters pertaining to government policies, the ruling families and other sensitive matters. Publications have been banned in recent years when the government's arbitrary guidelines were exceeded. The government uses the state-owned television and radio stations to espouse its views. Some stations augment their programming with CNN and other foreign broadcasts. All imported materials are reviewed by the Ministry of Information.

Permits are required for organized gatherings. Some emirates permit conferences where government policies are discussed, but all private associations must be strictly non-political. Islam is the official religion, and most citizens are Sunni Muslims. Shi'ite mosques are not permitted in Ras al-Khaimah. Dubai reportedly placed private mosques under government control in 1993. Non-Muslims can generally practice freely. There are no restrictions on internal travel, except near oil and defense facilities. Members of the small, stateless Bedouin population cannot receive passports.

Women can hold government positions and make up a large percentage of the enrollment at UAE University. However, in general, they face strong traditional pressure against entering the work force. They cannot hold majority shares in most businesses, and are legally disadvantaged in custody matters.

Workers lack the legal right to form trade unions or bargain collectively, and strikes by public sector employees are illegal. Foreign nationals employed as domestic help are occasionally abused by their employers, as was demonstrated by the case of 16-year-old Filipina domestic servant Sarah Balabagan in 1995. Accused of murdering her employer after he allegedly raped her, Ms. Balabagan was initially sentenced to death. Following diplomatic pressure from the Philippines, an appeals court reduced her sentence to 100 lashes, one year in jail and deportation upon payment of $41,000 to the man's family.

United Kingdom

Polity: Parliamentary democracy
Economy: Mixed capitalist
Population: 57,134,000
PPP: $17,230
Life Expectancy: 76.3
Ethnic Groups: English (82 percent), Scottish (10 percent), Irish (2 percent), Welsh (2 percent), Asian, African and Caribbean immigrants
Capital: London

Political Rights: 1
Civil Liberties: 2
Status: Free

Overview:

John Major's conservative government will probably give way to a Labor government led by Tony Blair after the elections in May 1997. While Tory leaders fought bitterly among themselves over the issue of European Monetary Union (EMU), Labor took a significant lead in opinion polls. Having abandoned the "tax and spend" policies of the past while limiting the influence of trade unions and endorsing market economics, Labor's popularity could be attributed to its new, more "conservative" image.

Adding to Major's woes was an EU ban on all products made with British beef, which came into effect in March after the announcement of a possible link between Bovine Spongiform Encephalopathy (BSE, or "Mad Cow Disease") and Creutzfeldt-Jacob disease (CJD) in humans. Though the ban was partially lifted in June, the British beef industry continues to suffer from plunging beef demand and prices.

The United Kingdom of Great Britain and Northern Ireland encompasses the two formerly separate kingdoms of England and Scotland, the ancient Principality of Wales and the six counties of the Irish province of Ulster (see Northern Ireland under Related Territories). The British Parliament has an elected House of Commons with 651 members chosen by plurality vote from single-member districts, and a House of Lords with over 1,000 hereditary and appointed members. A cabinet of ministers appointed from the majority party exercises executive power on behalf of the mainly ceremonial sovereign. Queen Elizabeth II nominates the party leader with the highest support in the House of Commons to form a government.

The Conservatives have held power since 1979. After taking over the party leadership from Margaret Thatcher, Major abandoned her unpopular poll tax, continued to privatize state industries, and attempted to assuage fears over the loss of national sovereignty while working towards closer European integration. However, by 1992, policy reversals and scandals, as well as division over Britain's role in the EU, began to erode Conservative support.

Since the ban on beef was imposed in March, Major has disrupted EU proceedings by vetoing most business requiring unanimous consent. His tactics, aimed at forcing a timetable for lifting the ban, have been ineffective and unsupported in the Union. Meanwhile, Britain is under pressure to expand plans to slaughter tens of thousands of cattle judged as high-risk. Fourteen cases of CJD were confirmed in the United Kingdom in 1996.

The Northern Ireland conflict came to the mainland this year, with the IRA claiming responsibility for seven bombs. Major has been blamed for stalling the Irish peace process by refusing Sinn Fein, the IRA's political wing, a seat at the Stormont talks pending decommissioning of IRA weapons. Major responded by arguing that the IRA needed to demonstrate its commitment to peace before being able to take part in the talks.

Political Rights and Civil Liberties: Citizens of the United Kingdom can change their government democratically. Voters are registered by a government survey and include both Irish and Commonwealth (former British Empire) citizens resident in Britain. British subjects abroad retain voting rights for 20 years after emigration. Wales, Scotland and Northern Ireland currently have no regional legislatures, but elect members to the House of Commons.

Britain does not have a written constitution. Civil libertarians have criticized a number of recent laws as dangerous to basic freedoms. The 1989 Prevention of Terrorism Act allowed police to detain suspects for eight days without charge. Under the Act, Kurdish MED-TV's offices were raided and equipment confiscated in September. In April 1996, citing fears of IRA terrorism on the eightieth anniversary of the Easter 1916 uprising, the government rushed through legislation that gives the British police the power to stop and search people on the streets without grounds for suspicion. These special powers were previously confined to Northern Irish law enforcement. Refusal to be searched could lead to imprisonment.

The case of Roisin McAliskey, a pregnant woman suspected of aiding in the bombing of a British Army barracks in Germany, has provoked international protest. Imprisoned in November outside London, Ms. McAliskey has no contact with other prisoners, does not have access to adequate medical care and is strip-searched twice a day. She has denied knowledge of the bombing and has no prior record of paramilitary involvement.

The Crown Prosecution Service (CPS) announced in August that no police officer is to be prosecuted for the death in custody in December 1995 of Wayne Douglas, a black man arrested for burglary. About 15 people a year die in police custody in Britain, though it is extremely rare for an officer to be suspended or dismissed as a result of a CPS investigation.

Though uncensored and mostly private, the British press is subject to strict libel laws. In April, a bill was introduced to create a new fast track for libel cases against newspapers and broadcasters handled by judges. The Defamation Bill is an attempt to weed out the large number of claims that now go to jury trial in hopes of massive awards. The British Broadcasting Corporation (BBC) is an autonomous public body which offers pluralistic views and airs both government and opposition political broadcasts, though it has at times submitted to government pressure to censor controversial items.

A Broadcasting Bill proposed in April would prevent newspaper groups with more than 20 percent of the national market from bidding for Independent

Television (ITV) licenses. Designed to prevent any one group from dominating the market, the bill sparked heated protest within the government, including the resignations of two Tory MPs as ministerial aides.

Freedom of movement is generally respected, though the Criminal Justice Act bars Roma (Gypsies) caravans from stopping at campsites. The Court of Appeals in June struck down a decision to remove the right of asylum-seekers to receive social security benefits. Legislation passed earlier in the year cut off benefits to some 8,000 people, but was found to conflict with existing legislation guaranteeing the right of asylum. In February 1997, British Home Secretary Michael Howard agreed to grant full citizenship to up to 8,000 Indian and Pakistani citizens of Hong Kong. Much concern has been raised about ethnic minorities who would become stateless following Hong Kong's handover to China in July 1997.

Trade unions remain active, despite having been financially and politically weakened in recent years. The Labour Party has promised not to repeal any of the labor laws that have been passed since 1980. With union power much reduced, membership has plummeted.

The existence of two established churches, the Church of England and the Church of Scotland, does not restrict religious freedom. State-financed schools' mandatory daily worship sessions are meant to be "broadly Christian" by law.

United States of America

Polity: Federal presidential-legislative democracy
Economy: Capitalist
Population: 265,182,000
PPP: $24,680
Life Expectancy: 76.1
Ethnic Groups: European (73 percent), black (13 percent), Hispanic (10 percent), Asian-Pacific (3 percent), native American (Indian, Eskimo/Inuit, Aleut) (1 percent), others
Capital: Washington, D.C.

Political Rights: 1
Civil Liberties: 1
Status: Free

Overview: **B**ill Clinton became the first Democrat to win reelection as president since Franklin D. Roosevelt was elected to his fourth term in 1944. But while Clinton won by an impressive margin over the Republican nominee, former Senate Majority Leader Bob Dole, his triumph was far from complete. Republicans retained control of both the House of Representatives and the Senate, and actually increased their majority in the latter. Thus the United States faces the prospect of at least two more years of divided government, with the Democratic Party holding the presidency and the Republicans maintaining control of the federal legislature.

Since 1789, the United States has had elected civilian rule under a constitution providing for a president, bicameral legislature, and independent judiciary headed by a Supreme Court. The 100-member Senate (upper house) consists of two members from each state, elected to staggered, six-year terms. Each state is guaranteed at least one member in the House of Representatives (lower house), with the remainder apportioned on the basis of the state's population. Currently, 435 representatives are elected biannually.

The president and vice president are elected to four-year terms via an electoral college. Voters in each state and the federal district, Washington, D.C., select a slate of electors, who usually give unanimous support to the candidate winning the popular vote in their jurisdiction. In the 1996 elections, Clinton won 379 electoral votes to 159 for former Senator Dole, and 49.2 percent of the popular vote to Dole's 40.7 percent. Billionaire independent candidate H. Ross Perot won no electoral votes but took 8.4 percent of the popular vote—a significant reduction in support from his showing in 1992.

Clinton's reelection represented an impressive turnaround for a president whose popular standing had reached its nadir one year before the balloting. His comeback was due to a number of factors. First, Bob Dole proved to be a weak opponent who failed to articulate an overarching theme or to convince the voters that a change in leadership was necessary. Moreover, it is highly unusual for a president to fail to win reelection under conditions of peace and prosperity, and under Clinton the United States had avoided involvement in serious foreign military ventures and had experienced steady, if unspectacular, economic growth.

The percentage of registered voters who participated in the 1996 election was one of the lowest this century, a fact which has triggered a debate over whether the turnout signals a decline in America's civic culture, or simply reflects American satisfaction with the status quo. The election results were not easy to characterize ideologically. Clinton, who had run as a champion of state intervention in 1992, was by 1996 proclaiming his devotion to a government with strictly limited objectives. A number of Republican candidates tended to distance themselves from the hard-edged conservatism of the past several years. This was a successful strategy in some cases, but not in others; if anything, liberal is lost with greater frequency than conservative ones. Overall, the composition of both Republican majorities was slightly more conservative than before. On the other hand, the Democratic composition of the House and Senate was slightly more liberal than before.

Americans clearly rejected the appeal of nativism, as reflected in the failed candidacy of Republican Patrick Buchanan. Although many predicted wide support for Buchanan's message of trade barriers, immigration control and an isolationist foreign policy, Buchanan's support during the Republican presidential primaries seldom exceeded 20 percent, and the issues he focused on were practically ignored during the general election campaign.

Nevertheless, the issue of immigration in American society was clearly of concern to many Americans. Although there was little support for the sweeping retrenchment proposed by Buchanan and others, Americans were troubled by the continued flood of illegal immigrants and the perceived political demands of certain ethnic groups for policies of multiculturalism in the schools and elsewhere. Although Congress did nothing to reduce the numbers of immigrants permitted into the United States, it did pass a law which denied certain social welfare benefits to legal non-citizen immigrants, an unprecedented move.

Race also continued to dominate American politics. The debate over affirmative action became rather heated during the referendum campaign on a California initiative to prohibit the state from carrying out policies of racial or gender preference; the measure passed by a 54-46 percent margin. Evidence purportedly showed that blacks do not need affirmative action to ensure adequate representation,. coming from congressional elections in districts which had previously been gerrymandered to favor black candidates. In several southern states, the Supreme Court struck down the use of race as a dominant criterion in congressional districting. Yet in almost every case, the black incumbent won reelection despite a racial breakdown that would supposedly have favored white candidates.

Nineteen-ninety-six also saw a notable decline in the activities of the militias and other radical organizations which thrive on conspiracy theories about the federal government. After a lengthy standoff, a group of militia men who had holed up in a cabin in Montana surrendered to the authorities; their activities seemed to garner little support, even among other militia organizations.

Political Rights and Civil Liberties:

Americans can change their governments democratically. U.S. citizens abroad may vote, as may resident aliens in some localities. The party system is competitive. Considerable concern has been voiced in recent years over the influence of campaign contributions from large corporations, trade unions and other special interests. This issue reached a climax during the recent election, when it was revealed that fundraisers for President Clinton and the Democratic Party had raised sizable sums from foreign financial sources, including corporations that had been involved in economic deals with the United States or had lobbied the government on certain issues of trade policy. In response, both President Clinton and leaders of the Republican Party have promised to enact new guidelines on campaign finance. Such pledges have often been made in the past.

The American media, though among the freest in the world, are facing new restrictions. Increasingly, newspapers and other media are confronted by demands for politically correct coverage of certain topics affecting racial minorities, gender issues and the like. Some large newspapers have imposed rules on the use of language and instituted racial quotas in hiring policies. At the same time, clear signs display mounting public disenchantment with the big media, most vividly reflected in legal decisions that found them guilty of slander or unethical practices. Media concentration is also troubling; the Telecommunications Act has encouraged buyouts and mergers of various large media and communications entities, as well as the creation of huge communications conglomerates.

Public debate and discussion in the United States is open and often freewheeling. In recent years, some concern has been voiced about the tone of the political dialogue in America. Conservative talk-show hosts on radio have been accused of creating a climate of anger. At the same time, minorities and radical feminists have been accused of trying to limit public discussion on racial and gender issues. Nonetheless, the 1996 presidential election was notable for its moderate and generally responsible tone.

The role of the federal judiciary is becoming increasingly controversial. Republicans have accused federal judges of usurping the authority of Congress in issuing decisions on such sensitive issues as abortion, affirmative action, homosexual rights, and school prayer. Of special concern were rulings which overturned laws adopted by state legislatures or decisions arrived at through public referenda.

The criminal justice system has also come under attack. Public concern over the high rate of crime has led to an increasing number of criminal defendants being sent to prison, which invariably leads to prison overcrowding. Another source of controversy is the issue of police brutality, particularly against black criminal suspects. Although disagreement exists among criminal justice experts as to whether the police are more prone to use excessive force than before, nobody questions that relations between urban police departments and the black community remain difficult. At the same time, a new trend has emerged in the legal system, known as jury nullification, which poses a potential threat to the public's faith in the legal system. Under jury nullification, attorneys for black criminal defendants adopt a deliberate strategy of appealing to the racial solidarity of minority jurors to persuade them to vote for acquittal even in cases where the evidence clearly indicates the defendant's guilt. Jury nullification is being employed in a growing number of criminal cases, the most notorious example being the acquittal of former football star O.J. Simpson.

Religious freedom is guaranteed, and a wide variety of religions are practiced in the United States. Supreme Court decisions that have limited religious displays on public property and prohibited organized prayer in public schools remain controversial.

America remains burdened by a large, primarily black, underclass plagued by unemployment, widespread drug addiction, rampant crime, female-headed households and illegitimate children. Changes in the welfare system, adopted by Congress and signed by President Clinton, place limits on the length of time a person can receive welfare assistance; the impact of the new legislation is as yet unclear. Nevertheless, a growing black middle class has made significant gains in housing, education and employment, and 1996 provided indications that the income gap between blacks and whites was narrowing somewhat.

Women have made notable gains towards economic, social and educational equality in recent decades. Although women still tend to hold a greater proportion of lower-paying jobs than do men, they have attained something close to equality in university enrollment, including graduate and professional schools.

The government restricts the freedom of movement to a few countries, notably Cuba. With certain exceptions, Americans wishing to visit Cuba must obtain a government license to spend money there.

The situation of Native American remains a problem, with poverty and joblessness at extremely high levels. Indian tribes have pressed for enhanced sovereignty, arguing that it would reduce their dependence on the federal government. In recent years, a number of tribes have grown wealthy through the sale of untaxed tobacco and through casino gambling. Many have cases in court charging federal violations of treaty provisions regarding control over land and resources.

Uruguay

Polity: Presidential-
legislative democracy
Economy: Capitalist-
statist
Population: 3,186,000
PPP: $6,550
Life Expectancy: 72.6

Political Rights: 1*
Civil Liberties: 2
Status: Free

Ethnic Groups: European (88 percent), mestizo (8 percent),
black and mulatto (4 percent)
Capital: Montevideo
Ratings Change: Uruguay's political rights rating changed from 2 to 1 due to
increasing popular participation in politics.

Overview:

Two journalists were put on trial and imprisoned in 1996
for defamation. In addition, the government imposed restrictions on the import of newsprint. These were unfortu-
nate violations of Uruguay's relatively free press traditions.

After gaining independence from Spain, the Republic of Uruguay was
established in 1830. The Colorado Party dominated a relatively democratic political
system through the 1960s. The 1967 constitution established a bicameral congress
consisting of a 99-member Chamber of Deputies and a 31-member Senate, with
every member serving a five year term. The president is also directly elected for a
five-year term. The recently-amended system of electoral lists had allowed parties
to run multiple candidates. The leading presidential candidate of the party receiving
the most votes overall was the winner. Congressional seats were allocated on the
basis of each party's share of the total vote.

An economic crisis, social unrest and the activities of the Tupamaro urban
guerrilla movement led to a right-wing military takeover in 1973. Civilian rule was
restored through negotiations between the military regime and civilian politicians.
Julio Sanguinetti won the presidential elections in 1984. In 1989 Luis Alberto
Lacalle of the centrist National Party was elected president. His popularity fell,
however, as he tried to liberalize one of the most statist economies in Latin America.

In the 1994 campaign Sanguinetti ran as a social democrat. The other main
contenders were the Broad Front's Tabare Vasquez, the popular mayor of Montevideo,
and the National Party's Alberto Volante. The 1994 election was Uruguay's closest
ever. The Colorodo Party won 31.4 percent of the vote, the National Party 30.2
percent and the Broad Front 30 percent. As the leading Colorodo vote-getter,
Sanguinetti was declared the winner. In the Chamber of Deputies the Colorodo
Party won 32 seats, the Nationals 31 and the Broad Front 28. In the Senate, the
Colorodo Party won 11 seats, the National Party ten and the Broad Front nine.

Sanguinetti gave numerous cabinet posts to the National Party, and thus
took office in March 1995 with considerable congressional support. He then pushed
through congress an austerity package that partially dismantled the country's
welfare state. This led to a series of labor stoppages and a sharp decline in

Sanguinetti's popularity.

On December 8, 1996, a plebiscite approved a constitutional amendment ending the system that allowed parties to field multiple presidential and legislative candidates for the same offices. Under the new system the top two presidential candidates will face a run-off if no candidate wins a majority in the first round.

Political Rights and Civil Liberties: Citizens of Uruguay can change their government democratically. Constitutional guarantees regarding free expression, freedom of religion and the right to form political parties, labor unions and civic organizations are generally respected. The former Tupamaro guerrillas now participate in the system as part of the Broad Front.

The press is privately owned, and broadcasting is both commercial and public. Numerous daily newspapers publish, many associated with political parties; there are also a number of weeklies. However, a May 1996 court ruling became a matter of concern. A publisher and a reporter of the leftist tabloid *La Republica* were sentenced to two years in prison under the national press law and constitution for accusing Juan Carlos Wasmosy, the president of Paraguay, of corruption. Wasmosy had sued the paper in March. The two journalists were provisionally released from jail, but by year's end their appeal was still pending. Furthermore, a number of publications have ceased production because of the government's suspension of tax exemptions on the import of newsprint. In addition, a June 1996 decree requires government authorization to import newsprint. The Inter-American Press Organization strongly criticized the decree. In a positive development, in October, a court rejected a case involving a libel suit filed by a former president on the grounds that it would impinge upon press freedom.

Political expression is occasionally hindered by the violence associated with hotly-contested political campaigns and labor disputes. In the 1994 electoral campaign a number of clashes erupted between party supporters; as a result, legislative candidates were attacked and two Colorodo Party offices were ransacked.

The judiciary is relatively independent, but has become increasingly inefficient in the face of escalating crime. The court system is severely backlogged and prisoners often spend more time in jail than they would were they to serve the maximum sentence for their alleged crime. Allegations of mistreatment, particularly of youthful offenders, have increased. In recent years, allegations of torture have been made, and a number of police personnel have been prosecuted for ill-treatment or unlawful killings. New measures to prevent such practices have been implemented but official investigations into abuses are not always effective. In June 1996 a commission on penal reform, created under the Public Safety Law, confirmed that prison conditions do not meet international standards.

In 1991, a decision by the Inter-American Commission on Human Rights of the Organization of American States ruled that the 1985 law which granted the military amnesty from rights violations during the years of dictatorship violated key provisions of the American Convention on Human Rights. The Amnesty Law authorizes the government to carry out investigations but the armed forces have firmly opposed such action.

Civic organizations have proliferated since the return to civilian rule. Numerous women's rights groups focus on violence against women, societal discrimination and other problems. The small black minority, estimated at 6 percent of the population, continues to face discrimination.

Workers exercise their rights to join unions, bargain collectively and hold strikes. Unions are well-organized and politically powerful. Strikes are often marked by violent clashes and sabotage.

Uzbekistan

Polity: Dominant party (presidential-dominated)
Economy: Statist-transitional
Population: 23,188,000
PPP: $2,510
Life Expectancy: 69.4
Ethnic Groups: Uzbek (71 percent), Russian (8 percent), Tajik, Ukrainian, Turk, others
Capital: Tashkent

Political Rights: 7
Civil Liberties: 6*
Status: Not Free

Ratings Change: Uzbekistan's civil liberties rating changed from 7 to 6 because the country, while still highly repressive, has seen growth in civic institutions.

Overview: In 1996, belying his reputation for political repression President Islam Karimov called for political reforms. He permitted the registration of external human rights organizations, sponsored two Organization for Security and Cooperation in Europe (OSCE) conferences on human rights, and released 80 prisoners, including members of the banned *Erk* (Freedom) Democratic Party. However, many human rights activists both inside and outside the country said the moves were geared to curry favor with the United States and to encourage foreign investment.

Among the world's oldest civilized regions, Uzbekistan became part of the Russian empire in the nineteenth century. In 1920, it became part of the Turkistan Soviet Socialist Republic within the RSFSR. Separated from Turkmenia in 1924, it entered the USSR as a constituent republic in 1925. In 1929 its eastern Tajik region was detached and also made a constituent Soviet republic.

Karimov, former first secretary of the Communist Party, was elected president on December 29, 1991, as head of the People's Democratic Party (PDP), the former Communist Party. He received 86 percent of the vote, defeating well-known poet Mohammed Salih of the Erk (Freedom) Democratic Party, who got 12 percent. The largest opposition group, the nationalist *Birlik* (Unity), was barred from registering as a party, and the Islamic Renaissance Party (IRP) was banned entirely, as was the Islamic Adolat group.

The 1992 constitution called for elections in 1994 for a new, 250-member legislature, the *Ulu Majilis*, to replace the Communist-era, 500-member Supreme Soviet. Throughout 1993 the regime curtailed all opposition. The December 1994 elections were marred by irregularities even though there was no real opposition to the government party. The PDP took 179 seats; nominally non-party but pro-government candidates gained 20 seats; and the *Vatan Taraqioti* (Fatherland Progress Party), nominally oppositionist but created by the government as a businesspersons' party, 6. In 1995, the PDP and its allies filled the remainder in by-elections.

In a February 1995 national referendum 99 percent of 11 million voters allegedly approved Karimov's plan to extend his term to coincide with that of parliament. Karimov personally controls everything from the secret industrial production plans to garbage removal in Tashkent, the capital.

The most significant political development in 1996 was Karimov's controversial June meeting with President Bill Clinton in Washington. Although the meeting was brief, it raised concerns among human rights groups. A month earlier, a Human Rights Watch Report accused the Karimov government of involvement in arbitrary arrests, disappearances, discriminatory dismissals from work, surveillance of homes and wire-tapping. Earlier, Washington had granted Uzbekistan Most Favored Nation (MFN) trade status with the United States. In an open letter to President Clinton, representatives of the exiled Birlik and Erk opposition parties objected to Karimov's visit.

While 80 political prisoners were released to coincide with Karimov's Washington trip, scores remained jailed. In August, exiled dissident Abdulmanop Pulatov, who was abducted by Uzbek agents while attending a conference in Kyrgyzstan in 1993 and subsequently forced to emigrate to the U.S., returned to Uzbekistan after Karimov had "personally guaranteed" his safety. The OSCE Human Rights Society conference took place in September despite strong objections from the interior and security ministries, but a Human Rights Watch representative was taken into detention, physically and verbally accosted, and held overnight. The group did not bother to send a representative to a second conference.

In November, Hasan Mirsaidov, son of Uzbek dissident Shukhurllo Mirsaidov, was abducted by three armed men, beaten, blindfolded, handcuffed and held for 12 hours before being freed. The government renewed its campaign to deport the family.

In economic issues, Karimov decreed the formation of a special committee to enforce the country's anti-monopoly legislation. In September, the government announced plans to sell off state shares in at least 300 medium-sized enterprises to newly-created investment funds. At year's end, a monetary crisis threatened to undermine the national currency, the som, leading the government to initiate a series of measures that restricted access to hard currency. Grain and cotton harvests were well below expectations, leading to the dismissals of several regional governors.

In May, a UN-sponsored conference on narcotics trafficking was held in Tashkent to discuss curbing the flow of drugs into the region, with a focus on drug corridors through Tajikistan, Kyrgyzstan and Uzbekistan.

Political Rights and Civil Liberties: Uzbekistan is a one-party de facto state dominated by former Communists, who have put severe restrictions on opposition political activity. The 1994 parliamentary elections were not free and fair, with only pro-government parties taking part.

The constitution, while enshrining a multiparty system, contains articles which undermine the right of parties to organize. Article 62 forbids "organized activities leading ...to participation in anti-government organizations."

In 1996, the government adopted a draft law that prohibits the formation of political parties on ethnic or religious lines, or for the purpose of advocating war or subversion of the constitutional order. Prospective parties must submit a detailed list of at least 5,000 members and register with the Justice Ministry, and may be banned by the Supreme Court if they are found guilty of persistent legal violations.

In 1996, several independent publications were launched, including a business magazine published by the Uzbek Central Bank, and *Kamalot*, a newspaper published by a youth organization by the same name. There were reports that two independent TV stations are operating in Samarkand. All of these ventures focus on business and culture, provide no political news, and are subject to state censorship. Indeed, a report in a state-run paper noted that if the media are to be true to their mission they must be "guided" by the state. There are 515 publications, including some in Korean and Russian, but all are controlled and distributed by national, regional or local governments. Independent political papers such as *Erk* and *Mustaqil hafatlik* (Independent Weekly) are banned. In March, an agreement between the BBC and the Uzbek Ministry of Communications permits the radio station to broadcast on medium wave, in addition to short-wave. Radio Free Europe/ Radio Liberty was scheduled to open an office in Tashkent.

Freedom of assembly, association and speech are seriously circumscribed. In June, the Open Society Institute, established by philanthropist George Soros in 1993, opened an office in Tashkent, and offers scholarships to young people to study abroad, promoting international contacts in the educational sphere. Freedom of religion is nominally respected in this largely Sunni Muslim nation, but the government controls the Muslim Religious Board. President Karimov's fear of Islamic fundamentalism has led him to make concessions to Muslims. While Samarkand's 20,000 Jews faced little overt persecution, many have left for Israel. German Lutherans, concentrated in Tashkent, have complained about the failure of the government to return properties confiscated under Stalin.

Ethnic Russians continued to leave in large numbers. The Russian Embassy reported that it was issuing 130-150 citizenship certificates a day, totaling more than 170,000 over the last several years. In all, over 500,000 people have left Uzbekistan for Russia, including Tatars, Jews and Bashkirs.

The judiciary is subservient to the regime, with the president appointing all judges, with no mechanisms to ensure their independence. The penal code contains many statutes intended to limit free expression and association. Article 60 bans "anti-state activities," Article 191 makes it a crime to defame the president, and Article 204, aimed at "malicious delinquency," has been used to stifle opposition activity. Despite freeing 80 political prisoners in June, scores remain imprisoned.

While trade unions are legal, their overall structure has been retained from the Soviet era and no independent unions operate. Women are underrepresented in high-level positions throughout society. Islamic traditions also undermine the rights of women.

Vanuatu

Polity: Parliamentary democracy
Economy: Capitalist-statist
Population: 170,000
PPP: $2,500
Life Expectancy: 65.4
Ethnic Groups: Indigenous Melanesian (90 percent), European, Vietnamese, Chinese, other Pacific islander
Capital: Vila

Political Rights: 1
Civil Liberties: 3
Status: Free

Overview:
Located in the southwestern Pacific Ocean, this predominantly Melanesian archipelago, formerly called the New Hebrides, was an Anglo-French condominium until it became independent in 1980. The condominium arrangement divided the islands into English-and French-speaking communities, creating rifts that continue today. The 1980 constitution vests executive power in a prime minister chosen by and from the members of a unicameral parliament, who are directly-elected for four-year terms. A largely-ceremonial president, currently Jean-Marie Leye, is elected for a five-year term by an electoral college consisting of the parliament and the six provincial council presidents.

The francophones were largely excluded from key posts in the first post-independence government, led by Prime Minister Father Walter Lini's anglophone, center-left Party of Our Land (VP). A number of islands initially faced brief secessionist movements.

The VP won subsequent elections in 1983 and 1987. In August 1991 the VP dumped Lini as its leader, charging him with running the party in an autocratic manner. Following December elections Maxime Carlot Korman's francophone Union of Moderate Parties (UMP) and Lini's new National United Party (NUP) shunted aside traditional Anglo-French animosities and formed a governing alliance, with Carlot as premier.

At the November 30, 1995, elections for an expanded 50-seat parliament, the Unity Front, a four-party opposition coalition headed by Donald Kalpokas, took 20 seats; UMP, 17; NUP, 9; two minor parties took one seat apiece and 2 independents. On December 21 the UMP's Serge Vohor, who had edged out Carlot as party leader, formed a coalition government with the NUP with Lini as deputy premier.

The rivalry between Vohor and Carlot for control of the UMP–and the government–continued in 1996. On February 20, Vohor resigned rather then face a pending no-confidence motion backed by eight dissident UMP MPs, and three days later parliament elected Carlot as prime minister. However, in September the Carlot government lost a vote of confidence, and in October parliament re-elected Vohor as premier.

On November 12, police arrested all but one of the 300-strong paramilitary Vanuatu Mobile Force (VMF) after nearly two months of rebellion over $980,000 in unpaid allowances. The crisis raised questions about how firmly the armed forces are under civilian control.

Political Rights and Civil Liberties: Citizens of Vanuatu can change their government democratically, although the government's strong influence over the media places the opposition at a disadvantage. Power is decentralized through six elected provincial councils.

Successive governments have undermined the integrity of the judiciary. Most recently, in late February 1996 the incoming Carlot government declared Roger de Robillard, an Australian lawyer who had represented Vohor before the Supreme Court in a challenge to Carlot's recent election, and Mauritian judge Jean-Claude Bibi, whom the Vohor government had brought to the country to serve on the Supreme Court, as "undesirable immigrants." Both left the country on March 2. According to the U.S. State Department the second Vohor government threatened to fire and expel the Supreme Court Chief Justice for seeking to issue warrants against leaders of the VMF mutiny, despite a political deal granting them immunity.

There is limited coverage of the opposition in the state-run media, which includes the AM Radio Vanuatu, an FM station, the *Vanuatu Weekly* newspaper, and a television station serving the capital, Port Vila, which began news coverage in June 1996. The private press includes two newspapers and several partisan newsletters.

In the last days of Vohor's December 1995-February 1996 government, the premier banned the broadcast media from covering the upcoming parliamentary vote that ultimately elected Carlot. In May the Carlot government banned Radio Vanuatu from broadcasting a statement by Vohor criticizing the Supreme Court decision upholding Carlot's election by parliament. Carlot's earlier government restricted media coverage of numerous issues and threatened to revoke the publishing license of one paper and to deport the publisher, and later to revoke the license of a second paper.

The independent Human Rights Forum, a nongovernmental organization, operates openly. Traditional norms limit women's opportunities for education and to hold land, which perpetuates their generally inferior status in society. Domestic violence is reportedly common.

The Carlot government set a precedent by politicizing the mid-level civil service. The country's five trade unions are all independent and are grouped under the Vanuatu Council of Trade Unions (VCTU). Collective bargaining is practiced in the formal sector. During a lengthy 1994 strike the government fired more than 1,200 striking civil servants, an action which reportedly has adversely affected union participation. An August 1995 law requires unions to give 30 days notice of intent to strike and to provide a list of proposed participants.

Venezuela

Polity: Presidential-
legislative democracy
Economy: Capitalist-
statist
Population: 22,311,000
PPP: $8,360
Life Expectancy: 71.8

Political Rights: 2*
Civil Liberties: 3
Status: Free

Ethnic Groups: Mestizo (67 percent), European (21 percent), black (10 percent), Indian (2 percent)
Capital: Caracas
Ratings Change: Venezuela's political rights rating changed from 3 to 2 because social and political upheaval receded along with the threat of the militarization of Caracas in the event of growing disorder.

Overview: In 1996, the government of aging President Rafael Caldera faced diminishing popular support as pessimism deepened amid persistent allegations of official corruption, increasing social unrest and rising crime. August opinion polls showed the president's popularity down to 24 percent from a high of 65 percent in November 1994, about a year after he became president, even as the government vowed to implement an ambitious privatization program and to reform a corrupt and inefficient judiciary.

The Republic of Venezuela was established in 1830, nine years after independence from Spain. Long periods of instability and military rule ended with the 1961 establishment of elected civilian rule. Under the 1961 constitution, the president and a bicameral Congress are elected for five years. The Senate has at least two members from each of the 21 states and the federal district of Caracas. The Chamber of Deputies has 189 seats.

Until 1993, the social-democratic Democratic Action (AD) party and the Christian Social Party (COPEI) dominated politics. Former President Carlos Andres Perez (1989-93) of the AD was nearly overthrown by nationalist military officers in two 1992 coup attempts. In 1993 he was charged with corruption and removed from office by Congress.

Rafael Caldera, a former president (1969-74) and populist who had broken with COPEI and railed against Perez's market reforms, was elected president in late 1993 at the head of the 16-party National Convergence, which included Communists, other leftists and right-wing groups. Amid coup rumors, Caldera was first past the post with 31 percent of the vote in a field of 17 candidates.

The 80-year-old Caldera's term has been marked by a national banking collapse (in 1994), the suspension of a number of civil liberties, mounting violent crime and social unrest and intermittent rumors of a military coup.

In 1995, Caldera's reputation for honesty was tarnished by allegations of corruption among his inner circle, including his sons and other relatives. With crime soaring, oil wealth drying up and the country in the worst economic crisis in 50 years, popular disillusionment with politics continued to deepen. In December state and local elections that saw pro-Caldera candidates crushed, 60 percent of voters stayed away from the polls, even though voting is mandatory.

In April 1996, the government launched an austerity-stabilization program to secure a $1.4 billion IMF stand-by loan. Many controls on prices and foreign exchange were removed. The market-oriented reforms were intended to reduce the country's budget deficit from 6.1 to 2 percent of GDP. Teodor Petkoff, the planning minister and former Marxist guerrilla, also announced an ambitious privatization program.

In the early autumn, the World Bank launched a $30 million program to reform Venezuela's notoriously corrupt, politicized and inefficient judiciary. Some human rights groups questioned the Bank's premise that the administration of justice could be made more effective through better management and training, because such an approach ignored the influence of political parties and corruption.

Political Rights and Civil Liberties:

Citizens can change their government democratically. However, Venezuela's institutions have been significantly eroded by decades of corruption and drug-trade penetration and also by two 1992 coup attempts. Trust in the political system has been in steep decline since the late 1980s. Voter abstention reached 60 percent in the 1995 state and local elections, the highest since the establishment of elected government. The elections themselves were marked by disorganization and allegations of fraud, which led to numerous riots.

The constitution guarantees freedom of religion and the right to organize political parties, civic organizations and labor unions. However, political expression and civil liberties are threatened by official antagonism towards the media and were undermined from mid-1994 to mid-1995 by the suspension of constitutional guarantees regarding arbitrary arrest, property rights and freedom of expression, movement and financial activity. The restoration of these guarantees, however, led to little change in security forces' repressive behavior against popular protests and labor strikes. Citizen security in general remains threatened by a drug-fueled crime wave that has resulted in hundreds of killings monthly in major cities and the rise of vigilante mob killings of alleged criminals. By May 1996, lynchings of purported criminals were averaging one a week, even as opinion polls showed broad support for vigilantism—a product of mass frustration with police corruption and inaction.

In 1996, Venezuelan and international human rights organizations continued reporting widespread arbitrary detentions and torture of suspects, as well as dozens of extrajudicial killings by military security forces and the notoriously corrupt police. Criminal suspects, particularly in poor areas and near the tense border with Colombia (a major drug-trafficking area that bases Colombian guerrillas), are subject to torture. Indigenous communities trying to defend their legal land rights are subject to abuses, including killings, by gold miners and corrupt rural police. Since the 1992 coup attempts, weakened civilian governments have had less authority over the military and the police, and rights abuses overall are committed with impunity. Police brutality and murder are rampant as crime increases.

The judicial system is headed by a Supreme Court and is nominally independent. However, it is highly politicized and undermined by the chronic corruption that permeates the entire political system. It is slow, ineffective and generally unresponsive to charges of rights abuses by police and security forces. The judiciary is further undermined by drug-related corruption, with growing evidence of bribery and intimidation of judges. A November poll found that 75 percent of Venezuelans distrust the judicial system. En Cambio, an advocacy group for judicial reform, proposed that all of the country's 1,109 judges be put on probation pending approval by an eminent jury in a public process.

Only 7,000 of Venezuela's estimated 25,000 prisoners have stood trial. Prisons are severely overcrowded and rife with drugs. Prison violence, virtually out of control, leads to hundreds of deaths annually. In October, at least 30 inmates were burned to death in a fire caused by a tear gas canister fired by guards.

A separate system of military courts has jurisdiction over members of the military accused of rights violations and common criminal acts. Military court decisions cannot be appealed in civilian courts. As a consequence, the military is rarely held accountable and most citizens view it as above the law.

The press is privately owned. Nearly a dozen daily newspapers, with Radio and television are mostly private, supervised by an association of broadcasters under the government communications ministry. The practice of journalism is restricted by a licensing law and threatened by government control of foreign exchange required to purchase newsprint and other supplies.

Since 1994 the media in general have faced a pattern of intimidation. Government and military officials, including the president, frequently attack the media verbally, and the Congress passed a series of restrictive laws involving the right of reply and journalistic conduct. Under one law, journalists must have a university degree and join the National Reporters' Guild, or face prison.

Labor unions are well-organized but highly politicized and prone to corruption. A new labor law in 1991 reduced the work week from 48 to 44 hours and made it illegal for employers to dismiss workers without compensation. However, the law is often disregarded. Security forces frequently break up strikes and arrest trade unionists.

Women face institutional and societal prejudice with respect to rape and domestic violence, which is very common and has been exacerbated by economic downturns.

Vietnam

Polity: Communist
one-party
Economy: Statist
Population: 76,580,000
PPP: $1,040
Life Expectancy: 65.5
Ethnic Groups: Vietnamese (85-90 percent), Chinese
(3 percent), Muong, Thai, Meo, Khmer, Man, Cham
Capital: Hanoi

Political Rights: 7
Civil Liberties: 7
Status: Not Free

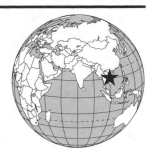

Overview: The Vietnam Communist Party (VCP)'s Eighth Congress in
June 1996 reaffirmed a policy of cautious market-oriented
reform while preserving the state sector as the foundation of
the economy. Authorities continued to crack down on peaceful political dissent and
religious activity.

The French colonized Vietnam in the nineteenth century. During World
War II a resistance movement led by Ho Chi Minh fought the occupying Japanese
and later the returning French. Vietnam won independence in 1954, and was divided
between a northern Communist government and a French-installed southern
government. Planned elections to reunify the country were never held, and military
forces and insurgent groups from the North eventually overtook the U.S.-backed
South in 1975 and established the Socialist Republic of Vietnam.

In 1986 the VCP launched a program of *doi moi* (renovation), which has
decentralized economic decision-making, encouraged small-scale private enterprises and largely dismantled agricultural collectivization while preserving the
central role of the state. In 1991 the VCP installed Do Moi as its party chairman. In
April 1992, the 395-seat National Assembly approved a new constitution that
codified many of the economic reforms and formally established the VCP as the sole
legal political party. Under the constitution the president is elected by, and from
within, the National Assembly. The July 1992 elections for the 395-seat National
Assembly brought in a crop of young technocrats. The Assembly subsequently
elected General Le Duc Anh as president, and re-elected Vo Van Kiet as prime
minister.

In October 1995 the National Assembly approved Vietnam's first civil
code, which delineated property rights, inheritance laws and other matters. The June
1996 party congress established a five-member Standing Board as the VCP's core
decision-making body, which includes the president, prime minister and party
chair.

**Political Rights
and Civil Liberties:**   Vietnamese citizens lack the means to change their government democratically. The VCP is the only legal party
and must approve all political candidates. The National
Assembly is unable to initiate or pass legislation the VCP opposes. The ruling
"troika" composed of the president, prime minister and party chair, lacks a system

of succession, a problem that was highlighted in November 1996 when President Anh was temporarily incapacitated by a stroke. Less than 3 percent of the population are party members, yet the party maintains tight control over all political, economic, religious and social affairs. Party membership is necessary for obtaining senior government positions and is a key factor in promotions in state companies.

Police and security forces carry out arbitrary arrests. Authorities routinely ignore legal safeguards such as time limits on pre-trial detention and the right to an attorney during interrogation. Credible reports indicate that security officials beat detainees, deny some prisoners visitation rights, and occasionally use prisoners as forced labor for commercial ventures. The judiciary is not independent. The VCP tightly controls the courts at all levels and instructs judges on rulings. Judges, appointed by the president, are selected based on their political reliability. In 1996 new courts were established to address abuse and corruption by state officials. Prison conditions are harsh and only rarely are prisons opened to international monitors.

In recent years the government has relaxed its monitoring of the population, although it maintains control through mandatory household registration, block wardens, informants and selective monitoring of communications. Freedom of expression is limited. Citizens enjoy greater latitude in criticizing government corruption and inefficiency, but are not free to advocate political liberalization or democratization. An estimated 200 political prisoners are believed to be held in "re-education camps." In the past two years at least five prominent dissidents have been arrested.

The government controls all media; there is no coverage of opposition views. In January 1995 authorities shut down two publications and in July 1996 three newspapers faced the threat of prosecution. It is illegal to publish anything that might incite opposition, undermine national unity, or contribute to adverse public opinion. Foreign journalists' activities are strictly circumscribed. In 1996 an Internet provider opened business, although the government is considering ways to regulate Internet content. During the year authorities issued strict laws regarding who can access foreign satellite television.

All assemblies require permits. Political protests are not permitted but the authorities occasionally tolerate small demonstrations over routine issues. The government does not permit independent elements of civil society.

Religious practice remains under tight VCP control. Only Buddhists belonging to the official Vietnam Buddhist Church are permitted to practice; the government continues to enforce its ban on the independent Unified Buddhist Church of Vietnam (UBCV). Authorities have arrested most of the UBCV's leadership, including their patriarch, Thich Huyen Quang. Major Buddhist temples are kept under surveillance and are occasionally raided by police. By law, religious activities, including the holding of meetings or training seminars, operating religious schools, or repairing places of worship, require official permission.

Catholic religious affairs are similarly controlled by the state-organized Catholic Patriotic Association. The government must approve Vatican appointments. In 1995 the authorities vetoed a Vatican-nominated clerical candidate, and the Cao Dai religious movement was prohibited from opening a seminary. The government has arrested Protestant clergy and other members of the minority

Montagnard ethnic group.

Ethnic minorities face restrictions regarding internal and international travel, education and employment. Violence and discrimination against women are widely practiced. Child prostitution and international trafficking of minors is increasing. The government urges limiting family size to two children and can penalize families that do not comply. Private human rights organizations are not permitted to operate and citizens are not allowed to contact international human rights organizations.

All unions must belong to the state-controlled Vietnam General Confederation of Labor (VGCL). In 1996 worker discontent rose as some employers failed to pay the minimum wage, refused to pay for overtime, and physically abused some workers. The VGCL does not serve as a true advocate of worker's rights, and less than six percent of workers are members. The 1994 labor code recognizes only a limited right to strike.

Western Samoa

Polity: Parliamentary democ- **Political Rights:** 2
racy and family heads   **Civil Liberties:** 2
Economy: Capitalist   **Status:** Free
Population: 179,000
PPP: $3,000
Life Expectancy: 67.8
Ethnic Groups: Samoan (93 percent), mixed, European, other
Pacific islander
Capital: Apia

Overview: Located 1,600 miles northeast of New Zealand, the western Samoan islands became a German protectorate in 1899. New Zealand claimed the islands during World War I and administered them until granting independence in 1962.

The 1960 constitution provides for a *Fono Aoao Faitulafono* (parliament) elected for a five year term and a head of state who must approve all legislation passed by parliament. Malietoa Tanumafali, one of the four paramount island chiefs, is head of state for life, although his successors will be elected by parliament for five-year terms.

In a 1990 referendum voters narrowly approved direct elections for parliament. Previously only the 25,000 *matai*, essentially heads of extended families, could vote. However, 45 of the 47 parliamentary seats are still reserved for matai, with the remaining two seats set aside for citizens of non-Samoan descent.

At the country's first direct elections in April 1991 Prime Minister Tofilau Eti Alesana led the ruling Human Rights Protection Party (HRPP) to victory with 30 of 47 seats in parliament. In early 1994 a controversial ten percent Goods and Services Tax (GST), which took affect during a severe economic downturn worsened by a taro blight which devastated the staple food crop, provoked large demonstrations. In December 1994 the chief auditor released a report on government corruption that implicated seven cabinet ministers.

At the April 26, 1996, national elections the HRPP won its fifth consecutive victory since 1982, but a large swing against it reflected voter anger over corruption and the GST. Final results gave the HRPP 24 seats; the Samoan National Development Party, 13; and independents, 12. On May 20 parliament re-elected Alesana as prime minister over opposition leader Tupua Tamasese Efi.

Political Rights and Civil Liberties: Western Samoans can change their government democratically, although only matai can sit in parliament (with the exception of two seats reserved for non-Samoans) and in the village *fonos* (councils of matai). Party affiliations are generally based more on individual loyalties than policies or ideology. Vote-buying was reportedly widespread during the 1996 election campaign. Following the elections, the Supreme Court overturned the results in four districts, and by-elections were held. Outside of the cities the village fonos are the main authority.

The judiciary is independent and defendants receive fair trials. However, many civil and criminal matters are handled at the local level by some 360 village fonos according to traditional law. The 1990 Village Fono Law affirmed this authority but provided some right of appeal to the Lands and Titles Courts and to the Supreme Court. Fonos occasionally order harsh punishments, including the burning of houses and banishment from villages.

The 1993 Newspapers and Printers Act requires journalists to reveal their sources in libel cases or face a $2,000 fine and a three-month prison sentence. The 1993 Defamation Act forbids journalists from publishing defamatory statements made in court that refer to a person not involved in the proceedings. It also requires editors to publish an apology when a member of a group that has been criticized in print requests it. Neither law has yet been applied, but they apparently contribute to some self-censorship among the private press. Two private radio stations broadcast, including the outspoken Radio Polynesia.

Freedom of assembly is generally respected. In February 1995 the government charged two former MPs with sedition over anti-government comments at a March 1994 rally against the GST. In June a magistrate dismissed all seven sedition charges for lack of evidence.

Village leaders often choose the denomination of their followers in this predominantly Christian country. The National Council of Churches and other religious groups freely comment on political matters and are highly influential.

A New Zealand-funded study of sexual abuse and domestic violence against women and children, released in spring 1996, reported that nearly 30 percent of the women surveyed had been victims of battery or sexual abuse. Traditional norms tolerate domestic violence and discourage women from reporting such abuse to the police. When abuses are reported, formal charges are sometimes dropped after the family of the perpetrator offers a traditional apology to the victim's family. Some domestic violence cases are adjudicated by village fonos. Women are underrepresented in politics since only matai can sit in parliament and the village fonos, and 95 percent of matai are men.

There are two independent trade unions, plus the Public Service Association which represents government workers, but overall the trade union movement is neither well-organized nor vigorous. Strikes and collective bargaining are legal but are practiced infrequently. Enforcement of occupational health and safety standards is weak.

Yemen

Polity: Dominant coalition (military-influenced)
Political Rights: 5
Civil Liberties: 6
Economy: Capitalist-statist
Status: Not Free
Population: 14,661,000
PPP: $1,600
Life Expectancy: 50.4
Ethnic Groups: Arab majority, African, Asian
Capital: Sanaa

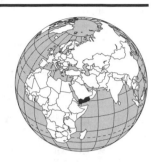

Overview:
The government's continued harassment of dissidents raised questions about the fairness of the parliamentary elections scheduled for April 1997.

The Republic of Yemen was formed in 1990 through the unification of North and South Yemen. North Yemen's Ali Abdallah Salih became president and South Yemen's Ali Salim al-Biedh vice-president.

The 1991 constitution provides for a 301-seat House of Representatives. In April 1993 parliamentary elections were held after a five month delay due to civil unrest. The General People's Congress (GPC) of former North Yemen won the most seats and formed a coalition with the Islamic fundamentalist, tribal-based *Islah* (Reform) Party, and the Yemeni Socialist Party (YSP) of former South Yemen. In October parliament formally elected Salih as president and al-Biedh as vice-president. However, al-Biedh boycotted the new government calling for demilitarization of the former north/south border, decentralization of authority and investigations into dozens of pre-election killings of YSP activists.

In April 1994 a civil war erupted between the northern and southern armies when the south attempted to secede. In July northern troops triumphed, and al-Biedh and other secessionist leaders fled the country.

In September 1994 parliament revised the constitution, broadening the powers of the chief executive. Parliament empowered itself to elect the next president and elected Salih to a fresh five-year term. Thereafter the president will be directly elected. In October the GPC and Islah formed a governing coalition. In February 1995, 13 opposition groups led by the YSP formed the Democratic Opposition Coalition.

Political Rights and Civil Liberties:
The 1993 parliamentary elections were reasonably free, but there were numerous irregularities and the ruling parties had significant advantages, including influence over the media. Power is now concentrated in the hands of the president and a small elite from his minority Shiite Zaydi sect. Tribal leaders wield considerable influence in some northern and eastern areas. Only political parties not contrary to Islam are

permitted. Parties are extended government financial support and are allowed to publish their own newspapers.

There continue to be numerous incidents of disappearance, harassment, beating, and arbitrary detention without charge or trial of those critical of the government. People, primarily those labeled 'secessionist,' are subject to the search of their homes and offices without warrants. Their personal communications are monitored. Security forces torture detainees accused of violent crimes to extract confessions and information. Prison conditions generally do not meet international standards. There are reports of extra-judicial prisons.

The judiciary is not independent. Judges are susceptible to bribes and government influence. There were, however, several instances in 1996 in which the courts challenged government abuses. In one case the court ruled that an academic who was released from his university post after writing a critical article be reinstated. In another case the court ruled against the government's attempt to shut down a weekly publication after it published an article criticizing the government.

Nonetheless, the government continued to obstruct the freedom of the press by shutting down or blocking distribution of media critical of the government. There were several cases of journalists being arrested, assaulted or detained for controversial reporting. The government owns the printing presses, radio and television stations. The press rarely offers pluralistic views.

Associations must register with the Ministry of Social Security and Social Affairs. The independent Yemeni Human Rights Organization operates openly. However, in 1994 the government dissolved a southern-based human rights group. The government allows international human rights observers relatively broad access.

Police and soldiers have violently dispersed protesters on several occasions. In February 1995, security forces broke up a demonstration in support of freedom of expression in the capital, Sanaa. In March, police forcibly dispersed protests against price increases, killing several people. In June 1996 police fired upon demonstrators protesting discriminatory statements made by a state prosecutor. Seventeen people were injured.

Islam is the state religion. The tiny Jewish population in the north faces fewer official restrictions than in previous years. Jewish citizens have limited employment opportunities. Church services are regularly held in the few existing churches in the south for the Christian population which is composed mostly of foreign residents. There are also Hindu temples in the south. The clandestine Islamic Jihad organization has carried out several violent attacks in the south, including deadly raids on wedding parties that feature dancing between men and women.

Citizens with a non-Yemeni parent (known as *muwalladin*), as well as members of the tiny *Akhdam* (servant) minority, face discrimination in employment opportunities. Women face legal discrimination in marriage and divorce matters. An estimated 80 percent of women are illiterate compared to 35 percent of men. Women enjoy the right to vote; however, only an estimated 20 percent of those eligible are registered to vote, compared to nearly 90 percent of the eligible men. Two women have been elected to parliament. Female genital mutilation is practiced in some areas; the government has not outlawed this practice.

The labor law permits only one union per enterprise and only one trade union confederation. State employees are prohibited from joining unions. The March 1995 law protects the right to strike and bargain collectively, but such activity is rare. Child labor is common.

Yugoslavia

Polity: Dominant party
Economy: Mixed statist
Population: 8,162,000
PPP: na
Life Expectancy: 72.6
Ethnic Groups: Serb (80 percent), Montenegrin (7 percent),
Sanjak Muslim (4 percent), Roma, Albanian, others
Capital: Belgrade

Political Rights: 6
Civil Liberties: 6
Status: Not Free

Overview: In 1996, Serbian President Slobodan Milosevic faced his biggest political crisis since assuming office in 1989 as massive, almost daily anti-government demonstrations---launched after his government nullified opposition victories in November's local elections—continued as the year drew to a close. The rallies, spearheaded by the three-party *Zajedno* (Unity) opposition, included students, pensioners and some workers frustrated at authoritarian and nationalist polices that had led to war in Bosnia, international condemnation and sanctions.

The reconstituted Federal Republic of Yugoslavia (FRY), formed in 1992 after the secession of Slovenia, Croatia, Macedonia and Bosnia-Herzegovina had left Serbia—which had seized control of the autonomous provinces of Kosovo and Vojvodina—and Montenegro as the only republics. The Serbian and Montenegrin legislatures accepted a constitution declaring the FRY a "sovereign federal state based on the principles of equality of its citizens and member republics."

The bicameral Federal Assembly (parliament) consists of the 42-member Chamber of Republics (divided evenly between Serbia and Montenegro) and the 138-seat Chamber of Citizens. In the December 1992 elections for the Chamber of Republics, Milosevic's Socialist Party of Serbia (SPS) won 47 seats; the ultra-nationalist Serbian Radical Party (SRS), led by suspected war criminal and paramilitary commander Vojislav Seselj, got 34; and the DEPOS opposition coalition, 20. Milosevic retained the Serbian presidency by defeating U.S. business-man and FRY non-party Prime Minister Milan Panic in a fraud-marred vote. In Montenegro, President Momir Bulatovic defeated Branko Kostic, a Milosevic ally, in a January 1993 run-off. Later that year, the Federal Assembly elected former Communist official and Milosevic ally Zorin Lilac as president. Milosevic then dissolved the 250-member Serbian parliament. Milosevic was strengthened after the December 19 elections, as the SPS won 123 seats, just shy of a majority. The SRS were the big losers, with the party's strength dropping from 73 to 39 seats. The charismatic Vuk Draskovic's Serbian Renewal Movement (SPO) held 46 seats, down from 50.

By 1995, Western sanctions had a deleterious impact on the Serb economy, leading to increased public weariness of the war in Bosnia. NATO air strikes, Croatian offensives that drove Serbs out of Western Slavonia and Krajina, and battlefield victories by Croat-Muslims forced Milosevic to sign the Dayton Accords that ended the fighting in Bosnia.

In 1996, with the war in Bosnia over and UN sanctions lifted, Yugoslavs focused on economic and domestic issues. Milosevic's reluctance to implement market reforms caused economic drift and increased disgruntlement. In May, 100,000 workers at the Serbian electronics group EI-Nis went on strike to press demands for overdue wages and a stake in the company. Milosevic and the ruling Socialists jettisoned the nationalists and fashioned an alliance with the newly-created United Left headed by Milosevic's wife, Mirjana Markovic, who was widely despised by Yugoslavs for her adherence to authoritarian Marxism.

Despite growing public discontent, fragmentation among the opposition helped the Socialists to victory in November 3 elections to the 138-member Federal Assembly. The media blockade of the opposition and a highly unfavorable election law passed in May also worked against the anti-Milosevic forces. The Socialist-United Left coalition won 64 seats and a likely ally, the Democratic Socialist Party (Montenegro's ruling party), won 20. The Zajedno coalition, consisting of Draskovic's SPO, the Democratic Party led by Zoran Djindjic, and the Civic Alliance headed by Vesna Pesic, took 22 seats, with 16 going to the nationalist SRS. The remainder were parceled out among six minor parties and coalitions. Barred from running for another term as Serbia's president, Milosevic hoped to position himself to be named federal president by parliament in late 1997.

The results of the local run-off elections on November 17 came as a shock to the government and the opposition, as the Zajedno alliance won 15 of 18 major cities, including Belgrade. After the government nullified the results, hundreds of thousands of demonstrators poured into the streets of Belgrade, Nis and other major cities. The pro-government local election commissions ignored court decisions ordering them to turn control over to the opposition in several cities. As the crisis escalated, the government closed the independent radio station, B-92, setting off international condemnation and the threat of punitive measure (it was allowed back on the air). Meanwhile, leaders of the staid Orthodox Church supported the opposition, as did leaders of Montenegro, frustrated by years of Serb dominance.

Demonstrations continued throughout December, with sporadic incidents of violence propagated by police, who refrained from a full-scale crackdown.

Political Rights and Civil Liberties:

Citizens of Yugoslavia can elect representatives to the federal and regional parliaments; both the president and prime minister are appointed by a parliament dominated by former Communists loyal to Serbian President Slobodan Milosevic.

The December 1993 elections to the Serbian republican parliament were marred by irregularities. Milosevic's control of the media, particularly state-run television, effectively shuts out opposition views and opposition access. Parliament violated the constitution and did not even bother to consult the Constitutional Court in ousting President Dobrica Kosic in 1993. The 1996 federal and local elections were marred by the government's refusal to provide the opposition with air-time on state-run radio and television.

Political parties are allowed to organize, but their activities are closely monitored by the government.

Freedom of assembly and expression are curtailed. In 1996, the massive demonstrations were not interfered with, but on several occasions police beat and roughed up protesters. Permits for the protest marches were denied. The government-controlled radio and television are subservient to Milosevic and the SPS, and are staffed by Milosevic loyalists. With independent newspapers expensive or unavailable outside Belgrade, television is the main source of news and commentary. In 1994, the government launched an insidious campaign to silence the independent press by moving to buy controlling interest in leading publications. In this way it took over *Borba*, the last newspaper critical of Milosevic. In 1995, ex-*Borba* journalists launched an independent *Nas* (Our) *Borba*, but the government cut off access to newsprint, distribution and printing facilities. Independent TV station Studio B was taken off the air and radio station B-92 has faced similar pressure.

Ethnic Muslims in the Sandzak region between Serbia and Montenegro have faced repression and persecution. Kosovo's Albanian majority faces severe persecution and oppression. Serbs and Montenegrins are overwhelmingly Eastern Orthodox and free to practice their religion. Serbian refugees from Croatia and Bosnia were denied entry into Serbia and the men were ordered to join the Bosnian Serb army. Entry into Serbia was made extremely restrictive, in violation of international refugee conventions.

The federal judiciary, headed by a Constitutional and a Federal Court, are subordinate to Serbia. The government has openly flouted the rule of law, ignoring statutes that barred the forced mobilization of refugees into military units and decisions mandating the government to recognize election results.

Federal and republican laws prohibit discrimination against women, but women remain underrepresented in high-level government and business sectors.

The independent Nezavisimost trade union has faced harassment and persecution, and most trade unions are directly or indirectly controlled by the government or the SPS. Despite restrictions and intimidation, workers have gone out on strike in several sectors over the last three years. Nongovernmental organizations such as professional and humanitarian groups operate, but political organizations face government harassment.

Zaire

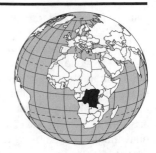

Polity: Presidential-military and interim legislative
Economy: Capitalist-statist
Population: 46,499,000
PPP: $300
Life Expectancy: 52.0
Ethnic Groups: Bantu tribes (80 percent), over 200 other tribes
Capital: Kinshasa

Political Rights: 7
Civil Liberties: 6
Status: Not Free

Overview: The crumbling of President Mobutu Sese Seko's dictatorship accelerated in 1996, as the central government's authority shrank further amidst widespread lawlessness and corruption, and as rebel forces began to seize large areas of the country's east from ill-disciplined and dispirited government forces. Serious human rights abuses persisted. President Mobutu Sese Seko manipulated the Rwandan refugee crisis in an effort to regain international stature. War broke out in November in northeastern Zaire. Mobutu's failing health further complicated already shaky plans to hold national elections by July 1997.

As the Belgian Congo, the vast area of central Africa that is today Zaire, the colony was exploited with a brutality astonishing even for the colonial period, and was left ill-prepared for independence when Belgium pulled out in 1960. The country became the site of Cold War competition until the then-Colonel Joseph Désiré Mobutu seized power in 1964. As a firm ally of the West, Mobutu was forgiven not only severe repression but also his kleptocratic excesses.

The Cold War's end left Mobutu bereft of allies, and domestic agitation for democratization and good governance forced the dictator to open the political process in 1990. Mobutu's Popular Revolutionary Movement (MPR), the sole legal party since 1965, and the Sacred Union of the Radical Opposition and Allied Civil Society (USORAS—a 200-group coalition) joined scores of other groups in a national conference that in December 1992 established a High Council of the Republic (HCR) to oversee a democratic transition. The national conference appointed USORAS leader Etienne Tshisekedi Wa Mulumba as prime minister. Mobutu dismissed Tshisekedi in 1993, however, and the current prime minister, Kengo wa Dondo, a longtime Mobutu ally, has introduced limited economic reforms but holds only limited real power.

Opposition disunity and Mobutu's political skill combined to delay and divert reforms. Another agreement in January 1994 initially called for multiparty elections under an interim constitution, the Transition Act, by July 1995. The polls have been delayed until at least July 1997, and many observers believe that date will pass without votes being cast.

Serious human rights abuses continued, including extrajudicial executions, torture, beatings and arbitrary detention. The security forces commit crimes with impunity, and soldiers and policemen are sometimes not paid for months and resort to an assortment of crimes to obtain the money to survive.

Mobutu allowed Hutu extremists, who had engineered the 1994 Rwanda genocide, to regroup and re-arm on Zairian soil, and to mount cross-border attacks in an effort to destabilize the Rwandan Patriotic Front government. Burundian Hutu rebels have also reportedly operated from Zaire.

Abuses occurred in northeastern Zaire, where citizens of Tutsi ethnicity, the Banyamulenge, were attacked by government troops while civilians were incited by local politicians. The imminent massacres sparked fierce resistance. In October, Banyamulenge fighters, reportedly aided by the Tutsi-dominated armies of Rwanda and Burundi, struck back against both Hutu militias and Zairian forces, and seized a large swathe of territory. Over a million Hutu refugees scattered from camps faced death from disease and starvation as aid workers fled the fighting.

In 1996, both France and Belgium resumed high-level diplomatic contacts with Mobutu and official aid to Zaire. Some analysts argued that Zaire would descend to utter anarchy without Mobutu's presence.

Political Rights and Civil Liberties:

Zaire's people cannot change their government through democratic and peaceful means. No properly-elected representatives serve, although the transitional parliament charged with overseeing new elections does reflect a broad array of public opinion. Mobutu won three presidential contests in 1970, 1977 and 1984 unopposed; the three legislative polls were only window-dressing for his authoritarian regime.

More than 300 political parties have been registered since their 1990 legalization. Many were involved in the national conference or are represented in the transitional parliament. The delineation of real power is often unclear, however, and remains fluid. Mobutu's control over most of the security forces is critical to his political survival.

Under Zaire's Transition Act, elections are required by July 1997, but it is uncertain that either the political will or the technical competence to conduct free and fair elections exists. In May 1995, the transitional parliament created a 44-member autonomous election commission charged with preparing and overseeing free and fair elections. But the government has not funded the autonomous commission and has created its own inter-ministerial election commission. An independent election commission has also been formed by nongovernmental organizations to monitor the official bodies.

Freedom of expression is guaranteed both by Zaire's constitution and the Transition Act. Extensive open debate and an energetic print media are existent, but newspapers hardly circulate outside the capital and a few large cities. The state-controlled radio network reaches a large number of people throughout the country, although church networks are increasingly important. Independent journalists are frequently threatened, sometimes resulting in self-censorship.

Numerous nongovernmental organizations are active, including several concerned with human rights issues. Among the most active were the Zairian Association for the Defense of Human Rights (AZADHO), the Zairian League of Human Rights and the Voice of the Voiceless (VSV). These groups produced reports highly critical of security forces and government actions, but were threatened and harassed and cannot function effectively. Other church-based and grassroots groups have undertaken civic-education projects. Freedom of assembly is restricted by various decrees and permit requirements, and security forces routinely break up anti-government demonstrations. Freedom of religion is respected in practice, although religious groups must register with the government to be recognized.

Zaire's judiciary is not independent and is grossly ineffective in protecting constitutional rights. Arbitrary detention is used to harass and intimidate political activists. Long periods of pre-trial detention in prisons where poor diet and lack of medical care can be life-threatening are common.

Women face de facto discrimination, especially in more traditional rural areas, despite an array of constitutional protections. Employment and educational opportunities are fewer for women than men, and equal pay is often not offered for equal work in the formal sector. Married women must receive their husband's permission to enter into many financial transactions.

The legalization of political parties in 1990 also led to an opening of the trade union movement. Previously, all unions had to affiliate with the National Union of Zairian Workers (UNTZA), which was part of the ruling MPR, despite constitutional guarantees of the right to form and join unions. Over 100 new unions are registered. Numerous strikes have been held to protest plummeting wages due to hyperinflation.

Zaire's formal economy has nearly ground to a halt. State-owned mining and railways corporations have declared bankruptcy. New business formation is difficult in a country where the rule of law is conspicuous by its absence and corruption has become the governing principle.

Zambia

Polity: Dominant party **Political Rights:** 5
Economy: Mixed statist **Civil Liberties:** 4
Population: 9,159,000 **Status:** Partly Free
PPP: $1,110
Life Expectancy: 48.6
Ethnic Groups: Bemba, Lozi, Lunda, Ngoni, others
Capital: Lusaka
Ratings Change: Zambia's political rights rating changed from 3 to 5 because of considerable irregularities in the October elections.

Overview:

Zambian President Frederick Chiluba was declared winner of a second five-year term of office in an October election rejected by independent monitors and opposition parties as neither free nor fair. The November vote was held under a new constitution adopted five months earlier by the MMD-dominated parliament that barred the most credible opposition candidate, former President Kenneth Kaunda, and weakened the judiciary. Problems in voter registration and other irregularities plagued election preparations, and state resources and state media were mobilized extensively to support Chiluba and the MMD. Several international observer groups refused to monitor the polls.

For over quarter of a century after achieving independence from Britain in 1964, Zambia was effectively ruled by President Kaunda and the United National Independence Party (UNIP) as a one-party state. Kaunda's regime grew increasingly repressive and faced security and economic difficulties during the long guerrilla wars against white rule in the neighboring countries, Rhodesia (now Zimbabwe) and Portuguese-controlled Mozambique. A stifling of free enterprise imposed by UNIP's socialist policies and a crash in prices for Zambia's main export, copper, significantly weakened the once-strong economy.

When Kaunda permitted free elections under international pressure in 1991, former union leader Chiluba won convincingly, and his MMD party took 125 of 150 seats in the National Assembly. Chiluba and the MMD failed to turn their popular mandate into a program for action. Liberalizing the long state-controlled economy is hindered by corruption and a drug trade that is estimated to be one of the most lucrative in Africa.

The free press is harassed by libel and defamation suits brought by the government and its ministers. The government threatened crackdowns against civic groups and parties which rejected Chiluba's re-election as fraudulent. The fraudulent elections may also hurt Zambia's economic recovery, as donors withhold aid to protest the country's slide back towards authoritarianism.

Political Rights and Civil Liberties:

Zambians have the constitutional right to change their government freely, but the 1996 presidential and parliamentary polls failed to meet credible standards as free and fair elections. Free and fair elections did take place in 1991, but President Chiluba and the MMD have steadily eroded the trust granted them.

Preparations for the November 1996 elections were marked by heavy use of state funds and state media to promote the government party, and by irregularities in voter registration. The basic question of how many of Zambia's roughly nine million people are eligible to vote was never answered before the election, and independent monitors claim that over two million people were effectively disenfranchised. The government's reaction to allegations of fraud was increasingly erratic. The Committee for a Clean Campaign and the Zambia Independent Monitoring Team, which denounced the way the elections were conducted, were alleged to have taken funds and directions from foreign aid donors. The European Union stated that election irregularities would lead to a "further decline in the previous standards of governance in Zambia."

The government dominates broadcasting, although some independent radio stations have begun operation. State media are increasingly closely-controlled by the government, and in November, six journalists were dismissed for allegedly accepting bribes to report unfavorably on election conduct. Government pressure on the independent press has taken the form of harassment through surveillance and denial of printing facilities as well as a spate of criminal libel suits in response to stories on corruption. The independent *Zambia Post* is the government's most persistent critic; its editor, Fred M'membe, faces 100 years in prison if convicted on all charges outstanding against him.

Other legislation restricts journalists' ability to report on governmental corruption and has sought to establish an official mandatory press union that would accredit all journalists, a move rejected by independent journalists.

Religious freedom is respected, and many nongovernmental organizations operate openly. Among groups engaged in human rights advocacy are the Zambian Civic Education Association and the Law Association of Zambia. The government human rights commission investigated complaints about police brutality, which are frequently made.

Severe conditions in Zambia's prisons have caused numerous prisoner deaths due to food shortages and a lack of health care. Many inmates are suspects who have been detained awaiting trial for five years or longer. Zambia's court system is overloaded, and it often takes years to bring a case to trial. Criminal cases are heard in government courts, but many civil matters are decided by customary courts whose quality and consistency vary greatly, and whose decisions are often at variance with both national law and constitutional protections. Discrimination against women is especially prevalent in such courts.

Women do not have the right to full economic participation and are not favored in rural lands allocation. Married women must have their husband's permission to obtain contraceptives. Women's rights advocates have also demanded concerted government action to curb spousal abuse and other violence against women. Societal discrimination remains a serious obstacle to realization of women's rights even when fair legislation exists.

Trade union rights are guaranteed by the Zambian constitution, and the country has one of Africa's strongest trade union movements. About two-thirds of the country's 300,000 formal sector employees are union members. The Zambia Congress of Trade Unions (ZCTU) is an umbrella for Zambia's 19 largest unions, and operates democratically without government interference. Collective bargaining rights are protected by the 1993 Industrial and Labor Relations Act (ILRA), and unions negotiate directly with employers.

Economic development is obstructed by high levels of corruption and inflation. Some economists believe distortions in the money supply are caused by large amounts of drug money circulating in the underground economy. People's ability to develop new businesses is limited by the country's overall economic weakness and a scarcity of investment capital. Restrictions on donor assistance following Chiluba's flawed re-election will also hurt investor confidence.

Zimbabwe

Polity: Dominant party
Economy: Capitalist-statist
Population: 11,515,000
PPP: $2,100
Life Expectancy: 53.4
Ethnic Groups: Shona (71 percent), Ndebele (16 percent), European, others
Capital: Harare

Political Rights: 5
Civil Liberties: 5
Status: Partly Free

Overview:
President Robert Mugabe's and his Zimbabwe African National Union-Patriotic Front (ZANU-PF) party swept to a deeply-flawed presidential election victory in March that reflected state powers of patronage and repression as the country edged closer towards becoming a de facto one-party state. ZANU-PF's firm grip on parliament and the security forces, electoral laws that strongly favor the ruling party, and decreasing opportunities for free expression further entrenched autocratic rule. Strikes by civil servants and doctors and nurses that closed down government offices and hospitals were expressions of a larger malaise that saw nearly two-thirds of Zimbabweans mired in poverty after 16 years of "majority rule."

Zimbabwe came into being in 1980 after a bloody guerrilla war against a white minority government—in what was then called Rhodesia—that had declared unilateral independence from Britain in 1965. From 1983-87, a civil war suppressed resistance by the country's largest minority group, the Ndebele, to the rule of Mugabe's majority ethnic Shona group. Severe human rights abuses accompanied the struggle, which ended with an accord that brought Ndebele leaders into the government, although several senior Ndebele figures have since died under suspicious circumstances. ZANU-PF has dominated Zimbabwe since independence, tailoring laws and constitutional amendments to cement its grip on power, including an annual state subsidy for its activities (in 1995-96 about $3.3 million)—for which no other party qualifies.

The 76-year old Reverend Ndabaningi Sithole, president of ZANU-Ndonga party and Mugabe's political rival for over three decades, holds one of only three opposition seats in the 150-member National Assembly, but is awaiting trial on charges of plotting to assassinate Mugabe in 1995. In December 1995, the alleged head of "Chimwenje," a guerrilla force reportedly aligned with ZANU-Ndonga and operating out of Mozambique, was sentenced to 15 years imprisonment as part of the Sithole plot. Chimwenje fighters are still operating along the Zimbabwe-Mozambique border, but are not a serious threat to the government.

Political Rights and Civil Liberties:
Zimbabweans' constitutional right to elect their representatives and change their government through democratic means has not been fully realized in practice. President Robert Mugabe won another six year term of office in 1996 by taking almost 93

percent of votes cast after his only two opponents announced their withdrawal from the race to protest what they called harassment and intimidation of their supporters. Less the one third of eligible voters turned out in an uncompetitive contest in which the opposition had no real chance of unseating Mugabe. The ruling ZANU-PF party significantly influences the entire electoral process and officially receives large state subsidies. Parliamentary elections and local polls in April and October 1995 entrenched ZANU-PF's de facto one-party rule. Amid widespread voter apathy and limited coverage of opposition viewpoints in the heavily state-controlled or state-influenced media, ZANU-PF swept nearly all the seats contested.

Deteriorating economic conditions and widespread perception of official corruption have brought disenchantment with the current electoral system. Voters have been intimidated in opposition strongholds. Voter registration, identification procedures and tabulation of results have sometimes been highly irregular. Twenty of the National Assembly's 150 members are presidential appointees, and ten others are traditional chiefs also beholden to the government. Only three oppositionists won seats in the 1995 parliament, and one has since been jailed. What remains has the form but little of the substance of representative government.

Election coverage in the media has been heavily slanted in favor of the government, with opposition statements either absent or censored. The small independent print media are thoroughly overshadowed by the state-run media. The government directly controls all broadcasting and several newspapers, including all dailies, and indirectly controls most others. An extended strike by 160,000 civil servants in August-September received nearly no coverage in the official media.

Self-censorship is extensive, prompted by the government's control over editorial policy and appointments. The small independent press is threatened by anti-defamation statutes and a wide-ranging Official Secrets Act. Defamation suits helped close the independent *Gazette* newspaper in 1995; a new newspaper founded by its editor, Trevor Ncube, in 1996, *The Independent,* could face similar difficulties. The Parliamentary Privileges and Immunities Act has been used to force journalists to reveal their sources to the courts and parliament.

The right of free assembly is constitutionally-guaranteed but generally respected only for groups the government deems non-political. Union demonstrations were violently dispersed in November. "The message sent by the Zimbabwean Government seems to be clear," an Amnesty International statement said "remain silent or risk arrest." Civic organizations critical of the government still operate but are closely scrutinized and sometimes harassed. Several groups focus on human rights, including the Catholic Commission for Justice and Peace, the Zimbabwe Human Rights Organization (Zimrights), the Legal Relief Fund and the Southern African Human Rights Foundation. Religious practice does not suffer from interference.

The judiciary remains largely independent, but its decisions protecting basic rights have been subverted by 13 constitutional amendments since 1980 that easily pass the ZANU-PF-controlled National Assembly. Government plans for land redistribution through seizure of white-owned properties have been challenged in the courts. Under existing laws, lands may be seized but not confiscated, and the government has lacked resources to make large-scale purchases.

Security forces, particularly the Central Intelligence Organization, often ignore basic rights regarding detention, search and seizure, and sometimes appear to act as an extension of the president's office or ZANU-PF.

Women's rights receive strong protection under law, although married women still cannot hold property jointly with their husbands. Especially in rural areas, access to education and employment for women is difficult, and few are fully aware of their legal rights or have the ability to pursue them. Domestic violence against women is common.

Private sector workers' rights are broadly protected by the Labor Relations Act (LRA), but public sector workers are barred from joining unions. Civil servants won a 20 percent pay increase only after a one-month strike. The Zimbabwe Congress of Trade Unions (ZCTU) is highly critical of the government's economic policies. The LRA also allows independent worker committees outside the unions, which labor leaders see as a government effort to dilute worker unity through parallel organizations.

Zimbabwe's economy has revived through improved crops following a long drought and expanded mining activities. A structural adjustment program fashioned by international donors and creditors has only been partially realized, and the government has yet to privatize numerous loss-making state enterprises. Real and perceived corruption is also considered a serious obstacle to business development. A typical example in 1996 was President Mugabe's sacking of the entire board of the state-owned Zimbabwe Electricity Supply Authority (ZESA), who had objected to a privatization deal with a Malaysian company imposed by the president. Western officials who criticized the deal, Mugabe added, could "go to hell." Mugabe's numerous international trips that disrupted the national airline were also criticized as a costly extravagance for a poverty-stricken country.

Armenia/Azerbaijan
Nagorno-Karabakh

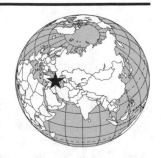

Polity: Armenian-occupied
Economy: Mixed statist
Population: 150,000
Ethnic Groups: Armenian (95 percent), Assyrian, Greek, Kurd, others

Political Rights: 6
Civil Liberties: 6
Status: Not Free

Overview:

President Robert Kocharian was re-elected in November 1996, as international mediation efforts again failed to resolve the status of the breakaway Armenian enclave within Azerbaijan. In December, the Organization for Security and Cooperation in Europe (OSCE) meeting in Lisbon endorsed Azerbaijan's territorial integrity, essentially rejecting Armenia's claim that the principle of self-determination includes its right to control 20 percent of Azeri territory, seized after eight years of bloody conflict that ended with a cease-fire in May 1994.

In 1921, Nagorno-Karabakh was transferred from Armenia and placed under Soviet Azerbaijani jurisdiction by Josef Stalin, then the commissar for nationalities. Subsequently, the Nagorno-Karabakh Autonomous Oblast (region) was created, with a narrow strip of land bordering Armenia proper. In 1930, Moscow permitted Azerbaijan to establish and resettle the border areas between Nagorno-Karabakh and Armenia.

In 1988, Azeri militia and special forces launched violent repression in response to Karabakh Armenians' call for greater autonomy. In 1991, the legislatures of Nagorno-Karabakh and Shahumyan voted for secession. Multi-party elections were held and on January 6, 1992, parliament's inaugural session adopted a declaration of independence and elected Artur Mkrtchian president. Following his assassination in April, Vice President Georgi Petrosian became president; he resigned in June 1993 and was replaced by Garen Baburian. During much of 1993-94, parliament did not meet, as many parliamentarians were fighting on the front lines. At the end of 1993, which saw military gains by the Karabakh Armenians, Azeri forces launched offensives in the northern, southern and eastern parts of the enclave.

In December 1994, the Karabakh Supreme Council—the executive body of parliament—elected Robert Kocharian, head of the state defense committee, to the post of president for a five-year term. The president appointed parliamentarian Leonard Petrossian as prime minister. In January 1995, President Kocharian created a governmental structure consisting of nine ministries, seven state departments and five state enterprises. Elections to a 33-member parliament were held in April and May, with an 80 percent voter turnout. Prior to the vote, a public organization, *Democratia*, was formed to assist all political parties, unions and other groups in preparation for the elections, which were generally free and fair.

Throughout the year, mediation efforts by the OSCE's so-called Minsk Group and by the Russians failed to yield results. The most contentious issue was the fate of the so-called Lachin corridor, which connects Nagorno-Karabakh with

Armenia and the city of Shushi. Public opinion polls indicated that 80 percent of Karabakh Armenians favored the deployment of Russian troops as peacekeepers, while 6 percent favored mediation by the OSCE.

The war left Karabakh with no functioning economy. It depends solely on aid from Armenia and from the Armenian diaspora. Armenians in the United States raised $12 million to improve the road through the Lachin corridor. The president announced a program to privatize small and medium-sized enterprises and to restructure the tax system to boost the economy.

Political Rights and Civil Liberties: Residents of Nagorno-Karabakh technically have the means to change their government democratically. Parliamentary elections in 1995 were generally free and fair. In the 1996 presidential election, Kocharian garnered 88.9 percent of the vote in defeating two challengers. Turnout was 80 percent. Prime Minister Petrosian retained his post. Government structures and a cabinet have been established. Several small political parties exist.

The undeclared state of war has impinged on rights and civil liberties. In January, parliament reaffirmed the extension of martial law in the republic through 1996, and conscription of eligible men up to age 45 continued. Border regions have been subjected to sporadic attacks. Freedom of movement has been curtailed by war, and there are restrictions on assembly and association, as well as self-censorship in the press. With Armenians making up 95 percent of the country, the Armenian Apostolic Church is the main religion, and the ethnic aspect of the war has constrained the religious rights of the few Muslims still left in the region. Although international efforts still include discussions about the return of Azeri refugees, Azeri homes and businesses have been expropriated, confiscated or destroyed, mosques have been leveled or remain abandoned, and Muslim graves have been desecrated. Armenians occupying Azeri territory have prevented the return of hundreds of thousands of internally-displaced Azeris.

China
Tibet

Polity: Communist one-party
Economy: Statist
Population: 4,590,000
Ethnic Groups: Tibetan, Han Chinese

Political Rights: 7
Civil Liberties: 7
Status: Not Free

Overview: In 1996 authorities continued their most severe crackdown on monasticism in Tibet since a martial law period in 1989 in an effort to limit the power of lamas and secular figures who openly support the Dalai Lama.

Prior to the Chinese invasion in 1949 Tibet had been a sovereign state for the better part of 2,000 years, coming under modest foreign influence only during brief periods in the 13th and 18th centuries. In late 1949 China invaded Tibet with 100,000 troops, and in 1951 formally annexed the country.

In 1959 popular uprisings against Chinese rule culminated in mass pro-independence demonstrations in Lhasa, the capital, in March. In the next several months China crushed the uprisings, killing an estimated 87,000 Tibetans in the Lhasa region alone. The Tibetan spiritual and temporal leader, the fourteenth Dalai Lama, Tenzin Gyatso, fled to Dharamsala, India, with 80,000 supporters.

In 1960 the International Commission of Jurists called the Chinese occupation genocidal, and ruled that prior to the 1949 invasion Tibet had possessed all the attributes of statehood as defined under international law. In 1965 China created the Tibet Autonomous Region out of an area containing less than half the territory of pre-invasion Tibet. The rest of Tibet had, since 1950, been incorporated into four southwestern Chinese provinces. By the late 1970s more than one million Tibetans had died as a result of the occupation, and all but eleven of 6,200 monasteries had been destroyed.

Between 1987 and 1990 Chinese soldiers forcibly broke up peaceful demonstrations throughout Tibet, killing hundreds and arresting thousands more. Since 1992 Beijing has expanded Tibet's road and air links with China, further facilitating the mass settlement of Han Chinese into Tibet.

In May 1995 the Dalai Lama identified six-year-old Gedhun Choekyi Nyima as the eleventh reincarnation of the Panchen Lama, Tibetan Buddhism's second most important religious figure. China rejected the Dalai Lama's authority and in late November organized a ceremony in Lhasa "selecting" Gyaincain Norbu, another six-year-old, as the Panchen Lama.

In 1996 there were at least four bombings in Lhasa and the northern village of Tsenden of official Chinese buildings, Chinese-owned shops and the residence of a Chinese sympathizer.

Political Rights and Civil Liberties: Tibetans cannot change their government democratically. China appoints compliant ethnic Tibetan officials to some key government posts to provide a veneer of self-rule but in reality controls all major policy decisions and sharply restricts basic rights and liberties.

A March 1996 report by the London-based Tibet Information Network (TIN) and Human Rights Watch said that arrests of political dissidents and torture in prisons had risen since July 1994, when Chinese officials held a high-level Third Work Forum on Tibet in Beijing and decided to tighten their political control over the region. The report listed 610 known Tibetan political prisoners as of January 1996 held for peacefully expressing political views or displaying symbols of Tibetan independence or cultural identity. More than half are monks and nuns. In December 1996 a court sentenced Ngawang Choepel, a Tibetan music expert who was arrested in August 1995 while conducting research on a Fulbright scholarship, to eighteen years in prison for alleged espionage.

An April 1996 report by the U.S.-based International Campaign for Tibet said that since July 1994, authorities have increased their monitoring of monasteries and other interference in Tibetan religious affairs. In March 1995 authorities placed a near total moratorium on the building of new monasteries and nunneries, placed stricter limits on the number of monks and nuns permitted in monasteries and nunneries, and limited the total number of clerics permitted in Tibet. Authorities have closed several monasteries and nunneries on political grounds. Religious figures are also banned from giving large public teachings and some politically active monks face internal travel restrictions.

In 1996 authorities purged hundreds of monks suspected of pro-Dalai Lama sympathies at three main monasteries and several smaller ones as part of a "patriotic re-education campaign." In a development reminiscent of the Cultural Revolution, in November TIN reported that authorities were forcing monks at key monasteries to attend political indoctrination sessions and take examinations on their political views.

In April 1996 China banned all photographs of the Dalai Lama from monasteries and residences, extending a 1994 ban on the sale of the Dalai Lama's photograph and on displaying his photograph in state offices. In May and June authorities detained at least ninety monks at the Ganden monastery east of Lhasa for protesting the ban; in a May incident security forces shot at least three monks, reportedly killing one. The official Radio Tibet reported that authorities were conducting house-to-house searches for photos.

The Chinese government's Sinification policy includes granting economic incentives and initiating development projects to lure ethnic Han Chinese into migrating to Tibet. This has altered the demographic composition of the region, displaced Tibetan businesses and reduced employment opportunities for Tibetans, and threatens to further marginalize Tibetan cultural identity.

China's attempts to indoctrinate Tibetan primary and middle school students include daily ceremonies which raise the Chinese flag and singing of the Chinese national anthem. Although China's draconian family planning policy ostensibly does not extend to Tibetans and other minorities, sources say the one-child rule is enforced in Tibet.

India
Kashmir

Polity: Indian-administered
Economy: Capitalist-statist
Population: 7,719,000
Ethnic Groups: Muslim majority, Hindu minority

Political Rights: 7
Civil Liberties: 7
Status: Not Free

Overview: The September 1996 state elections in Kashmir, the first since 1987, nominally ended federal rule but were marred by irregularities and were neither free nor fair.

Following the partition of India in 1947 the ruler of Kashmir, Maharajah Hari Singh attempted to preserve the predominantly Muslim, princely state's independence. Pakistani-backed tribesmen launched a revolt. The maharajah ceded control of the territory to India in return for protection and a guarantee of autonomy. Indian Premier Jawaharlal Nehru appointed Sheik Abdullah of the National Conference, a secular, left-wing party, as head of the territorial government. Nehru also promised a referendum on self-determination.

Following months of sectarian strife, a U.N. brokered cease-fire took effect in 1949. Pakistan retained control of the western third of Kashmir (today known as Azad [Free] Kashmir), while India maintained most of Kashmir and predominately Hindu Jammu, another ex-princely state.

Both India and Pakistan claim the predominantly Muslim Valley of Kashmir, which is in the area under Indian control.

Article 370 of India's 1950 constitution granted Kashmir substantial autonomy, although in practice this has been eroded. A 1952 accord gave Kashmir power over all areas except defense, foreign affairs and communications. In 1953, Nehru dismissed Abdullah's government, and in 1957, New Delhi formally annexed its territories as the state of Jammu and Kashmir, India's only Muslim majority state. The powers granted in the 1952 accord have slowly diminished.

In 1959 China occupied a portion of Kashmir, which it continues to hold. In 1965, and from 1971-72, India and Pakistan again fought in the territory.

During the 1960s and 1970s India continued to try and consolidate political control over Kashmir. In 1987 the Indian government rigged elections that brought a pro-Delhi coalition led by Sheik Abdullah's son, Farooq Abdullah, to power.

The rigged elections increased support for militant groups, divided between those seeking independence and those supporting incorporation into Pakistan and armed by Islamabad. The militants increased their attacks in 1989, leading to a major crackdown by Indian security forces. In 1990 New Delhi placed the state under federal rule.

Violence continued throughout the mid-1990s. On May 11, 1995 a two month stand off between several thousand Indian troops and 150 militants holed up in a fifteenth century mausoleum in the town of Charar-i-Sharief ended after a fire destroyed the shrine and most of the houses. Both sides accused the other of starting the blaze, and the increasingly unstable situation caused India to cancel state elections planned for July.

New Delhi allowed the state to participate in the April-May 1996 national elections. Muslim separatist groups called for a boycott in Kashmir Valley constituencies and threatened violence. The elections went off peacefully, but soldiers coerced many voters into participating.

The new United Front government in New Delhi subsequently called state elections over four dates in September. Most pro-Pakistan and pro-independence groups again called for a boycott. Militants vowed to kill candidates as well as transport operators not observing the strike. The National Conference contested the vote for the 87-seat assembly, the only Kashmir based party to do so, and took a majority of the seats. Soldiers and state-backed militants again coerced voter into participating. Farooq Abdullah returned as chief minister and pledged to recapture some of the guarantees of autonomy pledged in the 1952 agreement

Political Rights and Civil Liberties: India has never held a referendum on Kashmiri self-determination as called for in a 1948 United Nations resolution. Violence by militants and security forces has killed 20,000 people since the insurgency began.

Separatists urging a boycott of the 1996 national and state elections carried out terrorist attacks against candidates, campaign workers and other civilians, in some cases targeting Hindus. Soldiers and state-backed militias coerced Kashmiris into voting. Prior to the national elections state authorities imposed a ban on press coverage considered "prejudicial to the unity and integrity of the state and country" in an apparent effort to preclude articles calling for a boycott of the vote. Prior to and during the state elections authorities arrested leaders of the All Party Hurriyat Conference, a coalition of parties advocating a boycott. At least 20 people were killed in violence related to the state vote.

The 300,000 Indian soldiers, paramilitary troops and police in the territory carry out arbitrary arrests, detentions and torture against civilians and suspected militants, disappearances and reprisal killings of civilians, and disappearances and extrajudicial executions of suspected militants. Security forces are also responsible for the rape of Kashmiri women. In recent years soldiers have indiscriminately fired into crowds on several occasions, killing scores of civilians. Most security personnel responsible for abuses are either not prosecuted or are prosecuted on lesser charges, creating a climate of impunity.

The 1990 Jammu and Kashmir Disturbed Areas Act and the Armed Forces (Jammu and Kashmir) Special Powers Act allow authorities to search homes and arrest suspects without a warrant. Indian troops cordon off entire neighborhoods and conduct house-to-house inspections.

Kashmiri militants are responsible for grave human rights violations including the deaths of public employees, suspected informers, members of rival factions and civilians, often through indiscriminate bomb attacks in Jammu, Srinagar and other towns. At least 17 local legislators have been killed since 1989. Separatists also kidnap government officials, politicians and businessmen. The Al-Faran group kidnapped four foreigners in July 1995; their fate is unknown.

Since 1995 authorities have persuaded many ex-separatist militants to join irregular militias, which are armed by the government, operate without official accountability and carry out counterinsurgency operations against pro-Pakistani groups. A May Human Rights Watch report cited widespread abuses by these militias, known locally as "renegades," including attacks on journalists, human rights activists and medical workers. Security forces sometimes order the release of state-backed militants arrested by police.

The judiciary barely functions. Separatists routinely threaten judges, witnesses and the families of defendants. In June 1995 the Indian government agreed to allow the International Committee of the Red Cross (ICRC) to visit all persons arrested, detained or imprisoned in connection with the insurgency. In June 1996 the ICRC submitted a confidential report to authorities based on 36 visits to 27 places of detention.

Security forces and militants routinely harass local human rights activists, and have killed several since 1989. On March 27, 1996, villagers discovered the body of Jalil Andrabi, the chairman of the Kashmir Commission of Jurists. He reportedly had been detained by soldiers earlier that month.

India's 1971 Newspapers Incitements to Offence Act, which is only in effect in Jammu and Kashmir, allows a district magistrate to censor articles that could allegedly provoke criminal acts or other disturbances. In recent years the authorities have detained several journalists for reporting on militant groups. Six journalists have been killed since 1989. Sheik Ghulam Rasool Azad, an editor of two newspapers, was arrested in March 1996 and found floating in a river in April. Militants frequently harass or threaten journalists and coerce newspapers into suspending publishing. Police often forcibly break up demonstrations. Since 1990 more than 250,000 Hindu Kashmiris have fled the Kashmir valley. Many reported that militants had robbed families and raped women.

Indonesia
East Timor

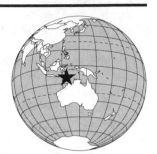

Polity: Dominant party (military-dominated)
Economy: Capitalist-statist
Population: 778,000
Ethnic Groups: Timorese, Javanese, others

Political Rights: 7
Civil Liberties: 7
Status: Not Free

Overview: The Portuguese arrived in Timor around 1520, and in the nineteenth and early twentieth centuries took formal control of the eastern half of the island. In 1974 Portugal agreed to hold a referendum on self-determination in 1975. In 1975 the pro-independence, leftist Revolutionary Front for an Independent East Timor (Fretelin) declared an independent republic. Indonesia invaded on December 7, and formally annexed East Timor in 1976 as the country's twenty-seventh province. By 1979 Indonesian soldiers had killed up to 200,000 Timorese. Skirmishes between Indonesian forces and Fretelin continued throughout the 1980s. Today Fretelin has fewer than 200 poorly-equipped fighters.

On November 12, 1991 Indonesian soldiers in the territorial capital of Dili fired on thousands of Timorese who were peacefully marching to the burial site of an independence supporter killed by security forces in October. Between 150 and 270 civilians were killed.

In a series of courts-martial in 1992, four officers and six enlisted men, charged only with assault or disobeying orders during the Dili massacre, received light terms ranging from eight to eighteen months. In separate proceedings eighteen East Timorese received terms ranging from six months to life imprisonment for alleged anti-government activities. In November Indonesian soldiers captured Fretelin leader Jose "Xanana" Gusmao. In May 1993 a court sentenced Gusmao to life imprisonment, subsequently reduced to twenty years, in a sham trial.

The October award of the Nobel Peace prize to East Timor Roman Catholic Bishop Carlos Felipe Ximenes Belo and Jose Ramos Horta, a leading exiled East Timorese independence activist, brought renewed international attention to official human rights violations in the territory.

Political Rights and Civil Liberties: The United Nations does not recognize Indonesia's 1976 annexation of East Timor. A referendum on self-determination, promised by Portugal in 1974, has never been held.

Freedoms of speech, press, assembly and association continue to be heavily restricted.

In 1996 security forces killed at least three civilians and continued to arbitrarily arrest, detain and torture civilians. Police clashed violently with demonstrators on several occasions. Authorities tolerate some non-violent assemblies but forcibly break up others, particularly those explicitly advocating East Timorese independence or criticizing the Indonesian government. In recent years courts have imprisoned several East Timorese for holding pro-independence demonstrations.

Authorities use state-organized youth gangs to harass and intimidate the local population. Fretelin guerrillas are responsible for killings and other abuses against migrants from other islands and pro-government Timorese.

The judiciary is not independent. Trials of political dissidents lack procedural safeguards. The trial of Jose "Xanana" Gusmao (see Overview) fell short of international standards in several respects. The court refused to allow Gusmao to choose his own attorney and instead appointed a defense attorney close to police and prosecutors; several witnesses against Gusmao were themselves detainees, raising the possibility they had been coerced; and the court refused to allow Gusmao to read most of his defense statement. Soldiers and police are generally not prosecuted for rights violations against civilians, and the few that have been tried and convicted have received relatively lenient sentences.

The government has closed schools that refuse to use the official Bahasa Indonesia as their primary language.

The Indonesian government's transmigration program, which uses financial inducements to encourage settlers from Sulawesi and other islands to migrate to East Timor, has slowed in recent years. However, other settlers continue to migrate on their own. The predominantly Muslim migrants' influence in the local economy has led to several violent conflicts, which often took on religious overtones in this predominantly Roman Catholic society.

Authorities restrict access by foreign journalists and human rights nongovernmental organizations to East Timor.

West Papua (Irian Jaya)

Polity: Dominant party **Political Rights:** 7
(military-dominated) **Civil Liberties:** 7
Economy: Capitalist- **Status:** Not Free
statist
Population: 1,700,000
Ethnic Groups: Mainly Papuan

Overview: By 1848 the Dutch controlled the entire western half of the island of New Guinea. In 1963 Indonesia assumed administrative responsibility for the territory under a United Nations agreement mandating that a referendum on self-determination be held by 1969.

In the mid-1960s the guerrilla Free Papua Movement (OPM) began fighting for independence. Rather than hold a popular referendum, in the summer of 1969 Indonesia convened eight hand-picked regional councils for a sham "Act of Free Choice." The predominantly Melanesian population seemed to favor independence, but the councils voted unanimously for annexation by Indonesia. The Indonesian military had a heavy presence in the territory, and the U.N. special observer reported that "the administration exercised at all times a tight political control over the population." Nevertheless, the U.N. accepted the referendum. In 1973 Indonesia renamed the land known locally as West Papua as Irian Jaya.

In 1984 an army offensive against the OPM sent hundreds of villagers fleeing into neighboring Papua New Guinea, and security forces murdered prominent intellectual Arnold Ap. In 1989 the army conducted another series of anti-OPM offensives.

In recent years human rights violations have been linked to the mining operations, including the giant Grasberg mine in the central highlands, of the local subsidiary of the U.S.-based Freeport McMoRan multinational. In April 1995 the Australian Council for Overseas Aid (ACOA) reported that several civilians had been killed by soldiers or had disappeared since the November 1994 killing of a Freeport employee by suspected OPM guerrillas. The ACOA accused Freeport of having abetted several killings through the army's use of the company's vehicles and facilities. In August the Roman Catholic Church of Jayapura made similar charges. In September Indonesia's official National Commission on Human Rights confirmed that the army had killed sixteen civilians and caused four "disappearances" in the area since October 1994.

In October 1995 the U.S. Overseas Private Investment Corporation canceled Freeport's $100 million political insurance risk policy, citing environmental concerns at Grasberg including potentially toxic mining tailings polluting the Aiwa River system. The local population receives no direct compensation from the mining operations, and the few homes and schools Freeport has built for the villagers are shoddy.

Local residents rioted in Timika and Tembagapura after a man was injured by a vehicle driven by a Freeport employee. March 18 and 19 rioting broke out in the territorial capital of Jayapura after the body of Thomas Wanggai, an independence activist, was returned for burial following his death in prison in Jakarta, apparently of natural causes. Police detained 130 people following the Jayapura rioting, most of whom were reportedly mistreated. In June the local Amungme and Komoro tribal leaderships rejected Freeport's plan to set up a trust fund for community works on the grounds that the money would be disbursed through the government. Rebels from the OPM and other insurgent groups took civilian hostages on four separate occasions in 1996, and killed several of their captives.

Political Rights and Civil Liberties: West Papuans lack the right to self-determination. The Indonesian government severely restricts freedoms of speech, press, assembly and association in the territory. Several OPM guerrillas and suspected supporters are incarcerated under Indonesia's harsh anti-subversion laws.

In September 1995 Indonesia's official National Commission on Human Rights accused the Indonesian military of violations in the territory including extrajudicial killings, torture, arbitrary arrest and detentions, "disappearances," widespread surveillance of the local population and destruction of property. Many of the violations occurred in the Timika district, where Freeport's Grasberg Mine is located (see Overview). The ACOA and the Roman Catholic Church of Jayapura have made similar accusations. The ACOA also reports that the army has burned numerous homes near Freeport's mines.

In 1996 fewer reports were made of abuses by security forces. In February a military court sentenced four soldiers to up to three years imprisonment for the deaths of three civilians in spring 1995. However no prosecutions have taken place for other killings by security forces in the 1994-95 period. According to the *Far Eastern Economic Review*, Freeport Indonesia will pay for barracks and other facilities for a 2,000 strong Indonesian military force that will handle security at the Grasberg mine.

Since the 1970s the Indonesian government has resettled more than 170,000 residents of Java and other overcrowded parts of the archipelago into West Papua under a controversial "transmigration" program. Irianese say the migrants have taken many of their jobs and seized indigenous lands. Although the transmigration program has slowed in recent years, in 1996 several violent clashes erupted between migrants and indigenous groups. According to Human Rights Watch/Asia, some logging companies have placed Irianese workers in a condition of de facto bonded servitude through debts allegedly run up at company stores. The government limits access to the territory for foreign journalists and restricts internal travel.

Iraq
Kurdistan

Polity: Dual leadership
Economy: Capitalist-
statist
Population: 4,000,000
Ethnic Groups: Kurdish majority

Political Rights: 6*
Civil Liberties: 6*
Status: Not Free

Ratings Change: Kurdistan's political rights and civil liberties ratings changed from 4 to 6 because rival factions broke the 1995 cease-fire.

Overview:

In August 1996 Kurdish rival factions broke the 1995 cease-fire drawing Iraqi forces into the fighting. Battles continued through the latter half of 1996 with the Kurdistan Democratic Party (KDP) and Patriotic Union of Kurdistan (PUK) vying for control over territories in northern Iraq.

In April 1991, the United States, Britain, France and Turkey established, and continue to maintain, a secure region with a U.S. enforced no-fly zone north of the 36th parallel in Iraq.

In May 1992, the inconclusive presidential elections resulted in a power-sharing deal between Massoud Barzani of the KDP and PDK leader Jalal Talabani. They also agreed to split the 100 at-large parliamentary seats (five are reserved for Christians) evenly and formed a coalition government. The position of president has yet to be filled. This has caused conflict over who should assume certain duties, such as certifying a death-penalty verdict.

No elections have taken place since 1992. Disputes over land and revenue issues as well as personal rivalry between Barzani and Talabani eventually led to a full scale civil war in late 1994. Since then, thousands of people have died in fighting between the two groups' *peshmerga* guerrillas (literally "those who face death"). Armed fighting among rival factions has replaced the electoral process.

Fighting resumed in August 1996 primarily over the PUK's demand for a share of the customs duties, as much as $250,000 per day, levied by the KDP on some 600 trucks crossing daily in and out of Turkey. On August 30, on the invitation of KDP leader Massoud Barzani, Iraqi forces entered the region and assisted in pushing PUK forces out of Kurdistan's capital, Arbil, occupying the city for three days. In October fierce fighting enabled the PUK to re-establish control over its previously held territory, save Arbil. In October the KDP and PUK signed a peace agreement that fell short of planning for new parliamentary elections, establishing a coalition government or unifying the region's financial revenues.

Political Rights and Civil Liberties:

The Kurdish people cannot elect their government democratically. Though relatively free and fair parliamentary elections were held in 1992, the post of president was never filled and no future elections are in sight.

The judiciary is not independent. The two leading political parties have run separate prisons and detention centers in which human rights violations have occurred. The death penalty is used for several crimes. Though no recent reports have been made of the death sentence being carried out, at least three people have been executed in an inhumane manner during the Kurdish administration of northern Iraq, and dozens of others are on death row.

In January 1995, Amnesty International accused the joint PUK-KDP administration of arbitrary detentions, torture of prisoners, summary trials and extra judicial executions of unarmed POWs, political opponents and demonstrators. It accused the fundamentalist Islamic Movement of similar violations.

The Islamic Movement (IMIK) has maintained independent control of some territory within Kurdistan. IMIK operates independent legal and judiciary systems, along with independent education, health and social services.

Iraqi laws passed prior to November 1991 remain in effect in Kurdistan, except for those judged by the National Assembly to be "against Kurdish interests."

The current political chaos has permitted the Turkish Kurdish Workers' Party (PKK) to further its goal of establishing a separate Kurdish homeland in Turkey by using Iraqi Kurdistan as a base from which to launch attacks on Turkey. The Turkish army launched operations in northern Iraq in an attempt to crush the PKK bases in 1992, 1995 and 1996. Some 13,000 Kurds who fled southeastern Turkey in 1994 remain in Kurdistan.

Observers report a generally open climate for dialogue on political issues. Numerous newspapers are available. The two major parties run television stations and news coverage is biased. Smaller parties operate radio stations. Traditional practices curtail the role of women in politics, education and the private sector. Religious groups practice relatively freely.

The Kurdistan Human Rights Organization operates openly despite repeated harassment, yet it is underfunded and understaffed. Several of its members have fled Kurdistan following personal threats. Each political party established its own human rights committees in the wake of human rights abuses in 1994. Each group monitors abuses against its own party members. Outside human rights organizations are not allowed to enter freely into Kurdistan.

Israel
Israeli-Administered Territories[a] & Palestinian Authority-Administered Territories [b]

Polity: Military and PLO administered
Economy: Capitalist
Population: 2,184,000
Ethnic Groups: Palestinian, Jewish

Political Rights: 6 [a]
Civil Liberties: 5 [a]
Status: Not Free

Political Rights: 5 [b]
Civil Liberties: 6 [b]
Status: Not Free

Overview: Palestinian self-rule in the West Bank and Gaza Strip expanded in January 1996 with elections for a new Legislative Council and for the head of the Council's executive authority. During the year the Palestinian authorities cracked down on the independent media and committed systematic human rights abuses.

The West Bank, Gaza Strip and East Jerusalem were part of the British Mandate between 1920-48. In 1948 Jordan seized East Jerusalem and the West Bank, while Egypt took control of Gaza. During the 1967 Six Day War Israel took the West Bank, Gaza Strip, East Jerusalem and the Golan Heights, which Syria had used to shell towns in northern Israel. Israel annexed East Jerusalem in 1967 and the Golan Heights in 1981.

In December 1987 Palestinians living in the West Bank and Gaza began attacks on mostly military targets to protest against Israeli rule in what became known as the *intifada* (uprising). A series of secret negotiations between Israel and the PLO yielded an agreement in August 1993 for a five-year interim period of Palestinian autonomy in the territories, beginning with the Gaza Strip and the West Bank town of Jericho.

By the end of 1994 Israel had transferred authority over education, health and other local services in the West Bank and Gaza to a new Palestinian Authority (PA), headed by Palestine Liberation Organization (PLO) chairman Yasir Arafat. A September 1995 agreement provided for Palestinian self-rule in most Palestinian population centers in the West Bank; and for a redeployment by March 1996 of Israeli troops in Hebron, a West Bank town with Jewish and Muslim holy sites; and a phased withdrawal of Israeli troops from most areas of the West Bank by September 1997. The remainder of the West Bank is to stay under Israeli army control pending further negotiations, although the PA will share responsibility for civil functions.

In the January 20, 1996, elections independents won 35 of the 88 Legislative Council seats, with Arafat's Fatah movement taking most of the remainder. In balloting for the head of the Council's executive authority Arafat won 88 percent of the vote against Samiha Khalil, a veteran social activist.

Between February 25 and March 4, terrorist attacks in Israel killed 62 people. The May 1996 Israeli elections brought a conservative coalition to power led by the Likud bloc and headed by prime minister Benjamin Netanyahu. Netanyahu, as did his predecessor, Shimon Peres, postponed the Hebron redeployment, citing the security needs of Jewish residents. The new premier also allowed a limited expansion of Jewish settlements in the territories.

In September, after Israel opened a second entrance to an ancient tunnel in Jerusalem's Old Quarter, the PA called for demonstrations. Ensuing clashes between Israeli and Palestinian security forces killed 58 Palestinians (including 11 security officers) and 16 Israeli soldiers.

Political Rights and Civil Liberties:

The January 1996 executive and legislative elections expanded Palestinian self-rule. Observers rated the January 1996 elections as reasonably free but not entirely fair. Arafat's Fatah movement reportedly pressured some independents to withdraw from legislative races, while the PA continued to harass the media and opposition figures. Arafat dominates government affairs and policymaking. Nevertheless, the Legislative Council does discuss a wide range of issues.

Under Israeli-Palestinian accords three separate jurisdictional delineations exist. In Zone A the PA has control over civil affairs and security; in Zone B the PA has jurisdiction over civil affairs and shares security responsibilities with Israel; in Zone C (the Israeli-Administered Territories in this report), which includes Jewish settlements, Israel shares responsibility for civil functions with the PA and is responsible for security.

An August 1996 Amnesty International report concluded that in areas under PA control there is a "climate of fear where gross human rights abuses are becoming systematic." During the year the Palestinian authorities arrested hundreds of Islamic militants, many for their association with the fundamentalist Hamas group rather than for specific acts. The arrests frequently came after terrorist attacks in Israel or on Jewish targets in the territories. Palestinian police also carried out arbitrary arrests of ordinary civilians. Prison conditions fall far short of international norms. Police routinely torture detainees and prisoners. At least four Palestinians died in Palestinian police custody. In three of the four cases courts convicted police in the deaths, although rights groups criticized some trials as unfair. Palestinian security forces used excessive force in breaking up demonstrations.

The PA judiciary, consisting of criminal, civil and state security courts, is not independent, and due process safeguards are often ignored. Judges lack proper training. The state security courts are generally used to try suspected Islamic militants. Trials are conducted in secret, often on short notice, and generally last only a few hours. There is no right of appeal, although Arafat can repeal verdicts.

In Israeli-controlled areas Israeli military courts try Palestinians accused of security offenses, and trials lack some procedural safeguards. The 150,000 Jewish settlers living in the West Bank and Gaza Strip are subject to Israeli law in Israeli courts.

Israeli district military commanders can order detention without charge or trial for up to 12 months, and such orders are renewable. Since an October 1994 terrorist attack in Tel Aviv that killed 22 Israelis, the Israeli government has empowered the head of Shin Bet, the Israeli intelligence service, to authorize investigators to use some physical force when interrogating suspects who might provide information about imminent terrorist attacks against Israelis. The April 1995 death of a suspected Islamic militant in Israeli custody highlighted the practice of violently shaking down suspects to extract confessions. A videotape in November 1996 showed Israeli security officers beating several Palestinian workers at a checkpoint in what local human rights say is a fairly routine practice. In 1996 Israeli military authorities destroyed several homes of suicide bombers or terrorist suspects.

In addition to the bombings in February and March, Palestinian militants carried out several smaller terrorist attacks against Israelis during the year. Israeli settlers harassed, and were responsible for the deaths of, several Palestinians.

During the year Palestinian authorities harassed and arrested journalists, pressured newspapers not to run certain stories and suspended newspapers on several occasions. A 1995 PA press law broadly bars the publication of "secret information" on Palestinian security forces or news that would harm "national unity" or incite violence. The press law also empowers the authorities to suspend a publication and fine and jail journalists. Palestinian authorities reportedly pressure the several small, private Palestinian radio and television stations to provide more favorable coverage of Arafat and the PA. Official Palestinian radio and television services function as Arafat's propaganda outlets.

Newspapers and magazines are still subject to Israeli military censorship on security matters, although such controls have eased since 1993. Israeli authorities prohibit expressions of support for Hamas and other extremist Islamist groups that call for Israel's destruction, but generally no longer enforce prohibitions on Palestinian nationalist symbols.

In recent years Israeli military authorities have applied an often prolonged policy of closure of the West Bank and Gaza Strip, sharply restricting entry into Israel from these areas, following Palestinian terrorist attacks. In spring 1996, following terrorist bombings that killed 58 Israelis, and again following the clashes between Israeli and Palestinian security forces in September, authorities imposed an "internal closure" preventing travel between West Bank towns, lasting about two weeks in each case. The policy has caused serious economic hardship.

Several Palestinian and Israeli human rights groups operate openly but face harassment. Palestinian women face considerable social discrimination, and violence against women is a problem. The September 1995 accords placed labor affairs in the West Bank under PA control, and new labor codes are being drafted.

Moldova
Transdniester

Polity: Presidential-parliamentary
Economy: Mixed-statist
Population: 700,000
Ethnic Groups: Ukrainian, Russian (60 percent);
Moldovan-Romanian (40 percent)

Political Rights: 6
Civil Liberties: 6
Status: Not Free

Overview: The president of the self-proclaimed Transdniester republic in Moldova, Igor Smirnov, was re-elected for another
five-year term in December 1996. Meanwhile, newly elected
Moldovan President Petru Lucinschi insisted that the election in the breakaway
region "cannot have any legal effect" until the status of the republic is negotiated.

In 1990, Slavs in the Transdniester region, a sliver of land that was part of
Ukraine until 1940 and joined to Moldova after Soviet annexation, proclaimed the
Dneister Moldovan Republic (DMR). Fighting in Transdniester, where local Slavs
were supported by Russian Cossacks, mercenaries and elements of Russia's 14th
Army, ended with a ceasefire in mid-1992. In 1994, Russia and Moldova agreed to
a three-year timetable for withdrawing the 14th Army. In March 1995 local
elections, 91 percent of Transdniester voters approved a referendum calling for the
approximately 8,000-man 14th Army to stay in Moldova. Russia, however, told the
Organization on Security and Cooperation in Europe (OSCE) that it planned to
honor its commitment to a three-year withdrawal process, regardless of the
referendum.

In 1996, despite mediation efforts by the OSCE, Russia and Ukraine,
Moldova and Transdniester did not sign a draft memorandum on normalizing
relations. While accepting Transdniester's autonomy, Moldovan officials insisted
in the sovereignty, territorial integrity and preservation of Moldova's borders, as
well as a single constitution, currency, foreign policy, army and security agency.
Leaders in Tiraspol, Transdniester's capital, insisted on a division of authority
between the region and Moldova. In November, the Russian Duma passed a
resolution of cooperation with Transdniester, leading to protests from Moldovan
leaders that Moscow was interfering in the internal affairs of Moldova.

**Political Rights
and Civil Liberties:**
Residents of Transdniester can elect their leaders democratically, and the 1996 presidential elections were relatively competitive. Incumbent Igor Smirnov defeated
challenger Vladimir Malakhov, a businessman, 72 percent to 20 percent. Turnout
was 57 percent, the lowest for the republic since its proclamation of sovereignty in
September 1990. In 1994, local authorities forbade residents from voting in
Moldova's parliamentary elections.

The media is pro-government and the free press is muzzled. Some 40
percent of Transdniester's 700,000 people who are not Russian or Ukrainian face
repression and have been prevented from voting in Moldova's elections. In 1995
parliamentary elections for the 67-seat bicameral legislature, parties coalesced

around the left-wing Bloc of Patriotic Forces and the moderate Movement for the Development of Dniester, which united centrist politicians and industrial bosses and backed the ruling Labor Movement of Dniester. Ballots did not refer to party affiliations.

The local judiciary is based on the Soviet-era model and is not independent. Unions are remnants of Soviet-era labor organizations. The United Council of Labor Collectives is influential in the government. Religious rights are generally respected, but freedom of movement and assembly have been circumscribed. Women nominally have the same rights as men, but are underrepresented in leadership positions in government and business.

Morocco
Western Sahara

Polity: Appointed governors
Economy: Capitalist
Population: 212,000
Ethnic Groups: Arab, Sahrawi

Political Rights: 7
Civil Liberties: 6
Status: Not Free

Overview: The mandate of the U.N. monitoring force (Minurso) to supervise a referendum on the future of the disputed and sparsely-populated territory of Western Sahara was extended for a further six months in November, but its now eight-year old mission seemed no closer to completion. Moroccan obstruction continued to block preparation for a vote on nationhood or integration into Morocco. The plan's failure to date raises fears of a return to the bloody guerrilla war that ravaged the territory from 1976 until a 1991 cease-fire. Yet direct talks between top Moroccan officials led by Crown Prince Sidi Mohamed, and Interior Minister Driss Basri and the Popular Front for the Liberation of Saguia el-Hamra and Rio de Oro (Polisario) in October, and the release of 66 Polisario prisoners, raised hopes that a negotiated solution to the long stalemate could still be achieved.

The coastal strip of the Western Sahara was claimed by Spain in 1888. The nomadic residents of the "Spanish Sahara" who ranged over its vast desert interior were only gradually subdued over the next five decades. Both Morocco and Mauritania laid claim to parts of the region after achieving their own independence from French rule in 1956 and 1960 respectively. When Spain withdrew from the colony in early 1976, local Sahrawis in the Polisario Front proclaimed the Saharan Arab Democratic Republic and launched a war against Morocco and Mauritania, with support and sanctuary provided by neighboring Algeria.

A 1975 opinion by the International Court of Justice ruled against Morocco. In 1979, Mauritania abandoned the costly conflict, leaving Morocco its third of the disputed territory. Moroccan security forces responded to Polisario's hit-and-run attacks with ferocity and quelled political opposition through arbitrary detention, torture and extra judicial killings. In 1984, the Organization of African

Unity (OAU) recognized the Saharan Arab Democratic Republic, provoking Morocco's withdrawal from the OAU.

The referendum process ground to a halt in 1995 over its threshold question: Who is a citizen of Western Sahara? Current voter registration procedures demand approval of two traditional sheiks for citizens to be recognized. Polisario argues that Morocco is registering tens of thousands non-Sahrawis while blocking Sahrawis. The U.N. describes Moroccan and Polisario positions as "irreconcilable" and has cut its presence by more than two-thirds, leaving less than 200 U.N. personnel in the territory.

Polisario leaders have warned that abandonment of a free and fair referendum process will lead to renewal of the war, including urban attacks in Morocco.

Political Rights and Civil Liberties: **S**ahrawis do not have the right to elect their own government. Since Spain's withdrawal, the territory has been under military occupation. Ten seats in the Moroccan parliament are reserved for Western Sahara residents, but integration into Morocco is rejected by Polisario. Moroccan non-cooperation has caused the U.N.-planned referendum on the territory's future to be repeatedly postponed, and it may never be held.

Civil liberties in the 85 percent of Western Sahara controlled by Morocco are restricted, and widespread human rights abuses have been reported. Moroccan immigrants face the same mix of authoritarianism and limited liberalization seen in Morocco itself. Several hundred Sahrawis detained by Moroccan security forces were released in 1994, but several hundred remain in captivity. Many may have been murdered, and sporadic arrests continue. Reports have been made of torture and other abuses by Polisario forces, but lack of access to areas they control makes verification difficult. Polisario released nearly 200 Moroccan prisoners-of-war in 1995, but reportedly still holds several hundred others.

Portugal
Macao

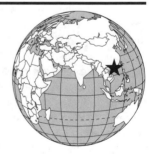

Polity: Appointed governor and partially elected legislature
Political Rights: 6
Civil Liberties: 4
Status: Partly Free
Economy: Capitalist-statist
Population: 447,000
Ethnic Groups: Chinese, Macanese, Portuguese

Overview: **P**ortugal established Macao in 1557. Consisting of a peninsula and two islands at the mouth of the Canton River, it is an entreport for trade with China and a gambling mecca. The 1976 Organic Statute serves as the territory's constitution. It vests executive powers in a governor appointed by the Portuguese president, and grants legislative powers to both the Portuguese government and Macao's Legislative Assembly. The Assembly has eight directly-elected members, eight named by businesses and other interest groups, and seven appointed by the governor.

The 1987 Sino-Portuguese Joint Declaration calls for China to assume sovereignty over Macao on December 20, 1999, with the enclave maintaining its legal system and capitalist economy for 50 years. In 1990 governor Carlos Melancia resigned over bribery charges. The current governor, General Vasco Rocha Viera, took office in 1991.

In the 1992 legislative elections pro-Beijing candidates swept all eight of the seats. In 1993 China's National People's Congress approved the Basic Law, Macao's post-1999 constitution. Pro-China candidates swept the September 1996 legislative elections.

Concern increases over the slow pace of the "localization" of the civil service. Portuguese expatriates and Macanese of mixed Chinese-Portuguese descent hold most judicial positions and the majority of the government posts, and along with many of the 6,000 Macanese civil servants, are expected to leave the territory or retire by 1999. Although Portuguese civil law, now being translated into Chinese, is to remain in effect after 1999, the expected exodus of these experienced judges and civil servants puts its application in doubt.

Political Rights and Civil Liberties: Citizens of Macao lack the democratic means to change their government. The governor is appointed by Portugal and only one-third of the legislature is directly elected. Although the legislature has the power to enact and veto laws, in practice the governor initiates the vast majority of laws, which are rarely contested. Due to the dearth of legal and political experience among the MPs, and Portugal's practice of deferring to China on key policy decisions, the legislature holds little power. The colony had no voice in the 1987 Joint Declaration ceding control to China in 1999. China maintains a dominant influence in Macao through its business interests and control of two key entities, the General Association of Workers and the General Association of Residences, a civic group.

The legal system is based on Portuguese Metropolitan Law, and citizens are extended the rights granted by the Portuguese constitution. The judiciary is independent and defendants receive fair trials. The government is training Chinese-speaking judges in the expectation that the Portuguese and Macanese judges currently serving will retire before 1999.

The government owns a controlling interest in the television and radio stations, although opposition viewpoints are generally aired. Newspapers are privately owned and most are blatantly pro-Chinese. Journalists practice self-censorship in reporting on China.

Women are active in both business and government. Equal opportunity legislation, enacted in 1995, mandated equal pay for equal work and made discrimination based on sex and physical ability illegal.

A ban on holding demonstrations within 50 yards of government buildings effectively bars protests from peninsular Macao, restricting them to the two islands. Although workers can join independent unions and hold strikes, there is no legal protection exists against retribution. Nearly all 7,000 unionized private-sector workers belong to the pro-Beijing General Association of Workers. Foreign workers, who comprise 16 percent of the workforce, often work for less than half the wages of Macao citizens, live in controlled dormitories and owe a significant amount of money to proxies for the purchase of their jobs.

Turkey
Cyprus (T)

Polity: Presidential par-liamentary democracy (Turkish-occupied)
Economy: Mixed capitalist
Population: 178,000
Political Rights: 4
Civil Liberties: 2
Status: Partly Free

Ethnic Groups: Turkish Cypriot, Turk, Greek Cypriot, Maronite

Note: See Cyprus (Greek) under country reports

Overview: **D**espite intense diplomatic efforts to settle the Cyprus dispute before the EU accession negotiations begin in mid-1997, the Greek and Turkish Cypriot communities remain divided, with almost no hope of reunification. Continuous violent provocation by Turkish Cypriots, an uncooperative Turkish government in Ankara, and Greek Cypriot plans to strengthen military defenses have exacerbated the already tense relations between north and south.

Britain, South Korea and the United States were among countries who sent delegations to the island in 1996 in search of an agreement. However, the new regime in Ankara seems less likely than previous secular governments to agree to concessions which would be unpopular with the army and the Turkish public. Meanwhile, Turkish Foreign Minister Tansu Ciller has said that a lasting settlement can occur only if Cyprus and Turkey are admitted to the EU at the same time. The EU is currently preparing to admit Greek Cyprus in 2000 or 2001. Greece is a full member of the EU, while Turkey as an associate member is not expected to gain full membership in the near future.

Turkish Cypriots are aware of their economic situation in comparison to the prosperous South. The North, which suffers from constant shortages and high unemployment, is supported by an estimated $200 million in annual assistance from Ankara. Due to its near total reliance on its Greek Cypriot neighbors for a free but diminishing power supply, the North suffers frequent outages of 12 to 14 hours per day. Turkish Cypriots know that a settlement with the south would ease shortages, while membership in the EU could bring substantial regional aid.

With 35,000 troops occupying the northern third of Cyprus, Turkey has traditionally enjoyed military superiority on the island. The Greek Cypriot admin-istration has sought to tilt the balance of power in its favor by upgrading the National Guard with new armaments, including a $600 million missile defense system to be purchased from Russia. The Turkish reaction has been to leak information about planned attacks on Greek Cypriot targets in order to pressure the Nicosia govern-ment to stop the build-up. Actual incidents occurred throughout the year, with Turkish troops firing on National Guard positions along the Green Line.

Ethnic violence in the second half of the year took the lives of four unarmed Greek Cypriots in the U.N.-controlled buffer zone. Three of the victims were killed by Turkish troops; one was beaten to death by armed demonstrators. The Cyprus government blamed Rauf Denktash, the Turkish Cypriot leader, and the mainland Turkish government for the incidents, and is expected to take at least two of the cases to the European Human Rights Commission.

Political Rights and Civil Liberties: Citizens of the Turkish Republic of Northern Cyprus (TRNC) can change their government democratically. The Turkish immigrants who settled in the North after the 1974 Turkish invasion have the right to vote in TRNC elections. The Greek and Maronite communities, numbering about 1,000, are disenfranchised in the North but maintain the right to vote in Cypriot Republic elections.

The judiciary is independent and trials are fair. Civilians deemed to have violated military zones are subject to trial in military courts, which maintain all rights of due process. In 1995, the TRNC allowed for the first time an investigation into the whereabouts of five American citizens of Greek Cypriot descent who disappeared during the 1974 invasion.

Advocates for Greek Cypriots living in Karpassia claim that these "enclaved" individuals are denied freedom of movement, speech, property, and access to the Greek press. In 1996, the European Court of Human Rights at Strasbourg held Turkey directly responsible for denying a Greek Cypriot refugee access to her property in the North since 1974. In doing so, the Court recognized Ankara, not the Turkish Cypriot administration, as having control of the North, and treated the internationally-recognized Republic of Cyprus as the sole legitimate government on the island.

Authorities control the content of Greek Cypriot textbooks, and many titles are rejected on the grounds that they "violate the feelings" of Turkish Cypriots. Turkish Cypriots enjoy freedom of speech and press, with a variety of newspapers and periodicals in print. Broadcast media are government-owned.

The majority Sunni Muslims and the minority Greek and Maronite Orthodox Christians, as well as foreign residents, practice their religions freely. With the exception of travel to and from the South, freedom of movement is generally respected. Workers are entitled to organize and to join independent trade unions.

forcibly deported several thousand Vietnamese. In May, Vietnamese resisting forcible deportation rioted at a detention center holding 8,600 detainees who had failed to secure refugee status.

In the New Territories husbands or male relatives frequently cast electoral ballots for women, according to local tradition. Workplace anti-discrimination legislation is inadequate and women are often openly discriminated against on the basis of age.

Northern Ireland

Polity: British administration and elected local
councils
(military-occupied)
Economy: Mixed capitalist
Population: 1,630,000

Political Rights: 4
Civil Liberties: 3
Status: Partly Free

Ethnic Groups: Protestant (mostly Scottish and English), (57 percent), Irish Catholic (43 percent)

Overview: **A** bombing in the London docklands on February 9, 1996 marked the end of the Irish Republican Army's 17-month cease-fire. Throughout the year, bombings, street violence and political infighting have dimmed hopes for the peace effort initiated in late-1994.

All-party talks on the future of Northern Ireland began on June 10 at Stormont without Sinn Fein. Though the IRA's political arm won a seat at the negotiating table through a special election in May, it has been banned from the talks by British Prime Minister John Major, who insisted that the IRA must declare an unequivocal cease-fire and renounce violence before Sinn Fein may join.

Northern Ireland comprises six of the nine counties of the Irish province of Ulster. At the insistence of the locally-dominant Protestants, these counties remained part of the United Kingdom after the other 26 predominantly-Catholic counties acquired Dominion status within the British Commonwealth in 1921. Catholics now constitute a majority in four of the six counties and 13 of the 26 local government bodies. The demographic trends have aroused anxiety within the Protestant population, which is largely descended from seventeenth-century Scottish and English settlers. Britain's 1920 Government of Ireland Act set up the Northern Irish parliament, which functioned until the British imposed direct rule in 1972. Subsequent attempts at Catholic-Protestant power-sharing have failed.

Disorder resulting from a nonviolent Catholic civil rights movement in the 1960s prompted the deployment of British troops which have occupied Northern Ireland to date. Amid sectarian violence beginning in the 1970s, divisions grew within both the primarily Protestant "Unionist" and the Catholic "Nationalist" or "Republican" communities. In addition to numerous political factions including the conservative Ulster Unionist Party, the hardline Democratic Unionist Party, the interdenominational unionist Alliance Party, the moderate pro-Nationalist Social Democratic and Labor Party and the pro-Nationalist Sinn Fein, paramilitary groups on both sides also engaged in acts of terrorism until September 1994.

Negotiations for a peace settlement have stalled over the issue of the decommissioning of terrorist arms as well as the seemingly intractable opposing claims of Republicans and Unionists. Anticipation of British parliamentary elections before the end of May 1997 has also fostered delay. Meanwhile, it is widely believed to be unlikely that the talks will produce any significant agreement without IRA representation.

The IRA claimed responsibility for seven bombs on the British mainland in 1996, severely damaging the credibility of Sinn Fein's commitment to peace. Further incidents included the bombing of a hotel in Enniskillen and two bombings at British army headquarters in Lisburn attributed to IRA splinter groups. The bombings, and the admitted involvement of the IRA in the shooting death of a police detective during a robbery in western Ireland, have called into question the unity of the Republican movement. More militant Republicans apparently do not support Sinn Fein leader Gerry Adams's efforts toward peace, and his ability to control Republican violence is in doubt.

After nearly two years of relative calm, Northern Ireland saw a gradual return to sectarian violence beginning in early summer. The "marching season" in June and July brought widespread unrest, including rioting and firebombing, as Catholic activists sought to block a traditional Protestant march from entering Catholic neighborhoods. Police had initially ordered the parade to re-route, but reversed their decision after a week of Protestant protests.

The loyalist role at Stormont was challenged in the wake of car bomb attacks and the attempted murder of two senior Republicans by loyalist paramilitaries in early 1997. The attacks unofficially ended the 27 month-old Protestant ceasefire, and prompted the British government to issue a stern warning to loyalist political representatives about their continued participation in talks.

Political Rights and Civil Liberties: The people of Northern Ireland can elect members to the British House of Commons and to local government bodies. The regional parliament was suspended in 1972 following the imposition of British direct rule. Unionists retain effective veto power over the North's unification with the Republic, causing Nationalists to claim that they lack the right to self-determination.

Freedom of movement improved markedly with the disappearance of British troops from the streets, the removal of checkpoints, and the revocation of exclusion orders by Northern Ireland Secretary Sir Patrick Mayhew last year.

In January, with the cease-fire still in force, Britain renewed the Emergency Provisions Act for another two years beginning in August 1996. The emergency legislation severely limits due process rights, compromising internationally accepted standards for detention, interrogation and the right to counsel. Under emergency law, suspected terrorists may be arrested without warrants and are denied trial by jury.

"Punishment beatings" by paramilitaries on both sides of the conflict continued in 1996. A renewed outbreak of antidrug murders committed by a group calling itself Direct Action Against Drugs (DAAD)—a suspected IRA front—also occurred. Seven such killings occurred in December 1995 and January 1996 before DAAD suspended its campaign for most of 1996, only to resume with another shooting death in September.

Sectarian unrest in the summer claimed the life of one man, a Catholic who was killed when a British army vehicle ran him down in Derry. Attacks by police in riot gear sent numerous people to emergency rooms for treatment.

United States
Puerto Rico

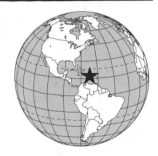

Polity: Elected governor and legislature
Economy: Capitalist
Population: 3,613,000
Ethnic Groups: Hispanic

Political Rights: 1
Civil Liberties: 2
Status: Free

Overview: Following approval by plebescite, Puerto Rico acquired the status of a commonwealth in free association with the U.S. in 1952. Under its terms, Puerto Rico exercises approximately the same control over its internal affairs as do the fifty U.S. states. Residents, though U.S. citizens, cannot vote in presidential elections and are represented in the U.S. Congress by a delegate to the House of Representatives who can vote in committee but not on the floor.

The Commonwealth constitution, modeled on that of the U.S., provides for a governor and a bicameral legislature, consisting of a 28-member Senate and a 54-member House of Representatives, elected for four years. A Supreme Court heads an independent judiciary and the legal system is based on U.S. law.

Pedro Rosello of the pro-statehood New Progressive Party (PNP) was elected governor in 1992, defeating Victoria Munoz Mendoza of the incumbent Popular Democratic Party (PPD). The PNP also won majorities in the House and Senate.

The election reflected anti-incumbency sentiment and immediate concerns over rising crime, high unemployment, government corruption and education. Still, the island's relationship with the U.S. remains a fundamental issue. In a nonbinding 1993 referendum, voters narrowly opted to retain commonwealth status. Commonwealth status received 48.4 percent of the vote, statehood 46.2 percent, and independence 4.4 percent. The vote indicated significant gains for statehood, which in the last referendum, in 1967, received only 39 percent of the vote.

Any vote to change the island's status would have to be approved by the U.S. Congress. A bill introduced in the House of Representatives in March 1996 called for a congressionally mandated plebescite by the end of 1998 that would offer Puerto Ricans a choice between statehood or independence. By year's end the bill had not come to a floor vote.

At the November 5, 1996, elections Rosello won re-election with 51.2

percent of the vote, defeating the PPD's Hector Luis Acevedo, who took 44.4 percent; the Puerto Rico Independence Party's (PIP) David Noriega Rodriguez took 3.8 percent. In the House the PNP won 37 seats; the PDP, 16; and the PIP, 1. In the Senate the PNP won 19 seats; the PPD, 8; and the PIP, 1.

A key issue continues to be the pending decision in Washington whether to retain Section 936 of the Internal Revenue Code, which gives major tax concessions and wage credits to U.S. companies located on the island. Rosello has backed phasing out Section 936 in favor of a tax-based job-creation program, arguing that such concessions are incompatible with statehood. The PPD has lobbied to retain Section 936 on the grounds that without it, the island's manufacturing base would shrink.

Political Rights and Civil Liberties: As U.S. citizens, Puerto Ricans are guaranteed all civil liberties granted in the U.S. The press and broadcast media are well developed, highly varied and critical. In recent years the Puerto Rican Journalists' Association (ASPRO) has charged successive governments with denying complete access to official information. Labor unions are well organized and have the right to strike.

The greatest cause for concern is the steep rise in criminal violence in recent years, much of it drug-related, and the Rosello government's response to it. Puerto Rico is now the Caribbean's main drug transshipment point. Since mid-1993, about 80 public housing projects, or about two-fifths of the total, have been under the control of the National Guard, the first time that U.S. military units have been routinely deployed to fight crime.

The Rosello government claims the projects have been "liberated" from drug traffickers. Critics point to civil rights abuses including unlawful search and seizure and other transgressions. The policy appears to have reduced crime in some categories, including homicide. Corruption and criminal activity within the police force are continuing concerns.

Yugoslavia
Kosovo

Polity: Serbian administration
Economy: Mixed-statist
Population: 2,018,000
Ethnic Groups: Albanian (90 percent), Serb, Montenegrin

Political Rights: 7
Civil Liberties: 7
Status: Not Free

Overview:

Kosovo, the predominantly ethnic-Albanian enclave within Serbia that had been an autonomous region in Yugoslavia, saw continued Serb repression of Albanians in 1996, despite an agreement between the Albanian shadow government and Serb authorities that ended a six-year Albanian boycott of state schools.

For Serbs, Kosovo is the historic cradle of the Serbian medieval state and culture. It was the site of the Battle of Kosovo Fields in 1389 between Serbian Prince Lazar and the Turks, which solidified Ottoman control over the Serbs for the next 500 years. Serbian President Slobodan Milosevic rose to power in 1987 over the issue of Kosovo's status. Central to his platform was the subjugation of the then-autonomous Yugoslav province (established by the 1974 constitution) to Serbian authority. Persecution by ethnic Albanians caused some 50,000 Serb and Montenegrin residents to flee Kosovo after the 1980 death of Yugoslav strongman Josip Broz "Tito."

In 1989-1990, Milosevic moved to abolish the provincial government and legislature and introduced a series of amendments to the Serbian constitution that effectively removed the legal basis for Kosovo's autonomy. Albanians elected a shadow president, Ibrahim Rugova, leader of the Democratic League of Kosovo (LDK), and a 130-member parliament in 1992 to underscore the illegitimacy of Serb rule. Bujar Bukoshi was named prime minister.

Serbian repression of Albanians is maintained by a 40,000-man army and militia force. Harassment, detention, intimidation and murder of Albanians is endemic. Since the Serb takeover, hundreds of thousands of Albanians have lost their jobs, and over 200,000 left for other parts of Europe and the United States. Serbs were placed in control of hospitals, universities, businesses, schools and government. While Albanian resistance has officially been non-violent, several Serbian policemen and militiamen were murdered in the last six years.

In 1996, ethnic Albanians continued to suffer arbitrary detention, police raids on shops and private homes, and the dragooning of young men into the Serbian army. In the early part of the year, a previously unknown terrorist group, the Kosovo Liberation Army (UCK), claimed responsibility for bombings at Serbian refugee camps, and for the shooting of Serb policemen and Serbian civilians, as well as the killing of an ethnic Albanian policeman. Some Albanian leaders speculated that the shadowy UCK was actually a Serbian provocation to violence. In April, four days of violence followed the killing of an Albanian student by a Serb civilian. The LDK sharply condemned "all types of violence."

In June, Serbs in Kosovo rallied after the head of the Serbian Academy of

Sciences and Arts made a speech indicating that Serbia may have to grant independence to Kosovo or consider a partition between Serbs and Albanians. The LDK rejected any notion of partition, arguing that with 90 percent of the population and one of the highest birthrates in Europe, Albanians would not settle for 50 percent of Kosovo's territory.

On September 3, President Milosevic and President Rugova signed an agreement for the return of ethnic Albanians to schools and the university, thus ending the parallel school system set up by Albanians after the abolition of the region's autonomy. By the end of 1996, however, the agreement had not been implemented, largely because of resistance from Serb academics and nationalist leaders in Kosovo. Some 200 schools continued to operate in private homes. Earlier, President Milosevic had allowed the United States Information Agency (USIA) to open an information center in Pristina, the capital.

The Albanians boycotted the November elections to rump-Yugoslavia's 138-member federal parliament, first elected in 1992, thereby conceding control of Kosovo's 13 seats to hard-line Serb nationalists, a strategy that angered the anti-Milosevic Serbian opposition. When mass protests broke out in Serbia after the government annulled opposition wins in local elections, the LDK waited three weeks before announcing on December 12 that it welcomed the demonstrations, but that they were an internal Serbian affair.

The demonstrations in Serbia, the failure to implement the school agreement, and continued repressions and arrests led to a possible challenge to President Rugova. Adem Demaci, a highly respected former political prisoner and head of the Kosovo Human Rights Council, announced that he was joining the Parliamentary Party, an LDK rival. But while Albanians might be impatient with Rugova's passive resistance, he continued to insist on Kosovo's independence; Demaci supports a new federation that would give Kosovo, the Muslim Sandjak region, and Vojvodina a constitutional status equal to that of Serbia and Montenegro.

In a December 1996 report, Human Rights Watch reported that at least 200 ethnic Albanians were in prison for political reasons after trials fraught with violations of due process. Police violence continued to be endemic, leading to several deaths of Albanians in custody. Beatings, torture and arbitrary arrest were common.

Political Rights and Civil Liberties: Kosovars cannot change democratically the *de jure* government imposed by Serbia. The Parliamentary Party and the Social Democrats are technically outlawed, while the LDK and its leaders have been targets of harassment and detention. Kosovo's democratically elected legislature and government were forced underground after the 1992 elections, which were not recognized by Serbia. Ultimate judicial authority lies with Belgrade.

Albanian TV and radio have been abolished. A Belgrade-based conglomerate took over the newspaper, *Rilindja*. The weekly *Zeri* continues to be published. In April 1996, police in Kosovo closed down the printing house of the Albanian-language weekly *Koha*. Albanian judges, policemen and government officials have all been replaced over the last four years. Freedom of movement and other fundamental rights have been circumscribed by the Serbs.

Albanian cultural identity has been suppressed. Over the last five yea Albanian monuments have been destroyed, streets have received Serbian name and signs in Cyrillic have replaced those in the Latin script. Serbian has supplantec Albanian as the official language. Since 1991, some 8,000 Albanian teachers have been dismissed. In 1993, Serb authorities shut down all 58 Albanian-language secondary schools and 21 of the 350-odd Albanian-language primary schools denying schooling to an estimated 63,000 children. A network of clandestine, underground schools have been set up in Albanian households. A September 1996 agreement between Presidents Milosevic and Rugova that would have returned Albanian students to state schools had not been implemented by the end of 1996.

The Independent Trade Unions of Kosovo (BSPK), an outlawed Albanian-language confederation, has been the subject of repression for refusing to affiliate with the official Serbian unions or sign collective agreements approved by these unions. Scores of union leaders were arrested in 1995 and 1996.

The Comparative Survey of Freedom—1996-1997 Survey Methodology

The purpose of the *Comparative Survey of Freedom* since its inception in the 1970s has been to provide an annual evaluation of political rights and civil liberties everywhere in the world.

The *Survey* attempts to judge all places by a single standard and to point out the importance of democracy and freedom. At a minimum, a democracy is a political system in which the people choose their authoritative leaders freely from among competing groups and individuals who were not chosen by the government. Putting it broadly, freedom is the chance to act spontaneously in a variety of fields outside the control of government and other centers of potential domination.

For a long time, Westerners have associated the adherence to political rights and civil liberties with the liberal democracies, such as those in North America and the European Union. However, there has been a proliferation of democracies in developing countries in recent years, and the *Survey* reflects their growing numbers.

Freedom House does not view democracy as a static concept, and the *Survey* recognizes that a democratic country does not necessarily belong in our category of "free" states. A democracy can lose freedom and become merely "partly free." Sri Lanka and Colombia are examples of such "partly free" democracies. In other cases, countries that replaced military regimes with elected governments can have less than complete transitions to liberal democracy. El Salvador and Guatemala fit the description of this kind of "partly free" democracy. (See the section below on the designations "free," "partly free," and "not free" for an explanation of those terms.) Readers should note that some scholars would use the term "semi-democracy" or "formal democracy," instead of "partly free" democracy, to refer to countries that are democratic in form but less than free in substance.

What the *Survey* is not

The *Survey* does not rate governments *per se,* but rather the rights and freedoms individuals have in each country and territory. Freedom House does not score countries and territories based on governmental intentions or constitutions but on the real world situations caused by governmental and non-governmental factors. The *Survey* does not quantify our sympathy for the situation a government finds itself in (e.g., war, terrorism, etc.), but rather what effect the situation itself has on freedom.

Definitions and categories of the *Survey*

The *Survey*'s understanding of freedom is broad and encompasses two sets of characteristics grouped under political rights and civil liberties. Political rights enable people to participate freely in the political process. By the political process, we mean the system by which the polity chooses the authoritative policy makers and attempts to make binding decisions affecting the national, regional or local community. In a free society, this means the right of all adults to vote and compete for public office, and for elected representatives to have a decisive vote on public policies. A system is genuinely free or democratic to the extent that the people have a choice in determining the nature of the system and its leaders.

Civil liberties are the freedoms to develop views, institutions and personal autonomy apart from the state.

The *Survey* employs checklists for these rights and liberties to help determine the degree of freedom present in each country and related territory, and to help assign each entity to a comparative category.

Beginning with the 1995-96 edition of the *Survey*, we reduced the number of questions on the political rights checklist from nine to eight. The ninth question was deleted because a lack of decentralization does not necessarily translate into a lack of freedom. The revised checklist also mandated changes in assignment of category numbers and freedom ratings (see below).

Political Rights checklist

1. Is the head of state and/or head of government or other chief authority elected through free and fair elections?
2. Are the legislative representatives elected through free and fair elections?
3. Are there fair electoral laws, equal campaigning opportunities, fair polling and honest tabulation of ballots?
4. Are the voters able to endow their freely elected representatives with real power?
5. Do the people have the right to organize in different political parties or other competitive political groupings of their choice, and is the system open to the rise and fall of these competing parties or groupings?
6. Is there a significant opposition vote, *de facto* opposition power, and a realistic possibility for the opposition to increase its support or gain power through elections?
7. Are the people free from domination by the military, foreign powers, totalitarian parties, religious hierarchies, economic oligarchies or any other powerful group?
8. Do cultural, ethnic, religious and other minority groups have reasonable self-determination, self-government, autonomy or participation through informal consensus in the decision-making process?

Additional Discretionary Political Rights questions

A. For traditional monarchies that have no parties or electoral processes, does the system provide for consultation with the people, encourage discussion of policy, and allow the right to petition the ruler?
B. Is the government or occupying power deliberately changing the ethnic composition of a country or territory so as to destroy a culture or tip the political balance in favor of another group?

When answering the political rights questions, Freedom House considers the extent to which each system offers a voter the chance to make a free choice among competing candidates, and to what extent the candidates are chosen independently of the state. We recognize that formal electoral procedures are not the only factors that determine the real distribution of power. In many Latin American countries, for example, the military retains a significant political role, and in Morocco the king maintains significant power over the elected politicians. The more people suffer under such domination by unelected forces, the less chance the country has of getting credit for self-determination in our *Survey*.

Freedom House does not have a culture-bound view of democracy. The *Survey* team rejects the notion that only Europeans and those of European descent qualify as democratic. The *Survey* demonstrates that, in addition to those in Europe and the Americas, there are free countries with varying kinds of democracy functioning among people of all races and religions in Africa, the Pacific and Asia. In some Pacific islands, free countries can have competitive political systems based on competing family groups and personalities rather than on European- or American-style parties.

The checklist for Civil Liberties

1. Are there free and independent media, literature and other cultural expressions? (Note: In cases where the media are state-controlled but offer pluralistic points of view, the *Survey* gives the system credit.)
2. Is there open public discussion and free private discussion?
3. Is there freedom of assembly and demonstration?
4. Is there freedom of political or quasi-political organization? (Note: This includes political parties, civic associations, ad hoc issue groups, and so forth.)
5. Are citizens equal under the law, with access to an independent, nondiscriminatory judiciary, and are they respected by the security forces?
6. Is there protection from political terror, and from unjustified imprisonment, exile or torture, whether by groups that support or oppose the system, and freedom from war or insurgency situations? (Note: Freedom from war and insurgency situations enhances the liberties in a free society, but the absence of wars and insurgencies does not in itself make an unfree society free.)

7. Are there free trade unions and peasant organizations or equivalents, and is there effective collective bargaining?

8. Are there free professional and other private organizations?

9. Are there free businesses or cooperatives?

10. Are there free religious institutions and free private and public religious expression?

11. Are there personal social freedoms, which include such aspects as gender equality, property rights, freedom of movement, choice of residence, and choice of marriage and size of family?

12. Is there equality of opportunity, which includes freedom from exploitation by or dependency on landlords, employers, union leaders, bureaucrats or any other type of denigrating obstacle to a share of legitimate economic gains?

13. Is there freedom from extreme government indifference and corruption?

When analyzing the civil liberties checklist, Freedom House does not mistake constitutional guarantees of human rights for those rights in practice. For tiny island countries and territories and other small entities with low populations, the absence of unions and other types of association does not necessarily count as a negative unless the government or other centers of domination are deliberately blocking association. In some cases, the small size of these entities may result in a lack of sufficient institutional complexity to make them fully comparable to larger countries. The question of equality of opportunity also implies a free choice of employment and education. Extreme inequality of opportunity prevents disadvantaged individuals from enjoying a full exercise of civil liberties. Typi-

The Tabulated Ratings

The accompanying Table of Independent Countries and Table of Related Territories rate each country or territory on seven-category scales for political rights and civil liberties, and then place each entity into a broad category of "free," "partly free" or "not free." On each scale, 1 represents the most free and 7 the least free.

Political rights

In political rights, generally speaking, places rated 1 come closest to the ideals suggested by the checklist questions, beginning with free and fair elections. Those elected rule. There are competitive parties or other competitive political groupings, and the opposition has an important role and power. These entities have self-determination or an extremely high degree of autonomy (in the case of related territories). Usually, those rated 1 have self-determination for minority groups or their participation in government through informal consensus. With the exception of such entities as tiny island countries, these countries and territories have decentralized political power and free sub-national elections. Entities in Category 1 are not perfect. They can and do lose credit for their deficiencies.

Countries and territories rated 2 in political rights are less free than those rated 1. Such factors as gross political corruption, violence, political discrimination against minorities, and foreign or military influence on politics may be present, and weaken the quality of democracy.

The same factors that weaken freedom in category 2 may also undermine political rights in categories 3, 4, and 5. Other damaging conditions may be at work as well, including civil war, very strong military involvement in politics, lingering royal power, unfair elections and one-party dominance. However, states and territories in these categories may still have some elements of political rights such as the freedom to organize nongovernmental parties and quasi-political groups, reasonably free referenda, or other significant means of popular influence on government.

Typically, states and territories with political rights rated 6 have systems ruled by military juntas, one-party dictatorships, religious hierarchies and autocrats. These regimes may allow only some minimal manifestation of political rights such as competitive local elections or some degree of representation or autonomy for minorities. Category 6 also contains some countries in the early or aborted stages of democratic transition. A few states in Category 6 are traditional monarchies that mitigate their relative lack of political rights through the use of consultation with their subjects, toleration of political discussion, and acceptance of petitions from the ruled.

cally, desperately poor countries and territories lack both opportunities for economic advancement and the other liberties on this checklist. We include a question on gross indifference and corruption, because when governments do not care about the social and economic welfare of large sectors of the population, the human rights of those people suffer. Government corruption can pervert the political process and hamper the development of a free economy.

How do we grade? Ratings, categories, and raw points

The *Survey* rates political rights and civil liberties separately on a seven-category scale, 1 representing the most free and 7 the least free. A country is assigned to a particular category based on responses to the checklist and the judgments of the *Survey* team at Freedom House. The numbers are not purely mechanical; they also reflect judgment. Under the methodology, the team assigns initial ratings to countries by awarding from 0 to 4 raw points per checklist item, depending on the comparative rights or liberties present. (In the *Surveys* completed from 1989-90 through 1992-93, the methodology allowed for a less nuanced range of 0 to 2 raw points per question. Taking note of this modification, scholars should consider the 1993-94 scores the statistical benchmark.) The only exception to the addition of 0 to 4 raw points per checklist item is the discretionary question on cultural destruction and deliberate demographic change to tip the political balance. In that case, we subtract 1 to 4 raw points depending on the situation's severity. The highest possible score for political rights is 32 points, based on up to 4 points for each of eight questions. The highest possible score for civil liberties is 52 points, based on up to 4 points for each of thirteen questions. Under the methodology, raw points correspond to category numbers as follows:

The Tabulated Ratings

Category 7 includes places where political rights are absent or virtually nonexistent due to the extremely oppressive nature of the regime or extreme oppression in combination with civil war. A country or territory may also join this category when extreme violence and warlordism dominate the people in the absence of an authoritative, functioning central government. Places in Category 7 may get some minimal points for the checklist questions, but only a tiny fragment of available credit.

Civil liberties

Category 1 in civil liberties includes countries and territories that generally have the highest levels of freedoms and opportunities for the individual. Places in this category may still have problems in civil liberties, but they lose partial credit in only a limited number of areas.

The places in category 2 in civil liberties are not as free as those rated 1, but they are still relatively high on the scale. These countries and territories have deficiencies in several aspects of civil liberties, but still receive most available credit.

Independent countries and related territories with ratings of 3, 4 or 5 have progressively fewer civil liberties than those in category 2. Places in these categories range from ones that receive at least partial credit on virtually all checklist questions to those that have a mixture of good civil liberties scores in some areas and zero or partial credit in others. As one moves down the scale below category 2, the level of oppression increases, especially in the areas of censorship, political terror and the prevention of free association. There are also many cases in which groups opposed to the state carry out political terror that undermines other freedoms. That means that a poor rating for a country is not necessarily a comment on the intentions of the government. The rating may simply reflect the real restrictions on liberty which can be caused by non-governmental terror.

Typically, at category 6 in civil liberties, countries and territories have a few partial rights. For example, a country might have some religious freedom, some personal social freedoms, some highly restricted private business activity, and relatively free private discussion. In general, people in these states and territories experience severely restricted expression and association. There are almost always political prisoners and other manifestations of political terror.

At category 7, countries and territories have virtually no freedom. An overwhelming and justified fear of repression characterizes the society.

The accompanying Tables of Combined Average Ratings average the two seven-category scales of political rights and civil liberties into an overall freedom rating for each country and territory.

Political Rights

Category Number	Raw Points
1	28-32
2	23-27
3	19-22
4	14-18
5	10-13
6	5-9
7	0-4

Civi Liberties

Category Number	Raw Points
1	45-52
2	38-44
3	30-37
4	23-29
5	15-22
6	8-14
7	0-7

After placing countries in initial categories based on checklist points, the *Survey* team makes minor adjustments to account for factors such as extreme violence, whose intensity may not be reflected in answering the checklist questions. These exceptions aside, in the overwhelming number of cases, the checklist system reflects the real world situation and is adequate for placing countries and territories into the proper comparative categories.

At its discretion, Freedom House assigns up or down arrows to countries and territories to indicate positive or negative trends, whether qualitative or quantitative, that may not be apparent from the ratings. Such trends may or may not be reflected in raw points, depending on the circumstances of each country or territory. Only places without ratings changes since the previous year warrant trend arrows. The charts also show up and down triangles. Distinct from the trend arrows, the triangles indicate changes in political rights and civil liberties caused by real world events since the last *Survey*.

free, partly free, not free

The accompanying map divides the world into three large categories: "free," "partly free," and "not free." The *Survey* places countries and territories into this tripartite division by averaging the category numbers they received for political rights and civil liberties. Those whose category numbers average 1-2.5 are considered "free," 3-5.5 "partly free," and 5.5-7 "not free." The dividing line between "partly free" and "not free" falls within the group whose category numbers average 5.5. For example, countries that receive a rating of 6 for political rights and 5 for civil liberties, or a 5 for political rights and a 6 for civil liberties, could be either "partly free" or "not free." The total number of raw points is the factor which makes the difference between the two. Countries and territories with combined raw scores of 0-28 points are "not free," and those with combined raw scores of 29-56 points are "partly free." "Free" countries and territories have combined raw scores of 57-84 points.

The differences in raw points between countries in the three broad categories represent distinctions in the real world. There are obstacles which "partly free" countries must overcome before they can be called "free," just as there are impediments which prevent "not free" countries from being called "partly free." Countries at the lowest rung of the "free" category (category 2 in political rights with category 3 in civil liberties, or category 3 in political rights with category 2 in civil liberties) differ from those at the upper end of the "partly free" group (e.g., category 3 in both). Typically, there is more violence and/or military influence on politics at 3,3 than at 2,3 and the differences become more striking as one compares 2,3 with worse categories of the "partly free" countries.

The distinction between the least bad "not free" countries and the least free "partly free" may be less obvious than the gap between "partly free" and "free," but at "partly free," there is at least one extra factor that keeps a country from being assigned to the "not free" category. For example, Lebanon, which was rated 6,5, Partly Free, in 1994, was rated 6,5, but Not Free, in 1995 (and again in 1996) after its legislature unilaterally extended the incumbent president's term indefinitely. Though not sufficient to drop the country's political rights rating to category 7, there was enough of a drop in raw points to change its category.

Freedom House wishes to point out that the designation "free" does not mean that a country has perfect freedom or lacks serious problems. As an institution which advocates human rights, Freedom House remains concerned about a variety of social problems and civil liberties questions in the U.S. and other countries that the *Survey* places in the "free" category. Similarly, in no way does an improvement in a country's rating mean that human rights campaigns should cease. On the contrary, we wish to use the *Survey* as a prod to improve the condition of all countries.

Readers should understand that the "free," "partly free," and "not free" labels are highly simplified terms that each cover a broad third of the available raw points. The labels do *not* imply that all countries in a category are the same any more than a bestseller list implies that all titles on it have sold the same number of books. Countries and territories can reach the same categories or even raw points by differing routes. We use the tripartite labels and tricolor maps to illustrate some broad comparisons. In theory, we could have eighty-five categories and colors to match the range of raw points, but this would be highly impractical.

The approach of the *Survey*

The *Survey* attempts to measure conditions as they really are around the world. This approach is distinct from relying on intense coverage by the American media as a guide to which countries are the least free. The publicity given to problems in some countries does not necessarily mean that unpublicized problems of other countries are not more severe. For example, while U.S. television networks are allowed into Israel and El Salvador to cover abuses of human rights, they are not allowed to report freely in North Korea, which has far less freedom than the other two countries. To reach such comparative conclusions, Freedom House evaluates the development of democratic governmental institutions, or lack thereof, and also examines the quality of civil society, life outside the state structure.

Without a well-developed civil society, it is difficult, if not impossible, to have an atmosphere supportive of democracy. A society that does not have free individual and group expressions in nonpolitical matters is not likely to make an exception for political ones. As though to prove this, there is no country in the *Survey* that places in category 6 or 7 for civil liberties and, at the same time, in category 1 or 2 for political rights. Almost without exception, countries and territories have ratings in political rights and civil liberties that are within two categories of each other.

The *Survey* rates both countries and related territories. For our purposes, countries are internationally recognized independent states whose governments are resident within their officially claimed territories. In the unusual case of Cyprus, we give two ratings, since there are two governments on that divided island. In no way does this imply that Freedom House endorses Cypriot division. We note only that neither the predominantly Greek Republic of Cyprus nor the Turkish-occupied, predominantly Turkish territory of the Republic of Northern Cyprus is the *de facto* government for the entire island. Related territories consist mostly of colonies, protectorates, occupied territories and island dependencies. However, the *Survey* also reserves the right to designate as related territories places within internationally recognized states that are disputed areas or that have a human rights problem or issue of self-determination deserving special attention. Northern Ireland, Tibet, and Kashmir are examples falling within this category. The *Survey* excludes uninhabited related territories and such entities as the U.S.-owned Johnston Atoll, which has only a transient military population and no native inhabitants. Since most related territories have a broad range of civil liberties and some form of self-government, a higher proportion of them have the "free" designation than do independent countries.

We provide only designations of "free," "partly free" and "not free" for the eight related territories with populations under 5,000, without corresponding category numbers. Notwithstanding, we will continue to score these territories according to the same methodology as the rest. They are: Cocos (Keeling) Islands, Rapanui (Easter Island), Falkland Islands, Niue, Norfolk Island, Pitcairn Islands, Svalbard and Tokelau.

This year there are no new countries, but there is a net gain of two additional related territories. Replacing the Occupied Territories and Palestinian Autonomous Areas (Israel) are two new entities: Israeli-administered Territories, and Palestinian Authority-administered Territories, both referenced in Related Territories under Israel. This reflects real-world differences in the political rights and civil liberties situations in the two areas, although it is not meant to endorse any political division or status. We have also added Transdniester as a related territory of Moldova, thus recognizing that Transdniester is essentially politically independent from Moldova, with its own governmental structures and army.

Tables and Ratings

TABLE OF INDEPENDENT COUNTRIES
COMPARATIVE MEASURES OF FREEDOM

COUNTRY	PR	CL	FREEDOM RATING	COUNTRY	PR	CL	FREEDOM RATING
Afghanistan	7	7	Not Free	Dominican Republic	3▲	3	Partly Free
Albania	4▼	4	Partly Free				
Algeria	6	6	Not Free	Ecuador	2	4▼	Partly Free
Andorra	1	1	Free	Egypt	6	6	Not Free
Angola	6	6	Not Free	↑El Salvador	3	3	Partly Free
Antigua and Barbuda	4	3	Partly Free	Equatorial Guinea	7	7	Not Free
				Eritrea	6	4	Partly Free
Argentina	2	3	Free	Estonia	1▲	2	Free
Armenia	5▼	4	Partly Free	Ethiopia	4	5	Partly Free
Australia	1	1	Free	Fiji	4	3	Partly Free
Austria	1	1	Free	Finland	1	1	Free
Azerbaijan	6	5▲	Not Free	France	1	2	Free
Bahamas	1	2	Free	Gabon	5	4	Partly Free
Bahrain	7▼	6	Not Free	The Gambia	7	6	Not Free
Bangladesh	2▲	4	Partly Free	Georgia	4	4▲	Partly Free
Barbados	1	1	Free	Germany	1	2	Free
Belarus	6▼	6▼	Not Free	Ghana	3▲	4	Partly Free
Belgium	1	2▼	Free	Greece	1	3	Free
Belize	1	1	Free	Grenada	1	2	Free
Benin	2	2	Free	Guatemala	3▲	4▲	Partly Free
Bhutan	7	7	Not Free	Guinea	6	5	Not Free
Bolivia	2	3▲	Free	Guinea-Bissau	3	4	Partly Free
Bosnia-Herzegovina	5▲	5▲	Partly Free	Guyana	2	2	Free
Botswana	2	2	Free	Haiti	4▲	5	Partly Free
Brazil	2	4	Partly Free	Honduras	3	3	Partly Free
Brunei	7	5	Not Free	Hungary	1	2	Free
Bulgaria	2	3▼	Free	Iceland	1	1	Free
Burkina Faso	5	4	Partly Free	India	2▲	4	Partly Free
Burma	7	7	Not Free	Indonesia	7	5▲	Not Free
Burundi	7▼	7	Not Free	Iran	6	7	Not Free
Cambodia	6	6	Not Free	Iraq	7	7	Not Free
Cameroon	7	5	Not Free	Ireland	1	1	Free
Canada	1	1	Free	Israel	1	3	Free
Cape Verde	1	2	Free	Italy	1	2	Free
Central African Republic	3	5▼	Partly Free	Jamaica	2	3	Free
				Japan	1	2	Free
Chad	6	5	Not Free	Jordan	4	4	Partly Free
Chile	2	2	Free	Kazakhstan	6	5	Not Free
China (P.R.C.)	7	7	Not Free	Kenya	7	6	Not Free
Colombia	4	4	Partly Free	Kiribati	1	1	Free
Comoros	4	4	Partly Free	Korea, North	7	7	Not Free
Congo	4	4	Partly Free	Korea, South	2	2	Free
Costa Rica	1	2	Free	Kuwait	5	5	Partly Free
Côte d'Ivoire	6	5	Not Free	Kyrgyz Republic	4	4	Partly Free
↓Croatia	4	4	Partly Free	Laos	7	6	Not Free
Cuba	7	7	Not Free	Latvia	2	2	Free
Cyprus (G)	1	1	Free	Lebanon	6	5	Not Free
Czech Republic	1	2	Free	Lesotho	4	4	Partly Free
Denmark	1	1	Free	Liberia	7	6	Not Free
Djibouti	5	6	Not Free	Libya	7	7	Not Free
Dominica	1	1	Free	Liechtenstein	1	1	Free

COUNTRY	PR	CL	FREEDOM RATING
Lithuania	1	2	Free
Luxembourg	1	1	Free
Macedonia	4	3	Partly Free
Madagascar	2	4	Partly Free
Malawi	2	3	Free
Malaysia	4	5	Partly Free
Maldives	6	6	Not Free
Mali	2	2▲	Free
Malta	1	1	Free
Marshall Islands	1	1	Free
Mauritania	6	6	Not Free
Mauritius	1	2	Free
Mexico	4	3▲	Partly Free
Micronesia	1	1	Free
Moldova	3▲	4	Partly Free
Monaco	2	1	Free
Mongolia	2	3	Free
Morocco	5	5	Partly Free
Mozambique	3▲	4	Partly Free
Namibia	2	3	Free
Nauru	1	3	Free
Nepal	3	4	Partly Free
Netherlands	1	1	Free
New Zealand	1	1	Free
Nicaragua	3▲	3▲	Partly Free
Niger	7▼	5	Not Free
Nigeria	7	6▲	Not Free
Norway	1	1	Free
Oman	6	6	Not Free
Pakistan	4▼	5	Partly Free
Palau	1	2	Free
Panama	2	3	Free
Papua New Guinea	2	4	Partly Free
Paraguay	4	3	Partly Free
Peru	4▲	3▲	Partly Free
Philippines	2	3▲	Free
Poland	1	2	Free
Portugal	1	1	Free
Qatar	7	6	Not Free
Romania	2▲	3	Free
Russia	3	4	Partly Free
Rwanda	7	6	Not Free
St. Kitts and Nevis	1	2	Free
St. Lucia	1	2	Free
St. Vincent and the Grenadines	2	1	Free
San Marino	1	1	Free
Sao Tome and Príncipe	1	2	Free
Saudi Arabia	7	7	Not Free
Senegal	4	4▲	Partly Free
Seychelles	3	3	Partly Free
Sierra Leone	4▲	5▲	Partly Free
Singapore	4▲	5	Partly Free

COUNTRY	PR	CL	FREEDOM RATING
Slovakia	2	4▼	Partly Free
Slovenia	1	2	Free
Solomon Islands	1	2	Free
Somalia	7	7	Not Free
South Africa	1	2	Free
Spain	1	2	Free
Sri Lanka	3▲	5	Partly Free
Sudan	7	7	Not Free
Suriname	3	3	Partly Free
Swaziland	6	5	Not Free
Sweden	1	1	Free
Switzerland	1	1	Free
Syria	7	7	Not Free
Taiwan (Rep. of China)	2▲	2▲	Free
Tajikistan	7	7	Not Free
Tanzania	5	5	Partly Free
Thailand	3	3▲	Partly Free
Togo	6	5	Not Free
Tonga	5	3	Partly Free
Trinidad and Tobago	1	2	Free
Tunisia	6	5	Not Free
Turkey	4▲	5	Partly Free
Turkmenistan	7	7	Not Free
Tuvalu	1	1	Free
Uganda	4▲	4	Partly Free
Ukraine	3	4	Partly Free
United Arab Emirates	6	5	Not Free
United Kingdom*	1	2	Free
United States	1	1	Free
Uruguay	1▲	2	Free
Uzbekistan	7	6▲	Not Free
Vanuatu	1	3	Free
Venezuela	2▲	3	Free
Vietnam	7	7	Not Free
Western Samoa	2	2	Free
Yemen	5	6	Not Free
Yugoslavia (Serbia and Montenegro)	6	6	Not Free
Zaire	7	6	Not Free
Zambia	5▼	4	Partly Free
Zimbabwe	5	5	Partly Free

PR and CL stand for Political Rights and Civil Liberties. 1 represents the most free and 7 the least free category.

⬆⬇ up or down indicates a general trend in freedom.

▲▼ up or down indicates a change in Political Rights or Civil Liberties since the last *Survey*.

The Freedom Rating is an overall judgment based on *Survey* results. See the "Methodological Essay" for more details.

* Excluding Northern Ireland.

TABLE OF RELATED TERRITORIES
COMPARATIVE MEASURES OF FREEDOM

COUNTRY	PR	CL	FREEDOM RATING	COUNTRY	PR	CL	FREEDOM RATING
Armenia/Azerbaijan*				New Zealand			
Nagorno-Karabakh	6	6	Not Free	Cook Islands	1	2	Free
Australia				Niue**			Free
Christmas Island	3	2	Free	Tokelau**			Free
Cocos (Keeling)			Free	Norway			
Islands**				Svalbard**			Free
Norfolk Island**			Free	Portugal			
Chile				Azores	1	1	Free
Rapanui (Easter			Free	Macao	6	4	Partly Free
Island)**				Madeira	1	1	Free
China				Spain			
Tibet	7	7	Not Free	Canary Islands	1	1	Free
Denmark				Ceuta	1	2	Free
Faeroe Islands	1	1	Free	Melilla	1	2	Free
Greenland	1	1	Free	Turkey			
Finland				Cyprus (T)	4	2	Partly Free
Aland Islands	1	1	Free	United Kingdom			
France				Anguilla	2	1	Free
French Guiana	1	2	Free	Bermuda	1	1	Free
French Polynesia	1	2	Free	British Virgin	1	1	Free
Guadeloupe			Free	Islands			
Martinique	1	2	Free	Cayman Islands	1	1	Free
Mayotte (Mahore)	1	2	Free	Channel Islands	2	1	Free
New Caledonia	3▼	2	Free	Falkland			Free
Reunion	2	2	Free	Islands**			
St. Pierre and	1	1	Free	Gibraltar	1	1	Free
Miquelon				Hong Kong	4	2	Partly Free
Wallis and	2	2	Free	Isle of Man	1	1	Free
Futuna Islands				Montserrat	1	1	Free
India				Northern Ireland	4	3	Partly Free
Kashmir	7	7	Not Free	Pitcairn Island**			Free
Indonesia				St. Helena and	2	1	Free
East Timor	7	7	Not Free	Dependencies			
West Papua	7	7	Not Free	Turks and Caicos	1	1	Free
(Irian Jaya)				United States of			
Iraq				America			
Kurdistan	6▼	6▼	Not Free	American Samoa	1	1	Free
Israel				Guam	1	1	Free
Israeli-Administered	6	5	Not Free	Northern Marianas	1	2	Free
Territories				Puerto Rico	1	2	Free
Palestinian Author-	5	6	Not Free	U.S. Virgin	1	1	Free
ity-Administered				Islands			
Territories				Yugoslavia			
Moldova				Kosovo	7	7	Not Free
Transdniester	6	6	Not Free				
Morocco							
Western Sahara	7	6	Not Free				
Netherlands							
Aruba	2	1	Free				
Netherlands	1	2	Free				
Antilles							

* Nagorno-Karabakh is disputed territory contested by Armenia and Azerbaijan.

** Micro-territories have populations of under 5,000. These areas are scored according to the same methodology used in the rest of the *Survey*, but are listed separately due to their very small populations.

TABLE OF SOCIAL AND ECONOMIC COMPARISONS

COUNTRY	REAL GDP PER CAPITA (PPP$)	LIFE EXPECTANCY	COUNTRY	REAL GDP PER CAPITA (PPP$)	LIFE EXPECTANCY
Afghanistan	800	43.7	Dominican Republic	3,690	69.7
Albania	2,200	72.0	Ecuador	4,400	69.0
Algeria	5,570	67.3	Egypt	3,800	63.9
Andorra	na	na	El Salvador	2,360	66.8
Angola	674	46.8	Equatorial Guinea	1,800	48.2
Antigua and Barbuda	5,369	74.0	Eritrea	na	na
			Estonia	3,610	69.2
Argentina	8,350	72.2	Ethiopia	420	47.8
Armenia	2,040	72.8	Fiji	5,530	71.6
Australia	18,530	77.8	Finland	16,320	75.8
Austria	19,115	76.3	France	19,140	77.0
Azerbaijan	2,190	70.7	Gabon	3,861	53.7
Bahamas	16,180	73.2	The Gambia	1,190	45.2
Bahrain	15,500	71.7	Georgia	1,750	72.9
Bangladesh	1,290	55.9	Germany	18,840	76.1
Barbados	10,570	75.7	Ghana	2,000	56.2
Belarus	4,244	69.7	Greece	8,950	77.7
Belgium	19,540	76.5	Grenada	3,118	71.0
Belize	4,610	73.7	Guatemala	3,400	65.1
Benin	1,650	47.8	Guinea	1,800	44.7
Bhutan	790	51.0	Guinea-Bissau	860	43.7
Bolivia	2,510	59.7	Guyana	2,140	65.4
Bosnia-Herzegovina	na	na	Haiti	1,050	56.8
Botswana	5,220	65.2	Honduras	2,100	67.9
Brazil	5,500	66.5	Hungary	6,059	69.0
Brunei	18,414	74.3	Iceland	18.640	78.2
Bulgaria	4,320	71.2	India	1,240	60.7
Burkina Faso	780	47.5	Indonesia	3,270	62.0
Burma	650	57.9	Iran	5,380	67.7
Burundi	670	50.3	Iraq	3,413	66.1
Cambodia	1,250	51.9	Ireland	15,120	75.4
Cameroon	2,220	56.3	Israel	15,130	76.6
Canada	20,950	77.5	Italy	17,160	77.6
Cape Verde	1,820	64.9	Jamaica	3,180	73.7
Central African Republic	1,050	49.5	Japan	20,660	79.6
			Jordan	4,380	68.1
Chad	690	47.7	Kazakhstan	3,710	69.7
Chile	8,900	73.9	Kenya	1,400	55.5
China (P.R.C.)	2,330	68.6	Kiribati	na	na
Colombia	5,790	69.4	Korea, North	3,000	71.2
Comoros	1,130	56.2	Korea, South	9,710	71.3
Congo	2,750	51.2	Kuwait	21,630	75.0
Costa Rica	5,680	76.4	Kyrgyz Republic	2,320	69.2
Côte d'Ivoire	1,620	50.9	Laos	1,458	51.3
Croatia	na	na	Latvia	5,010	69.0
Cuba	3,000	75.4	Lebanon	2,500	68.7
Cyprus (G)	14,060	78.7	Lesotho	980	60.8
Czech Republic	8,430	71.3	Liberia	843	55.6
Denmark	20,200	75.3	Libya	6,125	63.4
Djibouti	775	48.4	Liechtenstein	na	na
Dominica	3,810	72.0	Lithuania	3,110	70.3

COUNTRY	REAL GDP PER CAPITA (PPP$)	LIFE EXPECTANCY	COUNTRY	REAL GDP PER CAPITA (PPP$)	LIFE EXPECTANCY
Luxembourg	25,390	75.8	Slovakia	5,620	70.9
Macedonia	na	na	Slovenia	na	na
Madagascar	700	56.8	Solomon Islands	2,266	70.5
Malawi	710	45.5	Somalia	712	47.2
Malaysia	8,360	70.9	South Africa	3,127	63.2
Maldives	2,200	62.4	Spain	13,660	77.7
Mali	530	46.2	Sri Lanka	3,030	72.0
Malta	11,570	76.2	Sudan	1,350	53.2
Marshall Islands	na	na	Suriname	3,670	70.5
Mauritania	1,610	51.7	Swaziland	2,940	57.8
Mauritius	12,510	70.4	Sweden	17,900	78.3
Mexico	7,010	71.0	Switzerland	22,720	78.1
Micronesia	na	na	Syria	4,196	67.3
Moldova	2,370	67.6	Taiwan (Rep. of China)	na	na
Monaco	na	na			
Mongolia	2,090	63.9	Tajikistan	1,380	70.4
Morocco	3,270	63.6	Tanzania	630	52.1
Mozambique	640	46.4	Thailand	6,350	69.2
Namibia	3,710	59.1	Togo	1,020	55.2
Nauru	na	na	Tonga	na	na
Nepal	1,000	53.8	Trinidad and Tobago	8,670	71.7
Netherlands	17,340	77.5			
New Zealand	16,720	75.6	Tunisia	4,950	68.0
Nicaragua	2,280	67.1	Turkey	4,210	66.7
Niger	790	46.7	Turkmenistan	3,128	65.1
Nigeria	1,540	50.6	Tuvalu	na	na
Norway	20,370	77.0	Uganda	910	44.7
Oman	10,420	69.8	Ukraine	3,250	69.3
Pakistan	2,160	61.8	United Arab Emirates	20,940	73.9
Palau	na	na			
Panama	5,890	72.9	United Kingdom	17,230	76.3
Papua New Guinea	2,530	56.0	United States	24,680	76.1
			Uruguay	6,550	72.6
Paraguay	3,340	70.1	Uzbekistan	2,510	69.4
Peru	3,320	66.3	Vanuatu	2,500	65.4
Philippines	2,590	66.5	Venezuela	8,360	71.8
Poland	4,702	71.1	Vietnam	1,040	65.5
Portugal	10,720	74.7	Western Samoa	3,000	67.8
Qatar	22,910	70.6	Yemen	1,600	50.4
Romania	3,727	69.9	Yugoslavia (Serbia and Montenegro)	na	na
Russia	4,760	67.4			
Rwanda	740	47.2			
St. Kitts and Nevis	9,340	70.0	Zaire	300	52.0
St. Lucia	3,795	72.0	Zambia	1,110	48.6
St. Vincent and the Grenadines	3,552	71.0	Zimbabwe	2,100	53.4
San Marino	na	na			
Sao Tome and Príncipe	600	67.0			
Saudi Arabia	12,600	69.9			
Senegal	1,710	49.5			
Seychelles	4,960	71.0			
Sierra Leone	860	39.2			
Singapore	19,350	74.9			

Notes: Freedom House obtained the figures for purchasing power parities (PPP) and life expectancy from the U.N.'s Human Development Report 1996 (Oxford University Press, 1996). PPP's are real GDP per capita figures which economists have adjusted to account for detailed price comparisons of individual items covering over 150 categories of expenditure. The U.N. life expectancy figures represent overall expectancy, not differentiated by sex. In some cases not covered by the U.N., the chart lists a combined average of male and female life expectancy obtained from Rand McNally. For several countries the chart lists these combined averages.

COMBINED AVERAGE RATINGS: INDEPENDENT COUNTRIES

FREE
1.0
Andorra
Australia
Austria
Barbados
Belize
Canada
Cyprus (G)
Denmark
Dominica
Finland
Iceland
Ireland
Kiribati
Liechtenstein
Luxembourg
Malta
Marshall Islands
Micronesia
Netherlands
New Zealand
Norway
Portugal
San Marino
Sweden
Switzerland
Tuvalu
United States

1.5
Bahamas
Belgium
Cape Verde
Costa Rica
Czech Republic
Estonia
France
Germany
Grenada
Hungary
Italy
Japan
Lithuania
Mauritius
Monaco
Palau
Poland
St. Kitts and Nevis
St. Lucia
St. Vincent and
  Grenadines
Sao Tome & Principe
Slovenia
Solomon Islands
South Africa

Spain
Trinidad
United Kingdom
Uruguay

2.0
Benin
Botswana
Chile
Greece
Guyana
Israel
Korea, S
Latvia
Mali
Nauru
Taiwan
Vanuatu
Western Samoa

2.5
Argentina
Bolivia
Bulgaria
Jamaica
Malawi
Mongolia
Namibia
Panama
Philippines
Romania
Venezuela

PARTLY FREE
3.0
Bangladesh
Brazil
Dominican Republic
Ecuador
El Salvador
Honduras
India
Madagascar
Nicaragua
Papua New Guinea
Seychelles
Slovakia
Suriname
Thailand

3.5
Antigua and Barbuda
Fiji
Ghana
Guatemala

Guinea-Bissau
Macedonia
Mexico
Moldova
Mozambique
Nepal
Paraguay
Peru
Russia
Ukraine

4.0
Albania
Central African
  Republic
Colombia
Comoros
Congo
Croatia
Georgia
Jordan
Kyrgyz Republic
Lesotho
Senegal
Sri Lanka
Tonga
Uganda

4.5
Armenia
Burkina Faso
Ethiopia
Gabon
Haiti
Malaysia
Pakistan
Sierra Leone
Singapore
Turkey
Zambia

5.0
Bosnia-Herzegovina
Eritrea
Kuwait
Morocco
Tanzania
Zimbabwe

NOT FREE
5.5
Azerbaijan
Chad
Cote D'Ivoire
Djibouti

Guinea
Kazakhstan
Lebanon
Swaziland
Togo
Tunisia
United Arab Emirates
Yemen

6.0
Algeria
Angola
Belarus
Brunei
Cambodia
Cameroon
Egypt
Indonesia
Maldives
Mauritania
Niger
Oman
Yugoslavia

6.5
Bahrain
The Gambia
Iran
Kenya
Laos
Liberia
Nigeria
Qatar
Rwanda
Uzbekistan
Zaire

7.0
Afghanistan
Bhutan
Burma
Burundi
China
Cuba
Equatorial Guinea
Iraq
Korea, N
Libya
Saudi Arabia
Somalia
Sudan
Syria
Tajikistan
Turkmenistan
Vietnam

COMBINED AVERAGE RATINGS: RELATED TERRITORIES

FREE
1.0
Aland Islands (Finland)
American Samoa (U.S.)
Azores (Portugal)
Bermuda (U.K.)
British Virgin Islands
(U.K.)
Canary Islands (Spain)
Cayman Islands (U.K.)
Faeroe Islands (Denmark)
Gibraltar (U.K.)
Greenland (Denmark)
Guam (U.S.)
Isle of Man (U.K.)
Madeira (Portugal)
Montserrat (U.K.)
St. Pierre and Miquelon
(France)
Turks and Caicos
(U.K.)
U.S. Virgin Islands
(U.S.)

1.5
Anguilla (U.K.)
Aruba (Netherlands)
Ceuta (Spain)
Channel Islands (U.K.)
Cook Islands

(New Zealand)
French Guiana (France)
French Polynesia (France)
Guadaloupe (France)
Martinique (France)
Mayotte (Mahore)
(France)
Melilla (Spain)
Netherlands Antilles
(Netherlands)
Northern Marianas (U.S.)
Puerto Rico (U.S.)
St. Helena and
Dependencies (U.K.)

2.0
Reunion (France)
Wallis and Futuna Islands
(France)

2.5
Christmas Island
(Australia)
New Caledonia (France)

PARTLY
FREE
3.0
Hong Kong (U.K.)
Cyprus (Turkey)

3.5
Northern Ireland (U.K.)

5.0
Macao (Portugal)

NOT FREE
5.5
Israeli-Occupied Territories
(Israel)
Palestinian Authority-
Administered Territories
(Israel)

6.0
Kurdistan (Iraq)
Nagorno-Karabakh
(Armenia/Azerbaijan)
Transdniester (Moldova)

6.5
Western Sahara
(Morocco)

7.0
East Timor (Indonesia)
Kashmir (India)

Kosovo (Yugoslavia)
Tibet (China)
West Papua (Irian Jaya)
(Indonesia)
MICRO-
TERRITORIES
(ALL FREE)

Cocos (Keeling) Islands
(Australia)
Falkland Islands (U.K.)
Niue (New Zealand)
Norfolk Island (Australia)
Pitcairn Islands (U.K.)
Rapanui (Easter Island
(Chile)
Svalbard (Norway)
Tokelau (New Zealand)

Micro-territories have
populations of under
5,000. These areas are
scored according to the
same methodology used
in the rest of the
Survey, but are listed
separately due to their
very small populations.

ELECTORAL DEMOCRACIES (118)

Albania
Presidential-parliamentary democracy
Andorra
Parliamentary democracy
Argentina
Federal presidential-legislative democracy
Australia
Federal parliamentary democracy
Austria
Federal parliamentary democracy
Bahamas
Parliamentary democracy
Bangladesh
Parliamentary democracy
Barbados
Parliamentary democracy
Belgium
Federal parliamentary democracy
Belize
Parliamentary democracy
Benin
Presidential-parliamentary democracy
Bolivia
Presidential-legislative democracy
Bosnia-Herzegovina
Presidential-parliamentary democracy (transitional)
Botswana
Parliamentary democracy and traditional chiefs
Brazil
Federal presidential-legislative democracy
Bulgaria
Parliamentary democracy
Canada
Federal parliamentary democracy
Cape Verde
Presidential-parliamentary democracy
Central African Republic
Presidential-parliamentary democracy
Chile
Presidential-legislative democracy
Colombia
Presidential-legislative democracy (insurgencies)
Congo
Presidential-parliamentary democracy
Costa Rica
Presidential-legislative democracy
Croatia
Presidential-parliamentary democracy
Cyprus
Presidential-legislative democracy
Czech Republic
Parliamentary democracy
Denmark
Parliamentary democracy
Dominica
Parliamentary democracy
Dominican Republic
Presidential-legislative democracy

Ecuador
Presidential-legislative democracy
El Salvador
Presidential-legislative democracy (military-influenced)
Estonia
Presidential-parliamentary democracy
Fiji
Parliamentary democracy and native chieftains
Finland
Presidential-parliamentary democracy
France
Presidential-parliamentary democracy
Georgia
Presidential-parliamentary democracy
Germany
Federal parliamentary democracy
Ghana
Presidential-parliamentary democracy
Greece
Parliamentary democracy
Grenada
Parliamentary democracy
Guatemala
Presidential-legislative democracy (military-dominated)
(insurgencies)
Guinea-Bissau
Presidential-parliamentary democracy
Guyana
Parliamentary democracy
Haiti
Presidential-parliamentary democracy
Honduras
Presidential-legislative democracy (military-influenced)
Hungary
Parliamentary democracy
Iceland
Parliamentary democracy
India
Parliamentary democracy
Ireland
Parliamentary democracy
Israel
Parliamentary democracy
Italy
Parliamentary democracy
Jamaica
Parliamentary democracy
Japan
Parliamentary democracy
Kiribati
Parliamentary democracy
Korea, South
Presidential-parliamentary democracy
Kyrgyz Republic
Presidential-parliamentary democracy
Latvia
Presidential-parliamentary democracy
Lesotho
Parliamentary democracy (military- and royal-influenced)

Liechtenstein
Prince and parliamentary democracy
Lithuania
Presidential-parliamentary democracy
Luxembourg
Parliamentary democracy
Macedonia
Presidential-parliamentary democracy
Madagascar
Presidential-parliamentary democracy
Malawi
Presidential-parliamentary democracy
Mali
Presidential-parliamentary democracy
Malta
Parliamentary democracy
Marshall Islands
Parliamentary democracy
Mauritius
Parliamentary democracy
Micronesia
Federal parliamentary democracy
Moldova
Presidential-parliamentary democracy
Monaco
Prince and legislative democracy
Mongolia
Presidential-parliamentary democracy
Mozambique
Presidential-legislative democracy
Namibia
Presidential-legislative democracy
Nauru
Parliamentary democracy
Nepal
Parliamentary democracy
Netherlands
Parliamentary democracy
New Zealand
Parliamentary democracy
Nicaragua
Presidential-legislative democracy (military-influenced)
Norway
Parliamentary democracy
Pakistan
Presidential-parliamentary democracy (military-influenced)
Palau
Presidential-legislative democracy
Panama
Presidential-legislative democracy
Papua New Guinea
Parliamentary democracy (secessionist insurgency)
Paraguay
Presidential-legislative democracy (military-influenced)
Philippines
Presidential-legislative democracy
Poland
Presidential-parliamentary democracy
Portugal
Presidential-parliamentary democracy

Romania
Presidential-parliamentary democracy
Russia
Presidential-parliamentary democracy
St. Kitts-Nevis
Parliamentary democracy
St. Lucia
Parliamentary democracy
St. Vincent and the Grenadines
Parliamentary democracy
San Marino
Parliamentary democracy
Sao Tome and Principe
Presidential-parliamentary democracy
Seychelles
Presidential-legislative democracy
Sierra Leone
Presidential-parliamentary democracy
Slovakia
Parliamentary democracy
Slovenia
Presidential-parliamentary democracy
Solomon Islands
Parliamentary democracy
South Africa
Presidential-legislative democracy
Spain
Parliamentary democracy
Sri Lanka
Presidential-parliamentary democracy (insurgency)
Suriname
Presidential-parliamentary democracy
Sweden
Parliamentary democracy
Switzerland
Federal parliamentary democracy
Taiwan
Presidential-legislative democracy
Thailand
Parliamentary democracy (military-influenced)
Trinidad and Tobago
Parliamentary democracy
Turkey
Presidential-parliamentary democracy (military-influenced) (insurgency)
Tuvalu
Parliamentary democracy
Ukraine
Presidential-parliamentary democracy
United Kingdom
Parliamentary democracy
United States
Federal presidential-legislative democracy
Uruguay
Presidential-legislative democracy
Vanuatu
Parliamentary democracy
Venezuela
Presidential-legislative democracy
Western Samoa
Parliamentary democracy and extended family heads

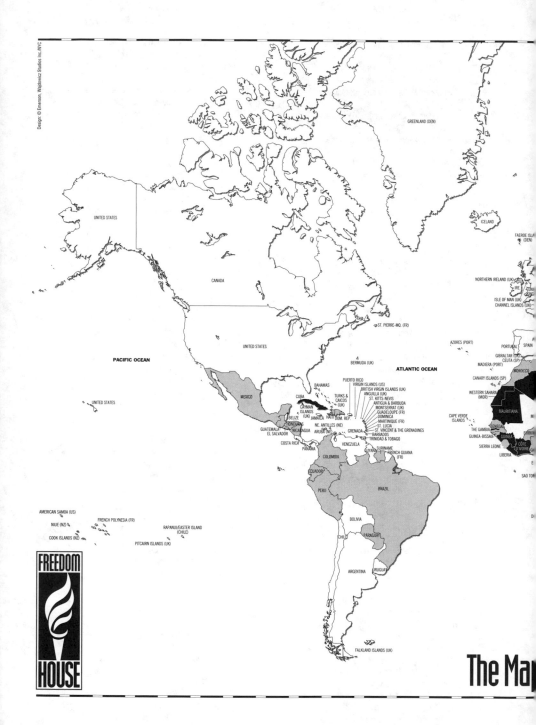

GREENLAND (DEN)

UNITED STATES

ICELAND

FAEROE ISL.
(DEN)

CANADA

NORTHERN IRELAND (UK)
IRE.
ISLE OF MAN (UK)
CHANNEL ISLANDS (UK)

ST. PIERRE-MQ. (FR)

AZORES (PORT)
PORTUGAL   SPAIN
GIBRALTAR (UK)
CEUTA (SP)
MADIERA (PORT)

UNITED STATES

BERMUDA (UK)

ATLANTIC OCEAN

MOROCCO

PACIFIC OCEAN

CANARY ISLANDS (SP)

WESTERN SAHARA
(MOR)

PUERTO RICO
VIRGIN ISLANDS (US)
BRITISH VIRGIN ISLANDS (UK)
ANGUILLA (UK)
ST. KITTS-NEVIS
ANTIGUA & BARBUDA
MONTSERRAT (UK)
GUADELOUPE (FR)
DOMINICA
MARTINIQUE (FR)
ST. LUCIA
BARBADOS
ST. VINCENT & THE GRENADINES
GRENADA
TRINIDAD & TOBAGO

MAURITANIA

MEXICO

CUBA

BAHAMAS

TURKS &
CAICOS
(UK)

CAYMAN
ISLANDS
(UK)

JAMAICA HAITI DOM. REP.

CAPE VERDE
ISLANDS

THE GAMBIA
SENEGAL
GUINEA-BISSAU   GUINEA

MI

UNITED STATES

BELIZE

GUATEMALA
EL SALVADOR

HONDURAS
NICARAGUA

COSTA RICA

NE. ANTILLES (NE)
ARUBA (NE)

SIERRA LEONE

CÔTE
D'IVOIRE

LIBERIA

PANAMA

VENEZUELA

GUYANA
SURINAME

E

FRENCH GUIANA
(FR)

COLOMBIA

SAO TOM

ECUADOR

PERU

BRAZIL

AMERICAN SAMOA (US)

NIUE (NZ)

FRENCH POLYNESIA (FR)

BOLIVIA

DI

COOK ISLANDS (NZ)

RAPANUI/EASTER ISLAND
(CHILE)

PARAGUAY

PITCAIRN ISLANDS (UK)

CHILE

ARGENTINA

URUGUAY

FALKLAND ISLANDS (UK)

The Ma

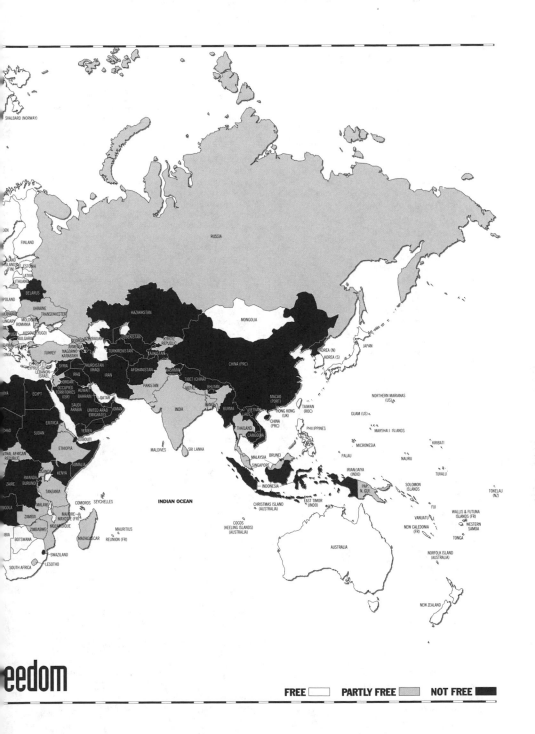

SVALBARD (NORWAY)

FINLAND

ICELAND
ISLANDS
(FIN)
LATVIA
LITHUANIA
POLAND
BELARUS
UKRAINE
TRANSDNIESTER
HUNGARY
MOLDOVA
ROMANIA
KOSOVO (YUGO)
BULGARIA
TURKEY
GEORGIA
AZERBAIJAN
ARMENIA
NAGORNO-
KARABAKH
CYPRUS (T)
CYPRUS (G)
LEBANON
ISRAEL
SYRIA
KURDISTAN
(IRAQ)
IRAQ
JORDAN
OCCUPIED
TERRITORIES
(ISR)
EGYPT
KUWAIT
BAHRAIN
SAUDI
ARABIA
UNITED ARAB
EMIRATES
QATAR
OMAN

RUSSIA

KAZAKHSTAN

MONGOLIA

UZBEKISTAN
KYRGYZ
REPUBLIC
TURKMENISTAN
TAJIKISTAN
AFGHANISTAN
KASHMIR
(INDIA)
TIBET (CHINA)
NEPAL
BHUTAN

KOREA (N)
JAPAN
KOREA (S)

CHINA (PRC)

PAKISTAN

INDIA

BANGLADESH
BURMA
MACAO
(PORT)
HONG KONG
(UK)
TAIWAN
(ROC)

NORTHERN MARIANAS
(US)

CHAD
SUDAN
ERITREA
YEMEN
DJIBOUTI
ETHIOPIA
SOMALIA

MALDIVES
SRI LANKA

LAOS
VIETNAM
THAILAND
CAMBODIA
CHINA
(PRC)

PHILIPPINES

GUAM (US)

MARSHALL ISLANDS

MICRONESIA

KIRIBATI

CENTRAL AFRICAN
REPUBLIC
UGANDA
KENYA
RWANDA
BURUNDI
TANZANIA
ZAIRE
MALAWI
ANGOLA
ZAMBIA
ZIMBABWE
MOZAMBIQUE
NAMIBIA
BOTSWANA

COMOROS SEYCHELLES
MAYOTTE
(FR)
MADAGASCAR
MAURITIUS
REUNION (FR)

MALAYSIA
SINGAPORE
BRUNEI

PALAU

INDONESIA

IRIAN JAYA
(INDO)

NAURU

TUVALU

INDIAN OCEAN

CHRISTMAS ISLAND
(AUSTRALIA)

COCOS
(KEELING ISLANDS)
(AUSTRALIA)

EAST TIMOR
(INDO)

PAP.
N. GUI.

SOLOMON
ISLANDS

FIJI

TOKELAU
(NZ)

WALLIS & FUTUNA
ISLANDS (FR)

VANUATU

NEW CALEDONIA
(FR)

WESTERN
SAMOA

TONGA

SWAZILAND
SOUTH AFRICA
LESOTHO

AUSTRALIA

NORFOLK ISLAND
(AUSTRALIA)

NEW ZEALAND

eedom

FREE ☐   PARTLY FREE ▨   NOT FREE ▮

Sources

Publications, organizations

AFL-CIO
Agence France Presse
American Institute for Free Labor Development
Amnesty International *Urgent Action Bulletins*
Amnesty International: *Report*
Armenian Information Service
Asian Bulletin
Asian Survey
Associated Press
The *Atlantic Monthly*
Azerbaijan International (U.S.)
Balkan Medja (Bulgaria)
Caretas (Lima)
Carib News
Caribbean Insight
Caribbean Review
Catholic Standard (Guyana)
Center for Strategic and International Studies
Centers for Pluralism: Newsletters (Poland)
Central America Report
Central Statistical Office, Warsaw (Poland)
Christian Science Monitor
Columbia Journalism Review
Commission on Security and Cooperation in Europe (CSCE):
    Implementation of the Helsinki Accords (Reports)
Committee to Protect Journalists *Update*
Dawn News Bulletin (All Burma Students Democratic Front)
Democratic Initiatives (Ukraine)
Eastern European Constitutional Review
The *Economist*
EFE Spanish news agency
El Financiero (Mexico City)
El Nuevo Herald (Miami)
Elections Canada
EPOCA (Mexico)
Equal Access Committee (Ukraine)
Ethiopian Review
Ethnic Federation of Romani (Romania)
Far Eastern Economic Review
Foreign Broadcast Information Service (FBIS):
    FBIS Africa
    FBIS China
    FBIS East Europe
    FBIS Latin America
    FBIS Near East & South Asia
    FBIS East Asia
    FBIS Soviet Union/Central Eurasia
    FBIS Sub-Saharan Africa
The *Financial Times*
Free Labour World
Free Trade Union Institute
The *Globe & Mail* (Toronto)
The *Guardian*
Hemisfile
Hemisphere
Himal
Hong Kong Digest
Immigration and Refugee Board of Canada
Index on Censorship
Indian Law Resource Center

Inter-American Dialogue
Inter-American Press Association
International Commission of Jurists
International Foundation for Electoral Systems (IFES)
International Republican Institute
The *Irish Echo*
The *Irish Voice*
Jeune Afrique
Journal of Commerce
Journal of Democracy
La Jornada (Mexico)
Latin American Regional Reports
Latin American Weekly Report
Lawyer to Lawyer Network (Lawyers Committee for Human Rights)
Los Angeles *Times*
Miami *Herald*
Middle East International
Milan Simecka Foundation (Slovakia)
Miist (Ukraine)
Monthly Digest of News from Armenia (Armenian Assembly of
    America)
The *Nation*
National Bank of Hungary (Monthly Reports)
National Democratic Institute for International Affairs
National Endowment for Democracy (U.S.)
New African
The *New Republic*
New York *Newsday*
New York *Times*
New Yorker
North-South Magazine
North-South Center (Miami)
Organization of American States
The *Other Side of Mexico* (Equipo Pueblo)
Pacific Islands Monthly
Political Handbook of the World: 1996-97
Proceso (Mexico City)
Reforma (Mexico)
Sposterihach (Ukraine)
State Department *Country Reports on Human Rights Practices for 1996*
The *Statesman* (Calcutta)
Statistical Handbook 1994: States of the Former Soviet Union
    (World Bank)
Swiss Press Review
The *Tico Times* (Costa Rica)
The *Week in Germany*
U.S. News and World Report
Ukrainian Center for Independent Political Research
Ukrainian Press Agency
Ukrainian Weekly
Uncaptive Minds (Institute for Democracy in Eastern Europe)
UNDP *Human Development Report*
UNICEF
U.S. Committee for Refugees (Special Reports)
Vuelta (Mexico)
Wall Street Journal
Washington *Post*
Washington *Times*
West Africa
World Population Data Sheet 1996 (Population Reference
    Bureau)

Human Rights Organizations

Amnesty International
Andean Commission of Jurists
Bangladesh National Women Lawyers Association
Caribbean Institute for the Promotion of Human Rights
Caribbean Rights
Child Workers in Nepal
Chilean Human Rights Commission
Civic Alliance (Mexico)
Committee of Churches for Emergency Help (Paraguay)
Council for Democracy (Mexico)
Croatian Democracy Project (Croatia)
Cuban Committee for Human Rights
Democracy After Communism Foundation (Hungary)
Fray Bartocomé de Las Casas Center for Human Rights
    (Mexico)
Free and Democratic Bulgaria Foundation
Group for Mutual Support (Guatemala)
Guyana Human Rights Association
Haitian Center for Human Rights
Honduran Committee for the Defense of Human Rights
Human Rights Commission (El Salvador)
Human Rights Organization of Bhutan
Human Rights Organization of Nepal
Human Rights Commission of Pakistan
Human Rights Watch
    Africa , Americas, Asia, Helsinki, Middle East
Inform (Sri Lanka)
Inter-American Commission on Human Rights

International Human Rights Law Group
Jamaica Council for Human Rights
Latin American Association for Human Rights
Latin American Commission for Human Rights and Freedoms of
    the Workers
Latin American Ombudsmen Institute
Lawyers Committee for Human Rights
Lawyers for Human Rights and Legal Aid (Pakistan)
Mexican Human Rights Academy
National Coalition for Haitian Refugees
National Coordinating Office for Human Rights (Peru)
Panamanian Committee for Human Rights
Peoples Forum for Human Rights, Bhutan
Permanent Commission on Human Rights (Nicaragua)
Permanent Committee for the Defense of Human Rights
    (Colombia)
Physicians for Human Rights
Reporters Sans Frontieres
Runejel Junam Council of Ethnic Communities (Guatemala)
Tibet Information Network
Tibetan Center for Human Rights and Democracy
Tutela Legal (El Salvador)
Venezuelan Human Rights Education Action Program
Vicaria de la Solidaridad (Chile)
Vietnam Committee on Human Rights
Washington Office on Latin America
Women Acting Together for Change (Nepal)
Women's Commission for Refugee Women and Children

Delegations/visitors to Freedom House

Africa/Middle East	Asia/Pacific	Former USSR
Egypt	Bangladesh	Russia
Eritrea	Bhutan	Ukraine
Ghana	Cambodia	
Mali	Hong Kong	**Western**
Mauritania	India	**Hemisphere**
Rwanda	Indonesia	Cuba
Tanzania	Malaysia	Venezuela
Turkey	Nepal	
Uganda	Pakistan	
Zimbabwe	Sri Lanka	
	Thailand	
	Tibet	

Delegations and On-Site Staff Investigations from Freedom House to:

Azerbaijan	Jordan
Bangladesh	Laos
Benin	Mexico
Canada	Nepal
Cambodia	Pakistan
Cote d'Ivoire	Palestinian Authority-Administered Territories (Israel)
Czech Republic	Philippines
Cuba	Russia
France	Singapore
Germany	Sri Lanka
Haiti	Suriname
Hong Kong	Switzerland
India	Thailand
Indonesia	Ukraine
Isreal	Vietnam